THE DOUBLE-FACING CONSTITUTION

This collection explores some of the many ways in which constitutional orders engage with, and are shaped by, their exteriors. Constitutional and legal theory often marginalize 'foreign' elements, such as norms originating in other legal systems, the movement of individuals across borders, or the application of domestic law to foreign affairs. In this book, these instances of boundary crossing lie at the heart of an alternative understanding of constitutions as permeable membranes, through which norms can and sometimes must travel. Constitutional orders are facing both inwards and outwards – and the outside world influences their interiors just as much as their internal orders help shape their surroundings. Different essays discuss the theoretical and historical foundations of this view (grounded in Kelsen, Hobbes, Locke, Rousseau and others) and its contemporary relevance for areas as diverse as migration law, the conflict of laws, and foreign relations law.

JACCO BOMHOFF is Associate Professor of Law at the Law Department of the London School of Economics and Political Science. He is the author of *Balancing Constitutional Rights: The Origins and Meanings of Postwar Legal Discourse* (Cambridge University Press, 2013).

DAVID DYZENHAUS is University Professor of Law and Philosophy at the Faculty of Law, University of Toronto, and a Fellow of the Royal Society of Canada. He is the author and editor of several books, including *Legality and Legitimacy* (1999) and *The Constitution of Law* (Cambridge University Press, 2006).

THOMAS POOLE is Professor of Law at the Law Department of the London School of Economics and Political Science. He is the author of *Reason of State: Law, Prerogative and Empire* (Cambridge University Press, 2015), and the editor, with David Dyzenhaus, of books on Hobbes, and on Oakeshott, Hayek and Schmitt.

THE DOUBLE-FACING CONSTITUTION

Edited by

JACCO BOMHOFF

London School of Economics and Political Science

DAVID DYZENHAUS

University of Toronto

THOMAS POOLE

London School of Economics and Political Science

CAMBRIDGE
UNIVERSITY PRESS

CAMBRIDGE
UNIVERSITY PRESS

University Printing House, Cambridge CB2 8BS, United Kingdom

One Liberty Plaza, 20th Floor, New York, NY 10006, USA

477 Williamstown Road, Port Melbourne, VIC 3207, Australia

314–321, 3rd Floor, Plot 3, Splendor Forum, Jasola District Centre, New Delhi – 110025, India

79 Anson Road, #06–04/06, Singapore 079906

Cambridge University Press is part of the University of Cambridge.

It furthers the University's mission by disseminating knowledge in the pursuit of education, learning, and research at the highest international levels of excellence.

www.cambridge.org
Information on this title: www.cambridge.org/9781108485487
DOI: 10.1017/9781108751483

First published 2020

Printed in the United Kingdom by TJ International Ltd, Padstow Cornwall

A catalogue record for this publication is available from the British Library.

Library of Congress Cataloging-in-Publication Data
Names: Dyzenhaus, David, editor. | Poole, Thomas (Thomas M.), editor. | Bomhoff, J. (Jacco), editor.
Title: The double-facing constitution / edited by David Dyzenhaus, University of Toronto; Thomas Poole, London School of Economics and Political Science; Jacco Bomhoff, London School of Economics and Political Science
Description: Cambridge, United Kingdom ; New York, NY, USA : Cambridge University Press, 2019. | Includes index.
Identifiers: LCCN 2019029314 (print) | LCCN 2019029315 (ebook) | ISBN 9781108485487 (hardback) | ISBN 9781108751483 (epub)
Subjects: LCSH: Constitutional law – Congresses.
Classification: LCC K3165.A6 D68 2019 (print) | LCC K3165.A6 (ebook) | DDC 342–dc23
LC record available at https://lccn.loc.gov/2019029314
LC ebook record available at https://lccn.loc.gov/2019029315

ISBN 978-1-108-48548-7 Hardback

CONTENTS

CONTRIBUTORS

HELMUT PHILIPP AUST is Professor of Law at the Freie Universität Berlin.

JACCO BOMHOFF is Associate Professor of Law at the London School of Economics and Political Science.

GENEVIÈVE CARTIER is Professor of Law at Sherbrooke University.

THEODORE CHRISTOV is Associate Professor of Honors, History and International Affairs at George Washington University.

EVAN FOX-DECENT is Professor of Law at McGill University.

DAVID DYZENHAUS is University Professor of Law and Philosophy at the University of Toronto.

DIETER GRIMM is Professor of Law Emeritus at the Humboldt University.

ASHA KAUSHAL is Assistant Professor of Law at the University of British Columbia.

KAREN KNOP is Professor of Law at the University of Toronto.

AUDREY MACKLIN is Professor of Law and Chair in Human Rights Law at the University of Toronto.

CAMPBELL MCLACHLAN is Professor of Law at Victoria University of Wellington.

THOMAS POOLE is Professor of Law at the London School of Economics and Political Science.

ALEXANDER SOMEK is Professor of Law at the University of Vienna School of Law.

1

Introduction

JACCO BOMHOFF, DAVID DYZENHAUS, THOMAS POOLE

This collection explores some of the many ways in which constitutional orders engage with the outside world – the world of other states, of foreign norms and of individuals who are in some sense 'strangers to the constitution'.[1] These various forms of foreignness we refer to as 'constitutional and legal exteriority'. The conceptual and normative understanding of constitutional orders as actively concerned with, and in part formed by, their exteriors, we call the 'double-facing constitution'.

Thinking about the double-facing constitution means thinking about constitutional orders in terms of both boundaries and boundary-crossings. It implies an understanding of the act of constitution 'as not an exclusionary but a liminal act'.[2] As one of us previously described this idea, the double-facing constitution envisages constitutional orders 'as having both an inner and an outer membrane. They face outwards as well as inwards and these two faces are related'.[3] These relations, this volume suggests, extend in two directions. On the one hand, 'the act of constituting the internal space of the state also necessarily affects the space outside of it as that space is constituted in relation to other constituted jurisdictions'.[4] On the other hand, 'how a constitutional order engages with the world outside it feeds back into how it constructs itself internally'.[5] At its broadest, as Karen Knop observes in this volume, the double-facing constitution calls attention to the many ways in which 'the existence of, dependence on and regard for the Other figure in the Constitution'.[6]

[1] Cf. Gerald L. Neuman, *Strangers to the Constitution: Immigrants, Borders, and Fundamental Law* (Princeton, NJ: Princeton University Press, 1996).

[2] David Dyzenhaus, 'The Janus-Faced Constitution', Chapter 2 of this volume.

[3] Thomas Poole, 'The Constitution and Foreign Affairs' (2016) 69(1) *Current Legal Problems* 143, 148.

[4] Dyzenhaus, 'The Janus-Faced Constitution', Chapter 2 of this volume.

[5] Thomas Poole, 'The Idea of the Federative', Chapter 3 of this volume.

[6] Karen Knop, 'The Spectre of Comity', Chapter 7 of this volume.

The relationship between domestic law and the outside world is not, of course, a new topic. The status of international law in domestic legal systems is a classic concern for legal theory and in public international law scholarship, while the role of domestic law in cross-border situations is the central preoccupation of private international law, or the conflict of laws. The categories of 'domestic' and 'international' have been in flux since at least the time of the League of Nations, and have since been joined by the 'transnational' and, more recently, the 'global'. The roles of territory and membership in law, and the role of law in the constitution of territory and membership, have been important topics in legal scholarship for many years, and in particular from the early 1990s onwards. The early 2000s saw a sustained debate in the United States over the legitimacy of judicial invocations of foreign norms – a dispute which drew attention to what one leading scholar labelled the 'multiple ports of entry' of constitutional orders – while legal scholars in Europe during the same period began to discuss related issues under the heading of 'constitutional pluralism'.[7] Judges and jurists have converged over the past decade in particular on the broad heading of 'foreign relations law' to engage with questions surrounding 'the legality of foreign affairs decisions by the executive' or 'the protection of the individual affected by the foreign exercise of public power'.[8]

The main strands of what we call 'double-facing constitutional law' are therefore familiar, even if they remain understudied. They concern principally, at a minimum, 'the relationship between national law and public international law; the relationship between states that gives rise to private international law; and the reach of the public law norms of a national order beyond the territorial limits of the state in the field of "foreign relations law"'.[9] The chapters in this collection draw on these various strands, while also suggesting new emphases and drawing new connections. In this Introduction, we explore some of the common themes and novel approaches to be found across this volume, before presenting the individual contributions in order.

[7] Judith Resnik, 'Law's Migration: American Exceptionalism, Silent Dialogues, and Federalism's Multiple Points of Entry' (2006) 115 *Yale Law Journal* 1564; Neil Walker, 'The Idea of Constitutional Pluralism' (2002) 65(3) *Modern Law Review* 317.

[8] Campbell McLachlan, *Foreign Relations Law* (Cambridge: Cambridge University Press, 2014). See also, most recently, Eyal Benvenisti and Mila Versteeg, 'The External Dimensions of Constitutions' (2018) 57(3) *Virginia Journal of International Law* 515; and Daniel S. Margolies, Umut Özsu, Maïa Pal, and Ntina Tzouvala (eds.), *The Extraterritoriality of Law: History, Theory, Politics* (Abingdon: Routledge, 2019).

[9] Dyzenhaus, 'The Janus-Faced Constitution', Chapter 2 of this volume.

Double-facing constitutionalism, firstly, suggests an understanding of the constitution as 'a membrane through which norms may and sometimes must travel'.[10] This 'permeable' conception of constitutional boundaries sustains attempts to move beyond a preoccupation with the classic questions listed above, in that it draws attention squarely, first, to the modalities and direction of this 'travel' and, second, to the character of the thresholds to be crossed. As to the former theme, the idea of the double-facing constitution calls for special consideration of the fact that 'it is not only the international that is piercing through the outer layers of the state, but it is also the inside of the state which is pushing its way outwards'.[11] The act of constitution, as David Dyzenhaus writes in this collection, 'is therefore Janus-faced – it looks both inwards and outwards'. This outward-facing dynamic is particularly central, for example, to Geneviève Cartier's exploration in this volume of the role of cities in foreign affairs. The latter theme – the character of the relevant thresholds – also plays a pivotal role in a number of chapters. Here too, the Janus-image is important, this time in his guise as the god of doorways and passages. In this vein, Karen Knop, for instance, examines 'a curious and little noticed threshold' between the domestic and the international in the form of 'the Supreme Court of Canada's recent characterization of "comity" as a principle of constitutional interpretation'. Audrey Macklin and Jacco Bomhoff, in their contributions, discuss the constructed character and changing nature of borders and other constitutionally salient jurisdictional and spatial boundaries. In this area, any binary oppositions suggested by the image of Janus or the 'double-facing' metaphor must themselves be kept under close review. 'Liminality', as Macklin wryly observes, 'is not so liminal anymore. Bordering is happening everywhere', whether 'a hundred miles inside the territorial United States' or 'at any visa office anywhere in the world'.[12] Notions of 'inside' and 'outside', as Bomhoff also notes, cannot be taken for granted but will instead have to be made themselves objects of constitutionalist concern.

The idea of the double-facing constitution aims to go beyond more familiar notions of extraterritoriality and foreign relations in a second way: by including within its scope a broad range of questions about how

[10] Dyzenhaus, 'The Janus-Faced Constitution', Chapter 2 of this volume.

[11] Helmut Philipp Aust, 'Shining Cities on the Hill? The Global City, Climate Change, and International Law' (2015) 26(1) *European Journal of International Law* 255, 260, cited in Geneviève Cartier, 'Double-Facing Administrative Law: State Prerogatives, Cities and Foreign Affairs', Chapter 11 of this volume.

[12] Audrey Macklin, 'The Inside-Out Constitution', Chapter 9 of this volume.

'the state's public law [governs] its interactions with non-citizens' – what Evan Fox-Decent calls in this volume 'the state's cosmopolitan law'. A large segment of these interactions is covered by the fields of immigration and citizenship law. One striking observation provoked by the contributions to this volume, however, is the extent to which the fields of immigration law and foreign relations law (and private international law, for that matter) have developed in isolation.[13] But questions of citizenship and alienage, of entry and exclusion, clearly have to be central to any conception of the double-facing constitution. Asha Kaushal's chapter addresses this issue of '*who* the constitution is facing' head on. 'When the constitution faces inward', she asks, 'who does it hold in its gaze? When the constitution turns outward, to whom is its face directed? The answers to these questions are found in the interstices of immigration law and constitutional law'.[14] After all, as Kaushal notes, 'both the membership and identity of the constitution's external and internal audiences are partly constituted by immigration law'. These 'interstices of immigration law and constitutional law' are fraught with dangers to constitutional rights protection, as both Kaushal's and Macklin's chapters make clear.

In many of the contributions to this volume, the 'double-facing' constitution figures as common shorthand for attention to a two-way traffic of constitutional normativity – from 'the local' as it faces outwards and from the constitution's exteriors as they seep into the polity. 'Double-facing' draws attention to the constructed character of boundaries and the close connections between what is deemed to be 'internal' and 'external' to the constitution – in contrast to a narrower, unquestioning focus on 'extraterritoriality' and 'foreign' affairs. It emphasises that there is 'no obvious or natural separation between one constitutional domain and the other',[15] that exclusionary dynamics may well operate deep inside the territories of nation states, but also that many familiar legal boundaries may well be 'more porous than is usually assumed'.[16] And it motivates the search for linkages between different fields that often lead

[13] See, for a similar integrated approach, the Symposium Issue on 'The External Dimensions of Constitutions' curated by Eyal Benvenisti and Mila Versteeg, in (2018) 57(3) *Virginia Journal of International Law*.

[14] Asha Kaushal, 'The Constitution in the Shadow of the Immigration State', Chapter 10 of this volume.

[15] Poole, 'The Idea of the Federative', Chapter 3 of this volume.

[16] Cartier, 'Double-Facing Administrative Law: State Prerogatives, Cities and Foreign Affairs', Chapter 11 of this volume.

separate lives – foreign relations law and immigration law; constitutional law and legal theory; public law and private law.

In the most general terms, as Karen Knop explains, 'exploration of the double-facing constitution might call for a certain amount of lateral thinking and methodological experimentation if it is to include a variety of thresholds – back doors, emergency exits, false doors, hidden passageways'.[17] Such experimentation is evident throughout the chapters that follow, particularly when it comes to questions of terminology and conceptual vocabulary. Bringing together immigration law and foreign relations law, for example, requires linking the language of 'the border' to that of 'jurisdiction', by foregrounding both the juridical character of the former and the materiality of the latter. To discuss Carl Schmitt alongside the jurisprudence of private international law invites reflection on how comity might relate to enmity and on the striking diversity of ways in which law distinguishes between insiders and outsiders. The invisibility of the local – cities – on the international plane is placed alongside the invisibility of the foreign – immigrants – in the sphere of domestic constitutional law. The question of who decides on the individuals 'we' are willing to let in is juxtaposed with the question of who determines the countries with which 'we' will cooperate – as well as, for both cases, the further question of how these decisions reflect back on any original 'us'. In a number of contributions, lost vocabulary or imported terms from seemingly very different contexts are invoked in efforts to capture the distinct conceptual nature and normative character of double-facing constitutionalism. In this spirit, Evan Fox-Decent turns to the idea of 'fiduciary' duties (to convey the legitimacy threshold for state action vis-à-vis citizens and outsiders alike), and Thomas Poole revisits the notion of 'the federative' (which Locke, drawing on Cicero, used to describe the state's foreign relations power).

In many of the contributions collected here, grappling with the double-facing qualities of constitutional normativity provokes reflection on foundational problems in jurisprudence and constitutional theory, some of which appear especially urgent today. Alexander Somek uses the work of Jean-Jacques Rousseau to rethink the connections between patriotism and cosmopolitanism, and Theodore Christov revisits Thomas Hobbes's conception of the state. David Dyzenhaus returns to the classic question of what constitutes a legal system in the work of H. L. A. Hart and Hans Kelsen. Helmut Aust, finally, connects theoretical salience to real-world

[17] Knop, 'The Spectre of Comity', Chapter 7 of this volume.

urgency in a particularly direct way, by framing his chapter as a response to the question of whether, and if so how, international cooperation can be made compatible with sovereignty and democracy.

That last, overarching, question points to some of the most pressing and difficult problems in contemporary scholarship and politics. The second decade of the twenty-first century has come to resemble an extended backlash against previously ascendant liberalising and cosmopolitan trends. Current scholarship, across a range of disciplines, is preoccupied both with the origins and character of contemporary 'globalism', *and* with the character and resurgent or continued appeal of localism, nationalism and nativism.[18] One assumption common to the chapters in this volume is that, as well as being the concern of historians, political scientists and lawyers more generally, these questions are also of specifically *constitutionalist* concern. Modern constitutionalism has to contemplate both dreams of 'taking back control' and reveries of a 'frictionless' world. Whatever its specific content, it must navigate between excesses of narrow parochialism and unmoored cosmopolitanism, finding a place for borders and jurisdictional boundaries as well as for permeability and transcendence. For the elaboration of such visions of constitutional ordering, we offer as a starting point the idea of 'double-facing' constitutionalism.

The contributors to this volume address the double-facing constitution from a range of different angles and in different registers. Chapters are divided into the following parts: (I) 'Theoretical Foundations', (II) 'Border Crossings: Comity and Mobility', and (III) 'The Foreign in Foreign Relations Law'.

I Theoretical Foundations

The volume opens with David Dyzenhaus's attempt, in Chapter 2, 'The Janus-Faced Constitution', to develop the theoretical basis for a 'permeable' conception of the constitution. This conception is developed by way of what

[18] See, e.g., Stephen Tierney (ed.), *Nationalism and Globalisation* (Oxford: Hart Publishing, 2015); Or Rosenboim, *The Emergence of Globalism: Visions of World Order in Britain and The United States, 1939–1950* (Princeton, NJ: Princeton University Press, 2017); Quinn Slobodian, *Globalists: The End of Empire and the Birth of Neoliberalism* (Cambridge, MA: Harvard University Press, 2018); Jean Comaroff and John L. Comaroff, *Theory from the South: Or, How Euro-America Is Evolving toward Africa* (Abingdon: Routledge, 2016); Glenda Sluga and Patricia Clavin, *Internationalisms: A Twentieth-Century History* (Cambridge: Cambridge University Press, 2017).

Dyzenhaus calls 'a rather deep dive into an arcane debate between the two great legal positivists of the last century, Hans Kelsen and H. L. A. Hart'. The purpose of that detailed analysis is to contrast the respective 'functional equivalents they propose to Hobbes's claim that a social contract explains the unity of political and legal order'. These alternatives are Hart's rule of recognition and Kelsen's basic norm. Favouring Kelsen's dynamic, monist conception of the relation between international and domestic law, and his commitment to the 'gaplessness' of legal order, Dyzenhaus ultimately turns to exploring the promise of this conception for an understanding of, both, the outward projection of public law norms of a domestic legal order beyond its borders and the reception, within that order, of norms originating elsewhere.

In Chapter 3, 'The Idea of the Federative', Thomas Poole makes a case for an account of the double-facing constitution which puts the idea of the federative at its heart. Locke used that term to designate the foreign relations power of the commonwealth. The argument builds on Locke's intuition, sourced from Cicero, that this power is concerned centrally with the capacity to effect compacts (alliances) with other political associations. One advantage of the perspective that ensues is that this compact-making power is demonstrably a juridical idea. It is an idea, moreover, that is open to the possibility of reciprocity and, by extension, the development of truly juridical structures of mutual recognition. In contrast to rival theories which have war or enmity as the focus of foreign relations, the federative theory relies on the generative properties of compact making and serves as such to de-centre war from this central position within the external constitution. The federative offers the prospect of escaping the paradox of the sovereign state, based on law and peace internally, but geared to prerogative and war externally, and unites the object of the internal and external aspects of the constitution – peace – and the means of achieving that object – law.

As the multitude of sovereign states emerged from a former world of empires, a common assumption has come to dominate the theory of statehood: that the spheres of the domestic and the foreign are fundamentally distinct from each other. The sovereign state has matured as Janus-faced, with one face looking inward, as a sovereign over its subjects, while the other face looks outward, as a sovereign among other sovereigns. Hobbes – and the 'Hobbesian tradition' he seems to have generated – is generally considered the originator of the dichotomy between home and abroad, the inside and the outside. Theodore Christov's Chapter 4, 'Hobbes's Janus-Faced Sovereign', traces

Hobbes's own thought on the nature of the sovereign state within the international sphere and disassociates him from such a common assumption. It argues instead that the domestic constitution of the Hobbesian sovereign is the precondition for the emergence of an international legal framework based in the consent of voluntary states and informed by their practice of the law of nations. The possibility for international legal compliance can be ensured only when states configure their domestic constitutions not as independently sovereign but as interdependently sovereign.

Evan Fox-Decent's Chapter 5, 'Jurisprudential Reflections on Cosmopolitan Law', is a defence of the basic claim that 'the state's public law governing its interactions with non-citizens – the state's cosmopolitan law – must have a certain outward orientation and representative character if it is to be law, properly so-called'. Drawing on earlier work with his frequent co-author Evan Criddle, Fox-Decent invokes the conceptual vocabulary of the 'fiduciary criterion of legitimacy' to denote the stipulation that state action ought always to be intelligible as 'action made on behalf of or in the name of the individual subject to it' if it is to be legitimate, regardless of whether this individual is a citizen or an outsider in some sense. Fox-Decent uses a discussion of Joseph Raz's notion of authority, and of the 'riveting and intractable' problem of 'the non-jurisdictional/jurisdictional distinction to distinguish de facto from legitimate authority', and on this basis constructs his case for the 'fiduciary criterion'. When it comes to the outer boundaries of the constitutional order, this criterion functions as a 'cosmopolitan threshold – not a barrier – that welcomes the entry of peaceful outsiders into sovereign states while empowering states to limit migration when conditions warrant'.

In Chapter 6, 'From Republican Self-Love to Cosmopolitan *Amour-Propre:* Europe's New Constitutional Experience', Alexander Somek uses Rousseau's famous notion of '*amour-propre*' – 'that form of self-infatuation which is mediated by shining in the eyes of others' – as a key towards mediating between patriotism and cosmopolitanism. Somek's defence of what he calls 'cosmopolitan *amour-propre*' against the prominent contemporary alternative of 'constitutional patriotism' leads him to a discussion of the Janus-faced dimensions of international peer review mechanisms for human rights compliance and, similar to Fox-Decent's argument for a 'fiduciary criterion' of legitimacy, to an emphasis on the importance of those outsiders 'legitimately excluded from the constituency'.

II Border Crossings: Comity and Mobility

In Chapter 7, 'The Spectre of Comity', Karen Knop takes up the question '[h]ow do we study doorways and the constitution?' and offers an answer in a deliberately 'explanatory and experimental vein'. Her contribution focuses on the curious introduction, by the Supreme Court of Canada, of 'comity' as a principle of interpretation for the Canadian Charter of Rights and Freedoms. Curious, because, as Knop writes, while the 'constitutionalization of comity is familiar', notably in the area of private international law, 'the "comitization" of the Constitution is not'. Knop analyses four leading decisions by the Supreme Court of Canada, each of which figured 'something(s) called "comity"' as 'a way in which the existence of, dependence on and regard for the Other figure in the Constitution'. Using these four cases, Knop is able to elaborate a history of 'cosmopolitanism introduced into the Constitution by comity', which both reaches further back and is richer – in including also private legal relations – than familiar accounts of the post–Second World War emergence of international human rights regimes in public international law.

Like Karen Knop – and like Audrey Macklin, in her chapter presented below – Jacco Bomhoff, in Chapter 8, 'Constitutionalism and Mobility: Expulsion and Escape among Partial Constitutional Orders', is also principally concerned with the character of constitutionally salient boundaries. In its first part, this chapter explores the contrast between, on the one hand, recognition of the legally mediated character of borders and jurisdictional boundaries in critical scholarship and, on the other hand, unquestioning determinations of 'inside' and 'outside' in judicial practice. The second part of this chapter, then, approaches the question of the character and effects of constitutional boundaries by way of a case study on mobility. Mobility, in its many different forms – its restriction and its excesses, for individuals and for corporations – lies at the heart of many pressing contemporary challenges. The legal treatment of mobility, however, is fragmented across many different specialised fields – from immigration law, to tax law, to international arbitration – in which constitutionalist concerns are rarely central. The chapter aims to address this lacuna by sketching the contours of an 'outward-facing constitutionalism' which could provide the conceptual and normative means to scrutinise the constitutional implications of the regulation of 'access' and 'exit' for both individuals and corporate actors.

In Chapter 9, 'The Inside-Out Constitution', Audrey Macklin engages with Canadian case law on the 'deportability' of non-citizen residents, as a case study on how the protection offered by constitutional rights guarantees is undermined in the field of immigration law. This project, she emphasises, 'is not a "whodunit" – everyone knows the culprit is sovereignty, conventionally understood'. The question to be explored rather is how this conception of sovereignty and its exclusionary effects are 'operationalized in a modern constitution, and at what cost'. Macklin explores this operationalisation of sovereignty in the case law on the state's right to exclude. The guiding image for Macklin's investigation is not so much the two-faced image of Janus but, following the sociologist Didier Bigo, the metaphor of the 'Mobius strip' – 'a rectangular ribbon that has been twisted and then joined'. Whether any claim for constitutional protection raises what Macklin calls an 'inside problem' for a constitutional order is a matter of perspective. Importantly, this alternative metaphor does not deny the existence of insides and outsides: 'it does not contemplate a borderless world, but rather one where borders are relational and perspectival . . . dynamic and contingent, but no less real'.

Asha Kaushal's Chapter 10, 'The Constitution in the Shadow of the Immigration State', also takes as its subjects the relationships between immigration law and constitutional law and between external and internal sovereignty. Kaushal focuses in particular on the importance of immigration to the constitution of 'the people'. As she writes: 'Immigration is both an external objective of the constitutional order and a modifier of that order.' Her chapter approaches these connections between outward projection and inward constitution by way of a conceptual and historical exploration of the relationship between citizenship and constituent power. These concepts, it turns out, surprisingly, are not often discussed in the same frame. Kaushal details what she calls the 'division of labour between immigration law and constitutional law' and the foundational role of the internal/external distinction in that division, through a rich historical overview ranging from Emer de Vattel's public international law to modern Canadian judicial decisions on the Charter's demands in the context of immigration law.

III The Foreign in Foreign Relations Law

In Chapter 11, 'Double-Facing Administrative Law: State Prerogatives, Cities and Foreign Affairs', Geneviève Cartier introduces cities 'as both subjects and agents on the international stage'. Traditionally seen as creatures of domestic law alone, cities are increasingly actively engaged in what is sometimes called 'local foreign policy'. The legal boundary crossings implicated in such local/foreign action require a form of 'normative mediation' between the different fields of law involved: local government, constitutional and international. She develops a double-facing conception of administrative law in which these boundaries do not disappear but are revealed to be 'more porous than is usually assumed'. The resulting processes of normative travel and transfer, as in several of the other double-facing analyses in this volume, go in two directions. External norms and practices affect the content of domestic understandings of city power, while cities rely on their traditional status in domestic law to shape their actions on the international stage.

This broad theme of the reconfiguration of the external and the internal and their interrelationship is also central to Helmut Philipp Aust's Chapter 12, 'The Democratic Challenge to Foreign Relations Law in Transatlantic Perspective'. Aust's topic is the connection between foreign relations law and domestic conceptions of democracy, and in particular the question of 'Who gets to decide on the international commitments of a state?' Populism and a broader inward-turn in the politics of many Western states, Aust writes, mean that 'there is a growing level of discontent with the way that the external sphere is impacting on the internal'. These changing perceptions of 'the international' filter through into different conceptions of foreign relations law, which, in turn, affect the ability of states to cooperate internationally. The chapter presents two variants of foreign relations law – a 'closed' version prevalent in the USA, and a German version traditionally more open to international cooperation. Through a comparative analysis, Aust shows how the openness to international cooperation that was long seen to lie at the heart of the German Basic Law is coming under increasing pressure.

If Geneviève Cartier's contribution looked at foreign relations law and – local – administrative law, and Helmut Aust's chapter at foreign relations law and democratic control, Campbell McLachlan's Chapter 13, 'The Double-Facing Foreign Relations Function of the Executive and Its Self-Enforcing Obligation to Comply with International Law', takes on the role of the executive. McLachlan's starting point is what he calls 'a neglected question that is central to an understanding of the operation of the "double-facing Constitution" in a dualist state' – meaning a state, like the United Kingdom, where domestic law and international law are thought of as operating on separate planes. The question is this: 'If the Constitution grants sovereign law-making power within the state to Parliament, and at the same time allocates the conduct of foreign relations to the executive, to what extent and, if so why, is the executive bound to comply with international law obligations that it has contracted on behalf of the state, but which have not been directly incorporated into domestic law?' Using a case study of the history of advice on international law provided by the Law Officers of the Crown and on recent changes to the wording of the so-called Ministerial Code in the United Kingdom, McLachlan argues that ministers are, and have long been, bound to comply with international legal norms. But he also shows that the content of this obligation to comply has to be clearly distinguished from the question of justiciability, or review by courts. Ultimately, McLachlan's chapter offers a revealing discussion of the intricate 'domestic' workings of foreign relations law and an argument for, and understanding of, the relationship between prerogative powers and constitutional obligations that advances the rule of law.

The theme of the relationship of the double-facing constitution to the rule of law is also central to Dieter Grimm's Chapter 14, 'The Various Faces of Fundamental Rights'. Grimm starts off with the claim that fundamental rights, at their origins, were double-faced – proclaimed as universal, but made positive only through, and in, the laws and territories of states. His contribution then shows how this double-faced character was lost from view, only to resurface in the era of legally binding international human rights instruments. The adoption of these instruments, Grimm argues, 'has changed the conditions under which fundamental rights in state constitutions operate . . . The national bills cannot be interpreted and applied anymore in a purely national perspective. As far as the rights from different sources overlap, both have to be taken into account and accommodated. This brings back the double-faced character to national fundamental rights', this time, though, within the realm of positive law. The focus of Grimm's chapter is on the work of domestic and international courts in accommodating these double-faced rights provisions and their demands, for example through the famous *Solange* jurisprudence of the German Federal Constitutional Court – a ruling that, as Grimm notes, in effect extended the scope of national fundamental rights beyond German territory and rendered them double-faced in the sense that they could now influence international law. Grimm concludes his chapter by returning to his own judicial experience with a variant of the overarching question raised by Helmut Aust: the question of how local institutions – local democracy, local rights protection – can coexist with 'hyperglobalisation'.

With regard to this fundamental dilemma, Grimm's chapter points to a clear diagnosis, in a sense summing up the volume as a whole. In those rare cases 'where inward and outward-looking perspectives converge', and local and global pressures line up neatly, jurists and judges face no great challenges. It is when they do not that matters become precarious and interesting. That is where we enter the much less firmly demarcated realm of Janus and Mobius; of federative alliances and fiduciary obligations; of comity and permeability. The realm, in short, of the double-facing constitution.

Most of the essays in this collection are based on papers presented at a workshop held in June 2017 at the *Wissenschaftskolleg zu Berlin*. We gratefully acknowledge the assistance of Vera Kempa in the organisation of this workshop, as well as the financial and logistical support provided by the *Wissenschaftskolleg*, and the financial support of the Faculty of Law of the University of Toronto, and the Law Department of the London School of Economics and Political Science. During the later stages of this project, we benefited from excellent editorial assistance provided by Mr Amitpal Singh in Toronto and from the support of Marianne Nield at Cambridge University Press.

PART I

Theoretical Foundations

2

The Janus-Faced Constitution

DAVID DYZENHAUS

> This is more than Consent, or Concord; it is a reall Unitie of them all, in one and the same Person, made by Covenant of every man with every man, in such manner, as if every man should say to every man, *I Authorise and give up my Right of Governing my selfe, to this Man, or to this Assembly of men, on this condition, that thou give up thy Right to him, and Authorise all his Actions in like manner*. This done, the Multitude so united in one Person, is called a COMMON-WEALTH, in latine CIVITAS. This is the Generation of that great LEVIATHAN, or rather (to speake more reverently) of that *Mortall God*, to which wee owe under the *Immortall God*, our peace and defence.
>
> Thomas Hobbes[1]

The constitution of the state demarcates a jurisdiction, an area in which the law commands by right. This idea of constitution is complex, first, because it is ambiguous between *constitution as act* and *constitution as achievement*. Contrast, for example, the idea in the social contract tradition that the state is the product of an actual contract between free and equal individuals with the idea of the German constitution, of the Canadian constitution and so on. To use terms currently popular, it is ambiguous between the idea of constituent power – 'we, the people' – and that of constituted powers – the artefact of 'we, the people'.

Second, as the epigraph from *Leviathan* tells us, the idea of constitution suggests not only that what is achieved is greater than the sum of its parts but also that there is an almost magical transformation in these parts that takes place between act and achievement. Here Hobbes picks up on a thought in the first pages of *Leviathan* that human individuals in making this 'Artificiall man' accomplish something that we can take to 'resemble that *Fiat*, or the *Let us make man,* pronounced by God in the Creation'.[2] There is an element of artifice as well as artefact in the creation of this artificial man, especially when, as Hobbes seems to

[1] Thomas Hobbes, *Leviathan*, ed. Richard Tuck (Cambridge: Cambridge University Press, 2014), 120.

[2] Hobbes, *Leviathan*, 9–10.

imply by 'as if' in talking of the covenant, we conceive of the covenant as hypothetical. The individuals should conclude that they had consented because, if they were reasonable, they would have consented.

Finally, the idea is complex because the act of constituting the internal space of the state also necessarily affects the space outside of it as that space is constituted in relation to other constituted jurisdictions. The act of constitution is therefore Janus-faced – it looks both inwards and outwards, which creates another ambiguity.

Janus is usually thought of as the Roman god of doors, and doors can be shut and barred against the outside. But he is also the god of door*ways*, thresholds, passages and transitions, which offers an alternative way of understanding the act of constitution as not an exclusionary but a liminal act. Such an act establishes not so much a barrier as a threshold or point of transition between both spaces and – to complicate things yet further – between times: between past and future. On this latter understanding, the act of constitution not only affects the space outside of it. It is also affected by the legal orders in that space, both with respect to the form in which it is constituted and in that the threshold marks a point which norms can and sometimes must cross to make their way from one space to another, or from one time to another.

I want to use these images to explore three legal relationships in which the Janus-faced aspect of the constitution of the state seems central: the relationship between national law and public international law; the relationship between states that gives rise to private international law; and the reach of the public law norms of a national order beyond the territorial limits of the state in the field of 'foreign relations law'.

If we think of legal orders as spheres,[3] there are two main candidates for understanding a constitution, the 'hermetic conception', which understands the constitution of a national order as establishing a kind of impermeable seal around the national order against the outside, and the 'permeable conception', which understands the constitution as a membrane through which norms may and sometimes must travel.[4] I shall argue for the permeable conception on the basis that it explains better all three legal relationships because it clarifies the ambiguity

[3] For use of the metaphor of spheres in this context, see Jacco Bomhoff, 'The Reach of Rights: The "Foreign" and the "Private" in Conflict-of-Laws, State-Action, and Fundamental-Rights Cases with Foreign Elements' in (2008) 71 *Law and Contemporary Problems* 39.

[4] For the idea of the constitution as a membrane, see Thomas Poole, 'The Constitution and Foreign Affairs' (2016) 69(1) *Current Legal Problems* 148.

between constitution as transformative act and constitution as achievement. More precisely, I shall show that the transformation creates not only the artificial person of the state but also the legal subject, who then can be retrojected as the author of the constitution – the constituent power.[5] She is both source and product of all three of the constitutional legal relationships just mentioned.

This argument seeks to set out the theoretical basis for the recent exploration by several authors of the potential in the methodology of private international law to explain the three relationships in accordance with, as I understand things, the permeable conception.[6] It requires a rather deep dive into an arcane debate between the two great legal positivists of the last century, Hans Kelsen and H. L. A. Hart. Section I sets out Hart's and Kelsen's candidates for what I shall refer to as the 'fundamental constitutional idea', the functional equivalents they propose to Hobbes's claim that a social contract explains the unity of political and legal order. Section II explores the merits of Hart's 'rule of recognition' and Kelsen's 'basic norm' when it comes to the public international law/national law relationship through the lens of the debate between monism and dualism. I argue that the rule of recognition is not up to the task, whereas the basic norm is, though the question then arises whether Kelsen's international law monism can respond to norm conflicts between, on the one hand, international law and national law, and, on the other, between different national orders' regimes of private law. Section III shows not only that Kelsen's position is responsive because he adopts a dynamic account of legal order but also that Hart's static account of legal order cannot perform the task he set for it of moving legal theory from an Austinian account of the commands of a legally unlimited sovereign, to an account of law as a matter of constituted authority. Section IV elaborates Kelsen's dynamic conception and explains why his commitment to the claim that legal order is gapless brings him

[5] As Hans Lindahl has argued, in, for example, 'Constituent Power and Reflexive Identity: Towards an Ontology of Collective Selfhood', in Martin Loughlin and Neil Walker (eds.), *The Paradox of Constitutionalism: Constituent Power and Constitutional Form* (Oxford: Oxford University Press, 2007), 9, 21–22.

[6] See Bomhoff, 'The Reach of Rights'; Karen Knop, 'Citizenship, Public and Private' (2008) 71 *Law and Contemporary Problems* 309; Karen Knop, Ralf Michaels, and Annelise Riles, 'International Law in Domestic Courts: A Conflict of Laws Approach' (2009) 103 *Proceedings of the Annual Meeting (American Society of International Law)* 268; Campbell McLachlan, 'The Allocative Function of Foreign Relations Law' (2013) *British Yearbook of International Law* 349; Campbell McLachlan, *Foreign Relations Law* (Cambridge: Cambridge University Press, 2014).

close to a Dworkinian theory of interpretation in which the assumption of gaplessness is made for ethical reasons. Section V indicates the promise of this method for an understanding of the reach of the public law norms of a national order beyond its borders.

I Rule of Recognition v. Basic Norm

'It is of course possible', Hart says in *The Concept of Law*, 'to imagine a society without a legislature, courts, or officials of any kind'.[7] Thus begins his parable of the emergence of legal order from this 'primitive' society in which the only rules that exist are customary public norms that impose duties on its members.[8] It emerges through the 'introduction ... of rules enabling legislators to change and add to the rules of duty, and judges to determine when the rules of duty have been broken' – 'a step forward ... as important to society as the invention of the wheel'.[9] It gives rise to the 'union' of the 'primary rules' that impose duties with the 'secondary rules' of 'change', 'adjudication' and 'recognition'.[10]

Of these three, the rule of recognition is the most important. It forges the union since it is the rule that specifies 'some feature or features possession of which by a suggested rule is taken as a conclusive affirmative indication that it is a rule of the group to be supported by the local pressure it exerts'.[11] It specifies, that is, the criteria for determining whether any rule, including the other secondary rules, are rules of the order; and its existence is determined as a matter of fact by looking to the accepted practice of legal officials.[12]

The rule of recognition thus seems the functional equivalent of Hobbes's fundamental constitutional idea: the act of constitution that gives rise to the 'reall Unitie of them all'. Hart reinforces this impression when he observes that 'if a system of rules is to be imposed by force on any, there must be a sufficient number who accept it voluntarily. Without their voluntary co-operation, thus creating *authority*, the coercive power of law and government cannot be established'.[13]

7 H. L. A. Hart, *The Concept of Law*, 2nd ed. (Oxford: Clarendon Press, 1994), 90.
8 Ibid., 93.
9 Ibid., 41–42.
10 Ibid., 94–97.
11 Ibid., 94.
12 Ibid., 110.
13 Ibid., 201(Hart's emphasis).

But even if there is this equivalence, most legal positivist philosophers would think that it goes no further than function, not least because, with Hart and his positivist predecessors Jeremy Bentham and John Austin, they utterly reject social contract theory. But more important is that both Hart and his followers suppose his account to amount to a revolutionary moment in the history of legal theory, one that allows much if not all of prior theoretical attempts to articulate the 'key to legal science' to be discarded.[14] It allows philosophy of law for the first time properly to explain legal order in terms of a constitutive, authority-creating idea other than the social contract, something that Bentham and Austin had failed to do because their command theory of law reduced law to the commands backed by coercion of a legally unlimited sovereign and so rejected the thought that legal theory needs a fundamental constitutional idea.

Austin, notably, argued that there is no such thing as constitutional law or international law.[15] What passes for these phenomena amounts, in his view, to rules of conventional morality, not legally binding rules. He substituted for the idea of social contract the fact of the 'habit of obedience' of the majority of those subject to the law. We identify the sovereign of a legal order by finding out who is habitually obeyed and does not obey any other person or body. All we need know about the habit is that there are sufficient sanctions attached to the sovereign's commands to motivate obedience. Hence, legal order can be fully explained as resting on coercion, in terms of might rather than right. But as Hart had argued in an essay in 1958, not only are sovereigns legally limited, but also law is a matter of authority as well as coercion – law 'surely is not the gunman situation writ large'.[16]

The claim that Hart had made this paradigm-shifting discovery of the legal equivalent of the invention of the wheel is, however, curious when

[14] For example, John Gardner, a successor to Hart in the Chair of Jurisprudence in Oxford, reports that Hart was in a state of high excitement when he came up with this idea, fully justified, in Gardner's view, because '[n]othing in the way law has been theorized has been the same since. It is an authentic "Eureka!" moment in the history of ideas'; 'Why Law Might Emerge: Hart's Problematic Fable', in Luis Duarte D'Almeida, James Edwards, and Andrea Dolcetti (eds.), *Reading HLA Hart's The Concept of Law* (Oxford: Hart Publishing, 2013), 81, 96. The idea of the key is to be found in Austin, as quoted by Hart in 'Positivism and the Separation of Law and Morals', in H. L. A. Hart, *Essays in Jurisprudence and Philosophy* (Oxford: Clarendon Press, 1983), 49, 58.

[15] John Austin, *Lectures on Jurisprudence or The Philosophy of Positive Law*, 2nd ed. Vol. 1 (London: John Murray, 1861), 177, 204.

[16] Hart, 'Positivism and the Separation of Law and Morals', 59.

one observes that Kelsen had articulated a similar idea some forty years before when he set out a theory of law in which legal order is a hierarchy of levels of norms at whose apex is a *Grundnorm* or basic norm. We thus need to complicate the trajectory just sketched: we get social contract theory, replaced by the command theory of law, replaced by the basic norm, replaced by the rule of recognition.

Unlike Hart's rule of recognition, the basic norm is not read off the practice of legal officials. It is stipulated by those who wish to make sense of legal order as a meaningful order of norms, as a unity rather than a plurality of competing authoritative demands. The basic norm for Kelsen is key to the science of jurisprudence because it explains how law transforms might into right.[17] Moreover, Kelsen, in the essay in which he first set out his hierarchical theory of legal order, explicitly recognised that the basic norm has a functional equivalence to the idea of the social contract in natural law theories.[18]

Now Hart was fully aware of Kelsen's candidate for the fundamental constitutional idea. But he dismissed it as redundant to an explanation of the authority of law. All one need observe is that there is as a matter of actual official practice a rule that stipulates criteria for the recognition of valid laws and officials manifest their acceptance of this rule by applying the criteria and criticising those who do not.[19] Hart's thought that one need look no further than the fact of accepted rule to explain law's authority is considered by his critics and by some of his followers to be wrong.[20] But there seems little interest in Anglo-American legal theory in investigating whether

[17] See, for example, Hans Kelsen, *Die philosophischen Grundlagen der Naturrechtslehre und des Rechtspositivismus*, where he says that the attempt by the positivist jurist to comprehend law as an objective order through the medium of the *Grundnorm* entails that 'in a certain sense might is transformed into right', in Hans Klecatsky, René Marcic, and Herbert Schambeck (eds.), *Die Wiener rechtstheoretische Schule: Hans Kelsen, Adolf Merkl, Alfred Verdross* Vol. 1 (Vienna: Europa Verlag, 1968), 281, at 339. I shall refer to the translation that appears as an appendix to Hans Kelsen, *General Theory of Law and State*, Anders Wedberg trans. (Cambridge, MA: Harvard University Press, 1945), 389, under the title 'Natural Law Doctrine and Legal Positivism', translated by Wolfgang Herbert Kraus. For the relevant passage, see 437, where 'die *Transformation der Macht zu Recht*' (Kelsen's emphasis) is blandly translated as 'the transformation of power into law'.

[18] Hans Kelsen, 'Die Lehre von den drei Gewalten oder Funktionen des Staates' [1924] in Klecatsky et al., *Die Wiener rechtstheoretische Schule*, Vol. 2, 1625, 1652.

[19] Hart, *The Concept of Law*, 293.

[20] Most prominently among his critics, Ronald Dworkin, and among his followers, Joseph Raz.

Kelsen's basic norm might do better.[21] I shall now conduct such an investigation in the context of the constitutional relationships sketched above.

II The Primitiveness of International Law

Kelsen and Hart seek to restore a fundamental constitutional idea to a central place in legal theory as an integral part of their attempt to explain law as matter of authority. With that idea in place, sovereignty in the sense of ultimate law-making power is understood as legally constituted and both constitutional law and international law are no longer ruled out as conceptual possibilities.

My argument for Kelsen's candidate for the fundamental constitutional idea of the basic norm adopts the lens of the monism versus dualism debate about public international law. In the history of legal theory, both monism and dualism respond to the position that public international law is not law properly so called because there is no world sovereign, in the sense of an ultimate law-making power not subject to anyone else's command, to whom every national state is subject, and who can enforce international rules by threatening and effectively implementing sanctions for non-compliance.

The first attempt to move away from this position was made at the end of the nineteenth century when legal theorists who sought to understand law both as a matter of authority and as the product of a legally unconstrained sovereign will held just this position. For them, there is the inward-looking face of sovereignty – the law of the sovereign that governs relationships between it and its subjects as well as between its subjects – and there is the outward-looking face: the law that governs its relationships with other sovereigns. With both national and international law, the law that binds the sovereign comes about because the sovereign chooses to be so bound. Public international law is, then, interstate law – the product of combined sovereign wills – that becomes part of a national legal order only when the sovereign of that order chooses to make it so.

[21] Though see Lars Vinx, *Hans Kelsen's Pure Theory of Law: Legality and Legitimacy* (Oxford: Oxford University Press, 2007) and Jochen von Bernstoff, *The Public International Law Theory of Hans Kelsen: Believing in Universal Law*, Thomas Dunlap trans. (Cambridge: Cambridge University Press, 2010), 116; Mathijs Notermans, 'Social Peace as *Conditio Tacita* for the Validity of the Positive Legal Order' (2015) 34 *Law and Philosophy* 201.

These theorists thus adopted dualism – a position that does not deny that public international law is law. Instead, it asserts that international and national law are distinct spheres, so that international law norms enter a national legal order only when they are expressly incorporated. There could be wholesale incorporation in a provision of the constitution, but when, as in Britain, Parliament is supreme, incorporation will be by explicit statutory provision. In other words, they adopted the hermetic conception of the constitution in which there is a seal between the two legal spheres that can be penetrated only when the sovereign permits.

Their argument fails as matter of theory, since it amounts to an uneasy compromise between the theoretical view that the sovereign is a legally unlimited entity and the recognition that, as a matter of fact, sovereigns can be legally bound by public law, whether national or international. Because Kelsen and Hart oppose this conception of sovereignty, they do not foreclose the conceptual space for public international law (or national constitutional law) to be genuine law. It could even be said that they argued that legal theory should rid itself to the greatest extent possible of the concept of sovereignty because in political and legal thought it is so bound up with the idea of a legally unlimited political entity. As Kelsen said at the end of his major work on sovereignty, the 'concept of sovereignty should be radically supressed'.[22] The question for both is whether the space opened by constructing sovereignty as a juridical concept permits a positive answer to the question whether public international law is law. Both answer 'yes' to the question, though they find international law problematic because it is 'primitive'.[23]

They also agree that while primitive societies lack legislatures and centralised law-enforcement agencies, the main mark of primitiveness is the lack of a judiciary – of officials who can make authoritative determinations of the law.[24] But they differ radically in that Hart supposes that this institutional lack shows that there is no rule of recognition, which entails for him that there is no legal order: 'there is no basic rule providing general criteria of validity for the rules of international law,

22 Hans Kelsen, *Das Problem der Souveränität* (1928, 2nd ed.) (Aalen: Scientia Verlag, 1981), 320. See Hart, *The Concept of Law,* 221 for similar doubts.

23 Kelsen is unabashed about the use of 'primitive' to describe the international legal order, while Hart is a little more wary, as I shall point out in the text below; see *The Concept of Law,* 227. For an excellent discussion, see Terry Nardin, *Law, Morality, and the Relations of States* (Princeton: Princeton University Press, 1983), 150–58.

24 For Hart, see *The Concept of Law*, 93–94. For Kelsen, see, for example, *General Theory of Law and State,* 327.

and . . . the rules which are in fact operative constitute not a system but a set of rules, among which are the rules providing for the binding force of treaties'.[25] Hence, the analogy with the primitive society, though Hart asserts that the analogy goes only so far: 'In form, international law resembles such a regime of primary rules, even though the content of its often elaborate rules are very unlike those of a primitive society, and many of its concepts, methods and techniques are the same as those of modern municipal law'.[26]

It is significant that Hart sets out his position on 'content, concepts, methods, and techniques' in order to forestall any thought that these 'formal differences between international and municipal law can best be described by classifying the former as "morality"'.[27] The first difference is that when states reproach each other for lapses from public international law they do not resort to the moral language of 'conscience', but to 'technical' arguments based on relevant legal materials.[28] Second, in public international law as in national law there are many rules of the sort 'drive on the left' or a 'valid will requires two witnesses' which are morally neutral but important in order to ensure predictability and certainty.[29] Third, one of the objections Hart had adduced earlier in his book to an analogy between national law and morality is that 'the very idea of change by human legislative *fiat* is repugnant to the idea of morality . . . because we conceive of morality as the ultimate standard by which human actions (legislative or otherwise) are evaluated'. But because there is no legislature for public international law, he said there is 'nothing similarly inconsistent with the idea that the rules might be subject to legislative change'.[30] Finally, while it is often said that the system as a whole must rest on 'a generally diffused conviction that there is a moral obligation to obey its rules', Hart thought that one can dismiss this claim for the same reason that he had dismissed it in the national context. While some states may indeed morally endorse public international law, there is a wide range of other reasons for endorsement – 'calculation of long-term interest, or . . . the wish to continue a tradition or . . . disinterested concern for others'.[31]

[25] Hart, *The Concept of Law*, 236.
[26] Ibid., 227.
[27] Ibid.
[28] Ibid., 228.
[29] Ibid., 228–30.
[30] Ibid., 230. For the earlier discussion, see ibid., 177.
[31] Ibid., 230–32.

This argument is rather strange.[32] Its direction suggests that public international law is law and not morality both because its subjects accept it as mandatory and engage in law-like arguments about its requirements. However, Hart had earlier denied that there is law in the primitive societies from which national legal orders emerge, despite such societies having customary, public rules maintained by criticism of lapses as well as by sanctions, albeit meted out inefficiently by self-help or collective group action.[33] Moreover, other than in two perfunctory endnotes to anthropological literature, Hart did not contemplate the possibility that where such customary norms exist in primitive societies, the group and individuals will deploy the kinds of legalistic techniques to determine their obligations that he finds in the international sphere.[34] Finally, his third reason – the lack of a legislature – speaks to an analogy not a disanalogy between the rules of public international law and those of morality and it is unclear why within his final reason 'disinterested concern for others' is not a moral motive, while 'long term interest' is surely a candidate for one.

Legal theorists sympathetic to Hart's general position, but critical of his treatment of international law, have sought to show that, contrary to his claim, public international law has much more developed secondary rules than he had detected.[35] The path not taken is Kelsen's, perhaps because it is thought that, while Hart may have botched his own argument, he had successfully shown why Kelsen's must fail.

Unlike Hart, Kelsen's path is via his fundamental constitutional idea – the basic norm. For Kelsen, a primitive society has a legal order so long as its members both accept the norms as binding and seek to understand

[32] See Jeremy Waldron, 'International Law: "A Relatively Small and Unimportant Part of Jurisprudence"', in D'Almeida, Edwards, and Dolcetti (eds.), *Reading HLA Hart's The Concept of Law*, 209.

[33] At 94 of *The Concept of Law*, Hart talks about the a 'step from the prelegal into the legal world'. It may seem that 'prelegal' is ambiguous between 'no legal order but law' and 'no law let alone legal order'. But Hart appears to disambiguate when he says on the same page that 'law may be most illuminatingly characterized as a union of primary rules of obligation with such secondary rules'.

[34] Ibid., 291–92. See A. Campbell, 'International Law and Primitive Law' (1988) 8 *Oxford Journal of Legal Studies* 169.

[35] This is Waldron's strategy, 'International Law: "A Relatively Small and Unimportant Part of Jurisprudence"'. For a more elaborate argument along these lines, see Mehrdad Payandeh, 'The Concept of International Law in the Jurisprudence of HLA Hart' (2010) 21 *European Journal of International Law* 967. As Payandeh points out, there is much better evidence for international law's institutional maturity some 40 years after Hart published *The Concept of Law*.

each norm as part of a meaningful unity, thus presupposing the basic norm. Similarly, so long as one can hypothesise a basic norm for the norms of international law, there is in place a legal order, and one that demands obedience from all those subject to it. In the international legal order, as in a primitive society, the subjects – states in the former and individuals in the latter – are at the same time the officials, responsible as they are for interpreting as well as enforcing the public norms of their order.

This difference in turn affects Hart's and Kelsen's answer to the question whether there is public international law. Hart's answer is 'Yes, there is public international law in the sense of discrete binding rules, but no international legal order', while for Kelsen there is public international law *because* there is international legal order.

It is precisely this conception of legal order that leads to Kelsen's opposition to dualism about the relationship between the international sphere, on the one hand, and the national spheres, on the other. But Kelsen also thought that when it comes to dualism about public international law and national law, legal science cannot itself decide between what I shall call 'national law monism' and 'international law monism'. The former insists that only one national legal order exists so that valid legal norms are only those norms that can trace their validity to its basic norm. In contrast, the latter states that there are many valid national legal orders, but they are all part of the international legal order and so trace the ultimate validity of their norms back to the basic norm of the international order. According to Kelsen, the choice between the two versions of monism is determined by political preference, which he thought should be for international law monism.[36] As he put it in his book on sovereignty of 1920:

> There is a generally accepted understanding of the nature and concept of international law that it constitutes a community of states with equal rights. The proposition of the coexistence of a multiplicity of communities, which despite their actual differences in size, population, and effective means of exercising power are of equal value and, when it comes to their mutually delimited spheres of power, are bound in a higher community is an eminently ethical idea and one of the few really valuable and uncontested components of contemporary cultural

[36] See for example, Hans Kelsen, *Introduction to the Problems of Legal Theory*, Bonnie Litschewski Paulson and Stanley L. Paulson trans. (Oxford: Clarendon Press, 1992), 116–17. This is the translation of Kelsen, *Reine Rechtslehre. Einleitung in der rechtswissenschaftliche Problematik* (1934).

> consciousness. But this proposition is only possible with the help of a juristic hypothesis: that above the communities understood as states stands a legal order that mutually delimits the spheres of validity of the individual states in that it hinders incursions by one into the sphere of the others, or at least subjects them all to equal conditions for such incursions.[37]

He concluded that 'when the primacy of international law fulfils this function, the concept of law is simultaneously perfected in a formal and substantive sense. The law attains the organization of humanity and thereby a unity with the highest ethical idea'.[38]

In *The Concept of Law*, Hart did not discuss this argument, presumably because he thought he had already shown that the basic norm is a redundant idea. He confined himself to the dismissive observation that one can do without the 'obstinate search for unity' once one sees that international law consists of discrete rules that states accept as binding.[39] But in two later essays, he attempted to refute Kelsen's international law monism, as well as Kelsen's opposition to dualism of any kind.

On Hart's understanding, Kelsen's 'central argument' for international law monism is the principle of effectiveness in public international law – the principle that so long as a state has an effective legal order, it will be recognised as a valid or legitimate order by international law. Hart called this relationship 'the relationship of validating purport': a norm of one order purports to validate the norms of another.[40] He thought that this argument can be quite easily shown to be wrong by the example of an English statute that purports to validate Soviet law. While this statute would validate Soviet law for the English courts, it would not validate Soviet law in the eyes of the Soviet legal order. Kelsen thus confused, Hart claimed, questions about the content of the law, with questions about the identity of legal systems, which turn not on the content of the law but on their 'mode of recognition'.[41] He concluded that Kelsen's theory 'has a juristic Midas touch, which transmutes all questions about laws and their relationship into questions of the content of law or questions

[37] Hans Kelsen, *Das Problem der Souveränität und die Theorie des Völkerrechts*, 204.
[38] Ibid., 205.
[39] Hart, *The Concept of Law*, 235.
[40] Hart, 'Kelsen's Doctrine of the Unity of Law', in Hart, *Essays in Jurisprudence and Philosophy*, 309, 317–21.
[41] Ibid., 319–21.

concerning what laws say; but the touch is perverse, for not all questions are of that kind'.[42]

But Hart's analysis is wide of the mark.[43] The principle of effectiveness is the principle of international law that validates the effective law of national legal orders. Hart's supposed counterexample is not a norm of public international law, but a positive law enacted in one of the plurality of national legal orders that purports to validate the law of another. It resembles more a choice of law rule in private international law than it does a norm of public international law.

Moreover, the principle of effectiveness is not the basis of Kelsen's argument for monism. Its function in Kelsen's argument is as a recognised norm of public international law that can't be explained as a matter of state consent since it explains why there is in the first place a state that can bind itself by consent. Its validity has therefore to be based on something other than a state-made law. The best explanation is that it is valid because it is part of the unified whole made up of the norms of public international law plus the norms of the different national orders. To conceive of those norms as a unified order, one must presuppose the basic norm of public international law.[44] Kelsen's argument is thus that for there to be a plurality of valid national legal orders, there must be in place an overarching legal order. In this regard, there is only one candidate – the international legal order.

For Hart, it transpires, the issue is whether a national legal order, because it is subject only to law certified by its rule of recognition, is

42 Ibid., 321.

43 For a robust, Kelsenian response to Hart, to which I am much indebted, see Lars Vinx, 'The Kelsen-Hart Debate: Hart's Critique of Kelsen's Legal Monism Reconsidered', in Jeremy Telman (ed.), *Hans Kelsen in America – Selective Affinities and the Mysteries of Academic Influence* (Switzerland: Springer, 2016), 59. My own response differs in that it seeks more to drive to the surface Hart's national law monism.

44 Jacco Bomhoff has challenged the claim that the only option is the international legal order on the basis that one could presuppose that the basic norm of each individual state legal order must be of some (unspecified) character that recognises the influx into that domestic order of some public international law norms and some foreign norms (a basic norm that itself has the character of a choice of law norm, not any posited domestic 'rule of validating purport'). I find this an intriguing possibility, though one would have to answer the question of what generates that necessity if it were not a higher order of legal obligation, i.e. international law. The answer might be that the necessity is generated through a higher law *internal* to each legal order of fundamental principles. This is in fact the position set out by Hermann Heller in his critique of Kelsen in 1927 – see Hermann Heller, *Sovereignty: A Contribution to the Theory of Public and International Law*, David Dyzenhaus (ed. and intro.), Belinda Cooper trans. (Oxford: Oxford University Press, 2019).

thereby sealed off from other national orders as well as from the list of international law norms. He thus not only mistook Kelsen's argument, but also begged the question in favour of dualism and the hermetic concept of the constitution. His example of laws of validating purport have no role in Kelsen's theory of law and are the product of his own mindset – one that adopts the hermetic conception of constitution, and so can only imagine the entry of a norm from one legal sphere into another by dint of a national law of validating purport.[45] Hence, he embraced the dualism of the late nineteenth- and early twentieth-century positivistic theories, despite his rejection of their conception of public international law as will-based interstate law, and his attempt to show against Austin that the positivist tradition is not committed to the denial of the legal status of international law.[46]

It is of course possible that neither the basic norm nor the rule of recognition helps to explain why public international law is valid law. But for the moment I wish only to register the point that if one wants, as Hart surely did, to account for both the fact that law is an authoritative or normative order and the fact of pluralism – of the existence of multiple national legal orders – Kelsen's argument is compelling that one should move up the legal hierarchy and opt for international law monism. Alternatively, one can subtract either factor and make do with just one. If one subtracts authority there is no problem coping with the fact of pluralism, but one gives up on the task of explaining international law as a matter of authority. And if one subtracts the fact of pluralism, one can be a national law monist.

This does not yet show that Kelsen's argument succeeds. It still needs to respond both to the fact that many legal orders are officially dualist and that evidence for dualism goes beyond any official stance because of the fact of norm conflicts between legal orders, whether between two national legal orders, or between the international legal order and a national legal order. But we can start by recognising that Kelsen, unlike Hart, follows through on the project of restoring the fundamental constitutional idea to legal theory by not giving up on that idea when it comes to public international law.

[45] See Alexander Somek, 'Kelsen Lives' (2007) 17 *European Journal of International Law* 409, 426–27.

[46] Hart, *The Concept of Law*, ch. X, 'International Law'.

III Norm Conflict in Private and Public International Law

In Hart's view, the fact of norm conflict between different legal spheres, as well as between the legal and moral spheres, is significant in showing that Kelsen's monism is mistaken.[47] However, Hart does not adduce conflicts between the private law norms of two orders as a problem for Kelsen's theory but for his own. I shall argue in part A of this section that his solution to this problem may presuppose Kelsenian international law monism, so that the question becomes whether that kind of monism can respond to norm conflicts between a national and the international spheres. In Part B, I argue that international law monism can respond appropriately to such conflicts. In the next section, I try to show how this response helps us to understand why Kelsen thought that monism can respond to norm conflicts between law and morality. In the final section, I indicate why Kelsen's response might help us to understand the reach of the public law norms of a national legal order beyond its territorial borders.

A Norm Conflict in Private International Law

Once Hart had 'refuted' Kelsen through the example of a law of validating purport, he turned to various problems that he thought attended his own account of the rule of recognition as a candidate for the fundamental constitutional idea. One such problem arises because '[a]ll civilized systems contain special rules for dealing with cases containing a foreign element . . . These special rules determine both when courts have jurisdiction to try cases with such foreign elements and which legal systems should guide the courts in the exercise of their jurisdiction'.[48]

The problem private international law poses for the rule of recognition is that it seems to invite the conclusion that Hart had rejected in Kelsen. It suggests that 'the laws of one country that are recognized and applied by the courts of another country belong to the legal system of the latter country as well as of the former'.[49] Hart's response to this problem is that when English courts apply the private law of another legal order they do not really '*apply*' the foreign law, 'but . . . a law of their own with a similar

[47] H. L. A. Hart, 'Kelsen Visited', in Hart, *Essays in Jurisprudence and Philosophy* (Oxford: Clarendon Press, 1983), 286, 302.

[48] Hart, 'Kelsen's Doctrine of the Unity of Law', in Hart, *Essays in Jurisprudence and Philosophy*, 309, 340–41.

[49] Ibid.

content to that of the foreign law that they recognize'.[50] According to Hart, this suggestion avoids the conclusion, destructive of the idea of the rule of recognition, that 'laws of one country that are recognized and applied by the courts of another belong to the legal system of the latter country as well as of the former'.[51]

Hart's solution might appear one by *fiat*, rather than by argument. Suppose that a couple gets married in state A, where the only marital property regime is community of property, and divorced in state B, where the only regime is separation of property. The wife argues to a court in B that the law of A should apply, while the husband argues that the law of B should. The court finds that the private international law rule of B is that on divorce the law of the state where the couple were married governs the division of property. Hart's suggestion seems to be that the court of B, in applying A's law of community of property is applying B's law of separation of property.[52]

Kelsen's solution is somewhat like Hart's, though Hart oddly does not refer to it given that it appeared in a book which is one of his main sources in his two critical essays. The difference is both that Kelsen supplies an argument and shows that the kind of solution to which Hart is drawn for norm conflicts in private international law supports international law monism. As a result, the question becomes whether Kelsen's solution is viable for the problem of conflicts in public international law.

[50] Ibid. Hart finds support in the work of W. W. Cook, *The Logical and Legal Bases of the Conflict of Laws* (Cambridge, MA: Harvard University Press, 1924) – see *The Concept of Law*, note 65 at 341.

[51] Hart, 'Kelsen's Doctrine of the Unity of Law', 340–41.

[52] Raz deals with the same problem by denying that the norms of another state become part of the law of the state in which they are applied, even though the courts are under a legal duty so to apply them, which he thinks buttresses his general argument that moral values do not become incorporated into law simply because judges give effect to them. See Joseph Raz, 'Incorporation by Law' (2004) 10 *Legal Theory* 1, at 10–11. For earlier references, see Joseph Raz, 'The Identity of Legal Systems', in *The Authority of Law: Essays on Law and Morality* (Oxford: Clarendon Press, 1983), 78, 97–102, 'The Institutional Nature of Law', ibid., 103, 119–20, 'Legal Validity', ibid., 146 at 149, and Raz, *Practical Reason and Norms* (Princeton: Princeton University Press, 1990, first published 1975), 152–54. There is a direct connection between Hart's claim about private international law and his later readiness to accept the argument of so-called 'inclusive legal positivism' that when a legal order incorporates genuine moral values, and when these determine results in contested cases, one should regard the result as fully determined by legal norms. See Hart's Postscript to *The Concept of Law*, 251–54. In light of the argument of my chapter, inclusive legal positivism is properly understood as another dualist attempt to make sense of legal facts that are at odds with a positivistic stance.

In terms of the example I offered, one can understand Kelsen's argument as follows. The courts of B are obliged to apply the law of A in a private dispute when and only when there is a rule validated by the constitution of B requiring them so to act. But then the 'reason of validity' of the law from A is that it is a 'norm of the legal system of that State', that is, of B.[53] There is no difference between this situation and that obtaining when a revolutionary constitution stipulates that some of the statutes of the old regime 'should continue to be in force under the new constitution'. 'Likewise the norms of so-called private international law prescribing the application of norms of a foreign law to certain cases "refer" to norms of another legal system instead of reproducing the contents of these norms.'[54]

The claim that private international law is 'so-called' is there solely to alert us to Kelsen's argument that there is no issue of international law at stake here, only a matter of what B's law requires. He also objected to the label 'conflict of laws' as, in his view,

> there is no conflict since the foreign law does not claim to be applied by the organs of the State whose private international law is in question; and the latter does not refuse the application. On the contrary. . . . the law of one state prescribes the application of the law of another State; and the latter does not object or demand it. It has no right to do so since it is not really its own law which is applied by the other State. The latter applies norms of its own law. The fact that these norms have the same contents as corresponding norms of another State does not concern the latter.[55]

Finally, Kelsen objects to the label 'choice of law' because there is no choice when a rule of one state requires its courts to refer to the law of another in resolving a dispute. Hence, he would prefer 'reference rules' or 'incorporation rules'.[56] Such a reference rule is distinguished from the 'norm to be applied' but, 'from a functional point of view, the one is essentially connected with the other. Only if they are taken together do they form a complete rule of law'.[57]

Notice that in Kelsen the reference rule, which need not be a statute, is not a rule of validating purport. It is not a rule that purports to confer validity, but a rule that does confer validity. It can be understood as such because B's reference rule validates another private rule of B's law, albeit

[53] Kelsen, *General Theory of Law and State*, 244.
[54] Ibid.
[55] Ibid., 246–47.
[56] Ibid., 247.
[57] Ibid.

one with a content similar to a private law of A, for B's jurisdiction only. Notice also that a consequence of this analysis of private international law is that it introduces a kind of legal pluralism to the legal order of B. Within B, community of property governs the couple married in A, while separation of property governs couples married in B. But that pluralism is made possible by the constitution of B, itself validated by the basic norm of the international legal order.

Things are quite different with international law, because there we move up a level. Indeed, on a Kelsenian conception of legal order, one needs to move up that level to understand why it might be the case that, if there are two national legal orders, one would expect to find that in both there are norms validated by their constitutions that require their courts to apply norms with the same content as the private law norms of the other jurisdiction. If Kelsen is right, the norms of private international law are not norms of international law. But that in all mature legal orders we find the same kinds of formal rules about how to deal with a dispute when an individual seems to be subject to the conflicting private law norms of two jurisdictions, tells us that these rules, albeit of different content, are necessary if that legal order is to take its place in the overarching order of legality.

Just as international law monism explains how we can understand the distribution of public law authority between states such that they are authorised to make law for those subject to their jurisdictions, so it explains why there will be in public international law rules that authorise states to make private international law rules for the adjudication of conflicts between the private law norms of one jurisdiction with another.[58] That is, if we are to make sense of the passage of private law norms from one national sphere to another that create such conflicts, we can do so only if we do not assume the truth of national law monism, which from B's perspective would require the denial of the existence of A as a separate sphere.

Nor can it happen, at least it could not happen as a matter of legal requirement, if the two spheres were, as dualism requires, seen as hermetically sealed solitudes. For if that were the case, some non-juridical explanation of why the sovereign permits entry would have to be supplied, which may account for the popularity of comity-based explanations these days, which are themselves likely relics of Austinian

[58] I am grateful for help in formulating this thought to Michael S. Green and his unpublished paper, 'Monism: An American History'.

positivism about public international law.[59] Indeed, dualism cannot be a coherent theory of how the private law of two national legal spheres relate *legally* to each other. Rather, it is a compromise forged by a national law monism that cannot ignore the fact of the existence of other legal spheres and so reaches for a non-juridical explanation of why there might be what we can think of as norm travel between spheres. Nor, as already suggested, can dualism be a coherent theory of how the law of any national legal sphere relates *legally* to the international law sphere – of how, that is, at least some norms of international law are authoritative for organs of national legal orders even though none of these organs has consented to be bound by them.

In sum, if we find that legal spheres relate to each not as hermetically sealed solitudes, but as separated only by porous membranes that permit or require the passage of norms from one to another, Hart's fundamental constitutional idea is of no help. I have diagnosed as the reason that it is an account of legal order suited to a national law monism that must resort to highly implausible explanations in a bid to account for the binding quality of norms from other legal spheres, for example, the non-juridical idea of comity or Hart's own attempt to understand international law in a way weakly analogous to the primitive society which he had claimed lacked law. But that these explanations are implausible does not show that Kelsen's argument for a legal relationship succeeds. Even if I am right that Kelsen can explain why conflicts between the private law of national legal orders are only apparent, nothing yet follows for conflicts between a national order and the international order.

B Norm Conflict in Public International Law

Since Kelsen's argument about private international law relies on what he thinks of as the 'reference rules' validated by the national constitution,

[59] See Hersch Lauterpacht, 'Diplomatic Protection and Criminal Jurisdiction over Aliens' (1947) 9 *Cambridge Law Journal* 330, at 331:

> This is not the proper occasion for enquiring in detail into the reasons of the fascination which the term 'comity of nations' has exercised over judges and practising lawyers. It is possible that the lingering influence of Austinian positivism which rejects the claim of the law of nations to be law 'properly so-called' may have given added attraction to a vague, non-committal and somewhat pretentious form of words which is on occasions strangely out of keeping with the reality of international relations. However that may be, it is suggested that the term 'comity of nations' is misleading and that there is no such antiquity about it as to make its abandonment impracticable.

which is in turn validated by international law, his position may seem vulnerable to exactly the criticism Hart levels against him.[60] In a legal order such as the UK's, where Parliament is supreme and can enact a law with any content, the constitution permits Parliament to enact a law with a content that contradicts the content of a norm of international law, and UK courts will regard themselves under a duty to uphold that law. For example, one identifies a valid norm, *X*, of the international legal order which requires protection of and a valid statutory norm of the national legal order, –*X*, which requires oppression of a minority and a court within the national order is under a duty to uphold the latter norm. Do we have here an example of norm conflict, created by a norm validated by the constitution, which testifies to the falsity of international law monism and hence to the superiority of Hart's fundamental constitutional idea?

Kelsen's answer is 'no' because this question presupposes an incomplete description of the situation. On the one hand, if one is a national law monist, there is no conflict because there is only one legal order. All norms that are not part of the order can gain entry only if explicitly incorporated, and *X* is not one such norm as shown by the existence of –*X*. On the other hand, if one is an international law monist, things are more complicated. If the claim that the national court must decide in accordance with –*X* depends, as it does in Hart, on the assumption that the UK Parliament is supreme in that it can enact any law it pleases, that assumption is made vulnerable by the basic norm of international law.[61] That basic norm states that Parliament itself gets authority to make law from a higher level of legality – the national constitution – and the constitution is not itself the final source of national authority. It must get its validity from somewhere; according to Kelsen, from the basic norm of international law.

As Kelsen argued, this situation is no more legally problematic than one in which there is a constitution that entrenches rights, but no institution within the legal order has the authority to invalidate a statute that violates one of the rights. Moreover, it is striking that in Britain today – in Hart's own legal order of parliamentary supremacy – this is precisely the situation when under the Human Rights Act (1998) a court may declare a statute incompatible with the state's obligations under the Act but Parliament and the government may choose to take no remedial action.

[60] Hart, 'Kelsen's Doctrine of the Unity of Law', 333–34.

[61] See Lars Vinx, 'The Kelsen-Hart Debate: Hart's Critique of Kelsen's Legal Monism Reconsidered'.

Eventually, the European Court of Human Rights will pronounce authoritatively on whether the state is in breach of its international obligations in leaving the breach of rights in place. But the point is that the situation is no more legally problematic than the one in which no institution within the legal order has the authority to invalidate a statute that violates a constitutional right, but not that it is legally unproblematic; and the fact that the statute is valid from the perspective of the national legal order does not tell us that it is legally unflawed. There is a legal problem in permitting the flawed act to continue to have the force it does which should, from the legal point of view, be remedied as soon as possible.

Kelsen can explain the nuances of this legally problematic situation in a way barred to Hart because, in contrast to Hart's static conception of law in which the law's content is whatever is identified at a particular moment by the rule of recognition, he offers a dynamic conception. The fact that a British court has to uphold the statute that requires at this point in time –*X* is not determinative of the claim that there is a conflict in the legal order that includes at the international level a norm prescribing *X*, because the legal process has not yet come to an end. As Kelsen says of such conflicts at the end of his discussion of international law monism:

> The specific function of juristic interpretation is to eliminate these contradictions by showing that they are merely sham contradictions. It is by juristic interpretation that the legal material is transformed into a legal system.[62]

With this dynamic view of the function of juristic interpretation, we can understand how international law may not only prescribe *X*, but also permit organs within a national order to prescribe –*X*. For it remains the case that while at the national level –*X* will prevail for the time being, at the international level the state is bound to bring its national law into line with international law. There might be no independent body that can pronounce definitively on this issue, nor a body other than another state that is entitled to and can force compliance. But that would show only that the international legal order is defective from the internal perspective of legality because it failed to provide the institutional resources that help to ensure that states will fulfil their obligations. Indeed, the dynamic process of interpretation, once unleashed by the presupposition of the basic norm, brings such institutional problems to the surface. And when

[62] Kelsen, *General Theory of Norm and State*, 375.

they are on the surface, they demand attention, both as problems that need immediate solutions and as problems that might require institutional reform to prevent their reoccurrence, so maintaining what we can think of as the rule-of-law project.

Notice that, as was the case with private international law, in order even to conceive of this kind of conflict, one must abandon national law monism. Far from denying the possibility of a conflict arising between norms from different legal orders, international law monism makes it possible to understand how there *could* be such a conflict in the first place by postulating an intrinsic connection between the orders because they are both *legal* orders.[63] This is not to say that states cannot be more or less dualist in practice, if all that is meant by this label is that states will have different ways of giving shape to their relationship with the order of public international law. From a theoretical perspective that seeks to understand law's normativity, however, this is not really dualism because international law monism is the theory that explains why states are under a prior obligation to give shape to that relationship. States can do a better or worse job of this, just as they can do a better or worse job of arranging their national constitutional order, or their rules of private international law under that order.

We must therefore be careful to distinguish between dualism as a description of actual state practice and dualism as a theory of international law. The former is an account of how many states in fact order their relationship with international law given an international monistic view of the obligation so to do. The latter, as in Hart, conflates that account with a theory of international law in a way that perpetuates the problems of the command theory of law. The choice for national law monism is not, then, as Kelsen suggested, suspect on grounds of political morality alone. Dualism as a theoretical position is an attempt to abandon national law monism without embracing international law monism. But that leaves it uneasily perched between a conception of sovereignty as prepolitical and thus legally unlimited, as in Austin's command theory of law, and a conception in which sovereignty is understood to be

[63] See, for example, the contrasting positions set out in Matej Avbelj and Jan Komárek (eds.), *Constitutional Pluralism in the European Union and Beyond* (Oxford: Hart Publishing, 2012) by Mattias Kumm, 'Rethinking Constitutional Authority: On the Structure and Limits of Constitutional Pluralism', 39, and Alexander Somek, 'Monism: A Tale of the Undead', 343.

legally constituted by one's candidate for the fundamental constitutional idea.[64]

Hart's difficulties with accounting for international law are, therefore, symptomatic of a more general problem with his candidate for a fundamental constitutional idea. It cannot perform the task he set for it of moving legal theory from Austin's reductive account of law as a matter of command and coercion to an account of law as a matter of constituted authority. As I shall now show, this problem persists into Hart's criticism of Kelsen when it came to the latter's opposition to dualism about another relationship – this time the relationship between what we can think of the legal and the moral spheres. From Kelsen's position on this issue, we can draw out the implications of the discussion so far for the legal relationship not yet addressed: the reach of the public law norms of one national order into the jurisdictions of other states.

IV Content, Concepts, Methods and Techniques

Recall that Hart said of public international law that '[i]n form it resembles . . . a regime of primary rules, even though the content of its often elaborate rules are very unlike those of a primitive society, and many of its concepts, methods and techniques are the same as those of modern municipal law'.[65] As we know, by 'form' Hart had in mind that because there is no rule of recognition for international law, the test whether a particular norm is law turns on whether it happens to be one of a list of discrete international law norms that happen to be accepted by the states that make up the international society of states. In that respect, he thought that the rules of international law are like the primary rules of a primitive society.

But, as Hart stated, he did not wish to push the analogy too far for two reasons. First, the content of the rules of international law is much more elaborate than those of a primitive society, presumably more akin to the legal rules of a national legal order. Second, again presumably, the practice of determining the content of these rules looks very much like that of national legal orders because sophisticated legal techniques are required and these are wielded by bodies of professional lawyers, including lawyers who staff the various international administrative bodies, judicial

[64] Hart, 'Positivism and the Separation of Law and Morals', 58–62. See Michael S. Green, 'Marmor's Kelsen', in Jeremy Telman (ed.), *Hans Kelsen in America*, 31, 41 note 18.

[65] Hart, *The Concept of Law*, 227.

bodies, arbitration courts, etc., when these exist. As we also know, Kelsen did not suppose that there is a difference in form. His formal requirement is not that there exists a judicial institution that can pronounce finally on whether a rule is a rule of international law. Rather, it is that those who wish to work out their legal obligations must presuppose that the norms that give rise to these obligations are part of a unified whole, which in turn requires presupposing the basic norm. Legal order is created when juristic interpretation of this sort can occur.

His position and Hart's are, then, similar in that they both see as a necessary but not sufficient condition for the existence of legal order that there are norms that are effective in that those subject to them comply with them most of the time. But they differ when it comes to the other necessary condition for there to be legal order. For Hart, it is acceptance by officials of a rule of recognition, while for Kelsen it is the ability to presuppose a basic norm. As I have suggested, this makes Hart's position incoherent as he asserts both that there is no law in primitive societies because there is no rule of recognition and that there is international law despite the fact that there is no rule of recognition. That leaves him unable to explain how states are under a legal obligation to obey international law since for him legal obligation presupposes the existence of a rule of recognition and there is no such rule in the international sphere. In contrast, Kelsen is not troubled by any incoherence. For him, there must be legal order before there can be law and the ability to presuppose the basic norm in attempting dynamic juristic interpretation, not any institutional fact, is all that is needed besides the sheer existence of effective norms.

Put in this way, Kelsen's emphasis on the dynamic nature of legal order, the importance of juristic interpretation in creating that order understood as a meaningful whole and the role of unity in the process of interpretation makes his legal theory look, perhaps surprisingly, quite similar to Ronald Dworkin's interpretative theory of law.[66] After all, for Dworkin, the key to legal theory resides in appreciating how judges in the process of deciding 'hard cases' – legal questions on which there is reasonable disagreement as to the outcome – seek to interpret the positive law in light of a guiding aim of showing how the legal order as

[66] For a rare discussion of the similarities between Kelsen and Dworkin, see Tony Honoré, 'The Basic Norm of a Society', in Stanley L. Paulson and Bonnie Litchewski Paulson (eds.), *Normativity and Norms: Critical Perspectives on Kelsenian Themes* (Oxford: Oxford University Press, 1998), 89, 109–12.

a whole lives up to an ethical ideal of 'integrity', which is Dworkin's candidate for the fundamental constitutional idea.[67]

Indeed, Dworkin, early in his career, noted an affinity between his theory and Kelsen's in a little-known response to Hart's critique of Kelsen's monism on the basis of conflicts between norms.[68] Dworkin argued that Hart had failed to properly recognise two different senses of validity at play in Kelsen's work. First, there is the sense that attaches to the statement that a norm is valid because it is created in accordance with the basic norm of a legal order; it has, that is, to do with the same kind of problem that the rule of recognition seems designed to solve. The second sense, Dworkin said, has to do with the 'dynamics of legal reasoning, and in particular with the structure of an argument that ends in the decision that some man or some official ought to do something, meaning not that he has good reasons for doing it, but that it is, on balance, what he must do'. Here validity attaches to a 'conclusory statement' that presupposes the validity of one basic norm, that is one norm that '"is binding" on the particular official and persons concerned'.[69]

Dworkin then offered his own analysis of a passage Hart objected to in which Kelsen, addressing possible conflicts between law and morals, said that 'an individual who regards law as a system of valid norms has to disregard morals as such a system . . . no viewpoint exists from which both morals and law may simultaneously be regarded as valid normative orders. No one can serve two masters'.[70] According to Dworkin, the 'key words here are "viewpoint" and "simultaneously"; Kelsen's view is that one person cannot regard both norms as valid in the sense of deciding the issue of what he ought to do on some occasion'. Hence, '[w]hen Kelsen says that if international law and municipal law conflicted, we could not speak of them both as valid at the same time, he means that someone who had to decide what he ought to do – a judge for instance – could not treat

[67] Ronald Dworkin, *Law's Empire* (London: Fontana, 1986), 110.

[68] H. L. A. Hart, 'Kelsen's Doctrine of the Unity of Law', in Howard E. Kiefer and Milton K. Munitz (eds.), *Ethics and Social Justice* (Albany: State University of New York Press, 1968), 171. Ronald Dworkin, 'Comments on the Unity of Law Doctrine (A Response)', in ibid., 200. As before, I shall refer to Hart's essay as reprinted in Hart, *Essays in Jurisprudence and Philosophy*, 309.

[69] Ibid.

[70] Hans Kelsen, *Pure Theory of Law*, Max Knight trans. (Cambridge, MA: Harvard University Press, 1945), 329.

them both as valid in the conclusory sense, could not, in Kelsen's phrase, serve two masters'.[71]

In making this point, Dworkin implicitly asserted a connection between Kelsen and his own (at this point still rather embryonic) theory of law. But we need to recall that Kelsen, like Hart, differed from Dworkin in that he did not offer a theory of adjudication – of how judges should decide hard cases – since such a theory was, he thought, a political theory beyond the scope of legal science. Like Hart, he emphasised that there is an irreducible moment of official creativity not only in legislation but also in interpretation and application of the law. Juristic interpretation for Kelsen is not therefore the same as judicial interpretation in Dworkin's legal theory, in which judges strive to find a theory that shows the relevant law in 'its best moral light' which then determines the 'one right answer' in a hard case.[72]

However, unlike Hart and his followers, Kelsen denied that there are gaps in the legal order.[73] On his account, a legal order provides seamlessly for an authorised official to solve by a legal procedure any problem raised within the legal order. In this respect, Kelsen's argument is again closer to Dworkin than it is to Hart's legal positivism, though he rejects a distinction that Dworkin relies on between legislation – the instrument of policy and the province of the legislature – and adjudication – the realm of principle and the province of the judiciary.[74] For Kelsen, the moment of creativity in legislation is much more heightened than in adjudication, but it is quantitatively rather than qualitatively different. Legislation is a legally authorised act that must respect the constitutional norms that govern its production. Similarly, the executive implementation of legislation requires official creativity, though a quantitatively smaller amount than legislation since it must respect both constitutional

[71] Dworkin, 'Comments on the Unity of Law Doctrine (A Response)', 201. (Dworkin is referring to the passage from Kelsen, *Pure Theory of Law*, 329 quoted in the text above.) His point shows, in my view, why Alexander Somek's illuminating work on these issues goes wrong in one fundamental respect. Somek says that legal positivists such as Hart fail to see that the relevant question for Kelsenian monism is always, 'What can happen next?' See Somek, 'Monism: A Tale of the Undead', 354–55. But Kelsen's question is not about prediction. It is: 'What *should* happen next?'

[72] Ibid.

[73] Hans Kelsen, *Pure Theory of Law*, 245–50.

[74] Ronald Dworkin, *Taking Rights Seriously*, 2nd ed. (Cambridge, MA: Harvard University Press, 1978).

norms and whatever legislated norms officials are charged with concretising.[75]

These rather subtle differences between Kelsen, on the one hand, and Hart's and Dworkin's legal theories, on the other, are important. Hart's legal theory is problematic because it consigns legislation and much adjudication and executive implementation of legal norms to an extra-legal realm. As I have argued elsewhere, the arbitrary individual at the apex of the political order – the legally unlimited sovereign of the command theory of law – is repressed, only to pop up whenever an official has to make a decision.[76] Dworkin's theory is often accused of falling prey to the opposite problem. Law's control becomes total as he equates law implausibly with the rule of liberal principles, as interpreted by judges, so that it is in his theory that Kelsen's ambition of the radical suppression of sovereignty is achieved. Kelsen, as I shall now explain, offers a theory that can navigate between these two extremes.

I sketched above Dworkin's criticism of Hart for having confused Kelsen's two distinct conceptions of validity: on the one hand, the conception that attends to certification of a norm as a valid member of a legal order, on the other, validity in the 'conclusory' sense that pertains to what an individual, apparently subject to the conflicting norms of two different normative orders, must do. In my view, his criticism of Hart is correct, but the two conceptions are better understood as two of the three dimensions of Kelsen's conception of validity.

First, and corresponding to validity as certification, there is the dimension of vertical validity, which can be understood as a ladder of formal authorisation that stretches from the lowest rung at which legal norms are concretised to the highest rung at which the most constitutional authorising norms reside. The second dimension of validity derives from the idea of the unity of the legal system, which tells us that an act must be more than formally authorised. Its content must be one that can cohere with the content of other relevant legal norms – substantive norms as well as formal authorising norms – within a unified field of legal meaning. This second dimension of validity thus accrues to a norm through being part of a unified field of meaning.

The third dimension of validity corresponds to the conclusory conception and it arises out of the way in which the other two dimensions

[75] See Lars Vinx, *The Guardian of the Constitution: Hans Kelsen and Carl Schmitt on the Limits of Constitutional Law* (Cambridge: Cambridge University Press, 2015), 48–49.

[76] See David Dyzenhaus, 'Positivism and the Pesky Sovereign' (2011) 22 *European Journal of International Law* 363.

work in combination. When a legal official is deciding on what someone must, legally speaking, do, the official's own duty is to justify the directive he issues – backed as it is by the state's coercive power – as being in accordance with the law. It is a necessary condition of such justification that the official in fact is legally authorised to issue that directive. But this procedural condition – the *ultra vires* condition specified by English administrative law – does not suffice. The content of the norm must also be substantively justifiable as a norm that fits within the unified field of legal meaning made up of substantive as well as formal norms. In other words, besides the ladder of formal authorisation there is what we can think of as the ladder of substantive concretisation.[77] When legal officials exercise their formal interpretative authority, they are also giving further content to the norm or norms they are interpreting, which requires an act of creative judgment. But, while creative, the judgment is constrained by the requirement that its content is understandable as a norm within a unified field of legal meaning. And that constraint distinguishes Kelsen's theory from Hart's legal positivism in which formal criteria of validity function as a kind of on/off switch for the certification of laws. For Kelsen, such criteria serve to identify the basis for a law-governed, though creative, process of interpretation which produces the content of the law.

Kelsen usually portrayed this requirement as epistemological, driven by the scientific need to demonstrate that the norms of the order cohere. But that suggestion raises the question of the audience for the demonstration, and the answer to that question shows that the requirement is an ethical one.[78] The first possible candidate is the officials themselves, which we should recall is the audience Hart identifies when it comes to the rule of recognition. According to him, only the officials need accept the rule of recognition. They must regard it as providing 'common standards of official behaviour and appraise critically their own and each other's deviations as lapses'.[79] But as Joseph Raz – Hart's most influential student – argued, the official perspective cannot be so confined. After all, the officials are applying rules to the other possible audience, the legal subjects, and in doing so placing the subjects under a duty to act which, should they not comply, makes them vulnerable to official sanctions. The officials thus must believe, or at least insincerely

[77] For my understanding of Kelsen on this topic, I owe much to Vinx, *Hans Kelsen's Pure Theory of Law: Legality and Legitimacy*, ch. 3.
[78] As Hermann Heller pointed out in 1927 in *Sovereignty*.
[79] Hart, *The Concept of Law*, 116–17.

manifest the belief, that the authority they wield is legitimate from the perspective of the legal subjects. Raz argued further that if legal theory is to understand law as a matter of authority, it should adopt this perspective and he found it articulated in Kelsen, in the figure he dubs 'Kelsen's legal man' who adopts 'the law as his personal morality, and as exhausting all the norms he accepts as just'.[80]

In response to Raz, Hart admitted that his account seems committed to the 'paradoxical', even confused, conclusion that 'judicial statements of a subject's legal duties need have nothing directly to do with the subject's reasons for action'. But he persisted with it because he regarded the moral component in Raz's account as too unsettling for his Separation Thesis which is committed to maintaining dualism in regard to the moral and legal spheres. The same worry manifests itself in Hart's first essay on Kelsen's legal theory in which he offers a response to Kelsen's 'alarming' claim that it is not possible to serve two masters when it comes to law and morality.[81] Hart said that while this point addresses the situation of conflict in which an individual has to act and is subject to duties by two conflicting norms he accepts as valid, it does not address the situation of an individual who wishes to make a moral criticism of the law for, say, requiring military service, even though he himself is not liable for such service.[82]

Hart has other criticisms.[83] But I shall focus on the thought he found 'alarming' that Kelsen's argument 'excludes the possibility of a moral

[80] Contrast Raz, 'Kelsen's Theory of the Basic Norm', in *The Authority of Law*, 142–43, and Stanley L. Paulson, 'The Weak Reading of Authority in Hans Kelsen's Pure Theory of Law' (2000) 19 *Law and Philosophy* 131. Paulson has argued elsewhere that Kelsen was not seeking to answer 'the classical question in political and legal philosophy: How is our obligation to obey the law justified?' Rather, his argument about normativity is located in the methodological disputes of his day, and he offers normativity as 'an alternative to psychologism and naturalism in legal science'. Stanley L. Paulson, 'A "Justified Normativity" Thesis in Hans Kelsen's Pure Theory of Law?: Rejoinders to Robert Alexy and Joseph Raz', in Matthias Klatt (ed.), *Institutionalized Reason: The Jurisprudence of Robert Alexy* (Oxford: Oxford University Press, 2012), 61, at 111. That Kelsen's theory of normativity was developed in this context does not of course tell us whether his conception was, perhaps despite himself, one of justified normativity and in this respect I side with Alexy and Raz, though I get to the Kelsenian idea of justified normativity by a different route.

[81] H. L. A. Hart, 'Kelsen Visited'. Hart refers to Kelsen, *General Theory of Law and State*, 373–75, 408–10. The discussion of national and international law is at 373.

[82] Hart, 'Kelsen Visited', 302–03.

[83] In my opinion, Hart's other main criticisms misfire. One is that Kelsen's account of a collision of duties is of a psychological collision, where a person thinks he is faced with conflicting duties when in fact he is not. Hart, ibid., 303–05. But Kelsen's point is that,

criticism of law'.[84] As he put it, '[n]o human being is *just* a lawyer or *just* a moralist. Some at least think about both moral and legal norms and consider their meaning as norms and find that they conflict'.[85] Hart's observation is of course right. Nevertheless, as Kelsen could have retorted, this is not his but Hart's problem: Hart cannot explain why this individual should experience any normative conflict in the first place, given his general view that legal norms do not of themselves have any morally binding force.

In fact, Raz's description of the legal subject in Kelsen is a little misleading. The question for Kelsen is precisely how to make sense of legal order from the perspective of an individual faced with a conflict between her 'personal morality' – the moral norms she herself holds dear – and the norms of her legal order, which she also accepts as valid. Moreover, in the perspective of a legal theory that understands law as a matter of authority, this individual is the legal subject, and so is not faced with an abstract conflict between the norms of two valid orders. Rather, she stands on the very particular ground of someone who needs to find out what her obligations are given that she is already subject to the rule of law – to the public order of law in which she happens to find herself. She must, that is, be able to find an answer to her question that also makes sense of the presumption that she should subject herself to the norms of that legal order even when these conflict with her personal morality.

This is a kind of relativism.[86] The legal subject accepts that the modern legal order is legitimate when some or even many of its norms do not correspond with her sense of right and wrong, and so she should regard

given that the person is not faced with an actual conflict, the conflict in pulls has to be explained psychologically, not as a matter of normative collision – Kelsen, *General Theory of Norm and State*, 375. Hart also says that there is no problem in asserting that there is a conflict between two ought statements of the sort 'there are good reasons for doing *A*', for example, 'there are good legal reasons for doing *A* and good moral reasons for not doing *A*'. Hart, 'Kelsen Visited', 307–08. But the issue for Kelsen is what must be presupposed by the person who must decide between doing *A* or not, as we saw Dworkin argue above. In my view, the same point undermines Hart's other objections. In general, Hart seems to assume that because we can, say, assert without contradiction that the law of country X requires *A* and the law of country *Y* requires -*A*, we can thereby identify a contradiction between two valid systems of norms. But, as I have argued, we need to ask that question not from the perspective of an external observer, but from the perspective of a judge faced with a dispute in private international law, who must decide which system's norms are valid for the purpose of determining the result.

84 Ibid., 302.

85 Hart, 'Kelsen Visited', 306 (Hart's emphasis).

86 See Raz, 'Legitimate Authority', in Raz, *The Authority of Law* 3, at 10–11, where he sketches in order to reject the idea of 'relativized authority', a way of referring to 'what

particular laws as binding on her whatever their content. She thus in this sense relativises her convictions in regard to both the convictions of her fellow subjects and the public judgements that are established as mandatory by the law. The idea here has something in common with Kelsen's well-known claim that the law can have any content as well as with Hart's suggestion that one of the features of 'authoritative legal reasons'[87] is that they are 'content-independent' – they are 'intended to function as a reason independently of the nature or character of the actions to be done'.[88] It differs, however, from Hart's account in respect of a feature that for Hart, and Raz following him, is implicit in the feature – that in order to function as a content-independent reason the content of the law has to be determinable as a matter of fact, that is, 'without using moral arguments'.[89] The difference, put somewhat paradoxically, is that on my understanding in order for a reason to function as a content-independent authoritative legal reason, its content must be both determinable and determined in such a way that the legal subject can make sense of her subjection to it.

This figure has much in common with the person Karen Knop has argued is at the heart of private international law. Standardly, private international law is taken to be a matter of working out the collisions between the private law norms from different systems. Knop suggests that this view has to be refined. In her view, private international law is about a private side of citizenship captured in the figure of the 'legal citizen' – the person who is entitled to sue and be sued in certain courts.[90] And she shows how what she calls private international law's 'cosmopolitan form' – its 'techniques' for dealing with the applicability of foreign law – allows it to bring a very concrete focus to contentious moral questions about 'inclusion and exclusion'.[91]

More recently, in a discussion of the application of international law norms by domestic courts, Knop (with Ralf Michaels and Annelise Riles) has argued that such techniques offer an alternative to the binary options

those people or societies accept or propose as legitimate authority without endorsing those views'.

[87] Hart, 'Commands and Authoritative Legal Reasons', in Hart, *Essays on Bentham: Studies in Jurisprudence and Political Theory* 244, 252–53.

[88] Ibid., 254.

[89] Raz, 'Legal Positivism and the Sources of Law', in Raz, *The Authority of Law*, 37, 47–48.

[90] Karen Knop, 'Citizenship, Public and Private' (2008) 71 *Law and Contemporary Problems* 309, 310. Here she relies on J. G. A. Pocock, 'The Ideal of Citizenship Since Classical Times' (1992) 99 *Queen's Quarterly* 33.

[91] Ibid., 313.

that courts must always apply such norms or not apply them unless required by national law to do so.[92] They call this alternative 'theory through technique':

> We do not resolve the question of whether international law applies in all circumstances, or even whether this international law applies in all circumstances. We seek to answer only the question of whether this international law applies to these litigants with respect to these specific legal rights and this particular dispute. For example, whereas countless scholars ask whether international law is democratically legitimate, we ask whether its application in the particular context is justified. This does not make the question small; it makes it concrete.[93]

In their view, this approach requires what they call a 'submission' to 'the constraint of legal form', though they add that their invocation of formalism should be understood in the spirit of L. Lon Fuller and his argument that legal fictions are devices we adopt not because we think them to reflect reality, but rather because we need them in our attempt to make sense of reality.[94] I shall now attempt to elaborate a little the idea of form that I believe to be at stake.

V Against Geographical Legality[95]

The lines just quoted from Knop, Michaels and Riles respond to an example of norm conflict that is a twist on the earlier example of an

[92] Karen Knop, Ralf Michaels, and Annelise Riles 'International Law in Domestic Courts: A Conflict of Laws Approach', 273, responding in part to Mattias Kumm, 'The Legitimacy of International Law: A Constitutionalist Framework of Analysis' (2004) 15 *European Journal of International Law* 907.

[93] The authors rely on the European Court of Justice's decision in *Kadi,* Case C–402/05 P and C–415/05, *P. Kadi and Al Barakaat International Foundation* v. *Council and Commission* [2008] ECR I–6351.

[94] Knop, Michaels, and Riles 'International Law in Domestic Courts: A Conflict of Laws Approach'. See Lon L Fuller, *Legal Fictions* (Stanford: Stanford University Press, 1967), and his reliance on Hans Vaihinger's 'as if' philosophy.

[95] In the course of his speeches in the cause of the impeachment of Warren Hastings, Governor-General of Bengal from 1773 to 1785, Edmund Burke famously protested against the view that morality is 'geographical' – the view that one set of public standards governed the way British public officials should act in Britain and another less exacting or hardly exacting at all governed their actions when abroad. On that view, Hastings should not be tried and convicted for his abuses of authority while in office because he was entitled to act in ways that would be regarded as violations of fundamental standards of law and morality at home. See Jennifer Pitts, 'Edmund Burke's Peculiar Universalism', in her *A Turn to Empire: The Rise of Imperial Liberalism in Britain and France* (Princeton: Princeton University Press, 2005), 59, especially 78–85, and Thomas Poole, *Reason of*

international law norm that requires –*X* (the morally admirable norm of non-discrimination) when a national law norm requires *X* (the morally repugnant norm of discrimination). In this new case, –*X*, a resolution of the Security Council, requires that individuals who are considered by a special committee of the Council to be connected to terrorist networks should be subject to criminal-like sanctions that affect important rights and interests without being offered any opportunity to contest or even to know the case against them. In contrast, *X* is the constitutional norm of the national order, generally agreed to be a universal norm of legality, that requires that no one should be subject to sanctions that affect important rights and interests unless he has first had an appropriate opportunity to contest the case against him before an impartial tribunal. A challenge is raised by an individual in a court of national jurisdiction A to a regulation enacted in that jurisdiction that implements the international law norm and in terms of which he has been subject to the sanctions.[96]

This example might seem to pose a problem for international law monism, if the position requires that international law norms always trump national law norms in cases of conflict. In that case, the court in A would have to apply the constitutionally repugnant norm in deciding a case within its national jurisdiction. But the example poses such a problem only if one visualises the union of the international legal order and national legal orders as existing on a plane levelled out by international law because its norms cause to be ejected from the plane any national law norm the content of which contradicts that of an international law norm. In this vision, the duty of a domestic court or any other law-applying and law-interpreting institution is to decide in favour of international law whenever such a conflict arises, and whatever the content of the norm.

But, as we can see from my discussion above of Hart on international law, this way of understanding the problem is not the product of the kind of international law monism developed here. Rather, it is the product of an international law monism that is the mirror image of a national law monism that seeks to come to terms with the fact of existence of international law, but whose static conception of law results in dualism and its dogma of incorporation. In both, all that matters is whether the content

State: Law, Prerogative and Empire (Cambridge: Cambridge University Press, 2015), 151–64.

96 See the discussion in Gráinne de Burca, 'The European Court of Justice and the International Legal Order after *Kadi*' (2010) 51 *Harvard International Law Journal* 1.

of a norm of the sphere to which it gives priority appears to contradict the content of a norm from another sphere that has a claim to be applicable in the matter. In that case, the norm from the privileged sphere must win. By contrast, an international law monism that adopts a dynamic conception of the law will not readily assume that there is a conflict between international law and national law in which one winner must emerge. Rather, the imperative to display overall unity drives a good faith interpreter to try to find a content for a conclusory norm that displays its identity with the relevant norms.

My emphasis on the dynamic aspect of this kind of international law monism is of course meant to alert us to the possibility that a court might find an interpretative way out of the problem. In the famous words of a common law judge in a case in 1863, where the legislation under review did not provide for a hearing prior to the state's demolition of property: 'although there are no positive words in a statute requiring that the party shall be heard yet the justice of the common law will supply the omission of the legislature'.[97] A judge may, that is, try to find a way to interpret the international law norm subject to the national constitutional norm with the result that no sanctions could be imposed without the person being given an opportunity to contest the case against him.

But this emphasis also alerts us to more than the interpretative option, as it is not the only one available, nor even – depending on the circumstances – the best one. The judge may find that the problem is not resolvable by interpretation at the national level, so it must be moved to the international level. She can attempt that move by making the equivalent of a declaration of incompatibility under the Human Rights Act. That is, she can recognise the formal validity of the regulation while pointing out very explicitly its constitutional flaw, which is, she should note, not a flaw merely because of a contingent feature of A's national constitution, but also a flaw from what we might think of as the very commitment to constitutionalism.

Now there are differences, notably, there is by assumption no national political body that can respond legislatively, nor any court at the international level that has authority to provide an interpretive solution. But there is the Security Council, the international body that issued the resolution, and which is capable of reforming the institutional set up for listing individuals in ways that conform to norms of fairness or due process. That body is under no legal obligation to respond in the sense

[97] Byles J in *Cooper* v. *Wandsworth Board of Works* (1863) 14 CB (NS) 180, 194.

that there is another body which can order it so to. But it is important to recall that we need not be confined in our understanding of fidelity to law by the theoretical blinkers of the command theory of law. As those who could make these reforms look down the ladders of formal authorisation and material concretisation, they will have to contemplate that national courts and other bodies are having constitutional and legal difficulty concretising the positive norm they have created. The criticism these difficulties elicit, as well as the occasional decision in which national or other courts find an interpretative solution that precludes application of the norm provide significant incentives for those who could make the reforms, *if* they wish to be seen as ruling by law and not by means of unmediated coercive power.[98]

Three features of dynamic international law monism fall out of this example. First, whichever solution seems appropriate – interpretative, institutional or some combination – its motivation is the regard that must be displayed for the legal subject whose interests are affected by an official decision, yet wishes to make sense of her subjection to law as a matter of authority or legal right rather than unmediated coercive power. Second, institutions located at the lower levels of the ladder of formal authorisation are under a duty to apply and interpret the law as if those with authority to enact legislative or quasi-legislative norms intended those norms to be interpreted as part of a unified field of meaning that includes constitutional norms of legality. Third, as this interpretative presumption suggests, the task of upholding the rule of law is not one that is exclusively the preserve of the judiciary, since it is as much the task of executive and legislative institutions. That judges are either not authorised to deal with a certain kind of dispute, or should not be authorised, in no way entails that the dispute is one to be settled politically, where 'political' settlement is equated with extra-legal action.

As Campbell McLachlan has pointed out in his work on the rule of law in foreign relations law, the fact that the judiciary might be excluded from a certain area of law may mean only that the law has allocated guardianship of rule of law in that area to some other institution, not that the institution has been permitted to enter some extra-legal space.[99] In addition, as I have suggested here, that the judiciary might be excluded from providing interpretative solutions for certain kinds of problems

[98] For an account and astute analysis of the actual story, see Devika Hovell, *The Power of Process: The Value of Due Process in Security Council Sanctions Decision-Making* (Oxford: Oxford University Press, 2016).

[99] McLachlan, *Foreign Relations Law*, 5.

does not mean that judges are excluded from enjoining in their judgments other institutions to perform their role of providing such solutions.

The term 'enjoinment', trading as it does on both 'urging' and 'compelling', is meant to capture something that 'comity' reaches for but stops short of – the legal obligation that exists albeit no institution exists that can force another to act. Those who claim to rule by law rather than by some other means can be held to the commitments implicit in that claim even if they cannot be forced to do so. The idea that a nation's conduct of its foreign affairs is law-governed and that one source of the legal norms that govern it is the nation's own public law or constitutional norms is anathema only to those who adopt the hermetic conception of the constitution. For them, the public law of a nation stops at its borders. But if one adopts the permeable conception, that 'geographical' understanding of the reach of public law norms must be rejected.

Recall the distinction between dualism as a description of actual state practice and dualism as a theory of international law. The former is an account of how many states in fact order their relationship with international law given international monism, whereas the latter conflates that matter of fact with the normative theory that seeks to justify the hermetic conception of the constitution. One cannot then be a national law monist and be committed to some form of extraterritorial reach of one's own legal norms, because to recognise such reach as a juridical matter is to be committed to international law monism. Similarly, international law monism is required to explain as a juridical matter the working assumption in many contemporary legal systems that the legal order is somewhat permeable and that the order has some, but not unlimited, external reach, not wholly determined by public international law since it is also determined by domestic constitutional law.[100]

With the geographical understanding rejected, we can begin the task of working up a legal theory that has at its centre a legal subject whose mark is that he or she is entitled to ask the question of a legal official, 'But, how can that be law for me?', and to get an answer that fully displays its legal basis, which may be in national law or international law, or both. As Knop's invocation of the 'legal citizen' suggests, this figure is not the citizen of the political community of a nation state, nor the subject of

[100] The problem here is analogous to that in international law theory when one recognises international law as genuine law at the same time as providing a legal theory that denies international law that status – see my 'Introduction: The Politics of Sovereignty', in Heller, *Sovereignty*.

democratic political theory. Rather, he or she is a member of what we can think of as a 'jural community' – the community of those who are bound together by legal right or *Recht*.[101]

The constitution of such a community will include the legal norms that are considered part of its national constitution, whether written or unwritten or both. But there are also the compulsory norms of public international law (*ius cogens* and 'general principles of international law'), as well as norms that a particular state has consented to be bound by, as well as norms that have some strong claim to be relevant to a dispute that arises within national public law. At the same time, the public law norms of the national legal order will presumptively apply to any challenge raised by someone who is directly subject to an act of state power, whether or not that individual is within the borders of the nation state. They must so apply if the state is to claim that it acts by authority rather than by unmediated coercive power, since to act with authority is to claim authorisation on the part of those subject to one's power, even if the authorising subject is, at least in part, constituted through the process of challenge; or, as I put it above, retrojected as the author of the constitution. And just as the legal subject is in a process of at least partial reconstruction, so is the constitution itself both act and achievement. As achievement, it provides the framework within which discussion must begin about what is legally required. As act, the conclusion as to the content of that norm may require adopting an innovative understanding of that framework.

While this requires immense complexity, it is hardly more than the complexity already in play in any actual private international law matter, when – as we saw Kelsen suggest – a norm from one order refers to a norm of another order in a bid to form a 'complete rule of law'. And, as Knop, Michaels and Riles suggest, this makes the problems of constitutionalism and legality explored here not little but concrete. That is to say, the problems have to be worked out creatively in practice. But the success of the solutions depends on having the correct conception of that constitution of that practice – the permeable conception advocated by international law monism.

[101] See Benjamin Straumann, *Crisis and Constitutionalism: Roman Political Thought from the Fall of the Republic to the Age of Revolution* (Oxford: Oxford University Press, 2016).

3

The Idea of the Federative

THOMAS POOLE

This chapter presents a juridical analysis of the double-facing constitution. It accepts the descriptive claim that how a constitutional order engages with the world outside it feeds back into how it constructs itself internally.[1] It defends a theory designed to account for those dynamics. That account rests on the 'federative', the term Locke took from Cicero and used to designate the foreign relations power as a distinct property of constitutional order.

I isolate as the core feature of the federative the capacity to enter into legal relations with other states. The implications of that proposition are worked out, using as a foil a rival approach which I call sovereigntist theory. Though elements of that theory are often relied upon by public lawyers, its essential structure was elaborated most decisively by Carl Schmitt. While Schmitt is recognised as a significant thinker on sovereignty, it is generally overlooked that he presents an account of the double-facing constitution. I reveal three specific flaws with Schmitt's sovereigntist theory – it is insufficiently juridical, it is unilateral, and it is geared to war not peace. These flaws relate to a more general deficiency: sovereigntist theory describes the solipsistic constitution incapable of engaging in juridical structures of mutual recognition with other constitutional orders.

In search of a different path, I trace the intellectual origins of the federative through Locke and back to Cicero. Excavating the federative's Roman roots uncovers a rich understanding of compact-making as a legal performance (*foedus*), a ritual jurisprudence of alliance etymologically and normatively related to the idea of good faith (*fides*), which aimed to constitute new juridical relationships between two previously opposed parties. That new relationship, defined by norms shared among

[1] On which see Thomas Poole, *Reason of State: Law, Prerogative and Empire* (Cambridge: Cambridge University Press, 2015).

independent entities, exists under the sign of Janus, the two-faced god who provides the figurehead for our collection.

These Roman sources on the federative are suggestive. But I explain the dynamics of the federative in more rigorous terms. In the terminology of speech act theory, law is the natural province of illocutionary acts (that is, things done through the act of saying things). The federative, in its original form, operates according to the logic of perlocutionary acts (things projected or desired in the course of saying something). It presents a relatively unstructured framework of exchange in which the person addressed has a choice about whether and, if so, how to respond. The resolution of the contestation, if it occurs, creates constitutive possibilities.

This equates in our context to jurisgenerative potential: the capacity not so much to fashion a new legal agreement but, through that agreement, to recast a relationship based previously, inasmuch as one existed at all, on enmity, into one grounded in good faith. The obverse of that process, less obvious but just as significant, is the reconstitution of the parties to the agreement. Juridical and moral character changes more or less subtly as a result of the new agreement. By extension, we can suggest that the federative is the means whereby states conceive of themselves as legal persons. It is the means whereby they acknowledge rights and duties that bind them and which they accept as standards against which their action will be judged. Sovereignty, we might say, is properly understood not as a matter of being unbound by laws, *legibus solutus* in the old formula, but as the *juridical* capacity to determine the laws to which one is bound.

The federative refers principally to a particular constitutional power and its exercise. It assumes by its nature the existence of a corresponding power in other political units (generally states). I call the juridical dimension created by the mutual exercise of the federative by a number of political units the 'federative terrain'. Repeated use of the federative by a plurality of constitutional orders opens up a new jural-political geographical consciousness which, especially once stabilised, is likely to have significant impact on the character of constitutional argument. We observe that as the federative matures, the conventions that surround its exercise tend to thicken, making its operations more routine. The classic perlocutionary structure of the federative continues, as does its capacity to form and re-form relations of alliance. But it also settles into more stable juridical forms, often becoming enmeshed in the body of public law principle, and liable to be used in the course of normal (or 'illocutionary') legal argument. Partly as a result, the potential for the state's external juridical interactions to loop back into the state increases.

I close by testing the explanatory power of this account of the federative against recent cases. Much of the relevant action occurs within the executive, but cases are particularly good at bringing out the issues of principle in allocation of functions questions relating to the external constitution. Two recent cases decided by the UK Supreme Court are analysed against this background. The first, *Belhaj*,[2] relates to the Act of State principle which concerns liability in UK courts for sovereign acts done by the UK in collaboration with its foreign allies. The second, *Miller*,[3] the Brexit case, decided that the foreign relations prerogative could not be used to notify the European Union of the UK's intention to withdraw since to do so would undermine Parliament's capacity to determine rights and obligations within the UK and to control constitutional change. Both cases come more clearly into focus, against the backdrop of federative theory, as being concerned with the construction of the external constitution. *Miller* also brings out the idea of the federative as a kind of airlock, regulating the space between the inner and outer membranes of the constitution and controlling the inward flow of normative material.

I The Sovereigntist Constitution

We carry in our heads a certain picture, more or less defined, of the character of the constitution. That picture is shaped by how we imagine the world around it to be constituted. Rarely do we give due attention to the relationship between the two. Like the dramatic use of chiaroscuro in baroque art, where the darkness of the peripheral shadow forces attention towards the painting's core, serving to intensify the central image, our picture tends to rely on a similar movement between the constitution's inside and outside. Our focal point is the state, conceived as a legal entity and assumed to be comprehensively regulated by laws that it has given itself. What surrounds the state is less clearly defined. But we tend often to assume that its subjection to law is at best nominal, while also having a relatively clear notion of the state as a legal actor in the international arena, the bearer of rights and duties in respect of other states.

2 *Belhaj* v. *Straw* [2017] UKSC 3.

3 *Miller* v. *Secretary of State for Exiting the European Union* [2017] UKSC 5.

Building on these assumptions, public lawyers often make use of a standard heuristic of a split-level structure in which inside and outside correspond to largely separable legal domains. That structure constructs the external frame as subservient to the internal in two ways. First, it claims that domestic law is superior to international law. International law is 'like it or not, a defective example of law', in John Finnis's estimation, and 'if we can speak of the Rule of Law in the international domain . . . it is only a Rule by imperfect analogy with the law of the land'.[4] Second, it assumes that domestic law is logically prior to international law. The state comes into existence first, giving birth to itself through a primordial act of self-authorship. Any law external to the state is taken to derive from this original jurisgenerative act. The basic conceit seems to be that international law is a sort of externality of the theory of constituent power, a theory intended to account for the national constitution as seen from the inside.[5] Martin Loughlin is committed to the proposition that public law only exists within state structures.[6] The state is a unique creation of the modern political imagination, he argues, which 'historically has been sustained by a civil religion that conceives the people as a unity', with (domestic) public law being the 'medium through which this institutional edifice is maintained'.[7]

Loughlin's account is instructive not only for the forcefulness with which he pressed the split-level case but also for making explicit the connection between such an approach and the theory of constituent power. Understood as the generative principle of modern constitutional arrangements,[8] constituent power is a theory of how constitutions derive from sovereign acts. It is appropriate, as such, to call the picture described here as the *sovereigntist* account of the relationship between the constitutional inside and outside. In a moment, I turn to Schmitt to elaborate this position. But before doing so, I want to note one of its important consequences. The split-level picture squeezes the external capacities of the state, especially the foreign relations power, into a remote corner of

[4] John Finnis, 'Ministers, international law, and the rule of law', Judicial Power Project (2 November 2015). See also Finnis, 'Brexit and the Balance of Our Constitution', Judicial Power Project (2 February 2018).

[5] Martin Loughlin and Neil Walker (eds.), *The Paradox of Constitutionalism* (Oxford: Oxford University Press, 2006).

[6] Martin Loughlin, 'The State – *conditio sine qua non*' (2018) 16 *International Journal of Constitutional Law* 1156.

[7] Martin Loughlin, 'The Misconceived Search for Global Law' (2017) 8 *Transnational Legal Theory* 353, 359.

[8] Martin Loughlin, *The Idea of Public Law* (Oxford: Oxford University Press, 2004), ch. 6.

the frame. We need to be careful throughout this analysis about what we mean by the word 'external' in this context. In an important sense it is a misnomer, since most of the relevant action occurs within the state's political and administrative structures. Even when some of the state's officials – e.g. diplomats and armed forces – operate abroad, we understand the state to be the true author of their actions for all relevant political, legal and moral purposes.

Pushing such 'external' powers to the edge of our frame means that they receive less attention than they merit. But they are marginalised in a more profound sense in that they are treated as constitutionally anomalous. The sovereigntist conception of the domain of activity that corresponds to these external powers as essentially strategic and only sparsely legal often coincides with the proposition that the external power be contained within a largely unstructured and discretionary prerogative authority.[9] Writers otherwise content to map state power in broadly familiar constitutional terms describe the external power as a kind of standing exception, within the normal constitution, to the principles they think ought to govern constitutional arrangements. Timothy Endicott argues that the Blackstonian virtues of unanimity, strength and dispatch continue to justify legally untrammelled but politically responsible prerogative action, especially in foreign relations. This is a general proposition: even in the context of the exercise of armed force, he argues, the requirement of prior parliamentary approval is 'useless'.[10] Speaking directly about more specific concerns, Endicott argues that the 'momentous' political nature of Brexit justifies an even greater centralisation, calling for 'scrutiny in extraordinary forms that respond to the extraordinary situation'.[11]

II Schmitt's Double-Facing Constitution

The exception tied especially to fraught moments of sovereign action; a decisionistic narrowing of the constitutional frame and the prioritisation

[9] This is a key part of what Campbell McLachlan describes as the dominance in foreign relations law of a 'Victorian acquis', a set of exclusionary doctrines structured around the two poles of 'uncontrolled executive prerogative power' and 'the rigid division between territoriality and extraterritoriality': *Foreign Relations Law* (Cambridge: Cambridge University Press, 2014), 14–15.

[10] Timothy Endicott, 'Parliament and the Prerogative: From the *Case of Proclamations* to *Miller*', Judicial Power Project (1 December 2016). See also Timothy Endicott, 'Lawful Power' (2017) 15 *New Zealand Journal of Public and International Law* 1.

[11] Timothy Endicott, 'This Ancient, Secretive Royal Prerogative', UK Constitutional Law Association, 11 November 2016.

of political necessity over constitutional form; a defence of legally unmediated prerogative in the field of foreign affairs – there are unmistakable parallels here with the constitutional theory of Carl Schmitt. Some of the writers I have identified as sovereigntists, notably Loughlin,[12] are heavily indebted to Schmitt.[13] Others, like Endicott, may not necessarily be influenced by Schmitt in their general thinking but fall into Schmittian mode when discussing the constitution's external powers. It is well known that Schmitt provides a developed sovereigntist theory of the constitution. What is less commonly appreciated is that this theory represents an account of the double-facing constitution. Reading across his output uncovers a relatively sophisticated, if flawed, understanding of the idea that what the state does externally is constructive of its internal constitutional character.

The place to start is Schmitt's post-war work on international law, *The Nomos of the Earth* (1950), an aspiration of which is to identify the preconditions of legal order. Schmitt thinks that it is hard for us, ensconced within functioning, almost hyper-developed legal systems, to appreciate the basic facts of legal life. To strip away the layers of modern false consciousness, Schmitt's returns to ancient Greece, isolating in particular the word *nomos*. We tend to think that the word means 'law', or more exactly law in the sense of *ius* as opposed to *lex*, that is, law as a normative system as opposed to law posited by a recognised authority. Originally, Schmitt claims, *nomos* derives from the verb *nemein* which had three meanings; namely to appropriate, to divide and to pasture.[14]

[12] See, e.g., Martin Loughlin, 'Why Read Carl Schmitt?' in Christoph Bezemek, Michael Potacs and Alexander Somek (eds.), *Vienna Lectures in Legal Philosophy*, Vol. 1 (Oxford: Hart Publishing, 2018).

[13] See also Eric A. Posner and Adrian Vermeule, *The Executive Unbound: After the Madisonian Republic* (New York: Oxford University Press, 2011); Adrian Vermuele, 'Our Schmittian Administrative Law' (2009) 122 *Harvard Law Review* 1095.

[14] Schmitt's reading is not supported by classical scholarship. In archaic Greece, 'the first semantic field of that term oscillated instead around the identification of a religious rituality, or customary principle, or even moral precept. In older Latin we would have to render the concept variously as *mos*, or perhaps as *ius* in its original meaning, but not as *lex*'. With the growth of democracy in the fifth century BC, however, *nomos* changed meaning, becoming charged with ideological connotations and indicating a paradigm of sovereign law-making (*lex*): Aldo Schiavone, *The Invention of Law in the West* (Cambridge, MA: Harvard University Press, 2012), 88–89 and 536. See also Martin Ostwald, *From Popular Sovereignty to the Sovereignty of Law: Law, Society, and Politics in Fifth-Century Athens* (Berkeley: University of California Press, 1986). Looking closely at the text of *Nomos*, it appears that Schmitt's interpretation is at odds with four of the five scholars he references on this point (Hans Erich Stier, Hans Niedermeyer, Alfred von Verdross and Felix Heinimann). The sole exception is a work written during the Second World War by Jost Trier, who

Schmitt understands these three meanings of *nomos* as forming a fixed relation, so that appropriation precedes division and division precedes production. No one 'can give, divide and distribute without taking', and in the beginning, 'there was no basic norm, but a basic appropriation'.[15] It follows that the first and original meaning of *nomos* signifies the constitution of 'the original spatial order, the source of all further concrete order and all further law' and that 'all subsequent law and everything promulgated and enacted thereafter as decrees and commands are *nourished* ... by this source'.[16]

Two salient points can be extracted. First, Schmitt regards the successful erection of borders in the aftermath of a land-appropriation – or perhaps more precisely the division (i.e. the delineation and earmarking) of territory so obtained – as the origin of all legal order. By 'origin', Schmitt means not just the beginning in a factual or historical sense but more importantly what he calls the 'reproductive root' or foundation in a conceptual and structural sense. The point is not that all public law rests ultimately on a series of land grabs, although this may be true.[17] It is rather that we do not understand public law unless we acknowledge the *continued* presence, however repressed or occluded, of these foundational moves of appropriation and division.[18] Hence the key word 'nourished', emphasised by Schmitt in the passage just quoted.

Second, *Nomos of the Earth* obviously relates an origins story, one that is played out on a global and intimidatingly *longue durée* scale. More precisely, it is an origins story of the double-facing constitution in its sovereigntist manifestation. Boundaries, borders and walls are so important in

perhaps coincidentally joined the Nazi Party in 1933 and viewed German philology in terms of Nazi ideology (72–75 and 325).

[15] Carl Schmitt, *The Nomos of the Earth in the International Law of the Jus Publicum Europaeum* G. L. Ulmen trans. (New York: Telos Press, 2003), 345.

[16] Schmitt, *Nomos of the Earth*, 48 (italics in the original). For analysis see Martin Loughlin, 'Nomos', in David Dyzenhaus and Thomas Poole (eds.), *Law, Liberty and State: Schmitt, Hayek and Oakeshott on the Rule of Law* (Cambridge: Cambridge University Press, 2015).

[17] Compare David Hume, *A Treatise of Human Nature*, ed. Ernst Campbell Mossner (London: Penguin, 1986), T.3.2.10.4: 'if we remount to the first origin of every nation, we shall find, that there scarce is any race of kings, or form of a commonwealth, that is not primarily founded on usurpation and rebellion, and whose title is not far worse than doubtful and uncertain'.

[18] See also *Nomos*, 78: 'all subsequent regulations of a written or unwritten kind derive their power from the inner measure of an original, constitutive act of spatial ordering. This original act is *nomos*. All subsequent developments are either results of and expansions on this act or else redistributions (*anadasmoi*) – either a continuation on the same basis or a disintegration of and departure from the constitutive act of the spatial order established by land-appropriation, the founding of cities, or colonization.'

that elaboration that, at times, they come close to being fetishised. Based on sacred orientations, '*nomos* can be described as a wall', Schmitt writes at one point, forming the 'force-field' of a particular order.[19] Such boundaries look simultaneously inward and outward, and generate norms in both directions. 'Land-appropriation thus is the archetype of a constitutive legal process externally (vis-à-vis other peoples) and internally (for the ordering of land and property within a country)'.[20] Schmitt's concern elsewhere in his output is the inward flow of politically salient information into the internal constitution, as we shall see. But here his interest is the outward movement, that is, the norming that occurs outside and as a result of these political boundaries. And the position he stakes out in this regard generalises the central sovereigntist contention that it is the self-generating polity (state) that gives itself law and juridically recognises itself as polity.

To be sure, there is room for mutual recognition in this picture. But the law that exists among states is imagined as thin or attenuated – Finnis's word 'defective' is not at all inapposite. The framework in which states operate, while not lawless, Schmitt says, may yet be described as 'anarchistic'.[21] The 'law' that emerges between states arises from the same *nomos*-driven 'constitutive processes and power manifestations that produce ... constitutions'.[22] The law of treaties is all but emptied of content through Schmitt's claim that since each sovereign person 'is the judge of his own affairs, he is bound only by his own treaties, whose interpretation is his own business'. This leaves war as just about the only meaningful feature of international legal order – on Schmitt's reading, it is certainly its paradigmatic feature. What states recognise is the equal right of other states to wage war (*jus ad bellum*) as opposed merely to inflict violence on each other: 'it was possible for each side to recognise the other as *justi hostes* [just enemy]. Thereby, war became somewhat analogous to a duel, i.e., a conflict of arms between territorially distinct *personae morales* [moral persons]'.[23]

This is international law under the sign of Heracles. The famous Pindar passage that speaks of *nomos basileus* – *nomos* as king – deals, on Schmitt's gloss, 'with the theft of cattle, an act of Heracles, the mythical founder of order, whereby, despite the violence of the act, he created law'. Primordial violence determines the texture of future legal

[19] Ibid., 70.
[20] Ibid., 47.
[21] Ibid., 147.
[22] Ibid., 82.
[23] Ibid., 142.

order. The authentic and paradigmatic behaviour of peoples is the carving up and carving out of territory. The moral person of the state equates to the recognition by other moral persons that it can fight on terms of formal equality. The law here, self-policed and auto-interpreted, is figured on the etiquette of the duel. It is little more, then, than a thin juridical overlay to obscure the more elemental behaviour of humankind. What we find in essence with the concept of *nomos* is 'precisely the full immediacy of a legal power not mediated by laws; it is a constitutive historical event – an act of *legitimacy*; whereby the legality of a mere law first is made meaningful'.[24]

We see this argument elsewhere in Schmitt. Given the language of the passage just quoted, the nearest example is probably the tract *Legality and Legitimacy* (1932),[25] which is cited at various points in *Nomos*. But on reflection much of Schmitt's earlier work explores the connection between the inside and outside of constitutional order. The central notion in that work is 'the political', the structural equivalent of *nomos* or 'legitimacy', by which Schmitt means a particular form of decision, one ideal typically unstructured by law and governed by the logic of the friend/enemy distinction.[26] That last idea – friend/enemy – provides the conduit through which the inward/outward dynamics that animate and define a constitutional order flow. The concept is fundamentally double-facing, since it postulates that a group self-identifies as a political unit *through* its decision as to who counts as enemy. Schmitt identifies the designation of enemy with a preparedness to fight. It is the very freighted quality of this designation, he thinks, that creates the peculiar density characteristic of political association. The political decision is thereby the mechanism through which a multitude becomes a unity. Its essence inheres in a double movement: establishing an external boundary between 'us' and 'them' instigates an internal boundary between the law that binds 'us' and the condition of non-law that relates to, or concerns our relations with, 'them'.[27]

Schmitt understood the inward dynamics that resulted from the enemy designation as a cascade, shaping the quality of the laws and decision-making within the shadow of those laws at the micro level as

[24] Ibid., 73.

[25] Carl Schmitt, *Legality and Legitimacy*, Jeffrey Seitzer trans. (Durham NC: Duke University Press, 2004).

[26] Carl Schmitt, *The Concept of the Political*, George Schwab trans. (Chicago: University of Chicago Press, 1996).

[27] See Eric L. Santner, *On Creaturely Life: Rilke, Benjamin, Sebald* (Chicago: University of Chicago Press, 2006), 13–14.

well as the macro, and on a daily basis as well as during larger constitutional moments.[28] The political decision must be able to radiate, he argued, in as unmediated a way possible throughout the constitutional order. Public law is ideally subject to and structured by the political, its content formed by determinations on the enemy made most naturally in the constitution's outward-facing dimensions. The dominant theme of the closest Schmitt got to a standard legal treatise, *Constitutional Theory* (1928), is precisely this prioritisation of this 'positive' concept of the constitution, 'the constitution of the complete decision over the type and form of the political unity', over the constitution in the normative sense, referred to dismissively as the bourgeois Rechtsstaat. 'The political decision, *which essentially means the constitution*, cannot have a reciprocal effect on its subject and eliminate its political existence. *This political will remains alongside and above the constitution*'.[29]

The other key concept that Schmitt drew on to make sense of the internal ramifications of the political decision is 'the exception'. The exception refers to a general category of constitutional theory and not merely a construct applied in emergency situations (though it is that too).[30] It nonetheless remains rather opaque, since it is applicable to a range of phenomena, and is in certain respects misnamed, since Schmitt insists that the 'exception' should also be infused within the 'normal'. For the sake of clarity, I reserve the term 'exception' for a constitutional moment or similar event in which the constitutional order undergoes radical change, especially as a result of extra-constitutional action, that is, through the operation of 'legitimacy' (in Schmitt's sense) not 'legality'. I use the word 'prerogative' to describe the phenomenon Schmitt describes as operating at the quotidian and micro level, that is, largely within the interstices of the legal.

Using prerogative to describe the everyday operation of the political largely within the domain of law has the author's sanction. Discussing the association between legal and theological concepts in *Political Theology*, Schmitt suggests that prerogative is 'analogous to the miracle in theology'.[31] Just as the miracle transcends the laws of the natural world,

[28] Exceptional moments 'bleed into the quotidian, in part because every quotidian moment is potentially existential': Nomi Claire Lazar, *States of Emergency in Liberal Democracies* (Cambridge: Cambridge University Press, 2009), 41.

[29] Carl Schmitt, *Constitutional Theory*, Jeffrey Seitzer trans. (Durham, NC: Duke University Press, 2008), 125–26 (emphasis added).

[30] Carl Schmitt, *Political Theology: Four Chapters on the Concept of Sovereignty*, George Schwab trans. (Chicago: University of Chicago Press, 1985), 5.

[31] *Political Theology*, 36.

he suggests, so does prerogative exceed the bounds of the 'normal' legal system. Both share the structure of a capacity for extraordinary intervention invoked by a powerful figure.[32] Indeed, it was precisely this term that Ernst Fraenkel reached for in order to describe the Schmittian orientation of the Nazi regime. That system operated according to the logic of the 'dual state', Fraenkel argued, in which 'the prerogative state', representing a special, floating, open-ended, politically driven jurisdiction, hovered over and ultimately cannibalised 'the normative state' or normal political and legal system.[33]

This clarification helps to reveal the connection between sovereigntist theory and the prerogative, controlled by a single supreme agent, as the institutional category containing the external power, something that was unclear in the earlier discussion of contemporary scholarship. On Schmitt's reading, the prerogative is the internal analogue of the political decision over who constitutes the enemy. Political decision and prerogative are Janus-faced elements of sovereignty. In fact, they are *constitutive* of sovereignty: 'Sovereign is he who decides the exception'.[34] Note how the prerogative agent is here as elsewhere figured by Schmitt as an individual man – the decisive leader,[35] whose decisions express the will of the people, channelling his 'principally unlimited authority'[36] above or against the existing legal framework to the extent that he thinks necessary.[37]

Schmitt's theory foregrounds constitutional moments, situations of crisis, emergency or upheaval. But it does so in order to describe the constitutionally normal. He sees these limit cases as showing us the way things really are. They uncover the pulsating life that we tend otherwise to stuff behind a juridical veneer. These elemental political moves animate the constitutional state through the radiating effect of prerogative.

[32] See Clement Fatovic, 'The Political Theology of Prerogative: The Jurisprudential Miracle in Liberal Constitutional Thought' (2008) 6 *Perspectives on Politics* 487.

[33] Ernst Fraenkel, *The Dual State: A Contribution to the Theory of Dictatorship*, E. A. Shills trans. (New York: Oxford University Press, 1941).

[34] *Political Theology*, 5.

[35] In the 1919 work *Political Romanticism*, Guy Oakes trans. (Cambridge, MA: MIT Press, 1991), Schmitt rather bathetically took Don Quixote as the exemplar of the free political agent, a man with 'the enthusiasm for a real knight of his rank' who, however absurd his battles, was at least 'capable of seeing the difference between right and wrong and of making a decision in favour of what seemed right to him': 147–48.

[36] *Political Theology*, 12.

[37] *Legality and Legitimacy*, 69: 'By his own discretion, the extraordinary lawmaker determines the presupposition of his extraordinary powers . . . and the content of the "necessary" measures.'

It is the means by which the exception becomes quotidian. But note that for Schmitt (a) prerogative is the internal manifestation of the political decision whose mark is a preparedness to go to war and (b) international legal relations are dominated by the concerns of interstate warfare. It seems to follow that war is what determines constitutional order. That does not mean that the constitution must be belligerent. But it is to insist that war is the mark of human collective action and the central criterion under which the constitution's internal and external dimensions are structured. 'War is neither the end nor the purpose nor even the very content of politics. But as an ever present possibility it is the leading presupposition which determines in a characteristic way human action and thinking and thereby creates a specifically political behaviour'.[38]

III The Paradox of the Sovereign State

The statist and unilateral aspects are so strong in Schmitt that it is easy to overlook that what he defends is actually a theory of the double-facing constitution. It reworks the Hobbesian doctrine of sovereignty which holds that 'the survival and greatness of a political community required the creation of an ultimate decision-making agency whose task was to devise adequate responses to external challenges and stop infighting at home with an iron hand'.[39] For a state to cohere, sovereign decisions cannot be isolated events taking place predominantly in the external domain. They must also have a radiating effect throughout the internal constitution. Prerogative is the essential mechanism to align the content of the internal constitution with the character-forming political decisions about whom we are prepared to fight.

Read as a theory of the double-facing constitution, there are three main weaknesses with Schmitt's account. (I suggest shortly that these are really three aspects of the same point.) First, the theory is insufficiently juridical. The pivot concept is the 'friend/enemy distinction', the criterion of which Schmitt says is a 'preparedness to go to war'. My objection here is not that the designation of another polity as friend or enemy is too imprecise to navigate the shifting and variegated terrain of international politics or too trivial to bear the conceptual weight Schmitt attaches to it,

[38] *Concept of the Political*, 34.

[39] Istvan Hont, 'The Permanent Crisis of a Divided Mankind: "Nation-State" and "Nationalism" in Historical Perspective', in Istvan Hont, *Jealousy of Trade: International Competition and the Nation State in Comparative Perspective* (Cambridge, MA: Harvard University Press, 2005), 464.

though both those things are true. The objection is more basic, relating to Schmitt's claim to have identified a juridical theory. If 'juridical' specifies a category concerned with legal relations – relations between legal persons each understood as 'an acting subject as the subject of obligations and rights'[40] – then the friend/enemy distinction has no more juridical content than if I imagine myself to be shouting 'I hate you'. It does not modify, or entail the modification of, existing legal rights or duties, nor does it create new ones. The party designated as friend or enemy is not an 'acting subject' in respect of the designation as it has no role to play in its making, being merely an object of it. Nor can that party be said to be under any obligation in respect of the designation once made. It may not even know that a designation has been made – since, being exceptional and so normless, no form attaches to it – and is under no obligation to accept a designation once it becomes known.[41]

The juridical inadequacy of Schmitt's account should not be surprising given the energy he spends on downgrading the legal (*qua* institutional normative order) and extolling the political (*qua* legally unstructured and uncontrolled discretionary power). The 'preparedness to go to war' criterion that Schmitt identifies as the distinctive quality that attaches to the political (friend/enemy) decision adds nothing in this regard. It is self-evidently not a juridical idea. What it might be is harder to determine. The trouble for Schmitt is that humanity has shown an impressively wide range of motivations for going to war – religious, ideological, cultural, racial, familial, for defence and acquisition, out of habit or sheer boredom. As such, the social phenomenon of 'readiness to go to war' cannot act as a criterion for distinguishing political from other forms of association.

The second criticism extends the first. For an account of the double-facing constitution, Schmitt's conceptual scheme is troublingly unilateral. It presents itself as relational – recognising, for instance, the logic of mutual recognition that grounds international law – but on examination

40 Hans Kelsen, *Pure Theory of Law*, Max Knight trans. (Berkeley: University of California Press, 1967), 290.

41 A similar criticism, that the friend/enemy distinction indicates nothing essentially political, was made by Hermann Heller in his essay 'Political Democracy and Social Homogeneity' [1928]: '"My friends are your friends, and your enemies should be my enemies", can apply just as well to the political friend as to any other friend who shares convictions – childhood friend, business friend, and bosom friend. Carl Schmitt is blind to the sphere of unity-formation within the state as politics', in Arthur J. Jacobson and Bernard Schlink (eds.), *Weimar: A Jurisprudence of Crisis* (Berkeley: University of California Press, 2002), 258.

it is relational, if at all, in a highly attenuated sense. The problem lies not only in the nature of the action – the friend/enemy distinction, already discussed – but also in the construction of the legal subject that is capable of bearing the rights and responsibilities associated with states. The theory seeks to sequester the constitutional order more or less exclusively within the domain of sovereign action. It is true that the theory assumes the existence of a legal order of states, albeit one conceived along the lines of a duelling club of a particularly murderous kind. But given the pivotal role it attaches to sovereignty, understood as legally untrammelled decision-making capacity, it is hard to see how its external-facing actions might give rise to rights and obligations. The theory is not prepared to recognise any meaningful species of right other than the one determined by sovereign decision, yet that decision can be binding *ex hypothesi* only in respect of the sovereign's legal subjects. We see this strongly in Schmitt's evisceration of treaty law on the altar of the right of sovereign auto-interpretation.

This opens up a more basic question: namely, how does a state become a state? (A state for the purposes of juridical analysis being an active subject of international law and as such the subject of obligations and rights that sound in international law.) Schmitt gives at best a partial answer. He has a theory of the self-authoring state, grounded in Sieyès's Hobbesian notion of constituent power, and an account of how the sovereign gives that state external agency. But that is only part of the story. The theory cannot properly explain the recognition of states by other states or how *legal* relations between states originate and are sustained. These matters are largely bypassed by Schmitt's conceptual scheme. Sovereignty, friend/enemy designation, preparedness for war, prerogative – these ideas, at least in the way Schmitt articulates them, do not provide a basis for connecting the state juridically to the world around it. What we have instead is the Grecian fable of the *Nomos of the Earth*. The idea, consistent with his Nazi-era expansionist writings on the *Großraum* theory of international law,[42] being that legal order rests on the acquisition and division of land. But this works only if you accept that international legal personhood is acquired through assertion and

[42] Carl Schmitt, 'The *Großraum* Order of International Law with a Ban on the Intervention for Spatially Foreign Powers: A Contribution to the Concept of the *Reich* in International Law', in Carl Schmitt, *Writings on War*, Timothy Nunan trans. (Cambridge: Polity, 2011). Indeed, Schmitt refers back to that idea at a number of points in *Nomos* (e.g. 55, 99, 243–44) – not surprisingly given that, though not published until 1950, the book was written in the early 1940s.

force alone. This is at best an incomplete account of the mutual recognition process that occurs between states, not least because it reduces the legal component of that process to a vanishing point.[43]

The third criticism is the most serious. We may have different views about the structure of international order, but we can agree that the constitution exists to secure a condition of peace, order and good government. Hobbes made the point with typical clarity. The commonwealth (i.e. constitutional state) is the solution to the problem of securing lasting peace, which corresponds to what Bernard Williams called the 'basic legitimation demand'.[44] We accept the binding force of its laws on that understanding. But the existence of these islands of domestic peace entails, Hobbes seems to suggest, a condition of competitive, watchful enmity between them: 'what else are many commonwealths, than so many camps strengthened with arms and men against each other; whose state, because not restrained by any common power, . . . is to be accounted for the state of nature; which is the state of war'.[45] This generates the passive-aggressive posture a constitutional order typically adopts in respect of the outside world. States exist, he says in *Leviathan*, 'in continual jealousies, and in the state and posture of Gladiators; having their weapons pointing, and their eyes fixed on one another; that is, their Forts, Garrisons, and Guns upon the Frontiers of their Kingdomes; and continual Spyes upon their neighbours, which is the posture of War'.[46]

Clear the distinction may be. But it often goes unnoticed that it introduces into Hobbes's account a tension between domestic conditions of peace and the international state of war that is never effectively resolved.[47] Why should not at least some portion of this competitive wariness bordering on hostility translate into the internal constitution?[48]

[43] Franz Neumann reached a similar conclusion when he observed 'the exception becomes the rule. There is no one international law but as many as there are empires, that is, large spaces. The *großdeutsche Reich* is the creator of its own international law in its own space': *Behemoth: The Structure and Practice of National Socialism, 1933–1944* (Chicago: Ivan R. Dee, 2009), 158.

[44] Bernard Williams, *In the Beginning Was the Deed: Realism and Moralism in Political Argument* (Princeton: Princeton University Press, 2005), 5.

[45] Thomas Hobbes, *On the Citizen* (*De Cive*) in Bernard Gert (ed.), *Man and Citizen* (Garden City, NY: Anchor, 1972), ch. 10, 234.

[46] Thomas Hobbes, *Leviathan*, ed. Richard Tuck (Cambridge: Cambridge University Press, 1991), 90.

[47] For a different view, see Theodore Christov's chapter in this volume, Chapter 4.

[48] In fact, I think Hobbes not only thinks that it does, to some extent, but that it *must*. Fear of invasion is one of the drivers for obedience to the sovereign. But on what basis does Hobbes assume that the internal constitution will take in the benefits but not the burdens

Indeed, since the Hobbesian sovereign is politically unchecked and legally unbound, what is to stop it from deciding to do so? What we might call the paradox of the Hobbesian sovereign state emerges more clearly when viewed through the prism of the double-facing constitution. Law reigns at home otherwise there is no real peace. Prerogative dominates externally otherwise there can be no real protection (and so no real peace). As we have seen, 'external' here is a juridical, not a geographical, expression and relates to dimensions of the constitution. It is not a simple matter to assign law and prerogative to separate spheres: law to the internal constitution, geared for peace; prerogative to the external constitution, geared for war. There is no obvious or natural separation between one constitutional domain and the other, and no reason why, within the interstices of the constitution, the demands of war should not allow prerogative to trump the law. The greater the scope for prerogative, however, the less the polity resembles a domain of law – the framework for sustaining conditions of peace – and the more it exists in a state of war, a 'camp of arms and men'.

Schmitt, who saw himself as the twentieth century Hobbes,[49] comes close to resolving the Hobbesian paradox. But he does so by extending the reach of prerogative far into the domain of law. Schmitt's double-facing constitution is more or less aligned as a result, but now both external and internal constitution are geared to war. To accept that war is 'the leading presupposition which determines . . . political behaviour' entails subordinating the internal constitution as well as the external constitution to the polity's war needs as determined at the sovereign's prerogative discretion. But this conceptual coherence comes at too high a price. Instead of the original Hobbesian bifurcations, Schmitt offers an internal 'dual' constitution in which prerogative dominates, and an external one patterned as a condition of competitive enmity between states.

IV Foundations of the Federative

We have given close attention to Schmitt because his theory attempts to work out the double-facing constitution in a way that is consistent with

(e.g. excessive use of prerogative; the security state; militarisation) from its external-facing side?

[49] See especially Carl Schmitt, *Leviathan in the State Theory of Thomas Hobbes: Meaning and Failure of a Political Symbol*, George Schwab and Erna Hilfstein trans. (Chicago: University of Chicago Press, 2008).

the assumptions many public lawyers today make about the inside and outside of the constitution. I have identified three weaknesses in this account: (1) it is insufficiently juridical, and so cannot make sense of legal relations (or the legal dimension of political relationships); (2) it is unilateral, and so cannot account for the existence of the state as a subject within a legal order that is not purely its own creation; and (3) it is oriented to war, and so cannot satisfy the basic requirement that constitution order represents a domain of peace (= law).

These criticisms are really aspects of a more general point, which is that the sovereigntist theory can only model what we might call the *solipsistic constitution*. Precisely because it is juridically impoverished, it is incapable of taking seriously any norms other than those it gives itself and so remains trapped in the circuitous logic of the sovereign self, unable to escape the hostile shadow it projects on to the outside world. A theory of the double-facing constitution must explain how a constitution realises itself at least in part through the process of mutual recognition with other constitutional orders. It must recognise the cardinal importance of constitutional self-authorship, to be sure, and the importance within that process of the continuous drawing of boundaries between us and them.[50] But it must be wired through a concept that, while identifiably a legal property of the state, is also capable of reaching outside the state and institute legal relations with other polities. Specifically, corresponding to criticism (1), this idea must be juridical, that is, capable of describing *legal* relations. Corresponding to criticism (2), it must be capable of describing the process whereby *reciprocal* legal relations between polities are established and cemented. Corresponding to criticism (3), its objective must be *peace*, understood not as a break in the fighting or the exhaustion that comes after conquest, but as the elaboration of a condition that is decent, ordered and lasting.

So where to begin? There is a clue lying half-submerged in a short and generally overlooked passage in Locke's *Second Treatise*. Locke shares Schmitt's interest in the cycles of disorder, violence and renewal that underpin constitutional orders. He is also interested in questions of constitutional design. Chapter XII of the *Second Treatise* continues a discussion of institutions that had begun in the previous chapter with an analysis of the supreme legislative power. Attention turns briefly to ordinary executive power which,

[50] Though, as Jacco Bomhoff points out in his contribution to this volume, boundary-drawing takes place in many different social spheres, a reality that Schmitt's homogenous friend/enemy binary cannot hope to capture.

though constitutionally subordinate to the legislature and formally charged with ensuring that the laws enacted are given constant and lasting force, retains considerable discretionary power. Exceptional executive power, discussed under 'prerogative' and which further extends the scope of executive discretion, gets a chapter to itself.[51]

Locke then identifies another power, distinct from both ordinary executive power and prerogative, which 'contains the Power of War and Peace, Leagues and Alliances, and all the Transactions, with all Persons and Communities without the Commonwealth'. He then names this power 'the Federative, if any one pleases'.[52] But having nudged open the door, Locke almost immediately closes it. Though distinct, he continues, the executive and the federative are intimately related. The former comprehends 'the Executive of the Municipal Laws of the Society within its self, upon all that are parts of it', while the latter corresponds to 'the management of the security and interest of the public without'. Partly for that reason, the two powers are 'always almost united', forming in effect two branches of the same office (the executive). Two connected reasons are given to explain this arrangement. The federative 'is much less capable to be directed by antecedent, standing, positive, Laws, than the Executive' and so it follows, Locke claims, that it must be 'left to the Prudence and Wisdom of those whose hands it is in, to be managed for the publick good'.[53]

This may not seem much to go on, but it nonetheless opens up a potentially productive seam. Locke isolates a formally distinct constitutional capacity, one appropriate to the particular operative conditions of state power in its external dimension. He also gives it, albeit tentatively, a name: the federative. Those, like Hobbes, who pattern interstate relations as a condition of war tend to see the external constitution in correspondingly war-oriented terms – 'the state and posture of Gladiators'. Locke sets us on a different path. The word 'federative' comes from the Latin *foedera* (sing. *foedus*) meaning agreements, compacts or treaties. Locke helps us to make the first decisive move, which is to suggest that, in identifying the federative as the constitutive element of foreign relations, the central feature of the external dimension of state power is not the capacity to wage war but the ability to make alliances with other polities paradigmatically through the juridical mechanism of the compact.

[51] *Second Treatise*, Chapter XIV, *Of Prerogative.*
[52] Ibid., s. 146.
[53] Ibid., s. 147.

V The Ritual Jurisprudence of Alliance

Locke took the term federative from Cicero, who was a major influence.[54] Reading Cicero reveals a sophisticated Roman tradition of law and practice on treaty-making powers.[55] War-making and treating-effecting powers inhabit the same juridical framework ('the laws of war and peace') which was in turn embedded within the republican constitution, as exemplified for instance in the rule that only the Roman people had constitutional authority to recognise a treaty as sacrosanct.[56] Such a position was consistent with a foundational belief that peace and not war was the natural condition amongst peoples.[57] For Cicero, it was precisely this inclination for peace, out of which came limitations and formalities attending war, that represented the difference between man and animal: 'in the case of a state in its external relations, the rights of war must be strictly observed. For since there are two ways of settling a dispute: first, by discussion; second, by physical force; and since the former is characteristic of man, the latter of the brute, we must resort to force only in case we may not avail ourselves of discussion'.[58]

[54] At his death, Locke possessed more copies of works by Cicero than any author other than Boyle and himself, including seven different editions of *De Officiis*. Locke had also at some point worked out an exact chronology of Cicero's life and works. The only other figure for whom Locke did this was Jesus Christ. See John Marshall, *John Locke: Resistance, Religion and Responsibility* (Cambridge: Cambridge University Press, 1994), 276.

[55] See in particular Marcus Tullius Cicero, 'Pro Balbo', in Cicero, *Orations: Pro Caelio, De Provinciis Consularibilis, Pro Balbo*, R. Gardiner trans. (Cambridge, MA: Loeb, 1958), v. 5, where Cicero praises Pompey's 'most remarkable knowledge of treaties, of agreements, of terms (*in foederibus, pactionibus, condicionibus*) imposed upon peoples, kinds, and foreign races, and, in fact, of the whole code of law that deals with war and peace (*in universo deinque belli iure atque pacis*)'. Grotius took the title of his masterpiece *De iure belli ac pacis* [1625] from exactly this passage.

[56] *Pro Balbo*, xiv.33: 'nothing can be sacrosanct save what has been enacted by the People or by the Commons [i.e. the *comitia populi* or the *concilium plebis*]'.

[57] In an interesting passage in *The Nomos of the Earth*, Schmitt takes issue with the enormously influential German classicist Theodor Mommsen to argue that 'Roman law, in its practice of international law, recognized a variety of wars, leagues, federations (*foedus aequum* [equitable federation] and *foedus iniquum* [inequitable federation], and foreign territories.' By the end of the same paragraph, he has returned to the theme of borders marking the edge of the legal: 'The purpose of such boundaries was to separate a pacified order from a quarrelsome disorder, a cosmos from a chaos, a house from a non-house, an enclosure from a wilderness' (51–52).

[58] Marcus Tullius Cicero, *De Officiis/On Duties*, Walter Miller trans. (Cambridge, MA: Loeb, 1913), I.xi.34.

The friendship paradigm was the key concept in the construction of ancient interstate relations.[59] But *foedera* did not just relate to foreign affairs. The concept was ubiquitous, carrying a moral and political resonance that fed on its use as a legal concept. Bill Gladhill identifies three main contexts where this 'script of alliance' operated: *foedera humana*, *foedera civilia* and *foedera naturae/mundi* (human *foedera*, political *foedera* and *foedera* of nature/the world). The original treaty-making *foedus* denotes not just the terms of an agreement between two polities, often to end hostilities and establish peaceful coexistence, but represents also the act of binding. Overseen by special priests called *fetiales*, alliances actualised *fides* (faith, loyalty, trust – originally the faith one is capable of radiating[60]) through ritual dialogue, songs and blood sacrifice.[61] 'In essence', Gladhill observes, '*foedus* is the performative and perfective side of fides, the completed action between two parties who grant and accept *fides*'.[62] The sacrificial element – typically involving striking a young piglet with a flint stone – links *foedus* both symbolically and etymologically not just to fides but also to *foeditas* (foulness). There seems to have been a connection in the Roman imaginary between the sacrificial acts of *foedera* and consequent bloodshed when they were violated.[63] Cicero reserves the term *foedifragus* (*foedus*-breaker) for the very worst type of political enemy, suggesting in so doing that individuals who break *foedera* become themselves foul.

Intriguingly, the image that hovers over this volume of the two-faced god Janus also links to *foedera*. Book 12 of Vergil's epic *The Aeneid* is devoted to a prolonged ritual alliance, concentrating on the *foedus* between Aeneas, Vergil's protagonist and on his telling, the founder of Rome, and Latinus, king of the Latins, the indigenous inhabitants of the

[59] Paul J. Burton, *Friendship and Empire: Roman Diplomacy and Imperialism in the Middle Republic (353–146 BC)* (Cambridge: Cambridge University Press, 2011), 25. See also Clifford Ando, *Law, Language, and Empire in the Roman Tradition* (Philadelphia: University of Pennsylvania Press, 2011), ch. 4.

[60] Schiavone, *The Invention of Law in the West*, 146.

[61] The connection between *foedus* and *fides* is picked up by Olivier Beaud in his important study of federalism. Drawing on the work of linguist Émile Benveniste, Beaud suggests that *fides* (good faith, trust) is central to *foedus*, but also that in antiquity the word tended to relate to two unequal contracting parties: *Théorie de la Fédération* (Paris: Presses Universitaires de France, 2007), 112.

[62] Bill Gladhill, *Rethinking Roman Alliance: A Study of Poetics and Society* (Cambridge: Cambridge University Press, 2016), 22.

[63] Clifford Ando extrapolates that the fetial ritual could also serve the function of inaugurating wars that the Romans regarded as just: *Law, Language, and Empire in the Roman Tradition*, 51.

area settled by the people who became the Romans. The significance the poem attaches to this moment suggests how natural it was for Romans to understand political association in terms of successive *foedera*. During the course of the ritual, Aeneas swears to keep the terms of the truce 'by Latona's twin offspring, and by two-faced Janus' (*Latonaque genus duplex Ianumque bifrontem* at *Aeneid* 12.198). As the ancient commentator Servius explains, Vergil's objective is to bring the first 'historical' treaty into alignment with the first 'mythical' treaty between Tatius, king of the Sabines, a rival tribe, and Romulus, twin-brother slayer and founder of Rome. After that treaty had been struck, Servius relates, Tatius and Romulus built a temple to Janus. The god's two faces symbolise treaty-making: 'the faces represent a *coitio* (meeting) of the two kings or symbolise the "reversion" to peace by parties who are about to embark on war'.

This gloss – Janus as the imago of *foedera* – explains the familiar association between the Temple of Janus and war and peace, underscoring the connection that we identified in Cicero between an alliance-fuelled peace being the natural or default normative condition. It also suggests an origins story, one quite different from the one offered by Schmitt, in which a single polity is able to reach beyond itself, even to the point of deep imbrication with another, through the ritual jurisprudence of alliance. The figure of Janus represents perhaps above all, then, 'the idea of making two nations one, the idea that this unification is the mixing of cultures into a novel syncretism'.[64]

VI The Concept of the Federative

Let us now strip away the more antiquarian elements to see whether it is possible to identify a conceptual scheme for the ordering of external relations, and by extension the internal constitutional ordering of the external relations power. This model rests on the conviction that peace, not war, is the natural condition among polities. That conviction is not naive – it is a proposition true in theory if not in fact – and may in fact be more pertinent in times like Cicero's when the doors of Janus's Temple never seem to be closed. The alternative, encapsulated in the 'realist' maxim that 'Man is a wolf to Man' in relations among peoples,[65] seems

[64] Gladhill, *Rethinking Roman Alliance*, 128–29.

[65] A phrase used by Plautus and Ovid famously applied to the law of nations by Hobbes in the dedication to *De Cive*. Hobbes's use is, in turn, favourably glossed by Schmitt in *The Nomos of the Earth* at 95 and 147.

almost to deny the possibility of effective escape from conditions of enmity and risks condemning us, in our inter-polity interactions, to the status of beasts.

This federative model juxtaposes a universe governed by force and fate to one that at least has the capacity to be patterned by human creations, paradigmatically compacts or *foedera*. Whereas the sovereigntist model holds that no compacts worthy of the name are possible outside the state, the federative presents a vision of order slowly mastering chaos through the consistent application of a 'script of alliance'. Peaceful coexistence, natural in a moral or normative sense, is not something that just happens but can only be achieved through artificial means, the creation of the human imagination allied with more or less consistent practical action. Many federative moments combine to form a web of alliances, each strand of that web acquiring normative significance ultimately on the basis of securing peace but proximately on the basis that it serves and secures trust (*fides*).[66] These demanding requirements, inescapably part of an ongoing process, are necessary given the precariousness of horizontal law-making. Compacts between polities being prone to collapse, the federative remains perched on the edge of foulness (*foeditas*). In schematic terms, while 'union' remains the distinctive property of states, the aim of the federative is to generate bonds of 'friendship' (*amicitia*) between particular states as a means ultimately of securing a more general condition of 'concord' (*concordia*) amongst peoples.

We have established the bare bones of the federative model. It isolates as its central case the capacity to make binding agreements or compacts with other polities. The decision to wage war (or, in Schmitt's looser and less juridical formulation, the decision as to the enemy) becomes almost an adjunct power, understood theoretically as a consequence of the deterioration of relations of trust engendered by compact-making. The model thus connects an important part of the constitution (the federative power) to a domain outside the state marked by the interaction between the federative powers of multiple constitutional orders (what we might call the federative terrain). But the more detailed elements of the model have yet to be specified. In particular, not least because of our criticism of

[66] Peace and pact are etymologically related. The chapter *De bellis* (On War), of Isidore of Seville's seventh century text *Etymologies* (18.1.11) closes with this observation: 'The term "peace" [*pax*] seems to be taken from *pactum*, pact. Moreover, a peace is agreed upon later; first, a *foedus*, a treaty is entered into. A treaty is a peace made between warring parties; it derives from *fides*, trust, or from *fetiales*, that is, the priests of that name.' Quoted in Ando, *Law, Language, and Empire in the Roman Tradition*, 60.

the sovereigntist model, we need to be clearer about what we mean when we say that the federative model is juridical in that it patterns legal relations between and among polities – relations, that is, which are understood as giving rise to rights and obligations among the relevant legal subjects.

1 The state has a capacity (intelligence and will) to identify its own best interest and to act with the intention of securing that interest externally.
2 Such action is exemplified by the operation of the state's power to effect compacts with other states so as to build alliances.
3 The ability to engage the compact-making power presupposes a legal capacity on the part of the state as an agent capable of assuming rights and duties in respect of other states.

These initial elements are in a sense unilateral in that, though they presume the identity of the state as a legal actor among other actors, they retain as the frame of reference the perspective of the singular state. A more complete, though still very basic, statement of the federative needs three additional elements that are not unilateral even in that thin sense.

4 The state is understood to have a capacity to identify which types of outside collectives or publics ('states') qualify as counterparties for federative-based compacts.
5 The state's compact-making power presupposes the existence of more or less developed conventions, in light of which commitments between federating parties can be made and made sense of.
6 The commitments undertaken by federating parties are understood by states (or a proportion of them) as patterning legal relations, that is, of generating rights and obligations.

VII The Formation of Constitutional Character

This initial formulation of the federative needs elaboration, but provides a place to start. We need in particular to reinforce the point where the federative (i.e. the perspective of the state considered singularly) meets the federative terrain (i.e. the perspective of the state considered relationally), that is, the 'join' between the first and last three elements listed above. The problem is that the federative might seem at first sight to be somewhat paradoxical. On the one hand (corresponding to elements 1–3), the federative is the property of the state constitution, and the federative terrain somehow created by an extension of that internal property. On the other hand (corresponding to elements 4–6), the federative as an internal constitutional property is (also) the creation of the communicative actions of external agents. In seeking to reconcile these two vectors – the state as both actor and acted upon – the danger to be avoided is on both sides: either a collapse back into solipsism, or else the watering down of the idea of the state as an actor in its own right.[67]

One starting point is to see the process as a structure of mutual recognition, so that the status of the constitutional order is confirmed – arguably even conferred – through its recognition by a legal order external to itself. And the status of that external or international order as law is itself confirmed – arguably conferred – through the acceptance as such by the states that are its subjects. Schematically, it would follow that a constitutional order comprises not just a unilateral Declaration of Independence but also a Constitution (in the name of 'We the People') and a Treaty of Paris (an external validation of the previous two moves). Ideal-typically, you need all three of these phases: an act of collective self-assertion, plus the instantiation of constituent authority together with the recognition of that instantiation by representatives of the external order.[68]

The point can be developed by drawing on the language of legal personhood, that is, the legal capacity to bear rights and duties.[69] We can detect in the operation of the federative a relational understanding of the development of the state as a legal person, one formed by its relations rather than by any inherent characteristic(s).[70] There is a point of comparison with Schmitt, who we saw also had a relational understanding of the state. On his account, the state develops by rubbing up against other political groupings, defining itself by a process of confrontation, if

[67] See, relatedly, David Dyzenhaus's discussion in Chapter 2 of this volume of Kelsen on monism and dualism.

[68] For elaboration, see Thomas Poole, 'The Constitution and Foreign Affairs' (2016) 69 *Current Legal Problems* 143.

[69] Richard Tur, 'The "Person" in Law', in Arthur Peacocke and Grant Gillett (eds.), *Persons and Personality: A Contemporary Inquiry* (Oxford: Blackwell, 1987), 121.

[70] Ngaire Naffine, *Law's Meaning of Life: Philosophy, Religion, Darwin and the Legal Person* (Oxford: Hart Publishing, 2009), 169: 'the way that law forms the person – relationally – directly reflects the way that the person is formed in society, likewise relationally; that is to say, the nature and form of legal relations, which make legal persons, mirror or picture . . . the nature and form of real human relations, which turn us into human subjects: into human persons'.

necessary through war. This account is flawed for reasons already given. The federative theory models a truly relational theory of sociability.[71] It understands the legal character of the state to develop as much exogenously as endogenously, rights and duties being simultaneously asserted by the agent and ascribed to it by other agents in the course of recognising it as a state. That character develops through the way it deploys those rights and duties over time, notably in respect of compact-making and related interactions. Just as Hume thought that human beings were dynamically inter-responsive, the minds of men being like 'mirrors' to each other, reflecting sentiments back and forth through an internal mechanism he called 'sympathy',[72] so may collective actors be said to be constructed through intersubjective relations, between political subjects who succeed in communicating with each other. Such successful communication in turn relies upon participants being able to reach a mutual agreement concerning what counts as a valid utterance.[73]

But this approach is still incomplete. It needs to be able to specify in more detail what is essentially a dynamic system, a set of processes that exist in a state of becoming. It must capture the feedback loops that define the double-facing constitution – outside from the constitutional order, back into it from outside – which themselves presuppose a continual assertion of jurisdictional boundaries between the internal and the external. Once again we can turn to Locke for inspiration, this time mixing more of our exegetical labour into the original text. One way to read the central thesis in the *Second Treatise* about the movement away from the natural to the civil condition is to understand it as a story about the progress of law.[74] The basic idea is that law-girded civil society is the way we get away from natural but problematic structures of rulership. This is first and foremost a story about law and liberty. But it is also about capacity building and identity forming – law and government as a special form of sociability. Locke's story, on this reading of it, has two threads – first, a narrative about how we came to rely on law in the first place and, second, an account of the genesis of the normative and

[71] On which see Paul Sagar, *The Opinion of Mankind: Sociability and the Theory of the State from Hobbes to Smith* (Princeton: Princeton University Press, 2018).

[72] Hume, *Treatise*, T.2.1.11.8 and T.2.2.6.21.

[73] Jürgen Habermas, *The Theory of Communicative Action, Vol. 2, Lifeworld and System: A Critique of Functionalist Reason*, T. McCarthy trans. (Boston: Beacon Press, 1987), 120.

[74] Jeremy Waldron, though not talking directly about the rule of law, highlights the historical or narrative aspects of the *Second Treatise* in 'John Locke: Social Contract Versus Political Anthropology' (1989) 51 *The Review of Politics* 3.

attitudinal structures necessary to sustain it. In other words, it is not enough to think in terms of the development of a particular artificial (legal) structure to replace older and more natural (human) forms of rulership. We must also find room for the development of an attendant culture – conceptual vocabulary, practices, institutions, conventions, habits of mind and so on – necessary to make that structure real.

VIII The Federative as Performance

We can condense Locke's point to the proposition that public law is not just form (the constitutional state) but also grammar (the language of law and government). It seems reasonable to assume that in their interactions, constitutional orders (states), as legal entities, speak through the language of law. I explore this idea of speaking through law in what follows, discovering a strong performative dimension to the federative. This should not be a surprise. Language, after all, is what makes it possible for us to project both backwards into the past, by processes of naming, remembering and reflecting, and forwards into the future, by declaring, promising and imagining.[75] But sovereigntists, conceiving the state's external power primarily in terms of decision, prioritise action over speech. We can agree for the sake of argument that force is the dark matter out of which polities are formed. But it can produce neither a compelling account of how complex political communities sustain themselves, nor a theory of how to do so.

This general idea of law as communicative action can be applied to our particular focus on the process of alliance making archetypically secured through compacts. Our earlier discussion of the Roman practice of concluding *foedera* with other political groups showed how a single polity could be understood as reaching beyond itself, even to the point of deep imbrication with another, through a ritual jurisprudence of alliance. The combination of 'ritual' and 'jurisprudence' is important.[76] Alliance was understood in juridical terms and not simply in terms of the operation of

[75] See Hobbes, *Leviathan*, 18: 'The most noble and profitable invention of all other, was that of SPEECH, consisting of *names* and *appellations*, and their connexion, whereby men register their thoughts; recall them when they are past; and also declare them one to another for mutual utility and conversation; without which, there had been amongst men, neither Commonwealth, nor society, nor contract, nor peace'. See the discussion of this passage in Karen S. Feldman, *Binding Words: Conscience and Rhetoric in Hobbes, Hegel, and Heidegger* (Evanston, IL: Northwestern University Press, 2006), 23–25.

[76] For an argument that contemporary public law ought to be thought of more in terms of ritual, see Jacco Bomhoff, 'Immanence and Irreconcilability: On the Character of Public

force. The *foedus* was as much performed as concluded, and more of a process than an event. First and foremost a faith-constructing exercise, the *foedus* can be understood as a process by which two previously opposed parties agreed to bind themselves to each other on the agreed terms. That process also entailed the recognition of a jurisdiction, in part the creation of the compact-making parties but also having an existence independent of them, in which the terms of the agreement could be said to be binding, that is, of containing legal rights and duties. 'The inherent moral sanction of *fides*', Paul Burton elaborates, 'had a constitutive effect on the international system, and reflects the concern of the Romans (and their competitors, but to a lesser extent) to alleviate the violent anarchy of the system in the interest of creating a more stable and controllable collective-security order'.[77]

We can clarify the exposition by deploying the speech acts taxonomy originally advanced by J. L. Austin.[78] The more developed iteration Austin provides in *How to Do Things with Words* distinguishes between the locutionary act (saying something meaningful), the illocutionary act (what is done *in* saying something), and the perlocutionary act (what is done *by* saying something). This scheme has been taken up, revised and rejected many times since. The way Stanley Cavell remodels it in the essay 'Performative and Passionate Utterance' is particularly valuable since it fills out the perlocutionary, not Austin's immediate focus, and clarifies the relationship between perlocutionary and illocutionary. As Cavell explains, 'to say the illocutionary "I promise, beseech, order, banish ... you" *is* to promise, beseech, order, banish ... you'.[79] We might say that law is the natural province of the illocutionary, so prevalent is its use. In law, words, often allied with dedicated procedures, are often used in this way, to effect a change in things (e.g. passing sentence, executing a will, concluding a contract). The ideal structure of legal argument might even be understood as a chain of something like illocutionary speech acts, one

Law as Political Jurisprudence', in Michael Wilkinson and Michael Dowdle (eds.), *Questioning the Foundations of Public Law* (London: Hart Publishing, 2018).

77 Burton, *Friendship and Empire*, 121.

78 J. L. Austin, *How to Do Things with Words* (Cambridge, MA: Harvard University Press, 1975).

79 Stanley Cavell, 'Performative and Passionate Utterance', in Stanley Cavell, *Philosophy the Day After Tomorrow* (Cambridge, MA: Harvard University Press, 2005), 173. The inclusion of banishment in this list is particularly interesting in the current context. Unlike the others in the list, banishment relies on a constructed community to make it effective. *I* don't banish you – *we* do. Perhaps banishment is more truly perlocutionary than the others.

leading inexorably to the next, until the final and dispositive illocutionary act is reached. Austin defined the perlocutionary act, by contrast, as one which produces 'certain consequential effects upon the feelings, thoughts, or actions of the audience, or of the speaker, or of other persons: and it may be done with the design, intention, or purpose of producing them'.[80]

Cavell elucidates the differences between the two categories. (1) The illocutionary act requires 'an accepted conventional procedure having a certain conventional effect, that procedure to include the uttering of certain words to certain persons in certain circumstances'. The perlocutionary act, by contrast, does not invoke a procedure but invites an exchange. Conventions of a sort may (almost certainly do) exist to structure that exchange, but they are more fluid and less determinative. (2) In the case of illocutionary acts, Austin had claimed, '[t]he "I" who is doing the action does ... come essentially into the picture'. But Cavell extrapolates that in perlocutionary acts 'the "you" comes essentially into the picture' – that is, as a potential subject in its own right and not purely the object of the utterance. The perlocutionary act (e.g. of alarming, horrifying, convincing) relies on *you*. (3) In the illocutionary act, the strong conventional procedure acts as a kind of *mise en scène*, setting the relationship between the participants. But in the perlocutionary act I must declare myself to have standing with you and single you out. (4) As an invitation to exchange, the perlocutionary leaves space, in a way the illocutionary does not, for an independent response from the addressee, who may contest my invitation to exchange for instance by denying that I have standing, or dismissing the demand for the kind of response I seek, or asking to postpone it.[81]

Cavell's interest in the perlocutionary stems from the category's monopoly on the ambiguous, open-ended – and emotionally charged – statement. His analysis is intended as a contribution to a wider view of expression, one which recognises language 'as everywhere revealing desire', put into the service of a moral theory based on a 'systematic recognition of speech as confrontation, as demanding, as owed'.[82] But Yarran Hominh has recently applied Cavell's reconstruction of speech act theory to the political context, reading the Declaration of Independence as a perlocutionary performative. Extending Cavell's analysis, Hominh argues (5) that the perlocutionary speech act does not rely

[80] Austin, *How to Do Things with Words*, 101.
[81] Cavell, 'Performative and Passionate Utterance', 177–82.
[82] Ibid., 187.

on an already-existing subject; rather it constitutes a plural subject – a 'We' – through the speech act itself. The creative potential of the perlocutionary arises from two of its distinctive features, *responsiveness* and *confrontation.* What is typically at stake in the perlocutionary confrontation 'is *our* relationship – a "We" has formed in the course of the confrontation. Importantly, this responsiveness turns on the history between us, on the existing "conventions".' A perlocutionary act, as an invitation to respond, enables history to be reinterpreted and reshaped. It is both contextual and creative of a new possibility. But Hominh also claims (6) that the individuals themselves ('you' and 'I') are effectively constituted through perlocutionary speech acts, 'because *who* each person is changes and develops through those relations that constitute the plural subject'.[83] Here we find the relational theory of sociability discussed earlier translated into the terminology of analytical philosophy.

IX Evolution of the Federative

Three persistent questions continue to trouble this elaboration of the federative. Incorporating our earlier findings into speech act theory, we may just be in a position to answer them. First: how does the operation of the federative, and the federative terrain, get going in the first place? Second: how does the federative terrain operate once established? Third: how does the operation of the federative in turn shape the juridical character of the constitutional order?

I address these questions by means of a stylised two-stage evolutionary story – the progress of the federative. Let us first stand alongside Aeneas and Latinus in a world largely devoid of compacts, where the 'script of alliance' capable of offering a set of conventional procedures into which to place our speech acts exists only in very rudimentary form. (Though even here, some kind of embryonic structure of mutual recognition must in play, a web of more or less shared meanings and conventions, whereby e.g. Aeneas knows that it is Latinus with whom he ought to treat.) Assume that Aeneas makes the first move. His peace offer initially reaches out to Latinus seeking a reciprocal response but knowing that none is guaranteed. He goes out on a limb where there is little or no normative support, only the possibility that such a support will be forthcoming if agreement is reached. If it is, then Aeneas's offer and Latinus's

[83] Yarran Hominh, 'Re-Reading the Declaration of Independence as Perlocutionary Performative' (2016) 22 *Res Publica* 423, 442, 438, 439.

acceptance will have effected a change in their relationship. On the understanding of the parties, reciprocal rights and duties exist where none existed before. By extension, we might say that their act of mutual recognition has created a new juridical framework, one neither Roman nor Latin, but a by-product of the alliance struck between them.

This scenario corresponds to the classic structure of the perlocutionary act. (1) There is no rigid conventional procedure. (2) The addressee, Latinus, 'comes essentially into the picture', not just the object of Aeneas's projections but as an agent in his own right. (3) Aeneas has no standing by right, but in inviting an exchange with Latinus declares himself to have appropriate standing. (4) Latinus has a choice about whether to respond in the desired way to the invitation. (5) The successful exchange produces a plural subject – in this case, an alliance. The participants acknowledge this, as evidenced by Aeneas's oath of fealty 'by Latona's twin offspring, and by two-faced Janus'. (6) The alliance also (re-) constitutes the individuals who conclude it, in that it produces the Romans and the Latins as *political* communities. Indeed, that seems to be the message Vergil wants us to draw from the poem.[84] Aeneas, the human person, led his people from Troy to Italy. But it was the compact with the Latins, concluded by Aeneas the Prince, that established Rome as a *civitas* – that is, in our terms, as a legal person.[85]

In the second phase of evolution, we are now in something like the world mapped out (or idealised) by Cicero, in which alliances of the sort concluded by Aeneas and Latinus are now commonplace features of international and domestic politics.[86] Conventional practices surrounding

[84] J. D. Reed, *Vergil's Gaze: Nation and Poetry in the Aeneid* (Princeton: Princeton University Press, 2007), 2: 'Roman identity – always reducible to some other nationality, depending on where the poem draws the boundary between nations – emerges as a synthesis (in a dialectical sense) of other national identities (analogous to the dialogue conducted by the Aeneid with its literary fore runners); there is no essence, no absolute centre, no origin that exclusively authorises Romanness'. See also Katherine Toll, 'Making Roman-ness and the *Aeneid*' (1997) 15 *Classical Antiquity* 34.

[85] In fact, Vergil's tale is denser – and the intermeshing of the previously warring groups more profound. 'According to the *Aeneid*, the Roman people sprang forth from the ashes of civil war . . . Though Aeneas won the battle against Turnus and his Italian allies, the Trojans [i.e. the group of Trojan exiles led by Aeneas] did not absorb the Latins. Rather, Troy and Trojan would disappear, and the Romans, born from Italian stock, became powerful through Italian virtue': Clifford Ando, *Imperial Ideology and Provincial Loyalty in the Roman Empire* (Berkeley: University of California Press, 2000), 53.

[86] Ando, *Law, Language, and Empire in the Roman Tradition*, 80: 'by the late first century B. C.E., theory and practice had evolved so that other parties to diplomatic exchange were treated as though they and Rome existed in a network of similarly ordered states'.

compact-making (*foedera*) are well established, and a more or less coherent and stable set of constitutional rules and attendant practices has emerged to govern them. Polities work to a conventionally agreed script of alliance. A federative terrain has emerged as a consequence in which (1) polities understand themselves as existing in a web of alliance built from ties of mutual obligation and (2) it has become meaningful to discuss the operation of that web of alliance in terms of a distinct body of law, neither mine or yours but ours, which has developed with the systematic operation of the script of alliance over time.[87] We have, in Cicero's phrase, though broadening his original meaning, 'the whole code of law that deals with war and peace'.

What does this more evolved federative look like using speech act theory? Despite all the developments, the basic perlocutionary structure of the classic federative remains intact. Any attempt to adjust in significant ways existing rights and duties through the federative will still take the form of an invitation to exchange – though such invitations now generally occur within the more settled framework of the mature federative. What is new is that the operation of the federative, now embedded within the normal texture of law, becomes more routine. Different types of speech act proliferate as a result. We see this in *Pro Balbo*, our main Ciceronian source on Roman treaty law, where during his speech Cicero makes a series of legal claims that are meant to lead to a particular dispositive result. On the basis of our earlier description of legal argument, we might say that these statements take something like illocutionary form. Some relate to domestic federative law: e.g. 'nothing can be sacrosanct save what has been enacted by the People or by the Commons'. Some to external federative law: e.g. 'How could greater ignorance be shown than by saying that states bound to us by treaty must "give consent"? For this is a condition which does not apply to states bound to us by treaty any more than to free states in general.' Others combine the two: e.g. 'if a saving clause makes admission to citizenship lawful, then, where there is no saving clause, admission must be lawful. Where, then, is there any saving clause in the treaty with Gades, under which the Roman People may not admit to citizenship any citizen of Gades?'[88]

[87] Ando, *Law, Language, and Empire in the Roman Tradition*, 79: 'It is, in fact, a notable achievement within Roman culture that it developed a conception of international law and that legal theorists so heatedly debated the source of its content and its force.'

[88] *Pro Balbo*, 667, 649 and 669.

The consequences of the original federative can be profound. In the compact between Aeneas and Latinus, the federative moment was constitutive. It simultaneously produced and confirmed Rome as a polity and established a new federative law, albeit one that was as yet very fragile and only bilateral. While not so elemental, the impact of the more mature prerogative is in a different sense equally profound as the feedback loops characteristic of the double-facing constitution become more common and more visible. We see this again in *Pro Balbo*. Cicero's primary concern on this score relates to what we might call the externalities of domestic political decisions, in particular those relating to the incentive structure for non-citizens who assist Roman interests.[89] He is concerned more generally here as elsewhere with ideas of good faith, justice and 'sacred obligation' that formed the moral structure of the federative terrain as he understood it,[90] and by extension with the possibility that illegal or injudicious use of the federative might corrupt Rome and undermine fundamental republican principles.

X The Contemporary Federative

This account of the evolution of the federative is not an attempt to write history. It is a stylised reconstruction that draws upon some of the materials we uncovered when tracing Locke's use of the federative back to Cicero. Even so understood, it might feel a little remote from current concerns. In the space remaining, I indicate how the idea of the federative elaborated here can illuminate important but poorly understood aspects of contemporary constitutional law and politics. In typical common law fashion, I examine recent cases whose meaning, I suggest, emerges more clearly when set against federative theory. More specifically, I show how the cases also show the relevance of the two-stage evolutionary analysis of the federative. That is, the modern federative can be seen as having both a perlocutionary aspect (i.e. more open-textured and capable of generating new norms) and an illocutionary aspect (i.e. more circumscribed and capable of grounding 'normal' legal claims).

89 *Pro Balbo*, 651: 'if neither our commanders, nor the Senate, nor the Roman People, are to be permitted, by offering rewards, to attract the bravest and best of our allies and friends from states bound to us by treaty to expose themselves to danger for our welfare, then, in dangerous and stormy times, we shall be deprived of a most valuable advantage and often of a most powerful aid'.

90 *Pro Balbo*, 673.

A Act of State: a Window into the Classic Federative

We characterised that classic (or perlocutionary) form of the federative as an invitation to exchange, central to which is a reaching out beyond jurisdictional boundaries in a search for recognition. The recognition often includes a kind of paralleling, with one party seeking the reassurance of another party on the rightness or appropriateness of a certain institutional arrangement or normative position. What can result from this exchange is a new normative understanding shared between two now (more) related but still independent participants. If this sounds esoteric, it should not. It is a pattern of behaviour that occurs constantly, often in minor ways. Much of it occurs within the executive branch (e.g. in the practice of the Foreign Office or equivalent), a topic explored in Campbell McLachlan's chapter in this volume. But all three branches of state play a role, including the legislature as we see shortly. Looking to the judicial branch can be revealing too. Especially in common law jurisdictions, judges often give voice to normative positions in a way that is not systematically true of the executive.

There has been a notable rise in cases in which this distinctive behaviour of reaching out or normative paralleling is visible, certainly in UK courts. This is partly a contextual matter, relating both to general trends towards greater international and cross-border interaction and also the specific post-2001 counterterrorism climate. An important trio of cases, handed down together by the UK Supreme Court, concerned the UK's complicity in the unlawful detention and rendition, assault, torture and cruel and inhuman treatment of individuals usually (in these actions) at the hands of officials of other states. The cases engaged the Act of State principle, a common law doctrine (or set of doctrines) that shelters from judicial oversight certain kinds of 'sovereign' acts done in the exercise of the foreign relations prerogative and the broadly comparable acts of other states. I concentrate here on one of those cases, *Belhaj* v. *Straw*.[91]

The Act of State doctrine is concerned with the construction of the federative power. It is part of domestic law, not public international law. As such, it is partly constitutive of the external constitution, that part of the state which comprehends and acts in the world outside it. This does not mean that argument in the case turned solely on domestic law. International law arguments, specifically on state immunity, were considered in *Belhaj*, an indication of how the federative and the

[91] [2017] UKSC 3.

international often dovetail.[92] Moreover, there is a very high incidence in dealing with the domestic law argument in the case of normative paralleling and related techniques. The judges frequently draw on foreign jurisprudence, often quite systematically, particularly of comparative jurisdictions ('allies') to see how they construct this aspect of the federative.[93] As well as looking outside for inspiration or confirmation, the judges sometimes do the opposite: that is, they project outwards in a way that seems to invite normative exchange. Take this passage from the lead judgment in *Belhaj*. Noting a potential problem with equating sovereignty with executive activity, Lord Mance continues:

> In states subject to the rule of law, a state's sovereignty may be manifest through its legislative, executive or judicial branches acting within their respective spheres. Any excess of executive power will or may be expected to be corrected by the judicial arm. A rule of recognition which treats any executive act by the government of a foreign state as valid, irrespective of its legality under the law of the foreign state . . . could mean ignoring, rather than giving effect to, the way in which a state's sovereignty is expressed.[94]

This is congruent with our criticism of the prerogative disposition of sovereigntist theory. But what is important here is that the statement projects outwards as well as looks inward. It is locutionary (it says something) and illocutionary (it does something in the course of saying something) in so far as it establishes the terms of English common law doctrine. But it is also perlocutionary (it projects or desires something in the course of saying something), and I think conceived as such, reaching out to other participants, especially foreign judges, seeking normative affirmation and reinforcement.

Belhaj gives us a small but fairly clear window into the federative. In this context, litigation brings to light an element of the external constitution, here the scope of the Act of State principle. That principle is federative to the core, being concerned largely with the legal consequences arising from the state's federative interactions with other states.

[92] See *Belhaj*, esp. paras. [12]–[31]. See also at [95]: 'It is true that the common law develops an responds to changing times and attitudes, and that a sharp division between the domestic and international legal sphere is less visible today than in the past' (per Lord Mance).

[93] In *Belhaj*, Lord Mance gave detailed consideration to US authorities (46–57); Lord Sumption considered French (at 201), US (209–12), Australian (246–47) and Canadian (264–65) authorities.

[94] *Belhaj* at [65].

In settling the question, the court sifts through the relevant legal materials. Given the context, it seems natural – and all but essential – to consider the way similar jurisdictions resolve similar questions. We may hope to see our preferred solution reflected back in constitutional practice of our allies. To the extent that it is not, it might cause us to pause and reflect some more.[95] Over time, though, this process is reciprocal. It is not just a matter of the UK court importing foreign material. It also exports normative material, whether as persuasive precedent or more direct normative propositions (of which Lord Mance's statement may be an example). This back-and-forth dynamic is characteristic of the federative in action, as we have seen. The focus may be very largely on internal ordering – on what laws we give ourselves – but the mirroring process may yet over time contribute, even if not intended as such, to a web of normative assumptions that exist on the federative terrain and pattern the relations between nations. There is no doubt that the judges in *Belhaj* were aware of this. The Act of State cases, they said, were part of the *jure imperii*, the law relating to sovereign acts.[96]

B Brexit and the More Developed Federative

The second stage in the evolution of the federative also contains the classic or perlocutionary federative. But what sets it apart is that the federative at this stage has also been increasingly normalised, as evidenced by the increased use of illocutionary statements grounded in the federative. (I do not mean to imply that these propositions are solely the province of the court. To the contrary, most will be advanced in the political branches of state, especially the executive.) The result is a thicker and more intricately patterned federative, in which both the frequency and visibility of feedback loops correspondingly increases.

Sticking with recent British cases, one example stands out: the Brexit case, *Miller* v. *Secretary of State for Exiting the EU*. Despite its novelty, *Miller* was argued in broadly familiar terms as a case on the exercise of prerogative power. (We shall see that the UK Supreme Court widened the inquiry to include a more deliberate focus on federative concerns.) Positions were drawn on correspondingly familiar lines. Some scholars supported the view that the government

95 See on this subject Kim Lane Scheppele, 'Aspirational and Aversive Constitutionalism: The case for studying cross-constitutional influence through negative models' (2003) 1 *International Journal of Constitutional Law* 296.

96 *Belhaj* at [199] (per Lord Sumption).

could effect the UK's notification of withdrawal from the European Union via the foreign relations prerogative, many of them drawing on sovereigntist theory.[97] Others agreed with the Court that the constitution required an Act of Parliament to be passed first, authorising notification, since withdrawal from the European Union would unsettle existing legal rights and duties, many of them statutory.[98]

This reading of the case as the latest in a line of great prerogative cases stretching back to early-modern times should not obscure the fact that *Miller* is fundamentally a case on the federative. This is obvious in one sense: the argument centred not on prerogative power in general terms, but specifically on the foreign relations prerogative, the main (if not the only) category through which federative power is organised and exercised in the constitution. *Miller*, as the leading case on the foreign relations prerogative in living memory, is certain to affect how that power is understood. It may be possible elsewhere to see this power in operation in more or less its classic form, say in the forging of new compacts. But in *Miller* we encounter the operation of the foreign relations power in a setting dense in law. So dense in fact that one of the more interesting aspects of the judgments is how they propose to separate contiguous sources of law, UK and EU.

Faced with this reality, the sovereigntist assumptions that animated the pro-prerogative position proved to have little traction. Sovereigntist theory assumes a split-level world, as we have seen, in which the terrain outside the state is taken to be sparse in law and interactions between states essentially strategic. Any law that does manage to emerge from this normative wasteland is seen as special ('deficient') since it is bound up with the logic of sovereign decision. But the situation that emerged in *Miller* – and subsequently the whole Brexit process – is one marked not by a paucity of law but the opposite. This is not just a matter of the variety of legal sources in play (UK, EU) but also the way in which they function in recognisably normal ways: that is, they ground illocutionary propositions and conclusions. In terms of our evolutionary schema, *Miller* inhabits the realm of the more developed federative, belonging to the world of Cicero not Aeneas. What was in play more specifically – just as it was in *Pro Balbo* – was what, given our frame of reference, we can call the

[97] See, e.g., Endicott, 'This Ancient, Secretive Royal Prerogative', discussed earlier.

[98] See, e.g., Thomas Poole, 'Devotion to Legalism: On the Brexit Case' (2017) 80 *Modern Law Review* 696.

relevant federative terrain (e.g. EU treaties),[99] the internal federative (e.g. the European Communities Act) and the nexus between them (e.g. rules relating to parliamentary sovereignty and the foreign relations power).

It is perhaps not surprising, when outlined in these terms, that a substantial majority of the UKSC in *Miller* rejected a sovereigntist position, just as it was rejecting similarly motivated arguments in the Act of State cases. That rejection is perhaps clearest in the majority's response to Lord Carnwath's dissent which, in its articulation of a 'balance of power' position between executive and Parliament as justifying the use of prerogative in the exceptional context of Brexit, closely tracked the sovereigntist argument advanced by Endicott and others. The majority judges saw this position as 'a potentially controversial argument constitutionally', since it justified 'all sorts of powers being accorded to the executive, on the basis that ministers could always be called to account for their exercise of any power'.[100] One way of interpreting this position is to see it as a rejection of the argument that the exception ought to trump the norm, the effect of so doing incidentally being to reinforce the constitutional norm. But we can also read it as responding to the dangers inherent in a position that seeks to transfer a strongly prerogative mindset in respect of the external constitution into the internal constitution.

In fact, when you start looking for them, *Miller* is full of feedback loops, as one would expect in an important decision on the more developed federative. It is not just an awareness of the negative effects of the transference from outside to inside noted in respect of Carnwath's 'balance of power' argument. It is also visible in the way the majority reflected on the UK's membership of the EU as having effected a significant change on the fundamental constitution. The European Communities Act had introduced 'a new constitutional process for making law in the United Kingdom'. That process radically altered UK laws, but it also helped to reshape the UK constitution, not least because the new source of law had precedence over all other sources of domestic law including statute. Essential to this process was how 'a dynamic,

[99] Of course, the federative is only one, necessarily limited, perspective on a political and legal entity as complicated as the European Union. A more classic legal perspective on the subject can be obtained from reading Dieter Grimm's chapter in this volume, Chapter 14. The strength of the federative is that it draws attention to what the world looks like from the perspective of the state. It also tells us something about the connection between the juridical creations that populate the federative terrain – the products of the plural exercise of the federative capacity – and the individual state, and by extension the way that terrain helps to shape the juridical construction of the state.

[100] *Miller* at [92].

international source of law was grafted onto, and above, the well-established existing sources of domestic law: Parliament and the courts'.[101] This goes to the heart of the majority position since it followed, on its view, that Parliament and not the executive should now be responsible for the decision to shut down that constitutional process.

This dimension of the case, predictable enough given our elaboration of the federative, tends to be overlooked by commentators. But what *Miller* is particularly good at bringing into view is the federative's role as a kind of constitutional airlock, determining how norms that derive from the federative terrain get into the constitution and on what basis. Seen in these terms, the Court's task was to determine the allocation of functions that pertain in the space between the inner and outer membranes of the constitution. The rejection of the claim that the withdrawal notification could be given as a matter of executive prerogative is well understood as a decision to reinforce parliamentary sovereignty. More specifically, in my view, it was a decision to ensure that the exercise of prerogative did not undermine Parliament's federative capacity, i.e. that part of its role as ultimate guardian of constitutional order which is concerned with what comes into that order from external sources.[102]

XI Concluding Observations

The chapter has made a case for an account of the double-facing constitution which has the idea of the federative at its heart. Locke used that term to designate the foreign relations power of the commonwealth. I have built on Locke's intuition that this power is concerned centrally with the capacity to effect compacts (alliances) with other political associations. One advantage of the perspective that ensues is that this compact-making power is demonstrably a juridical idea. It is an idea, moreover, that is open to the possibility of reciprocity and, by extension, the development of truly juridical structures of mutual recognition. Just as important, it also serves to de-centre war from the central position many writers accord it within the external constitution. As such, the federative offers the prospect of escaping the paradox of the sovereign state: based on law and peace internally, but geared to prerogative and war externally. The federative unites the object of the internal and

[101] *Miller* at [90].

[102] Parliament's federal capacity was recognised and somewhat enhanced by Part 2 of the Constitutional Reform and Governance Act 2010.

external aspects of the constitution – peace – and the means of achieving that object – law.

The federative theory relies on the generative properties of compact-making. To be more exact, it rests ultimately on the capacity of a political entity to recognise the capacity of like entities to effect compacts. The compact emerges from this inquiry as the essential generative structure in the construction and elaboration of juridical relations. For most of the chapter, we travelled outwards from that starting point, seeking to map the double-facing constitution. We sought in particular to show how the structure of mutual recognition among compacting states delineates the state as a juridical character whose identity correlates with the sum of its interactions with other political entities.

We might just as easily have turned our attention inward. Compact-making abounds *within* domestic constitutions, not only in states recognised as federations. I have so far refrained from observing that the term used most frequently as the embodiment of the federative – compact – is precisely the word Hobbes used to describe the structure of agreement by means of which the commonwealth is instituted. If we are prepared to recognise the compact as conceptually necessary for establishing domestic constitutional order – in effect as the axiom undergirding political life – why would we not recognise the same power as necessary for establishing juridical relations between orders so constituted? The case for doing so is stronger to the extent that we share Hume's intuition that, politically speaking, the external predates the internal. 'I assert the first rudiments of government to arise from quarrels, not among men of the same society, but among those of different societies'.[103]

Naturally, not all of the implications of the position opened up in this investigation have been explored. The most important of these omissions concerns the nature of sovereignty.[104] We have touched on that most vexed of constitutional subjects, challenging the coherence of a popular split-level conception which juxtaposes the sovereign's internal duty as law-maker with the strategic action through prerogative that is thought to characterise the exercise of its external functions. But our analysis

[103] *Treatise*, T.3.2.7.3.

[104] Another omission, obvious given the prominent inclusion of Cicero in the narrative, relates to the question of power imbalances in the operation of the federative, specifically the relationship between the historical development of the federative and the rise and fall of empire – on which see, e.g., Lauren Benton and Lisa Ford, *Rage for Order: The British Empire and the Origins of International Law, 1800–1850* (Cambridge, MA: Harvard University Press, 2016).

opens up a more direct point of attack. For Hobbes, the precondition of a constitutional order determining its own laws was a capacity to remain free from law. Schmitt took that idea of unboundedness to new heights, generalising the imagined moment of ecstatic release from normative constraint in his elaboration of the 'exception'. These positions remain trapped in the solipsistic state. What, then, about this alternative gloss as a basis for future reflection? Sovereignty is not being unbound by law. It is the juridical capacity to determine the laws by which one is bound. That capacity is constructed rather than asserted, the product of external interaction as much as internal action.

4

Hobbes's Janus-Faced Sovereign

THEODORE CHRISTOV

There are two maxims which are surely both true: Man is a God to man, *and* Man is a wolf to Man. *The former is true of the relations of citizens with each other, the latter of relations between commonwealths.*

Thomas Hobbes, *De Cive*[1]

Introduction

Today most of us live as citizens of specific states with jurisdiction over every inhabitable corner of the globe. Unimaginable a mere two centuries ago, the state emerged from a former world of empires and rapidly accelerated over the past seven decades or so to claim sovereignty over our most basic form of civil association.[2] As a universal dictum of political organisation, the state defines us as citizens and delineates our duties to each other, not only as fellow citizens of the same state but also how we relate as foreigners and members of different states. We may be citizens of specific states, but we also relate to one another as equal persons transcending the confinement of our own state. Despite recent claims to the universality of humanity and widespread celebrations of cosmopolitan citizenship, however, we do remain fundamentally defined by our belonging to a territorially bound and constitutionally specific state, subject to its particular laws. Even our globalised sentiments are still rooted in the recognition that the state does persist as the basic unit in which we choose to organise ourselves. Widespread and contagious, the state also remains stubborn: no matter how we choose to talk about politics, we axiomatically grant its powers.

But what we mean by the state can be, at best, deeply contentious, as the writings of one of its original proponents show. Disagreement

[1] Thomas Hobbes, *De Cive*, ed. Richard Tuck and Michael Silverthorne (Cambridge: Cambridge University Press, 1998), 3–4.

[2] Since the founding of the United Nations in 1945, the number of states has increased fourfold.

emerges over methodology (where we disagree over the best approach of how to think about the very concept of the state, assuming, of course, that we reach a consensus over its definition) and periodisation (when we are continually divided over its boundaries, whether natural or artificial). At worst, the quest for a neutral – if not, ambitiously, transhistorical – definition of the state (as largely practised, for example, in the quantitative branch of political science) remains merely illusory, and, for that reason alone, it remains an empty aspiration.[3] From its earliest days, when Thomas Hobbes originally formulated it, the concept of the state has invariably been entangled in deeply ideological debates over the nature and practice of politics – particularly, how the domestic relates to the international – and hence the subject of ongoing contestations over its very essence.

And yet, if we turn to the early beginning of how the sovereign state was first theorised, well before its practice became widespread, we can bring to light a normative understanding of the state that was originally committed to the twin goals of securing an enduring domestic peace first, so that it can subsequently serve as a vehicle for promoting international peace. The Hobbesian sovereign stood in a twofold relation: how its own citizens – as natural persons – covenant with each other to institute the artificial person of the state, and then how such artificial persons, in turn, interact with one another in the absence of a global sovereign. This twofold relation is generally illustrated through an analogy between the interpersonal and international state of nature, which indeed lies at the heart of the Hobbesian project. While essential, as I shall argue, the analogy between the relations between individuals and the relations between states is incomplete and bears limitations.

States are independent not only in relation to one another, but also because of the absence of a sovereign above them all. And because they are fiercely autonomous, they are also seen as generally hostile. With no sovereign above all sovereigns, their relations largely seem to be determined by the use of force and the dynamics of power relations. Their hostility proceeds from their competitive nature in the same way, as the analogy is widely accepted, as raw individuals in a state of lawless nature. But such a straightforward application of the analogy between the domestic and the international, as the chapter argues, is ultimately mistaken: Hobbes's conflation of the law of nature and the law of nations

[3] Quentin Skinner, 'A Genealogy of the Modern State' (2009) 162 *Proceedings of the British Academy*, 325–70.

does not support such a straightforward parallel between individuals and states. While essential in its feature of autonomous agency, the analogy between the internal and external domains remains incomplete: the insecurity of individuals outside of sovereignty is, in a strict sense, incomparable to that of states in a world of no global leviathan.

While the internal and external dimensions of Hobbesian sovereignty are generally recognised, their precise relationship continues to be the subject of debates, and there is a strong tendency to accept that a great divide separates the two. The pronounced dichotomy of home and abroad, the inside and the outside, with which we have customarily come to characterise sovereign states today, has only tended to sharpen their binary nature, rather than seek to affirm their original symbiotic relationship.[4] At its inception, sovereignty – as Hobbes claimed – served as the political glue to bind citizens with one another domestically inasmuch as it also facilitated, through the procurement of safety internally, the general amelioration of relations among sovereigns externally. International peace feeds on domestic peace.

Over time, however, the two faces of the sovereign have continually grown apart: the internal is widely regarded as creating peacefulness and order from within, whereas the external is seen as perpetuating warfare from without. Because of their divergent goals, the two, we are persistently told, are difficult, if not impossible, to reconcile. The domestic consolidates peace, whereas the international invites the sword.[5] To

[4] Howard Williams, *International Relations and the Limits of Political Theory* (New York: St. Martin's Press, 1996); David Boucher, *Political Theories of International Relations: From Thucydides to the Present* (Oxford: Oxford University Press, 1998); Richard Tuck, *The Rights of War and Peace: Political Thought and the International Order from Grotius to Kant* (Oxford: Oxford University Press, 1998); Philip Bobbitt, *The Shield of Achilles: War, Peace, and the Course of History* (New York: Knopf, 2002).

[5] Joseph Margolis, 'War and Ideology,' in Virginia Held, Sidney Moregenbesser, and Thomas Nagel (eds.), *Philosophy, Morality, and International Affairs* (New York: Oxford University Press, 1974); Richard Falk, 'The World Order Models Project and Its Critics: A Reply' (1978) 32(2) *International Organization*, 531–45; Hedley Bull, *The Anarchical Society: A Study of Order in World Politics* (London: Macmillan, 1977); Hedley Bull, 'Hobbes and the International Anarchy' 41 *Social Research*, 717–38; Friedrich Kratochwill, 'The Force of Prescriptions' 38(4) *International Organization*, 685–708; T. Airaksinen and M. A. Bertman (eds.), *Hobbes: War among Nations* (Aldershot: Ashgate Publishing, 1989); Laurie M. Johnson, *Thucydides, Hobbes, and the Interpretation of Realism* (DeKalb: University of Illinois Press, 1993); Laurie Johnson, 'Mathematici versus Dogmatici: Understanding the Realist Project through Hobbes', in David Clinton (ed.), *The Realist Tradition and Contemporary International Relations* (Baton Rouge, LA: Louisiana State University Press, 2002), 96–116; Raino Malnes, *The Hobbesian Theory of International Conflict* (Oslo: Scandinavian University Press, 1993);

speak of the Hobbesian sovereign, therefore, is to call attention to a persistent dilemma over how to relate the domestic legal order and the international legal order. On the one hand, as the holder of domestic sovereignty, the state is the bearer of order and security. But on the other hand, the plurality of such states creates an international state of nature with no overarching sovereign. There, then, is the puzzle. How can the Hobbesian sovereign have two faces – internal and external – and, moreover, how do the two relate to each other?

The chapter examines the internal and external dimensions of the state. It focuses on Hobbes's conception of the state by relating its internal, domestic, or municipal capacities to those encompassing the relations between states. The goal is to offer a novel interpretation of the infamous state of nature and how it informs our understanding of artificial persons without a sovereign above them all. The sovereign state is examined as Janus-faced, with one face looking inward, as a sovereign over its subject, while the other face looks outward, as a sovereign among other sovereigns. Rather than regarding these two faces as coexisting in a tense relationship, I argue that their relationship is mutually reinforcing by showing just how central international relations were to Hobbes's domestic theory of the state. This approach will offer a new way of thinking about the genealogy of sovereignty by uniting the two crowns of state: domestic and international.

My argument is that the sovereign state is Janus-faced, with one face looking inward over its domestic constitution, while the other face is looking outward over its relations with other sovereigns. It faces inward, calling the citizen to perform one's duties for others, to the need to uphold the social bond, and to the commitment to '*ought to endeavour Peace*', as Hobbes's 'Fundamentall Law of Nature' dictates.[6] And yet, just as clearly, it also faces outward, inviting other sovereigns of good

Laurie Johnson, 'Thucydiean Realism: Between Athens and Melos', in Benjamin Frankel (ed.), *Roots of Realism* (London: Frank Cass & Co, 1996), 169–93; Chris Brown, 'Contractarian Thought and the Constitution of International Society', in David Mapel and Terry Nardin (eds.), *International Society* (Princeton, NJ: Princeton University Press, 1998), 132–43; Kurt Taylor Gaubatz, 'The Hobbesian Problem and the Microfoundations of International Relations Theory' (2001) 11(2) *Security Studies*, 164–86; Daniel Deudney, 'Left Behind: Neorealism's Truncated Contextual Materialism and Republicanism' (2009) 23(3) *International Relations*, 341–71; Ian Hall, 'The Triumph of Anti-liberalism? Reconciling Radicalism to Realism in International Relations Theory' (2011) 9(1) *Political Studies Review*, 42–52.

[6] Thomas Hobbes, *Leviathan*, ed. Richard Tuck and Michael Silverthorne (Cambridge: Cambridge University Press, 1996), 92.

judgment to the need to work for the common good of humanity and thereby provide a focal point for peace among other states. Perhaps most strikingly, the double-faced state serves to define one sovereign against other sovereigns in the absence of any higher authority. International peace proceeds from and feeds on domestic peace.

I Between the Inside and the Outside

Of the many facts about the contemporary world that we tend to take for granted, one of the most pervasive is, of course, that it is a world of separate states. The sovereign state fundamentally defines the political universe we inhabit: it is not only stubborn, for its persistent hold on our political existence. It is also contagious, for it has spread its jurisdiction over every inhabitable corner of the world. The groundwork for a recognisably modern theory of the sovereign state had already been laid by the middle of the seventeenth century. Central to this development was, as we all know, the figure of Thomas Hobbes, whose aim was 'to make a more curious search into the rights of states and duties of subjects'.[7] While it is undeniable that Hobbes is widely accepted as the first modern theorist of the sovereign state (for his theory of the state is partly our own theory today), it is far from clear that we hold a unanimous view about his justification for the institution of sovereignty, and the nature of the subsequent multitude of leviathans across the globe.

In fact, a strange, if not puzzling, imbalance begins to emerge if we look at studies of Hobbes in the history of political thought, on the one hand, and in the history and theory of international relations, on the other hand. For most historians of political thought, Hobbes is regarded as the founder of the theory of domestic sovereignty, where the state is sovereign over its subjects. For historians of international thought, Hobbes is a canonical figure for his theory of the state as a sovereign among other sovereigns.[8] While no student of political thought or international relations can possibly afford to disregard Hobbes's contribution to both fields, we, as scholars and teachers, are clearly confronted with a problem. If Hobbes's contribution to international thought was so fundamental – and to many, he is the founder of the "Realist" theory of

[7] *De Cive*, Preface, xiv.

[8] David Armitage, 'Hobbes and the Foundations of Modern International Thought', in James Tully, Annabel Brett and Holly Hamilton-Bleakly (eds.), *Rethinking the Foundations of Modern Political Thought* (Cambridge: Cambridge University Press, 2006).

international politics – how could it have been ignored for so long? Moreover, how did he come to be accepted as canonical in international thought if his thoughts on the subject were so few and, to many, unsystematic? The answers to these questions will have profound consequences for how we understand, and teach, both the history of political thought and international relations theory. I seek to address these questions by examining the corpus of Hobbes's writings, including various editions of his work.

So let us ask ourselves: what is so puzzling about the asymmetry between the political theory Hobbes and the international relations Hobbes? Within the canon of political theory, the name of Hobbes has come to be synonymous with order and there are two basic assumptions that go with this view (both of which I will contest). In the first assumption, Hobbes is widely regarded as a radical individualist, who denies sociability and for whom the state of nature is defined as the condition where humans live outside groups.[9] In the second assumption, Hobbes is generally seen as a theorist of 'civil science', or domestic politics. His 'civil science' examines the state solely in relation to its internal organisation and has nothing to say about its role as an international agent.[10] From this perspective, the Hobbesian state is examined as a sovereign over its subjects rather than as a sovereign among sovereigns.

This relative silence of commentators in political theory on the international dimension of Hobbes's work contrasts starkly with his canonical position among the founding fathers of international theory. No student of international relations, as we all know, can possibly afford to disregard Hobbes's lasting impact to that field. Within the canon of international relations, the name of Hobbes has become an easy synonym with anarchy. In the first assumption, Hobbes directly inspired the conception of

[9] Alan Ryan *The Making of Modern Liberalism* (Princeton, NJ: Princeton University Press, 2012), 186. Similarly, C. B. Macpherson, *The Political Theory of Possessive Individualism: Hobbes to Locke* (Oxford: Oxford University Press, 1962), 40; Leo Strauss, *Natural Rights and History* (Chicago: University of Chicago Press, 1965), 278; Carole Pateman, *The Problem of Political Obligation: A Critique of Liberal Theory* (Berkeley: University of California Press, 1979), 39; Ian Shapiro, *The Evolution of Rights in Liberal Theory* (Cambridge: Cambridge University Press, 1986), 51; Carole Pateman, *The Sexual Contract* (Stanford: Stanford University Press, 1988), 43–44; David Johnston, *The Idea of a Liberal Theory: A Critique and Reconsideration* (Princeton, NJ: Princeton University Press, 1994), 83; Richard Flathman, *Thomas Hobbes: Skepticism, Individuality, and Chastened Politics* (Oxford: Oxford University Press, 2002), 5.

[10] Richard Tuck, *Philosophy and Government: 1572–1651* (Cambridge: Cambridge University Press, 1993); Quentin Skinner, *Liberty Before Liberalism* (Cambridge: Cambridge University Press, 1998).

the relations between states as fundamentally anarchic, where states, in the absence of a superior power, are unconstrained by any norms. On this account, the view of Hobbes the anarchist was simply an extension of his domestic theory.

In the second assumption, shared particularly by classical Realists, such as E. H. Carr and Hans Morgenthau, Hobbes was, after Machiavelli, the second great Realist. The consensus, however, that established Hobbes as a preeminent Realist is in fact rather new: it did not emerge until the early twentieth century and was a product of exogenous intellectual developments which had absolutely nothing to do with Hobbes himself. So how did his contribution inspire 'a discourse of anarchy' if his central intellectual concern – as argued here – was to establish the conditions of peace?

So my aim here is threefold, and accordingly, there will be three parts to what follows. I describe Hobbes's conception of the interpersonal state of nature in order to show the various manifestations 'nature' can take. I then consider the Hobbesian sovereignty over subjects and how it is to be distinguished from the state of war. And, finally, I examine the implications of sovereignty for the international sphere. I draw two main conclusions: domestically, Hobbes's sovereign is surprisingly fragile and has to learn to live with the imminence of its possible dissolution. Internationally, perhaps even more surprisingly, sovereigns relate a cooperatively and relatively peacefully.

II States of Nature

Between the early seventeenth and early nineteenth centuries, major political thinkers conceived for the first time the possibility of a world of states, where a multitude of sovereign states would eventually emerge from a former world of empires. The earliest moment in which we find recognisably modern discussions of statehood – the nature of its powers and the scope of its authority – occurs around the turn of the seventeenth century and rapidly takes off later in that century. Rightly regarded by many as the first modern theorist of the sovereign state, Hobbes has come to occupy the position of originator of the concept. The formation of early modern theories of the state occurred during a period in which the rights of persons – whether natural or artificial – to govern themselves were affirmed in the idea of autonomy. The sovereignty of the state was subsequently modelled after the autonomy of the individual: each arose from the need to provide protection and establish independence.

Through arguments about the varieties of human nature, political thinkers theorised an international state of nature comprised of sovereign states as morally equivalent to autonomous persons: to many of them, the most meaningful way to understand the state – what provokes one to wage a war and what makes one seek peace – was to construct an analogy between persons and states.

Once instituted as an artificial person, a commonwealth, in Hobbes's fine language, 'hath the same Right, in procuring the safety of his People, that any particular man can have, in procuring his own safety'.[11] Commonwealths analogously take on the qualities and attributes of the natural individuals who comprised them in the first place: the intellectual move is always from the natural to the artificial person, rather than the other way around. To wish to describe the characteristics of pre-civil persons by way of transposing those of states back to the very individuals who originally constituted them would assume the very conclusion of the argument to be proven. The analogy between natural and artificial persons, while essential in its capacity to evoke the qualities and attributes of sovereign states from those of human beings, remains at the same time incomplete in its inability to make the reverse analogous move.

While the analogy helps characterise the domestic nature of the state, it also places interstate relations at the very centre of debates over the moral basis for international warfare and commitments to the pursuit of peace. From Grotius, through Hobbes and Pufendorf, to Rousseau, Vattel and Kant, the relations between states instantiate the rights and duties of the individual writ large. Empirically observable, the international domain of sovereigns without a sovereign above them all manifests the interactions between autonomous agents, except on a much larger scale. These authors were all keenly aware that, while their arguments emerged in response to the calamities of internecine conflict and civil war, they also sought to solve the international state of nature, where states themselves take on the characteristics of self-defensive and fearful individuals.

The quest for peace was not limited to the domestic sphere, but extended to the foreign domain as well: the symbiosis between 'home' and 'abroad' would become a major preoccupation in the political thought of early modern political thinkers. The idea that the international arena is itself a state of nature defines the development of the modern concept of the state, and Hobbes's view on the subject is generally regarded as foundational and drawn in its support. Artificial

[11] *Leviathan*, 244.

persons are analogous to natural persons: states stand in relation to one another parallel to how individuals act outside sovereignty, and, in the absence of a common superior to enforce the rules of conduct, war is the natural state of affairs.

As descriptive of the life of man outside civility, the Hobbesian state of nature presents, in part, an ahistorical and purely fictional situation as a condition of the social contract: it is intended to serve as a conceptual apparatus in imagining how autonomous agents would act outside the contingency of human experience. But it also can be said to manifest the historical (rather than cultural) development of societies: Hobbes consistently draws on the example of the small families of North America as existing in a state of nature not on account of their primitivism, but because of their absence of full-fledged sovereignty. He also imagines the international domain of autonomous states as the best instantiation – and not merely a manifestation – of the natural condition par excellence: the international state of nature follows the interpersonal one. The foreign domain also reveals the most fundamental tenet of Hobbes's civil science: the state of war and the state of peace cohabitate the same space and enmity and amity exist side by side. The link between nature and sovereignty, savagery and civility, war and peace, death and life itself remains fragile and tenuous.

The frontispiece of Hobbes's *De Cive* captures the central message of his political project: the distance between the state of war and the state of peace is far narrower than their opposition might suppose and their relationship is invariably tense. Comprised of three equal panels, the middle of which is – crucially – veiled, the lower half of the engraving illustrates the contrast between the anarchy of nature and the order of the city. *Libertas*, on the right, is an Algonquian woman of Carolina whose long arrow in her right hand points downward, as if anticipating the damnation of Christ's final judgment depicted in the upper *Religio* panel. The state of war behind *Libertas* impresses precisely with the absence of everything that *Imperium* on the left makes possible. Barren uncultivated lands with a few scattered huts fill the background of the state of war: frightened men, chased by hunters with arrows, run for their lives. Their anxious faces express the agonising experience of survival in a warlike environment, where everyone is free to exercise one's natural right to self-preservation, even if that entails the killing of another in order to remain alive. Far removed from any ordinary experience the reader may be familiar with, the visual depiction of war includes its most extreme form: cannibals have gathered around a fire roasting human flesh from the hanging limb of a human victim. Primitive savagery distinguishes life outside sovereignty: unbounded in their natural right to take the life of another in extreme cases of survival, natural men are perpetual warriors who fight simply to remain alive. Life in the state of nature is not only precarious, but is also definitive of war itself.

Outside of nature, life could not be any more peaceful: order and serenity reign on the left panel. The toga-clad and regal-looking *Imperium*, reminiscent of a free Roman citizen, balances the scales of justice in her right hand in the embodiment of orderliness and legitimacy. Holding a sword in her left hand pointing upwards, she dispenses justice not only through wise judgment but also through fear of punishment, as if to indicate that no one who disobeys her authority, will be spared Unlike the barrenness of nature, life in *civitas* abounds in the cultivation of civic life: industrious people till the land, while the spires of the churches in the background beckon them to tower above their daily chores in the experience of the divine. Through religion and agriculture, the primitivism of war and the solitude of fighting have been banished and nature has been transformed into an oasis of peace and prosperity.

While nature and civility reinforce the usual opposition between war and peace, they overlap, seemingly, in the middle panel. The space between *Libertas* and *Imperium*, occupying an equal third of the lower half of the panel, is veiled by a curtain: were one to lift it, it would appear that no radical break exists between war and peace, and their dichotomy is largely imaginary. How can, then, nature and sovereignty, savagery and civility, war and peace, coexist in the same space? The question of their relationship will become the central question of the entire tradition of natural law, originating with Thomas Hobbes and his Dutch predecessor Hugo Grotius at the beginning of the seventeenth century, through their followers Samuel Pufendorf and John Locke, to the middle of the eighteenth with the Swiss Jean Jacques Rousseau and Emer Vattel.

Foundational to how we have come to regard modern politics, these thinkers used interpersonal relations analogously to the international affairs between sovereigns. Eminently observable in interstate interaction, the international domain is a blown-up illustration of how individuals would interact in the absence of any intervening authority over them. Rather than derived from the rights and duties of individuals from such an analogy, political agency writ large is merely described through their actions, since states need individuals in the first place. In turn, war and peace – the subject of the relations between states – provide the domestic theory of the state with the most compelling example of how independent agents act interdependently.

The intellectual transition from the war of savagery to the peace of the commonwealth requires the idea of a state of nature: it alone can possibly justify the establishment of the modern state. Outside of any political commitments or social environment, a bare individual, stripped of any prior obligation, can be imagined to consent to submission to authority and enter into a social contract. For many, if not all, contractarian thinkers, the laws of nature as applied to natural persons – or the laws of nations when enacted by artificial persons – circumscribe the minimalist character of the natural rights tradition. The interaction of individuals, with the capacity to exercise their own wills, can be applied to that of states. Commonwealths emerge as persons writ large: the international state of nature follows the interpersonal one.

In this common narrative, the radical dissociation of nature's war and sovereignty's peace eliminates the possibility for their mutual coexistence: the institution of the sovereign is largely regarded as the irreversible end of the state of nature, and where the state enables all the commodities of life that peace brings. But for many early modern political thinkers, as Hobbes's frontispiece of *De Cive* indicates, the relationship between war and peace should be seen less as diametrical and more as coextensive: a state may be at peace internally and yet in conflict externally. As a sovereign over its subjects, the state commands peace, whereas as a sovereign among sovereigns, the state remains in a state of nature internationally. The close association between a state's domestic organisation and how it conducts itself externally lies at the heart of the early modern history of peace: the construction of the commonwealth proceeds from the larger view of ameliorating the international domain by way of pacifying the domestic realm. A peaceful international order is best promoted through domestic peace.

The international arena, which not merely manifests but preeminently instantiates the state of nature, is the domain where the state of war and the state of peace cohabitate the same space: enmity and amity exist side by side in a world of states. The institution of leviathans, as international relations reveal, by no means ends the state of war: it simply solves the domestic dilemma of peace, while it simultaneously creates an international state of nature, where states themselves take on the same qualities of self-preservation that had defined those of natural individuals. The state of nature is, par excellence, observable in international relations: even as citizens of states, we remain in a perpetual state of war. While sovereignty emerges in response to the miseries accompanying the natural condition and solves conflict between private individuals, it simultaneously creates an international state of nature with states without a sovereign either between them or over them.

And yet, the analogy between men and states, while essential, remains only incomplete: unlike natural persons, who remain vulnerable because of their perfect equality, artificial states do not face the same level of insecurity (and hence any argument in favour of extending the leviathan to a global one fails on account of the safety provided by states themselves). The urgency of constituting a civic commonwealth has no equivalent in establishing a global or a world state, were it even possible to construct one. Any peace between states, however long-lasting, marks only a temporary cessation of hostilities, rather than a permanent solution to their warlike disposition. The German philosopher G. W. Leibniz perceptively captures the volatile character of international peace as 'a breathing-space of two gladiators', reflecting Hobbes's infamous reflections how 'in all times, Kings, and Persons of Soveraigne authority, because of their Independency, are in continuall jealousies, and in the state and posture of Gladiators; having their weapons pointing, and their eyes fixed on one another; that is, their Forts, Garrisons, and Guns upon the Frontiers of their Kingdomes; and continuall Spyes upon their neighbours, which is a posture of War'.[12] In his *Codex Iuris Gentium Diplomaticus* (1693), a major work on the law of nations, Leibniz concludes that the assertion made by 'the subtle author of the *Elementa de Cive*' of warlike international relations 'is not altogether absurd, provided it refer not to a right to do harm, but to take proper precautions'. Among nations, inclined to pursue peace even by means of war, 'breathing time' and 'breathing space' is the surest peace that can be obtained in a world competing for more security.

The war that defines the natural condition imposes the imperative to exit from it, whereas the gladiatorial posture among sovereigns makes no such demands. Even the character of war and peace – whether among natural or artificial persons – would seem to differ on the basic level of how each is experienced. The state of nature, for Hobbes, manifests itself variously, and, depending on the nature of the conflict, it ranges from the more familiar and less violent to the less common and more warlike. Whether it can be eminently observed among some Amerindian tribes,

[12] G. W. Leibniz, *Political Writings*, ed. Patrick Riley (Cambridge: Cambridge University Press, 1988), 166; Hobbes, *Leviathan*, 90.

or mercenary soldiers, or factions during civil war, or among irreconcilable ideological doctrinaires, what characterises such a condition is the absence of any sovereign authority: outside sovereignty, reign the miseries of war. Unique among all manifestations of the state of war, international relations alone serve as more than a mere example of the miseries that accompany the state of war: they are themselves the state of nature in its most original and actual sense, for they always fall outside sovereignty, regardless of how secure domestic order may be. All other manifestations simply show the state of war as a possible and contingent condition: we may fall into it (as is the case of civil war), or we may exit from (as Amerindians may do so eventually). As a permanent state of war, on the other hand, international relations stand out as both an actual and ongoing state of affairs: precisely because sovereigns seek to organise themselves in a world of independent states, they will continually find themselves in a condition of enmity.

III The War Within

That anarchy is by nature and sovereignty by convention is a widely received interpretation of Hobbes's theory of the state, where a thick impenetrable wall separates the order of the city from the disorder outside of it. The exit from anarchy is irreversible and the design of the commonwealth requires a consenting individual to obligate oneself to a common power: the movement is typically seen in the ascending direction from political absence to political fullness. Commentators have supposed that the modern problem about political obligation can be traced back to Hobbes's famous formulation of the opposition between nature and sovereignty and the single move from one to the other: he justifies political obligation unequivocally in order to leave no recurrence to anarchy, chaos, rebellion or civil war. In exiting from barbarism and submitting itself to the law, man's humanity is somehow 'acquired' in 'embarking on the venture of civilization', and, in one influential account, 'the transition from the state of nature to civil society … [occurs] with the conclusion of the social contract': man's 'leaving the state of nature and establishing civil society [is seen] as a kind of revolt of man against nature'.[13] Such a one-time 'transition' from animality to humanity – or a 'leap', or a 'lifting process' – establishes the covenant as a foundational contract that suddenly creates political

[13] Leo Strauss, *Natural Rights and History* (Chicago: University of Chicago Press, 1965), 272.

power from vacuum.[14] On this popular account, sovereignty emerges as the definitive antipode to nature, extinguishing its predecessor and fierce enemy: once the social contract has been 'concluded', nature has been conquered and anarchy vanquished. Even Leibniz complains about absolute 'Hobbesian empires' which 'exist neither among civilized peoples nor among barbarians, and I consider them neither possible nor desirable, unless those who must have supreme power are gifted with angelic virtues': Hobbes's 'fallacy' denies 'some middle road' between the unity of sovereignty and the lawlessness of nature, which 'experience has shown' to be a common practice.[15] The reason why we like to turn to Hobbes for an answer in exploring the genealogy of the state is because of the perennial question: how do we 'transition' from nature to sovereignty?

Inasmuch as the Hobbesian commonwealth removes the fear of anticipation, it simultaneously instills a new, and more powerful fear: that of its own dissolution. While much of the theoretical construction of the leviathan is indeed devoted to the 'transitional' move of turning natural residents into obedient citizens, Hobbes's *objective* is rather the opposite: how to prevent the reverse move from civility to nature. In emphasising the starkness of the opposition between civility and its absence, Hobbes radicalises the reversibility of moving from the established order to the chaos of war. While he is undeniably preoccupied with the erection of the commonwealth, he is in fact rather anxious about the seeds of its own ruin. Once we shift the focus away from the standard emphasis on the foundational contract to the possible commingling of barbarity and civility, then his theory is designed, above all, to address the pernicious destruction of the leviathan, rather than its meticulous construction. If Hobbes were so anxious to warn against the possible crumbling of political order, we could reasonably ask, why does he not draw a more obvious parallel between nature and sovereignty? The most convincing answer would be that the paranoia that the natural and the civil may somehow be seen as coextensive, with a porous boundary between the

[14] John Rawls, *Lectures on the History of Political Philosophy* (Cambridge, MA: Harvard University Press, 2007), 90. Similarly, Hanna Pitkin, *The Concept of Representation* (Berkeley: University of California Press, 1967), 29; Norberto Bobbio, *Thomas Hobbes and the Natural Law Tradition* (Chicago: University of Chicago Press, 1993), 17; T. H. Green, *Lectures on the Principles of Political Obligation* (Clark, NJ: The Lawbook Exchange, 2005), 72; Carole Pateman and Charles Mills, *Contract and Domination* (Cambridge: Polity, 2007).

[15] Leibniz, *Political Writings*, 120.

two, haunts Hobbes and, quite understandably, he seeks to mute any argument that potentially might challenge their carefully sculpted opposition. His pedantic insistence on the antagonism between the two serves him a pedagogic and instructive purpose in collective memory building, particularly in the aftermath of the English Civil War. It is also used as a powerful mnemonic device designed to remind readers of the fullness that only political life in the commonwealth can provide: nations should never forget how fragile their peace is.[16]

Accepting the particular concept of anarchy as the absence of dominion, the argument establishes that natural men continually weave, as it were, a tapestry of rights transferals by tying and untying contractual bonds amongst themselves, just as they seek to increase from a few to many in their number. Through a common language, they are all made equal in their capacity to enter into a covenant, and in such a worded nature of saviours and saved protection is secured for as long as obedience is provided. No one wishes to be a slave, but everyone, by nature, desires to be a servant and saved through servitude, so that the greater obedience servants render their masters, the greater their liberty grows: the practice of 'cyclical dominion' of voluntary renouncing and regaining of dominion ensures the liberty of servants. Moreover, the most common covenant in nature, that of cohabitation, is commonly practised in families. As 'small commonwealths', families have been stripped of any biological meaning, subsumed into the larger theory of dominion acquisition, and endowed with two features we normally attribute to civility: they are covenanted and multitudinous. The family provides the same basic model for states, where the civil obedience of fully grown citizens proceeds from their earlier household discipline as children. The formation of large commonwealths originates in the dominion of families, and the natural could be said to persist into the civil. The Hobbes without anarchy endorses a civilised nature and a naturalised civility.

Hobbes is renowned for the idea that life in the state of nature is '*solitary*, poor, nasty, brutish and short, that there is no society therein'.[17] If solitude is a central characteristic of the natural state, it

[16] Hobbes affirms the ancients' knowledge that 'Memory begets Judgement, and Fancy' and praised them for making 'memory the mother of the Muses', Thomas Hobbes (1971) 'The Answer of Mr. Hobbes to Sr. William D'Avenant's Preface', in William D'Avenant, *A Discourse upon Gondibert. An Heroick Poem Written by Sr. William D'Avenant with an Answer to It by Mr. Hobbes*, ed. David F. Gladish (Paris, 1650).

[17] *Leviathan*, 89.

would seem that groups are precluded and that humans are radically individualist. Some of the most influential twentieth-century accounts of the origins of the social contractarian tradition in fact take this position: contractual bonds, they say, must start with a view of the 'raw' individual, stripped of *any* social connections. On their account, Hobbes, unlike Aristotle in the *Politics*, takes the constituents of the state to be *asocial* individuals rather than individuals embedded in fundamental social relations. But is this picture of Hobbes correct?

Hobbes ultimately does accept a form of natural human association; he nonetheless insists that a human is not born *fit* for political society because a civil society is not a mere social congregation but requires contractual bonds. He acknowledges a natural human desire for society: 'we discern', he claims in *De Cive* I.2 n, 'all desirous of congress, and mutual correspondence . . . it is true indeed that, to Man, by nature, or as Man, as soon as he is born, solitude is an enemy . . . wherefore I deny not that men (even nature compelling) desire to come together'. Even the 'savage people' in America come together in the concord of 'small families', through the mutuality of their desires. At the very least, there is in the state of nature 'the natural inclination of the sexes one to another and to their children' (Leviathan xx.4).

The power of Hobbes's argument stems not from a denial of the elements of sociability, but from the fact that his analysis does not require innate sociability: the desire to come together is not sufficient to guarantee political sovereignty (as it had been for the ancients, particularly Aristotle). But he recognises that sociability will lead to natural groupings, outside of the structure of the state, and that even without such sociability, natural groupings will arise from strategies of defence and conquest. In the absence of sovereignty there can be human interaction and social aggregation; people may develop socially oriented passions by habituation within their family, conquest group, or league (these are the three types of groups). If we find jarring the admission of a social passion in Hobbes before the advent of sovereignty and for that same reason insist on a supposed radical individualism, this may be because our view of the natural condition requires revision. Instead, the tendency has been to revise Hobbes; in other words, to misinterpret Hobbes.

The solitude and lack of society, to which Hobbes occasionally refers, are not assumed starting points – preconditions of the state of nature; instead, he regards them as the effects of the time of war, particularly in the political upheaval of the English Civil War. In this sense, the state of nature is meant above all to illustrate the post-political state of affairs (the crumbling of sovereignty), rather than the pre-political state of affairs (the instituting of a sovereign). Solitude and want of all things proceed from the dissolution of existing political order. Rather than being the cause of war and hence anteceding it, 'solitude' in fact follows the destruction of peace and is, therefore, 'consequent to a time of Warre' (Leviathan XIII.9). Apart from a single rhetorical use, 'solitude' was altogether absent from the original description of natural life in *De Cive*: in fact, 'solitude' would make its way only for a second, and last, time in Leviathan (but not in any of the six editions of *De Cive* during Hobbes's lifetime).

In a shift that is especially notable between the first edition of *De Cive* and *Leviathan*, Hobbes increasingly comes to view the natural condition as a relation that exists between any two persons with no authority over themselves. Thus, and this is a crucial point, one is solitary insofar as one is in the state of war; but one might be in a state of war with one person and not with another. What begins to emerge is a basic distinction between those of the same grouping and those outside of it. And let's recall that there are three types of social relations: those based in the family, in the conquest group (captured in war), and in leagues (in voluntary submission). Let me briefly examine the first one only, the family.

With respect to families, Hobbes admits that they all have a natural urge for company as expressed in ties of affection, and he goes as far as maintaining that familial authority is coeval with earliest humanity, rather than a later development. Even the continued existence of a human implies a family-type authority, for 'infants have need of others to help them live' (*De Cive* note i.1). So a given person at a particular time can be inimical to some people and amicable to others of one's group, while still in nature. Thus there may be a state of nature between groups such as families (an example might be the rivalry relations between the Medici and Soderini families), but not within those families. It even seems that Hobbes entertains the notion of sovereignty outside the commonwealth. He says that before offspring are born, we can already be assured of 'the obedience . . . owed to their parents; who have sovereign power over their children' (Leviathan xxvi.40). Because these family-sovereigns have no sovereign over they themselves, their fear of one another justifies the commencement of war. Even the primaeval natural condition is a condition of war among families. If we regard the family, as Hobbes does, as part and parcel of the natural condition, then authority, obedience, security, and perhaps even quasi-sovereignty must be admitted as significant elements of the natural condition.

Groups, then, are a necessary part of the logic of the Hobbesian state of nature, and they provide an important justification for its existence and character. A natural condition, which somehow had no groups, would naturally develop such groups. In short, the notorious war of each against all is immediately transformed into the war of some against others. Hobbes's nature endures neither as a war of each, nor as a war against all. Rather, it is a shifting condition of group formation. Because they are restless security seekers, natural men are group initiators and group sustainers by nature; they actively and persistently 'seek allies' (*De Cive* I.13), in whose company they find temporary respite. '[N]o man is of might sufficient ... of preserving himself thereby', Hobbes perceives, and 'reason therefore dictateth to every man for his own good ... to strengthen himself with all the help he can procure, for his own defense against those, from whom such peace cannot be obtained' (Elements of Law I. xiv.14). Outside the alliance of a grouping, natural man lacks the resources he needs to anticipate an evil, and hence preempt a future threat. In failing to secure the services and advantages of associating, such a hypothetical unaided monad simply disappears in the abyss of nature.

To sum up, the natural condition is essentially one of groups. What is more, Hobbes indicates that the natural condition of war exists because of groups: that is, the Hobbesian state of nature presupposes and depends upon people banding together. Moreover, a rigid distinction between nature and sovereignty as two antipodes, of the kind advanced by the painters of the caricature Hobbes, is erroneous. In highlighting only one (sociability) of the several similarities that nature and sovereignty share, we begin to see the proximity between the two: rather than seeing the sovereign state and the natural condition as two strangers, we should see them as first cousins with striking feature resemblances. In consequence, the question, how do we transition from nature to sovereignty, is not Hobbes's question. Instead, his question is quite the inverse: given the sovereignty of established political order, how do we prevent it from erupting into the violent flames of its own dissolution. His sovereign remains delicately fragile because the solution to the greatest political evil, civil war, has opened up a graver theoretical problem – that of sovereignty's imminent dissolution. And it is only in the interactions among sovereigns that Hobbes finds hope for a more enduring peace.

IV Peace from Without

The state of war in the international domain stands out as categorically distinct from any other instantiation of the state of nature. The experience of war and peace, correspondingly, differs from Hobbes's 'perpetuall War' found among natural individuals and the 'publique Peace' maintained within leviathans.[18] The realm of international relations does not suffer from an impending all-out war, although neither does it ever hope of attaining the security of peace possible domestically. It merely functions as an armed peace. The analogy between men and cities (and for Hobbes cities are artificial persons endowed with the same attributes as natural men) affirms the claim that both natural and civil persons are virtually indistinguishable with respect to how they interact with one another: they are all in a state of nature among themselves. The international arena populated by sovereigns can be described in exactly the same way as the domain of natural persons: the same characteristics that define self-defensive natural men and the same natural laws that operate among them can be transferred to civil persons. Individuals can be used to characterise states, but not the other way around, since artificial persons require natural persons in the first place. For that reason, the analogous relationship between men and states is imperfect and incomplete, of course, because it signifies a movement from natural to civil persons but not conversely.

Hobbes's insistence that interactions among Leviathans constitutes the clearest manifestation of the natural condition looks unsurprising, but it highlights the possible *coexistence* between anarchy and sovereignty, war and security. Moreover, the admitted existence and utility of interstate treaties suggests that the international state of nature allows a considerable degree of cooperation and mutual protection *even* between the supposedly warring parties. The *absence* of a single will among sovereigns as that among civil men, does not preclude the possibility of adherence to the law of nations. Such adherence is derived from reciprocal voluntary relationships, in which states enter through agreements.

Some commentators, particularly from international relations, have asked why the mechanism of contract whereby individual parties institute a sovereign could not function also among nations, bringing them to institute a super-sovereign, ending international conflict. Hobbes,

[18] Hobbes, *De Cive*, 30, and Hobbes, *Leviathan*, 133, respectively.

however, does not agree that the situations are necessarily the same in the relevant respects; it seems, therefore, that the logic of the state of nature will potentially be multiple rather than single. Whereas individuals may be obligated by the law of nature to contract their way out of the state of nature, states remain in their condition of separateness: 'it is not only lawful for sovereigns to send out spies, to maintain soldiers, to build forts, and to require monies for these purposes, but also, not to do thus, is unlawful' (*De Cive* xiii.8). The ameliorative nature of the international domain proceeds not from states' shared benevolence to unite into a single sovereign body, but from reciprocal agreements in their acknowledged desire for peace.

In his infamous description of the international arena as gladiatorial, Hobbes makes explicit what he had argued implicitly: instituted sovereigns continually remain in a state of war, which is not merely like a state of nature, but a state of nature itself. But, crucially, 'because they [sovereigns] uphold thereby, the Industry of their Subjects; there does not follow from it, that misery, which accompanies the Liberty of particular men'.[19] Hobbes considers external peace central to – if not a prerequisite for – domestic safety and hence lists it as the foremost enjoyment that sovereignty enables by making citizens 'safe from foreign and civil war'.[20] If the essential analogy between natural and civil persons is to hold true for Hobbes, commonwealths as artificial persons are subject to the laws of nations in the same manner as individuals are subject to the laws of nature.

'As for the law of nations', Hobbes concludes his The Elements of Law, 'it is the same with the law of nature. For that which is the law of nature between man and man, before the constitution of the commonwealth, is the law of nations between sovereign and sovereign, after'.[21] His understanding of the law of nations, and how it relates to the law of nature and civil law, reflects his commitment to locate the fundamental precepts of what has later come to be known as 'international law' firmly within the boundaries of natural law. Hobbes was certainly not the first one to situate the province of *jus gentium* within the domain of *jus naturalis*. His contemporary, Richard Zouche, Alberico Gentili's successor and the holder of the Regius Chair in Civil Law at the University of Oxford, similarly sought to establish the foundations of the law of nations within

19 *Leviathan*, 90.
20 *De Cive*, 144.
21 Hobbes, *The Elements of Law, Natural and Politic* (London: Cass Publishing, 1969), 190.

a natural law framework and the language of ancient Roman law, and by the middle of the seventeenth century, the shift from *jus commune* to *jus naturalis* had already taken place.[22]

Hobbes's naturalist theory of *jus gentium* would later earn him Vattel's accusation that he was ultimately mistaken for his straightforward application of the law of nations exactly as the natural law when applied to nations, because the law of nature must 'suffer' a 'necessary change' once 'applied to states or nations'.[23] '[T]he Law of Nations, and the Law of Nature', Hobbes observes in Leviathan, 'is the same thing' and the two are indistinguishable only by virtue of their subjects, whether natural individuals or artificial persons.[24] His firm division of natural law between that of men and that of commonwealths would become standard in all of his mature political writings and lead to strengthening the analogy between the interpersonal and international domain.

Regardless of whether persons are natural or artificial, the precepts dictating their conduct derive their force, crucially, from the same natural law of self-preservation. While individuals have a primary obligation to care for their basic necessities and physical survival, all sovereigns have the secondary duty to abide by the law of nations and provide for their citizens' flourishing and improvement. As the principal actors under the law of nations, commonwealths emerge not simply as guarantors of domestic peace but also as promoters of a commodious life. The development of the arts and sciences, distinguishing 'the modern world from the barbarity of the past,' contributes to 'a commodious living', where 'the enormous advantages of human life have far surpassed the condition of other animals'.[25] It is the duty of sovereigns not only to establish the safety and security of citizens and promote peace but also to pursue growth and prosperity through robust commerce as a vehicle for peace. Robust commercial relations with other states and a general openness of international trade are all part of the universality of the law of nations and practised as a right of nations.

While frugality and economic foresight determine domestic prosperity, commercial relations with other states transform a state from a self-sufficient political entity to a partner for peace and strategic ally: states would far more likely engage with it in the quest for international peace.

[22] On Zouche, see Carlo Focarelli, *International Law as Social Construct: The Struggle for Global Justice* (Oxford: Oxford University Press, 2012), 100.

[23] Emer Vattel, *The Laws of Nature and Nations* (Indianapolis: Liberty Fund, 2008), 8–9.

[24] *Leviathan*, 244.

[25] *De Cive*, 4; *De Homine*, in Hobbes, *Man and Citizen*, ed. Bernard Gert (Atlantic Highlands: Humanities Press, 1972), 4 and 39.

The law of nations dictates the promulgation of free traffic in the conduct of indiscriminate commerce and a universal observance of equality in dealing with diverse states. A failure to apply the law of nature of impartiality in international affairs is manifestly a declaration of hatred, which is effectively a condition of war: 'For he that alloweth that [free commerce] to one man, which he denieth to another, declareth his hatred to him, to whom he denieth; and to declare hatred is war.'[26] The laws of nature compel states to have their ports open and their markets free to all equally with a certain guarantee of safety for a peaceful interaction. In general, those states that respect the dictates of the law of nations can expect a high degree of cooperation, and, in a world of competing states with conflicting interest, economic exchange can be beneficial for peace through demands for mutual respect and reciprocation of trade agreements.

Communication, in consequence to commerce, must be free and equally accessible to all regardless of citizenship 'for without this there would be no society among men, no peace'.[27] As communicative creatures, endowed with the capacity to engage peacefully with others, all men have a right by nature to roam the corners of the world unhindered as long as they respect the laws and customs of the first inhabitants and do not dispossess them of their land against their will. The natural right of free passage for Hobbes is part of the law of nature, 'That all messengers of peace, and such as are employed to procure and maintain amity between man and man, may safely come and go', and allows for negotiation to occur.[28] 'By the mere law of nature', as Samuel Pufendorf later echoes Hobbes, 'envoys . . . are inviolable' and, as messengers of peace, they should be allowed free access especially in times of war. 'Mediators of Peace should have immunity', Hobbes observes, for 'Peace cannot be had without mediation, nor mediation without immunity.'[29] The natural right of free passage, both in the unhindered crossing in peaceful times and in the mediation during conflict, extends to all nations across the globe, since it is derived as a dictate of natural reason, and hence exerts the same force everywhere. It, therefore, properly belongs to *jus gentium*, which reason alone, in the observance of justice, prescribes to everyone in general. In their pursuit of the 'Fundamentall Law of Nature; which is, to

[26] *Elements of Law, Natural and Politic*, 87.
[27] *Leviathan*, 40.
[28] *The Elements of Law, Natural and Politic*, 87.
[29] *De Cive*, 51.

seek Peace, and follow it', sovereigns enter into alliances for mutual protection without instituting a common power above them all.[30]

Although mutual vulnerabilities and interests lead individuals to give up their liberties in the state of nature in exchange for protection, the miseries that accompany a plurality of sovereigns are not as onerous, hence there is no political basis to move towards a global leviathan. In Hobbes, we find, I think, the first articulation of the argument that a world government or a world state is unnecessary, although he does envisage that the development of a lawful international order is not only possible, but also politically desirable. The rise of an international Leviathan to somehow liberate commonwealths from the dangers of the state of nature in the same way as the institution of the sovereign protects individuals is incomparable, 'because states uphold thereby, the Industry of their Subjects; there does not follow from it, that misery, which accompanies the Liberty of particular men' (*Leviathan* xiii.9). Unlike some modern arguments for the inevitability of a world state, defended on grounds of the inescapable struggle for recognition, Hobbes insists on the mutual interdependence of sovereigns and the efficacy of leagues founded on long-term interests: 'Leagues between Commonwealths, over whom there is no human Power established, to keep them all in awe, are not only lawful, but also profitable for the time they last' (286). This emphasis on the interdependence of states through treaties and agreements, rather than their independence and autonomy, is a key point that renders Hobbes not merely a domestic theorist of the state, but also an international political theorist.

Meaningful covenants can, and do, exist in the international state of nature – not just within warring commonwealths, but also between them – and yet this does not prevent it from being a state of nature. These covenants do not set up an overarching sovereign power and therefore may be unstable, easily rendered invalid, and insufficient for the security of the parties to the covenant. As Hobbes explains in *De Cive*, the international situation is not just like a state of nature, rather it is a state of nature par excellence: 'For the state of commonwealths, considered in themselves, is natural' (*De Cive* xiii.7). For that reason, *De Cive* opens not with a portrait of an interpersonal state of nature, but rather with the state of nature of international relations. After having concluded the work, however, he remarks in the Preface, that his main concern is the state of nature of civil war, rather than international war (this is hardly surprising given

[30] *Leviathan*, 92.

that the Preface was written in late 1641, just months before the outbreak of the English Civil War). It seems that his earlier efforts, particularly the two decades between the early 1620s and the early 1640s, were more concerned with international war. Most prominent of those efforts to grapple with the state of international conflict is of course his first ever, and still unrivalled, English translation of Thucydides's *History of the Peloponnesian War* of 1629. Part of his interest in international relations developed during his reading of Bacon and translating letters from the correspondence between Bacon's literary agent in Venice, Fulgenzio Micanzio, and the second Earl of Devonshire.

Hobbes's interest in international affairs would sustain him in his main political works *De Cive* and *Leviathan*. Ironically, those scholars in the field of international relations, who identify a form of perpetual realism in Hobbes, turn to the notorious Chapter 13 of *Leviathan*. The general picture that emerges, from Hobbes's own considerations, however, is one of cooperation and exchange between states. States are talkers and the more they communicate, the more likely they are to lessen conflict amongst themselves. Hobbes would not even approve a state's engagement in wars of aggression or conquest: 'military activity', he writes, 'was once regarded as a gainful occupation under the name of piracy or raiding. And before the formation of commonwealths, when the human race lived dispersed in families, it was considered just and honorable . . . military activity is like gambling; in most cases it reduces a person's property; very few succeed'. (*De Cive* xiii.4). Acquisition and expansion, he admits, may temporarily secure domination and even establish short-lived hegemony; however, they can never serve as the pillars of a politically and economically prosperous society whose reputation lies not in actual military exploitation but in prudential capability to project power abroad. International relations is the domain where sovereigns can fulfill their primary duties of procuring their survival, contentments of life, and industry of the people.

Hobbes not only discounts the extension from a single to a global leviathan as illogical; he also ardently defends the proposition that states remain in the international state of nature by all means necessary. The need for self-preservation, which requires a natural person to enter into a contract with another solely for one's survival, carries no compelling obligation when extended to civil persons. Since for Hobbes the primary duty of sovereigns is to procure the survival of their citizens and 'have their industry protected', any transfer of rights to an entity outside one's own state amounts to renouncing one's allegiance to the sovereign.[31] And if all citizens were to renounce their state allegiance, they would find themselves in a condition of self-inflicted despotism and a return to the state of war. A sovereign above all sovereigns, as desirable for world peace as it may seem to be on account of its broad appeal to global security, is greatly resisted by both Hobbes and Pufendorf, who remain fearful of any claims to universal authority, whether political or religious.

Eighteenth-century critics of Hobbes, including the Prussian Christian Wolff, have dismissed the inconvenience of rival polities and the inevitable proneness to a politics of war among them. Their proposals for a world state – such as Wolff's *civitas maxima* – would only lead to the fragmentation of sovereignty and result in the compromising of states' liberty in the external domain. Firmly rejecting the idea of a world superstate with an authority over the component member states, Vattel affirms the principle of equality as consistent with the law of nations and relies on Hobbes to make 'clear that there is by no means the same necessity for a civil society among nations as among individuals'.[32] The rejection of a supreme sovereign and reaffirmation of the voluntary practice of the law of nations underlie Hobbes's tenet: just as individuals in nature interact in accordance with the laws of nature – especially the "Fundamentall Law of Nature; which is, to seek Peace, and follow it" – even outside any juridical authority, so do commonwealths follow the laws of nations in the absence of a common power above them all.[33]

Even in the most extreme circumstances of warring princes, where 'every Soveraign hath the same Right, in procuring the safety of his People, that any particular man can have, in procuring his own safety', the law of nations prescribes the duties and obligations of states not only in times of peace, but also during war.[34] The perennial quest for international peace, in Hobbes's view, frames the relations between commonwealths, rather than any foreign aggression for the sake of aggrandisement, which would likely endanger their own preservation. Should defensive wars become necessary when survival itself is at stake, they also ought to be conducted in accordance with the law of nations and generally recognised duties in warfare. While sovereign states may not have the assurance of permanent security in their external relations, and may at any time resort to defensive war in providing for their own

31 *Leviathan*, 189.
32 *The Laws of Nature and Nations*, 9.
33 *Leviathan*, 92.
34 *Leviathan*, 244.

safety, they yield a great advantage in the active engagement with other states for mutual benefit and peaceful relations. Samuel Pufendorf, one of Hobbes's infamous successors, espouses the general position that the international arena instantiates the state of nature among sovereigns. Similar to most thinkers in the tradition of *jus gentium*, he does not regard the state of natural liberty of states as descriptive of extreme isolationism: instead, the foreign mirrors the domestic, where each individual is part of a web of agreements and alliances.

V Conclusion

What should be obvious by now is that the contrast between nature and sovereignty is not as great as it is often thought. Elements usually associated exclusively with the Hobbesian sovereign (such as groups) are already present in the state of nature. Moreover, the contrast is also blurred from the other side: elements usually associated with the Hobbesian state of nature (such as insecurity) are still to be found within a well-ordered state. The birth of the state is not the end of war (and this conclusion allows us to lift the curtain entirely). If anything, the state of nature is an actual situation (as opposed to hypothetical or primitive), a point which Hobbes was keen to emphasise in his correspondence with one of his French admirers, Peleau. 'What?' Hobbes fumed in his November 1656 response to Pelau's suggestion that the state of nature never existed, 'Don't we see this in the war of minds?' (Hobbes is here referring to the conflicts of intellectual opinions in the republic of letters).[35]

Further, the state of nature is not only actual; it is also composite. It will not be easy to accept this sort of 'mixing' of the natural and the civil conditions. But if we grant that Hobbes is trying to construct and reinforce, rather than merely describe, a division between state of nature and civil society, we can see why we have the feeling that Hobbes insists that they are far apart, and yet ultimately admits that they can be quite close to one another. And finally, we need to recognise that the state of nature is meant to function as a reminder of why we want to avoid war, and why we should do our part to ensure it does not return. In pursuing this end, Hobbes highlights

[35] Noel Malcolm, *The Correspondence of Thomas Hobbes*, vol. I (Oxford: Clarendon Press, 1994), 300–10 and 450–51. On this point, see Tuck, *The Rights of War and Peace*, 138, 214.

how bad it can be, and tends to describe what is highly tenuous in the state of nature as if it were altogether absent.

And finally, today it is all the more evident that the concept of the state is undergoing a welcome change towards a greater awareness of the cohabitation between its domestic and foreign dimensions: sovereignty affirms as much its right to command obedience internally as it claims jurisdiction over its external relations with other states. In challenging the division between the domestic and the foreign, Hobbes transgresses intentionally their borderline and intensifies their porousness. A return to his understanding of the Janus-faced sovereign constitutes a major piece in the genealogy of the modern state. The false dichotomy between the domestic and the global – against which Hobbes had warned – has increasingly diminished, as current transformations of the international order demand fresh considerations of the formative period of state theory. Individuals no longer remain detached citizens of particularised political communities, but they increasingly participate in a larger network of ethical commitments and moral responsibilities that transcend the local.

The world of states thus grew out of a vision of a world of men, in which they did share obligations to one another and fundamental commitments to justice. The kind of normative architecture of world order we find in Hobbes calls for a political universalism that recognises global principles to act in accordance with equity. It would be a mistake to assimilate Hobbes to a purported tradition of domestic sovereignty alone, one that derives its inspiration from establishing domestic order rather than international peace. A return to Hobbes affirms the symbiotic relationship between the inside and outside of the Janus-faced sovereign, and brings him closer to some of the political values of inclusion and openness we should all aspire to acquire.

5

Jurisprudential Reflections on Cosmopolitan Law

EVAN FOX-DECENT*

Introduction

States assert jurisdiction to announce and enforce law against citizens and non-citizens within their territory. I will argue that the state's public law governing its interactions with non-citizens – the state's cosmopolitan law – must have a certain outward orientation and representative character if it is to be law, properly so-called. Drawing on previous work on international law with Evan Criddle,[1] I deploy a criterion of legitimacy we develop for interpretative and normative purposes to make a conceptual claim in this chapter about the nature of law. This criterion stipulates that for a state's action to be legitimate with respect to a given individual, it must be intelligible as action made on behalf of or in the name of the individual subject to it, even if the state's action sets back the individual's interests.[2] I will refer to this norm as the 'fiduciary criterion of legitimacy', or where context warrants, simply the 'fiduciary criterion'. The fiduciary criterion is both normative and conceptual, and here I will argue that it can help explain and inform the conceptual claim that,

* I thank for helpful comments the participants of the following events: 'The Double-Facing Constitution' symposium at the Wissenschaftskolleg in Berlin, June 22–23, 2017; a Work-in-Progress workshop of the Research Group on Constitutional Studies at McGill University in Montreal, October 12, 2017; the Canadian Immigration Law Scholars Conference at the Université du Québec au Montréal (UQAM) in Montreal, March 1–2, 2018; the Berlin Colloquium on Global and Comparative Public Law at Humboldt University, Berlin, April 18, 2019; the Kadish Workshop in Law, Philosophy, and Political Theory at University of California at Berkeley, May 3, 2019. I am particularly grateful for comments from Joshua Cohen, Seth Davis, David Dyzenhaus, Mattias Kumm, Dan Lee, Tom Poole, and Steve Ratner.

[1] Evan J. Criddle and Evan Fox-Decent, *Fiduciaries of Humanity: How International Law Constitutes Authority* (Oxford: Oxford University Press, 2016).

[2] Ibid., 3, 99–100, 131, 217, 240, 268, 288.

according to Joseph Raz, all legal systems necessarily make; i.e., the claim to possess legitimate authority.[3] On this view, it is an existence condition of a legal system that it claims to possess legitimate authority. I will refer to this existence condition from Raz's legal theory as 'Raz's conceptual claim'. It follows from his conceptual claim that legal systems either have (and claim) legitimate authority or they possess merely de facto authority while claiming but not having legitimate authority. A further corollary of his conceptual claim, Raz says, it that law 'must be capable of possessing authority'.[4]

Raz of course is not the first theorist to notice the intimate relationship between law and authority. Hobbes famously declared that '*Auctoritas non Veritas facit Legem*'.[5] But Raz's theory is an important touchstone and foil for the argument I develop because, as I now explain, Raz's conceptual claim grounds the best attempt in the Anglo-American positivist tradition to explain law's relationship to authority. Although the attempt in my view fails, engaging with it seriously will help illuminate the point and content of the anti-positivist theory I later defend.

Within the Anglo-American positivist tradition, the four most important figures are Jeremy Bentham, John Austin, H. L. A. Hart, and Joseph Raz. Bentham and Austin defended a command theory under which law was defined as the commands of a legally unlimited sovereign backed by force.[6] Hart criticised the command theory for its failure to explain power-conferring rules, such as the rules underlying contracts, wills, and marriage. Unlike sovereign commands, these rules invoke 'the coercive framework of the law' only at the behest of individuals who wish to invoke it.[7] For Hart, the command theory mischaracterised law as 'the

[3] Joseph Raz, 'Authority, Law, and Morality', in *Ethics in the Public Domain: Essays in the Morality of Law and Politics* (Oxford: Clarendon Press, 1994), 210, 215 (arguing that 'every legal system claims that it possesses legitimate authority'). Raz use phrases such as 'the law claims' or 'legal systems claim' to indicate that legal officials or institutions implicitly or explicitly make certain claims *qua* legal authorities. For a defence and extension of Raz's view, see John Gardner, 'How Law Claims, What Law Claims', in *Law as a Leap of Faith* (Oxford: Oxford University Press, 2012), 125. Gardner extends the view to assert that law claims authority vis-à-vis legal officials as well as subjects.

[4] Raz, 'Authority, Law, and Morality', 215. Following Raz, I will use 'legitimate authority' and 'authority' interchangeably, and distinguish both from non-legitimate authority with 'merely de facto authority'.

[5] Thomas Hobbes, *Leviathan* (1651) reprinted in Noel Malcolm (ed.), *Thomas Hobbes: The English and Latin Texts* (i) Vol. 2 (Oxford: Oxford University Press, 2012), ch. 26, at 431. Latin version, trans: 'authority not truth makes law'.

[6] See, for example, John Austin, *The Province of Jurisprudence Determined* (1832).

[7] H. L. A. Hart, *The Concept of Law* 3rd ed. (Oxford: Oxford University Press, 2012), 27.

gunman situation writ large'.[8] The individual subject to the gunman's threat could be obliged to hand her money over, but, Hart said, 'we should misdescribe the situation if we said . . . that [the individual] "had an obligation" or a "duty" to hand over the money'.[9]

Hart's solution was a theory of law premised on the union of primary and secondary rules.[10] Primary rules are object-level rules of private law and public law. Secondary rules are meta-level rules governing the identification, change, and adjudication of primary rules. Hart's rule of recognition, for example, is the secondary rule that lets officials distinguish certain rules as legal rules and determine their validity. However, although Hart's main complaint against the command theory was that it did not account for the way law purports to be authoritative, he did not think legal subjects generally had to accept or even have knowledge of 'the legal structure or of its criteria of validity [i.e., its rule of recognition]'.[11] For officials 'there should be a unified or shared acceptance of the rule of recognition', whereas for subjects the 'indispensable minimum' for a legal system to exist was merely that the system's laws were 'obeyed by the bulk of the population'.[12] Hart thought that officials must share 'the internal point of view accepting rules as standards for all to whom they apply', whereas the 'ordinary citizen' could obey the law 'out of fear of consequences, or from inertia, without thinking of himself or others as having an obligation to do so and without being disposed to criticize either himself or others for deviations'.[13] In short, for Hart the 'two minimum conditions necessary and sufficient for the existence of a legal system' were that (i) its primary rules must be 'generally obeyed' by legal subjects, and (ii) 'its [secondary rules] must be effectively accepted as common public standards of official behaviour by its officials'.[14]

Importantly, the legal subject does not inhabit the domain of officialdom from which law's authority is said to arise. And, it is law's authority – its normative standing to announce and enforce public rules – that is supposed to distinguish legal directives that give rise to legal obligations from the gunman's normatively inert commands. For the Hartian subject

[8] Ibid., 5.
[9] Ibid., 82.
[10] Ibid., 92–99.
[11] Ibid., 114.
[12] Ibid.
[13] Ibid., 114–115.
[14] Ibid., 115.

who obeys a directive purely 'out of fear of consequences', the directive's claim to be law would not be undermined simply because the directive came from a putative legal system that ruled its subjects through terror while making no claim to possess legitimate authority. For a rule-based terror regime to rank as a genuine legal system under Hart's theory, its officials must accept the prevailing secondary rules as 'common public standards of official behaviour'. There is, however, no obvious conceptual bar to those standards enabling systemic wickedness in a manner that would reduce the regime to a merely coercive order of a kind incapable of possessing legitimate authority.[15] Although Hart's theory does not embody 'the gunman situation writ large' in anything like the way the command theory does, it nonetheless does not disqualify a regime from counting as a legal order merely on the grounds that the regime is in fact a gunman writ large. A terror regime such as this – one that in principle is incapable of possessing legitimate authority – would find its legal credentials under stress for the very reasons Hart invoked to discredit the command theory: unmediated coercion of the gunman variety is inconsistent with legal obligation.

Raz offers a way forward by linking authority to law at the conceptual level, but in a way that lets illegitimate regimes with merely de facto authority count as legal systems so long as in principle it is possible for them to possess legitimate authority. The lynchpin of Raz's strategy is his separation of the law's *claim* to legitimate authority, on the one hand, from the question of whether the law *is* a legitimate authority, on the other. Regarding the law's claim to authority, Raz argues that the claim 'is manifested by the fact that legal institutions are officially designated as "authorities", by the fact that they regard themselves as having the right to impose obligations on their subjects, by the claims that their subjects owe them allegiance, and that their subjects ought to obey the law as it requires to be obeyed'.[16] Not only, however, does Raz's conceptual claim stipulate an existence condition on which the designation 'legal' depends. The content of the claim is such that it applies comprehensively to the relationship of ruler and ruled, official and subject.

[15] I consider in Section III the reply that any system of putative but wicked legal rules is in principle capable of possessing legitimate authority because all that needs to change for authority to be present is the contingent content of the rules. For now my purpose is merely to suggest that Hart's theory is hard-pressed to answer the kind of criticism he lays against the command theory.

[16] Raz, 'Authority, Law, and Morality', 215–16.

Implicit to the law's claim to authority is the idea that the law's officials and institutions are in a relationship of authority with their legal subjects, since claims to authority presuppose relations of authority. As will become evident when we bring Raz's service conception of authority into the picture, the law's claim to be in an authority relation with its subjects entails that the law must also claim that its raison d'être is to help legal subjects act on the basis of reasons which apply to them independently. Whereas for Hart a legal system can exist without concerning itself with the legal subject beyond ensuring that its primary rules are obeyed on any grounds by 'the bulk of the population', for Raz a constitutive element of a legal system is that it must claim that its coercive framework of rules helps its subjects comply with reason. In this sense, Raz's conceptual claim is comprehensive in scope across officials and subjects because it implies that law claims to be in an authority relationship between ruler and ruled, a relationship whose justification lies in its service to the ruled. As we shall see, a central issue for present purposes is whether Raz's conceptual claim implies that a certain form of wicked regime – a slave-owning regime – is disqualified from ranking as a legal system. More specifically, the question we will address is whether a slave-owning regime can satisfy the corollary Raz identifies as following from his conceptual claim; i.e., that law 'must be capable of possessing authority'.

Let me now offer a roadmap of the argument I intend to make. To bring Raz's conceptual claim into contact with the fiduciary criterion of legitimacy, I look first to the legal effects of peremptory or *jus cogens* norms of international law. Those norms bar inconsistent provisions of international treaties from having legal effect; in essence, invalidating the offending provisions. While such provisions may have impeccable legal sources or pedigree, their infringement of peremptory norms precludes them from having binding legal effect. Put another way, the legal validity of international treaty provisions depends on their consistency with international law's peremptory norms.

I then consider a particular *jus cogens* norm of international law – the prohibition on slavery – and use it to show how the fiduciary criterion can serve conceptual as well as normative purposes. Roughly, the argument is that no regime that maintains slave laws can be understood to assert those laws on behalf of the individuals held in slavery, and therefore a slave regime cannot possibly claim to assert legitimate authority over slaves. Such laws manifestly violate the fiduciary criterion and show themselves to lack moral legitimacy. The more controversial claim I'll make, with Kristen Rundle, is that slave laws violate Raz's conceptual claim as well as the fiduciary criterion.[17] Slave laws thereby show themselves to be instruments of mere coercive force rather than law. I suggest that Raz's own views on the relation between law and slavery are ambivalent, and that there is good reason to amend Raz's conceptual claim so that it incorporates the representational requirement from the fiduciary criterion of legitimacy.

The next step will be to show that if the state's cosmopolitan law does not satisfy the fiduciary criterion in relation to outsiders, then the state treats them as possessing a status akin to slaves. Such a state would interact with outsiders as Hart's gunman writ large. If this argument is sound, it will show that slavery is not a special case of a failure of law. Similarly, if the outsiders-as-slaves argument is persuasive, it will strengthen the case in favour of positing the fiduciary criterion of legitimacy as the content of the law's claim to authority. With this content, the law would be understood to claim to possess the normative standing adequate to entitle it to speak in a fiduciary or representative capacity for everyone subject to its jurisdiction.[18]

Let me introduce now how this argument relates to the idea of a double-facing constitution. In his chapter in this collection, David Dyzenhaus suggests that Janus should be appreciated as a god of doorways, and that a doorway denotes the idea of a threshold rather than a barrier. A threshold marks a physical or conceptual space through which passage is possible, but passage (or passage of a certain kind) is usually subject to conditions. If those conditions are satisfied, the person or thing or idea meeting them typically becomes transformed in some way for having crossed the threshold. For example, if someone comes to the unattended gate of a park, she may decide to enter without paying the token admission requested by a sign at the gate. But, other things being equal, she cannot decide to enter the park without paying and also be a friend of the park. Our free rider is no friend of the park precisely

[17] For previous arguments against the legality of slave laws, see Evan Fox-Decent, 'Is the Rule of Law Really Indifferent to Human Rights' (2008) 27 *Law & Philosophy* 533, 563–65; Evan Fox-Decent, *Sovereignty's Promise: The State as Fiduciary* (Oxford: Oxford University Press, 2011), 253–54; Evan Fox-Decent, 'Unseating Unilateralism', in Lisa Austin and Dennis Klimchuk (eds.), *Private Law and the Rule of Law* (Oxford: Oxford University Press, 2014), 116, 118–19; Kristen Rundle, 'Form and Agency in Raz's Legal Positivism' (2013) 32 *Law & Philosophy* 767.

[18] See Paul Miller, 'Fiduciary Representation', in Evan Criddle, Evan Fox-Decent, Andrew Gold, Sung Hui Kim, and Andrew Gold (eds.), *Fiduciary Government* (Cambridge: Cambridge University Press, 2018), 21. Miller argues that the fiduciary's capacity for representation is the golden thread that unites private and public fiduciaries.

because she uses the park but refuses to contribute her fair share. Compare her position with the park user who pays admission. By doing her fair share, this second person is transformed from a mere park user into a park friend, since she has satisfied the threshold condition we stipulated for becoming a park friend. A threshold does not, therefore, necessarily pose a barrier to entry into a given physical or conceptual space, but it typically does affect the status of a person, thing or idea that has crossed it. Where attributions of status are definitive of the kind of person, thing or idea an entity is (e.g. a mere park user or a park friend), the threshold's attribution of status is also constitutive of the kind of person, thing or idea the entity becomes.

I will suggest that the fiduciary criterion of legitimacy sketched above can be understood as a threshold of a type familiar to public lawyers in the common law tradition. The threshold of the criterion is jurisdictional in nature, and therefore marked by considerations of what falls within and outside the scope of a given legal power. While authorities can make certain kinds of errors and still have their directives regarded as morally binding, they cannot make jurisdictional errors and have their directives regarded as binding, since in those cases they have no authority – they lack jurisdiction – to give directives of that kind. Now, the distinction between non-jurisdictional and jurisdictional error is one of the most riveting and intractable problems of both administrative law and philosophical discussions of authority. Riveting because the distinction provides a basis for distinguishing genuine assertions of authority from counterfeits. Intractable because once one concludes that an authority has made an error of any kind, there is no obvious way to resist the inference that the authority has exercised a power not delegated to it (or in the case of an inherent authority, a power not part of its inherent authority). And once this inference is made, it seems that every error an authority commits can be counted as a jurisdictional error – i.e., as an exercise of a power not confided to the authority – thus dissolving the distinction with which we started.

I cannot hope to resolve this puzzle here. Nor must I. My theoretical aim is to suggest that the representational fiduciary criterion must ultimately rely on the non-jurisdictional/jurisdictional distinction to distinguish de facto from legitimate authority when an authority's decisions are called into question. Here too Raz's views will serve as a helpful foil to illuminate how jurisdictional considerations can lend structure to a cosmopolitan threshold that reflects a double-facing constitution involving national and supranational law. When deploying the jurisdictional distinction to the case of outsiders, we shall see that the fiduciary criterion implies that national officials adopt a solicitous attitude towards international human rights law and other legal sources that recognise the outsider as a free and equal legal subject. The aim is to show that the fiduciary criterion requires a cosmopolitan threshold – not a barrier – that welcomes the entry of peaceful outsiders into sovereign states while empowering states to limit migration when conditions warrant.

In the final section I argue that when the fiduciary criterion in the context of cosmopolitan law is construed as a jurisdictional threshold, the assessment of validity it makes possible is necessarily substantive rather than formal, and porous to international norms. From this it follows that the fiduciary criterion is in tension with the exclusive positivist sources thesis that the existence and content of law can be identified by reference to institutional sources and without recourse to moral considerations. I begin, however, with a few words to clarify what is meant by cosmopolitan law and *jus cogens*.

I Cosmopolitan Law and *Jus Cogens*

With respect to cosmopolitan law, I adopt with some qualification Kant's idea of a *ius cosmopoliticum* that governs relations between states and foreign nationals or outsiders.[19] Kant recognised that the law of nations provided norms appropriate to international legal order, and that municipal law was adequate to the task of providing domestic legal order by regulating interactions between citizens (domestic private law) and between citizens and the state (domestic public law). But even taken together, the law of nations and ordinary municipal law leave a gap, since neither contemplate the legal regime appropriate to relations between the state and outsiders. Kant called this regime a 'law of world citizenship', and understood it to include various duties of hospitality, including the right to enter, visit, conduct commerce, and travel within and through foreign states.[20] Today, international human rights law and international humanitarian law adopt Kant's foundational premise that all human beings – including outsiders – have various rights against domestic and foreign states with which they interact.

While foreign nationals living within a state's territory are subject to most of the same laws as citizens – ordinarily, the primary rules of criminal law, private law and public law – various legal regimes govern threshold

[19] See Immanuel Kant, *Perpetual Peace* (1795) (New York: Cosimo Classics, 2005).
[20] Ibid., 20.

issues that apply uniquely to non-citizens. These distinctive regimes govern entrance at the border, the naturalisation process, and access to the state's public institutions and social safety net (e.g. health care, social assistance, education, technical and professional certification). These interactions between the state and outsider have a threshold quality because in each there arises a boundary question concerning, in one way or another, whether the state will allow the outsider in. This is most evident at the border, but it applies to naturalisation through the question of whether the outsider will be allowed into the political community as a citizen, and it applies to public institutions through eligibility conditions that determine access as a threshold requirement of receiving health care, education, a license to practice a profession, etc. These various regimes that govern territorial frontiers, naturalisation and access to public institutions are the focus of this chapter. I will call them cosmopolitan regimes because structurally they involve threshold interactions between states and outsiders, notwithstanding that in many cases these regimes are deliberately hostile to newcomers and in a good sense *anti*-cosmopolitan. Consider now the nature and effect of international law's peremptory norms.

Peremptory or *jus cogens* norms of international law were described by Alfred Verdross as compulsory rules of international law that preclude states, independently of their consent, from agreeing to binding treaty provisions inconsistent with them.[21] Treaties inconsistent with *jus cogens*, Verdross said, would include agreements 'binding a state to reduce its police or its organization of courts in such a way that it is no longer able to protect at all or in an adequate manner, the life, the liberty, the honour, or the property of men on its territory'.[22] Other agreements contrary to *jus cogens* would include treaties that purport to bind 'a state to close its hospitals or schools, to extradite or sterilize its women, to kill its children, to close its factories, to leave its field unploughed, or in other ways to expose its population to distress'.[23]

Peremptory norms are now recognised in the Vienna Convention on the Law of Treaties, Article 53 of which provides that '[a] treaty is void if, at the time of its conclusion, it conflicts with a peremptory norm of general international law'.[24] Article 53 goes on to define a peremptory

[21] Alfred Verdross, 'Forbidden Treaties in International Law' (1937) 31 *The American Journal of International Law* 571.

[22] Ibid., 574.

[23] Ibid., 575.

[24] Vienna Convention on the Law of Treaties, opened for signature May 23, 1969, 1155 UNTS 331, 8 ILM 679 (hereinafter VCLT), Art. 53.

norm as 'a norm accepted and recognized by the international community of States as a whole as a norm from which no derogation is permitted and which can be modified only by a subsequent norm of general international law having the same character'.[25] The VCLT, however, does not specify which norms of international law count as *jus cogens*, nor how such norms are to be identified. Nor does the VCLT specify the ultimate justification or theoretical basis of these norms.[26]

While the VCLT's silence on these questions has led to heated debates, a common reference point regarding the specification of peremptory norms is the *Restatement on Foreign Relations of the United States (Restatement).*[27] The *Restatement* defines *jus cogens* to include, minimally, prohibitions against genocide, slavery, the slave trade, systemic racial discrimination, murder or disappearance of individuals, prolonged arbitrary detention, torture or other cruel, inhuman, or degrading treatment or punishment, and the use of military force not authorised under the United Nations Charter.[28]

Criddle and I argue that a helpful way of thinking about peremptory norms is that they arise as relational features of the fiduciary or trust-like relationship in which all public authorities stand vis-à-vis the persons amenable to their jurisdiction.[29] On our view, the fiduciary principle that underlies fiduciary relations generally both authorises and requires the state to establish a regime of secure and equal freedom for everyone subject to the state's authority. The state fulfills this duty, in part, by governing through norms that conform to two intermediate and regulative principles: the Kantian ideal of non-instrumentalisation (persons cannot be treated as mere means) and the republican ideal of non-domination (persons cannot be made to live subject to arbitrary power). The principles are *intermediate* because they fall between the state's abstract duty to guarantee secure and equal freedom, on the one hand, and more determinate obligations such as those flowing from

[25] Ibid.; see also Ibid., Art. 64: ' If a new peremptory norm of international law emerges, any existing treaty in conflict with the norm becomes void and terminates.'

[26] For the suggestion that *jus cogens* has a natural law basis and was able to underpin the human rights revolution in international law only because its natural law foundation was never clearly articulated, see Jens David Ohlin, 'In Praise of Jus Cogens' Conceptual Incoherence' 63 *McGill Law Journal* (in press).

[27] Restatement (Third) of Foreign Relations of the United States.

[28] Ibid., § 702 cmts. d-i, § 102 cmt. k (1987).

[29] Criddle and Fox-Decent, *Fiduciaries of Humanity*, ch. 3; see also Evan J. Criddle and Evan Fox-Decent, 'A Fiduciary Theory of Jus Cogens' (2009) 34 *Yale Journal of International Law* 331.

international human rights law, on the other. The principles are *regulative* because the Kantian and republican injunctions are expressly normative and therefore proscribe some policies while encouraging others.

The fiduciary theory also suggests more substantive relational principles drawn from the trust-like nature of the state-subject fiduciary relationship: i.e., integrity (a prohibition on using public offices for private ends), formal moral equality (all must be treated with equal respect), and solicitude (legitimate interests must be taken seriously). And it incorporates the formal principles of Lon L. Fuller's internal morality of law, such as publicity, clarity, and non-retroactivity of penal sanctions.[30] Ultimately, the fiduciary theory brings together Fuller's formal principles with the substantive relational principles mentioned above, and presents them as more hard-edged instances of the Kantian and republican ideals. Criddle and I claim that this model can explain the norms of international human rights law and *jus cogens*. We also suggest that the fiduciary theory can distinguish the relatively narrow set of international law's peremptory and absolute norms from the much more expansive set of non-absolute norms that are subject to limitation and derogation under international law (e.g. international human rights to freedom of assembly or expression).

To distinguish peremptory norms from others, Criddle and I deploy a variant of the fiduciary criterion of legitimacy. On our telling, a norm that conforms to the fiduciary theory's principles will count as non-derogable *jus cogens* if its infringement would always be inconsistent with the state's basic duty to secure legal order (a regime of secure and equal freedom) on behalf of every person subject to it. The fiduciary principle entitles every individual to be treated as an equal co-beneficiary of legal order, and therefore prohibits policies that inherently and intractably instrumentalise or dominate individuals touched by them.[31] Any

[30] Lon L. Fuller, *The Morality of Law*, 2nd ed. (New Haven: Yale University Press, 1969). Fuller defends as an internal morality of law the formal principles of generality, publicity, non-retroactivity, stability over time, consistency, susceptibility to compliance, clarity and fidelity to the law's spirit and letter.

[31] One need not adopt the fiduciary conception of public law to be persuaded by the central argument of this chapter. Various liberal and republican theories demand that individuals be treated with equal moral concern. Part of the point of the fiduciary theory is to show how the demand for equal concern can flow from a legal relationship and therefore have a distinctively legal as well as political quality. But, common law constitutionalists, for example, may be able to draw legal principles supportive of equality and human rights

state that adopts such policies is to that extent illegitimate. This is the corollary of the fiduciary criterion of legitimacy which, to reiterate, affirms that every legitimate state action must be intelligible as action taken on behalf of every person subject to it. Action that deliberately abuses or dominates individuals with impunity cannot be understood as action taken on their behalf, even if many others or the state would benefit greatly.

On the fiduciary theory, then, international law examines the on-the-ground relationship between state authorities and those who are subject to them, and extracts principles from the general features of that relationship to explain the norms of international human rights law and jus cogens, as well as provide a basis for their critique, interpretation, and extension.[32] In this manner, concrete features of the national level explain and inform norms of international law that then descend to the national level with the aspiration of bringing state conduct into the deepest possible conformity with what Mattias Kumm calls the 'the trinitarian formula of the constitutionalist faith' – human rights, democracy, and the rule of law.[33] The double-facing constitution of global constitutionalism can thus be seen to embody a mutual and fruitful sharing of norms between national and supra-national levels.

Let us consider now how the fiduciary criterion of legitimacy can explain the prohibition of slavery as a peremptory norm, and the possible connection between this criterion and Raz's conceptual claim, including its corollary that law must in principle be capable of possessing authority.

II Slavery and Law's Conceptual Claim as a Claim to Represent

Under the fiduciary theory, international law delegates sovereignty to states by recognising within them the operation of a power-conferring

from the common law and international adjudication, and then use those to explain *jus cogens*. It may be awkward to deploy the fiduciary criterion of legitimacy without a theory to explain the centrality of representation to legitimacy (a core tenet of the fiduciary theory), but democratic theory and theories on corporate structure may be adequate to the task. Of course, these latter theories are in reality different kinds of fiduciary theory.

32 Criddle and I, for example, critique the alleged peremptory norm against piracy, arguing that it is merely a common crime, and we extend the typical canon of *jus cogens* to include a prohibition on corruption. Criddle and Fox-Decent, *Fiduciaries of Humanity* at 110–11.

33 Mattias Kumm, 'Constitutionalism and the Cosmopolitan State' (2013) New York University Public Law and Legal Theory Working Papers, Paper 423 at 5.

fiduciary principle that authorises states to establish legal order on behalf of every individual amenable to their jurisdiction.[34] As a principle of legality, the fiduciary principle must treat like cases alike, though of course there may be disagreement regarding which cases count as 'like cases'. But even assuming that certain assessments of likeness will be controversial, it follows from the like-cases maxim that the fiduciary principle has no normative capacity to discriminate arbitrarily between individuals subject to the same fiduciary power, since such a capacity would be inconsistent with the maxim.

Individuals within a state are subject to the same fiduciary power. They therefore enjoy co-equal status as beneficiaries of the fiduciary principle's authorisation of state authority. One of the entitlements of co-equal status is that the state is not entitled to discriminate arbitrarily between individuals, because to do so would violate the like-cases maxim. As a consequence, if the state recognises some individuals within its jurisdictions as legal persons, it must recognise all as such. And if the state must recognise all individuals as legal persons, it cannot regard any as slaves, since slavery is precisely the denial of legal personhood. The inexorable effect of a systematic denial of legal personhood is comprehensive, incurable domination with impunity. Even if the slave regime treats its slaves in wholly benevolent ways, under the republican conception of freedom as non-domination the slaves remain unfree merely by dint of their subjection to arbitrary power.[35] Thus, under the fiduciary model, the peremptory norm against slavery is explained, first, by the fiduciary principle's incapacity to authorise the arbitrary discrimination presupposed by slavery and, second, by the theory's rejection of domination.

This explanation is confirmed by the fiduciary criterion of legitimacy, which avers that slave regimes cannot be understood to maintain slavery on behalf of or in the name of the slaves. Slave regimes do not represent slaves. They instead enable masters to possess them as property, as things the master may destroy with impunity if he or she so wishes. In ancient Rome, for example, Barry Nicholas observes that '[i]n law the slave was a thing . . . he himself had no rights: he was merely an object of rights, like an animal'.[36] Consequently, the slave was incapable of being the subject

[34] This does not mean that states owe every person amenable to their jurisdiction identical duties. For example, states do not owe transient non-citizens political rights related to voting, though they do owe them duties related to due process if the state detains them.

[35] Philip Petit, *Republicanism: A Theory of Freedom and Government* (Oxford: Oxford University Press, 1997).

[36] Barry Nicholas, *An Introduction to Roman Law* (Oxford: Clarendon Press, 1962), 69.

of a relationship of authority because the slave, like an animal, was denied the possibility of having either legal rights or obligations. As a conceptual matter, then, Roman law could not claim to possess legitimate authority over slaves because in principle it could not possess *any* authority over them. The absence of an authority relation was also evident from the standpoint of the slave's possible reasons for doing as instructed. Regarded in law as 'an animal' subject to arbitrary power, the slave might obey to curry favour or avoid punishment. The slave could not obey as a matter of legal duty, however, since the slave was denied the status required in order to have such duties.

In his well-known article *The Rule of Law and Its Virtue,* Raz endeavours to cut the rule of law down to exclusive positivist size, insisting at one point that the rule of law is consistent with slavery.[37] As Kristen Rundle points out, however, there is considerable tension between this claim from *Rule of Law* and his writing on authority.[38] In his writing on authority, Raz clearly distinguishes de facto from legitimate authority. Contrary to what one might expect from reading *Rule of Law* and its view of slavery, Raz in his work on authority never claims that a legal system could consist of merely de facto authority (much less mere coercive authority). When discussing authority, Raz's emphatic view is that a de facto authority *must* claim to possess legitimate authority in order to be a legal authority. And as also noted above, Raz takes it to be an implication of his conceptual claim that all legal systems in principle must be capable of possessing legitimate authority. Rundle astutely remarks that 'it is difficult to see how the precondition of the capacity for legitimate authority over a subject that Raz suggests is part of the nature of law, and something which it cannot fundamentally fail to possess, could be satisfied if the law designated that subject as a slave'.[39]

Raz might reply that when he said that putative legal systems must be capable of possessing legitimate authority, he only intended to exclude laws that don't apply to human conduct, such as the laws of natural science applicable to volcanoes, and entities that cannot have authority, such as trees.[40] Slave regimes, he might say, are just one type of wicked regime that with adequate abolitionist reform could possess legitimate

[37] Joseph Raz, 'The Rule of Law and Its Virtue', in *The Authority of Law: Essays on Law and Morality* (Oxford: Clarendon Press, 1979), 211 (hereinafter *Rule of Law*).

[38] Rundle, 'Form and Agency'.

[39] Ibid., 797.

[40] Raz, 'Authority, Law, and Morality' at 216–17 (excluding 'a set of propositions about the behavior of volcanoes'); Ibid., at 217 ('Trees cannot have authority over people').

authority, or at least some measure of it. The Antebellum South of the United States and ancient Rome are examples of this. They were wicked, but they were also perfectible normative systems that governed human conduct. Thus, it is possible, in the relevant sense, for slave regimes to possess legitimate authority, since slavery is a contingent institution that can be abandoned. Like many de facto regimes that lack legitimate authority, slave regimes could become legitimate if adequate reform policies were adopted. Thus, Raz might say, so long as slave regimes are de facto authorities that also claim to possess legitimate authority (e.g. the Antebellum South and ancient Rome), they qualify as legal regimes. They are wicked and do not actually possess legitimate authority, but on Raz's theory this is not a bar to them counting as legal orders.

There is, however, a compelling rejoinder. The notion of a slave regime persisting over time and becoming legitimate is misleading because the only way a slave regime can become legitimate is by ceasing to be a slave regime. If we ask the question, 'Can a slave regime *as a slave regime* possess legitimate authority over slaves?', the answer is plainly 'no'. Because slaves are denied personhood, they cannot possess the duties of subjects or otherwise occupy the position of subjects within an authority-subject relation. The incompatibility of slavery and authority is also suggested by Raz's own service conception of authority.

The heart of Raz's theory is the 'normal justification thesis', which asserts that a person will ordinarily count as an authority if following her directives will lead a subject to comply better with moral and prudential reasons applicable to him than he would if he decided matters for himself.[41] If we plug the normal justification thesis into Raz's conceptual claim, then, as noted in the introduction, the result is that law necessarily claims that (ordinarily) it issues directives that help its subjects comply better with reason than they would on their own. It is hard to see, however, how the typical directives of a slave regime directed towards a slave could help her comply better with moral and prudential reasons that apply to her. Another element of Raz's theory of authority – the dependence thesis – makes this plainer still. According to the dependence thesis, 'all authoritative directives should be based on reasons which already apply independently to the subjects of the directives'.[42] I doubt there are any reasons underlying slavery-creating directives that 'apply independently' to the slave targeted by those directives.

[41] Joseph Raz, *The Morality of Freedom* (Oxford: Clarendon Press, 1986), 53.
[42] Ibid., 47.

A Razian might counter that the fact that officials of slave regimes had de facto authority and claimed to possess legitimate authority is enough to say that there was a legal system in place, albeit a very wicked legal system. The Razian could agree that the officials of the regime are deluded in thinking their regime is legitimate. But that is what they believe and claim, and those beliefs and claims explain why their regime is a legal system, whereas a purely de facto slave regime in which officials do not claim legitimate authority is not a legal system.

In my view, there is something misguided about a conceptual approach to law that relies on moral delusion to distinguish legal from non-legal systems of rule. It is counterintuitive to think that officials can in effect wish a legal system into existence by claiming a legitimacy the system does not and cannot possess, at least 'cannot' while remaining a certain kind of wicked regime, such as a slave regime. I am, in other words, convinced by Raz himself when he writes that '[w]e cannot create reasons just by intending to do so and expressing that intention in action. Reasons precede the will'.[43] If this is true of reasons, then it is true of authorities, at least on Raz's account. The point of authorities for Raz is that they play a mediating role between the subject and her ultimate reasons for action, making it more likely that she will comply with those ultimate reasons while saving her the trouble of reasoning down to first principles every time she acts.

My hope is to improve on Raz's conceptual claim that legal systems necessarily claim to possess legitimate authority, but to do so in a way that does not see the proposed improvement collapse into 'old school' natural law under which any unjust law is disqualified as law. And that means conceptual space must be provided for a range of legal regimes with (relatively) wicked policies (of some kinds, but not others) to actually count as legal regimes. My suggestion is that we substitute the representational fiduciary criterion of legitimacy, suitably modified, for Raz's conceptual criterion that legal systems necessarily claim to possess legitimate authority. The substitution yields the following: all legal systems necessarily represent – they necessarily act on behalf of or in the name of – every person subject to their authority.[44] On this theory, it is

[43] Ibid., 84 (chastising consent as a foundation of authority).

[44] I am using a broad understanding of 'represent' that includes cases where one person administers, manages, or simply acts on behalf of another in some way that treat's that other person's interests as primary. On this broad understanding, agents plainly represent their principals. But trustees also represent their beneficiaries, on this understanding, when they manage the trust's assets.

part of the nature of law that all legal systems must be intelligible as normative systems that can credibly claim to represent the persons subject to their authority. The laws of science governing volcanoes and trees cannot count as these kinds of normative systems, but neither can slave regimes.

The representational or fiduciary criterion is both weaker and stronger than Raz's conceptual claim. It is weaker in the sense that the power to represent someone, ordinarily, is weaker than the possession of legitimate authority over them. In Raz's hands, legitimate authority is a moral power, the correlative jural concept of which is a liability that crystallises ultimately (when the power to rule is exercised) in a duty to obey.[45] The moral power to represent, without more, does not entail a duty to obey. The representational claim is stronger, however, because it includes a standard of adequacy that Raz's conceptual claim does not. Whereas Raz simply looks to see whether legal officials have claimed legitimacy, with the ambiguous rider that the claim must be possible to realise, the representational criterion asserts that the words and conduct of legal officials must be intelligible as representing the people subject to their authority. It is not enough for officials to simply wish or say that they are acting for the people subject to their authority. There has to be some basis for believing that they are really doing so. If there is such a basis, then even if their policies fall short of establishing a fully legitimate regime, they will nonetheless have established a legal system.

The case of slavery, as discussed at the beginning of this section, is a relatively easy case, since it is not credible to think that a slave regime acts on behalf of the slaves.[46] Reaching this conclusion does not require

[45] Raz, *The Morality of Freedom*, 24.

[46] Some might think that the public rules of slave regimes are not law for the slaves, but that some of the regime's rules are law for slave owners, notwithstanding the odiousness of slavery. Law might guide and structure the lives of slave owners vis-à-vis one another much as it guides and structures private interactions in non-slave-holding societies. These are complex matters I cannot pursue properly here. It is arguable that the apparently innocent private law of slave owners is akin to fruit of the poisonous tree. The slave owners' private law is a standing and institutionalised reminder of his unjust privilege, and a social construction that facilitates his extraction, possession and use of value from slaves. The legality of the slave owners' law may also be challenged by analogy to fiduciary law that renders void decisions a fiduciary is not competent to make or which are made *ultra vires* the fiduciary's mandate. The purported authorisation of a slave-owning regime may be void *ab initio* on grounds that the fiduciary principle has no normative capacity to make or sanction such an authorisation. Alternatively, one might think that some measure of legality may be in place for some in a society while absent for others. Even this more restrained view, however, marks a significant departure from the positivist

a searching moral assessment of slave regimes. All that is required is an inquiry to determine whether the facts disclose a relationship between ruler and ruled in which the ruler can be said to act in the name or on behalf of the slaves. Still, some may think slavery is a special case. It may appear that because slave regimes so comprehensively deny the slave's legal personhood and the very possibility of legal entitlements, those regimes must enforce slavery through force alone. In the next section I argue that outsiders at the boundaries of the state's territory, political community, and public services are at risk of being treated as slaves, since they are at risk of being subjected to a public power that cannot be said to represent them. The theoretical takeaway is that the fiduciary criterion of legitimacy can facilitate more fine-grained distinctions within analytical jurisprudence than those necessary to eliminate slave regimes from the set of regimes that rank as legal orders.

III Outsiders and Law's Claim to Represent

For the sake of simplifying, I limit discussion in this section to issues related to the state's purported entitlement to establish a regime of unilateral border control. The regime is unilateral in the sense that states take themselves to be legally empowered to use irresistible force to deny entry to peaceful migrants for any reason or for no reason at all. With relatively minor adjustment, what I say about the boundary interaction at the border applies to other cosmopolitan contexts too (i.e., contexts where the relevant interaction is between states and foreign nationals, and the issue is access to citizenship or access to public services and institutions).

I have argued elsewhere that with respect to peaceful outsiders – not just asylum seekers, but ordinary migrants too – a border regime is legitimate from a normative point of view only if the state governing it is required to give a substantial justification for decisions to exclude outsiders, a justification that demonstrably takes seriously migrant interests.[47] I suggested some possible, context-dependent justifications for exclusion, such as the threat of large-scale and rapid migration into a smaller state of lesser abundance. In principle, limits might also be set

thesis that the identification of a legal rule is always possible without recourse to moral considerations.

47 Evan Fox-Decent, 'Constitutional Legitimacy Unbound', in David Dyzenhaus and Malcolm Thorburn (eds.), *Philosophical Foundations of Constitutional Law* (Oxford: Oxford University Press, 2015), 119.

with a view to protecting a vulnerable culture or a comprehensive social welfare system sensitive to a sudden incursion of migrants. But, I claimed, such justifications would have to be reviewable by an independent public body, such as a national or international court. The default position, in the absence of an overriding and reviewable public justification, would be open borders to peaceful migrants.

Skating over many details, the argument begins with the observation that in practice the present regime of unilateral state border control produces a context of pervasive domination between ascendant states and vulnerable outsiders. At the border, the foreign national is at the state's mercy and subject to its coercive force. States may build physical walls or electrical fences across their frontiers. They may use tear gas or more extreme forms of violence to deny entry. They may tear apart undocumented families, separating small children from their parents and then holding those children incommunicado at undisclosed locations. More powerful states may threaten to impose crippling economic measures against weaker states that decline to use example-setting force against individuals who appear prepared to cross without authorisation the more powerful state's border. States may engage in extra-territorial interdiction on the high seas for the purpose of denying migrants access to the state's courts. States may inflict these and other dystopian consequences on outsiders for nationalist or populist reasons, or for no discernible reason at all, and with relative impunity. They may do so while formally subject to international human rights law and municipal legal regimes that demand better treatment of outsiders than in practice they generally receive. Overwhelmingly, migrants at the border are subject to arbitrary and often capricious power that states may use against them without fear of meaningful sanction. In other words, states ordinarily dominate peaceful outsiders who arrive at their borders. I will argue below that the position of the outsider resembles that of the slave: both suffer entrenched domination.

Against the view that citizens have a collective right to self-determination that justifies a general right to exclude outsiders, I argued previously that a right of self-determination does not imply that states have normatively legitimate claims to unilateral jurisdiction over their borders. Although the state is a public entity authorised by international law to govern and represent its people, if the state in practice has a liberty right to do as it pleases with foreign nationals who come to its border, then it effectively confronts the outsider in a state of nature. The state appears to the outsider at the border not as a public authority, but as a lawless giant, a soulless Leviathan of which she is not a member.

To overcome the legitimacy deficit at the border, I suggested that we can think of states as occupying two roles. At the local level, they are fiduciaries of the people within their territory, authorised by international law to govern and represent their people. At the global level, they are fiduciaries of humanity, and as such entrusted with collective stewardship of the earth's surface. So conceived, states are entitled to favour the interests of their own people. Within reciprocal legal limits, states may legitimately bargain hard on behalf of their people in treaty negotiations. In less formal settings of foreign or transnational affairs, they may advocate for their people and institutions. And they may rightly limit migration for the good of their people, so long as they provide a substantial and reviewable justification that takes seriously the interests of outsiders. In sum, states can treat their people as their primary moral concern, but their people's interests cannot be their exclusive moral concern.[48] Because states are fiduciaries of humanity charged with stewardship of the earth's surface, outsiders have a call on that stewardship and an entitlement to migrate where they wish in the absence of reasons adequate to justify their exclusion. The right to a justification is supported by the view of Rainer Forst that individuals are generally entitled to 'justifying reasons for the actions, rules, or structures to which he or she is subject'.[49] There is no reason to think this principle runs out at the border.[50] Indeed, its salience at the border suggests that the proper focus of legality is not the citizen, but the legal subject.

[48] See Evan J. Criddle and Evan Fox-Decent, 'Guardians of Legal Order: The Dual Commissions of Public Fiduciaries', in Evan Criddle, Evan Fox-Decent, Andrew Gold, Sung Hui Kim, and Andrew Gold (eds.), *Fiduciary Government* (Cambridge: Cambridge University Press, 2018) (arguing that fiduciaries commonly have multiple mandates to distinct beneficiaries, such as the lawyer's duty of zealous advocacy to her client and her often competing duty of candour to the legal system as an officer of the court).

[49] Rainer Forst, *The Right to Justification: Elements of a Constructivist Theory of Justice* (New York: Columbia University Press, 2011), 209.

[50] The principle already applies to goods subject to the trade regime administered by the World Trade Organization. As Joseph Weiler puts it, 'in the GATT, obstacles to trade, even if nondiscriminatory, may be prohibited unless a rational justification may be invoked'. Joseph Weiler, 'Epilogue: Towards a Common Law of International Trade', in Joseph Weiler (ed.), *The EU, The WTO and the NAFTA* (Oxford: Oxford University Press, 2000), 202. See Appellate Body Report, *European Communities – Measures Concerning Meat and Meat Products (Hormones),* WT/DS26/AB/R, WT/DS48/AB/R, adopted 13 February 1998, DSR 1998:I, p. 135.

The key point for present purposes, however, is that conceiving of states as fiduciaries of humanity allows them and foreign nationals to exit the state of nature and enter a cosmopolitan condition of legality with one another. As fiduciaries of both their people and humanity, states can credibly claim to represent both constituencies, and act on behalf of both, including when outsiders appear at their border. Put another way, the fiduciary premise gives the receiving state the opportunity to achieve *standing to rule* relative to outsiders. The receiving state can realise this opportunity if it treats the outsider's request to enter with solicitude, rejecting that request only if there is a substantial justification to do so, and only if the state's justification is capable of surviving independent review. Without the standing to rule this cosmopolitan legal framework provides, the receiving state interacts with the outsider as at best a de facto authority, with force aplenty, but not the force of law.

Let us now gather some of the implications of these ideas in relation to the fiduciary criterion of legitimacy, and then consider two important objections. On the view essayed immediately above, if a state arrogates to itself unilateral power to control its border, it cannot be said to represent or act on behalf of outsiders, and therefore, with respect to outsiders, the state's legal system would fail to satisfy the representational fiduciary criterion of legitimacy that all putative legal systems must satisfy to be actual legal systems. Because the law, on this assumption, does not speak for the outsider, it is not the outsider's law, but force channelled through a merely coercive de facto authority.

One objection to this analysis is that nationalist-populist states make no claim to represent outsiders, nor aspire to do so. The objection confuses contingent facts with the conceptual criteria of an analytical framework. It makes no difference whether a state explicitly claims or denies that it acts in the name of, or on behalf of, foreign nationals. All that matters is the substance of the policy the state adopts and whether it offers reasonable grounds for inferring that the state in some sense acted in the name of or on behalf of outsiders. For instance, if a state raised the number of migrants it was willing to accept in a given year because the reasons justifying a lower number no longer applied, the policy shift would be a basis for inferring that the state had taken outsider interests seriously and acted on behalf of migrants as well as its own people. This inference remains valid even if the actual reason for the pro-migrant policy was that it served the government's immediate political interest. The actual reason for the policy is irrelevant because the point of the inquiry is merely to determine whether the policy can be interpreted objectively, in the manner one might interpret a statute, as law made on behalf of outsiders as well as the state's people.[51]

The second objection challenges the claim that if a state arrogates to itself unilateral power to govern the border in a manner indifferent or hostile to peaceful outsiders, then it fails to satisfy the fiduciary criterion of legitimacy and thereby fails to meet the demands of legality. If the unilateralist state abides by the relevant rules of international law – rules that include international human rights law but which permit the state to exclude non-necessitous outsiders – is that not enough to meet the demands of legality? No, it is not. Although international law has brought a measure of legality to state-outsider border relations through discrete but overlapping legal regimes that aim to protect asylum seekers, children, and family life, as well as ensure humane treatment and due process,[52] there remains an important sense in which international law governing borders has yet to catch up to its underlying presuppositions. On the view defended here, the crucial underlying presupposition is that part of what it means to be a public authority is to stand in a representational capacity vis-à-vis the individuals subject to the authority's power, since it is this capacity that produces the normative standing that entitles the authority to rule. To appreciate the implications of international law's failure to institutionalise this presupposition at the border, compare the position of the peaceful outsider in respect of a hostile receiving state and the position of the slave vis-à-vis a slave regime.

In both cases, the vulnerable party is subject to an arbitrary power that can be exercised against her capriciously and with impunity. Although the contemporary outsider benefits from international human rights protections, human rights to association, assembly, and movement have yet to dent the state's asserted prerogative to determine unilaterally

[51] The point might be easier to see with Raz's conceptual claim. Suppose an official explicitly denied that a just, reasonable, solicitous, and otherwise good legal institution implicitly claimed to possess legitimate authority. So what? We would evaluate the institution and its implicit claim on the merits, and possibly question the official's understanding of his role.

[52] In addition to international refugee law, in some cases international human rights law has dented the state's claim to unilateralism. The right to family life and the best interests of children have led some courts to quash deportation orders and allow outsiders to remain. See, e.g., *Baker* v. *Canada (Minister of Citizenship and Immigration)*, [1999] 2 SCR 817 (referring to the Convention on the Rights of the Child and setting aside a Minister's decision to refuse to grant discretionary relief from a deportation order to a mother of four Canadian-born children).

whether non-asylum seeking peaceful migrants may enter and remain within their territory. If a peaceful outsider has no family within the receiving state or prior connection to it, and cannot make a case for refugee status or *non-refoulement*, then ordinarily she will find herself without legal recourse and at the mercy of the receiving state. The state may adopt a benevolent policy and allow her to enter and remain, but under the prevailing understanding of the prerogatives of state sovereignty, the state is not under any obligation to do so. From the conventional perspective, the state is entitled to use coercive force – even lethal force – against peaceful migrants, for no discernible reason or even capricious reasons. In this fundamental respect, the position of the peaceful outsider resembles that of the slave: both are subject to domination – arbitrary power exercisable with impunity – backed up by the threat and possible use of force.

One might object that there is nothing especially perverse or unusual about the state's use of coercion to enforce its laws. The state is entitled to use coercive force on a subject who disobeys a lawful order from a police officer, but the subject's status before the law is not akin to the status of a slave. There are significant differences, however, between the relationship of police officer and subject, on the one hand, and border guard and outsider, on the other. The police officer acts on behalf of the state of which the legal subject is a member, and thus in principle the officer can also be said to act on behalf of the subject, consistent with the fiduciary criterion of legitimacy. The same cannot be said of the border guard and the outsider, at least not under the conventional unilateralist assumption. Similarly, in issuing a lawful order the police officer implicitly relies on a legal warrant traceable to law made in the subject's name. Not so in the case of the border guard and the migrant. Finally, in practice, police officers who use force are more likely than border guards to be subject to meaningful review and accountability procedures. In the standard case, then, individuals subject to police coercion are also subject to authority, whereas migrants subject to border enforcement are subject to domination.

Nonetheless, some may think that the comparison of migrants to slaves is hyperbole, since slavery involves not merely a practical denial of the slave's personhood, but the use of legal machinery to make the denial effective. In this respect too, however, there are parallels. As we shall see, in *Jennings* v. *Rodriguez*,[53] a 2018 decision of the US Supreme

[53] 138 S. Ct. 830 (2018) (hereinafter *Jennings*).

Court, the US government argued that undocumented migrants are not entitled to constitutional protections because, so far as the law is concerned, they are not persons within the United States.

Rodriguez is a Mexican citizen and permanent resident of the United States. Immigration authorities incarcerated him following a 2004 conviction while seeking his removal. In 2007, while litigating his removal, he filed a habeas corpus petition as a class action representing three groups of non-citizens detained and awaiting determination of their residency status: asylum seekers, immigrants with a criminal conviction who served their sentence, and immigrants claiming an entitlement to remain for reasons unrelated to persecution. Rodriguez claimed that the statutes under which he and the class he represented were detained did not authorise prolonged detention in the absence of periodic bond hearings. The US Supreme Court had held in *Zadvydas* v. *Davis* in 2001 that the Fifth Amendment's Due Process Clause protected deportable aliens held without a hearing, and construed the relevant statute to limit detention to six months.[54]

In *Jennings*, Justice Alito, writing for a 5–3 majority, interpreted the statute to provide for the indefinite detention of all three groups without bail hearings, and sent the case back to the lower court to redetermine the constitutional due process question. He panned *Zadvydas*, and without solicitation from the government, suggested that the lower court dissolve the class, forcing every plaintiff to litigate his or her case individually.

Justice Breyer wrote for the dissent. He took the extraordinary step of reading his opinion from the bench. Relying on *Zadvydas*, he interpreted the relevant statute to require a bail hearing after six months. Breyer J held that the Due Process Clause foresees eligibility for bail as part of due process, and that it applies to 'all persons within the territory of the United States'.[55] Breyer J was especially anxious to denounce the government's argument that 'the law treats arriving aliens as if they had never entered the United States', and thus they are not 'persons' within its territory and cannot avail themselves of constitutional protections.[56] Breyer J warned that the government's position would strip away personhood and legal protections in a manner that recalled slavery and the vulnerability to arbitrary cruelty slaves suffered:[57]

[54] 533 US 678 (2001) (hereinafter *Zadvydas*).
[55] *Jennings*, at 7 (per Breyer J, dissenting).
[56] Ibid.
[57] Ibid.

> No one can claim, nor since the time of slavery has anyone to my knowledge successfully claimed, that persons held within the United States are totally without constitutional protection. Whatever the fiction, would the Constitution leave the Government free to starve, beat, or lash those held within our boundaries? If not, then, whatever the fiction, how can the Constitution authorize the Government to imprison arbitrarily those who, whatever we might pretend, are in reality right here in the United States? The answer is that the Constitution does not authorize arbitrary detention.

Admittedly, Breyer J overstates. Someone – a US appellate judge – has claimed as recently as 2017 that undocumented migrants 'are totally without constitutional protection'.

In *Rochelle Garza* v. *Eric Hargan*,[58] Judge Henderson of the US Court of Appeals for the District of Columbia Circuit found that a pregnant, undocumented 17-year old held in custody was not entitled to the protection of the Due Process Clause. In her dissenting judgment, Judge Henderson held that the woman was not entitled to access an abortion, a right protected under the Due Process Clause. She explained: 'Despite her physical presence in the United States, J. D. has never entered the United States as a matter of law and cannot avail herself of the constitutional rights afforded those legally within our borders.'[59] That is, having failed to enter the United States 'as a matter of law', she is not deemed to be a person within its territory, and therefore, like Dred Scott, she is denied standing to assert constitutional rights. Under this doctrine, undocumented migrants would be in a worse constitutional position than detainees at Guantánamo Bay who enjoy constitutional protections such as habeas corpus. While Justice Alito in *Jennings* remanded the case to the Ninth Circuit for redetermination, his evident sympathy for the government's position rivals Judge Henderson's. The United States is just that close to formally entrenching its practical domination of undocumented outsiders by stripping them of their personhood.

From a normative point of view, the denial of migrants' personhood is egregious. But once we appreciate the implications for legality of the state's assertion of unilateralism at the border, we can see that the proposed policy is just the chickens coming home to roost. Nativist institutional norms are chasing nativist practices that are made possible, in part, by the state's assertion of unilateral authority at the border that international law

58 No. 17-5236 (D.C. Cir. 2017).

59 Ibid., at 8 (per Henderson, dissenting).

sanctifies. Although the connection between nativist practices and personhood-stripping norms is not one of logical entailment, nativist practices arguably lend plausibility and acceptability to nativist norms. Of course, defenders of unilateral border authority can resist the descent into nativism, and do have a more positive argument on offer.

A familiar defence of borders is that if the migrant is not an asylum-seeker fleeing persecution, then by definition there is somewhere else she can go without threat to her human rights. This being so, international law may be thought to allocate properly territory to states that can have sovereignty in the sense of robust self-determination and self-government only if their citizens are entitled, as a general matter, to determine the terms under which peaceful migrants may enter and gain membership. I have suggested elsewhere that this defence of unilateral border control conflates public territory with private property, and that the argument cannot bear the weight it attempts to shoulder.[60] But its deeper weakness is that it presupposes that the state alone is the arbiter of the purported scope and legal consequences of its alleged right to exclude. This unilateralist presumption puts the state and the outsider in a state of nature with one another because the state's assertion of unilateralism just is an assertion that it alone sits in final judgment of the migrant's claim to enter, as Austin's uncommanded commander. In this context, the state cannot plausibly be said to be acting in the name of or on behalf of the migrant, and as explained above, the fact that the state may strenuously deny that it in any way represents or acts on behalf of migrants subject to its coercive power is irrelevant. It follows that under the fiduciary theory's representational criterion of legitimacy, the unilateralist state that uses force against migrants – e.g. physical restraint, forcible confinement and detention, or forcible transportation – does so extra-legally, since the statutes and regulations relied on by the unilateralist state to mobilise force against migrants are in no way implemented in their names.

As noted already, the state can avoid this descent into lawlessness by taking seriously its global role as a fiduciary of humanity as well as its local role as a fiduciary of its people. Taking these dual roles seriously means being prepared to justify publicly and submit to independent review decisions to exclude. The state's participation in this exercise of public justification and review would allow the state to defend, as a fiduciary of its people, its understanding of the significance of its community's identity, as well as its conception and preferred means of

[60] Fox-Decent, 'Constitutional Legitimacy Unbound', at 129–31.

self-determination. By engaging in public reason in this way, the state would enter a cosmopolitan state of right with the outsider, and treat her as a legal subject rather than as a stranger or enemy. Although the state's advocacy of its conception of its citizens' interests may pit it against the outsider, the state's participation on an equal legal footing with the outsider in an institutional regime of public justification and impartial adjudication is itself a way for the state to act on behalf of the outsider. Public administrative authorities do not, as a rule, owe favourable outcomes to all who come before them. But ordinarily they owe individuals a reviewable justification if they propose policies that will be backed with the threat or use of force. This is part of what it means to be a public fiduciary. Put another way, the representational criterion of legitimacy requires at the border a cosmopolitan threshold – not a barrier – that permits entry to peaceful outsiders unless states can offer a persuasive and reviewable justification for exclusion.

Let us consider now the sense in which the fiduciary criterion of legitimacy can play a heuristic role as a jurisdictional *grundnorm* of cosmopolitan legal order. The criterion can play this role because, like the norms of *jus cogens*, it polices the validity of state action, implicitly limiting what the state can do and authorise through law in its interactions with outsiders (e.g. no torture or deportation to a place of danger), and the manner in which the state can do those things (e.g. no deportation without a public and reviewable justification). These limits are jurisdictional by nature, since they delimit, even if imprecisely, the scope of the state's lawful authority vis-à-vis outsiders. But for any such account of authority to be practicable, we need to be able to distinguish jurisdictional errors that render purportedly authoritative decisions or directives invalid from non-jurisdictional errors that do not. Raz's discussion of jurisdiction and its relationship to authority will help us grasp the stakes involved. With those stakes in view, I will tentatively suggest that the norms of representation may help to draw the jurisdictional/non-jurisdictional distinction. With the contours of some of these norms in place, we will return, in the following section, to the sense in which the representational fiduciary criterion of legitimacy works as a threshold in a service of peaceful outsiders who are also the subjects of cosmopolitan law.

IV The Jurisdiction of Cosmopolitan Legality

Along with the normal justification and dependence theses mentioned above, Raz's conception of authority involves a third thesis, the pre-emption thesis. According to this thesis, authoritative rules or directives replace the dependent reasons the subject had to act in a certain way before the rule or directive came into existence.[61] To illustrate, Raz gives the case of an arbitrator whose decision is 'meant to replace the reasons on which it depends'.[62] Thus, 'reasons that could have been relied upon to justify action before his decision cannot be relied upon once the decision is given'.[63] Having appointed an arbitrator, the parties must accept his decision and decline to act on the reasons they believe applied to them before the decision. Otherwise, there would be no point to the arbitration. Moreover, authorities are entitled to make mistakes, Raz says, and have their directives treated as binding, since second-guessing would defeat the mediating role authorities are supposed to play (via the pre-emption thesis) between action and the ultimate reasons for action.[64] Thus, Raz claims that 'the legitimate power of authorities' is not 'generally limited by the condition that it is defeated by significant mistakes which are not clear'.[65]

Nonetheless, he admits that the pre-emption thesis 'depends on a distinction between jurisdictional and other mistakes'.[66] Raz recognises, for example, that an arbitrator's decision can be challenged or disregarded under certain jurisdiction-forfeiting circumstances: if the arbitrator 'was bribed, or drunk while considering the case, or if new evidence turns up, each party may ignore the decision'.[67] And mistakes that authorities make 'about factors which determine the limits of their jurisdiction render their decisions void'.[68] In other words, when authorities make these kinds of mistakes, they do so as de facto rather than legitimate authorities, since their decisions are 'void' and therefore have no capacity to bind their subjects. The decisions of authorities who lack jurisdiction are not really decisions of authorities *on those matters*, and are invalid *ab initio*. The legal validity of public, authoritative decision-making depends on the decision-making body having jurisdiction to make the relevant decision. Rather than offer an account of how to distinguish jurisdictional from other mistakes, however, Raz simply

61 Raz, *The Morality of Freedom*, at 57–59.
62 Ibid., 42.
63 Ibid.
64 Ibid., 61.
65 Ibid., 62.
66 Ibid.
67 Ibid., 42.
68 Ibid., 62.

notes that if the distinction were difficult to make, 'most other accounts of authority would come to grief'.[69]

For the reason given in the introduction, however, distinguishing jurisdictional from non-jurisdictional mistakes is notoriously controversial. An authority's interpretation of virtually any provisions or terms of its mandate can be recast as an interpretation that 'determines the limits' of the authority's jurisdiction. Consider, for example, the famous Canadian case *CUPE* v. *NB Liquor Corporation*.[70] At issue was the meaning of the term 'employee' within the Public Services Labour Relations Act,[71] and more specifically, whether management personnel were to count as 'employees' for the purpose of determining whether they could lawfully replace striking workers. Interpretative arguments pulled in both directions. Management argued that 'employee' was a defined term under the Act. The union argued that the Act prohibited management personnel from replacing striking workers as the quid pro quo for the Act's prohibition of union picketing.[72] The lower courts held that determining the meaning of 'employee' was a matter of legal interpretation and jurisdictional, and therefore the board had to get the interpretation right to have jurisdiction to determine whether management personnel were unlawfully replacing strikers. In other words, the lower courts treated the interpretive question as one involving Raz's 'factors determining the limits' of the board's jurisdiction. Having determined the crucial issue to be jurisdictional, the lower courts reviewed the board's decision on a standard of correctness, ultimately quashing it.

Dickson J (as he then was), for a unanimous Supreme Court of Canada, sought to rein in judicial interventionism in labour law by admonishing reviewing courts not to 'brand as jurisdictional, and therefore subject to broader curial review, that which may be doubtfully so'.[73] According to Dickson J, the interpretive issue did not go to jurisdiction, and so review of the board's decision was to proceed on the deferential standard of patent unreasonableness. In the result, he upheld the board's decision. Dickson J did not, however, declare a ban on jurisdictional review. Nor did he explain how courts were to determine if a question of legal interpretation was or was not jurisdictional.

[69] Ibid.
[70] [1979] 2 SCR 227 (hereinafter *CUPE*).
[71] RSNB 1973, c. P-25 (hereinafter the Act).
[72] *CUPE*, at 240.
[73] Ibid., 233.

The representational fiduciary criterion of legitimacy offers pointers towards a framework to guide inquiry on the question of whether an issue is jurisdictional. Roughly, the idea would be to use institutional norms that attend representation as signposts for whether an issue goes to a public decision-maker's jurisdiction. Some of the constraints are familiar. For example, we would expect the decision-maker to be disinterested in the outcome and impartial in her deliberations. The thornier issues are like those in *CUPE* and involve contentious legal interpretations of the public body's enabling statute. The norms of representation suggest the following sorts of inquiries. Has the board in *CUPE* interpreted its statute in a manner that takes seriously the interests of the parties before it? Has the board interpreted the statute in a way that is consistent with the statute's general purpose and the board's role within the statutory scheme? The first question pays close attention to the legitimate interests of the parties for whom the board is acting. The second question seeks to determine whether the board is making decisions related to the purpose for which it was established, for the benefit of the public at large as well as for the benefit of the parties. The idea is to adopt a restrictive approach to jurisdictional review by limiting the relevant questions to those that concern fairness between the parties and the board's raison d'être as a public actor. Far more would have to be said, however, to show that this framework does not suffer from the same weaknesses as others; specifically, that it does not invite the collapse of all questions of law into jurisdictional questions.

With that caveat in place, a weaker claim that will serve for present purposes is that norms related to representation plausibly have a place in whatever framework is ultimately best for distinguishing jurisdictional errors from other mistakes. We can also concur with Raz that theories of authority generally, including the fiduciary theory and its representational criterion of legitimacy, must be able to distinguish jurisdictional from other mistakes if the theory is to be capable of specifying the conditions under which directives are binding (i.e. the twin conditions of when the decision-maker has not made a mistake and when the decision-maker has made a mistake but it does not go to jurisdiction). At the risk of some repetition, this feature of the theory is crucial because the jurisdiction of a given authority is constitutive of its legal powers and their limits, and so without a grasp of an authority's jurisdiction we lack understanding of the nature and limits of its public power.

It is time now to consider the relationship between the representational fiduciary criterion as a jurisdictional threshold that is porous to peaceful outsiders, and the sources thesis according to which the existence and content of law can always be identified by reference to social sources alone.

V Law's Moral Claim to Represent and the Sources Thesis

In the border context, the representational fiduciary criterion is a jurisdictional *threshold* in the sense that it supplies a standard of adequacy the receiving state must meet for its interactions with peaceful migrants to conform to the demands of legality. The threshold is *jurisdictional* because its standard of adequacy provides the power-conferring conditions the state must satisfy to have de jure authority over outsiders. These power-conferring conditions – the procedural and structural threshold requirements of cosmopolitan legality – are public justification and independent review. But it is important to recognise that the justification of these formal requirements presupposes that the outsider's interests will be taken seriously, both at first instance and on review.

A state that chooses to exclude peaceful outsiders might be expected to offer a proportionality analysis to show that exclusion is a necessary or at least proportionate policy in light of legitimate state concerns. Moreover, the state's justification would be expected to take seriously international norms such as international human rights law. These norms expressly recognise outsiders as both legal subjects and persons, and thereby resist the nativist call to strip migrants of their personhood. And, because international norms transcend states and their encounters with migrants, they can contribute to a cosmopolitan and double-facing constitution from which the just state can garner legitimacy through public justifications that strive to accommodate fairly the state's local and global responsibilities. While these justifications would be context-dependent, they would also be substantive and jurisdictional, since they would explicitly refer to and establish the limits of a state's authority to exclude outsiders. Public justifications that pass independent review demonstrate a valid exercise of the state's limited power to exclude, while justifications that fail to survive scrutiny under review are legal nullities.

Let me briefly retrace our steps and then assess the sources thesis in light of this framework for cosmopolitan legal order. We began by noting that norms of *jus cogens*, such as the prohibition on slavery, supervise the validity of international treaties (offending treaties or treaty provisions are of no legal effect). The representational fiduciary criterion of legitimacy allows us to identify *jus cogens* norms; these are norms the violation of which could never be lawful because slavery, genocide, racial discrimination, etc. could never be intelligible as policies implemented in the name of or on behalf of the people subject to them. I then argued that under the prevailing understanding and practice of state sovereignty, outsiders at the border occupy a position akin to slaves: both are subject to comprehensive domination, and mere coercive force rather than law. For states to have legal authority over outsiders, I suggested they have to take seriously their position as fiduciaries of humanity, and institute a legal framework premised on a double-facing constitution that includes substantial public justification and meaningful review. The framework makes the receiving state's implementation of exclusionary policies intelligible as action that takes seriously the interests of the outsider, precisely because the state must offer a justification and subject it to review. It is this submission to legality that makes it plausible to say that the state's action, filtered through legal channels in which the outsider enjoys legal equality, is action taken on behalf of the outsider as well as the state's citizens. When the state occupies its dual roles as a fiduciary of its people and a fiduciary of humanity, there is arguably a sense in which it unifies institutionally the internal and external aspects of the double-facing constitution.

This conception of legality is in significant tension with the sources thesis. The tension arises from the fact that the fiduciary criterion of legitimacy makes demands on the receiving state that flow from norms of representation. These norms are not source-based in any ordinary sense, but rather arise from a morality of role intrinsic to the representative nature of public institutions. On the theory defended here, the norms of representation are constitutive of legality and have ineliminable moral content, such as the duty to justify adverse decisions. In the cosmopolitan context, these norms are drawn from the global and local roles of fiduciary states charged with stewardship of the double-facing constitution.

6

From Republican Self-Love to Cosmopolitan *Amour-Propre*: Europe's New Constitutional Experience

ALEXANDER SOMEK

Introduction

This contribution draws conspicuously on Rousseauvian terminology. Insiders may find this both unimaginative and bewildering. What, if anything, is the organising principle of the so-called *Second Discourse* if not the distinction between the pre-social form of self-love – *amour de soi-même* – and that form of self-infatuation which is mediated by shining in the eyes of others – *amour-propre*?[1] Why trade in commonplaces? At the same time, there is no obvious connection between these forms of love and the distinction between a bounded and an unbounded political temperament. So, what's the point?

As is well known, in the context of Rousseau's theory of modernity, the former, pre-social self-love, plays the role of an innocuous primitive impulse whereas the inflamed love of one's self, *amour-propre*, is the source of many social evils, such as status-competition, inequality of wealth, condescension or self-aggrandisement.[2] Indeed, both appear to be mediated by different forms of self-assertion. There is, on the one hand, the self giving itself to spontaneous gratification, for example, by enjoying a hearty meal or taking a warm bath; and then there is, on the

[1] See Jean-Jacques Rousseau, *The Discourses and other early political writings*, Victor Gourevitch trans. (Cambridge: Cambridge University Press, 1997), at 218. For an illuminating interpretation, see, in particular, Frederick Neuhouser, *Rousseau's Theodicy of Self-Love: Evil, Rationality, and the Drive for Recognition* (Oxford: Oxford University Press, 2008).

[2] See also Neuhouser's second work on this topic, *Rousseau's Critique of Inequality: Reconstructing the Second Discourse* (Cambridge: Cambridge University Press, 2014).

other, the self whose love of itself depends on the judgment of others.[3] The latter is, in other words, the self of subjectivity. It is the self of self-consciousness that, as Hegel memorably stated, exists only as recognised.[4] In the case of *amour-propre*, or the love of one's self, one's esteem of oneself is utterly dependent on external recognition. That is, the self could not perceive its value if it were not judged favourably by other selves. With regard to the source of recognition it is essentially outside of itself.

Without having to delve into the complexity of how personal self-love can be related to the love of one's country[5] – 'patriotism',[6] that is – it should be apparent to the discerning eye how this elementary distinction helps to elucidate current attitudes towards constitutional law. For example, it is plausible to view the late Justice Scalia's views[7] on the exceptional character of the American constitutional tradition as expressing Republican self-love, for he deliberately and provocatively dissociates the appreciation of American constitutional law from recognition by other constitutional cultures. Echoing Scalia's outlook, patriotic Americans might even proclaim that, yes, they do have the death penalty and, yes, they have recently reinvigorated the constitutional right to bear arms. Americans are allowed to hoist a swastika to their flagpole and even, should they fancy to do so, to burn a cross in their backyard. They are disposed to take pride in their freedoms, even if others find these weird and wacky, for they don't give a damn about what others think.

Contrast such audacious complacency with the timidity with which constitutional traditions on the European continent are expected to join the train of evolutive interpretation of the European Convention in order

[3] See Neuhouser, *Rousseau's Theodicy of Self-Love*, at 13, 33, 43.

[4] See G. W. F. Hegel, *Phänomenologie des Geistes*, Heins-Friedrich Wessels and Heinrich Clairmont (eds.) (Hamburg: Meiner, 1988), at 127.

[5] See the illuminating analysis by Neuhouser, *Rousseau's Theodicy of Self-Love* at 232–43, showing that Rousseau's own texts remain ambivalent on this point. While Rousseau presents patriotism as something that is based on extending the self in order to include others such that their fate becomes inextricably intertwined with one's own, there are also indications in his writings that patriotism reflects the desire to be honoured by compatriots on the ground of one's ability to take the position of each when determining the general will. The motive of garnering the respect that may be rightfully demanded from others for successfully embracing the general will likens patriotism more to *amour-propre*, however, in a manner that does not amount to a socio-psychological pathology.

[6] See Maurizio Viroli, *For Love of Country: An Essay on Patriotism and Nationalism* (Oxford: Oxford University Press, 1995) at 2–6.

[7] See, for example, 'A conversation between U.S. Supreme Court justices' (2005) 3 *International Journal of Constitutional Law*, at 519–41.

not to count as backwaters in the eyes of their peers.[8] There is not much room left for Republican self-love. Rather, what matters is that one passes as being up to speed. Obviously, republican self-love has been replaced with some cosmopolitan *amour-propre*, for it is the opinion of others that counts.

I Nationalism and Patriotism

But isn't this a cause for celebration? The old world of constitutional law was based upon a dangerous belief, namely, the idea that the people are the wellspring of all constitutional authority. This idea is inextricably entwined with nationalism and, hence, conjoined with sentiments that feed into practices of exclusion and aggression. Or this is what contemporary liberals would have us believe.[9]

Bernard Yack has perceptively observed that within our modern political language 'the people' denote two different ways of being together.[10] Synchronically understood, the people constitutes the sum total of those who are permanently subject to the exercise of sovereign power. By contrast, diachronically understood, the people are nothing short of the nation, which is a community reflecting on how it extends over time. The special obligations that are believed to originate from nationhood arise from sharing certain memories.[11] Evidently, it is the problem haunting the concept of nationhood that it is never quite clear by virtue of which alchemy the sharing of memories is able to generate, let alone rationally underpin, mutually binding commitments. Be that as it may, once people conceive of themselves as nationals they come to regard themselves as

[8] For a useful introduction, see Kanstantsin Dzehtsiarou, 'European Consensus and the Evolutive Interpretation of the European Convention on Human Rights' (2011) 12 *German Law Journal* 1730–45.

[9] See, for example, also Mattias Kumm, 'The Best of Times and the Worst of Times: Between Constitutional Triumphalism and Nostalgia', in P. Dobner and M. Loughlin (eds.), *The Twilight of Constitutional Law: Demise or Transmutation?* (Oxford: Oxford University Press, 2010), at 201–19.

[10] See Bernard Yack, *Nationalism and the Moral Psychology of Community* (Chicago: University of Chicago Press, 2012), at 106–12.

[11] It should be noted, though, that such memories are created and sustained at a level that is largely unrelated to world of ordinary life. In the case of the author's country, the culture and politics of the period marked by the reign of Austria's last emperor, Kaiser Franz Joseph, is to this day of great significance for its national identity. At the same time, it is completely detached from how people live today and what they care about. The memories merely provide a focal point for the belief that Austrians are tied to one another in virtue of their common history.

part of a larger whole and as participants in a historical project for the success of which they have, by virtue of belonging to the nation, shouldered a joint responsibility. Awareness of a national history is the origin and permanent cement of political loyalties, such as the attachment to a republican government and respect for the accomplishments of founders and ancestors.[12]

The sentiment by which people express, and mutually assure each other of, their national belonging is patriotism, i.e., the love of the fatherland. People loving their fatherland feel good about living among their compatriots and are generally not indifferent to their fate. As Rousseau clearly believed,[13] they take an active interest in whether the government pays heed to their rights, for nobody would reasonably feel at home in a place where rights are in jeopardy. Moreover, they do not turn a blind eye to hardship suffered by other nationals. The love of their fatherland allows citizens to transcend the narrow focus on their own well-being and to become virtuous. Yet, this is possible, apparently, only within *particular* communities, such as nations. Republican self-love presupposes the distinction between 'us' and 'them'.

II Constitutional Patriotism

Much contemporary liberal political theory is prepared to expose nationhood as a myth.[14] While this lends theorising an enlightened appearance, it creates a problem at the tail end of political philosophy where conditions of stability have to be identified. What could mediate the broad support necessary in order to sustain a constitutional democracy in the long term if it were not for nationhood?[15] After all, enabling and upholding a reasonably just constitutional regime requires some form of

[12] Halbertal has identified correctly the danger that resides in investing deeds with value simply because they involved sacrifice. Putting one's life at stake for the sake of a cause is not a way of establishing the value of that cause. See Moshe Halbertal, *On Sacrifice* (Princeton: Princeton University Press, 2012), at 99, 113.

[13] See, in particular, the 'Discourse on Political Economy', in Alan Ritter and Julia Bondanella (eds.), *Rousseau's Political Writings* (New York: Norton & Co, 1988), 58 at 69–70.

[14] For a critical historical perspective, see Patrick J. Geary, *The Myth of Nations: The Medieval Origins of Europe* (Princeton: Princeton University Press, 2002).

[15] See, for example, Gertrude Himmelfarb, 'The Illusion of Cosmopolitanism', in Joshua Cohen (ed.), *For Love of Country* (Boston: Beacon Press, 1996), 72; Charles Taylor, 'Why Democracy needs Patriotism', in Joshua Cohen (ed.), *For Love of Country* (Boston: Beacon Press, 1996), at 119.

emotional attachment. Could there be an alternative to old-fashioned patriotism?

The reply given by liberal political theory to this predicament is to present constitutional patriotism as the preferred post-national vehicle of loyalties.[16] The attitude is substantially anchored in the conditions under which citizens are able to justify political rule to one another. These conditions materialise in 'constitutional essentials', that is, the fundamental principles of a constitutional democracy and the culture investing them with life in particular contexts.[17] The mode of attachment that is supposedly adequate to constitutional patriotism is decidedly not faith or pride in a mission or a project, but rather something more 'reflexive'[18] and, quoting from Müller, 'critical, or even ambivalent'. Instead of pride one is likely to encounter 'shame, righteous indignation, and even anger and guilt'.[19] These emotions are negative and betray reactive attitudes. If anything, they reflect disappointment.[20] The reason for sustaining a regime is the belief that the best realisation of the principles of constitutional democracy 'through reasonable disagreement' requires a permanent effort.[21]

The notion of constitutional patriotism reveals contemporary liberalism's unease with the flesh and, in particular, the blood of communal loyalties.[22] Constitutional patriotism is the political equivalent of so-called 'Platonic' love on a personal level. It advocates a chaste devotion to constitutional principles. Evidently, it involves a substitution of the diachronic perspective on the people. The enchanting immersion in

[16] On the following, see Jan-Werner Müller, 'Towards a general theory of constitutional patriotism', www.princeton.edu/~jmueller/I-CON-CP-JWMueller-March2007.pdf, accessed July 30, 2019. See also Viroli, *For Love of Country* at 171–85.

[17] Müller, 'Towards a general theory' at 13; 16: 'The kinds of conversations, controversies, and disagreements that characterize constitutional cultures are necessarily related to particular national and historical contexts.' As Yack, *Nationalism* at 36, correctly observes, it is by virtue of culture that nationality is reintroduced through the back door. For it is the culture of constitutional democracy that invites individuals to conceive of themselves as members of nations.

[18] Müller, 'Towards a general theory' at 19.

[19] Ibid., at 21.

[20] Ibid., at 22: '[W]hat is certainly not compatible with the picture of a complex post-traditional society, however, are unquestioned pride and linear or homogeneous narratives of heroes and victories. In that sense, a post-traditional constitutional culture is indeed a post-heroic one; and it is post-nationalist, rather than post-national.'

[21] Ibid., at 20.

[22] The flesh and the blood are ethnic and cultural reasons of feeling connected. See Jürgen Habermas, *Faktizität und Geltung: Beiträge zur Diskurstheorie des Rechts und des demokratischen Rechtsstaats* (Frankfurt aM: Suhrkamp, 1992), at 636.

a people's history is replaced with the commitment to principles that happen to require particular contexts for their realisation. But in this context the particular is always a source of embarrassment, not something that may be joyfully embraced as an inheritance. It adds impurity to immaculate universals. In this vein, constitutional patriotism is at pains to underscore that the constitution must not be viewed as lending expression to an underlying national core of identity.[23] Constitutional patriotism attaches itself to universal norms and principles,[24] not to the particular. It is averse to particularising historical narratives. It embraces the particular merely because of its indispensability.

III Losing the Particular

This explains why constitutional patriotism must remain unpersuasive. If patriotism is a sentiment that is essentially partial[25] – one loves one's own country more than any other – constitutional patriotism is *entirely* unpatriotic, for it cannot give us any reason not to feel attached to all constitutions fitting the same universal type equally. It merely advocates sustaining and improving various particularisations of universal constitutional essentials. Consequently, there is no reason to conclude that expressing one's concern over the violations of human rights and the erosion of democracy in another country should not pass as constitutional patriotism, for it is critical of how one particular realisation of constitutional essentials might be going off the rails.[26]

If that observation is correct, then the attitude underlying such a concern is not a manifestation of patriotism. Rather, it represents a specific form of cosmopolitanism. It is not the type of cosmopolitanism that associates itself with the constitution of a global federation of republics or with principles allocating authority within a multilevel system; on the contrary, this type of cosmopolitanism views any national constitution that embraces universally valid 'constitutional essentials' (democracy, the rule of law, separation of powers, fundamental rights) as a constitution that is worthy of support. There is no reason to limit the

[23] Müller, 'Towards a general theory' at 14.
[24] Ibid., at 17.
[25] See Alasdair MacIntyre, *Is Patriotism a Virtue?* (Lawrence: University of Kansas Press, 1984), at 4, 9.
[26] Ibid., at 4, 9; Ulrich Wagrandl, 'Transnational Militant Democracy' (2018) 7 *Global Constitutionalism* 143.

attachment to the country to which one happens to belong. Actually, if there were such a limit, this cosmopolitanism would commit the sin of particularism without resort to narratives which appeal to the virtue of individual patriotic self-transcendence.

Not surprisingly, however, constitutional patriotism cannot deliver what we expect. It fails to account for the *particularising* emotional element underpinning legitimate forms of attachment. It is submitted, here, that only a theory of cosmopolitan *amour-propre* can provide us with that.

IV From the People to Peoples

In order to arrive at such a theory, one needs to take stock of the fundamental shift that constitutional authority has undergone in the course of the ascendancy of human rights.[27] Legitimate constitutions are no longer viewed as idiosyncratic expressions of a popular sovereign. Rather they are understood to be acts of moral recognition. They are based upon the recognition of human dignity, the demands of which are further spelled out in a set of fundamental rights. From that angle, any constitution that commits itself to the realisation of human rights is as good as any other.

The people are divested of their authorising role in constitutional law. Yet, constitutional authority cannot float freely. It needs to take root in some historical factor that can plausibly claim to be a reliable voice of reason. Since philosopher kings or elite parties have only rarely been considered to be great options, the most plausible candidates for this critical task are those whom constitutional democracies have reason to regard not only as equals, but also as equally committed to the same enterprise. The quest of constitutional legitimacy shifts, therefore, from the vertical to the horizontal dimension, namely, from the acclaim garnered in referenda to the judgment of one's peers.[28] The central question can no longer be whether the populace are contented, but whether one's conduct could pass muster in the eyes of other equally valuable constitutional regimes. Who these others are and how many of them count is left in a remarkably indeterminate state. This is the

[27] On the following, see Alexander Somek, *The Cosmopolitan Constitution* (Oxford: Oxford University Press, 2014).

[28] This is a shift that inflames the constitutional passion of American constitutionalists for whom the disappearance of the people is an outrage. See Jed Rubenfeld, 'Unilateralism and Constitutionalism' (2004) 79 *New York University Law Review* 1971.

fundamental conundrum of Europe's new constitutional experience. We shall return to it below.

This sea change is by now a well-known fact, in particular, in the context of the European Convention System. In order to appreciate it fully, one merely needs to focus more closely on who these others are whom one regards as peers. Even though they have to be, in order to count as such, engaged in the same type of constitutional enterprise, they are first and foremost *foreigners*. Hence, a truly cosmopolitan constitution is one that accords foreigners some voice and makes their views relevant to one's own constitutional law; more radically, such a constitution conceives of the authority of constitutional law from the perspective of outsiders. From this perspective, it is possible, however, to reconstruct the relevance of the particular that constitutional patriotism surreptitiously abandons. The type of constitution that commits itself to realising human rights and accords relevance to the judgment of those whom it recognises as being engaged in the same enterprise is a cosmopolitan constitution. The relevance of peoples rather than 'the' people implies a replacement of republican self-love with cosmopolitan *amour-propre*.

V The Margin of Appreciation

The most elementary step taken by a cosmopolitan constitution consists in considering the judgment of peers relevant for one's own constitutional experience. Such a granting of relevance can appear in different guises, ranging from constitutional borrowing[29] to accepting, even if only grudgingly, the relevance of an international monitoring body, such as the Venice Commission.[30]

There is a Janus-faced dimension inherent in taking this step. From the perspective of a national constitutional system, introducing international mechanisms of mutual monitoring or adjudication adds another layer to a scheme designed to stabilise constitutional democracy at home.[31] At the same time, by introducing mechanisms such as an international human

[29] See Sujit Choudhry (ed.), *The Migration of Constitutional Ideas* (Cambridge: Cambridge University Press, 2006).

[30] See www.venice.coe.int/webforms/events/, accessed August 6, 2018.

[31] See, in particular, Andrew Moravcik, 'The Origins of Human Rights Regimes: Democratic Delegation in Postwar Europe' (2000) 54 *International Organization* 217.

rights tribunal, the national constitution becomes, in a sense, denationalised, for it exposes itself to censure by other nations.[32]

At first glance, this elementary step seems merely to invite a *detached* inquiry into whether one would consider a constitutional system legitimate *as a foreigner*, that is, from a point of view of someone who is essentially *uninvolved* and merely asking whether the constitution is good enough for people that are committed to certain traditions (for the French, the Italians, etc.). It may be suspected that a detached inquiry of this type might underpin what the European Court of Human Rights has memorably introduced in the *Handyside* case as the 'margin of appreciation'.[33] But one needs to be circumspect at this point.

In this case, the Court established that where, for want of convergent practices, no common European concept denotes a ground of restricting fundamental rights,[34] it is left to the signatory states to use such a concept by their own lights and, in particular, to assess the necessity of an interference.[35] One can read this idea as saying that in certain instances and within limits, which are scarcely ever specified,[36] it is left to the democratic process of the participating state to determine the right balance between fundamental rights, on the one hand, and legitimate grounds of restriction, on the other. In *Handyside* the Court adopted, memorably, the attitude of an outside institution that is out of touch with the 'vital forces of society'.[37] Hence the Court appears to state that from the perspective of a foreigner it is permissible for particular national systems to have their way. Arguably, the Court said to the country

[32] See Dieter Grimm, 'The Constitution in the Process of De-Nationalization' (2005) 12 *Constellations* 447.

[33] See *Handyside* v. *United Kingdom*, [1976] ECHR 5, 1 EHRR 737.

[34] The grounds for derogation are explicitly listed in the Convention.

[35] As is well known, the concept of the margin of appreciation has made a long career in the case law of the European Court of Human Rights and found its application even outside of the rights to which the Convention explicitly adds grounds of derogation (Articles 8-11). See David Harris, Michael O'Boyle, and Edward Bates and Carla Buckley (Harris, O'Boyle and Warbrick), *Law of the European Convention on Human Rights*, 3rd ed. (Oxford: Oxford University Press, 2014), at 15.

[36] It is a frequently voiced complaint that the circumstances specifying the applicability of the margin of appreciation are never clearly specified in the case of law of the Court. Hence, the doctrine is *unpredictable* and *unclear*. See, for example, Dominic McGoldrick, 'A Defense of the Margin of Appreciation and an Argument for Its Application by the Human Rights Committee' (2016) 65 *International and Comparative Law Quarterly* 21, at 38; see also Luzius Wildhaber, Arnaldur Hjartarson and Stephen Donnelly, 'No Consensus on Consensus? The Practice of the European Court of Human Rights' (2013) 33 *Human Rights Law Journal* 248, 252.

[37] *Handyside*, at [48].

concerned 'if you want it, you can have it' and abstained from passing judgment on the subject.

At the same time, the elementary step entails another one. The margin of appreciation does not particularise in the sense of allowing a people to go forward as long as they leave everyone else alone. The margin is supposed to define a human rights standard, and this implies that what the country does must still be universally acceptable. The margin stands for *universally acceptable particularity*. This means that the attitude of those who do not partake of the vital forces of society is not that of entire indifference. The acceptance is not mediated by an equivalent to the harm principle. If that were the case, people would be free to use torture in emergency situations as long as they limited its use to nationals. Rather, universally acceptable particularity reflects the attitude of outsiders who would deny constitutional recognition to the relevant law or practice at home, but who nonetheless find it acceptable abroad even if it were applied to them as visitors. They have no reason to reject what others made into law for those subject to their jurisdiction, for such a protest would be tantamount to denying them recognition. If that is correct, it follows that not only residing in your home country and, as it were, at a safe distance give you reason to respect the outcome of another national democratic process, you also have no reason to complain about it on constitutional grounds if the relevant law happens to be applied to you. While the law in question may not pass constitutional muster in your own country, it is unassailable when your actions are within the compass of its scope of application somewhere else. Owing to the margin of appreciation you have to admit that such a law is not only acceptable for others viewed *from the perspective of* an uninvolved foreigner ('If they are happy with it, I don't care'), but that it is also legitimate *for* you *as a* foreigner ('I am not the co-author of these laws, but I respect their authority'). While the first perspective is, using Hartian parlance, external, the second is internal.

VI Virtual Representation

Such acceptability *for a foreigner* is much stronger than what would follow from the principle of *volenti non fit injuria*. According to this principle, someone moving to another country can be presumed to have succumbed implicitly to foreign authority by tacit consent. Such consent may even extend to dictatorial regimes.

In order to perceive the difference, it needs to be borne in mind that the European convention establishes a system of peer review. The relevant group is composed of democratic societies, which explains why restrictions are permissible only if they are, as the text of the Convention repeatedly suggests, necessary in a democratic society. What mediates the legitimacy of the restriction is, aside from the relaxed proportionality requirement in the case of the margin of appreciation,[38] the fact that the laws have been arrived at by democratic means. The acceptability for foreigners is not by accident, but, indeed, *essentially* linked to the law emerging from a reasonably democratic political process.

This means, more precisely, that from their perspective it is not *active* participation that mediates democratic legitimacy. This raises the question under which condition laws can be regarded as democratically legitimate even if the persons affected did not participate in the process leading to its adoption. The classical, and highly contested, answer to this question is *virtual* representation.[39] While the idea is clearly preposterous vis-à-vis people who are denied the franchise for wrong reasons, it is perfectly sound when it comes to those who are legitimately excluded from the constituency. Foreigners fit that description. They are not actually represented, for they do not participate in the election of representatives. Nevertheless, they can be *virtually* represented in a democratic political process that meets the following conditions:

1. The representative process must not violate equal civil rights. Otherwise it would amount to the tyranny of the majority.
2. Political rights that ensure that the views of non-represented outsiders can be given a voice have to undergird the process. More precisely, it must be possible within the system of representation to articulate the *type of interest* that foreigners might have.

[38] It is, of course, true that the existence of a margin of appreciation implies a more relaxed, possibly only procedural, standard of review on the part of the European Court of Human Rights. See McGoldrick, 'A Defense of the Margin of Appreciation' at 34–35. Yet, staying within the margin of appreciation must not be confused with passing the proportionality test no matter how strict or relaxed it might be. The latter reflects a wrong understanding of the margin that is, alas, also found in the jurisprudence of the Court. See George Letsas, *A Theory of Interpretation of the European Convention of Human Rights* (Oxford: Oxford University Press, 2008), at 87–88.

[39] See Melissa S. Williams, 'Burkean "Descriptions" and Political Representation: A Reappraisal' (1996) 29 *Canadian Journal of Political Science* 23.

3 The outcome must not discriminate on the grounds of nationality, or at least it must not unduly do so.[40]

Evidently, these conditions of virtual representation would have to be fleshed out in greater detail in order to establish their soundness. But this need not detain us here. What matters is that cosmopolitan constitutionalism envisages legitimacy from the perspective of virtual representation.

Hence, the step following the elementary step is of momentous significance since it signals a seismic shift in the foundations of democratic constitutionalism. Democracies have to be legitimate in the eyes of foreigners. This approach is the *only* consistent alternative to the national outlook of constitutional theory, for it renders belonging to a national community secondary without – in contrast to constitutional patriotism – dismissing it as inessential. Any citizen body, regardless of whether it happens to be your own or another, mediates the democratic legitimacy that renders laws acceptable for those who either are *or* conceive of themselves as foreigners. This second condition is important since it explains why from the cosmopolitan perspective one's own body of citizens is merely a placeholder for the foreigners that sustain democratic polities somewhere else in this world. Compatriots are deputy foreigners. Only with such a turn of perspective can constitutionalism be dissociated from the homely warmth of nationality. At the same time, however, it has to make room for national polities, not least because they are indispensable locales facilitating virtual representation.

Lest the argument be misunderstood, it is not limited to cases in which states benefit from the margin of appreciation. The margin is a helpful stepping stone when it comes to explaining the shift in constitutional authority that is brought about by approaching constitutional legitimacy from the horizontal perspective of peers. It results in a denationalised account of national law.

VII Fundamental Boundaries

We have not yet accounted for the particular in a manner that doesn't only perceive it as a mere detractor, that is, as something that is essentially privative or negative. There are two ways of remedying this shortcoming.

[40] On equality as a principle that is representation-reinforcing, for it forces actors to respect the interests of discriminated against groups, see John Hart Ely, *Democracy and Distrust: A Theory of Judicial Review* (Cambridge, MA: Harvard University Press, 1980), at 85–86, 98, 100.

The first highlights the dialectic – mutual presupposition and mutual repulsion – of the universal and the particular, the second focuses on particularity itself. We shall begin with the first.

The universal could not become real if it were not for the particular. Hence, not only is the difference between the particular and the universal itself universal, the particular is essential for the universal to inhabit the real. Particularity is universally necessary.[41]

This explains why cosmopolitan peer review systems have to be sufficiently pluralistic. If they were not and expected all participants to converge on contested issues, that which purports to be universal would take the place of the particular and, consequently, eliminate the condition on which its realisation depends. The universal is not tantamount to uniformity, but a unity that is preserved in diversity.

The implication for a constitutionalism that puts rights at the centre is quite momentous and real. It means that fundamental rights have to be complemented with fundamental boundaries. At this point, the first way of accounting for particularity blends immediately into the second. J. H. H. Weiler memorably remarked that while 'fundamental rights are about the autonomy and the self-determination of the individual, fundamental boundaries are about the autonomy and self-determination of communities'.[42] He adds that the relevance of fundamental boundaries is expressive of a 'vision of humanity which vests the deepest values in communities'[43] and stems from acknowledging the social nature of humankind. Weiler attempts to accentuate the positive side of particularity. In his view, it is of relevance to understanding fundamental rights in three different ways. First, different levels in the protection of human rights are not a question of more or less; rather, they *reveal* something about the identity of nations, for example the relative weight that

[41] In the case of a system of fundamental rights the relevance of the particular is quite straightforward. Fundamental rights necessarily have to be amenable to interference on grounds having to do with the pursuit of public interests and the protection of other rights. The relative weight attributed to the enjoyment of rights or countervailing considerations reflects evaluations that are informed by culturally specific perceptions of their worth. Speech that is merely intended to hurt can be considered to be either of next to no value or of at least some value to those who are able to endure listening to it. See John Durham Peters, *Courting the Abyss: Free Speech and the Liberal Tradition* (Chicago: University of Chicago Press, 2005). The important point is that if it were not for these particular traditions no intelligible balance could be struck in the cases of interference.

[42] Joseph H. H. Weiler, *The Constitution of Europe: 'Do the New Clothes Have an Emperor?' and Other Essays on European Integration* (Cambridge: Cambridge University Press, 1999), 104.

[43] Ibid.

a majority is prepared to accord to either liberty or dignity when it regulates offensive speech. Second, the pursuit of governmental objectives is not in and of itself inimical to liberty, but conducive to the protection of liberties of others (such as the prevention of crimes) and of a way of life. Weiler therefore accords to governments a right to make social choices by striking a balance between rights and public interests. Indeed, it would be injurious to deny them that choice:[44]

> Fundamental boundaries are designed, thus, to allow communities and polities to make and live by those difference [sic] balances which they deem fundamental.

In his view, an international tribunal, such as the European Court of Human Rights, is tasked with protecting a minimal standard below which no particular country is permitted to fall.[45] It is left to the participating states, however, to protect greater liberty if they desire to do so.

VIII Two Readings of What the Margin Is All About

Weiler's observations present us with an appreciation of particularity that does not merely perceive it as a privation, albeit necessary, of universality. Rather, the particular offers a different perspective on who we are.[46] It renders us not as isolated individuals but as beings who believe what they believe and are what they are by virtue of belonging to certain places where a majority of people share a normative perspective on certain issues.[47]

While Weiler is undoubtedly correct in inviting our attention to our social nature, he nonetheless does not state clearly what the very point of the margin of appreciation is. In his view, the European Court of Human Rights defines with this doctrine 'the area within which fundamental boundaries may be drawn'.[48] This formulation suggests that the margin is

44 Ibid., at 106.

45 For a critique, see Paul Martens in *Dialogue between Judges* (Strasbourg: Council of Europe, 2008).

46 See Alasdair MacIntyre, *After Virtue*, 2nd ed. (Notre Dame: University of Notre Dame Press, 1984), at 221: '[T]he story of my life is always embedded in the story of those communities from which I derive my identity. I am born with a past; and to try to cut myself off from that past, in the individualist mode, is to deform my present relationships. The possession of an historical identity and the possession of a social identity coincide. Notice that rebellion against my identity is always one possible mode of expressing it.'

47 On this 'constitutive' conception of community, see Michael J. Sandel, *Liberalism and the Limits of Justice* (Cambridge: Cambridge University Press, 1982), at 150.

48 Weiler, *The Constitution of Europe*, at 107.

first and foremost some discretion carved out for the signatory states. Yet, the doctrine also hints at the *reason* why the participating states may legitimately claim such space. It thereby also indicates what particularity is all about.

The margin of appreciation with regard to attributing meaning to grounds of restriction is available to states if and so long as no European consensus on the significance of these grounds in certain cases has arisen.[49] Arguably, there is no common European understanding of 'morals', nor a shared view of the 'rights of others'. One way of looking at the margin of appreciation suggests that whether it obtains or not is eventually a matter of empirical fact. Should a large majority of participating states converge on certain understandings, the leeway would evaporate into thin air. This, at any rate, is what a *weak reading* of the doctrine suggests. It says that the social facts of diversity and pluralism create the right to have – within unspecified limits – one's national way. What this doctrine does not clarify, however, is the reason why diversity and pluralism in the field of fundamental rights might be also desirable. If the Germans enjoy less freedom of speech than the British, this seems to pose a problem from a human rights perspective.[50]

The *strong reading* of the doctrine attempts to show how it points to the nature of particularity that actually accounts for the legitimacy of variation.[51] The Court arrives at an implicit conception of particularity by establishing the link between divergent understandings of grounds of restriction, on the one hand, and the *necessity* component of the proportionality principle, on the other. Since this component is the principle's most important part,[52] it cannot come as a surprise that it is also relevant to the determination of the margin of appreciation. States have leeway to *regard* certain measures as *necessary* for the attainment of an objective.

49 On the rather unclear nature of the consent condition, see Wildhaber et al., 'No Consensus on Consensus', at 252; McGoldrick, 'A Defense of the Margin of Appreciation', at 38.

50 For related critiques of the margin of appreciation, see McGoldrick, 'A Defense of the Margin of Appreciation', at 37–38.

51 Lack of consensus would thus be only one factor explaining why the margin of appreciation is wide. Other factors that can be identified in the case law of the Court are whether the matter concerns an important aspect of individual identity or existence (consequence: the margin is narrower) or whether it affects social or economic or environmental or moral legislation or affects the transition to democracy (consequence: the margin is wider). See McGoldrick, 'A Defense of the Margin of Appreciation' at 24–28; Harris et al., *Law of the European Convention*, at 16.

52 See Berhard Schlink, *Abwägung im Verfassungsrecht* (Berlin: Duncker & Humboldt, 1976).

They may legitimately *believe* that there is no less intrusive means available to satisfy a ground of restriction.

At first glance, this may appear mystifying. A means is either necessary or it is not. Aren't we talking about matters of fact? Why should there be any room for evaluation left at all?

Yet, the mystery disappears once we realise that dealing with interferences with fundamental rights is essentially a matter of risk regulation.[53] Speech that either praises or exculpates National Socialism is illegal in Germany and Austria. The relevant criminal statutes address the risk of seeing homemade Fascism return to power. One might wonder whether, for example, suppressing any public doubt as to the magnitude of the Holocaust, *i.e.* the number of people killed, is indeed necessary to attain this objective. The authorities in these countries may believe so, for in their view allowing people to claim that the number of people killed amounted to 'merely' one million would already come perilously close to countenancing the whitewashing of an evil regime. One must not open the floodgate for more, since nothing good is likely to come from it.

It is of utmost importance to be clear about how judgments of this type work.[54] Moral evaluations often come in the guise of anticipating doom as a consequence of transgression. Such thinking is old and deeply engrained in human culture.[55] Risk assessments lend expression to what we fear. The seriousness of the perceived risk depends, however, on how much or little value we attribute to the acts that are likely to give rise to some concatenation of events. The committed socialist is alarmed by a sudden downturn in the stock market and immediately begins to develop doomsday scenarios. When a government decides to adopt a ban on hate speech, a libertarian already has forebodings of totalitarianism. Conversely, judgments that say what is necessary to avert a danger or to manage a risk *reveal* the strength of certain moral beliefs since these beliefs are articulated in the form of risk assessments. For the Puritan, any kind of polluting behaviour (sex, cigarettes, alcohol) creates the high risk that something really bad will come from it. Even scientists trying to

[53] See generally on constitutional law from that perspective, Adrian Vermeule, *The Constitution of Risk* (Cambridge: Cambridge University Press, 2014).

[54] On the following, see Dan M. Kahan, Donald Braman, John Gastil, Paul Slovic, C. K. Mertz, 'Culture and Identity-Protective Cognition: Explaining the White-Male Effect in Risk Perception' (2007) 4 *Journal of Empirical Legal Studies* 465.

[55] See Mary Douglas and Aaron Wildavsky, *Risk and Culture: An Essay on the Selection of Technological and Environmental Dangers* (Berkeley: University of California Press, 1982), at 88, 187.

determine probable outcomes are prone to sift evidence and conceivable effects depending on the magnitude of evil that they believe to inhere in certain acts. What else might explain that all expertise is bound to remain controversial?[56]

The explanation for such a roundabout way of articulating the normative is relatively simple. First, the anticipation of a bad future precipitated by malign acts is a way of asserting the binding force of an offended norm. Indeed, perhaps there is no more natural way of expressing bindingness than by suggesting that some superior power will intervene in some manner and punish disobedience. If something is really binding one should not delude oneself into believing in one's power to escape its grip. Second, pointing out that something even worse will follow from bad acts is the best way of sounding persuasive in the face of divergent deontological commitments. For liberals and libertarians, doing business is an inherently good thing, while such doing has a slightly dubious nimbus for genuine conservatives. The former are prone to discount the future adverse consequences of business dealings. Nonetheless, they might listen when they are confronted with the prospect of irreversible environmental disaster.

Most importantly, however, judgments about what is considered necessary to avoid some public evil lay bare what a majority truly believes in. They render explicit what its members, perhaps even unwittingly, find deeply disturbing and repugnant, such as the oppression of women, nudity on TV, smoke-filled rooms or getting drunk in public. The more terrified they are by certain prospects the more inclined they will be to regard precautionary measures 'necessary'. The measures considered necessary in a democratic society to protect the rights of others, morals, public health and safety reveal the *Sittlichkeit* of that society. They express commitments. In the eyes of those claiming their necessity doing anything less than what they demand would jeopardise the goods that are at stake. The protection of public health is so important that permitting the advertisement of tobacco products would create an unreasonable risk of increasing the incidents of preventable death. It is, hence, within the compass of the margin of appreciation that peoples demonstrate to one another what their communities stand for and what they deem necessary in order to realise the goods inherent in a system of fundamental rights. Within the margin they assert that particularity

[56] Ibid., at 80. See also Dan M. Kahan, 'The Cognitively Illiberal State' (2007) 60 *Stanford Law Review* 115.

which defies universalisation, but which is nonetheless indispensable for the realisation of any system of rights. And if others, speaking through the Court, respect the margin within which particularity may have its way, the cosmopolitan *amour-propre* of countries is given reassurance without inflaming patriotic passion.

IX The Question of Indeterminacy

The universal is what unites us. Particularity is what sets us apart. We all believe in freedom of expression, but different national constitutional systems are not likely to protect the same set of expressive acts. There will be both overlap and divergence. The particular allows us to get to action, for it is by virtue of particular evaluative outlooks[57] that people can confidently cope with the concerns that they share. Some collective body may find it necessary in a democratic society to erect a wall in order to protect ordinary citizens against attacks by the violent rabble. Another collective body may find it necessary to curb the consumption of alcoholic beverages in order to rein in the adverse social consequences of drinking. The risk perceptions underlying regulations may frequently reflect what has remained stuck in the collective memories of peoples. They reveal the relevance of national narratives to the evaluative outlook of societies.

In a cosmopolitan context, however, asserting the *Sittlichkeit* of a democratic society loses its seemingly self-authenticating force. It can no longer simply pass as a quasi-natural expression of republican self-love. Nevertheless, cosmopolitan constitutionalism respects collective *amour-propre*. It endorses the mutual recognition of indispensable particularity. Not surprisingly, patriotism becomes recast in a different format. As a dangerous source of pride in one's alleged superiority or exceptional nature, it becomes superseded by the more modest admission that public concerns have to be addressed by drawing on one's own tradition, for it is the only way of inviting confidence in solutions. Societies have to cope with risks in a manner that their members are comfortable with. Tradition permits societies to set themselves into time and to exist in a narrative form that regenerates the hope that challenges

[57] An evaluative outlook comes to the fore in how moral judgment tacitly draws on holistic visions of how people have to live in order to live in the right way. See my book *The Legal Relation: Legal Theory After Legal Positivism* (Cambridge: Cambridge University Press, 2017), at 115. It is that which has been mistakenly shed by modern moral theory according to MacIntyre, *After Virtue* at 204.

can be commonly met while being reassured by the memory of past successes.

Of course, shifting to cosmopolitan *amour-propre* – to the mutual recognition of diverse evaluative outlooks – invites adopting an external perspective on one's collective memory. The views of the deputy foreigners that happen to be one's compatriots may even begin to appear strange. They are contingent. *Sittlichkeit* becomes infused with irony.[58] The cosmopolitan perspective invites self-relativisation, as a result of which societies have the opportunity to become milder in the long term.

Undeniably, the most disturbing question raised by the margin of appreciation concerns its scope. The margin is all about the central question of fundamental rights law, namely the application of the necessity component of the proportionality test. The persistent lack of clarity with regard to where it exists and where, if it exists, it comes to an end, in addition to the pertinent disagreement among members of the Court,[59] suggests that determining the margin may well be a matter of converging on a bundle of standards over time. Arguably, the matter has to be left on the level of working with precedents. For it seems to be in the nature of that margin that its scope defies conceptual clarification.

In order to understand this final point, it is necessary to raise the matter to that level of higher generality to which it truly belongs.

X Reasonable Disagreements

It has been argued by some authors that the legal relation is a reply to the existence of reasonable disagreements.[60] Rights stand for the proposition that others may do what we would never consider someone, including ourselves, to have reason to do. While we recognise their freedom of action socially, we persist in disagreeing substantially. Nonetheless, we mutually accept that our substantive disagreement must not stand in the way of our actions. This is the point of granting one another rights. What people end up doing, hence, is taken to reflect what we, and they, refer to as their 'choices'.

[58] See Richard Rorty, *Contingency, irony, and solidarity* (Cambridge: Cambridge University Press, 1989), at 68.

[59] See McGoldrick, 'A Defense of the Margin of Appreciation' at 38–39.

[60] See, for example, Jeremy Waldron, *Law and Disagreement* (Oxford: Oxford University Press, 1999); Samantha Besson, *The Morality of Conflict: Reasonable Disagreement and the Law* (Oxford: Hart Publishing, 2005). See also my book cited in note 57.

We permit disagreement within the confines of what we take to be mutually for granted. Rights are based upon existing laws. But the laws are not simply derivative of human nature. Our laws are also the result of political choices. We allow these political choices to go forward – we yield to what they demand from us – as long as they honour the fundamental principles of freedom, equality and reciprocity.

In order to realise these principles political processes are constitutionalised. But constitutions are not expressions of natural law either. The import of the fundamental principles and what it takes to protect them is itself subject to reasonable disagreement. Therefore, constitutions are, again, based upon decisions. We expect these to respect some elementary precepts of reasonableness that are not infrequently articulated in the language of unamendable constitutional law.[61]

What runs through these levels of determining the legal relation – rights, laws and constitutions – is the extension and absorption of reasonable disagreement. Such disagreement consists, at its core, of the recognition of the reasonableness of others even if it must appear to be the other of the reasonableness that we attribute to ourselves. It represents that which is foreign to us and owing to its foreignness also somewhat strange ('*They* think that it is a good idea to create a European Banking Union'). Not all disagreements are reasonable. The agreement on that which is unreasonable limits the scope of reasonable disagreements. Evidently, it is often unclear on which side some view has to fall. For example, some societies believe that consensual sexual intercourse between a 15-year-old and an 18-year-old should be a punishable criminal offence. Is this view inside or outside the zone of reasonable disagreement? Evidently, some procedure and decision are needed in order to clarify the issue.

XI The Contrast to the Federal System

Against this background, the significance of the indeterminacy of the margin of appreciation can be best understood by redescribing, if only hypothetically, the convention system in a manner congenial to how scholars of public international law sometimes assimilate mere conventional practices to constitutional structures.[62] The weak reading of the margin of appreciation suggests that some majority of signatory states is

[61] For an elementary exposition, see Yaniv Roznai, *Unconstitutional Constitutional Amendments: The Limits of Amendment Powers* (Oxford: Oxford University Press, 2017).

[62] They would then likely add that the relevant phenomenon is 'in the process of constitutionalization'.

necessary in order to make the margin disappear. The signatory states can be understood as the equivalent of a federal legislature in which is invested the power to preempt state legislation. The convention system thus seems to anticipate a federal system. It appears to be headed into that direction.

Such an analogy, however, misses the point that the contours of margin necessarily have to remain indeterminate. As we have seen above, all determinations within the zone of reasonable disagreements are legitimate subject to certain conditions. In the course of determining these conditions, however, the reach of reasonable disagreements becomes extended to include these conditions. Our law is thoroughly political.[63] The conditions for the exercise of rights are rules that respect freedom, equality and reciprocity. Since the substance of these rules is subject to reasonable disagreement it needs to be settled by means of political choices. Since the conditions for political choices are also subject to reasonable disagreement we need constitutions. Since the substance of constitutions is subject to reasonable disagreement acts of constitution making are required to establish what it is.

XII Conclusion: Past Sovereignty

What has been hitherto taken for granted in constitutionalism is that the subject of constitutional decision-making is the people. In other words, the power to overcome the ultimate reasonable disagreement was seen to be vested in sovereign authority. Now that sovereignty is dispersed and the authority of the people is diffused into peoples, the margin must remain indeterminate. Neither is it clear what the peoples have to converge on, nor is established how many of these peoples would count. There is neither a sovereign subject left nor any natural law. Without either it can never become clear where the margin comes to an end or whether it exists.[64]

The margin of appreciation is the final condition for the justification of the legal relation. The 'vital forces of society' are one more instantiation of that particular which one encounters also in the guise of individual will

[63] See Martin Loughlin, *Political Jurisprudence* (Oxford: Oxford University Press, 2017).

[64] Lest we forget, constitutions can work by leaving matters of vital importance unsettled. There was no rule determining the succession of the Roman *princeps*, and the empire was able to cope with this situation for a relatively long period of time.

or the democratic majority. Within the legal relation, the particular may have its way subject to generally indeterminate conditions that have to be spelled out case-by-case. While the margin is not nothing, it is not something either.

Isn't this the most amazing feature of the cosmopolitan constitution?

PART II

Border Crossings: Comity and Mobility

7

The Spectre of Comity

KAREN KNOP[1]

> Janus is usually thought of as the Roman god of doors . . . But he is also the god of door*ways*, thresholds, passages and transitions, which offers an alternative way of understanding the act of constitution as not an exclusionary but a liminal act. . . . On this latter understanding, the act of constitution not only affects the space outside of it. It is also affected by the legal orders in that space, both with respect to the form in which it is constituted and in that the threshold marks the point which norms can and sometimes must cross to make their way from one space to another . . .[2]

How do we study doorways and the constitution? For the past two decades, public international lawyers have been fascinated by the proliferating ways in which international law enters domestic law.[3] Much of this scholarship has been prompted by what judges are actually doing or, by extension, could do. Some focuses on how judges have misunderstood or taken liberties with the rules of reception, while other scholars are interested in identifying and theorising new points of entry to be found in the cases.

In discerning new thresholds, passages or transitions, the classical debate in public international law about whether international law and domestic law are one system (monism) or two (dualism) only goes so far. For instance, once the domestic legal system is taken as separate, dualism does not tell us whether it receives international law as law or as something else. Legal philosophers like Hans Kelsen and H. L. A. Hart, who took opposing sides in the monism/dualism debate, both considered international law to be law and therefore did not pursue alternative characterisations that would create different kinds

[1] The author gratefully acknowledges the comments of Jacco Bomhoff and David Dyzenhaus and the support of the Social Sciences and Humanities Research Council of Canada.

[2] David Dyzenhaus, 'The Janus-Faced Constitution', Chapter 2 of this volume, 18.

[3] See, e.g., André Nollkaemper and August Reinisch (eds.), *International Law in Domestic Courts: A Casebook* (Oxford: Oxford University Press, 2018).

of passageways.[4] Strong international law sceptics are inclined to grant international law entry into the domestic legal system only through politics. At the other end of the spectrum are those who analyse international law in domestic courts as empirical evidence of universal values or natural law. Yet others see international law as a mirror rather than a threshold: it applies insofar as comparison with international law reveals our own domestic law to us more clearly. These various domestic characterisations usually assume that the international law in question is binding as between states; that is, in the international legal system. Yet existing practices of reception also include cases in which some sublevel of government binds itself domestically to an international law that is binding internationally – but not on that state. Monism/dualism has little to say, as well, about such unilateral 'implementation' of international law. A well-known example is US cities that have passed municipal laws implementing international treaties, notably the United Nations Convention on the Elimination of All Forms of Discrimination Against Women, to which the United States is not a party.[5] This strategy fits neither monism nor dualism well because the Convention is binding international law and the city's law is binding domestically, but there is no legal tie between the states party to the Convention and the city.

If Janus is the god of doorways, then, our exploration of the double-facing constitution might call for a certain amount of lateral thinking and methodological experimentation if it is to include a variety of thresholds – backdoors, emergency exits, false doors, hidden passageways. In perceiving and arguing for emerging thresholds, scholars have often thought through analogies with other fields of law.[6] For example, approaching other legal systems as a mirror is familiar from comparative law methods, while ideas of informal or non-state law animate studies of sub-state and grassroots adoption of international treaties. Of particular relevance to this chapter is the comparison between the international law-domestic law relationship and the relationship between domestic law and foreign law in private international law, which animated Kelsen and Hart in

[4] See Dyzenhaus, 'The Janus-Faced Constitution'.

[5] See, e.g., Karen Knop, 'International Law and the Disaggregated Democratic State: Two Case Studies on Women's Human Rights and the United States', in Claire Charters and Dean R. Knight (eds.), *We, the People(s): Participation in Governance* (Wellington: Victoria University Press, 2011), 75.

[6] See Neil Walker, *Intimations of Global Law* (Cambridge: Cambridge University Press, 2015), ch. 3.

their day. Private international law is the branch of a state's law that determines when its courts will take jurisdiction over a private law case with a foreign element, and if a court takes jurisdiction, whether it applies the foreign law rather than its own. In addition to jurisdiction and choice of law, private international law determines when a court will recognise and enforce the judgment of a foreign court. Why a domestic court would ever apply a foreign law or recognise a foreign judgment, when it would do so and how, are all questions that parallel the international law-domestic law relationship. And insofar as private international law defers to foreign law domestically in the absence of an international obligation to do so, it can reflect legal internationalism without international law, not unlike the US cities that choose to ally their law with a treaty.

As distinct from emerging patterns discernible through analogy, thresholds can also be illuminated archaeologically, as Audrey Macklin does in her chapter on the state's right to exclude or expel a non-citizen.[7] By tracing the doctrinal question of how this power of the sovereign, part of the common law, has come to circumscribe the individual's constitutional rights instead of vice versa, she uncovers that the power may, in fact, operate as a transmuted right between states under public international law rather than a prerogative power over individuals that rests with the state under domestic constitutional law. Because it makes the state a rights bearer in constitutional rights jurisprudence, the transformation of 'an external norm of sovereignty into an ersatz internal norm of sovereignty' both refutes the individual's claim of a constitutional right not to be expelled and frees the state from the requirements of legality that accompany its exercise of a power.[8]

While analogical approaches tend to be structural and forward-looking, Macklin reveals a particular transition that would not have been apparent without her archaeological approach. Undertaken in an exploratory and experimental vein, the current chapter has something in common with both approaches, as well as with the turn to private histories in public international law. It begins with a curious and little-noticed threshold introduced over a decade ago by the Supreme Court of Canada's characterisation of 'comity' as a principle of interpretation for the Canadian Charter of Rights and Freedoms, Canada's constitutional bill of rights.[9] While the Court referenced international comity in private

[7] Audrey Macklin, 'The Inside-Out Constitution', Chapter 9 of this volume.

[8] Ibid., 261–62, 273–75.

[9] *R* v. *Hape*, [2007] 2 SCR 292. On the uses of comity by common-law courts, see, e.g., Adrian Briggs, 'The Principle of Comity in Private International Law' (2011) 354 *Recueil*

international law and other discrete areas of the Canadian legal system, it cited no precedent for applying comity between states to the interpretation of constitutional rights. The constitutionalisation of comity between provinces is familiar; this 'comitization' of the Constitution is not. Searching for earlier uses of the term 'comity' in constitutional interpretation by the Supreme Court of Canada, this chapter uncovers a spectral parallel with issues well known in public international law.[10]

Ranging from the turn of the century to the present, the four sets of cases discussed differ in the meaning assigned to comity and in its interpretive role vis-à-vis the Constitution. Comity by nature is two-faced. Authors have referred to it as a principle of recognition and a principle of restraint, or a bridge and a wall.[11] Comity is also a shape-shifter over time.[12] Moreover, while comity 'retain[s] its vitality in the jurisprudence of Canadian courts', the Supreme Court has also acknowledged that 'comity has proven a difficult concept to define in legal terms'.[13]

All of the cases, however, show something(s) called 'comity' to be a way in which the existence of, dependence on and regard for the Other figure in the interpretation of the Constitution. This contrasts both with the modern tendency observed by Thomas Poole among British public law scholars to conceive of the constitution in isolation[14] and with the starting point of sovereign independence notionally assumed in public international law. In a striking passage from a 1907

des cours 65; William S. Dodge, 'International Comity in American Law' (2015) 115 *Columbia Law Review* 2071; Thomas Schultz and Jason Mitchenson, 'Navigating Sovereignty and Transnational Commercial Law: The Use of Comity by Australian Courts' (2016) 12 *Journal of Private International Law* 344.

[10] As of 1 December 2018, a search of the Supreme Court of Canada (Lexum) database for 'comity' turned up 110 cases since Confederation. The chapter takes account of all of these cases, but concentrates on the small number that are constitutional cases and have used comity to interpret the Constitution (as opposed to vice versa, about which much has been written). For cases in this subset prior to 1949, when the Judicial Committee of the Privy Council ceased to be Canada's ultimate appellate court, the chapter takes account of Privy Council appeals.

[11] See Dodge, 'International Comity in American Law', 2079; Joel R. Paul, 'Comity in International Law' (1991) 32 *Harvard International Law Journal* 1, 3–7.

[12] See, e.g., Roxana Banu, *Nineteenth Century Perspectives on Private International Law* (Oxford: Oxford University Press, 2018); Dodge, 'International Comity in American Law'; Paul, 'Comity in International Law'.

[13] *Spar Aerospace Ltd* v. *American Mobile Satellite Corp.*, [2002] 4 SCR 205, 218. See also ibid., 217–19 (tracing the history and criticisms of the notion of international comity).

[14] Thomas Poole, *Reasons of State: Law, Prerogative and Empire* (Cambridge: Cambridge University Press, 2015), 9–11.

judgment, Idington J wrote that in interpreting the Constitution, 'regard ought to be had, and I venture to think, was had, to . . . the manifold relations of every kind then had with foreign neighbours whether as individuals or as states'.[15] Whereas the role played by the recognition of others in the cosmopolitan constitution described in Alexander Somek's chapter is a post–Second World War achievement which relates to the rise of the international human rights system,[16] the cosmopolitanism introduced into the Constitution by comity has a longer history. The mobility of individuals, corporations and other private parties across internal and external borders that gives rise to comity, and the value of history, also chime with Jacco Bomhoff's chapter. Bomhoff argues that the constitutionalist preoccupation with whether people or events are inside or outside constitutionally salient boundaries should yield to a more immediate focus on instances of mobility. He writes critically:

> We do not have a constitutional discourse that is able to encompass not just the individuals of immigration law, but also the corporations of tax law or commercial arbitration; not just mobility across borders, but also within countries; and not just denials of entry, or enforced immobility, but also opportunities for exit, all together, within one frame. We also mostly lack a robust historical awareness.[17]

I Private Histories of International Law

The point of departure for this chapter is two types of threshold between domestic and foreign legal systems read into the Constitution by the Supreme Court of Canada in a 2007 case. In *R* v. *Hape* the issue was whether the Charter of Rights and Freedoms applied to searches and seizures conducted by Canadian police officers in another country.[18] The Supreme Court relied on principles of public international law to reach the conclusion that the Charter could not apply extraterritorially, meaning that Canadian authorities acting outside Canada's borders would henceforth be operating in what one critic termed 'Charter-free zones'.[19] As commentators have noted, this is an ironic win for international law: 'the

[15] *Canadian Pacific Railway Co.* v. *Ottawa Fire Insurance Co.* (1907), 39 SCR 405, 453.

[16] Alexander Somek, 'From Republican Self-Love to Cosmopolitan *Amour-Propre*: Europe's New Constitutional Experience', Chapter 6 of this volume.

[17] Jacco Bomhoff, 'Constitutionalism and Mobility: Expulsion and Escape Among Partial Constitutional Orders', Chapter 8 of this volume, 3.

[18] *R* v. *Hape*, [2007] 2 SCR 292.

[19] See Kent W. Roach, '*R v. Hape* Creates Charter-Free Zones for Canadian Officials Abroad' (2007) 53 *Criminal Law Quarterly* 1. For possible exceptions, see below at 200.

Canadian Supreme Court's openness to international law leads to lesser constitutional protection abroad than the narrower use of international law by the U.S. Supreme Court in interpreting the Bill of Rights – a result few international lawyers would have predicted'.[20] Much attention has been paid not only to the Supreme Court's restrictive analysis of the international law of jurisdiction, but also to the Court's categorical assertion that the Charter is presumed to conform with international law – a rule of statutory interpretation that until *Hape* had not applied to the Constitution as well.[21] At play is both the relationship between domestic and foreign legal systems (jurisdiction according to public international law) and the relationship between public international law and the Constitution (the presumption of conformity according to constitutional law).

In addition, *Hape* introduced a rule of constitutional interpretation that has attracted little attention despite being unexpected, perhaps because it furnishes only a supporting reason for the judgment: 'Where our laws – statutory and constitutional – could have an impact on the sovereignty of other states, the principle of comity will bear on their interpretation'.[22] The Supreme Court defined comity as 'informal acts performed and rules observed by states in their mutual relations out of politeness, convenience and goodwill'.[23] When Canada's lawful exercise

[20] Pierre-Hugues Verdier, 'Case Comment: *R v Hape*' (2008) 102 *American Journal of International Law* 143, 148.

[21] See, e.g., Amir Attaran, 'Have Charter, Will Travel? Extraterritoriality in Constitutional Law and Canadian Exceptionalism' (2008) 87 *Canadian Bar Review* 515; John H. Currie, 'Weaving a Tangled Web: *Hape* and the Obfuscation of Canadian Reception Law' (2007) 45 *Canadian Yearbook of International Law* 55; John H. Currie, '*Khadr's* Twist on *Hape*: Tortured Determinations of the Extraterritorial Reach of the Canadian *Charter*' (2008) 46 *Canadian Yearbook of International Law* 307; Noemi Gal-Or, '*R. v. Hape*: International Law Before the Supreme Court of Canada' (2008) 66 *Advocate* 885; François Larocque and Martin Kreuser, 'L'incorporation de la coutume international en common law canadienne' (2006) 44 *Canadian Yearbook of International Law* 173, 215–20; Chanakya Sethi, 'Does the Constitution Follow the Flag? Revisiting Constitutional Extraterritoriality After *R v Hape*' (2011) 20 *Dalhousie Journal of Legal Studies* 102; Verdier, 'Case Comment'.

A number of other legal systems also contain the concept that André Nollkaemper calls the 'consistent interpretation' of domestic law with public international law. André Nollkaemper, 'General Aspects', in Nollkaemper and Reinisch (eds.), *International Law in Domestic Courts*, 1, 22–27.

[22] *Hape*, 320. For commentators who include some discussion of comity in *Hape*, see Currie, '*Khadr's* Twist on *Hape*', 315 n. 49, 322–23; H. Scott Fairley, 'International Law Comes of Age: *Hape v. The Queen*' (2008) 87 *Canadian Bar Review* 229, 234–36, 238–39; Kerry Sun, 'International Comity and the Construction of the *Charter*'s Limits: *Hape* Revisited' *Queen's Law Journal* (in press, 2019).

[23] *Hape*, 320.

of its jurisdiction would conflict with the jurisdiction of another state, then comity counsels self-restraint in the application of Canadian law.

The existence of a familiar public international law passageway and an overshadowed counterpart associated with private international law resonates more generally. In public international law, 'private histories' are having a moment.[24] Martti Koskenniemi argues that histories of international law should expand from the law of sovereignty to include the law of property and their relationship with one other as the 'yin and yang of global power'.[25] By approaching the history of international law in terms of states – war, diplomacy, treaties, institution-building – international lawyers cordon off the private-law relations that underlie and support those actions. Koskenniemi writes evocatively:

> Any international legal history would say something about the abolition of the slave trade but little if anything about the contractual form through which that trade was connected with Caribbean sugar production and the export of arms and manufactures to Africa. Its account of North American colonization would rarely include an analysis of the charters under which private companies and individual proprietors would rule the thirteen colonies.[26]

To this, private international lawyers add that public international lawyers also frequently ignore private international law, whereas historians of private international law are usually very aware of the relationship.[27]

[24] See, e.g., B. S. Chimni, 'Prolegomena to a Class Approach to International Law' (2010) 21 *European Journal of International Law* 57; James Thuo Gathii, *War, Commerce, and International Law* (New York: Oxford University Press, 2010); Martti Koskenniemi, 'Empire and International Law: The Real Spanish Contribution' (2011) 61 *University of Toronto Law Journal* 1; Doreen Lustig, *Corporate Regulation in International Law: A History of Failure?* (Oxford: Oxford University Press, in press, 2019); Luigi Nuzzo, 'Territory, Sovereignty, and the Construction of the Colonial Space', in Martti Koskenniemi, Walter Rech and Manuel Jiménez Fonseca (eds.), *International Law and Empire: Historical Explorations* (Oxford: Oxford University Press, 2017), 263; Ileana M. Porras, 'Constructing International Law in the East Indian Seas: Property, Sovereignty, Commerce and War in Hugo Grotius *De Iure Praedae* – The Law of Prize and Booty, or "On How to Distinguish Merchants from Pirates"' (2006) 31 *Brooklyn Journal of International Law* 756.

[25] Martti Koskenniemi, 'Expanding Histories of International Law' (2016) 56 *American Journal of Legal History* 104, 112.

[26] Ibid., 109. See also Martti Koskenniemi, 'Histories of International Law: Significance and Problems for a Critical View' (2013) 27 *Temple International and Comparative Law Journal* 215, 235 (arguing that the law of contracts as well as the law of property should be included).

[27] See Ralf Michaels, 'Private Lawyer in Disguise? On the Absence of Private Law and Private International Law in Martti Koskenniemi's Work' (2013) 27 *Temple International and Comparative Law Journal* 499, 512. See also Alex Mills, *The Confluence of Public and*

Koskenniemi's argument is about context: by neglecting private law, historians of international law produce only a partial account of how power operates through international legal concepts and institutions. With regard to private international law, Robert Wai argues similarly that by neglecting the internationalist policy consciousness underlying the development of the Supreme Court of Canada's modern private international law jurisprudence because there is no treaty or customary international law involved, commentators produce only a partial account of how foreign relations operates through Canadian legal concepts and institutions.[28] Canadian private international law, for example, is explicitly based on the modern need to facilitate the flow of wealth, skills and people across borders.

The Supreme Court of Canada's characterisation of comity as a principle of constitutional interpretation in *Hape* illustrates not only that foreign policy objectives can be read into a constitution but that they can diffuse from private law. Some constitutions include explicit objectives. The Brazilian Constitution, for instance, presses the country to 'seek the economic, political, social and cultural integration of the people of Latin America, with a view towards forming a Latin-American community of Nations'.[29] The Constitution of South Sudan calls for 'promotion of international cooperation, specially within the United Nations family . . . for the purposes of consolidating universal peace and security,

Private International Law: Justice, Pluralism and Subsidiarity in the International Constitutional Ordering of Private Law (Cambridge: Cambridge University Press, 2009), 71; Alex Mills, 'The Private History of International Law' (2006) 55 *International and Comparative Law Quarterly* 1. Private international lawyers interested in the present suggestiveness of this historical moment include Diego P. Fernández Arroyo, 'Réflexions autour du besoin réciproque entre le droit international privé et le droit international public' in *Le 90e anniversaire de Boutros Boutros-Ghali: Hommage du Curatorium à son Président* (London/Boston: Martinus Nijhoff, 2012), 113; Roxana Banu, *Nineteenth-Century Perspectives*; Nikitas Hatzimihail, 'Reflections on the International Dimension of Private International Law' in Rafaël Jafferali, Vanessa Marquette and Arnaud Nuyts (eds.), *Liber Amicorum Nadine Watté* (Brussels: Bruylant, 2017), 287; Mills, *The Confluence of Public and Private International Law*; Mills, 'The Private History of International Law'; Horatia Muir Watt, 'Private International Law Beyond the Schism' (2011) 2 *Transnational Legal Theory* 347; Joel R. Paul, 'The Isolation of Private International Law' (1988) 7 *Wisconsin International Law Journal* 149.

[28] Robert Wai, 'In the Name of the International: The Supreme Court of Canada and the Internationalist Transformation of Canadian Private International Law' (2001) 39 *Canadian Yearbook of International Law* 117, 120.

[29] Art. 4, sole paragraph, Brazilian Constitution.

[and] respect for international law'.[30] In the EU context, a recent study argues that foreign policy objectives codified in the constitution are not merely a 'wish list for a better world' or a 'political candy box' but should be taken seriously as norms of constitutional law.[31] The 'comitization' of the Canadian Charter of Rights and Freedoms is all the more striking for a Constitution like Canada's that is silent on foreign relations.

The rise of private histories of public international law stems both from an interest in context and from the hypothesis that private law relations undergird public international law not only materially but structurally. A classic example is Sir Hersch Lauterpacht's early work on private law sources and analogies in public international law.[32] In Canadian law, comity has a longer and richer history in private international law than in cases like *Hape* involving public international law and foreign relations. This is also true more generally.[33] Comity arose in private international law to address the problem that the rise of exclusive territorial sovereignty following the 1648 Peace of Westphalia created for the safeguarding of foreign rights. According to the seventeenth-century Dutch jurist Ulrich Huber, one sovereign was to act by way of comity such that the rights acquired within the limits of the government of another retained their force everywhere, so far as they did not cause prejudice to the power or the rights of the government or of its subjects.[34] Unlike international law, comity was not binding, but neither was it

[30] Art. 43(a) Transitional Constitution of South Sudan, 7 July 2011, https://wipolex.wipo.int/en/text/250715, accessed 1 August 2019.

[31] Joris Larik, *Foreign Policy Objectives in European Constitutional Law* (Oxford: Oxford University Press, 2016), 3.

[32] Hersch Lauterpacht, *Private Law Sources and Analogies of International Law (With Special Reference to International Arbitration)* (London: Longmans, 1927).

[33] Historical literature on comity and which schools of private international law subscribed to some conception of comity as foundational includes G. Blaine Baker, 'Interstate Choice of Law and Early-American Constitutional Nationalism: An Essay on *Joseph Story and the Comity of Errors: A Case Study in Conflict of Laws*' (1993) 38 *McGill Law Journal* 454; Friedrich K. Juenger, 'A Page of History' (1984) 35 *Mercer Law Review* 419; Gerhard Kegel, 'Story and Savigny' (1989) 37 *American Journal of Comparative Law* 39; Arthur Nussbaum, 'Rise and Decline of the Law-of-Nations Doctrine in the Conflict of Laws' (1942) 42 *Columbia Law Review* 189; Paul, 'Comity in International Law'; Thomas Schultz and David Holloway, 'La *comity* dans l'histoire du droit international privé' (2012) 139(2) *Journal du Droit International* 571; Alan Watson, *Joseph Story and the Comity of Errors: A Case Study in Conflict of Laws* (Athens, GA: University of Georgia Press, 1992); Hessel E. Yntema, 'The Comity Doctrine' (1966) 65 *Michigan Law Review* 9.

[34] Ulrich Huber, *De Conflictu Legum Diversarum in Diversis Imperiis* (1689), reprinted and translated in Ernest G. Lorenzen, 'Huber's *De Conflictu Legum*' (1919) 13 *Illinois Law Review* 375, 403.

merely courtesy. Huber wrote, 'nothing could be more inconvenient to commerce and to international usage than that transactions valid by the law of one place should be rendered of no effect elsewhere on account of a difference in the law'.[35] Canonical authors differ on whether comity was a choice-of-law rule as well as a theory of why one state would submit to another state's private law. Blaine Baker argues that 'in Huber's scheme of interstate conflicts doctrine, comity was a substantive principle that provided an all-embracing rule which made detailed choice-of-law rules superfluous', whereas for the influential late nineteenth-century US scholar Joseph Story, 'comity was not a value or policy relevant to the content of choice-of-law rules'.[36]

We can see here how the structure of cosmopolitanism in private international law differs from the idea of the cosmopolitan constitution that Somek develops in his chapter. In Somek's account, universal human rights can legitimately be particularised differently in the constitutions of different states, as the 'margin of appreciation' in European human rights law suggests. Universalism is not uniformity. He expresses the test for universally acceptable particularity as whether someone who would deny constitutional recognition to a given law or practice in her own country would nevertheless find it acceptable in another country were it to be applied to her as a visiting foreigner.[37] In private international law, the analysis does not begin with overarching universalism and move to the question of acceptable particularisation, but proceeds from the presumption that diverse legal systems will be recognised for the reasons that Huber gives. Unlike in Somek's scenario, the foreign rights 'travel' to us by coming into contact with our legal system, as opposed to his hypothetical of a person travelling to another state and being subjected to their constitution. The limit of recognition in private international law is, classically, when the foreign rights prejudice 'the power or rights of the government or of its subjects'. Known as the public policy exception in common law systems, this limit is judged relative to our own legal system's fundamental values, which may, but need not, be universal.

Although comity is a cosmopolitan idea and an idea that has migrated transnationally, as a doctrine of domestic law it is found in common law and not civil law systems (the Canadian system being mixed common

[35] Ibid.
[36] Baker, 'Interstate Choice of Law', 497.
[37] Somek, 'From Republican Self-Love to Cosmopolitan *Amour-Propre*', 162.

law, civil law and Indigenous law).[38] The wider interest of this chapter is not to argue for comity as a principle of constitutional interpretation, but to argue for private histories of the double-facing constitution by way of illustration. As the chapter's title suggests, such histories may be spectral, both relative to public international law and in the nature of the Other-regarding construct. Compared to the roles played by treaty or customary international law, comity can be evanescent, as will be seen, but it is also not simply a judicial foreign policy preference or view of international relations. Comity has a spectral quality because the mutuality of relations comes from acts performed by one state in the conjured expectation that others will share the same sense of appropriateness and behave likewise. And being a relationship that one legal system conjures rather than negotiates with another, it can vanish when a court in that system substitutes a national vantage point on the relationship that turns regard for the Other into regard for the Self. Even when another vantage point is ultimately substituted, however, comity provokes a style of legal encounter in constitutionalism that can contribute to the internal form of the state (Section II), the nature of its external relations (Section III), the model of internal relations between subunits (Section IV) and the reach of the constitution (Section V).

The value of private histories is also in identifying when private sources or analogies run out. In Section V, which returns to *Hape*, comity is shown to be more influential than its presentation as a supporting reason and a non-binding norm indicate. At the same time, the judgment's treatment of comity as a unified concept masks the introduction of foreign relations comity as a general type both distinct from the private international law tradition and in potential tension with it.

II The Other and the Internal Form of the State

The first series of Supreme Court of Canada cases on 'comity' and the Constitution arose from the power of other states to affect the internal

[38] See William S. Dodge, 'International Comity in Comparative Perspective', in Curtis A. Bradley (ed.), *Oxford Handbook of Comparative Foreign Relations Law* (Oxford: Oxford University Press, 2019), 701. Dodge compares the principle of comity with that of 'mutual trust' in the jurisprudence of the Court of Justice of the European Union. In Canada, the principle of comity also underlies the private international law rules codified in the Québec Civil Code. See *Spar Aerospace Ltd*, 220-221, 233. Regarding Indigenous law, see *Beaver v. Hill*, 2018 ONCA 816, para.17 (For constitutional purposes, Aboriginal rights or Indigenous law do not constitution 'foreign law' even in the conceptual sense.).

form of the state by recognising the private laws of different levels of government and the rights they establish.

Unlike this effect, the parallel potential in public international law is a well-known controversy in federal states. When a federal government enters into an international treaty on subjects over which the subunits have jurisdiction domestically, the state is responsible under public international law for compliance with the treaty regardless of whether the constitution gives it the power to implement those obligations domestically. In some federations, the federal government has the power to implement any treaty, with the result that it can ensure compliance internationally and also increase its jurisdiction domestically by entering into a treaty concerning a subfederal subject area. In other federations, the federal government does not, which leaves it vulnerable to non-compliance by the subunits. Addressing this risk of non-compliance can lead to constitutional conventions or practices that give the subunits a say in treaty-making that they do not have according to the constitutional division of powers. Either way, a treaty may have the consequence – unintended from that treaty's point of view – of altering the federal division of power inside a state. From a constitutional perspective, the issue is whether international law can be an indirect way to change the state's federal structure. For Canada, the Judicial Committee of the Privy Council in the 1937 *Labour Conventions* case famously answered no.[39] The Privy Council ruled unconstitutional federal legislation seeking to implement several International Labour Organisation conventions because the legislation dealt with provincial matters.

As a 1913 dissenting judgment from this first snapshot of comity makes clear, comity raised a parallel concern about the potential of outside legal orders to alter the internal form of the state: 'Comity, whatever may be the legal meaning of the word in international relations, cannot operate between the provinces so as to affect the distribution of legislative power between the Dominion [the federal authority] and the provinces.'[40] In a series of Supreme Court cases beginning in 1903, comity was central to a protracted federal-provincial contest over whether the provinces and not just the Dominion could create companies that operated throughout Canada and abroad.[41]

[39] *Attorney-General for Canada* v. *Attorney General for Ontario*, [1937] AC 326.

[40] *In re Companies* (1913), 48 SCR 331, 339–40 (Fitzpatrick, CJ).

[41] See F. W. Wegenast, Annotation to the *Companies Case* (Judicial Committee of the Privy Council) (1916), 26 DLR 294.

What did comity signify in this episode? An earlier non-constitutional case on winding up a company provides some context. In this 1885 Supreme Court of Canada case, Strong J applied, in *obiter,* the rule of interpretation that a statute should be construed so as not to conflict with 'well-established rules of international law'.[42] Included in international law were 'the rules and canons which govern the comity of nations and make up what is called Private International Law'.[43] In the late nineteenth century, a number of influential scholars subscribed to the unity of public and private international law, some of them advancing arguments that aimed to make private international law rules obligatory under public international law, as opposed to a matter of comity.[44] While Strong J did not go this far, he treated private international law under the 'rules of international law'. Finding that English, American and Continental authority agreed on the principle that a company or partnership is only to be wound up in the forum of its domicile, he concluded that the statute in question did not authorise a Canadian court to wind up a company domiciled in England.[45] Thus, although private international law was a branch of domestic law, Strong J looked to the private international law rules of other countries, which were in agreement and presumably made the rule 'well established'. The 'comity of nations' was a way of referring to the terrain of private international law, but in context it also carried the sense of confidence that comity was more than 'mere courtesy and good will', as an often-cited US Supreme Court case of the time put it,[46] and that the rules and canons of private international law would be followed despite the lack of an international obligation between states.

The British North America Act ('BNA Act') of 1867 (the law passed by the British Parliament creating the Dominion of Canada, now known as the Constitution Act 1867) gave both the Dominion and the provinces the power to create companies. Dominion companies had the status of domestic companies throughout Canada and operated in all provinces as

[42] *Merchants' Bank of Halifax* v. *Gillespie* (1885), 10 SCR 312, 325 (Strong J). See also *Canadian Pacific Railway Company* v. *Western Union Telegraph Company* (1889), 17 SCR 151, 163–67 (citing US cases stating that the rules of comity 'have the controlling force of legal obligation' until modified by local law and that 'comity is presumed from the silent acquiescence of the State').

[43] *Merchants' Bank of Halifax*, 325.

[44] See Banu, *Nineteenth-Century Perspectives,* ch. 2.

[45] *Merchants' Bank of Halifax*, 325.

[46] *Hilton* v. *Guyot*, 159 US 113 at 163–64 (1895). *Hilton's* formulation of comity is adopted by the Supreme Court of Canada in a number of cases, including *Morguard Investments Ltd* v. *De Savoye*, [1990] 3 SCR 1077, 1096, discussed in Section IV below.

of right. In contrast, the provinces could make laws relating to the incorporation of companies 'with provincial objectives', a phrase in the BNA Act that the federal government ever since Confederation had interpreted as restricting the existence of provincially incorporated companies to the territory of the province.[47] That other provinces and other states would recognise provincial companies as *foreign* companies by virtue of comity formed part of arguments to the contrary. Without this likelihood, the constitutional issue would have been of no practical relevance. Moreover, whether comity won or lost the day was of considerable economic importance because the fees for the incorporation of companies brought in substantial revenue for the provinces.[48]

In the 1907 case *Canadian Pacific Railway Co.* v. *Ottawa Fire Ins. Co.*, the Supreme Court of Canada held that a provincial fire insurance company was not inherently incapable of entering into an insurance contract outside the province concerning property also outside the province.[49] Whereas the dissent objected that comity would effectively give provincial corporations powers coextensive with Dominion corporations,[50] Idington J, who wrote one of the majority judgments, reasoned that the doctrine of the comity of nations must have formed part of the common knowledge of the constitutional framers and the Constitution must therefore be read accordingly:

> The very word corporation implies and implied in England at the passing of 'The British North America Act,' a right to trade abroad for the purposes for which the corporation was created, unless restricted, just as much as the words 'free citizen' implies in modern times his right to go abroad.
>
> . . . [A]ny state creating a corporation without restricting its power is supposed to know as a matter of international law that the same kind of business it enables it to do can then legally be done abroad by this creation, in states that choose to accord it recognition.[51]

Indeed, the case for a presumption of conformity with international law (in which Idington J included comity) was even stronger for the Constitution than for an ordinary statute:

[47] *Canadian Pacific Railway Co.* v. *Ottawa Fire*, 414–15.

[48] Wegenast, Annotation, 303. Taking out a Dominion charter would have been a simple solution to the problem of territorial limits, but many provinces required Dominion companies to obtain authorisation to operate in the province and to pay fees approximately equal to those that would have been charged for a provincial charter. Ibid.

[49] *Canadian Pacific Railway Co.* v. *Ottawa Fire*. This case was not appealed to the Privy Council. Wegenast, Annotation, 302.

[50] Ibid., 412–13 (Fitzpatrick, CJ).

[51] Ibid., 452–53.

> When statesmen frame a law, its language must be read in light of that international law and unless clearly repugnant thereto or expressly excluding its operation both must be read together.
>
> It becomes more imperative to do so in the case of a piece of legislation that itself is in its fundamental nature akin to what is commonly known as international law. An instrument such as 'The British North America Act' is essentially of this character.[52]

In the 1913 *Companies Reference*, Anglin J also took up Idington J's comity line of reasoning, maintaining that vague language in the BNA Act such as 'provincial objectives' could not be grounds to conclude that the Constitution was intended to deny to provincial legislatures the right to endow their 'corporate creatures' with the capacity to avail themselves of 'privileges accorded by international comity'.[53] To the contrary, Davies J expanded on the federalism objection made in dissent in *Canadian Pacific Railway Co.* that reading comity into the Constitution would contradict both the cardinal principle restricting the exclusive powers of the provincial legislatures to the province alone and the rule of construction prohibiting doing indirectly that which cannot be done directly.[54]

Reprised by the Supreme Court in *Bonanza Creek Gold Mining Co.* v. *The King*,[55] the debate was finally settled by the Privy Council in the *Bonanza Creek* appeal.[56] But whereas '[a] great deal was said about the comity of nations and the right of a company to do business in a foreign state by virtue of that comity', as one of the Supreme Court justices put it,[57] the Privy Council did not dwell on comity at all. Indeed, the Privy Council judgment gives scarcely a hint that comity was ever part of the arguments.

We can see here how comity is a ghostly passageway. In the absence of a treaty, transnational legal persons are a discretionary co-creation. The home jurisdiction can create a company with the capacity to exist outside its territory, but whether that company does, depends on the particular foreign jurisdiction's domestic rules on recognition. Supreme Court of Canada judges such as Idington J were sufficiently convinced of the comity of other provinces and states to make the effect on the federal-

52 Ibid., 453. See similarly *In re Insurance Act, 1910* (1913), 48 SCR 260, 283-84 (Idington J).
53 *In re Companies*, 454–55.
54 Ibid., 352.
55 *Bonanza Creek Gold Mining Co.* v. *The King* (1915), 50 SCR 534.
56 *Bonanza Creek Gold Mining Co.* v. *The King*, [1916] 1 AC 566 (UK JCPC).
57 *Canadian Pacific Railway Co.* v. *Ottawa Fire*, 430 (Davies J, dissenting).

provincial division of powers a focus (that is, the Other): the 'doctrine of the comity of nations, carrying with it . . . this recognition of a foreign corporation, is as firmly embedded in . . . international law as anything can well be'.[58] In contrast, the Privy Council focused purely on capacity (that is, the Self). Whereas Idington J looked outward and maintained that the constitutional drafters must have had regard to 'the manifold relations of every kind then had with foreign neighbours whether as individuals or as states',[59] the Privy Council looked inward and applied to the BNA Act the principle for interpreting the powers of a corporation created by statute.[60]

III Mirroring the Other as External Relations

The next historical episode in which comity intersects with the Canadian Constitution involves provincial powers and the nature of external relations. As in the previous episode, the parallel issue in public international law is much better known. The US Constitution, for example, provides that no US state shall enter into any treaty, alliance or confederation and that the consent of Congress is needed for a state to enter into any agreement or compact with another US state or with a foreign power.[61] In Canada, the Constitution is silent. It is generally accepted that provinces have no treaty powers, there is a long-standing difference of opinion between the federal government and Québec regarding the power to negotiate treaties relating to provincial areas of jurisdiction.[62] In this episode on comity in constitutional interpretation, the issue is whether a province's mirroring of a foreign statute on private international law is analogous.

The 1955 Supreme Court of Canada case *Attorney General for Ontario v. Scott* involved an unsuccessful challenge to the constitutionality of a provincial family law statute.[63] Patterned upon an English act, the Ontario *Reciprocal Enforcement of Maintenance Orders Act* provided a way to register foreign maintenance orders between reciprocating states without the need to initiate proceedings for their enforcement.[64] Under the

[58] Ibid, 448.
[59] Ibid, 453.
[60] *Bonanza Creek Gold Mining Co.* (UK JCPC), 577–78.
[61] US Constitution, Art. I, Section 10.
[62] See, e.g., Hugo Cyr, *Canadian Federalism and Treaty Powers: Organic Constitutionalism at Work* (Brussels, P. I. E. Peter Lang, 2009), 13–33.
[63] *Attorney General for Ontario v. Scott*, [1956] SCR 137.
[64] Ibid., 150.

English legislation, Elizabeth Scott, an English resident, applied before an English magistrate for a maintenance order on the ground that her husband, a soldier in the Canadian Army stationed in Ontario, had wilfully neglected to provide reasonable maintenance for her and their children. The magistrate's order was provisional only and would have no effect unless and until confirmed by a competent court in Canada. Under the corresponding Ontario legislation, Mr Scott received a summons reciting the terms of the English order and directing him to appear before an Ontario judge to show cause why the order should not be confirmed.[65]

As opposed to implementing a treaty between Ontario and England, the Ontario statute simply mirrored the English statute. To quote from the majority judgment of Rand J: 'The enactments of the two legislatures are complementary but voluntary; the application of each is dependent on that of the other: each is the condition of the other; but that condition possesses nothing binding to its continuance.'[66] Among the constitutional challenges raised by Mr Scott was that the legislation was, in effect, an international treaty, which was not within provincial competence.[67] Rand J rejected the characterisation of the Ontario and English statutes together as a treaty on the basis that a treaty's essence is its binding effects between the parties.[68]

The relationship of mirror statutes was also challenged as concerning international comity, another federal matter.[69] The work done by the concept of comity in *Scott* differs from the provincial companies cases, in which comity could be read as a predictor of other states' behaviour and thus as effectively augmenting provincial power. In *Scott*, the accent was on comity as involving the application of foreign law. Whatever its nature, Rand J wrote, the comity of nations 'ordinarily signifies the respect paid by one state to the laws and to civil rights established by them of another'.[70] Rand J rejected the comity challenge in *Scott* by rejecting the idea that the Ontario Act recognised a foreign right. The right of the wife was created not by English law, but by Ontario law with reference to English law.[71] Properly understood, the true nature of the arrangement was as follows:

[65] Ibid., 148–49.
[66] Ibid., 142.
[67] Ibid., 139.
[68] Ibid., 142.
[69] Ibid., 139. In the two concurring judgments, the treaty challenge is not separated from the comity challenge. See ibid., 147 (Abbott J), 153–54 (Locke J).
[70] Ibid., at 140.
[71] Ibid.

> The province, recognizing the practical difficulty of enforcing the rights of a wife so placed, has intimated its willingness to exercise its authority over the husband by compelling him to the performance of a duty which both countries recognize as an incident of the marriage status. In carrying this out, the province has adopted provisions which the law of England prescribes for the relief of the deserted wife. The effect is to vest in the wife a right to enforce the duty in Ontario in accordance with the provisions adopted.[72]

Despite the different inflection of comity in *Scott*, it again proves a ghostly passageway between legal systems. The 'vested right not comity' shift in *Scott* resembles the 'common law not comity' shift that makes the passageway disappear in the Privy Council's judgment resolving that earlier episode. Nonetheless, it is the comity challenge that gives shape to what 'external' relations the provinces can conduct.

IV International Comity as a Model of Internal Relations

In the early 1990s, the Supreme Court of Canada brought constitutional law to bear on private international law.[73] The next snapshot of comity discusses the first in this line of cases, *Morguard Investments Ltd* v. *De Savoye*. Whereas the major story of *Morguard* is the constitutionalisation of private international law, the 'private history' focus adopted in this chapter turns our attention to the role of comity in first interpreting what the Constitution means. In *Morguard*, international comity between states serves as a lens on constitutional relations between provinces, paralleling the more familiar comparison between interstate relations in public international law and federalism.

The issue in *Morguard* was an asymmetry in the common-law rules inherited from England on the recognition and enforcement of judgments, which extended to the judgments of other provinces as well as of foreign countries. The bases of jurisdiction for a court to hear a case (known as jurisdiction simpliciter) were wider than the bases of jurisdiction recognised in that court by courts abroad for the purposes of enforcing its judgment. In *Morguard*, an Alberta court had jurisdiction simpliciter under Alberta law. According to the traditional approach to recognition, however, the basis on which it took jurisdiction would not be recognised

72 Ibid., at 140.

73 *Morguard*; *Amchem Products Inc.* v. *British Columbia (Workers' Compensation Board)*, [1993] 1 SCR 897; *Hunt* v. *T & N plc*, [1993] 4 SCR 289; *Tolfoson* v. *Jensen*, [1994] 3 SCR 1022.

by a British Columbia court for the purposes of enforcement, and the Alberta judgment would therefore not be enforceable against the defendant in *Morguard* who had moved to British Columbia and ignored the case against him. The British Columbia Court of Appeal rejected this approach, as did the Supreme Court of Canada, which held that so long as the court of one province had taken jurisdiction on the basis of a 'real and substantial connection' with the action, then its judgment should be recognised and be enforceable in another province.

Rather than reason directly from constitutional law, the Supreme Court began by setting out its view of the foundations of private international law as between states and then, in this light, determined that Canadian constitutional arrangements and practices were an even stronger reason to discard the existing rules on the recognition of judgments between provinces. Comity was central to the Court's reasoning because it identified the principle of comity, together with the principles of order and fairness, as underlying private international law between states. 'The considerations underlying the rules of comity', La Forest J wrote in a unanimous judgment, 'apply with much greater force between the units of a federal state'.[74] The nineteenth-century English rules that recognised narrower jurisdiction in foreign courts than English courts took themselves 'fly in the face of the obvious intention of the Constitution to create a single country' with a common citizenship that ensures mobility between provinces and a common market in which barriers to interprovincial trade are removed.[75] Moreover, the arrangement of the Canadian judicial structure addresses any real concerns about differential quality of justice among the provinces.[76] Whereas some federal constitutions, including Australia and the United States, have a 'full faith and credit' clause that requires mutual recognition of judgments across the federation, La Forest J did not go so far as to read in such a clause, noting that *Morguard* was not argued in constitutional terms.[77] For him, the integrating nature of the Canadian constitutional arrangements he identified made a 'full faith and credit' clause unnecessary. It was sufficient to conclude that 'the rules of comity or private international law as they apply between provinces must be shaped to conform to the federal structure of the Constitution'.[78] In subsequent

[74] *Morguard*, 1098.
[75] Ibid., 1099.
[76] Ibid., 1099–100.
[77] Ibid.,1100–101.
[78] Ibid., 1101.

constitutional cases, the Supreme Court anchored the 'real and substantial connection' solidly in constitutional law.[79]

Thus, it was the comparison with international comity that led La Forest J to assemble the pieces of the constitutional picture that, in turn, changed the rules on recognition of judgments between provinces. Nathan Hume observes that La Forest J repeated this international-to-constitutional interpretive strategy in his two other landmark private international law judgments of the early 1990s, even when purely interprovincial disputes were at issue, and Hume criticises the comparison for simplifying and distorting the relevant picture of the federation.[80] Similar to the provincial companies episode and the *Scott* episode, international comity disappears in the result because it is the contrast that does the work in the *Morguard* reasoning. International comity is a mirror held up to the Constitution that reveals something latent in the constitutional structure of the federation, as opposed to a model that is applied. Nevertheless, as Hume traces, the exercise of comparison has an influence on the constitution.

In contrast, in a recent Indigenous rights case, comity is a remainder of the historical relationship between nations in public international law, as opposed to acting as a mirror. The Supreme Court used the term 'comity' to capture the relationship of the Canadian Crown to Indigenous peoples in a case on the Crown's constitutional and legal duty to consult before an independent regulatory agency authorised a project that could impact Indigenous treaty rights. In discussing the significance of written reasons, the Court quoted from an Alberta trial court judgment that reasons are 'a sign of respect [which] displays the requisite comity and courtesy becoming the Crown as Sovereign toward a prior occupying nation'.[81] Here, comity was read into the constitutional duty to consult.

As will be relevant to the chapter's next snapshot of comity, *Morguard* is also significant for its analysis of the nature of international comity. La Forest J reasoned that whereas comity had been understood as based on formal respect for the dictates of other sovereigns, it also reflects the necessity of such a doctrine where legal authority is divided among states.[82] Comity is a principle that serves a purpose: 'the need in modern

[79] See *Hunt*, 324, 328.

[80] Nathan Hume, 'Four Flaws: Reflections on the Canadian Approach to Private International Law' (2006) 44 *Canadian Yearbook of International Law* 161, 208–09, 224–45.

[81] *Clyde River (Hamlet)* v. *Petroleum Geo-Services Inc.*, [2017] 1 SCR 1069, 1092 (quoting *Kainaiwa/Blood Tribe* v. *Alberta (Energy)*, 2017 ABQB 107, para. 117 (CanLII)).

[82] *Morguard*, 1096.

times to facilitate the flow of wealth, skills and people across state lines in a fair and orderly manner'.[83] In an earlier judgment re-interpreting territorial jurisdiction in criminal law, La Forest J wrote of states: 'we are all our brother's keepers'.[84] In *Morguard*, this vision of interdependence also underpins international comity. 'Modern states, however, cannot live in splendid isolation', La Forest J maintained in rejecting the rules on recognition of judgments adopted from England.[85] It follows that comity is dynamic and changes over time – indeed, it must be decolonised:

> the content of comity must be adjusted in the light of a changing world order. The approach adopted by the English courts in the 19th century may well have seemed suitable . . . at a time when it was predominantly Englishmen who carried on enterprises in far away lands [and] there was an exaggerated concern about the quality of justice that might be meted out to British residents abroad . . .[86]

On the one hand, international comity in *Morguard* does important framing work: it aligns private international law with public international law, internationalism and a view of the field as deciding conflicts of jurisdiction between sovereigns, as opposed to aligning it with, for example, private law, national interests and/or the individual as the unit of analysis.[87] As Roxana Banu argues, there are strong echoes of the comity of nations theory which reached its zenith in late nineteenth century continental private international law scholarship.[88] On the other hand, the relationship between comity, order and fairness fluctuates in subsequent cases,[89] and comity may matter less as a principle than as a locus. Already in *Morguard*, La Forest J stated 'I do not think it much matters whether one calls these rules of comity or simply relies directly on the reasons of justice, necessity and convenience'.[90] In keeping with

[83] Ibid.

[84] *Libman* v. *The Queen*, [1985] 2 SCR 178, 214. See also *United States of America* v. *Cotroni*, [1989] 1 SCR 1469, 1486 (La Forest J) (extradition law); *R* v. *Finta*, [1994] 1 SCR 701, 772 (La Forest J, dissenting) (jurisdiction over war crimes).

[85] *Morguard*, 1095.

[86] Ibid., 1097–98.

[87] See Roxana Banu, 'Assuming Regulatory Authority for Transnational Torts: An Interstate Affair? A Historical Perspective on the Canadian Private International Law Tort Rules' (2013) 31 *Windsor Yearbook of Access to Justice* 197 (discussing *Tolofson*, which built on *Morguard*).

[88] Ibid. (discussing *Tolofson*).

[89] See Hume, 'Four Flaws', 188–200.

[90] *Morguard*, 1098. See also *Hunt*, 325.

comity as a locus, the Supreme Court has also adjusted what some critics considered its naive internationalism and over-emphasis on relations between states.[91] The Court wrote in a 2006 case: 'Comity is a balancing exercise . . . [it] concerns not only respect for a foreign nation's acts, international duty and convenience, but also the protection of a nation's citizens and domestic values.'[92]

Comity seems to assume a firmer shape in contemporaneous public law cases, notably in the area of extradition, which is governed mainly by bilateral treaty and interlocking domestic legislation. A 1991 Supreme Court of Canada judgment identified comity, reciprocity and respect for differences in other jurisdictions as the principles governing extradition law,[93] and these principles continue to be cited by the Court.[94] The Supreme Court does not dwell on the nature of comity in extradition cases or relate it to comity in private international law or other contexts. Rather, comity here implicitly takes on meaning relative to its companion principles of reciprocity and respect for difference, being perhaps more solidaristic than the tit-for-tat relations of reciprocity. As in *Morguard*, these principles serve a purpose. In recent constitutional cases involving extradition, the Court has stated that in addition to fulfilling Canada's treaty obligations, they achieve the pressing and substantial domestic objectives of protecting the public against crime, bringing fugitives to justice and ensuring that international borders do not impede the rule of law. These broad purposes of extradition, according to the Court, must be carefully balanced with the rights and interests of persons sought for extradition,[95] from which it follows that there is a difference with comity in private international law. In extradition cases, comity is part of a balancing exercise, rather than itself being a balancing exercise. This presumably also means that the meaning of comity in extradition law is solely about interstate relations and less fluid than in private international law.

V International Comity and the Reach of the Constitution

The final snapshot of comity involves the reach of constitutional rights. In *R v. Hape*, the 2007 case that served as the point of departure for this

[91] See Banu, 'Assuming Regulatory Authority for Transnational Torts'; Hume, 'Four Flaws', 219; Wai, 'In the Name of the International'.
[92] *Pro Swing Inc.* v. *Elta Golf Inc.*, [2006] 2 SCR 612, 631, 637.
[93] *Kindler* v. *Canada (Minister of Justice)*, [1991] 2 SCR 779, 844.
[94] See, e.g., *India* v. *Badesha*, [2017] 2 SCR 127, 141.
[95] See, e.g., *India*, 141-42; *M.M.* v. *United States of America*, [2015] 3 SCR 973, 993.

chapter, the issue was whether the Charter of Rights and Freedoms applied to searches and seizures conducted by police officers abroad. The Supreme Court of Canada could have interpreted the Charter provision on its scope of application relative to the Constitution alone, considering the ordinary meaning of the words, purpose of the provision, context, drafters' intentions and so on.[96] Instead, it relied on principles of public international law, supported by the principle of comity, to conclude that the Charter could not apply extraterritorially.

Whereas international law has been the target of most commentary on *Hape*, the analysis offered here continues the chapter's 'private history' by focusing on comity. It suggests first that although not presented as such, comity as a choice of law methodology might account for what appears convoluted, if not outright contradictory, to public lawyers about *Hape's* approach to extraterritoriality. Then again, the value of private history is also to show where private sources and analogies run out. The analysis of *Hape* in this section suggests, second, that despite presenting a unified meaning of comity, LeBel J's majority judgment in *Hape* implicitly adds to Canadian constitutional interpretation, and Canadian law more broadly, a generalised 'foreign relations' comity in potential tension with comity in private international law.

In *Hape*, LeBel J crafted an approach to the extraterritoriality of the Charter from principles of customary international law that is radically different from – and categorically narrower than – precedent and unfamiliar from other international and domestic jurisdictions.[97] The lower courts relied on the precedent of *R* v. *Cook*, a Supreme Court of Canada judgment on the extraterritorial application of the constitutional right to counsel.[98] In *Cook*, the majority held that the Charter applied unless it created an objectionable extraterritorial effect – what might be called a 'Charter unless' approach to its extraterritorial application. While the foreign state had territorial jurisdiction, Canadian officers could exercise concurrent jurisdiction on the international law basis of nationality so

[96] Compare *R* v. *Cook*, [1998] 2 SCR 597, 642 (L'Heureux-Dubé J, dissenting):

> [T]he question of when the *Charter* applies is not properly determined by looking to the intricacies of extraterritoriality in international law, nor can ordinary principles of statutory interpretation be used ... What is at issue, instead, is the interpretation of the Constitution ...

[97] See Attaran, 'Have Charter, Will Travel?' 545.

[98] *Cook*. The principle of comity is not applied in *Cook*. See ibid., 616–27 (Cory and Iacobucci JJ).

long as it did not interfere, on the facts, with the jurisdiction of the foreign state.

LeBel J concluded that *Cook* was wrong in finding overlapping jurisdiction. Canadian police officers abroad are exercising jurisdiction to enforce Canadian law, whereas the analysis in *Cook* was based on prescriptive jurisdiction.[99] Because enforcement jurisdiction is narrower and strictly territorial, the Charter could not apply outside Canada according to international law. But the Charter also did not prevent Canadian government officials from acting extraterritorially, thereby producing what were referred to earlier as 'Charter-free zones'.[100] However, in addition to the possibility that a foreign state might consent to the application of the Charter,[101] LeBel J left open the possibility that the participation of Canadian officers in investigations in another country that violate Canada's international human rights obligations might justify a Charter remedy.[102] He also stressed that Charter protections could affect the admissibility of evidence obtained abroad in a Canadian trial.[103]

Commentary on *Hape* tends to concentrate on the public international law dimensions of the reasoning: the relationship between public international law and Canadian law as well as the understanding of jurisdiction.[104] In using customary international law to interpret the Charter, the Supreme Court finally explicitly endorsed the adoptionist doctrine that prohibitive rules of international custom are part of the common law without any need for legislative implementation.[105] In addition, the Court extended the presumption of conformity with international law from a principle of statutory interpretation to the interpretation of the Charter.[106] Yet the Court's equivalent statement about comity has gone virtually unremarked: 'Where our laws – statutory and

[99] *Hape*, 340–41.

[100] See Roach, '*R v. Hape* Creates Charter-Free Zones for Canadian Officials Abroad'.

[101] *Hape*, 351–52.

[102] Ibid., 349–50.

[103] Ibid., 352–55.

[104] Commentary on *Hape* has argued that the case 'might better have been treated as one of concurrent prescriptive jurisdiction, subjecting the Canadian agents to both Turks and Caicos law and Canadian law – including the Charter'. Verdier, Case Comment, 147.

[105] *Hape*, 316.

[106] Ibid., 324. But see *Health Services and Support – Facilities Subsector Bargaining Assn.* v. *British Columbia* [2007] 2 SCR 391, 412, 433–34, 438 (released the day after *Hape* and not applying its presumption of conformity). See also Currie, 'Weaving a Tangled Web', 84–85.

constitutional – could have an impact on the sovereignty of other states, the principle of comity will bear on their interpretation.'[107]

In *Hape*, comity supports the principles of international law that prevent the extraterritorial application of the Charter: in LeBel J's words, 'comity reinforces sovereign equality and contributes to the functioning of the international legal system'.[108] Comity in this coordinating mode must yield where it would undermine 'peaceable interstate relations and the international order'.[109] However, as Kerry Sun emphasises, comity is more than a supporting reason. Citing the two faces of comity, he argues that it is actually the linchpin of the judgment because comity also promotes international cooperation beyond that required by international law.[110] To quote LeBel J again, 'the principle of comity encourages states to co-operate with one another in the investigation of transborder crimes even where no treaty legally compels them to do so'.[111] Comity here means that a state requesting legal assistance in criminal matters from another state must respect the way in which the other state decides to provide assistance within its territory. In this cooperative mode, comity must yield where it would be inconsistent with international law and fundamental human rights.[112]

We thus have in *Hape* what might be called a 'comity unless' approach to the extraterritorial application of the Charter, as opposed to *Cook's* 'Charter unless' approach. This approach becomes clearer in *Canada (Prime Minister)* v. *Khadr*, a subsequent Supreme Court of Canada case in which a unanimous Court applied the international human rights exception suggested in *Hape*.[113] *Khadr* concerned a Canadian citizen taken prisoner in Afghanistan and detained by the US military at Guantánamo Bay. Canadian intelligence agents had questioned him on matters connected to murder and other terrorism-related charges that were pending against him and had shared the results of these interviews with US authorities. The US Supreme Court had already ruled that the Guantánamo detainees had illegally been denied access to habeas corpus and that the procedures for their prosecution violated the Geneva Conventions. The Supreme Court of Canada concluded that the US

[107] *Hape*, 320.
[108] Ibid., 322
[109] Ibid.
[110] Sun, 'International Comity and the Construction of the *Charter's* Limits'.
[111] *Hape*, 322. See also ibid., 348.
[112] Ibid., 322.
[113] *Canada (Justice)* v. *Khadr*, [2008] 2 SCR 125.

holdings were sufficient to trigger the *Hape* exception[114] and, applying the Charter, that Canadian participation in the Guantánamo Bay process violated the constitutional right to life, liberty and security of the person.

The 'comity unless' approach seen in *Khadr* has been criticised as convoluted or opaque in a number of respects. Describing *Hape* as a 'tangled web' and *Khadr* as 'tortured' reasoning, public international lawyer John Currie argues that the Supreme Court failed to explain '*how* or *why* Canada's participation abroad, in a process that is inconsistent with its international legal obligations, leads to the applicability of the *Charter* to that participation'.[115] He unpacks these questions into a series of questions left unaddressed by the Court, of which I will take up two.

A key passage in *Hape* states:

> The permissive rule that allows Canadian officers to participate even when there is no obligation to do so derives from *the principle of comity*; the rule that foreign law governs derives from *the principles of sovereign equality and non-intervention*. But the principle of comity may give way where the participation of Canadian officers in investigative activities sanctioned by foreign law would place Canada in violation of its international obligations in respect of human rights.[116]

Currie argues that by assigning the permissive rule to comity, which is non-binding, this passage makes it seem obvious that the permissive rule allowing participation must give way to Canada's binding obligations in international human rights law. But, Currie observes, comity in *Hape* merely provides additional support for conclusions reached on the basis of binding international law. It follows that an explanation, or even an acknowledgement, is needed for why the international law forbidding the extraterritorial application of the Charter must yield to other international law.[117] Second, 'even assuming that violations of some of Canada's international legal obligations oust the constraining effects of other obligations that would otherwise exclude the *Charter*'s application abroad, why does it necessarily follow that the *Charter* in fact applies abroad?'[118]

Currie illustrates that it is possible to address these concerns in terms of public international law and its relationship to the Constitution. International law has hierarchies of norms and other ways of resolving

114 Ibid., 129, 134–36.
115 Currie, 'Weaving a Tangled Web'; Currie, '*Khadr's* Twist on *Hape*', 324.
116 *Hape,* 349 (emphasis added).
117 Currie, '*Khadr's* Twist on *Hape*', 326.
118 Ibid.

conflicts between its norms. It follows that any conflict could be worked out by international law, and the result read into the Charter in accordance with the presumption of conformity with international law. Alternatively, LeBel J's pervasive references to comity may be a clue that he saw no inconsistency to be addressed. A typical choice of law rule in Canadian private international law is *lex loci delicti*: in the case of a tort with connections to multiple jurisdictions, the governing law is the law of the place where the tort occurred. *Lex loci delicti*, like all choice of law rules, is subject to a general public policy exception. Thus, if *lex loci delicti* points to foreign law, a court will not apply that law if it violates the forum's fundamental notions of justice and morality. In that case, the court will apply its own law instead. For some private international law authors, comity is about the possibility that a state would ever choose to apply the law of another (illustrated by the *lex loci delicti* rule). For others, it is about the possibility that it retains to not apply that law (the public policy exception).

The passage from *Hape* quoted above presents a sort of choice of law rule: the law of the place governs unless X (in which case apply the Charter). As a public international lawyer, Currie pursues the idea that public international law generates the entire rule 'the law of the place governs unless X' where X is international human rights law, and that this rule is read into the Charter. The rule and the exception interrelate in the sphere of international law. Alternatively, the parallel with choice of law suggests that the rule and the exception occupy separate spheres: public international law generates the rule 'the law of the place governs', while X is akin to the general public policy exception or the discretion that a state retains even with respect to international law. International human rights law is not the exception; rather it populates the domestic sphere of exception.

This choice of law parallel also sheds some light on Currie's second question: why the Charter could end up applying even though LeBel J began by finding its extraterritorial application to be impossible under the international law of jurisdiction. This is not to say that the parallel is a normatively satisfying answer, but that its sensibility may explain why the question was not acknowledged – about which Currie also wonders.[119] In choice of law, the application of forum law (by analogy

[119] According to Horatia Muir Watt, this transposability from private to public is typical of unilateralist private international law methodology, which prospers in common law settings, as opposed to the alternative methodologies she describes as multilateralist (advancing a 'grand plan' based on universalisable criteria and exemplified by EU private

here, the Charter) may represent a run-of-the-mill pragmatic solution or, more bluntly, an acceptable analytical failure. If the foreign law is ruled out through the public policy exception and the forum law therefore applies, the forum will often be the jurisdiction with the second closest connection to the facts of the case. But a common law court does not ask this question; it does not inquire whether the forum has a closer connection than some third jurisdiction such that its laws should apply. Instead, the court simply applies its own law. Similarly, it will apply its own law if the applicable foreign law has not been pleaded or its content has not been established. To maintain the choice of law logic in the case of failure of proof, the application of the forum law was traditionally explained by the presumption that the foreign law was identical, but the Supreme Court of Canada, in a Québec civil law case, recently discarded this presumption in favour of the practical need to clarify the legal norm that applies to the dispute before the court.[120]

The second point to be made about the value of private history in appreciating the role of comity in *Hape* concerns the limits of private sources and analogies. On the one hand, Kerry Sun demonstrates continuities between the Supreme Court of Canada's underlying vision of the world order in *Hape*, a foreign relations case, and the vision introduced in the *Morguard* line of private international law cases.[121] On the other, private history equips us to be sceptical about *Hape's* integrated account of comity. Prior to *Hape*, the Supreme Court's analysis of comity in areas of law involving public international law or foreign relations was usually confined to the area in question. Unlike in its private international law jurisprudence, the Court did not elaborate on comity as a general concept. Furthermore, foreign relations cases did not tend to cite private international law cases on comity.[122] In contrast, the *Hape* majority presents an overarching view of comity with different fields of law serving

international law) and neoliberal (based on the principle of party autonomy). Horatia Muir Watt, 'Theorizing Private International Law', in Anne Orford and Florian Hoffmann (eds.), *The Oxford Handbook of the Theory of International Law* (Oxford: Oxford University Press, 2016), 862, 871, 874, 877.

For an argument that analogies with private international law can normatively as well as conceptually illuminate issues in fundamental rights cases with a foreign element, see Jacco Bomhoff, 'The Reach of Rights' (Summer 2008) 71 *Law and Contemporary Problems* 39.

120 *Barer* v. *Knight Brothers LLC*, 2019 SCC 13, at para. 76 (Gascon J, majority judgment).

121 Sun, 'International Comity and the Construction of the *Charter's* Limits'.

122 There is some cross-citation in private international law cases on comity. See, e.g., *Morguard*, 1095; *Pro Swing Inc.*, 642.

as citations and illustrations. *Morguard* is cited alongside *The Parlement Belge*.[123] Whereas *Morguard* is the landmark private international law judgment on comity, Sir Hersch Lauterpacht dates English references to comity in public international law cases to the 1880 *The Parlement Belge* – and deplores such references as misleading where the norms are, in fact, binding as international law.[124]

It might be thought that Lauterpacht would have had no cause for concern in *Hape*: International law principles of sovereign equality and non-intervention govern, and comity plays an explicitly reinforcing role. Subsequent developments, however, demonstrate that *Hape* has introduced free-floating foreign relations comity into argument, and that foreign relations comity can detract from international human rights law – and therefore the application of the Charter. Despite being presented as synthetic, LeBel J's account of comity implicitly adds to Canadian case law a notion of 'foreign relations' comity at large. Tracing cross-cultural developments, Horatia Muir Watt differentiates foreign relations comity from the private international law tradition of comity as follows:

> unilateralist [private international law] methodology usually calls for a balancing or mediating principle. The doctrine of 'comity' plays this role. Historically, comity provided an explanatory principle grounded not in deference but in enlightened cooperation, for considering the laws of other sovereigns (with a view to reciprocity). By contrast, however, it is used today to justify non-intervention. In this respect, it can appear as a form of protectionism to the extent that it is a decision *not* to discipline national champions which might otherwise be subject to regulation. Thus, disputes over the demands of comity are at the heart of contemporary debates about the social responsibility or conduct regulation of multinational private actors.[125]

Because the 'comity unless' structure elaborated in *Hape* and *Khadr* involves determining whether Canadian officials are participating in a foreign process that violates international human rights law, the potential to offend the other sovereign – that is, foreign relations comity – can be a reason that courts should refrain from such determinations. This concern is not raised in *Hape*, but *Khadr* can be read as acknowledging it. In *Khadr*, the Supreme Court appeared to rely on the US Supreme Court's holdings both to determine that the conditions under which

[123] *Hape*, 320.
[124] Hersch Lauterpacht, 'Allegiance, Diplomatic Protection and Criminal Jurisdiction Over Aliens' (1947) 9 Cambridge Law Journal 330, 330–31.
[125] Muir Watt, 'Theorizing Private International Law', 870.

Khadr was held and was liable for prosecution were illegal under international law (thereby triggering the *Hape* exception and the application of the Charter) and to avoid disrespect to the United States. The following statement in *Khadr* seemed to have the latter in mind: 'Issues may arise about whether it is appropriate for a Canadian court to pronounce on the legality of the process at Guantanamo Bay under which Mr. Khadr was held', but they need not be resolved in this case because the US Supreme Court has found the process illegal.[126]

Foreign relations comity could thus seriously narrow the international human rights exception and thereby the extraterritorial application of the Charter. In addition, it can feed back into private international law in the way that Muir Watt describes. In a tort case currently before the Supreme Court of Canada,[127] Eritrean refugees allege that a Canadian corporation developing a gold, copper and zinc mine in Eritrea engaged the Eritrean military and Eritrean military-controlled corporations and was complicit in the use of forced labour at the mine, conscripted under Eritrea's National Service Program. The corporation argues that *Khadr* demonstrates the existence of the 'act of state' doctrine in Canadian law and that this doctrine precludes a Canadian court from judging the legality of the sovereign acts of a foreign state within its own territory. In support, the corporation points to the fact that the UK Supreme Court has referred to *Khadr* as an act of state case.[128] The fact that the doctrine has never been applied in Canadian law enables the corporation to argue for a strong form that absent a prior finding by a foreign or international court with jurisdiction, such as by the US Supreme Court in *Khadr*, a Canadian court should not undertake the task of applying international law to the acts of a foreign state, including because it would violate comity.[129] In opposition, one of the interveners argues that the Supreme Court of

[126] *Khadr*, 134. See Sun, 'International Comity and the Construction of the *Charter*'s Limits'.

[127] *Araya* v. *Nevsun Resources Ltd*, argued before the Supreme Court of Canada in January 2019 www.scc-csc.ca/case-dossier/info/dock-re.g.i-eng.aspx?cas=37919, accessed 2 August 2019.

[128] Factum of the Appellant Nevsun Resources Ltd, SCC File Number 37919, at para. 42, www.scc-csc.ca/WebDocuments-DocumentsWeb/37919/FM010_Appellant_Nevsun_Resources_Ltd.pdf, accessed 2 August 2019.

[129] Ibid., para. 53. The appellant also argues that it would violate international law, but in the United Kingdom and the United States, where the act of state doctrine has long been applied, the courts have made clear that the doctrine is not required by international law. See, e.g., *Belhaj* v. *Straw*, [2017] UKSC 3, para. 200 (Lord Sumption); Curtis A. Bradley, *International Law in the U.S. Legal System* 2nd ed. (Oxford: Oxford University Press, 2015), 10–13.

Canada should not establish the act of state doctrine, but instead reason directly from, inter alia, the overarching principle of comity.[130] Cited in support is the Court's private international law jurisprudence describing comity as 'flexible'.[131]

These pleadings show that *Hape's* integrated account of comity does not hold. By encompassing foreign relations comity at large, it opens the door to the establishment of foreign relations doctrines such as act of state. And by citing *Morguard* in its account of comity, *Hape* invites litigants to use private international law thinking about comity as a way to resist foreign relations reasoning. In *Hape*, comity lines up cleanly with the interstate principles of sovereign equality and non-intervention in public international law. This is particularly so because there can be no concurrent jurisdiction between the territorial state (Turks and Caicos) and the foreign state whose government agents are operating in that territory (Canada), and any application of the Canadian Constitution therefore amounts to intervention. There is none of the ability to narrow the conflict to particular subissues or to the particular facts as is typical of private international law discourse and of the *Cook* 'Charter unless' approach, which asked whether an objectionable extraterritorial effect was actually, as opposed to formally, created. In *Hape*, considerations such as convenience or protection of individuals are treated as external to comity.[132] Campbell McLachlin argues that *Hape* misunderstands the doctrine of jurisdiction in international law (which LeBel J presented as supported by comity) as existing for the benefit of other states, whereas it also exists to benefit individuals.[133] Comity in private international law is more flexible and more capacious.

Differences can be overdrawn, of course. For instance, both the *Morguard* line of cases and *Hape* have been criticised for their legalistic internationalism.[134] In his separate opinion in *Hape*, Binnie J disagreed with the rigidity of the majority judgment because it took insufficient account of the heterogeneous post-9/11 world order and the wide range

130 Factum of the Intervener, International Human Rights Program, University of Toronto Faculty of Law, SCC File Number 37919, at paras. 19–22, www.scc-csc.ca/WebDocuments-DocumentsWeb/37919/FM030_Intervener_International-Human-Rights-Program-University-of-Toronto-Faculty-of-Law.pdf, accessed 2 August 2019 (citing cases on comity in both public and private law).

131 Ibid., para. 20.

132 *Hape*, 341–42.

133 Campbell McLachlan, *Foreign Relations Law* (Cambridge: Cambridge University Press, 2014), 316.

134 See Hume, 'Four Flaws', 219; Wai, 'In the Name of the International'.

of global contexts in which Canada was already acting.[135] The examples of comity that LeBel J gave feature extradition and mutual legal assistance,[136] but extradition treaties and mutual legal assistance treaties pre-approve the states to which Canada shows comity. In originally setting out comity, reciprocity and respect for differences in other jurisdictions as the principles on which extradition is based, the Supreme Court of Canada wrote: 'we require a limited but not absolute degree of similarity between our laws and those of the reciprocating state'.[137] In principle, at least, the dynamic conception of comity set out in *Morguard* can adapt to address the sorts of concerns that Binnie J raised. Since *Morguard*, the Supreme Court of Canada has continued to take this view of comity with respect to private international law, reiterating in 2015 that 'the doctrine of comity (to which the principles of order and fairness attach) "must be permitted to evolve concomitantly with international business relations, cross-border transactions, as well as mobility"'.[138]

In the US context, where foreign relations comity is well developed, Donald Childress argues that US courts using the doctrine of international comity in non-private international law cases ignore its historical position as a private international law doctrine and ought instead to resituate comity within this tradition. For Childress, the wrong turn taken by the courts was to turn comity into a doctrine of deference to foreign sovereigns as opposed to a doctrine designed to ameliorate conflict between sovereigns through attention to the specific sovereign interests at stake in a case.[139] His solution is particular to the US private international law tradition, in which comity was long ago abandoned as a theory of the field, but the role of sovereign interests in comity was revived in modern form as governmental interest analysis.[140] It is also specific to the US concern with the separation of powers. Nonetheless,

[135] *Hape*, 386–87.

[136] Ibid., 320–22.

[137] *Kindler*, 845 (McLachlin J). Relatedly, see Gal-Or, '*R. v. Hape*: International Law Before the Supreme Court' (noting that the *Hape* majority's section on 'The Globalization of Criminal Activities and the Need for International Cooperation' disregards the increasing number of treaties concerning international cooperation in criminal matters).

[138] *Chevron Corp.* v. *Yaiguaje*, [2015] 3 SCR 69, 115 (quoting *Beals* v. *Saldanha*, [2003] 3 SCR 416, 436). There is also some precedent for such an approach outside private international law. See *Libman*, 197–98, 214 (a case of criminal jurisdiction in which La Forest J referred to 'the realism that must prevail in approaching the notion of comity nowadays' and considered the respective interests of the two states involved).

[139] Donald Earl Childress III, 'Comity as Conflict: Resituating International Comity as Conflict of Laws' (2010) 44 *University of California, Davis Law Review* 11, 34.

[140] Ibid., 45–46.

Childress's argument illustrates the potential of the private international law tradition of comity to be mobilised against foreign relations comity.

VI Conclusion

The point of departure for this chapter was a surprising yet overlooked doorway – 'comity' as a principle of constitutional interpretation – opened by the Supreme Court of Canada in *Hape*. Where did this doorway come from? Perhaps the closest case to a precedent is *Daniels* v. *White*, which applied to a constitutional amendment the rule of construction that Parliament is not presumed to legislate 'in breach of a treaty or in any manner inconsistent with the comity of nations and the established rules of international law'; however that case did not deal with comity.[141] Moreover, as seen in this chapter, 'comity' in the presumption may have referred to the rules of private international law rather than comity as used in *Hape*. Alternatively, perhaps LeBel J generated comity as reinforcing or necessary to the interpretive presumption of conformity with international law.[142] As just discussed, this justification, too, would only go so far because comity does not neutrally support all of international law. Whatever the derivation of comity as a principle of Charter interpretation, we may have concerns about applying to the Constitution either a more formal foreign relations approach or a more flexible private international law approach to determining comity – indeed, about applying comity at all.[143]

As these puzzles confirm, the elegance of the monism/dualism debate has difficulty comprehending some of the curious passageways created by courts. But, as we saw, there is also something more systematic to be turned up by searching for comity's impact on the constitution. Scholars

141 *Daniels* v. *White*, [1968] SCR 517, 541 (Pigeon J). The presumption in *Daniels* is quoted by LeBel J in *Hape* and also cited previously by him as 'well-established' in *Society of Composers, Authors and Music Publishers of Canada*. However, neither reference is in the context of comity, and none of the additional citations that follow in *Hape* refers to comity. *Hape*, 323; *Society of Composers, Authors and Music Publishers of Canada* v. *Canadian Association of Internet Providers*, [2004] 2 SCR 427, 485.

142 See *Hape*, 322. Compare *Kazemi Estate v. Iran*, [2014] 3 SCR 176, 194 (LeBel J pairing comity with state sovereignty as underpinning state immunity); *Wakeling* v. *United States of America*, [2014] 3 SCR 549, 584 (Moldaver J, LeBel and Rothstein JJ concurring, pairing comity with state sovereignty as the foundation on which 'Canada pursues its objectives on the international stage').

143 Compare *Cook*, 677 (Bastarache J); Currie, 'Weaving a Tangled Web', 77–81 (problematising the parallel presumption of conformity with international law as applied to the Charter).

of global law are increasingly interested in private international law as a form of or analogy for global governance.[144] Historians of international law are increasingly investigating private law and private international law as a significant context and underpinning for public international law. By way of an experiment in the private history of the double-facing constitution, this chapter traced the role of 'comity', a concept originally associated with private international law, in the interpretation of the Canadian Constitution. As seen, the resulting narrative is better understood as a series of ghost stories than a continuous line of jurisprudence. Nonetheless, the cases showed that comity contributed to the legal working out of the state's internal form, the nature of external relations, the relationship between its subunits and the reach of its constitution. In each of these episodes, comity was a legal reminder that the state depends on other states and that its legal system exists in juridical relation to other legal systems. This recognition is not at the grand level of a new state in public international law or an enemy or ally in international relations, but points to a different layer of recognition and outlook as generative of the double-facing constitution.

[144] See, e.g., Horatia Muir Watt and Diego P. Fernández Arroyo (eds.), *Private International Law and Global Governance* (Oxford: Oxford University Press, 2014).

8

Constitutionalism and Mobility: Expulsion and Escape among Partial Constitutional Orders

JACCO BOMHOFF*

Introduction

If we are to imagine what a more encompassing contemporary constitutionalism could look like and what it might demand, then it could be tempting to start with some idea of 'the border'. Nation state borders, such thinking might go, mark the line from which constitutional commitments can be either projected inwards or outwards. And it is this latter, 'outward-facing', dimension, that has most often been ignored in the past, and that is now most urgently in need of appraisal and re-invigoration. Such an approach is especially tempting because the urgency it invokes is real. It is precisely in zones in some way 'beyond' the border, or 'outside' the state's jurisdiction – the spheres of 'extraterritoriality' and 'foreign relations', of 'aliens' and immigration, or of 'transnational contexts' – that constitutional commitments have often been most feebly felt and most haphazardly enforced. '*[E]ven in the sphere of foreign affairs*', Justice Kennedy of the US Supreme Court wrote in his concurrence in the 2017 Travel Ban case, '[i]t is an urgent necessity that officials adhere to ... constitutional guarantees ... *so that freedom extends outwards,* and lasts'.[1] This rousing admonition, however, did nothing to stop the US government from implementing a measure with regard to foreigners abroad that was far removed from anything the US Constitution would have permitted with regard to citizens at home. Surely, then, *this* is where a more robust form of 'outward-facing' constitutionalism could have most purchase, and so, surely again, this is where reflection on the meaning of a 'double-facing constitution' should start.

* I am very grateful to Karen Knop, Emmanuel Voyiakis, David Dyzenhaus, and Tom Poole for their comments on earlier drafts. The usual disclaimer applies

[1] *Trump* v. *Hawaii* 585 US ___ (2018) 138 S. Ct. 2392 (Kennedy, J, concurring) (slip op, at 2).

Well, I want to suggest in this chapter, yes, and no. The first main argument offered here is that this temptation – to start from state borders, and to move swiftly outwards, into discussions of jurisdiction, foreign affairs law, immigration, or extraterritoriality – should be resisted, at least in part, for two main reasons. The first of these has to do with the constructed character of any border or other constitutionally relevant boundary. Whether any individual, any governmental action, or any rights claim comes 'within' or remains 'outside' the reach of any particular constitutional order, is always itself a legally mediated question. The first task for a re-invigorated 'outward-facing' constitutionalism will have to be to scrutinise precisely these processes of demarcation, and thus the very constitution of the boundaries of the polity. 'Extraterritoriality', for example, can be shorthand for an outcome in constitutional law; for a determination that someone or something lies outside constitutional coverage. It cannot, without more, serve as an input for such a conclusion.[2] This argument has been made before, notably in the fields of immigration law and conflict of laws, some of which this chapter surveys, or in discussions of Internet governance. It is, however, only beginning to be made a central element of more general reflections on what might be called 'constitutional exteriority'.[3]

Borders, in other words, cannot be taken as given. They also cannot, without more, be taken *as special*. The second reason for why reflection on outward-facing constitutionalism should not focus solely on borders is that many of the social and economic dynamics, governmental techniques, and individual experiences commonly associated with state borders, have important equivalents and parallels deep inside the territories of modern nation states. This is true in a number of different ways. The policing of state borders, first of all, is sometimes redesigned so as to effectively take place within states' territories.[4] But beyond border policing in even this broader sense, local regulations, such as restrictive

[2] See, e.g., Joanne Scott, 'Extraterritoriality and Territorial Extension in EU Law' (2014) 62 *American Journal of Comparative Law* 87; Hannah L. Buxbaum, 'Territory, Territoriality, and the Resolution of Jurisdictional Conflict' (2009) 57 *American Journal of Comparative Law* 631. See further Sections I and II.

[3] The terms of 'legal' and 'constitutional exteriority' have recently also been invoked by Raza Saeed, with special attention to colonial and tribal contexts. See Raza Saeed, 'Contested Legalities, (De)Coloniality and the State: Understanding the Socio-Legal Tapestry of Pakistan', unpublished PhD thesis, University of Warwick, School of Law (2014).

[4] See Ayelet Shachar, 'The Shifting Border of Immigration Regulation' (2009) 30 *Michigan Journal of International Law* 809; Kate Huddleston, 'Border Checkpoints and Substantive Due Process: Abortion Rights in the Border Zone' (2016) 125 *Yale Law Journal* 1744.

zoning ordinances, can also produce exclusionary effects that are functionally similar to immigration restrictions. And there is one still more general and more fundamental point. As Kunal Parker has written, with regard to US constitutional history: 'Designation as foreign is not a function of coming from the territorial outside. It is a political strategy that has been used inside *and* outside the country and to multiple ends'.[5] If this is true, and if the aim is to grow the reach of constitutionalism, specifically by way of the further development of its 'outward-facing' dimension, then it seems that this dimension itself may have to be made to reach further *inwards* – back into the polity, as it were – than an exclusive focus on borders and on the outer limits of jurisdiction would allow. In short: the first main argument of this chapter, to be developed in Sections I, II and III below, is that preoccupation with the question of whether people or events come within, or fall outside of, constitutionally salient boundaries, cannot offer a solid foundation on which to elaborate a more consciously 'outward-facing' form of constitutionalism.

This chapter's second main argument, set out in Section III, is that we should replace this concern with what lies 'inside' or 'outside' of constructed boundaries, with a more immediate focus on instances of *mobility*. Mobility – alongside, crucially, its denial – figures at the heart of many highly visible contemporary conflicts that require more intense engagement from within constitutionalist thought. From travel bans to 'frictionless trade', one recurrent contemporary theme is the stark contrast between virtually unrestrained possibilities of 'escape' for wealthy individuals and corporate actors – what we might broadly call the 'hypermobility' of capital – on the one hand, and individuals stuck in 'peripheries', or even at risk of 'expulsion' – from cities and countries, neighbourhoods and livelihoods – on the other.[6] In all such cases, it is mobility, both within and across bounded territories, as well as enforced immobility, that in fact contribute to the production and reproduction of socially, politically and economically – and thus constitutionally – salient space itself.[7] 'Mobility', as a recent newspaper report on the French yellow-vests protests put it, 'is the story of globalization and its inequities.

[5] Kunal M. Parker, *Making Foreigners: Immigration and Citizenship Law in America, 1600–200* (Cambridge: Cambridge University Press, 2015), ix.

[6] Saskia Sassen, *Expulsions: Brutality and Complexity in the Global Economy* (Cambridge, MA: Belknap Press, 2014).

[7] See on this idea more generally, Philip E. Steinberg, 'Sovereignty, Territory, and the Mapping of Mobility: A View from the Outside' (2009) 99(3) *Annals of the Association of American Geographers* 467.

Mobility means more than trains, planes and automobiles, after all. It also includes social and economic mobility – being too poor to afford a car, being rich enough to transfer money out of the country'.[8]

But if social scientists and journalists have begun to explore these themes of expulsion and escape, and of physical and constructed, literal and metaphorical mobility together, constitutional theory has not kept up.[9] The idea of 'exit', for example, figures prominently as a guarantor of freedom in traditions of liberal, republican and libertarian thought.[10] But it is not clear that classical, liberal constitutionalism has the resources to readily address, say, runaway transnational corporate autonomy. One important reason for this, I would argue, is that we lack an appropriate conceptual and normative vocabulary in which to conduct this kind of reflection. We do not have a constitutional discourse that is able to encompass not just the individuals of immigration law, but also the corporations of tax law or commercial arbitration; not just mobility across borders, but also within countries; and not just denials of entry, or enforced immobility, but also opportunities for exit, all together, within one frame. We also mostly lack a robust historical awareness. We miss a historical perspective that could remind us of how, in the United States for example, domestic migration was made free only fairly recently, and of how out-of-state corporations were still regularly 'ousted' from doing business in target jurisdictions, as recently as a century ago.[11]

Notable partial exceptions to this fragmented landscape do of course exist. Kunal Parker, who was cited earlier, has investigated parallels and symmetries among a wide range of different 'ways of rendering foreign' across four centuries of American history. And Timothy Zick has brought together a variety of territorial restrictions or denials of individual liberties under the heading of 'constitutional displacement'. Neither

[8] Michael Kimmelman, 'France's Yellow Vests Reveal a Crisis of Mobility in All Its Forms' *The New York Times*, A4, 21 December 2018 (citing the work of French geographer Christophe Guilluy).

[9] For an early social-theoretical and ethnographical analysis of different forms of movement and immobility (legal and illegal, physical and constructed) across the fields of international migration, inter-country adoption, and global finance, see Susan Bibler Coutin, Bill Maurer, Barbara Yngvesson, 'In the Mirror: The Legitimation Work of Globalization' (2002) 27(4) *Law & Social Inquiry* 801.

[10] See notably Robert S. Taylor, *Exit Left: Markets and Mobility in Republican Thought* (Oxford: Oxford University Press, 2017); Chandran Kukathas, *The Liberal Archipelago: A Theory of Diversity and Freedom* (Oxford: Oxford University Press, 2003), on Locke's 'freedom of exit'; Michael Otsuka, *Libertarianism without Inequality* (New York: Oxford University Press, 2003), on the importance of 'costless exit'.

[11] See further Section IV.

of these projects includes corporations, however. Robert Wai has usefully coined the terms of 'lift-off' and 'juridical touchdown' to describe transnational corporate activity, but then his study does not look at individuals, or at mobility within jurisdictions.[12] Mostly, then, mobility is not seen as one broad, unifying concern in constitutional thought. And where it is, its theorisation and regulation are often displaced upwards, towards federal or international levels.[13] But that vantage point one-up, as it were, tends to come with its own imperatives of 'liberalisation', and its rejection of most local impediments to mobility as suspect 'balkanisation' or 'parochialism'. But just as exclamations of 'extraterritoriality' cannot settle issues of constitutional reach, neither can simple denunciations of 'parochialism'. Nor, I would argue, the mere invocation of an unanchored, cosmopolitan notion of 'freedom' or 'autonomy'.

What is missing, therefore, turns out to be something fairly specific. We lack a constitutionalist vocabulary that can institute more encompassing aspirations while remaining conscious of its own inevitably incomplete, partial character.[14] A constitutionalism that is simultaneously local – relative to other possible scales of legal or constitutional ordering – and outward-facing; one that does not take the illusory certainty of determinations of 'inside' or 'outside' for granted, but that speaks rather to governmental control over mobility across any constitutionally salient boundary; and that does so with regard to both individuals and corporate actors. Such a constitutionalism would indeed be 'double-facing' in that it would demand and sustain ongoing deliberation over whether the commitments that make up the polity's core are being lived-up to at its margins, wherever these may be found. It is to the elaboration of the outward-facing dimension of such a form of constitutional thought that this chapter seeks to make a contribution.

The chapter proceeds as follows. Sections I, II, and III develop the first argument set out above. Section I first introduces the theme of constitutional exteriority and then turns to the centrality of the domestic/foreign distinction in liberal thought. Sections II and III then seek to undermine

[12] Parker, *Making Foreigners*; Timothy Zick, 'Constitutional Displacement' (2009) 86 *Washington University Law Review* 515; Robert Wai, 'Transnational Liftoff and Juridical Touchdown: The Regulatory Function of Private International Law in an Era of Globalization' (2001–2002) 40 *Columbia Journal of Transnational Law* 209.

[13] See, e.g., the literature on European Union citizenship, or the recent Symposium on 'Framing Global Migration Law' (2018) 111 *American Journal of International Law Unbound*.

[14] See further Section I.

this distinction. Section II first develops a critique the artificiality of determining 'presence' and 'foreignness' in law, while also revealing the continued importance of precisely these techniques in current jurisprudence. Section III.A questions the naturalness of our principal received constitutional boundary: the border of the territorial state, while Section III.B interrogates the emergence and effects of new constitutionally salient boundaries. Section IV then moves to the second argument set out above, suggesting a focus on 'mobility' as an – incomplete – answer to the critique of the inside/outside distinction developed earlier. This section, finally, offers up a provisional grid of ways in which constitutionalism and mobility can intersect, looking at 'access' and 'exit', of both individuals and corporate actors.

I Discovering Constitutional Exteriority

Constitutional law and theory, it seems, *should* be able to say something of value about the 'outside' of constitutional orders. No such order, after all, finds itself alone in this world. 'When individuals bind together to form a political community . . . they also create a collective agent that holds an inevitable relationality with *other* collective agents.'[15] Even just as a conceptual matter, then, constitutionalism would seem to have to address these relations. But there is also a strong case that, as the type of normativity that both institutes and limits the autonomy of political communities, constitutionalism *ought* to be concerned also with the project of generating responsibilities in these autonomies themselves, towards other communities as well as towards individual outsiders.[16] And to make matters more complicated still, some of these outsiders – resident aliens, notably – stake their claims on constitutional orders well within these orders' own territories. For, as Robert Meister reminds us, 'self-governing citizens have never exhausted the cast of characters who populate liberal states'.[17]

The classic questions in relation to constitutional exteriority are those concerned with the constitutional order's territorial reach, with admission to and exclusion from the polity, and with the status and rights of aliens once admitted. Typically not addressed in written constitutional

[15] Douglas A. Kysar, 'Global Environmental Constitutionalism: Getting There from Here' (2012) 1 *Transnational Environmental Law* 83, 90–91.

[16] Gunther Teubner, *Constitutional Fragments* (Oxford: Oxford University Press, 2012), 3.

[17] Robert Meister, 'Sojourners and Survivors: Two Logics of Constitutional Protection' (1996) 3 *University of Chicago Roundtable* 121, 121.

documents, these questions were also, in the past, largely ignored in constitutional legal scholarship. In a path-breaking 1985 article, Louis Henkin could still refer to these three topics as 'several small related subjects which have been largely neglected' in US constitutional scholarship.[18] That characterisation, though, certainly no longer holds true. In the decades since Henkin wrote, legal scholars have engaged with precisely these questions ever more intensively, prompted in particular by post–Cold War trade liberalisation, by restrictive turns in the immigration policies of many Western countries beginning in the mid-1990s, and by the 'war on terror' since the early 2000s.[19] And so, while it is certainly true that 'the domain of . . . constitutionalism has *always* been contested', in the USA as well as elsewhere,[20] it does seem clear that interest in how constitutionalism might speak to what happens beyond the boundaries of legal and constitutional orders has intensified more recently.[21]

Animating this growing interest appears to be increased recognition of the idea that a constitutionalism that does not address the exteriors of constitutional orders is, in an important sense, radically incomplete. A constitutionalism that does not offer normative resources to scrutinise, say, projections of military power abroad, or denials of membership at home, is increasingly seen as *partial* – in a way analogous to how earlier generations of scholars came to see a constitutionalism that did not

18 Louis Henkin 'The Constitution as Compact and as Conscience: Individual Rights abroad and at Our Gates' (1985) 27 *William & Mary Law Review* 11, 11. As a general note: Most of the examples in this chapter will be taken from US constitutional law. The arguments developed, however, do seek a broader application.

19 See, e.g., Saskia Sassen, *Losing Control: Sovereignty in the Age of Globalization* (New York: Columbia University Press, 1996); Gerald Neuman, *Strangers to the Constitution* (Princeton, NJ: Princeton University Press, 1996). For overviews, see, e.g., Kal Raustiala, 'The Geography of Justice' (2005) 73 *Fordham Law Review* 2501; Daniel Kanstroom, 'Alien Litigation as Polity-Participation: The Positive Power of a Voteless Class of Litigants' (2012) 21 *William & Mary Bill of Rights Journal* 399.

20 Neuman, *Strangers to the Constitution*, 3 (emphasis added).

21 See in particular the contributions to the Symposium on 'The External Dimensions of Constitutions', convened by Eyal Benvenisti and Mila Versteeg (2018 *Virginia Journal of International Law* Symposium); Daniel S. Margolies, Umut Özsu, Maïa Pal, and Ntina Tzouvala (eds.), *The Extraterritoriality of Law: History, Theory, Politics* (London: Routledge, 2019); Ran Hirschl and Ayelet Shachar 'Spatial Statism' (2019) 17(2) *International Journal of Constitutional Law* 387–438; Chimène I. Keitner, 'Rights Beyond Borders' (2011) 36 *Yale Journal of International Law* 55; Galia Rivlin, 'Constitutions Beyond Borders: The Overlooked Practical Aspects of the Extraterritorial Question' (2012) 30 *Boston University International Law Journal* 135.

address (domestic) abuses of private power as partial.[22] The discourse of 'constitutional black holes' and 'constitution-free zones' is a good examples of this development. The 'black hole' metaphor is by no means new to constitutional jurisprudence. American scholars had for some decades been using this expression, as well as that of 'constitution-free zones', from time to time, to refer to sites of perceived gaps in constitutional coverage that were entirely domestic – such as labour relations or criminal trials – and often in some sense 'private' – such as family relations and schools.[23] With the advent of the 'war on terror' and the turn to 'black sites' and the prison at Guantanamo, the 'black hole' and 'free zone' metaphors were seamlessly, and with increased power, transferred to 'extra-territorial' sites of public-law lawlessness.[24]

Addressing these newly apparent gaps in constitutional coverage is proving difficult, though. One important reason for this is that liberal constitutional orders are partial also in a second sense. Constitutionalist discourse, even when often profoundly aspirational in terms of its substance, is commonly biased towards the status quo in terms of its formal reach – notably towards current distributions of membership, and towards existing zones of responsibility.[25] Both forms of partiality are reflected and embodied in the inside/outside – domestic/foreign – distinction in public law. This dichotomy is central to the modern liberal way of ordering the world.[26] Giving voice to the contrasting commitments towards insiders and outsiders that lie at the heart of liberal thought, Michael Walzer has famously argued that '[n]eighborhoods

[22] I borrow this vocabulary from Cass R. Sunstein, *The Partial Constitution* (Cambridge, MA: Harvard University Press, 1993), which deals extensively with the public/private distinction. From the perspective of international relations, and in descriptive terms: while any ordering effect stemming from domestic state constitutions could only ever be partial, any global ordering itself is also only partially realised. See notably Robert A. Keohane, *Power and Governance in a Partially Globalized World* (London: Routledge, 2002).

[23] For a well-known example from employment law, see James Gray Pope, 'Labor and the Constitution: From Abolition to Deindustrialization' (1987) 65 *Texas Law Review* 1071, 1074–76.

[24] See, e.g., Michel Rosenfeld, 'Judicial Balancing in Times of Stress: Comparing the American, British, and Israeli Approaches to the War on Terror' (2006) 27 *Cardozo Law Review* 2079.

[25] Neil Walker calls this 'demarcation constitutionalism'. See Neil Walker, 'Sovereignty and beyond: The Double Edge of External Constitutionalism' (2018) 57 *Virginia Journal of International Law* 799.

[26] See, e.g., Michael Walzer, *Spheres of Justice: A Defense of Pluralism and Equality* (New York: Basic Books, 1986); Linda Bosniak, 'Being Here: Ethical Territoriality and the Rights of Immigrants' (2007) 8(2) *Theoretical Inquiries in Law* 389; Meister 'Sojourners and Survivors', 121.

can be open only if countries are at least potentially closed'.[27] For Walzer, as Linda Bosniak has commented, '[b]oundedness governs at the community's edges, while inclusiveness prevails within'. And these 'dual commitments', crucially, are not seen as contradictory.[28] The inside/outside distinction, then, almost exclusively in its guise of the domestic/foreign demarcation, is foundational to liberal thought, and with it to liberal constitutionalism. The question, though, is whether it can hold.

In his well-known history of the 'stages of decline' of the public/private distinction, Duncan Kennedy sums up the telltale signs indicating that a particular legal dichotomy is 'no longer a success'. 'Either people can't tell how to divide situations up between the two categories', he writes, 'or it no longer seems to make a difference on which side a situation falls'.[29] What, then, we might ask, would an assessment, of the contemporary state of the inside/outside distinction in constitutional legal thought and practice look like, applying Kennedy's criteria? How do constitutional legal orders attempt 'to divide situations up' between the two categories of 'inside' and 'outside'? Do such allocations still matter to the constitutional imagination, and what level of commitment do they garner when implemented in constitutional legal practice?

More concretely, Kennedy's analysis raises three broad types of question when transposed to the context of the domestic/foreign distinction: with regard to legal method, normative principle and societal implications. First, as to method, Kennedy prompts us to ask whether, and if so how, faith is maintained in the techniques of 'jurisdictional division' that sustain polities' contrasting commitments to insiders and foreigners.[30] Second, in terms of principle, the question is how a double-facing stance can avoid becoming *two-faced*, in the sense of normatively inconsistent and complacent? And third, empirically, we have to ask whether nation state borders, and other outer limits to state jurisdiction, are still the boundaries that matter, or whether their exclusionary effects are as likely

[27] Walzer, *Spheres of Justice* 38.

[28] Bosniak, 'Being Here', 395. See also Seyla Benhabib, *The Rights of Others: Aliens, Residents, and Citizens* (Cambridge: Cambridge University Press, 2004), 118–20.

[29] Duncan Kennedy, 'The Stages of Decline of the Public/Private Distinction' (1982) 130 *University of Pennsylvania Law Review* 1349, 1349. The public/private distinction, Kennedy argued, together with other binary oppositions such as those between state and society, and property and sovereignty – and, he allowed, 'maybe some more I'm not thinking of' – constituted 'the liberal way of thinking about the social world'; a way of thinking that, in his diagnosis at least, was in long-term decline.

[30] Cf. Bosniak, 'Being Here', 397.

to be dispersed or replicated elsewhere, possibly deep inside or even far outside the polity.

There are good reasons to be sceptical on these points. As Linda Bosniak explains in a passage worth quoting at length, the 'splitting strategy' of 'jurisdictional division' between inside and outside,

> is based on empirical premises about the possibility of maintaining separation between the community's inside and its edges that simply do not hold. . . . Exclusion functions also inside the territory . . . – the 'border' – conceived as regulatory sphere – follows the immigrant into the national geographic space and shapes her experience there. . . . The point, in short, is that the normative divide between the community's inside and its edges that the territorialists presume possible – that, indeed, is foundational to them – is *chimerical.*[31]

This sense of boundaries that are 'chimerical', but that still appear able to sustain a constitutional jurisprudence that is itself arguably 'schizophrenic',[32] poses a difficult dilemma for the elaboration of any form of 'outward-facing' constitutionalism. This is the problem of how to redirect attention in constitutional thought towards engagement with the 'outside' of constitutional orders, without at the same time subscribing to the substance and location of any particular inside/outside demarcation in current constitutional law. The challenge, in other words, of taking constitutional exteriority seriously, without at the same time accepting such exteriority at face value. This is the challenge that is taken up in the following sections.

II Being 'Here' and 'There'

This section addresses Kennedy's first sign of decline for pivotal distinctions in law: the sense that it is no longer possible to know 'how to divide situations up between the two categories'. Its aim is to demonstrate a striking tension between longstanding acknowledgment of the artificiality and circularity of determinations of 'here' or 'there' in legal theory, on the one hand, and continued uncritical reliance on precisely such determinations in practice.

The critique of the artificiality of judicial efforts to allocate cases to different localities and their legal orders goes back at least to the American Legal Realists, and in particular to the work of Walter

[31] Ibid. (emphasis added).

[32] Parker, *Making Foreigners*, 204.

Wheeler Cook. In his '*Logical and Legal Bases of the Conflict of Laws*', Cook, with evident relish, called out judges for their qualifications of litigants as '"*constructively*" absent' – or constructively present – within different relevant jurisdictions.[33] For example, when discussing court decisions on cross-border shootings, Cook pointed out that courts sometimes regarded shooters as – constructively – 'accompanying the [canon] ball, and as being represented by it, up to the point where it strikes', while at other times taking a diametrically opposing approach. Cook wrote he was 'tempted to add' that, apparently at least in some cases, shooters were deemed also to have 'constructively returned' to their home state, 'as soon as [they] had accomplished the purpose for which [they] constructively accompanied the bullet'.[34] In a similar vein, a few years later, another noted Legal Realist, Felix Cohen, used the question 'Where is a corporation?' – which he compared in usefulness to the scholastic question of 'How many angels can stand on the point of a needle?' – as his opening example of what he famously came to call 'transcendental nonsense' in the law.[35] These critiques then, are early gestures at the more general idea that what is deemed to be 'inside' or 'outside' of any particular legal order – the 'fact', we could say, misleadingly, of 'being here' – is always a matter of construction.

This idea has been developed much more fully in legal scholarship of the past two decades or so, some of it animated by advances in critical geography. Most of this development has taken place in immigration law studies, with Linda Bosniak, Ayelet Shachar, and Leti Volpp among the main authors. Volpp's work, for example, addresses the question of how space is 'legally imagined' in immigration law.[36] 'Being here', she insists, 'can mean many different things', and the legal doctrines determining whether a person is '*inside* particular territorial borders [or] standing *outside* at the gates', are 'complicated and paradoxical'.[37] Echoing Walter Wheeler Cook's writings, Volpp catalogues cases within US immigration law where, as she puts it, 'noncitizens who surely are in some sense "here" are met by government arguments that they in fact,

[33] Walter W. Cook, 'The Logical and Legal Bases of the Conflict of Laws' (1924) 33 *Yale Law Journal* 457, 463.

[34] Ibid.

[35] Felix S. Cohen, 'Transcendental Nonsense and the Functional Approach' (1935) 35 *Columbia Law Review* 809, 810–11.

[36] Leti Volpp, 'Imaginings of Space in Immigration Law' (2012) 9(3) *Law, Culture & the Humanities* 456, 456.

[37] Ibid., 456–57 (emphasis in original).

are not here'.[38] As a mirror image of this scenario, we could think of claims arising out of the conduct of military agents abroad as similarly situated in a twilight zone of quasi-presence and quasi-absence. When such foreign conduct is subjected to foreign law only, rather than also to the constitutional-legal constraints of the agents' home country, is this not akin to claiming that the agents involved were never truly 'there', in the place where they exercised force under colour of official authority – at least not 'there' as public officials, representing their home polity, and acting within limits set by its constitutional order?

In all these instances, it turns out, on reflection, that people – their lives, injuries, and grievances – are really only 'foreign' to a constitutional order when that order *makes* them so. This, it seems, has been clear, at least on some level, for decades. We know enough not to fall into 'the facile trap of fetishizing space, of allowing our sense of what we owe to neighbors and do not owe to strangers to turn on something as crude as "pure" physical presence or absence, which . . . is always politically and legally mediated'.[39]

And yet, this is precisely what happens regularly in judicial practice. The judicial determinations of 'inside' and 'outside', or 'here' and 'there', in the context of cross-border shootings, jurisdiction over foreign corporations, and divorce proceedings, that Cook and Cohen were concerned with, have their contemporary analogues in debates on the jurisdictional reach of constitutional rights protection. In these more recent constitutional cases, circularity and artificiality are still on full display. An analysis of US constitutional rights jurisprudence shows how labels like 'outside' and 'inside' – or 'extraterritorial' and 'domestic' – cannot be applied in any neutral or mechanistic way, principally because the localisation of any rights infringement that such a distinction requires itself already depends on a background notion of what it is the relevant right is meant to protect in the first place.[40] We can take the Fourth and Fifth Amendments to the US Constitution as examples. Only once it is already decided that a violation of the prohibition on unreasonable searches in the Fourth Amendment is 'fully accomplished' at the time of the actual search itself – regardless of whether any evidence found will be invoked in a subsequent trial – only then does a case involving a police search abroad become

[38] Ibid., 460 ('a noncitizen can be spatially here, but not doctrinally here'. See at 463, discussing the case of individuals 'paroled' into the United States).

[39] Parker, *Making Foreigners*, 16.

[40] This point is analogous to Cook's own famous critique of the circularity involved in the so-called 'vested rights' doctrine in choice of law.

a 'foreign' case, outside the scope of constitutional protection.[41] Conversely, it is only once it has already been decided that the Fifth Amendment's privilege against self-incrimination is a 'fundamental trial right' which 'applies' 'in American courtrooms', that a case involving testimony compelled abroad by foreign officials becomes, seemingly naturally, a 'domestic' case, squarely within the realm of local constitutional protection.[42] But then again, on that reading, a case involving *US* officials, compelling a *US* citizen, to testify against him or herself, in domestic proceedings, would become a 'foreign' case, if that testimony was only likely to be used in criminal proceedings abroad, brought by a foreign sovereign.[43] This, then, despite the fact that the Fifth Amendment refers to 'any person' and 'any criminal case' in setting out the privilege, and despite the fact that all relevant governmental conduct in such a case would occur within the territorial boundaries of the USA.[44] If, on the other hand, US courts were to read the privilege against self-incrimination as 'a rule of conduct generally to be followed by our Nation's officialdom' – as Justice Ginsburg did in her dissent in the case this discussion is based on – then any foreignness would dissipate, and the case would revert to being an ordinary, 'domestic' constitutional rights case.[45]

The artificiality of such wholesale designations of 'inside' our 'outside', in cases such as these, was on especially stark display in recent decisions involving, as did Cook's discussions a century earlier, cross-border shootings. In *Mesa* v. *Hernandez*, a US border patrol officer on the US side of the border shot and killed an unarmed Mexican teenage boy

[41] *United States* v. *Verdugo-Urquidez*, 494 US 259 (1990).
[42] *United States* v. *Allen*, No. 16–898 (2nd Cir. 2017).
[43] *United States* v. *Balsys*, 524 US 666 (1998).
[44] Note that the outcome would have been the same had Balsys been a US citizen. By way of context, as one critic of the decision pointed out at the time: 'until *Balsys*, no case had ever held that a US citizen or lawful resident alien would not be protected from otherwise unconstitutional governmental conduct within the fifty states'. See Daniel J. Steinbock, The Fifth Amendment at Home and Abroad: A Comment on *United States v. Balsys* (2000) 31 *University of Toledo Law Review* 209, 216.
[45] Justice Ginsburg, dissenting opinion in *Balsys*. These difficulties involved in allocating 'cases' and 'claims' to a domestic or a foreign sphere may also arise outside the rights context. Helmut Aust's chapter in this collection furnishes a nice example. The US Supreme Court was asked to review an executive decision with regard to a statute regarding the registration of 'Jerusalem, Israel' as place of birth in US official documents. Was this, as Chief Justice Roberts wrote, simply a case of a US citizen, in the USA, seeking vindication of a statutory right – 'a familiar judicial exercise' –, or was this rather a case arising ' in the field of foreign affairs', as Justice Breyer held in dissent? See the discussion of *Zivotofsky* in Helmut Aust, 'The Democratic Challenge to Foreign Relations Law in Comparative Perspective', Chapter 12 of this volume.

playing on the Mexican side.[46] Previous case law strongly suggested that, had the case involved a similar shooting entirely within the territory of the USA, a private right of action against the agent would have been available to his relatives. And yet, the majority found that the 'transnational context' and 'extraterritorial aspect' of this case cautioned against 'extending' such a remedy 'for injuries to foreign citizens on foreign soil'.[47] In fastening its gaze exclusively on the point of injury – a foreign citizen, on foreign soil – the majority was able to invent a 'transnational context' for this case, with all that such a mode of framing brings along: a presumption against extraterritorial extension of US law, fear of diplomatic incidents, etc. A case which, as the dissenters noted, 'simply involves a federal official engaged in his law enforcement duties acting on United States soil who shot and killed an unarmed fifteen-year-old boy standing a few feet away', is made foreign.[48] There is real pathos in the dissenters' invocation of *Marbury* v. *Madison*'s appeal to 'the very essence of civil liberty' as 'the right of every individual to claim the protection of the laws, whenever he receives an injury'.[49]

It is in cases like *Mesa*, that an outward-looking constitutionalism could have real bite, connecting commitments at a community's core to claims voiced at its outer edges. An outward-facing constitutionalism would recognise that there can be no prior stage of constitution-free determinations of 'jurisdiction' or 'reach'. It would demand a more disaggregated assessment of the different connections to the polity in any given case, and a more searching reflection on how such connections ought to, or ought not to, count. Such a perspective could be put into operation, for example, by way of a presumption in favour of constitutional coverage – even if such a presumption would be rebuttable, just as current presumptions *against* extraterritoriality are. Such an approach would have the benefit of demanding explicit engagement with the important underlying question of whether the constitutional community's 'vision of harmonious self-ordering could be made to be more inclusive' – even if it is accepted that the answer to that question will not always be a fully cosmopolitan 'yes'.[50] In any case, whatever approach is

[46] *Hernandez* v. *Mesa*, 885 F 3d 811 (3rd Cir. 2018).

[47] Ibid., at 817. See also at 823 (citing Judge Kavanaugh's discussion of the 'presumption against extraterritoriality' in *Meshal* v. *Higgenbotham*, 804 F 3d 417 (DC Cir. 2015), at 425–26, 430).

[48] Ibid., at 825 (dissenting opinion of Judge Prado).

[49] Ibid., at 832.

[50] Kysar, 'Global Environmental Constitutionalism', 90.

chosen in any given polity, what matters is recognition of the pretence involved in claiming that merely 'localizing' individuals and their claims can somehow, as a matter of legal logic, settle their status. That, any robust form of outward-facing constitutionalism, cannot allow.

III Boundaries That Matter

'Success' for a legal distinction, in Kennedy's scheme cited earlier, had two dimensions: it should not only be 'possible to make the distinction', that distinction must also 'make a difference'.[51] How does the inside/outside dichotomy in constitutional law fare on this second criterion? This section addresses this question by looking at how a double-facing constitutionalism can ensure scrutiny of those boundaries between insides and outsides that matter most today. This involves interrogating both *which* boundaries matter, and *how* they matter. The analysis, accordingly, proceeds in two steps. First, Subsection III.A interrogates the contingent and constructed character of what is by far the most prominent inside/outside boundary in modern constitutional law: the territorial border of the nation state. Subsection III.B then looks in more detail at changes in the character of state borders, and at the emergence of new constitutionally salient boundaries and cleavages – many of them crisscrossing the inner domains of states – and their effects. Section IV will then go to analyse these effects in terms of their impact on the mobility of individuals and corporations.

A *The Constitution of 'Domestic' and 'Foreign'*

A double-facing constitutionalism should scrutinise the constructed and contingent character of the vantage points from which determinations of inside and outside are made. This means, principally, interrogating the construction of the nation state border as *the* paradigmatically meaningful boundary for liberal polities. As geographers have noted, this involves questioning two powerful assumptions. First, the so-called 'territorial trap', 'wherein the inside of the territorial state is assumed to be a timeless fundamental sociopolitical entity'. And second, a view of 'the outside' as merely some 'residual space remaining after declaring the inside'. For, as Philip Steinberg observes, '[i]f that is the prevailing image

[51] Kennedy, 'The Stages of Decline of the Public/Private Distinction', 1349.

of the outside it is an image that is itself constructed in tandem with the construction of a particular image of the inside'.[52]

Opening up these images for scrutiny – of the constituted inside, the empty outside, and their radical separateness – can follow different tracks. Gerald Frug, for example, has developed a pioneering critique of the way liberal political thought has long devaluated the idea of 'real local power', by casting forms of regulation at infra-state levels as 'local selfishness and protectionism'.[53] In a way taken up only some years later by geographers, Frug's work called attention to the question of the 'missing scale' – those levels of government and those jurisdictions that do not exist, or exist only in enfeebled form, and whose absence has an impact on those levels that current legal or ideological frameworks do empower.[54] Other work challenges the radical separation of inside and outside in contemporary constitutional thought, by recovering lost connections. Such scholarship might point out, for example, that the model of federalism adopted for what was to become the interior of the United States was developed on the basis of contemporary understandings of relations between states in the law of nations.[55] At the same time, and in the opposite direction as it were, as David Golove and Daniel Hulsebosch have recently argued, 'the revolutionary generation conceptualized, drafted, and institutionalized their new constitutions not only for domestic constituencies but also for foreign audiences'. In this way, many of the Founders 'conceived of the Federal Constitution in particular as a promise to foreign nations'.[56] Domestic and foreign, then, were intertwined during the founding era in ways that look rather different from the strict modern liberal inside/outside distinction.

But the vision of an undifferentiated, homogenous interior, on which the contemporary character of the state's outer border depends, finds

52 Steinberg, 'Sovereignty, Territory, and the Mapping of Mobility', 472, 477.

53 Gerald E. Frug, 'The City as a Legal Concept' (1980) 93 *Harvard Law Review* 1057, 1066–67.

54 Dennis R. Judd, 'The Case of the Missing Scales: A Commentary on Cox' (1998) 17 *Political Geography* 29, 30, cited in Allan Erbsen, 'Constitutional Spaces' (2011) 95 *Minnesota Law Review* 1168, 1177.

55 Edwin D. Dickson, 'The Law of Nations as Part of the National Law of the United States' (1952) 101 *University of Pennsylvania Law Review* 26. See also Meister 'Sojourners and Survivors', 124.

56 See Daniel Hulsebosch, 'Being Seen Like a State: How Americans (And Britons) Built the Constitutional Infrastructure of a Developing Nation' (2018) 59 *William & Mary Law Review* 1239; David M. Golove and Daniel J. Hulsebosch, 'A Civilized Nation: The Early American Constitution, the Law of Nations, and the Pursuit of International Recognition' (2010) 85 *New York University Law Review* 932.

perhaps its strongest support in a constitutional ideal of unrestricted domestic mobility – even if such an ideal is only patchily realised in practice. This is so especially when such a vision is contrasted with the stringent regulation of migration across the nation state border. Interrogating the role of the citizen/foreigner distinction in immigration regulation, in other words, can also adopt the track of revisiting the foundations and history of internal migration, and with it the elaboration of a unified, national conception of citizenship. Developing this point requires a brief excursus.

If we take the USA as a case study, it is clear that *local* barriers to free movement were indeed both prevalent and significant, until really rather recently. Many of the most widely used local regimes for 'keeping people in their place' – some with histories going back to Elizabethan England – were only abolished in the period between the 1930s and the mid-1970s. Significantly, these earlier regimes, such as vagrancy statutes or Welfare Codes prohibiting the migration of indigent persons, typically did not distinguish between domestic and foreign migrants. With millions of mostly poor Americans on the move during the middle decades of the twentieth century, the US Supreme Court came to take tentative steps towards the recognition of a constitutional right to 'free movement', and provision for the indigent slowly became a federal concern.[57] As Elisa Minoff has noted, it was only over the course of this period, and in large part as a result of precisely these developments that *national* citizenship became, for the first time, the primary mode of identification for many Americans.[58] Strikingly, though, as Minoff also writes, 'the interest in internal migration during these years and its profound consequences for the formation of the American state and the evolution of thinking about rights and citizenship has been all but forgotten'.[59]

But if free domestic migration is a comparatively recent invention, so too is the construction of a powerful, centralised regime to control immigration from outside the country.[60] And just in the way that the foundations of free internal migration are today largely forgotten, there is also

[57] See Karen M. Tani, *States of Dependency: Welfare, Rights, and American Governance, 1935–1972* (Cambridge: Cambridge University Press, 2016); Parker, *Making Foreigners*; Elisa Alvarez Minoff, 'Free to Move? The Law and Politics of Internal Migration in Twentieth-Century America', unpublished Doctoral dissertation, Harvard University (2013). For a contemporary source, see, e.g., Leonard B. Boudin, 'The Constitutional Right to Travel' (1956) 56 *Columbia Law Review* 47.

[58] Minoff, 'Free to Move?', iv.

[59] Ibid., 7.

[60] Parker, *Making Foreigners*, 204ff.

today, in the words of one leading immigration law scholar, 'surprisingly little opposition to or discussion of the basics of the U.S. immigration system'.[61] This notably includes the most basic immigration law principle of all: the categorical demarcation of 'aliens' from insiders.[62] These twin trajectories of construction, neglect, and forgetting have produced the unique character of the domestic/foreign distinction in constitutional law. When the history of the vulnerability of 'insiders' is forgotten, and the present vulnerability of 'outsiders' is left unquestioned, what emerges is an understanding of the country's current external borders as constituting a natural boundary – one that has no specific history and does not require any special justification. It is this boundary that sets apart today's immigrant as 'the ultimate outsider' – 'a lonely legal subject . . . uniquely marked with a set of distinct legal and territorial disabilities that he or she once shared with many insiders'.[63]

B *From the Border, to the Edge*

One key challenge for a double-facing constitutionalism, then, is to encourage reflection on how the processes of constitution and exclusion, of government and neglect, have come to be associated almost exclusively with the outer boundaries of the nation state – with its borders and with the furthest reaches of its jurisdiction more generally (Section III.A, above). Another task, as was seen earlier, is to interrogate the juridical techniques by which these processes are put in operation (Section II, above). What remains to be discussed is one further challenge: to demand vigilance in the face of the emergence of new boundaries, and to changes in the character of familiar ones. Today's immigrants may well be 'ultimate outsiders' in many ways. But if governmental strategies and individual experiences of exclusion are being replicated within our polities, then, a genuinely double-facing constitutionalism must stand ready.

There are indeed signs of changes afoot in the character and location of the boundaries that matter. As the anthropologists Jean and John

[61] T. Alexander Aleinikoff, 'Towards a Global System of Human Mobility: Three Thoughts' (2017) 111 *American Journal of International Law Unbound* 24, 24.

[62] See, e.g., Bosniak, 'Being Here', 399 (on the common rejection as 'utopian' of open-border arguments). For important recent reflections on the philosophical foundations of migration regulation, see the contributions to Sarah Fine and Lea Ypi (eds.), *Migration in Political Theory: The Ethics of Movement and Membership* (Oxford: Oxford University Press, 2016); and in particular, on the role of the basic insider/outsider distinction, the contribution by Sarah Fine on 'Immigration and Discrimination' in the same volume.

[63] Parker, *Making Foreigners*, 11.

Comaroff note, 'the lines that count nowadays seem less and less coterminous with geopolitical boundaries'.[64] This is true in at least two ways. First, national borders themselves increasingly exhibit the paradoxical character of being 'simultaneously open *and* closed': 'permeable to business from the outside ... yet closed to aliens', embodying in this way 'the contradiction between globalised *laissez-faire* and national priorities, protections, and proprieties'.[65] As another collective of anthropologists has detailed, these contradictory jurisdictional regimes actively facilitate some types of 'border crossings' – such as notably those of international finance, but also those involved in inter-country adoptions, for example – while others are made difficult, rendered suspect, or are criminalised.[66] At the same time, though, 'internal frontiers *within* countries tend increasingly to reinforce racial and ethnic cleavages, seeking to secure the "homeland" by dividing citizens from outsiders wherever they might be'.[67] Racial profiling, mass incarceration, and a wide range of other forms of spatial and economic exclusion, combine to create a '*de facto* border' that 'crisscrosses the country'.[68] Taken together, these changes amount to the rise of a new 'archetype': of the state as 'citadel', and of borders as 'elusive lines to be drawn and redrawn within the polity and beyond'.[69]

These emerging parallels, between outer boundaries and inner cleavages, border patrols and prisons, aliens and marginalised citizens, have recently been given a distinctive sociological frame by Saskia Sassen. Like Comaroff and Comaroff, Sassen goes back to the 1980s to locate the roots of what she calls the emergence of 'new logics of expulsion'.[70] This term indicates societal dynamics – made up of much more than just governmental action – by which people are expelled from societies or economies. These dynamics operate not just, or not even principally, at national borders, but are rather the manifestation of 'global trends inside countries'.[71] Logics of expulsion take hold at '*the systemic edge*' of whatever system is in play – 'economic, social,

64 Jean Comaroff and John L. Comaroff, *Theory from the South: Or, How Euro-America Is Evolving toward Africa* (London: Routledge, 2012), 28, 104.
65 Ibid., 27.
66 Bibler Coutin, Maurer and Yngvesson, 'In the Mirror', 801.
67 Comaroff and Comaroff, *Theory From the South,* 104.
68 Ibid., 104, 106.
69 Ibid., 107.
70 Sassen, *Expulsions*, 1.
71 Ibid., 7.

biospheric', and can as easily lie inside a country as at its outer borders.[72] As Sassen emphasises, the systemic edge 'is foundationally different from the geographic border in the interstate system'.[73]

In addition, then, to identifying the emergence of domestic boundaries that are equivalent, in functions and impact, to state borders, these accounts by social scientists make two further important contributions. They point to the importance of including corporations, and private law instruments more generally, in any discussion of borders and jurisdiction; and they suggest that alongside 'exclusion', some forms of 'escape' will also have to be counted among the constitutionally salient effects of legal boundaries. These two points are closely related. Many corporations, Sassen writes, 'have sought to free themselves from constraints, including those of local public interests'. They have made use in particular of 'global freedoms of movement' and of 'private contractual arrangements that can bypass state regulations *lawfully*, so to speak'.[74] This is, of course, the same observation Felix Cohen made back in 1935, when he remarked on 'the practice of modern corporations in choosing their sovereigns'.[75] If corporations and their assets are free to move, however, it should not be forgotten that it is state law that gives capital its mobility.[76]

But even if it is state practices that 'render people and property mobile' – just as it is state practices that make people foreign, as seen earlier – the resultant threat of escape changes the character of the boundaries around our polities. As Comaroff and Comaroff write, many states today 'act as if they were constantly subject *both* to invasion from outside *and* to the seeping away of what, like offshore commerce, jobs, and human capital, ought properly to remain within'.[77] Sassen brings these themes together under an overarching heading of extreme inequality in a passage worth quoting in full:

> Inequality, if it keeps growing, can at some point be more accurately described as a type of expulsion. For those at the bottom, or in the poor middle, this means expulsion from a life space; among those at the top,

[72] Ibid., 211. Note: Such 'edges' need not, strictly speaking be spatial in character, but the discussion here will be limited to those that operate at least to some extent in spatial terms.
[73] Ibid.
[74] Ibid., 213, 23.
[75] Cohen, 'Transcendental Nonsense and the Functional Approach', 810.
[76] Bibler Coutin, Maurer and Yngvesson, 'In the Mirror', 809.
[77] Comaroff and Comaroff, *Theory from the South*, 98 (emphasis added).

> this appears to have meant exiting from the responsibilities of membership in society via self-removal . . . .[78]

These, I would argue, are precisely the tendencies contemporary constitutionalism must concern itself with to remain relevant. This is where the newest and most urgent gaps in constitutional coverage are to be found. And so this is where thinking about a double-facing constitutionalism could be most productive. As our foremost public vocabulary for expressing collective aspirations and responsibilities, constitutionalism has to be able to speak to themes such as expulsion and escape; to 'hypermobility' for capital, and 'stagnant' mobility for individuals;[79] and to the ever-growing chasm between our 'global cities', our 'peripheries', and our deserts. When returning foreign fighters have their citizenship revoked; when homeless individuals are expelled from city parks; or when registered sex offenders are excluded from so many neighbourhoods that no place remains for them to live, it does make at least intuitive sense to cast all these governmental practices and individuals' experiences of them as 'banishment'.[80] If that intuition points to a plausible case that these and other phenomena of expulsion and of escape are indeed connected – that there could indeed be meaningful connections between how a diesel tax affects the 'mobility' of poorer citizens, and a wealth tax the 'mobility' of the rich – then there is a challenge for constitutional theory to answer. This is not to say that constitutionalism ought to necessarily conceive of, say, prisoners and aliens in equal terms, or treat 'social' and 'physical' mobility as raising the exact same difficulties in each case. But, and this is the main point: an appropriately outward-focused constitutionalism will at least make it harder to lazily assume any categorical difference.

IV Constitutional Mobility: Varieties of Expulsion and Escape

Over the course of the twentieth century, liberal constitutionalism has had to come to terms – however haltingly and incompletely – with

[78] Sassen, *Expulsions*, 15.

[79] Ibid., 25 (on 'hypermobility').

[80] Katherine Beckett and Steven Kelly Herbert, *Banished: The New Social Control in Urban America* (Oxford: Oxford University Press, 2010); Audrey Macklin and Rainer Bauböck, 'The Return of Banishment: Do the New Denationalisation Policies Weaken Citizenship?,' Robert Schuman Centre for Advanced Studies, EUI Discussion Paper 2015/14; *Galvan* v. *Press*, 347 US 522, 530 (1954) (on deportation as akin to 'banishment or exile').

private spheres previously thought of as akin to a foreign country. Today's 'new constitutional question' requires renewed engagement with another range of zones that are again 'foreign' to constitutional orders, this time in a more literal sense.[81] A 'double-facing' constitutionalism can do this. But, as the previous sections have sought to demonstrate, efforts to rethink constitutionalism's reach go wrong if they start from the nation state border and simply seek to project constitutionalist ideals and responsibilities outwards. A 'double-facing' constitutionalism *does* need to do that, but its aspirations should run much deeper.

A more encompassing, 'double-facing', constitutionalism cannot start from the state border, but must scrutinise how boundaries, of any kind, are legally and politically constructed in the first place. It cannot take 'extraterritoriality' or 'transnational contexts' as given, but has to interrogate how individuals and their claims come to be relegated to constitutional exteriors to begin with. It has to ask how people and places are 'made foreign', and whether in doing so, the constitutional order is being true, at its peripheries, to the commitments that make up its core. If constitutional orders are necessarily and often justifiably partial, then a 'double-facing' constitutionalism must take this partiality as its starting point. If experiences of expulsion and banishment turn out to show so many similarities across different societal scales – from local zoning measures to national laws revoking citizenship – then a 'double-facing' constitutionalism has to at least encourage reflection on whether these phenomena should not also be placed in the same constitutionalist frame.[82] If transnationally organised spheres of private – corporate – activity are expanding ever more deeply into the interiors of nation states, severely restricting the ability of local polities to assert themselves, then a 'double-facing' constitutionalism could aim to check these 'expansionist tendencies' and the 'centrifugal dynamics of subsystems in global society'.[83]

This, of course, remains all rather abstract. But I do want to suggest that a first challenge for thinking about the outside of constitutional orders has to be to confront the sheer range of forms of constitutional exteriority – of forms of 'foreignness' either actively pursued or tolerated by governments or private actors, and variously experienced by a diverse

[81] Cf. Gunther Teubner, *Constitutional Fragments: Societal Constitutionalism and Globalization* (Oxford: Oxford University Press, 2012), 1.

[82] On this topic, see notably Peter J. Spiro, 'Expatriating Terrorists' (2014) 82 *Fordham Law Review* 2180; and Leti Volpp, 'Citizenship Undone' (2007) 75 *Fordham Law Review* 2580.

[83] Teubner, *Constitutional Fragments*, 4.

cast of constitutionally marginalised individuals.[84] Cataloguing ways of 'rendering foreign', therefore, has to be useful in itself. And so, the very breadth of the examples given before is partly the point. It may well be that, on further reflection, there are good reasons for treating nation state borders as special, at least in some circumstances and for some purposes. To some degree, 'banishing' registered sex offenders from parks, and 'banishing' returning ISIS fighters from their states of origin, really can be very different things. Immigration control with regard to aliens and the regulation of 'extraterritorial' government action will always be areas of special concern to any form of outward-facing constitutionalism. But the cases and literature surveyed above offer sufficient indications to suggest that if the aim is to make our constitutional thinking more inclusive, much work remains to be done both abroad *and* at home, both at the level of transnational activity *and* in local settings.

But if a first task for this chapter was to expand the potential range for what should become a more encompassing constitutionalism, then what remains to be carried out is the opposite move of finding some narrower starting point to make this project more concrete. This is what this final section will try to do, by suggesting an approach that focuses, not on finding the – illusory – answer to the question of whether natural or legal persons 'are' within or outside the reach of any particular constitutional domain, but rather engages directly with these persons' *mobility* across constituted boundaries. The relevant parameters for such an approach, as developed over the preceding sections, are as follows. The aim is to develop a vocabulary and conceptual tools for an outward-facing constitutionalism (1) that can operate not just at state borders but at any relevant boundary or 'edge' where individuals risk expulsion or collectives risk undermining through escape; (2) that looks to the edges of constitutional domains that are partial, both in the sense that they are incomplete and in the sense that they – to an extent justifiably – attach value to membership and other forms of counting as insider; (3) that is able to interrogate in particular how these domains have come to be constituted, and with what sorts of exclusionary or centrifugal effects; (4) and that is able to take in not just individuals but also corporate actors and the mobility of capital. Finally, in order to avoid again hypostatising these boundaries simply via a different route, the focus of this approach should be, not on the 'fact' of moving from

84 These individual experiences deserve much fuller consideration, in particular by way of ethnographic fieldwork, than is possible here.

A to B, but on the combination of governmental measures – aimed at forcing, allowing, or restricting mobility – and on individual experiences of mobility – in the form of expulsion, as escape, or through the denial of freedom to move.[85] This combined focus on governmental strategy (to keep out, to keep in place, to allow to leave) and individual experience (being kept at bay, being kept in place, being allowed to leave) should allow us to distinguish 'the mechanisms' through which the various forms of a status of 'in' or 'out' are shaped, from that status itself.[86]

Engaging with governmental measures and individual experiences centred on mobility could bring a number of benefits. It could help create an initial sense of what types of cases may have to be thought of together, as part of the same frame of reference, in the development of an outward-facing constitutionalism. It could also help introduce a much-needed historical awareness. One thing that is especially striking about some of the governmental strategies to be discussed in the provisional typology below, is how certain types of measures to control mobility were, at one time, absolutely dominant, often to the point of normality, but then disappeared astonishingly quickly. This becomes very clear if we look at how some of the relevant vocabulary has disappeared from practice; think of terms such as 'locomotion', 'ingress' and 'egress', 'ouster', and banishment'. Such a historical overview, however, can also reveal how some of these measures, thought to have been banned for good, were sometimes swiftly reintroduced, using different legal techniques, but with very similar impact on individual experiences.[87] Finally, elaborating a grid of measures and experiences of mobility forces us to face up squarely to the manifold and stark ways in which the law treats natural persons and corporations differently. This was not always the case. An outward-facing constitutionalism concerned with the mobility of all sorts of

[85] As Bibler Coutin, Maurer and Yngvesson, 'In the Mirror', demonstrate, in addition to facilitating or hindering movement, state laws can make movement appear as non-movement.

[86] Saskia Sassen, 'The Repositioning of Citizenship and Alienage: Emergent Subjects and Spaces for Politics' (2005) 2 *Globalizations* 79, 81, cited in: Kanstroom, 'Alien Litigation as Polity-Participation' at 407.

[87] See, e.g., Beckett and Herbert, *Banished* (detailing the hybrid public-private law character of local regulations in Seattle); Harry Simon, 'Towns without Pity: A Constitutional and Historical Analysis of Official Efforts to Drive Homeless Persons from American Cities' (1991–1992) 66 *Tulsa Law Review* 631, 634 (US Supreme Court decisions 'changed the form, but not the substance, of official efforts to control the homeless').

actors and in all sorts of forms can help address this gulf, by allowing us to imagine and recover an 'immigration law for corporations' or 'frictionless movement for people'.

Here, then, is what a provisional grid of instances of constitutional mobility could look like.

A *Natural Persons – Access*

The paradigm cases of governmental measures limiting access for natural persons, of course, are immigration and citizenship laws. *Within* contemporary liberal polities, on the other hand, it is much more difficult to think of legal limits on individual movement. Such limits do exist, but it is also certainly true that they were much more prevalent in the past. Prime examples from historical and current practice include local zoning regulations and private limitations on housing – so called 'restrictive covenants' – and a wide range of local government ordinances that could broadly be called 'anti-vagrancy' measures.[88]

If we think of these together, as all concerned with inward individual mobility, the following points emerge. First, as discussed in earlier Section III.A, the radical distinction between internal migrants and foreign immigrants is a historically contingent phenomenon, and a creation in particular of the era since the Great Depression. Second, these nominally very different types of restraints show a revealing symmetry in their relationship to constitutional sources. Critics have commented on a profound '*incoherence* in the relationship of immigration law to the Constitution'.[89] In the absence of any foundations for a federal power to control immigration, this power has been found to simply 'inhere' in the scheme of the US Constitution – an approach that has resulted in extensive authority and minimal judicial oversight. At the same time though, even within the domestic sphere, the US Supreme Court has never been able to agree on a clear and coherent foundation for a domestic 'right of free movement'. Instead, such a 'right of locomotion' was found to be 'a right so elementary [that it] was conceived from the beginning to be a necessary concomitant of the stronger Union the

[88] On the prominence – until very recently – of this latter category, see Risa Goluboff, *Vagrant Nation: Police Power, Constitutional Change, and the Making of the 1960s* (Oxford: Oxford University Press, 2016).

[89] Jennifer Gordon, 'Immigration as Commerce: A New Look at the Federal Immigration Power and the Constitution' (2018) 93 *Indiana Law Journal* 653, 656 (emphasis added).

Constitution created'.[90] And in this area, as discussed above, many previously prevalent measures have since been held to fall foul of constitutional constraints. One closely related striking further parallel is that when courts have intervened, in either area, they have often done so on more procedural 'rule of law' grounds, such as the excessive 'vagueness' of the relevant legislation, rather than on any substantive justification specific to human mobility and its limitation by governments.[91]

In both areas, then – of the 'plenary power' over immigration, and the 'inherent' right of locomotion – the best argument courts have been able to muster is a kind of purported obviousness: Of course countries must be able to control their borders; of course, domestically, individual mobility should be free.[92] The divergence between the two regimes of domestic and cross-border movement really came about only once such purportedly obvious arguments – such as the designation of paupers as a 'moral pestilence', and the conception of barriers to their entry as part of a 'sacred right of self-defence' – were held to no longer apply in the domestic context.[93] The upshot of these symmetries and divergences, however, remains troubling. Not only is governmental power over immigration radically under-determined by constitutional standards, but also internal mobility of citizens, residents and others, is itself not as securely protected constitutionally as it should be. And so, local governmental strategies to keep people out that once seemed definitively beyond the constitutional pale, are able to resurface again, in different formal guises, but with the same harsh effects.[94] In conclusion, and to reiterate once more: The argument of this subsection is not that domestic migration and immigration are entirely equivalent, from a constitutionalist standpoint, and that citizens and foreigners ought to be treated the same way in all cases. Whether and when that is so will have to depend on the

[90] *Shapiro* v. *Thompson*, 394 US 618, 630–31 (1969), quoting *United States* v. *Guest*, 383 US 745, 758 (1966). See further Simon, 'Towns without Pity'.

[91] See, e.g., Gordon, 'Immigration as Commerce', 655 (on the role of 'vagueness' in immigration jurisprudence); *Papachristou* v. *City of Jacksonville*, 405 US 156 (1972) ('vagueness' and vagrancy laws). For extensive discussion of this line of attack on vagrancy regulations, see Goluboff, *Vagrant Nation*.

[92] See, e.g., *Saenz* v. *Roe*, 526 US 489, 498 (1999) (on the constitutional right to travel as 'a virtually unconditional personal right, guaranteed by the Constitution to us all').

[93] *Edwards* v. *California*, 314 US 160 (1941) (overruling *New York* v. *Miln*, 36 US 102 (1837)). Parallel tensions in European law – in part related to EU citizenship – have to remain outside the scope of this chapter.

[94] See, e.g., Paul Ades, 'The Unconstitutionality of "Antihomeless" Laws: Ordinances Prohibiting Sleeping in Outdoor Public Areas as a Violation of the Right to Travel' (1989) 77 *California Law Review* 595.

constitutional commitments each polity is willing to make. The argument is, however, that the current, unthinking, radical bifurcation between domestic migrants and immigrants 'from abroad' makes it that much more difficult to organise systematic reflection on whether those commitments are being lived up to, in both types of cases.

B Natural Persons – Exit

A long tradition in republican thought has seen the right of 'exit' – previously constrained by sovereign prerogative – as central to meaningful conceptions of freedom. Today, in liberal democracies, there is little in public law that directly limits the possibilities for individuals to leave. Constraints do exist, but they commonly take less direct forms, for example through the domestic criminalisation of foreign conduct, the refusal to recognise statuses obtained abroad, or the denial of public benefits to citizens residing out-of-state.[95] One striking example from recent history concerns efforts by countries to extraterritorially regulate access to abortion abroad. In one well-known episode, the Irish courts granted an injunction designed to prevent a pregnant Irish teenager from traveling to the United Kingdom for an abortion. Around that same time, in the early 1990s, West German customs officials engaged in 'compulsory gynecological examinations' at the German-Dutch border, in order to seek out and be able to prosecute German women whom had obtained abortions in The Netherlands.[96]

A few decades earlier, we find striking examples of how law can also aid individuals' attempts at escape, in the context of the American civil rights movement. For lawyers representing civil rights activists in southern US states of the late 1950s and early 1960s, a key challenge was 'freeing their clients from the shackles of the state system'.[97] The US Supreme Court responded to state court hostility with a series of seminal jurisdictional rulings that 'reshaped the boundaries between federal and state courts'.[98]

[95] See, e.g., Zick 'Constitutional Displacement', 536; Lea Brilmayer, 'Interstate Preemption: The Right to Travel, The Right to Life, and the Right to Die' (1993) 91 *Michigan Law Review* 873.

[96] See, e.g., Seth Kreimer, 'But Whoever Treasures Freedom . . . : The Right to Travel and Extraterritorial Abortions' (1993) 91 *Michigan Law Review* 907; Gerald Neuman, 'Conflict of Constitutions – No Thanks: A Response to Professors Brilmayer and Kreimer' (1993) 91 *Michigan Law Review* 939, 942.

[97] Robert J. Glennon, 'The Jurisdictional Legacy of the Civil Rights Movement' (1994) 61 *Tennessee Law Review* 869.

[98] Ibid., 870.

These allowed litigants to seek relief in lower federal courts and thus, effectively, to escape the southern states' jurisdictional reach. If we are willing to consider these cases as relevant instances of constitutional mobility – under the heading of 'exit' or 'escape' – as I want to suggest we should, then three facets of these jurisdictional innovations of the Warren Court era are especially interesting. First, these cases illustrate really how broad the range of legal instruments with potential effects on meaningful mobility can be. 'Jurisdiction' is a mostly helpful general heading, but the relevant techniques ranged widely, and included doctrines of 'removal', 'abstention', 'exhaustion', and habeas corpus, to name just a few.[99] Second, it is important to note that most of the relevant cases in fact concerned denials of access to segregated public facilities. And of course, 'escape' from the reach of southern administrations was achieved only through 'entry' into a different constitutional order – that of the Federal Constitution. This means that these cases are also illustrative of how closely intertwined strategies and experiences of expulsion and escape may be in practice.[100] The third point is this. When it comes to civil rights claims brought by individuals, many of these jurisdictional innovations were rolled back from the mid-1970s onwards.[101] This means that, for individuals in the USA, the Warren Court era in many ways marks the high point of their freedom to 'opt out' of local public regulation. A similar rollback, however, never took place for corporate actors. Instead, the freedom for legal persons to escape, opt out, achieve 'lift-off' from the constraints of local public law has never stopped expanding.[102]

C *Corporations – Exit*

Picking up on this last point: It is indeed today extremely easy for corporate actors to escape the reach of local public regulation. This is true, for example, with regard to the laws determining their internal organisation (by way of the transfer of their corporate 'seat'); with regard

[99] Ibid.

[100] It is important to re-emphasise that what matters is not the 'fact' of mobility from an unambiguous 'here' to an equally unambiguous 'there', but, in this case, the individual experience of being able to leave one legally constituted realm for another (the 'private' lunch counter, for example, for the 'public' sphere of constitutional rights; oppression allowed or mandated under state law, for constitutional relief under federal law).

[101] See, e.g., Glennon, 'The Jurisdictional Legacy of the Civil Rights Movement', 871.

[102] Jacco Bomhoff, 'Back to The Bremen (1972): Forum Selection and Worldmaking', in Horatia Watt, Lucia Bíziková et al. (eds.), *Global Private International Law: Adjudication without Frontiers* (Cheltenham: Elgar, 2019), 16.

to corporate liability (through the use of local subsidiaries); or in the field of taxation (by way of transfer-pricing techniques, for example). What is especially striking, though, is how the contrasting idea of limiting 'exit' possibilities for corporations has become almost unthinkable. Efforts to do so are typically short-lived, and swiftly denounced as 'parochial' and unworkable. This was the fate, in particular, of efforts by local governments in the USA in the 1980s to stem the tide of corporations moving out-of-state and offshore. During that time, many state governments passed so-called 'plant closing statutes' which would allow local authorities to condemn – that is: expropriate by way of eminent domain – businesses on the verge of relocation.[103] Critics quickly labelled these statutes as 'the embodiment of economic parochialism'.[104] They were difficult to apply effectively in practice and were soon thought be in violation of the federal constitutional imperative of unrestrained interstate commerce.[105]

Of great practical relevance to the scope of corporate 'lift-off' today, is the concept of party autonomy in private international law. Party autonomy is what allows individuals and corporations to opt out of local legal systems, by choosing a foreign court or a foreign applicable law, or by electing to have their disputes settled in arbitration. Party autonomy has become the predominant feature of both jurisdiction law and choice of law in the post–World War II era.[106] While it is true that party autonomy can benefit both individuals and corporations, it is corporate actors in particular that have been able to use this 'escape device' to evade local regulations on a massive scale. The phenomenon of 'hypermobility', mentioned earlier, is largely a creation of this form of autonomy from local law. And yet, as Ralf Michaels has noted, '[g]iven the radical character of party autonomy, it is surprising how little theoretical discussion there is on its

[103] Edward P. Lazarus, 'The Commerce Clause Limitation on the Power to Condemn a Relocating Business' (1987) 96 *Yale Law Journal* 1343; Michael H. Abbey, 'State Plant Closing Legislation: A Modern Justification for the Use of the Dormant Commerce Clause As a Bulwark of National Free Trade' (1989) 75 *Virginia Law Review* 845.

[104] Abbey 'State Plant Closing Legislation', 879.

[105] Lazarus 'The Commerce Clause Limitation on the Power to Condemn a Relocating Business'; Abbey, 'State Plant Closing Legislation'.

[106] See, e.g., Horatia Muir Watt, '"Party Autonomy" in International Contracts: From the Makings of a Myth to the Requirements of Global Governance' (2010) 3 *European Review of Contract Law* 250; Peter Nygh, *Autonomy in International Contracts* (Oxford: Oxford University Press, 1999).

theoretical foundations'.[107] As any other foundational discussion on the balance between individual freedom and public authority, such reflection, it is submitted, will require some grounding in constitutional theory and experience. The same corporate autonomy, for example, that allows multinational corporations today to operate around the world while remaining out of the reach of most local laws, was invoked by the NAACP – technically a New York corporation – as a shield to protect its members and activities in southern states, during the civil rights era discussed above.[108] The idea of constitutional orders as both partial and outward-facing, with a stake in, and some legitimate say over, the determination of their own reach, may offer a useful way forward.

D Corporations – Access

State-imposed obstacles to access for foreign corporations are as rare today as efforts to limit immigration of individuals are commonplace. Many countries rather go out of their way to attract foreign business. Examples of such barriers can be found, however. In Europe, for example, a series of decisions by the Court of Justice of the European Union over the past two decades has enforced limits on the ability of EU member states to impose local company law standards on foreign corporations as a condition for their local recognition.[109] For more direct and more dramatic examples of state regulations seeking to impose conditions on the 'privilege' of doing business for out-of-state corporations, we do have to go back quite a while, however: to the United States of the late nineteenth and early twentieth century. At the time, many US states, in particular in the Midwest, had extensive lists of conditions that they imposed only on out-of-state corporations, for the privilege of 'doing business' within the forum. As a typical decision of an Alabama court of the era put it, conditions such as the obligation for foreign corporations to appoint an in-state resident as an agent for service of court documents, were 'just as much a police regulation for the

[107] Ralf Michaels, 'Party Autonomy in Private International Law – A New Paradigm Without a Solid Foundation?' (2013) 15 *Japanese Yearbook of Private International Law* 282, 283. See, more recently, also Alex Mills, *Party Autonomy in Private International Law* (Cambridge: Cambridge University Press, 2018).

[108] *NAACP* v. *Patterson*, 357 US 449 (1958).

[109] See, principally, the now classic decisions in Case C-212/97 (*Centros*); Case C-208/00 (*Überseering*); and Case C-167/01 (*Inspire Art*).

protection of the property and interests of its citizens as a law forbidding vagrancy among its inhabitants'.[110] Many of these limits were gradually struck down by the US Supreme Court, under a newly developed doctrine of 'unconstitutional conditions'.[111] In fact, virtually all of the early cases on what Robert Lee Hale came to call 'the conditioning power of the state' were such out-of-state corporations cases; a fact that reveals the intimate connection between the character of constitutional limits on governmental power more generally and the theme of (corporate) mobility more specifically. These state efforts to 'oust' corporations have been largely forgotten. But they may well be worth revisiting. For one, as Naomi Lamoreaux and William Novak note in their recent *Corporations and American Democracy*, they belie the image of the Gilded Age as a uniformly '*laissez-faire*' era.[112] Still more importantly, these instances of local assertiveness could serve as inspiration for an outward-facing constitutionalism that is able to mediate between a boundless liberalisation, on the one hand, and an absolutely bounded parochialism, on the other.

V Conclusion

The history of the interplay of constitutionalism and mobility seems littered with practices that are today either virtually forgotten, or so widespread to seem almost completely natural. 'Corporate ouster' and 'vagrancy laws' are examples of the former; 'party autonomy' and immigration restrictions, of the latter. Our constitutional jurisprudence seems caught in stark binaries, such as between a power over immigration that is supposedly 'plenary', and a domestic right of free movement that is purportedly 'obvious'. Absent from these two strands of purported obviousness is a more nuanced legal and constitutional vocabulary in which to discuss old and new questions of what was long known as the right of 'ingress and egress'. The lack of such a constitutional language is an important part of why it is so difficult to talk about reasserting local public autonomy vis-à-vis transnational private autonomy without

110 *American Union Telegraph Company* v. *Western Union Telegraph Company*, 67 Ala. 26 (1880), cited in Gerard C. Henderson, *The Position of Foreign Corporations in American Constitutional Law* (Cambridge, MA: Harvard University Press, 1918), 125.

111 See in particular Robert L. Hale, 'Unconstitutional Conditions and Constitutional Rights' (1935) 35 *Columbia Law Review* 321.

112 Naomi R. Lamoreaux and William J. Novak (eds.), *Corporations and American Democracy* (Cambridge, MA: Harvard University Press, 2017), 17–19.

facing immediate objections of 'local selfishness and protectionism';[113] or, conversely, to discuss limits to local sovereignty from a position other than that of a 'citizen of nowhere'.

This chapter has suggested that if liberal constitutional thought is to address these challenges, it will have to be through a more robust development of its outward-facing dimension. This means investing in a form of constitutionalism that demands and scrutinises commitment to greater inclusivity, while remaining conscious of the partial character of whatever local domain it institutes. Much about such a brand of constitutionalism remains to be elaborated. But the argument offered in this chapter does at least suggest some pitfalls to be avoided. An outward-facing constitutionalism should not be preoccupied with what 'is', or is not, inside any particular jurisdiction or polity. It should not limit itself to the level of national borders. And it should not be concerned only with the rights of individuals. Instead, I have suggested, an outward-facing constitutionalism should look at the widest possible range of forms of mobility and enforced immobility. It should scrutinise the constitution and effects of any kind of legally meaningful boundary to such mobility. And it should encompass both natural persons and corporate actors.

Questions of individual and corporate mobility – relating to experiences of being forced out, allowed in, permitted to exit, or of simply being 'stuck' – are found time and again at the heart of pressing contemporary issues. And constitutional thought simply has not kept up. Instead, the legal treatment of mobility has been fragmented across a wide range of specialised fields of regulation and scholarship, in which constitutionalist concerns rarely play any central role. An outward-facing constitutionalism may work to bring these strands together, and, in so doing, offer a home for reflection on the profound contemporary challenge of how to 'broaden the benefits of openness while enhancing democratic accountability'.[114]

113 Frug 'The City as a Legal Concept', 1067.

114 Mark Carney, 'The Global Outlook', Speech of 12 February 2019, available at www.bankofengland.co.uk/-/media/boe/files/speech/2019/the-global-outlook-speech-by-mark-carney, accessed 5 August 2019.

9

The Inside-Out Constitution

AUDREY MACKLIN

> One of the rights possessed by the supreme power in every State is the right to refuse to permit an alien to enter that State, to annex what conditions it pleases to the permission to enter it, and to expel or deport from the State, at pleasure, even a friendly alien, especially if it considers his presence in the State opposed to its peace, order, and good government, or to its social or material interests. Vattel, *Law of Nations*, book 1, s. 231; book 2, s. 125.
>
> *AG Canada* v. *Cain (Reference re: Alien Labour Act, s. 6 (Can.))*, [1906] AC 452, at [5]

Introduction

Evoking a Janus-faced constitution makes it easy not to notice the role of constitutional jurisprudence in generating the boundary that animates the metaphor. The image trades on spatiality, which in turn aligns with territoriality as the principal basis of sovereign jurisdiction. It risks downplaying the way constitutions project horizontally across space (inside/outside), but also vertically according to status (citizen/non-citizen), and even backward across time (past/present). The constitutional gaze is splintered along many vectors.

Immigration law is concerned with stabilising and managing boundaries that are not only legal, but also political and social. Liberal political theory posits closure as the originary moment of constituting political community and legal order, and the capacity to include and exclude validates and reenacts that founding in perpetuity. Every decision to admit, refuse and expel replays in microcosm the power to define and enclose the political community.

States insist that border control is the ultimate metric of sovereignty, made more vital than ever because other indicia have been traded away. The liminality of the non-citizen is definitive, unalterable and an existential requirement of statehood.[1] As Bas Schotel puts it, exclusion 'is essential and constitutive [of] the legal order to the extent that it is inescapably beyond justification'.[2]

The opening quotation invites attention to territory and status. Temporality is latent in the text but made patent in a dictum of the US Supreme Court that the state's entitlement to deport 'foreigners who have not been naturalized' is as 'absolute and unqualified as the right to prohibit and prevent their entrance to the country'.[3] In constitutional time and space, the non-citizen is perpetually arriving at the border for the very first time.[4]

Despite the obvious and even irresistible attraction of binary metaphors in any discussion of migration and citizenship, I hesitate at extending it to the constitution, even where, as here, its invocation is immediately accompanied by appropriate and nuanced qualification. First, liminality is not so liminal anymore. Bordering is happening everywhere: a hundred miles inside the territorial United States, at airport lounges and departure gates, on Christmas Island, at pre-clearance zones in Dublin and Toronto, and at any visa office anywhere in the world. Bordering is not only performed by state actors, but by airline employees, landlords, health providers, educators and all those deputised by the state to scrutinise the immigration status of passengers, tenants, patients, employees and students. Liminality also operates through the proliferation of statuses between citizen and non-citizen – mono-citizen, plural citizen, EU citizen, denizen, permanent resident, temporary resident, refugee, asylum seeker, stateless – each with their own criteria for transition in and out. The gaming of borders and status by states is by now a familiar tactic for exerting power and evading accountability, and data sharing may be the least visible and most pervasive of all instruments: State A and state B's constitutional constraints on the surveillance of their own citizens/denizens can be circumvented through interstate

[1] Bas Schotel describes the argument for the inherent power over inclusion and exclusion as 'the exclusion thesis'. Bas Schotel, *On the Right of Exclusion: Law, Ethics and Immigration Policy* (Routledge: New York, 2012), 54.

[2] Ibid., 88.

[3] *Fong Yue Ting* v. *United States* 149 US 698 (1893) at 707.

[4] Importantly, successive US immigration statutes have, in fact, conferred greater procedural and substantive protection against expulsion of lawful permanent residents than exclusion of first-time entrants. Similarly, resident non-citizens enjoy various constitutional rights under the Bill of Rights in respect of state action not directly in the service of expulsion. These are among the reasons why President Trump's Second Executive Order dropped the measures against lawful permanent residents and visa holders.

cooperation if each state surveilles foreigners on their territory and then swaps information with the foreigners' countries of nationality.[5] A model of constitutionalism that trades on borders will necessarily regard liminality as anomalous, but it is not. And it is not anomalous in ways that matter for constitutional law and interpretation.

International political sociologist Didier Bigo has long contested the border between the 'outside' of security and the 'inside' of law and order. He uses his empirical investigation of high-ranking members of French police, military intelligence, armed forces, customs and immigration officials to ground a new 'topology of security'.[6] The functional and institutional continuities between the logics guiding agents inside and outside the boundary enclosing the state – the production, circulation and governance of risk, insecurity and unease – undermine the unity and coherence of the boundary itself. As a means of liberating the imagination and provoking critical reflection, Bigo offers the image of the Mobius strip as alternative to the circle defined by a line demarcating the internal and external.

The Mobius strip is a rectangular ribbon that has been twisted and then joined. Importantly, the Mobius strip metaphor does not deny that there is an inside and an outside – it does not contemplate a borderless world, but rather one where borders are relational and perspectival. The mathematical label for this is 'non-orientable'. An observer of entities moving along the strip would identify some as inside and others as outside, but this sorting into insiders and outsiders will change as the observer moves. The border is dynamic and contingent, but no less real.

The metaphor's appeal lies partly in its invitation to denaturalise without refusing bordering and boundaries. It thus offers a way of thinking about the constitutional significance of various configurations of space, subjectivity and temporality that does not relegate them *ex ante* to categories of normal or exceptional. This is attractive to migration law scholars precisely because the conspicuous weakness or absence of constitutional protections available to non-citizens in practices of exclusion and expulsion is shared across domestic legal orders. Just as liminality is not so liminal, immigration exceptionalism is not so exceptional. The

[5] See, generally, Valsamis Mitsilegas, 'Surveillance and Digital Privacy in the Transatlantic "War on Terror": The Case for a Global Privacy Regime' (2016) 47 *Columbia Human Rights Law Review* 1.

[6] Didier Bigo, 'The Möbius Ribbon of Internal and External Security(ies)', in Albert Mathias, David Jacobsen and Yosef Lapid (eds.), *Identities, Borders, Orders: Rethinking International Relations Theory* (Minneapolis: University of Minnesota Press, 2001) 91, 113.

much-maligned US plenary power doctrine presents as a paradigmatic instance of the infolding of external sovereignty. In its original formulation, it exempts immigration from constitutional scrutiny on the premise that migration control is a sub-category of foreign relations; any check on the exclusion or expulsion of non-citizens would make the United States 'to that extent subject to the control of another power'.[7] Contemporary US scholarship on plenary power doctrine tilted in the direction of the doctrine's demise in the face of competing constraints imposed by other constitutional norms, or by statutory encroachment, especially with respect to resident non-citizens. The Supreme Court's 2018 decision in *Trump* v. *Hawaii* upholding President Trump's anti-Muslim travel ban changed that.[8]

This paper attends to the contemporary Canadian version of immigration exceptionalism formulated by the Supreme Court of Canada in its interpretation of section 7 of the Canadian Charter of Rights and Freedoms. I reveal the mechanics of the doctrinal techniques that eviscerate constitutional rights protection in immigration law. This is not a 'whodunit' – everyone knows the culprit is sovereignty, conventionally understood.[9] The question I want to explore is how it is operationalised in a modern constitution, and at what cost. I do this through a close reading of jurisprudence regarding the deportability of the non-citizen

[7] *Chae Chan Ping* v. *United States*, 130 US 581 (1889) at 609. For further discussion of plenary power and other 'discretionary doctrines', see Colin Grey, *Justice and Authority in Immigration Law* (Oxford: Hart Publishing, 2015), 44–46.

[8] *Trump* v. *Hawaii*, 585 US ___ (2018). The travel ban commenced with President Trump's 2017 Executive Order, but and ended with a third iteration. Each version targeted citizens of majority Muslim countries varied the scope of coverage based the traveller's immigration status in the United States. The first Executive Order's treatment of lawful permanent residents (LPRs) and visa holders conflicted with the statutory rights extended by Congress to these classes. LPRs also enjoy a certain degree of constitutional procedural due process protection that the Executive Order ignored. The second Executive Order banning citizens of named majority Muslim states did not apply to visa holders and LPRs. The third Executive Order did not alter the content of the measures, but confined them to first-time entrants not protected by existing statutory provisions or (by virtue of plenary power) the Constitution. In other words, the revised Executive Order did not resile from discriminatory exclusion. Instead, each successive version confined its application to the rightless.

[9] This point was made most explicitly in *Mitchell* v. *Canada (MNR)*, 2001 SCC 33, an Aboriginal rights case, where the Grand Chief of the Mohawk nation claimed an extinguished Aboriginal right under s. 35 of the Constitution to mobility of goods and persons across the US border. In his concurring judgment, Binnie J quotes Vattel, Blackstone and US cases before declaring simply that the 'international trading/mobility right claimed by the respondent as a citizen of the Haudenosaunee (Iroquois) Confederacy is incompatible with the historical attributes of Canadian sovereignty'. *Mitchell*, at[163].

resident in order to illustrate the role of a type of aggrandised prerogative power in – depending on one's perspective – locating the non-citizen inside the legal order (*qua* subject of law) while simultaneously placing the non-citizen outside the constitution (*qua* object of sovereign power).[10] While my focus is on Canada and its particular articulation of immigration exceptionalism, I believe that the analysis resonates broadly across the domestic variants of other jurisdictions.

I Immigration Exceptionalism, Canadian Edition

The epigraph that opens this chapter declares the absence and presence of right: the non-citizen has no right to enter or remain; the state has a right to exclude or expel the non-citizen. A casual reader might assume the latter proposition is merely the corollary of the former; as I explain later, this is erroneous. In any case, Commonwealth judges intone one or the other formulation so habitually in any migration case – often for no apparent reason – that it has (in its various forms) become a mantra – what I will henceforth call the Principle. The positive version that extols the right of states to exclude and expel was most famously enunciated in *AG Canada* v. *Cain*, where the Privy Council simply quoted with approval eighteenth century international jurist Emmerich Vattel.[11] The negative version, foregrounding the absence of a right to enter or remain, also appears in contemporary case law as a common law principle.[12] The eventual effect of the Principle was to insulate deportation 'as such' from substantive constitutional scrutiny under section 7 of the Charter.[13]

Section 7 states that:

> Everyone has the right to life, liberty and security of the person, and the right not to be deprived thereof, except in accordance with the principles of fundamental justice.

The structure of a section 7 analysis requires that a court first consider whether the impugned state (in)action engages or impairs life, liberty and

[10] Elsewhere, I have discussed the parallel role of the prerogative over foreign affairs in draining the content of constitutional protection of the non-resident citizen (Omar Khadr) 'Comment on *Canada (Prime Minister)* v. *Khadr*', (2010) 51 SCLR (2d) 295–331.

[11] *AG Canada* v. *Cain (Reference re: Alien Labour Act, s. 6 (Can.))* [1906] AC 542 at [5].

[12] *R* v. *Pentonville Prison, ex p Azam* [1974] AC 18 at 27; *Canada (Minister of Employment and Immigration) v. Chiarelli* [1992], 1 SCR 711, at 733.

[13] These are the franchise/right to stand for office (s. 3) and the right to enter and remain (s. 6).

security of the person. These terms have generally been interpreted broadly to include a range of important interests not confined to pre-existing legal rights. If life, liberty or security of the person is infringed, the next question is whether the deprivation accords with 'fundamental justice' in substantive or procedural terms. The complexity of a section 7 analysis is compounded by the fact that protection of the stipulated right is internally limited by principles of fundamental justice, but also by a general provision applicable to all Charter rights. Section 1 'saves' Charter-violating state action if it survives a proportionality test.

'Everyone' under section 7 includes non-citizens, but infringements to life, liberty and security of the person do not include deportation 'as such'. So, non-citizens are not denied the substantive protection of section 7 of the Charter unless they face expulsion. Chiarelli's version of the Principle – 'the most fundamental principle of immigration law is that non-citizens do not have an unqualified right to enter or remain in the country'[14] – has been recited over a hundred times in subsequent jurisprudence.[15]

The Principle is the doctrine that incarnates immigration exceptionalism in Canadian law. The plenary power doctrine performs a similar function in US constitutional law, and Marie-Benedicte Dembour has elegantly depicted a parallel move in European Court of Human Rights case law, which she dubs the 'Strasbourg Reversal'.[16] The argument I develop here is that Canadian constitutional jurisprudence has internalised a rights-annihilating Principle within the nucleus of a rights-generative bill of rights, with necrotising effect.[17] I mean by this that the Principle has corrosive spill-over effects on legality and rights protection.

The paradigmatic case animating my intervention concerns the long-term permanent resident who arrives in Canada as a child, grows up without obtaining citizenship, commits one or more criminal offences, and is ordered deported as a consequence. To the extent that a person is formed by the society and circumstances in which he or she grows up, such individuals – criminal offenders included – are products of Canada. Their familial and other attachments are (more or less) all

[14] *Chiarelli*, at 733.

[15] *Chiarelli*, based on a CanLII search of the phrase.

[16] Marie-Benedicte Dembour, *When Humans Become Migrants* (Oxford: Oxford University Press, 2015), 4–6, 185–87.

[17] See Robert M. Cover, 'The Supreme Court, 1982 Term – Foreword: Nomos and Narrative' (1983) 97 *Harvard Law Review* 4 for an account of legal judgment as variously jurispathic and jurisgenerative.

located in Canada, yet they face (more or less) automatic deportation to their country of citizenship if convicted and sentenced to a term of imprisonment of at least six months.[18] The individuals may never have left Canada since arriving as children, may or may not speak the language of the country of origin, and have few if any meaningful connections to the country of origin. However, the risks the individual might face upon deportation do not amount to persecution, torture or death. The harm subsists in the expulsion of the individual from the place that is, in functional terms, their only home. I label the harm of deportation in such cases 'deracination,' by which I mean a profound uprooting. Deracination is not a harm recognised under the Charter.[19]

A *The Road to* Chiarelli

The Supreme Court of Canada's early Charter jurisprudence radiated openness to non-citizens' rights claims. In *Singh*, an unsuccessful refugee claimant challenged the process of refugee determination laid out in the Immigration Act.[20] Wilson J wrote for three of six judges who heard the case and decided that section 7 of the Charter applied and that the process did not comport with fundamental justice. The other three judges ruled that the process violated the Bill of Rights, but all judges agreed that it was unlawful. Today, the Charter decision is regarded as the controlling precedent.

It is tempting to interpret *Singh* as guaranteeing a Charter right to refugee protection. Elements of the judgment could support a claim of that nature, but taken as a whole, the actual decision is more circumspect or, as Cass Sunstein would have it, minimalist.[21]

18 Immigration and Refugee Protection Act, Statutes of Canada 2001, c. 27, as am., s. 36(1).

19 Importantly, it has been recognised by the Human Rights Committee as a violation of Art. 12(4) of the ICCPR's right to enter and remain in one's 'own country' and, arguably, the right to protection of family and private life under the International Covenant on Civil and Political Rights and European Convention of Human Rights jurisprudence. See, e.g., *Jama Warsame* v. *Canada*, Comm. No. 1959/2010, UN Doc. CCPR/C/102/D/1959/2010 (2011); *Nystrom, Nystrom & Turner* v. *Australia*, Comm. No. 1557/2007, UN Doc. CCPR/C/102/D/1557/2007 (July 18, 2011).

20 *Singh* v. *Canada (Minister of Employment and Immigration)*, [1985] 1 SCR 177; Immigration Act, 1976–77, c. 52, s. 1.

21 Cass R. Sunstein, *One Case at a Time: Judicial Minimalism on the Supreme Court* (Cambridge, MA: Harvard University Press, 1999). For a further exploration of Wilson J's judgment in light of subsequent jurisprudence, see Colin Grey, 'Thinkable: The Charter and Refugee Law after Appulonappa *and* B010' (2016) 76 *Supreme Court Law Review* (2d)87.

Wilson J acknowledges at the outset of her judgment that section 6 of the Charter guarantees mobility rights only to citizens, and then adds that 'at common law an alien has no right to enter or remain in Canada except by leave of the Crown'.[22] But here, the Principle is of no constitutional moment because, as Wilson J continues to explain, statute supersedes common law, and the statute created a right to remain in the form of protection against *refoulement* (return). Wilson J did not need to consider what the Charter would require had the Immigration Act made no provision for refugee protection. All the Court needed to address was the process for determining access to the extant statutory right to refugee status, and this enabled Wilson J to caution that was 'unnecessary for the Court to consider what it would do if it were asked to engage in a larger inquiry into the substantive rights conferred in the Act'.[23]

Having delimited the bounds of the inquiry, Wilson J addresses the two elements of a section 7 analysis: Was Singh's life, liberty or security of person imperilled by the process of refugee determination? Did the actual process comport with fundamental justice?

Wilson fends off the attempt to limit section 7 to citizens and affirms that 'everyone' under section 7 'includes every human being who is physically present in Canada and by virtue of such presence amenable to Canadian law'.[24] Territoriality appears to trump status; a more tantalising (but unresolved) question is whether subjection to Canadian law is sufficient to bring an individual under the aegis of the Charter.[25]

Wilson J finds that security of the person is engaged by refugee determination, even if *refoulement* presents only a risk rather than a certainty of persecution, and even though the proximate agent of persecution is the state of nationality, not Canada:

> 'security of the person' must encompass freedom from the threat of physical punishment or suffering as well as freedom from such punishment itself. I note particularly that a Convention refugee has the right under s. 55 of the Act not to ' . . . be removed from Canada to a country where his life or freedom would be threatened . . .' In my view, the denial of such a right must amount to a deprivation of security of the person within the meaning of section 7.[26]

[22] *Singh*, at [13].
[23] Ibid., at [55].
[24] Ibid., at [35].
[25] For a cogent argument in favour of the non-territorial position, see Donald Galloway, 'The Extraterritorial Application of the Charter to Visa Applicants' (1991) 23(2) *Ottawa Law Review* 335–72.
[26] *Singh*, at [47].

In coming to this view, Wilson J. looks to the consequences of state action for the person concerned. The potential impact of *refoulement* for a refugee makes this an easy case in her estimation:

> [I]f the appellants had been found to be Convention refugees as defined in s. 2(1) of the Immigration Act, 1976 they would have been entitled as a matter of law to the incidents of that status provided for in the Act. Given the potential consequences for the appellants of a denial of that status if they are in fact persons with a 'well-founded fear of persecution,' it seems to me unthinkable that the Charter would not apply to entitle them to fundamental justice in the adjudication of their status.[27]

This conclusion then grounds the Court's assessment of why the existing determination process failed to accord with fundamental justice, and the imposition of a minimum set of required procedures, such as disclosure of the evidence upon which the Minister relies, and an oral hearing to test credibility.

Wilson J thus leaves dangling the important question of whether the Charter guarantees a section 7 right to refugee protection independent of the contingent existence of the statutory rights set out in the Immigration Act.[28] In other words, if a government repealed the statutory regime of refugee protection in Canada, could a refugee claimant standing at (or inside) the border claim a Charter right against *refoulement*? Wilson J's earlier emphasis on the consequences of a denial of refugee status make it 'unthinkable' to deprive a claimant of fundamental justice in the determination of that status, incline towards an affirmative answer.[29] After all, the same concern about the consequences of *refoulement* that animates her insistence that principles of fundamental justice apply to refugee determination militates towards a finding that *refoulement* violates a right to security of the person. But, as noted earlier, the Court does not to venture down that path, leaving an unresolved tension in the judgment.[30]

B The Chiarelli *Decision*

Singh challenged the process leading to recognition of refugee status, which confers a statutory right to remain in Canada on a non-citizen who

[27] Ibid., at [52].
[28] The Immigration Act already granted to refugees a statutory right not to be refouled to a country where they would face a well-founded fear of persecution, a permit entitling them to remain in Canada, and the right to appeal a deportation order.
[29] *Singh*, at [52].
[30] Colin Grey, 'Thinkable'.

otherwise has no legal basis for entering or remaining in Canada. Chiarelli challenged the process leading to deportation of a permanent resident from Canada. Permanent residents are entitled to enter and remain in Canada indefinitely (and to eventually apply for citizenship), subject to certain conditions. Breach of those conditions may lead to loss of status and expulsion. In contrast to Singh, Chiarelli did not allege a risk of persecution if deported, and unlike Singh, he enjoyed a relatively secure immigration status (permanent residence) in Canada for about a dozen years.

Joseph (Giuseppe) Chiarelli immigrated to Canada from Italy at age 15. At age 24, he was convicted of uttering threats and possession of a narcotic for purposes of trafficking. He received a sentence of six months imprisonment. Criminality is a ground of inadmissibility for permanent residents, and so Chiarelli was subject to loss of status and deportation because of his criminal convictions and subsequent sentence. Ordinarily, Chiarelli could have sought a discretionary reversal of the deportation decision in light of humanitarian and compassionate considerations (H&C).[31]

In broad terms, the exercise of H&C discretion assesses the consequences to the individual of removal from Canada, and of return to the country of nationality, as well as the likely impact to Canada of his or her continued presence in Canada. Relevant factors include the length of residence in Canada, the range and depth of familial and other personal relationships, social and economic integration, severity of actual offences and prospects for rehabilitation (where criminality is at issue), and personal, linguistic, cultural and other connections to the country of citizenship.[32]

Chiarelli was statute-barred from asking the Immigration Appeal Division to exercise humanitarian and compassionate discretion in his case because he was allegedly engaged in organised crime and thus subject to a separate and stricter 'security certificate' regime.[33] Chiarelli challenged the regime as a violation of section 7. He contended that deportation infringed his liberty through coercive, permanent, physical

[31] Immigration Act 1976, s. 72(1)(b).

[32] See *Ribic, Marida* v. *M.E.I.* (IAB T84-9623), D. Davey, Benedetti, Petryshyn, August 20, 1985.

[33] Ibid., s. 19(1)(d)(ii). A subsequent iteration of the security certificate regime was found unconstitutional in *Charkaoui* v. *Canada (Citizenship and Immigration)*, [2008] 2 SCR 326 (*Charkaoui*). Its successor was upheld in *Canada (Citizenship and Immigration)* v. *Harkat*, [2014] 2 SCR 33.

expulsion from Canada and transfer to another state. Doing so without regard to his personal circumstances was arbitrary and disproportionate, and failed to accord with a substantive conception of fundamental justice.[34]

The Court's analysis adopts an idiosyncratic approach to section 7 that finds no support in prior or subsequent section 7 jurisprudence outside the domain of immigration. The Court does not begin in the usual way by assessing whether a section 7 interest is engaged by deportation. Instead, the Court leapfrogs over the question of whether deportation violates life, liberty or security of the person, and finds that it does not matter anyway, because there could be no breach of fundamental justice in deporting a permanent residence for breach of the conditions upon which status was contingent:

> The appellant correctly points out that the threshold question is whether deportation per se engages s. 7, that is, whether it amounts to a deprivation of life, liberty or security of the person. . . . I do not find it necessary to answer this question, however, since I am of the view that there is no breach of fundamental justice.[35]

No other Charter jurisprudence detours around the first step of the section 7 analysis and heads straight to fundamental justice.

Turning to the breach of fundamental justice, the Court does cite earlier jurisprudence in support of the proposition that the 'principles of fundamental justice are to be found in the basic tenets of our legal system'.[36] Sopinka J repeatedly invokes the centrality of 'context' and a 'contextual approach' in determining the scope of fundamental justice, which leads him to state that the relevant context consists of the principles and policies underlying immigration law:

> Thus in determining the scope of principles of fundamental justice as they apply to this case, the Court must look to the principles and policies underlying immigration law. The most fundamental principle of immigration law is that non-citizens do not have an unqualified right to enter or remain in the country. At common law an alien has no right to enter or remain in the country.[37]

[34] The procedural deficiencies concerned the process for issuing a security certificate in existence at the time (which differed significantly from the process that was successfully challenged in 2007 in *Charkaoui*).

[35] *Chiarelli,* at 731–32.

[36] Ibid., at 732.

[37] Ibid., at 733. Sopinka J also offers extradition jurisprudence as an example of the same principle in action.

Sopinka J then presents section 6 of the Charter, which guarantees only to citizens the right to enter and remain, as the constitutional instantiation of the common law principle.

Viewed against this legal landscape, the Immigration Act simply specifies in statutory form those qualifications on the right of non-citizens to enter and remain. One of those conditions is that the permanent resident not be convicted of a crime punishable by more than five years' imprisonment. This is 'a legitimate, non-arbitrary choice by Parliament'.[38] Those found inadmissible for criminality have deliberately violated a condition of permanent residence. This justifies rescission of status and removal from Canada. Accordingly, compliance with fundamental justice does not require one to look beyond this fact to other 'aggravating or mitigating circumstances',[39] including the personal circumstances of the individual. Later in the judgment, Sopinka J reiterates the same conclusion, this time focusing on an appeal as the vehicle for injecting individualised factors into the adjudicative process.

It is useful to contrast his genealogy of the conditions on the statutory right of the individual to enter and remain with his genealogy of constraints on the state's power to deport. According to the Court, the former derives from a timeless principle embedded in the common law. The latter lacks any such normative anchor in the tenets of the legal system, and simply reflects the vagaries of legislative choice by successive parliaments. Thus, attention to individualised considerations as an element of a deportation decision is a contingent feature of the legislation in its various iterations, rather than the expression of a deeper normative principle regarding fair treatment of the legal subject. And, as Sopinka J notes 'there has never been a universally available right of appeal from a deportation order' on 'all the circumstances of the case'.[40]

[38] Ibid., at 715

[39] Ibid., at 715.

[40] Ibid., at 741. This focus on a 'right' to an appeal is an unfortunate distraction. The central issue is whether deportation of a long-term permanent resident potentially violates s. 7 and thus requires consideration by a decision-maker, not whether that consideration happens by way of appeal or other procedure. Prior to 1967, only the Minister possessed broad discretion to provide relief from deportation. Thereafter, the independent, quasi-judicial Immigration Appeal Board had jurisdiction to quash a deportation order on the basis of 'all the circumstances of the case', but this discretion could be overridden by the Minister of Immigration and the Solicitor General if it would be 'contrary to the national interest to provide such relief'. Immigration Appeal Board Act, SC 1966–67, c. 90, s. 15; s. 21.

For present purposes, *Chiarelli* can be distilled to the following propositions. Access to fundamental justice can be determined independently of whether, how, or to what extent a right to life, liberty or security of the person has been breached. Since aliens have no unqualified right to enter and remain, a legitimate, non-arbitrary qualification on the right of aliens to remain – like criminality – cannot violate a principle of fundamental justice. Consideration of individual circumstances is a policy choice of legislators, not a legal principle rooted in basic tenets of the legal system. Though the Court is not explicit on this point, a necessary inference is that it is not arbitrary to deport a permanent resident without regard to personal circumstances.[41] It should be noted, however, that the meaning of both arbitrariness and gross disproportionality under section 7 of the Charter has evolved considerably since *Chiarelli* was decided and, most importantly, requires attention to the specific impact of the impugned law on the individual.[42]

C *After* Singh *and* Chiarelli

I offer here a truncated tour of Charter-related immigration jurisprudence after *Singh* and *Chiarelli.* Though it wanders astray from the common law principle that launched the inquiry, these cases enable us to assay its effects.

Neither *Singh* nor *Chiarelli* directly resolve the question of whether an otherwise lawful deportation breaches liberty or security of person. The

[41] It should be noted that Chiarelli was decided when non-arbitrariness as a principle of fundamental justice was relatively undeveloped, and whether the same inference would flow today is debatable See, e.g., *Carter* v. *Canada (Attorney General)*, [2016] 1 SCR 13 (*Carter)* and *Canada (Attorney General)* v. *Bedford*, [2013] 3 SCR 1101 (*Bedford*). In the former, the Court explained '. . . arbitrariness targets the situation where there is no rational connection between the object of the law and the limit it imposes on life, liberty or security of the person' at [83]. *Chiarelli's* s. 12 and s. 15 challenges were cursorily dismissed. While the Court affirmed pre-Charter jurisprudence insisting that deportation was not punishment, it granted that deportation constituted 'treatment' for purposes of s. 12. Nevertheless, automatic deportability of a permanent resident convicted of a criminal offence punishable by five years' imprisonment was not 'grossly disproportionate'. *R* v. *Smith*, [1987] 1 SCR 1045 at 1072, [1987] SCJ No 36, cited in *Chiarelli*, at 735–36. Indeed, Sopinka J opined that it would outrage standards of decency if 'individuals granted conditional entry into Canada were permitted, without consequence, to violate those conditions deliberately'. (at 736).

[42] See, e.g., *Carter*; *Bedford*. In the former, the Court explained '. . . gross disproportionality compares the law's purpose, "taken at face value," with its negative effects on the rights of the claimant, and asks if this impact is completely out of sync with the object of the law' ([89]).

Court in *Singh* did not need to, because the Immigration Act provided refugees with a statutory right against removal, and the issue concerned the procedures for determination of that statutory right. *Chiarelli* did not need to since, as the Court saw it, aliens had no unqualified right to enter and remain and so fundamental justice was not implicated in the content of 'legitimate and non-arbitrary' conditions on the statutory right to remain.[43]

In *Medovarski* v. *Canada (MCI)*,[44] the Supreme Court directly answered the question. The appellants were permanent residents ordered deported for serious criminality, having received custodial sentences of more than six months.[45] They were caught in a transition between a system that permitted them to appeal the deportation to the IAD on 'all the circumstances of the case' and amendments that excluded them from an equitable appeal.[46] The Charter arguments took up four short paragraphs in the judgment. Medovarski argued that deportation 'removes her liberty to make fundamental decisions that affect her personal life, including her choice to remain with her partner'.[47] Security of the person was engaged because of the 'state-imposed psychological stress of being deported'.[48]

The Court disposes of the section 7 claim by invoking the Principle:

> The most fundamental principle of immigration law is that non-citizens do not have an unqualified right to enter or remain in Canada: *Chiarelli v. Canada (Minister of Employment and Immigration)*, [1992] 1 S.C.R. 711, at p. 733. Thus the deportation of a non-citizen in itself cannot implicate the liberty and security interests protected by s. 7 of the *Canadian Charter of Rights and Freedoms*.[49]

Recall that in *Chiarelli*, the Court did not find it necessary to determine whether deportation breached the section 7 right to liberty and security of the person because the common law principle meant that fundamental justice was not engaged anyway. Now, the Principle is the reason that deportation does not implicate liberty or security of the person. If this is the case, it is unclear why the Court did not simply say so in *Chiarelli*. If nothing else, it is analytically more coherent to simply deny that a section

[43] *Chiarelli* at 734.
[44] [2005] 2 SCR 539 (*Medovarski*).
[45] Immigration and Refugee Protection Act, SC 2001, c. 27, s. 64.
[46] Ibid., s. 196.
[47] *Medovarski* at [45].
[48] Ibid.
[49] Ibid., at [46].

7 interest is engaged than to contend that even if deportation breaches a section 7 right, no principle of fundamental justice constrains the process or substance of that rights deprivation. The flaw in the latter approach is that the demands of fundamental justice are linked to the nature and intensity of the infringement, and cannot be determined without a prior inquiry into whether life, liberty or security of the person is infringed.

Evidently, the Principle does important normative work: That non-citizens do not enjoy an unqualified right to enter and remain pre-empts the section 7 inquiry first (in *Chiarelli*) in respect of fundamental justice, and subsequently (in *Medovarski)* in relation to the section 7 right. Once uttered, it obviates Charter accountability for direct effects caused by the state's exercise of the deportation power.[50]

In later jurisprudence, the Supreme Court presses on the qualifier contained in *Medovarski*, namely that deportation does not *in itself* implicate liberty or security of the person. The Court leaves open the possibility that even if forcibly transferring a person from one country to another does not implicate liberty or security of the person, incidental or consequential features of deportation may do so. So far, the Supreme Court has found that section 7 is engaged where detention is incidental to deportation[51] and where the consequence of expulsion is a substantial risk of torture.

So, in *Suresh* v. *Canada*,[52] the Court attended to torture as possible consequence of deportation. Here, the Court conceded that section 7 is engaged by deportation where it exposes a non-citizen to a substantial risk of torture in the destination country.[53] Recognition that return to torture breaches section 7 rights initially looks like a simple variation on the reasoning in *Singh*, where the Court found that returning a refugee to the risk of persecution engages security of the person. The important difference is that in *Singh*, the statute created the positive right to refugee protection for a person in Singh's situation, provided he came within the refugee definition. In *Suresh*, the Court finds that deportation to a substantial risk of torture engages section 7, even though the statute authorises the Minister to deport where the Minister deems the refugee to pose a threat to national security. The Court in *Suresh* concludes that

[50] The qualification 'direct' acknowledges that at least one indirect consequence (torture) engages s. 7; it remains unclear whether persecution does.

[51] *Charkaoui*, at [13]–[14].

[52] [2002] 1 SCR 3 (*Suresh*).

[53] Ibid., at [77].

there is a free-standing Charter right not to be returned to torture unless 'exceptional circumstances' exist.[54] Because persecution encompasses more than torture, *Suresh* did not resolve whether *refoulement* to persecution short of torture violates section 7 or, put in other terms, whether the Charter guarantees a right to refugee protection. In *Febles* v. *Canada (MCI)*, however, the Court declared that removal may be prevented 'where Charter-protected rights may be in jeopardy'.[55] At the same time, the Court also declared in *obiter* 'the Charter does not give a positive right to refugee protection'.[56] The court is still out, so to speak, on where and when section 7 of the Charter is engaged

II What Is the Legal Status of the Principle?

A *Seeing Like a State, Feeling Like a Person*

In the course of her judgment in *Singh*, Wilson J addresses the constitutional relevance of the traditional common law characterisation of immigration as a privilege and not a right. She rejects it as determinative of whether a right to life, liberty or security of the person is engaged under section 7. Her narrow justification is that refugee protection is a statutory right, in contrast to a discretionary benefit such as parole. The more expansive claim is that the formal, *ex ante* classification of an interest as right or privilege from the state's perspective is the wrong methodology for evaluating an infringement on life, liberty or security of the person. Wilson J insists that the inquiry must focus on the impact of state action on the life, liberty or security of the person in functional terms, from the perspective of the rights bearer. This means that infringement of a legal right (e.g. property ownership) will not necessarily engage life, liberty or security of the person, while infringement of an interest falling short of a legal right may do so, depending on the effect on the rights bearer. So, describing an interest in formal terms as a privilege does not foreclose the section 7 inquiry, nor does describing it as a legal right dictate the outcome of a section 7 inquiry.

This impact-based approach is consistent with prior and subsequent trends in administrative law, such as *Baker* v. *Canada (MCI)*.[57] Mavis Baker lived in Canada for over a decade with no lawful status, not even

[54] Ibid., at [78].
[55] [2014] 3 SCR 431 at [67] (*Febles*).
[56] Ibid., at [68].
[57] [1999] 2 SCR 817 (*Baker*).

a claim to refugee protection. All she could request was a favourable exercise of humanitarian and compassionate discretion to exempt her from deportation to Jamaica based on the impact that deporting her from Canada would have on her, and her children. Insofar as humanitarian and compassionate discretion exempts a person from the enforcement of immigration law, Mavis Baker was seeking a privilege from the Minister, not claiming a right. Yet administrative law jurisprudence had long conceded that the duty of fairness applied to humanitarian and compassionate discretion because, as the Court notes, it is a decision of 'exceptional importance to the lives of those with an interest in the result – the claimant and his or her close family members'.[58]

Indeed, this attention to the substantive impact of a discretionary decision as against its formal character as privilege can be traced back to the 1959 SCC judgment *Roncarelli* v. *Duplessis*.[59] The formal approach is driven by the character of the relationship between state and legal subject, as viewed from the perspective of the state. It asks how the state sees the individual who is the object of the decision. The legal category to which the state assigns the individual (rights bearer, benefit seeker, license holder, etc.) is comprehensive, exhaustive and determinative. The substantive approach adopts the perspective of the legal subject. It asks how the individual experiences the decision.[60]

In *Chiarelli* and then *Medovarski*, the work performed by the Principle is to deny that deportation implicates life, liberty or security of the person. That is the same work done historically by the common law right-versus-privilege dichotomy in blocking procedural fairness and unfettering the exercise of discretion in deportation decisions. As deployed by the Supreme Court, the Principle restates the claim that immigration is a privilege, not a right, and restores to that dichotomy the juridical force that *Singh* sought to divest from it.[61]

[58] Ibid., at [31].

[59] [1959] SCR 121, [1959] SCJ No 1. See generally David Dyzenhaus, 'The Deep Structure of *Roncarelli v. Duplessis*' (2004) 53 *University of New Brunswick Law Journal* 111.

[60] Compare *Chieu* v. *Canada (Minister of Citizenship and Immigration)*, [2002] 1 SCR 84 at [57], where the Court quotes approvingly from *Prata* v. *Minister of Manpower and Immigration*, [1976] 1 SCR 376 the assertion that a person appealing a lawful removal order 'does not, therefore, attempt to assert a right, but, rather, attempts to obtain a discretionary privilege' at 380.

[61] S. 6 of the Charter, which guarantees only to citizens the right to enter and remain, only bolsters the argument if one reads all citizens' right to remain under s. 6 as defeating any non-citizen's claim to a right to remain under s. 7. This would be akin to arguing that since s. 10(b) guarantees all criminal accused a right to legal counsel, no person who is not

One might object that I am mixing apples and oranges here. After all, in both *Singh* and *Baker*, the statute created a mechanism (refugee status or humanitarian discretion respectively) for enabling otherwise inadmissible/removable non-citizens to remain in Canada. The Court's attention to the consequences of removal was oriented solely towards how those decisions would be made, both procedurally and substantively, not towards whether the individuals were entitled to such a mechanism in the first place. At the heart of the appellants' claims in *Chiarelli* and *Medovarski*, however, is a claim that the Charter mandates individualised justification for the initial decision to exclude/expel.[62] Neither *Singh* nor *Baker* endorse the relevance of impact for that purpose. And so, *Chiarelli* and *Medovarski* are superficially reconcilable with *Singh* and *Baker* on the rationale that the human impact of deportation is legally relevant to the lawful exercise of the power to deport if and only if Parliament has already decided to qualify the power to deport on that basis.

The hazard with this containment strategy is normative spill-over – or perhaps the cognitive dissonance required to repel leakage. Once a court recognises that deportation as such can affect 'in a fundamental manner the future of individuals' lives',[63] and that exposing a person to certain risks consequent to deportation – persecution, torture – may impair life, liberty or security of the person,[64] switching off that awareness via the Principle in relation to the same or other potential harms of deportation strains against the integrity of judicial reasoning. One way of illustrating this is to notice how the Court toggles between status and personhood in constituting the non-citizen. The non-citizen is a rights bearer under section 7 yet she can lay no claim as rights bearer when it comes to coercion in the form of deportation. Why? Because she is a non-citizen. She has been re-assigned from 'everyone' in section 7 to 'alien' under the

a criminal defendant has a right to counsel. Yet the Supreme Court of Canada rejected this logic when it found that in certain circumstances, s. 7 mandates the provision of state-funded legal counsel in child apprehension proceedings: *New Brunswick (Minister of Health and Community Services)* v. *G(J)*, [1999] 3 SCR 46, [1999] SCJ No 47 (*G(J)*). More generally, in one of the Court's earliest dicta, Dickson CJ remarked that the Charter 'is intended to constrain governmental action inconsistent with those rights and freedoms; it is not in itself an authorization for governmental action'. *Hunter* v. *Southam*, [1984] 2 SCR 145 at 156.

[62] The Court in *Chiarelli* submerges this issue beneath an inquiry into whether Chiarelli had a Charter right to a particular institutional vehicle for addressing the consequences, namely an equitable appeal examining 'all the circumstances of the case' at 741.

[63] *Baker*, at [15].

[64] *Singh*, at [44].

common law. Note that this disengagement from section 7 is not the equivalent of a determination that the harms of deracination in a given case do not rise to the level of a section 7 infringement. Nor is it tantamount to concluding that fundamental justice is not breached by deportation because of countervailing concerns. To engage in a balancing exercise, one must first recognise a rights infringement, assess the nature and intensity of the infringement and then notionally weigh it against the state interest.

Chiarelli does none of those things. Instead, Sopinka J short-circuits the analysis by refusing to inquire into the circumstances that may reveal a rights infringement:

> This condition [criminal inadmissibility based solely on length/severity of crime] represents a legitimate, non-arbitrary choice by Parliament of a situation in which it is not in the public interest to allow a non-citizen to remain in the country. All persons falling within the class of permanent residents described [as inadmissible for serious criminality] have deliberately violated an essential condition under which they were permitted to remain in Canada. Fundamental justice is not breached by deportation: it is the only way to give practical effect to the termination of a permanent resident's right to remain in Canada. Compliance with fundamental justice does not require that other aggravating or mitigating circumstances be considered.[65]

It is undeniable that the common law recognises and attaches considerable weight to interests that do not count under the Charter. Property rights spring to mind as an example. But it is more difficult to explain how the impact of deportation could count for so much in *Baker*, and for nothing in *Chiarelli*.[66] Severing an individual's connection to Canada, even where that person is deeply embedded in a web of familial, personal, linguistic, cultural, social, political and economic relationships, does not sound as a possible infringement of liberty or security of the person because the Court has covered its ears.

The doctrinal puzzle is this: How does a common law declaration of sovereign power come to circumscribe a Charter right, instead of vice

[65] *Chiarelli*, at 715.

[66] This differential treatment is distinguishable from the solicitude towards property rights in administrative law and their exclusion from the Charter: The common law exerts influence in administrative law but doesn't control how the Charter regards property. In the case of deportation, the common law doesn't control how administrative law regards the impact of deportation, but it seems to control how the Charter regards the impact of deportation.

versa? After all, the Charter is not supposed to take orders from the common law. The Constitution is the supreme law.

B The Principle and the Common Law

Chiarelli's version of the Principle distils a dictum from the English Court of Appeal in *R* v. *Governor of Pentonville Prison, ex parte Azam.*[67] The Court of Appeal in *Azam* was concerned with three non-status migrants, citizens of India and Pakistan, who entered the UK clandestinely and remained and worked unlawfully for up to three years before coming to the attention of authorities. Lord Denning noted that until 1962, a Commonwealth citizen 'could come as of right into this country [and] could not be deported, not even if he was an habitual criminal, nor even if his presence here was very obnoxious to the rest of the people'.[68] He contrasted the situation of the Commonwealth citizen with that of the alien at common law:

> At common law no alien has any right to enter this country except by leave of the Crown; and the Crown can refuse leave without giving any reason. If he comes by leave, the Crown can impose such conditions as it thinks fit, as to his length of stay, or otherwise. He has no right whatever to remain here. He is liable to be sent home to his own country at any time if, in the opinion of the Crown, his presence here is not conducive to the public good[.][69] [citations omitted]

In *Pentonville Prison*, the common law status of the alien is a historical reference inserted for comparative purposes. The case offers up two disparate insights. First, the pre-1962 right of 'Commonwealth citizens' to enter was clearly a residue of empire, suggesting that a transnational imperial formation (with its non-contiguous inside and outside) muddles the apparent clarity of the common law position.[70] Indeed, the 1906 Privy Council judgment in *Attorney General* v. *Cain* concerned the new

[67] *Azam*, cited in *Chiarelli*, at 733. *Chiarelli* does not mention another oft-cited case about the power to exclude and expel aliens, namely *Attorney General for the Dominion of Canada* v. *Cain*, [1906] UKPC 55. That case stands for the proposition that the power to make laws governing entry, exclusion and expulsion is a 'supreme power in every State' which the Imperial Government could, and did, delegate to the Dominion Government of Canada (at 3).

[68] *Azam*, at 27, aff'd *Azam* v. *Secretary of State for the Home Department* [1973] UKHL 7.

[69] Ibid.

[70] Notably, Lord Denning did not explicitly rely on the prerogative to do any work in his judgment; he introduced it along with the pre-1962 legal position of Commonwealth citizens in order to situate the appellants' current legal position, which was determined by

Dominion of Canada's authority over borders, not the UK's. Secondly, *Pentonville Prison*'s extravagant depiction of the Crown's authority makes patent that the obverse of the alien's rightlessness at common law is the absolute power of the sovereign to exclude and expel.

In *Chiarelli*, this Principle is invoked to supply 'context' for the interpretation of section 7, and for this purpose, it matters that neither Lord Denning nor Sopinka J affixed the Crown's authority at common law with a label. For what they describe looks, in essence, like an executive prerogative over immigration. The conceptual foundations and precise definition of a prerogative power remain disputed. A dominant account provided by Dicey describes it as 'the residue of discretionary or arbitrary authority which at any time is left in the hands of the Crown'.[71] Matching Dicey's general definition against Lord Denning's account of the Crown's authority over aliens under common law reveals a close fit. In the absence of immigration law, it is not the case that borders are open; rather, the Crown allegedly possesses plenary and unfettered power to admit, exclude or expel the alien.[72]

The persistence of prerogative powers raises obvious democratic and rule of law objections: the Crown may exercise a prerogative without prior legislative authority and, until recently, judicial review of prerogative powers was less oversight than perfunctory glance. The insulation of the prerogative from judicial review has diminished but not disappeared over time. Because prerogative powers are rooted in the common law, the courts adjudicate the existence and ambit of a given prerogative, but courts remain diffident about genuinely scrutinising the actual exercise of a prerogative.[73]

Canadian courts' unease with prerogative powers is reflected in techniques that shrink and curtail them. One is the doctrine of displacement.

1968 reforms to UK law that significantly restricted rights of entry and residence of Commonwealth citizens.

[71] Peter W. Hogg, Patrick J. Monahan and Wade K. Wright, *Liability of the Crown* 4th ed. (Toronto: Carswell, 2011) at 19 citing A. V. Dicey, *The Law of the Constitution* 10th ed. (London: Macmillan, 1959). For a comparison of the Diceyan version with those of Blackstone and Locke, as well as more general administrative 'third source' powers, see Thomas Poole, 'The Strange Death of Prerogative in England' (2018) 43(2) *University of Western Australia Law Review* 42.

[72] Lord Denning's account would likely fit Blackstone's or Locke's concept of the prerogative equally well.

[73] See Audrey Macklin, 'Comment on *Canada v. Khadr*' (2010) 51 *Supreme Court Law Review* (2d) 295–331.Thomas Poole concludes that the conceptual distinctiveness of the prerogative is waning in England and that the range of executive powers that attract that designation (and relative deference) is shrinking. See Poole, 'Strange Death' at 59–66.

According to the 'abeyance principle' of English law, a prerogative power may be extinguished by statute, and 'once a statute has occupied the field formerly occupied by the prerogative, the Crown must comply with the statute'.[74] A displaced prerogative cannot be revived by repeal of the statute. Indeed, recent UKSC jurisprudence confirms that the Immigration Act 1971 extinguished whatever prerogative existed with respect to aliens in the UK, except for enemy aliens in wartime.[75] One could reasonably assume the same of any prerogative over aliens under Canadian law, in light of more than a century of immigration statutes authorised under section 91(25) of the Canadian Constitution Act, 1867. Indeed, the evidence that any prerogative over immigration has been displaced by legislation seems incontrovertible. But even if one is not persuaded by the argument for abeyance, the Supreme Court of Canada has ruled that prerogative powers in Canada are subject to the Charter anyway.[76]

So if the Principle is really an extinguished prerogative, why is it intruding into constitutional adjudication to negate a claim to fundamental justice? The Court does not identify it as (an extinguished) prerogative, but introduces it as a resource for interpreting the scope of section 7. But it is not merely *a* source of context, it is the *only* source of context for thinking about the constitutional rights of non-citizens in relation to deportation.

In so doing, the Court omits consideration of any other common law resources that are directly apposite to contemporary immigration law. For example, domicile is a common law concept that links an individual to a jurisdiction through a combination of residence and the subjective intention of the individual to make that place the centre of his or her existence. It is not formally bestowed by the state in the form of

74 Hogg et al., *Liability of the Crown* at 21. The original English case is *Attorney-General v. De Keyser's Royal Hotel Ltd* [1920] AC 508.

75 *Munir* v. *Secretary of State for the Home Department*, [2012] UKSC 32; *Alvi* v. *Secretary of State for the Home Department*, [2012] UKSC 33. The judgments emphasise that the prerogative never applied to Commonwealth citizens anyway, since they owed allegiance to the Crown and were therefore not 'aliens'. However, in *R (XH)* v. *Secretary of State for the Home Department* [2017] EWCA Civ 4, the Court of Appeal ruled that the UK Terrorism Prevention and Investigation Measures Act 2011 had not displaced the royal prerogative to issue, rescind and cancel passports. In Canada, the issuance of passports is acknowledged as a prerogative power, but the exercise of that power is still subject to the Charter. *See Abdelrazik* v. *Canada*, 2009 FC 580.

76 *Operation Dismantle* v. *The Queen*, [1985] 1 SCR 441; *Canada (Prime Minister)* v. *Khadr* 2010 SCC 3; *Abdelrazik*.

permanent resident status. Rather, it is legal recognition of the de facto functional and subjective attachment by the individual to the jurisdiction: it is home.[77] The common law declares domicile to come into existence when the 'facts on the ground' support it, and formal state recognition is neither an element nor prerequisite of domicile.[78] It recognises that time and ties matter. Consistent with other common law principles, domicile tacitly acknowledges that the strength of a claim to a benefit increases the longer one has enjoyed it.

Importantly, for most of the twentieth century, immigrants who were domiciled in Canada for at least five years were virtually non-deportable, even though they were not naturalised as British subjects of Canada or (after 1947) as Canadian citizens.[79] The common law of domicile was incorporated into immigration law and tacitly recognised a functional membership (or at least social attachment) between individual and jurisdiction that crystallised independent of status, and which warranted protection from severance. Up until the 1976 Immigration Act, Canadian immigration law regarded those with domicile as entitled to greater protection from removal than those immigrants or even naturalised Canadians who had either not acquired or had relinquished Canadian domicile.[80]

Apart from immigration-specific concepts and doctrines in the common law, constitutional jurisprudence offer various resources that would be germane to determining whether deportation of a long term permanent resident engages life, liberty and security of the person. These include the recognition of state-imposed psychological stress, and the harm occasioned by loss of custody of children. And if the hurdle of 'life, liberty and security of the person' is cleared, principles of fundamental justice such as disproportionality and individualised assessment also come into play.

[77] As Lord Cranworth stated over 150 years ago, 'by domicile, we mean home, the permanent home'. *Whicker* v. *Hume*, [1858] HLC 124.

[78] Domicile currently operates mainly in private law, but it also operated in Canadian immigration law until the late 1970s.

[79] The criminal grounds for deportation of domiciled immigrants fluctuated over the years; the law that the 1976 Immigration Act replaced restricted deportation to subversion, disloyalty, and certain narcotics offences (s. 19). Non-domiciled immigrants were deportable for any offence for which the actual sentence was six months.

[80] See, e.g., *R* v. *Hall*, (1983), 3 DLR (4th) 135; 44 O.R. (2d) 45 (domiciled non-citizen immune from deportation for crime committed before 1976 Immigration Act, but deportable as permanent resident for same offence committed after Immigration Act in force).

My point is that if the Principle is really there to provide context for the interpretation of section 7, it could and should have been accompanied by other contextually relevant considerations drawn from the common law, international law, and constitutional jurisprudence. More importantly, it would have been followed by an acknowledgement that common law qualifications on the non-citizen's right to enter and remain are still subject to the Charter. That non-citizens, and only non-citizens, can be deported is not responsive to an argument that the actual laws governing deportation violate life, liberty or security of the person. Nor does it answer the question of whether any such violation comports with fundamental justice.

To the extent that a common law principle may inform interpretation of the Charter, it is not by dint of its mere existence, but rather because it embodies or expresses deeper principles and values animating the Charter. In *Re BC Motor Vehicle Act*, Lamer J cautioned that contenders for section 7 principles of fundamental justice must be 'recognized as elements of a system for the administration of justice which is founded upon a belief in the human dignity and worth of the human person ... and on the rule of law'.[81] In *R* v. *Oakes*, Dickson CJ summarised the values underpinning the Charter as 'respect for the inherent dignity of the human person, commitment to social justice and equality, accommodation of a wide variety of beliefs, respect for cultural and group identity, and faith in social and political institutions which enhance the participation of individuals and groups in society'.[82]

To reprise, if the Principle is meant to channel an ordinary common law prerogative, that prerogative would have been extinguished a century ago and even it was not, it would still be subordinate to the Charter.[83]

But perhaps this prerogative over aliens can't really have been extinguished after all; maybe it has been undead all along. For instance, in *Chiarelli*, the Supreme Court quotes with approval the following passage from its 1976 judgment in *Prata* v. *Minister of Manpower and Immigration*,[84] which concerned residual Ministerial discretion to overrule a contrary decision by an immigration tribunal and order the removal of a non-citizen in light of national security or criminal intelligence reports:

[81] [1985] 2 SCR 486 at [30], [1985] SCJ No 73.
[82] [1986] 1 SCR 103 at [64], [1986] SCJ No 7.
[83] See, e.g., *Operation Dismantle* v. *The Queen*, [1985] 1 SCR 441; *Canada (Prime Minister)* v. *Khadr*.
[84] [1976] 1 SCR 376.

> The effect of s. 21 is to reserve to the Crown, notwithstanding the powers conferred upon the Board by the Act, the right, *similar to the prerogative right which existed at common law*, to determine that the continued presence in Canada of an alien, subject to a deportation order, would not be conducive to the public good.[85]

Despite the rule that statute displaces prerogative, this zombie prerogative haunts immigration law, seemingly indestructible and immortal. Consider the *Suresh* exception. The Court had before it a discretion akin to section 21 in *Prata*. Section 53(1)(b) of the Immigration Act permitted the *refoulement* of a refugee where the Minister was 'of the opinion that the person constitutes a danger to the security of Canada'.[86] Suresh was a refugee found inadmissible on national security grounds. He faced a substantial risk of torture if deported to Sri Lanka. Confronted with the question of whether deportation to torture violates section 7 of the Charter, the Court could have said yes, or no. Instead, it said 'yes, unless there are exceptional circumstances'.[87] And it managed to say so without mentioning *Chiarelli* or uttering the Principle.

Elsewhere, I have asked what exceptional circumstances could justify deportation to torture.[88] The standard hypothetical justification for torture – the ticking bomb scenario – clearly has no relevance to a decision to expel a non-citizen. And if evidence showed that the person was extremely dangerous, the expansive powers of Canadian anti-terrorism law could confine him. My powers of imagination failed to conjure up any scenario where the benefits to national security of deporting a person exceeded the harm of torturing that person, no matter how heinous the individual. Indeed, the more demonstrably heinous the individual, the more certain the availability of alternative means of containment – including criminal prosecution.

I now believe that the *Suresh* exception does not exist to accommodate a hypothetical case where deportation to torture could be justified according to any rational calculus. Rather, I suspect that the Court simply could not bring itself to judicially impose an absolute limit on the executive's power to deport, no matter the gravity of the rights violation, even if it meant flouting international law, and despite precedents from

[85] Ibid., (emphasis added).
[86] RSC 1985, c I-2.
[87] *Suresh* [2002] 1 SCR 3, at [78].
[88] Audrey Macklin, 'Still Stuck at the Border', in Craig Forcese and François Crépeau (eds.), *Terrorism, Law & Democracy: 10 Years After 9/11* (Ottawa: Canadian Institute for the Administration of Justice, 2012) 261 at 274–85.

the European Court of Human Rights and elsewhere.[89] Instead, the Court fashioned and delivered to the executive a new prerogative, the power to deport a non-citizen to torture in exceptional circumstances. This authority resembles a prerogative more than an ordinary grant of discretion in two respects. First, it is a judicial creation in the tradition of the common law's authority to identify and delimit the prerogative. It is not a statutory discretion legislated by Parliament. Secondly, it is inherently impervious to the discipline of legality. No technique of judicial review, not even under the rubric of deference, could furnish a principled account of a decision to deport to torture as a proportionate rights violation.[90]

This zombie prerogative also has the pernicious knock-on effect of propagating further distortions of legality upstream in the process: In *Belmarsh*, the UK House of Lords ruled, inter alia, that the impossibility of deportation to torture discredited the government's argument that confinement of non-citizens deemed security threats did not constitute indefinite detention. Detention in the service of facilitating deportation lost its rationale if detention was not foreseeably practicable, and became indefinite and arbitrary. In *Charkaoui*, the Court found that the hypothetical possibility of lawful deportation to torture meant that detention of persons named in security certificates was not detached from the ultimate purpose of deportation.[91] So, the Canadian Supreme Court tolerates a species of indefinite detention that the UK court does not because the former clings to the possibility that the detention may be a prelude to a lawful deportation to torture, whereas the UK court has foreclosed that possibility.[92]

This judicial diffidence in the face of the executive will to expel tracks extradition jurisprudence.[93] In the 1991 *Ng* and *Kindler* judgments,[94] the

[89] See, e.g., *Chahal* v. *United Kingdom* (1996), ECHR 54, 25 EHRR 33; *Saadi* v. *Italy*, No 37201/06, [2008] ECHR 179 [GC], 47 EHRR 17; *Attorney General* v. *Zaoui*, [2005] NZSC 38.

[90] Macklin, 'Still Stuck'.

[91] The Australian High Court took the same position in *al Kateb* v. *Godwin*, 2004 HCA 37, concerning the indefinite detention of a stateless Palestinian.

[92] See Rayner Thwaites, 'Discriminating Against Non-citizens Under the Charter: Charkaoui and Section 15' (2009) 34 *Queen's Law Journal* 669.

[93] See Catherine Dauvergne, 'How the Charter Has Failed Non-citizens in Canada: Reviewing Thirty Years of Supreme Court of Canada Jurisprudence' (2013) 58(3) *McGill Law Journal* 663 at 722. In her survey of thirty years of Supreme Court jurisprudence on the Charter and non-citizens, Dauvergne arrives at the conclusion that the Court prefers to create a '"constitutionalized' space for discretionary decision-making, rather than make a hard rights-based response'.

[94] *Kindler* v. *Canada (Minister of Justice)*, [1991] 2 SCR 779, [1991] SCJ No 63; *Reference re Ng Extradition (Canada)*, [1991] 2 SCR 858, [1991] SCJ No 64.

Court ruled that the Charter did not require the Canadian government to request assurances from the USA that extradited individuals would be spared the death penalty. In *Chiarelli*, Sopinka J quotes from *Kindler* in support of the 'right and duty of the state to keep out and expel aliens from this country if it considers it advisable to do so'.[95] A decade later, the Supreme Court of Canada reversed itself in *Burns and Rafay*.[96] Henceforth, the Canadian government was 'constitutionally required in all but exceptional cases' to seek assurances that the extradited person would not be subject to the death penalty.[97] Here again, the Court narrows but does not eliminate executive discretion. As with torture, one struggles to conjure up a scenario that would justify a refusal to request assurances.[98] One surmises that, as with torture, the Court gambled on never being called on to judicially review the unreasonableness of the undecidable. But what I wish to underscore here is simply the distinctiveness and sheer tensile strength of the Principle.

C Can Reason of State Rescue the Principle?

As described above, my position is not that the Principle is an ordinary prerogative.[99] I concur with Thomas Poole's observation that for at least three decades, 'the judiciary has been waging a fairly consistent campaign to bring prerogative power within the ambit of "normal" judicial review',[100] albeit the judiciary displays considerable deference towards exercises of prerogative power within that ambit. Though writing about the UK, his assessment is equally if not more apposite to Canada, especially since the Supreme Court of Canada has ruled explicitly that the prerogative is subject to the Charter. This does not preclude deferential outcomes, but they are presented as justified rights infringements, not as formally beyond the reach of judicial accountability.

95 *Kindler*, at 834, cited in *Chiarelli*, at 733.

96 *United States* v. *Burns* [2001] 1 SCR 283 (*Burns and Rafay*).

97 Ibid., at [8].

98 It is noteworthy that the Court in *Burns and Rafay* did not rely on the appellant's Canadian citizenship as a distinguishing factor. The ruling applies equally to citizens and non-citizens.

99 I note here that while prerogative powers are subject to the Charter, the Court has approached their review with extraordinary deference. See Audrey Macklin, 'Comment on *Canada (Prime Minister) v Khadr* (2010)' (2010) 51 *Supreme Court Law Review* (2d) 295.

100 Thomas Poole, *Reason of State: Law, Prerogative and Empire* (Cambridge: Cambridge University Press, 2014), 265.

Poole's analysis of the prerogative, however, plays a secondary role in the project of recuperating 'reason of state' as a conceptual category capable of conceding 'the existence of an exceptional domain that is necessarily part of the stable ordering of the state', without renouncing modern constitutionalism's insistence that 'even in these more exceptional contexts the basic reasoning and justification obligations on those who exercise state power are not obviated'.[101] Poole's objective is at least partly to provide an alternative theoretical framework to Agamben's (via Schmitt and Arendt) Manichean state of exception model, the more prosaic typology of states of emergency, or indeed the common law prerogative power. He explicates the ways in which reason of state is embedded in recent constitutional jurisprudence, why liberal rights constitutionalism can never fully suppress or eliminate it, and how the counterforce exerted by reason of state can be better managed within law in light of the values underpinning the modern liberal state. I find his account cogent and nuanced in many respects, and I approach it not for purposes of broad critique, but more as a foil to probe the question of how what I label as a zombie prerogative is putatively rationalised within a constitutional bill of rights.

Poole's contemporary definition of reason of state is the culmination of a journey through the history of the idea over time. For present purposes, I want to isolate three features: First, reason of state 'presupposes a situation in which state action moves from one register, based on law and right, to another, based on interest and might', because of the 'assertion that state's vital interests are at stake'.[102] Second, 'vital interests' are implicated in many aspects of apparently ordinary (as opposed to exceptional) governance. In contrast to the existential crisis that precipitates the state of exception, 'reason of state usually operates on a slightly less dramatic plane – war, diplomacy, safety, security – and in ways that are often rather quotidian'.[103] Finally, Poole posits an isomorphism between the inward and outward facing constitution – the 'internal construction of the state and its external actions'[104] – and the domains of legality and power respectively. But Poole also recognises that the 'way in which a state engages with the world outside feeds back into the way it constructs itself internally',[105] and further that 'given the

[101] Ibid., 279.
[102] Ibid., 3-4.
[103] Ibid., 5.
[104] Ibid., 9.
[105] Ibid.

prevalence of rights and risk in modern government, the exceptional is now as often as not folded up in, and all but indistinguishable from, the normal'.[106]

Poole does not identify immigration regulation as a domain of 'reason of state' but as soon as one reframes it as border control, it seems a likely candidate. Protecting the state and its citizens from the menacing foreign threat is a standard trope of statecraft. And, of course, US plenary power doctrine is predicated on tethering migration control to the conduct of foreign affairs.

The easy case for the operation of 'reason of state' arises where deportation concerns a deemed terror suspect. Here, I wish to focus on a stylised dialogue that Poole imagines in order to illustrate the sequence of 'trade-offs' between reason of state (government) and rule of law (judges) in the post-*Belmarsh* procession from terror suspect to detainee to deportee. He starts and finishes with the following admonitions from court to government:

> We (the court) have decided that you (the government) cannot have non-national terrorist suspects interned without trial (*Belmarsh*). But you *can* have control orders, so long as they do not infringe the right to liberty (*JJ, E*). . . . If you *have to* deport non-national terrorist suspects, you can only do so to problematic receiving countries once there is a sufficiently strong and believable memorandum of understanding in place.[107]

I want to pause and draw attention to this imaginary court's concession that the state 'has to' deport non-national terrorist suspects. Where does this necessity come from? This necessity to deport cannot flow from the designation of the individual as terror suspect, because citizen terror suspects are non-deportable. The state has no choice but to manage them through other means.[108] Therefore, the necessity can only derive from the fact that the suspect is a non-national. Reason of state must attach to alienage then, and not to security as such.

Migrants, of course, embody the liminality where reason of state and rule of law occupy the same field yet remain immiscible. Poole describes the governance of diplomacy as liminal, 'operating in the space between

[106] Ibid., 261.
[107] Ibid., 285 (italics in original; underline added).
[108] I leave aside here the possibility that if the terror suspect is a dual citizen, he may be deprived of UK citizenship when it conduces to the public good. If anything, this only reveals how the propagation of reason of state can lead to ever greater deformations of legality.

the ordinary and the internal, to which constitutional principles might be said to attach in a relatively uncomplicated way, and the exceptional and external, which always remain at least somewhat outside the grasp of those ordinary principles'.[109]

One might understand the migrant in the same terms, especially the migrant who seeks entry based on the state's external – yet legal – commitments (such as the Refugee Convention) or the migrant already residing within the state, that space where constitutional protection supposedly attaches.[110] The resident non-citizen is simultaneously inside the state and entitled to its protection (rule of law), and external to the polity and so the object of power and interest (reason of state).

What are the criteria for assigning a sphere of state action to the reason of state's remit? Border control could, I think, fit comfortably within the category 'reason of state'. But even if one is persuaded that rule of law absolutists should reconcile themselves to some version of it rather than attempt to suppress it, there remains the challenge of taxonomy. With the ascendance of governance through risk, it requires only moderate gifts of imagination on the part of those so inclined to populate 'reason of state' with an ever growing list of policy domains that implicate 'the health and well-being' of the people or the 'vital interests' of the state. I struggle to discern what (if any) norms ought to guide classification. The allowances made for 'reason of state' raise the stakes on designation, and so the question of what belongs to 'reason of state' becomes contestable in normative (and not only analytical) terms.

Assigning contemporary border control to 'reason of state' seems descriptively plausible but normatively disquieting. First, it capitulates to the assertion of securitisation as the defining trait of migration regulation. Second, I fear that it replicates (rather than resolves) the problem that the Principle exposes. That is to say, it adopts the state perspective as the basis of classification and suggests that a unified legal response should govern matters within the class. If we regard the legal subject (rather than the state) as the launching point for the inquiry instead, one might concede that an individual may act in myriad ways that engage or imperil the 'vital interests' of the state. But to return to my earlier example, what distinguishes the legal response to the citizen terror suspect and the alien terror suspect is not whether vital interests of the state are at stake.

[109] Poole, *Reason of State*, at 269.

[110] For an exploration of this in the US context, see Linda Bosniak, *The Citizen and the Alien* (Princeton: Princeton University Press, 2007).

My pragmatic explanation for the disparity is that the legal system's historic and core preoccupation with the liberty deprivation entailed by imprisonment makes it harder to ignore the liberty deprivation of immigration detention. The *Belmarsh* court clearly sees immigration detention as an inside problem for UK constitutionalism. The Supreme Court of Canada locates it elsewhere along the Charter's Mobius strip. Deportation, however, is uniquely and singularly applicable to non-citizens; without a citizen comparator, judicial recognition of deportation's damaging impact on long-term residents is easier to suppress: It's easier for all courts to see it as an outside-the-constitution problem.

III Conclusion

Having invested in the label 'zombie prerogative' to explain the mechanics of immigration exceptionalism, I want to finish by suggesting that it may not be operating as a prerogative *power* at all. The quotation from Vattel that opens this chapter declares the 'right' of the state to exclude and expel the alien.[111] More recently, the European Court of Human Rights in *Jeunesse* v. *Netherlands* rejected a claim that deportation of a long-term permanent resident with a Dutch spouse and Dutch children would breach her right to family life under Article 8 of the European Convention on Human Rights. The European Court of Human Rights restates Vattel's claim that 'a State is entitled, as a matter of well-established international law and subject to its treaty obligations, to control the entry of aliens into its territory and their residence there'.[112] But the Court then draws the following inference:

> The corollary of a State's right to control immigration is the duty of aliens such as the applicant to submit to immigration controls and procedures and leave the territory of the Contracting State when so ordered if they are lawfully denied entry or residence.[113]

As a statement of international legal rights and duties, this cannot be correct. At the risk of overweaning formalism, one must differentiate between parties to legal relations at international law and under domestic law.[114] At international law, states possess sovereign rights as against other states, not against individuals. The right of states to exclude or expel

[111] See the epigraph at 243.
[112] 2014 ECHR 12738/10, October 3, 2014, [100].
[113] Ibid.
[114] I do not undertake a Hohfeldian analysis here.

non-citizens is a right notionally asserted against the other state of nationality. If state X has a right to exclude a national of state Y, the obverse is that state Y has no right to foist its national onto state X. And if state X wishes to expel a national of state Y, state Y has the corresponding duty to (re)admit its national. Individuals are the objects, not the agents, of these transactions. The larger point is that exclusion and expulsion are rights of states against other states – not against individuals – at international law. Thus, the corollary of a state's right to exclude a non-national at international law is the state of nationality's duty to (re) admit that national, not a duty of the alien.

That is not to deny the obvious facts that states exercise power in and outside their territory to exclude and expel foreigners, and aliens are bound by those domestic laws. Under domestic constitutional law, the relevant relationship is not state-to-state, but rather state-to-legal subject. States exert power, albeit power that depends on legal authorisation; individuals do or do not possess rights that constrain the exercise of that power. More specifically, the Constitution Act 1867 is the source of federal jurisdiction over immigration in the Canadian legal order, and whatever rights individuals possess that limit that power are located in public law norms and the Charter.

Without saying so explicitly, the Principle confounds the distinction between state rights under international law and state powers under domestic constitutional law by treating the state's domestic constitutional *power* over aliens to expel them as a domestic constitutional *right* of states to expel aliens. How does the Principle do this and why does it matter? If all the statement 'an alien has no unqualified right to enter and remain' means is that the state has the power to exclude and expel aliens, the Principle would be unexceptionable. But it would also fail to do any work. No legal case I know advances the argument that aliens have an unqualified right to enter and remain; the argument is always about the legality of the qualifications.

What the Principle does instead is declare that an alien has no unqualified right to enter and remain and *therefore* the deportation of an alien does not engage the constitutional or human rights of the person. But the first proposition does not generate the second as a necessary consequence. That the state possesses a given power does not answer (much less defeat) a claim that the exercise of that power violates the right of an individual in a particular case.

But if the state *does* have a domestic constitutional right as against aliens to expel, the state's right would indeed refute a claim of constitutional right not to be expelled. And then it would make sense to proceed from the right of the state to deport, to the absence of an alien's right not to be deported, to the conclusion that deportation cannot be a rights-violating act. Significantly, the assertion of a right requires no reasoned justification. Of course, it may be limited by public interest considerations, but the burden of justification lies on the one who seeks to limit the right, not on the rights holder.

In contrast to assertion of right, the assertion of public power within a legal order is answerable to a call for reasoned justification addressed to the one over whom power is exercised. The confounding feature of the Principle is that it allows a power to behave like a right, unencumbered by a duty to justify itself to the non-citizen. In so doing, it both stifles the individual right, and repudiates the commitment to reasoned justification that Poole posits as the requirement for accommodating 'reason of state' within a framework of legality. In effect, the Court imports an anthropomorphic conception of the state as rights bearer into the *Charter*, and sets up deportation as a contest of 'state right' versus 'individual right', where the state and the individual are juridical equals. This is simply wrong. The figure of a rights-asserting state is intelligible when a state asserts a right against another state, but is incompatible with the internal architecture of a constitutional bill of rights or, at any rate, the Canadian Charter.[115] States have power; people have rights.

So, the Principle beguiles and deceives by transforming an external norm of sovereignty into an ersatz internal norm of sovereignty. Sovereign equality between states (the external norm) underwrites the right of states to exclude and expel under international law. The Principle converts this sovereign equality of states into juridical equality between state and non-citizen under domestic constitutional law. This move is distinct from the equal subjection of state actor and individual to the rule of law within a domestic legal order, and inimical to the normative foundation of a constitutional bill of rights.[116] There is no such internal norm of juridical equality between state and legal subject in Anglo-American law. And yet, there it is, hiding in plain sight, in public law

[115] This fetishisation of border-control explains why the s. 7 doctrine in this field appears aberrant when situated alongside other s. 7 jurisprudence. See, e.g., Hamish Stewart, *Fundamental Justice: Section 7 of the Canadian Charter of Rights and Freedoms* (Toronto: Irwin Law, 2012), 280–84.

[116] Nothing I have said entails accepting that non-citizens do have an unqualified right to enter or remain. Nor do I develop an argument about a potential constitutional challenge to the alleged right to exclude (as opposed to expel).

and constitutional jurisprudence in Canada, the USA and the UK. We just don't face it.

This chapter does not follow-up critical analysis with affirmative prescription. The normative point is that the Principle wrongly denies a class of legal subjects access to accountability for the exercise of state power in the form of deportation. At least some of those deportations would not withstand meaningful constitutional scrutiny. To that extent, non-citizens are unjustly expelled from the constitutional terrain, despite formal recognition as rights bearers. Genuine recognition of the non-citizen as a rights-bearing subject would not preclude deportation, but it would rule out-of-court the 'we do it because we can' legitimation of force that underwrites the Principle. Like any other rights-infringing exercise of power, deportation would be answerable to the call for individualised justification.[117] Advancing that normative project would require tackling the claim that sovereign power to admit, exclude and expel, whether in the name of self-determination or self-preservation, is appropriately regarded as existential and transcendent. On this account, it constitutes the state and so, accordingly, cannot or should not be fully subject to the discipline of a national constitution. If this is an acceptable view, we should be troubled, not only because of the harm it inflicts on non-citizens, but because of the damage it inflicts on the rule of law.

[117] For an extended argument about why states owe a legal duty of justification in respect of exclusion, see Bas Schotel, *On the Right of Exclusion*.

10

The Constitution in the Shadow of the Immigration State

ASHA KAUSHAL

Introduction

The two-faced constitution conjures the image of a constitution with an external and an internal face. The theoretical value of that image lies in its ability to enhance our understanding of the constitution and its politics. This chapter intervenes in the discussion over constitutional visages to query *who* the constitution is facing. When the constitution faces inward, who does it hold in its gaze? When the constitution turns outward, to whom is its face directed? The answers to these questions are found in the interstices of immigration law and constitutional law. Because both the membership and identity of the constitution's external and internal audiences are partly constituted by immigration law, this chapter focuses on how the faces of the constitution are conceived and justified in the theoretical frameworks of both fields. Once we place these frameworks in conversation – and once we think about immigration decisions as threshold citizenship matters – it is clear where immigration law meets the constitutional theory of constituent power. The image of the two-faced constitution reveals that the internal and external faces of the constitution are inextricably tied to immigration law and the project of constituting the people.

Immigration is both an external objective of the constitutional order and a modifier of that order. This chapter explores immigration law as a specific channel of external projection, which also constitutes the internal constitutional order. This is what I will refer to as the concept of *constitutive duality*. Immigration laws face both inwards and outwards. Their primary function, though, is to project outward what will ultimately constitute the state internally ('the people'), locking the external projection of immigration laws and the internal constitution of society in an ongoing constitutive circuit. In terms of the double-facing constitution, immigration law offers insights into constitutional identity because of the force of this constitutive duality. Immigration policy reflects constitutional identity 'by mirroring not only the qualities that "we" value in others, but also by reflecting what defines "us" as a nation'.[1] It is equally important as a pivot upon which constitutional subjectivity turns, especially where subjectivity is understood as marking constitutional rights holders. Constitutional norms of non-discrimination, limits on deprivations of liberty in detention and deportation settings, and the division of powers all touch the margins of immigration law but they do not address its core legal distinctions or statuses. Constitutional subjects are often identified by citizen status, and yet immigration is largely outside of the constitution.

The nexus between the constitution and immigration law is a revealing site. Hanna Pitkin suggested that 'to understand what a constitution is, one must look not to some crystalline core or essence of unambiguous meaning but precisely *at* the ambiguities, the specific oppositions that this specific concept helps us to hold in tension'.[2] Taking this to heart, and tracing the juridical relationship between immigration and the constitution over time, several oppositions are rendered. The story of the relationship begins with a very old internal/external distinction from international law publicist Emer de Vattel, which was enfolded into constitutional law with enduring consequences. Several countries of immigration incorporated this distinction – itself based on a particular melding of natural and positive law – into early cases that grant the executive branch broad powers to exclude and remove non-citizens. This jurisprudence relies on obsolete notions of internal and external spheres of action to make immigrants 'strangers to the constitution'.[3] As the rights revolution progressed, the relationship between immigration and the constitution began to be articulated through certain constitutional rights. The external/internal distinction plays a key role in the reach and scope of those rights to immigrants. In particular, the right to life, liberty,

[1] Liav Orgad, *The Cultural Defense of Nations: A Liberal Theory of Majority Rights* (Cambridge: Cambridge University Press, 2015), at 86–87: '[D]efining the "we," setting criteria for identifying the desired "they", and finding the core to which "they" should subscribe to become part of "us".'

[2] Hanna Fenichel Pitkin, 'The Idea of a Constitution' (1987) 37 *Journal of Legal Education* 167 (emphasis in original).

[3] Gerald Neuman, *Strangers to the Constitution: Immigrants, Borders and Fundamental Law* (Princeton: Princeton University Press, 1996).

and security of the person in section 7 of the Canadian Charter of Rights and Freedoms turns out to be a significant source of law about immigration and the faces of the constitution. It is through the contextual approach to the principles of fundamental justice in section 7 that the key oppositions suggested by immigration law are both made material and held in fragile balance.

This discussion of the constitution and immigration, of constituent power and citizenship, requires some precision about the audience of the double-facing constitution. The alien functions as a concept that limits the internal and external aspects of the constitutional order. The term 'alien' is used in international law as well as some municipal law systems, including the United States, to denote a person who is not a national or citizen. In Canada, we prefer the terms 'foreign national' or 'permanent resident'. There are gradations of alien status – temporary or permanent, documented or undocumented – but the underlying concept describes the status of non-citizen and thus non-member. Sitting on the threshold between inside and outside – typically inside the state but not a citizen-member, often marked for external deportation – the alien captures several dynamics of the constitutional 'us' and 'them'. In constitutional law cases, alien status is often the pivot upon which rights often turn. By parsing where immigration law meets the constitution, it is clear that the external face of the constitution is partial out there beyond state borders, where it effectively leaves immigration law to its own devices, while its internal face is only fully focused on citizens. That the constitutional order enfolds the core concepts of immigration law to delimit its reach and content should not be surprising.[4] Both constitutional and immigration law depend on concepts of closure and membership.

The constitution treats aliens in various ways. In terms of constitutional rights, the language of the Canadian Charter of Rights and Freedoms is mixed, referring to 'everyone', 'every citizen', 'a permanent resident', 'any person', 'every individual', 'any member of the public in Canada', and 'anyone'.[5] Indeed, while most of the fundamental rights and freedoms are available to those present on Canadian soil, this is not the whole picture.[6] This chapter examines the way that the Constitution

4 It is worth noting that immigration law is not the only body of law that performs this kind of work. See, e.g., Indian Act, RSC, 1985, c. I-5.

5 Canadian Charter of Rights and Freedoms, Part I of the Constitution Act 1982, being Schedule B to the Canada Act 1982, c. 11 (UK), ss. 2–24.

6 Some rights, like voting rights, some mobility rights, and minority language rights, are reserved to citizens. On the limits of the constitutional text, see also Catherine Dauvergne,

treats aliens under section 7 of the Charter, which is the provision most often invoked by aliens to challenge legal actions related to their alienage, such as detention and deportation proceedings. These cases reveal the Supreme Court of Canada reckoning with the circle of membership in the adjudication of rights. In this reckoning, the Court reframes the facially inclusive language of the Charter by making alienage relevant in other sites of constitutional analysis. In section 7 cases about refugees and immigrants, the Court accomplishes this by drawing on the specific context presented by immigration to limit the reach of constitutional rights. These cases reveal the complicated position of the alien in the constitutional order: someone whom the constitution seeks to address and subject but not to fully protect.

In immigration law, citizenship is the standard bearer for delimiting issues of membership and constitutional coverage. In constitutional law and theory, constituent power is the conceptual foundation of legitimacy, as well as constitutional coverage. These are both concerned with 'the people' of the constitutional order. As we shall see, these concepts overlap but they are not the same, nor do they perform the same disciplinary theoretical work.[7] This chapter is focused on the people – loosely understood as the body politic – in the context of an existing constitution. While the concept of constituent power crosses pre-constitutional and post-constitutional time, this chapter begins from the immigration perspective and, consequently, is concerned with the construction of the people after the constitution has been made. This is perhaps obvious in a discussion about who the constitution faces when it is turned internally or externally. The insights implicate the broad temporality of constituent power to the extent that they speak to how constituent power moves through time and how it binds future addressees but that is not their primary focus.

The chapter proceeds in five sections. First, it surveys the concepts of constituency in immigration law and constitutional law. This section locates the common conceptual base of citizenship and constituent

'How the Charter Has Failed Non-citizens in Canada: Reviewing Thirty Years of Supreme Court of Canada Jurisprudence' (2013) 58 *McGill Law Journal* 663.

7 There is a definition of 'constitution' (in its constitutive function) where citizenship and constituent power perform the same function of delimiting membership in constitutional state. But, as time passes and each category expands, they each come to mean more than that. On the constitutive function of the constitution, see Stephen Holmes, 'Constitutions and Constitutionalism', in Michel Rosenfeld and Andras Sajo (eds.), *The Oxford Handbook of Comparative Constitutional Law* (Oxford: Oxford University Press, 2012), 189.

power through the lens of the double-facing constitution. It argues that these fields rely on a division of labour for their boundaries and coherence. Second, the chapter analyses the relationship between immigration and the constitution. It takes an historical approach, beginning with an old distinction between external and internal obligations from the classical international law publicists. After tracing the genealogy of that distinction as it travelled into constitutional law, this section examines its contemporary manifestation in section 7 of the Charter. The chapter concludes with the narrative suggested by the section 7 cases, and how it fits into the division of labour between immigration law and constitutional law. It returns to Pitkin's constitutional oppositions to argue that all of these pieces come together against the backdrop of the double-facing constitution in motion and that the dynamic constitution reveals the relationship between the internal and external faces of the constitution.

I The View from Where? Concepts of Constituency

The concept of constituency is panoptic; it is used here to connote the people who count for the relationship between immigration and the constitution. This section explores the disciplinary concepts of constituency that underwrite the people in immigration law and constitutional theory. It is by now well established that communities rest on boundaries and that, at some point, boundaries imply closure.[8] Both immigration law and constitutional law are about constituting the people of the constitutional order. What concepts do immigration law and constitutional theory use to construct and reinforce those boundaries? Immigration and citizenship law are concerned with access to membership and how to extend and curtail it. Constitutional theory is concerned with the legitimacy of the constitutional order and who is included in it. One uses the concept of membership *qua* citizenship; the other uses the concept of constituent power.

The problem that immigration presents for constituent power is temporal: how does constituent power incorporate new members? The problem that the constitution presents for immigration is status: how

[8] Michael Trebilcock and Ninette Kelley, *The Making of the Mosaic: A History of Canadian Immigration Policy* (Toronto: University of Toronto Press, 1998), 1; Michael Walzer, *Spheres of Justice: A Defense of Pluralism and Equality* (New York: Basic Books, 1984); Rogers Brubaker, *Citizenship and Nationhood in France and Germany* (Cambridge: Harvard University Press, 1992).

can there be partial constitutional subjects who are not part of the people? The result is a division of disciplinary labour. Immigration law gives constitutional law its constituency. Constitutional law depends upon immigration law's structural concepts of inclusion (such as status) to demarcate its own content and reach, as well as immigration law's role in 'managing' people so that the constitutional membership may be replenished. It is immigration law that constitutes the constitutional order in the most basic sense: it marks and enforces the boundaries of the people through its concepts of status. But this dependence is not only functional; it is also normative. Constitutional studies, like citizenship studies, rely on the premise of closure that immigration executes in order to avoid questions about the reach of justice and the scope of moral identifications.[9]

Immigration law lives in the shadow of citizenship; this is why the constitutional cases turn on the citizen/non-citizen distinction. Citizenship, also called nationality, is the legal concept of the legal status of belonging to a state.[10] In fact, the principles of fundamental justice cases are easily understood as turning on citizenship and subjectivity. In them, membership status is the basis for 'categorical, status-based distinctions that legitimize government action against non-citizens that would be unacceptable if applied to citizens'.[11] Linda Bosniak explains the co-dependent relationship between immigration and citizenship:

> The regulation of immigration presumes the noncitizenship of national outsiders; it is their lack of citizenship that allows the state to limit and otherwise place conditions on their territorial ingress and membership. Immigration control is thus the policy expression of bounded citizenship in its purest form.[12]

As Rogers Brubaker argued, the concept of citizenship that immigration law requires citizenship to be 'at once universal and particularistic, internally inclusive and externally exclusive'.[13] Once we think about immigration decisions as *threshold* citizenship matters, it is clear where immigration law meets constituent power.

[9] Linda Bosniak, *The Citizen and Alien: Dilemmas of Contemporary Membership* (Princeton: Princeton University Press, 2008).

[10] Catherine Dauvergne, *Making People Illegal* (Cambridge: Cambridge University Press, 2008).

[11] Daniel Kanstroom, *Deportation Nation: Outsiders in American History* (Cambridge: Harvard University Press, 2007), 48.

[12] Bosniak, *The Citizen and Alien*, 33.

[13] Brubaker, *Citizenship and Nationhood*, 72.

The constitution, meanwhile, lives in the shadow of constituent power. Constituent power is the principle that power vests in the people.[14] It is the self-referential claim of constitutional authority: those subject to power are also its authors. This concept of constituent power – the people – internalises the constitutional collective. These are the people who count for the constitution. Yet it is immediately apparent that 'to postulate the people as the bearer of constituent power . . . only begs the question about its identity'.[15] The value of constituent power for collective life lies in the concept of self-rule. Self-rule in this frame means the 'identity of the governed and the governing' so that the rulers and the ruled are the same.[16] This identity raises the puzzle of form. James Tully suggests that constitutional forms include the people, the nation, representative democracy, modern citizenship, federalism, self-determination, participatory democracy, and revolution.[17] But in the triangle of constituent power, the constitution, and constituted power, which form realises dynamic inclusion so that the 'self' in self-rule is coincident with the constitutional population?

Immigration intervenes here, bringing new citizens and thus new constituents to the constitution. This is the circuit of constitutive duality: the immigration state externally projects to attract and cull potential immigrants. Then, the resulting immigrants modify both the internal and external faces of the constitution through their identities and demands. They participate in society, acquire citizenship, vote in elections, make rights claims, and ultimately remake immigration and constitutional laws in their contemporary image. Immigration often forces a reckoning over constitutional identity in terms of rights and values. This is because immigration is not a singular event; it is the ongoing negotiation of the terms of entry and settlement. The stages of

[14] Martin Loughlin, 'The Concept of Constituent Power' 2014 13(2) *European Journal of Political Theory* 218.

[15] Zoran Oklopcic, 'Joel Colon-Rios, Weak Constitutionalism, Book Review' (October 15, 2012), *ICON-nect Blog* www.iconnectblog.com/2012/10/joel-colon-rios-weak-constitutionalism-democratic-legitimacy-and-the-question-of-constituent-power-london-routledge-2012/, accessed August 6, 2019.

[16] Hans Lindahl, 'Constituent Power and Reflexive Identity: Towards an Ontology of Collective Selfhood', in Martin Loughlin and Neil Walker (eds.), *The Paradox of Constitutionalism: Constituent Power and Constitutional Form* (Oxford: Oxford University Press, 2007), 9.

[17] James Tully, 'The Imperialism of Modern Constitutional Democracy', in Loughlin and Walker (eds.), *The Paradox of Constitutionalism: Constituent Power and Constitutional Form*, 315.

immigration begin with immigrant selection but move quickly to laws which 'shape the transition and integration of immigrants to degrees of membership'.[18] In negotiating those degrees of membership, immigration law engages ideas of the constitutional order's self and identity in order to exclude external others.

Constitutional constituent power thus runs into the problem of identifying its constituency. This is implicit in the push to find a unity.[19] No matter the approach, constituent power must still distinguish members and thus still rely upon citizenship law. Hans Lindahl argues that constituent power can only be resolved by recourse to reflexive identity, that constitutional acts can only be viewed retroactively – and provisionally – as an act by the collective.[20] He marries retroactivity with reflexive identity to suggest that no collective self exists independently of the individuals who compose it, but that the self to which they attribute these acts is a political unity.[21] This conception still chafes against questions of who gets to act. It rests on members or at least individuals capable of exercising rights – which the alien cannot. He argues, for example, that members of a collective body must retroactively accept this attribution by exercising the powers granted to them by a constitution. Whenever individuals exercise constitutional rights, they take up the 'people' perspective of the constitution. Clearly, this is not for individuals on the margins. Indeed, if constituent power is perceptible in the 'evolution of the fundamental laws of a particular society'[22] then the principles of fundamental justice are a telling example of how immigration law's unbounded discretion has been enfolded into a constitutional principle to the detriment of the alien.

Immigration law is a productive lens on constitutional identity and rights precisely because of the constituent duality. When the two fields are placed side by side, it is possible to see the constitutive duality in motion. Immigration law externally projects the requisite qualities for joining the people (which are based on notions of the constitutional self and its values), and those external projections loop back into

[18] Hiroshi Motomura, 'Looking for Immigration Law' (2015) 38(8) *Ethnic & Racial Studies* 1305, 1308.

[19] Ulrich K. Preuss, 'Constitutional Powermaking for the New Polity: Some Deliberations on the Relations between Constituent Power and the Constitution' (1992) 14 *Cardozo Law Review* 639.

[20] Lindahl, 'Constituent Power'.

[21] Ibid.

[22] Alexander Somek, 'Constituent Power in a Transnational and National Contexts' (2012) 3 *Transnational Legal Theory* 31, 36.

constitutional identity. The identity of the constitutional order – the terrain of constituent power – is projected outward and then revised by the people who are admitted to the order. Immigration is said to define the self as much as the other.[23] Indeed, the section 7 cases examined below show that constitutional law marks out its subjects and thus in large part its identity in quiet conversation with immigration law about the status of the alien.

There is yet another layer to this: immigration law projects externally and constitutional law constitutes internally. Immigration's work in culling the masses for citizenship – *membership* decisions, in other words – is also performed in constitutional law settings.[24] Constitutional law does not do this formally – by extending the status of citizenship or not – but rather substantively by ensuring that non-citizens do not get rights or protections reserved for citizens. Constitutional law relies on immigration law and its concepts of status to carve out a set of non-subjects outside of constituent power and thus not protected by constitutional concerns about legitimacy or democracy or self-rule. This is significant because within the *polis* constitutional law is generally considered non-discriminatory and robust, but closer examination of how constitutional law internalises immigration law's concepts and principles reveals the extent to which the former relies upon the status of the alien to mark out the parameters of constitutional subjectivity. It is to the details of this shared labour of delimiting the people that the chapter now turns.

II The Relationship between Immigration and the Constitution in Three Acts

The interface between the two-faced constitution and the relationship between immigration and the constitution is located in the question of *whom* the constitution is facing. The constituency inquiry highlights the division of labour between immigration law and constitutional law. Moreover, the constitutive duality observed earlier explains the trajectory of immigration in constitutional law from absolute discretion to more a nuanced narrative towards aliens. That duality is a source of constitutional dynamism but it also requires constant constitutional reckoning with immigration and particularly aliens. The external face of the

[23] Michel Rosenfeld, *The Identity of the Constitutional Subject: Selfhood, Citizenship, Culture and Community* (New York: Routledge, 2010).

[24] David Scott Fitzgerald and David Cook-Martin, *Culling the Masses* (Cambridge: Harvard University Press, 2014).

constitution is not external only in territorial orientation, pointed outside of state borders, but also external in personal orientation, pointed towards aliens inside state borders. The internal face, meanwhile, is directed towards citizens but over time has come to include pieces and slices of others in its gaze.

This section traces the evolution of the relationship between immigration and the constitution in Canada over time. The first part explores the lineage of the constitutional doctrine of absolute discretion in immigration law. This doctrine, present in Canadian as well as US and UK law, underwrites constitutional law's stance towards aliens. The second part examines how this doctrine has been incorporated into the specific constitutional phrase found in section 7: 'the principles of fundamental justice'. Three key conceptual cases are examined for their interpretative stance towards those principles in immigration law cases. The focus is on the judiciary's contextual approach to those principles and how that approach embodies the disciplinary division of labour.

A *The Internal/External Distinction from Emer de Vattel*

Aliens begin as outsiders to the state and its society.[25] They are external to the state, either nationals of other states or stateless on the international plane. When and under what conditions may an alien enter the state? The immediate answer to this question is contained in national immigration laws. The historical and theoretical basis for those laws, however, comes from the classical publicists of international law. The movement of people across borders was a preoccupation for these publicists, including Francisco de Vitoria, Hugo Grotius, and Emer de Vattel; key parts of immigration law remain anchored in their writings.[26]

The historical inquiry on the international plane focused on the extent to which a state was required to admit aliens. It turned on the line between the sovereign's absolute, unfettered right to exclude aliens and the qualifications of that right. Christian Wolff, and later his disciple Emer de Vattel, suggested an internal/external dichotomy rooted in the natural law tradition. This distinction might seem archaic but it has achieved traction as the foundation for contemporary immigration

[25] Neuman, *Strangers to the Constitution*, 10, 11.

[26] Vincent Chetail, 'The Human Rights of Migrants in General International Law: From Minimum Standards to Fundamental Rights' (2014) 28 *Georgetown Immigration Law Journal* 225, 225–26.

law.[27] Writing in 1758, Vattel argued that there was a distinction between the sovereign's internal natural law obligation to admit aliens and its external right to exclude aliens.[28] The sovereign *obligation* to admit aliens is a natural obligation, which means it is only internally binding on a sovereign's conscience. It is not recognised in international law and thus not enforceable.[29] The internal obligation of admission, then, amounts to a moral imperative.

> A sovereign sometimes had a natural obligation to permit aliens to enter the territory, particularly when the alien's need was great or the entrance could be permitted without significant disadvantage.[30]

Apart from its internally limited nature, the obligation to admit is also read down by the sovereign *right* to decide whom to admit and under what conditions. This right is external, which means it is rooted in the law of nations and thus enforceable. Vattel distinguished:

> [T]he internal law of nations, rooted in natural law, from the external law, rooted in what today one might call positivism. Internal law establishes sovereign duties as a matter of conscience and principle, whereas external law establishes sovereign rights as a matter of will.[31]

According to classical international law, then, states are morally or internally bound to admit aliens when there is no harm to their interests. James Nafziger argues that this is the correct reading of the publicists: there is a general obligation to admit except where national interests would be threatened.[32] His tentative rule of customary international law, based on a close reading of the classical publicists and case law, is: 'a state may exclude aliens if, individually or collectively, they pose serious danger to its public safety, security, general welfare, or essential institutions'.[33] However, as Gerald Neuman points out, states evaluate that harm and those interests themselves.[34] States were internally bound

[27] Neuman, *Strangers to the Constitution*, 13.

[28] Emer de Vattel, *The Law of Nations, Or, Principles of the Law of Nature, Applied to the Conduct and Affairs of Nations and Sovereigns, with Three Early Essays on the Origin and Nature of Natural Law and on Luxury*, Béla Kapossy and Richard Whitmore (eds.) (Indianapolis: Liberty Fund, 2008).

[29] Neuman, *Strangers to the Constitution*.

[30] Ibid., at 11.

[31] James A. R. Nafziger, 'The General Admission of Aliens under International Law' (1983) 77 *American Journal of International Law* 804, 812.

[32] Ibid.

[33] Ibid., 832.

[34] Neuman, *Strangers to the Constitution*, 14.

to admit but externally permitted to exclude for compelling reasons. These worked together: the internal conscience balanced by external conditions.

The internal/external distinction, rooted in the natural law and positive law traditions, has been carried forward in immigration law jurisprudence. Like a children's game of telephone, though, the ultimate legal meaning is not the same as the original one, partly due to the exigencies of the setting. Nafziger explains how Wolff fashioned a principle of free movement out of the statements of Grotius, Vitoria, and others, which was subject to 'several stipulated exceptions within the discretion of states'.[35] Vattel then drew from both camps – natural law and positivism – to posit an interpretation of sovereign duties as well as rights. Nafziger argues that immigration law has misinterpreted Vattel's position, ignoring 'both the subtleties on the duty side and his qualifications of the sovereign "right" to exclude foreigners'.[36] In the result, by making the internal sphere the preserve of conscience and making the externally enforceable right the site of exigencies and conditions, the modern translation of the distinction ensures that the immigration power is unconstrained.[37] It also excises the alien from the reach of international law when it comes to admission. There is a large body of international law on diplomatic protection and the minimum standard of treatment, but the admission of aliens is exclusively a matter of domestic jurisdiction.

B *The Case Law Genealogy*

At the heart of immigration law, then, is this doctrine of near-absolute discretion anchored in the external/internal distinction of the international law publicists. This unqualified sovereign right to exclude aliens appears in several late nineteenth century and early twentieth century cases.[38] In the United States, the Supreme Court transformed this characterisation of international law into the constitutional doctrine of plenary power that operates in immigration matters.[39] Its most common formulation is found in the second of the *Asian Exclusion* cases:

35 Nafziger, 'General Admission of Aliens', 811.
36 Ibid., 814.
37 Ibid., 804.
38 See Neuman, *Strangers to the Constitution*; Nafziger, 'General Admission of Aliens'; Colin Grey, *Justice and Authority in Immigration Law* (Oxford: Hart Publishing, 2015).
39 Ibid.

> It is an accepted maxim of international law, that every sovereign nation has the power as inherent in sovereignty, and essential to self-preservation, to forbid the entrance of foreigners within its dominions, or to admit them only in such cases and upon such conditions as it may see fit to prescribe. Vattel, lib. 2, §§ 94, 100; 1 Phillimore (3d ed.) c. 10, §220.[40]

The cases rely on the classical publicists to ground the unqualified right to exclude.[41] Vattel's internal/external distinction was selectively translated into the plenary power doctrine, forming the basis for the maxim that sovereign discretion over immigration matters is unconstrained. Stated conversely, by discarding sovereign duties towards aliens, the translation made limits on the sovereign power over aliens into internal matters. Arguably, the international law publicists, Vattel included, intended those limitations to be matters for positive international law; instead the judiciary displaces them onto domestic public law.[42]

Canadian case law can trace a similar trajectory, starting with *Attorney-General for Canada* v. *Cain* in 1906. In *Cain,* Lord Atkinson explained the admission and treatment of aliens as a matter of sovereign discretion, citing Vattel's *Law of Nations*:

> One of the rights possessed by the supreme power in every State is the right to refuse to permit an alien to enter that State, to annex what conditions it pleases to the permission to enter it, and to expel or deport from the State, at pleasure, even a friendly alien, especially if it considers his presence in the State opposed to its peace, order, and good government, or to its social or material interests: Vattel, Law of Nations, book 1, s. 231; book 2, s. 125.[43]

Although the aliens in that case were US citizens, the scaffolding was in place for the broad discretion that places immigration law beyond close judicial oversight. Almost ninety years later, in a case about extradition, the Supreme Court of Canada relied on *Cain* to reiterate the 'basic state power' described by Lord Atkinson:

> The Government has the right and duty to keep out and to expel aliens from this country if it considers it advisable to do so. This right, of course, exists independently of extradition. If an alien known to have a serious criminal record attempted to enter into Canada, he could be refused

[40] *Nishimura Ekiu* v. *United States* 26 Stat. 1084 (1891).

[41] Nafziger argues these international law publicists never suggested there was an unqualified right.

[42] I am grateful to David Dyzenhaus for this clarification.

[43] *Attorney General for Canada* v. *Cain*, [1906] AC 542 (Privy Council) at 545–46.

> admission. And by the same token, he could be deported once he entered Canada.[44]

The contours of the Vattel distinction are present here. The exclusion of aliens is a matter of external right and a prerogative of sovereignty. Moreover, that right includes the power to decide whom to admit and on what terms; here, Justice La Forest describes a serious criminal record as the basis for exclusion or deportation. The distinction assumes its full modern form in the Canadian case of *Chiarelli*. This seminal case is the foundation stone of Canadian immigration law:

> The most fundamental principle of immigration law is that non-citizens do not have an unqualified right to enter or remain in the country.[45]

The court made this statement in the deportation context. Supporting its statement was the British common law articulation of the absolute discretion of the Crown in *R* v. *Governor of Pentonville Prison*:

> At common law no alien has any right to enter this country except by leave of the Crown; and the Crown can refuse leave without giving any reason: see *Schmidt v. Secretary of State for Home Affairs* [1969] 2 Ch. 149 at 168. If he comes by leave, the Crown can impose such conditions as it thinks fit, as to his length of stay, or otherwise. He has no right whatever to remain here.[46]

These cases carve out the sovereign state's near-unfettered power over the alien.[47] They mark the evolution of the Vattel distinction into a principle that contains no sovereign duties or obligations, natural or otherwise. The problem that this genealogy reveals is that, as natural law has waned, the entire basis for the duty or obligation to admit has also faded away. Divorced from the constraints of natural law rights and obligations, only the sovereign discretion part of the distinction remains and is carried forward. This makes the constitution the sole preserve for any moral or humanitarian duty or obligation of hospitality: either to admit foreigners in need or, even more broadly, to admit foreigners

44 *Kindler* v. *Canada (Minister of Justice)*, [1991] 2 SCR 779 at 834.

45 *Canada (Minister of Employment and Immigration)* v. *Chiarelli*, [1992] 1 SCR 711.

46 *R* v. *Governor of Pentonville Prison*, 747, cited in *Prata* v. *Minister of Manpower & Immigration*, [1976] 1 SCR 376. The Court then supported this position by referring to *Kindler*, to section 6 of the Charter (the mobility rights provision which reserves the right 'to enter, remain in, and leave Canada' to citizens), and various provisions of the immigration statute.

47 Catherine Dauvergne, 'Sovereignty, Migration and the Rule of Law in Global Times' (2004) 67 *Modern Law Review* 588–615, 591.

whenever the state's interests are not threatened.[48] This heightens the protective role of the constitution in immigration law, which has internalised the doctrine of absolute discretion untethered to its former limitations, but is now also the site of protections and rights.[49]

The contours of this executive discretion look different in different states. It is nonetheless accurate to describe the selective domestic incorporation of the Vattel distinction as turning immigrants into 'strangers to the constitution'.[50] By enfolding the Vattel distinction as the doctrine of absolute discretion, the constitutional order gives the nation state its primary instrument for drawing and policing boundaries and membership. It also has the consequence, as Neuman points out, of placing immigration outside of normal constitutional reasoning.[51] This makes reconciling immigration law with constitutional norms a tricky task and compounds the harm of being outside of constitutional reasoning – because that is also the location of rights. The Vattel distinction, then, morphed from a moderately generous, albeit two-faced, stance towards aliens into a singular sovereign discretion to exclude. This turn is obviously troubling for aliens, but it is also theoretically troubling. Using the lens of the double-facing constitution, it is possible to see how this singular discretion redoubles on itself, at work in immigration law as well as constitutional law.

C Section 7 and the Principles of Fundamental Justice

This section explores the contemporary relationship between the Constitution and immigration through the lens of a particular constitutional concept: the principles of fundamental justice. The principles of fundamental justice are contained in section 7 of the Charter, as a qualifier for the 'open-textured' right to life, liberty, and security of the person.[52] This is the place where the Vattel distinction makes its most frequent appearance, and is the most often invoked constitutional

48 States admit humanitarian migrants under their immigration laws but this is not because of any *national* obligation or duty (although it may be because of an international one – i.e. the 1951 Refugee Convention).

49 International human rights are another source of protection, but it has been well-remarked that international law generally does not reach admission and, in any case, international human rights may be difficult for aliens to enforce.

50 Neuman, *Strangers to the Constitution*.

51 Ibid.

52 Nadar R. Hasan, 'Three Theories of "Principles of Fundamental Justice"', (2013) 63 *Supreme Court Law Review* (2d) 339–75.

provision by aliens appearing in Supreme Court of Canada jurisprudence. The translation of the Vattel distinction into the doctrine of absolute sovereign discretion in immigration law raises the question of outer limits. Even if there is no natural law obligation to admit anyone, regardless of need or interest, what restrictions does constitutional law place on the field of immigration law? Although the relationship between immigration and the constitution continues to be structured by alienage, recent cases appear to contemplate some kind of moral imperative with respect to aliens in egregious circumstances. This section explores the principles of fundamental justice in three seminal cases.

i The Principles of Fundamental Justice

Section 7 of the Charter contains the principles of fundamental justice:

> Everyone has the right to life, liberty and security of the person and the right not to be deprived thereof except in accordance with the principles of fundamental justice.

Section 7 applies to everyone physically present in Canada and 'protects an individual's most basic interests . . . by requiring any state action affecting those interests to comply with the principles of fundamental justice'.[53] To make out a section 7 claim, one must demonstrate that section 7 applies to the matters at issue and that the state conduct does not conform to the principles of fundamental justice.[54] Canadian courts have interpreted section 7 broadly and the Supreme Court has never upheld a violation under section 1 (the constitutional limiting provision).[55] Section 7 is 'a powerful tool for the protection of rights through litigation'.[56] Yet, in cases involving non-citizens, the fact of alienage cuts against this protective function, and the principles of fundamental justice are the vehicle for this undercutting.

The principles of fundamental justice do not constitute a protected standalone right, but rather qualify the right not to be deprived of 'life, liberty and security of the person'. Stated conversely, the principles of fundamental justice provide authorisation for the deprivation of legal

[53] See *Singh* v. *Minister of Employment and Immigration*, [1985] 1 SCR 177; Hamish Stewart, *The Principles of Fundamental Justice* (Toronto: Irwin Law, 2012), 18.

[54] Upon application, the individual must demonstrate: standing, state conduct, and effect on life, liberty or security of the person. Ibid., 22.

[55] Ibid., 18. There has been at least one appellate court exception to this statement in the lower courts: *R* v. *Michaud*, 2015 ONCA 585.

[56] Stewart, *Principles of Fundamental Justice*.

rights: so long as the deprivation is in accordance with the principles of fundamental justice, the state *may* infringe the right to life, liberty and security of the person. The Charter does not specify the principles of fundamental justice, nor provide guidance as to how to determine their content.[57] Before turning to the language that the Supreme Court has developed to work out these principles, it is helpful to investigate the potential relationship between concepts of natural law and natural justice and the meaning of the principles of fundamental justice.

As *Re BC Motor Vehicle Act* established, the phrase does not have 'a single incontrovertible meaning'.[58] The preexisting Canadian *Bill of Rights* guaranteed the right to a fair hearing *in accordance with the principles of fundamental justice*, where the phrase was understood to be synonymous with natural justice.[59] The rules of natural justice have a more settled content, generally comprising a hearing, unbiased adjudication, and a fair procedure.[60] According to Peter Hogg and Barry Strayer, among others, the legislative history of section 7 confirms that the framers intended for 'fundamental justice' to mean 'natural justice'.[61] Natural justice, in turn, is derived from natural law. Bernard Schwartz argues that natural law underwrites the field of public law: 'it is, indeed, not too much to assert that modern public law is founded upon the work of the eighteenth-century law of nature jurists'.[62] In this broad procedural sense, natural law permeates the principles of fundamental justice. However, in *Re BC Motor Vehicle Act*, the Supreme Court of Canada interpreted the fundamental principles of justice, contra this procedural tilt, to encompass both substantive and procedural protections.[63] As I explore below, it is arguable that this expansive interpretation of fundamental justice has indirectly truncated the reach of section 7 in immigration cases.

The Supreme Court of Canada has tried to breathe life into the fundamental principles with guiding frameworks and criteria. The

57 Jonathan MacFarlane, 'Thomas Hobbes on Section 7 of the Charter: How Are the Fundamental Principles of Justice Fundamental?' (2007), available online: www.cpsa-acsp.ca/papers-2007/MacFarlane.pdf, accessed August 6, 2019.

58 *Re BC Motor Vehicle Act*, [1985] 2 SCR 486 at [25].

59 Peter Hogg, *Constitutional Law of Canada* (Toronto: Carswell, 2015), 47–20 (emphasis added).

60 Ibid.

61 Ibid. See also Barry Strayer, *Canada's Constitutional Revolution* (Edmonton: University of Alberta Press, 2013).

62 Bernard Schwartz, 'Administrative Procedure and Natural Law' (1953) 28 *Notre Dame Law Review* 169 at 172.

63 Stewart, *Principles of Fundamental Justice*.

principles of fundamental justice are recognised as 'essential elements of a system for the administration of justice which is founded upon a belief in the dignity and worth of the human person and the rule of law'.[64] Over time, the Supreme Court has both articulated and rejected various specific fundamental principles.[65] In 1985, the Supreme Court of Canada wrote the blueprint for their analysis in *Re BC Motor Vehicle Act*:

> [T]he principles of fundamental justice are to be found in the basic tenets of our legal system. They do not lie in the realm of general public policy but in the inherent domain of the judiciary as guardian of the justice system.[66]

Then, in *Rodriguez*, Justice Sopinka constructed the scaffolding of their contemporary framework:

> Discerning the principles of fundamental justice with which deprivation of life, liberty or security of the person must accord, in order to withstand constitutional scrutiny, is not an easy task. A mere common law rule does not suffice to constitute a principle of fundamental justice, rather, as the term implies, principles upon which there is some consensus that they are *vital or fundamental to our societal notion of justice* are required. Principles of fundamental justice must not, however, be so broad as to be no more than vague generalizations about what our society considers to be ethical or moral. They must be capable of being identified with some precision and applied to situations in a manner which yields an understandable result. They must also, in my view, be legal principles.[67]

In 2004, the Supreme Court compressed the notion of societal justice into three criteria, establishing the test that endures today:

> [A] 'principle of fundamental justice' must fulfill three criteria . . . First, it must be a legal principle . . . Second, there must be *sufficient consensus that the alleged principle is 'vital or fundamental to our societal notion of justice'* . . . The principles of fundamental justice are the *shared assumptions* upon which our system of justice is grounded. They find their meaning in the cases and traditions that have long detailed the basic norms for *how the state deals with its citizens. Society views them* as

[64] *Re B.C. Motor Vehicle Act*, at 503, citing Preamble to Canadian Bill of Rights and Charter, respectively.

[65] Some rejected principles include the harm principle and the best interests of the child; some accepted principles include that the law must not be overly vague, overbroad, arbitrary or grossly disproportionate. See Stewart, *Principles of Fundamental Justice*.

[66] *Re B.C. Motor Vehicle Act*, at 513.

[67] *Rodriguez* v. *British Columbia (Attorney General)*, [1993] 3 SCR 519 at 590–91 (emphasis added). See also *R* v. *Malmo-Levine*; *R* v. *Caine*, [2003] 3 SCR 571.

> essential to the administration of justice. Third, the alleged principle must be capable of being identified with precision and applied to situations in a manner that yields predictable results.[68]

The phrases 'sufficient consensus', 'societal notion of justice' and 'shared assumptions' describe or modify the norms for 'how the state deals with its citizens'. The problem with this interpretation is that it tasks society with identifying the basic tenets of the legal system and the basic norms of the administration of justice. Hamish Stewart, troubled by the Supreme Court's allusion to public opinion as the basis for the principles of fundamental justice, has explained that the consensus is based on the higher order values of dignity and rule of law.[69] While this may circumvent the difficulty of uncovering the legal content implicit the societal consensus, it does not avoid the problem posed by the Court's contextual approach, examined next.

As the Supreme Court said in *Lyons*, 'it is also clear that the requirements of fundamental justice are not immutable; rather, they vary according to the context in which they are invoked'.[70] In *Wholesale Travel Group*, Justice Cory confirmed the contextual approach:

> It is now clear that the *Charter* is to be interpreted in light of the context in which the claim arises. Context is relevant both with respect to the delineation of the meaning and scope of *Charter* rights, as well as to the determination of the balance to be struck between individual rights and the interests of society.[71]

To discern this context, the judiciary will look to 'the applicable principles and policies that have animated legislative and judicial practice in the field'.[72] This judicial instruction directs courts to look to ordinary statutes and common law practices to ascertain the demands of fundamental justice in each case. In the case of an alien, the principles of fundamental justice have their referents in immigration law, with dramatic repercussions for aliens. As Catherine Dauvergne points out, 'the ruling that principles of fundamental justice vary with context, and that for immigration matters a key feature of that context is that non-citizens have no right to remain in Canada' has come to overshadow the rights

[68] *Canadian Foundation for Children, Youth and the Law* v. *Canada (Attorney General)*, [2004] 1 SCR 76 (emphasis added).
[69] Stewart, *Principles of Fundamental Justice*, at 108–109.
[70] *R* v. *Lyons*, [1987] 2 SCR 309 at [85].
[71] [1991] 3 SCR 154 at 226.
[72] *R* v. *Beare; R* v. *Higgins*, [1988] 2 SCR 387 at [30], referring to *Lyons*.

that non-citizens do have.[73] In immigration and refugee cases about the principles of fundamental justice, the Supreme Court resort to the context of immigration law *reduces* the level of protection required by the principles of fundamental justice and leads to the absurd result that the same act or set of acts can be characterised as a deprivation of section 7 rights in one legal context but not another.[74] The problem with the Court's turn to context lies in its malignant result: it is not simply the benign migration of norms from the field of immigration law into the field of constitutional law, but rather the use of norms from one field of law to attenuate the reach of norms in another, higher-order, field of (constitutional) law.

ii The Immigration Cases: *Chiarelli*, *Suresh*, *Charkaoui*

In 1985, shortly after the Charter came into force, the Supreme Court of Canada decided *Singh* v. *Minister of Employment and Immigration*, a case about the refugee status determination procedure in Canada.[75] The Court found that the procedural defects of the determination process breached the principles of fundamental justice. In order to reach that finding, Justice Wilson determined that section 7 applied to 'every human being who was physically present in Canada'.[76] This seemed to inaugurate a broadly protective interpretation to Charter rights.[77] The *Singh* case sets the ambit for the principles of fundamental justice in two important ways: first, it ensured that most immigration claims would invoke section 7; and second, it anchored the procedural emphasis that the fundamental principles receive in immigration cases.[78] This section examines three cases that establish the conceptual relationship between immigration and the constitution through the principles of fundamental justice.

[73] Catherine Dauvergne, 'Non-citizens and the Charter of Rights and Freedoms, *In Due Course*' (March 2014), available at http://induecourse.ca/non-citizens-and-the-charter-of-rights-and-freedoms/, accessed August 6, 2019 .

[74] Gerald Heckman, 'Revisiting the Application of Section 7 of the *Charter* in Immigration and Refugee Protection' (2017) 68 *University of New Brunswick Law Journal* 312, 331–32.

[75] [1985] 1 SCR 177.

[76] Ibid., at [35].

[77] Ibid. *But see* Audrey Macklin, Chapter 9 of this volume, for the limits of the Court's decision.

[78] Although *Singh* was decided the same year as *Re B.C. Motor Vehicle Act*, the *Singh* decision preceded the latter's pronouncement that the fundamental principles of justice went beyond natural justice by eight months, which perhaps explains its procedural emphasis.

1 Chiarelli [1992] Giuseppe Chiarelli was a permanent resident convicted of serious crimes in Canada.[79] Under the governing immigration legislation, those convictions required his deportation. Chiarelli challenged his deportation. The Supreme Court of Canada first established immigration as a contractual relationship with the state, which contract may be breached by committing a crime. Justice Sopinka went on to make two important findings about section 7 and the principles of fundamental justice in immigration settings. First, *Chiarelli* articulates the force of the contextual approach in the immigration setting for the first time.[80] This context is marked by a sharp distinction between citizen and non-citizen. After setting out the contextual approach, Justice Sopinka referred to *Kindler* for the maxim that the fundamental justice standard for extradition should be based on 'the principles and policies underlying extradition law and procedure'.[81] For *Chiarelli,* then, the relevant sources for the principles of fundamental justice in deportation were located in immigration law:

> Thus in determining the scope of principles of fundamental justice as they apply to this case, the Court must look to the principles and policies underlying immigration law. *The most fundamental principle of immigration law is that non-citizens do not have an unqualified right to enter or remain in the country.*[82]

This statement is simply a restatement of the mistranslated Vattel distinction in the vernacular of section 7. Ninette Kelley explains that relying on the immigration law context to determine the content of a constitutional right, rather than using the values underlying the constitution and Charter, 'effectively denied the supremacy of the *Charter*' and 'accorded complete deference to the legislature'.[83] The principles of fundamental justice thus set up a symbiotic relationship between constitutional standards and immigration law, where the content of the former depends upon the latter.

The second significant finding in *Chiarelli* is, in fact, a non-finding. Justice Sopinka notes that section 7 is a two-part provision: 'the threshold question is whether deportation *per se* amounts to a deprivation of life,

[79] *Canada (Minister of Employment and Immigration)* v. *Chiarelli,* [1992] 1 SCR 711.
[80] Dauvergne, 'How the Charter Has Failed Non-citizens'.
[81] *Chiarelli.*
[82] *Chiarelli* (emphasis added).
[83] Ninette Kelley, 'Rights in the Balance: Non-citizens and State Sovereignty Under the Charter', in David Dyzenhaus (ed.), *The Unity of Public Law* (Oxford: Hart Publishing, 2004), 266.

liberty or security of the person'.[84] The issue of whether deportation is a deprivation of liberty is fraught, to say the least, and courts have twisted themselves in knots to find that it is not. The crux of that knot lies in the alien/citizen distinction. In *Chiarelli*, Sopinka J did not find it necessary to answer the liberty question because he was of the view that 'there is no breach of fundamental justice'.[85] He came to that view because permanent residents in Chiarelli's situation had violated 'an essential condition under which they were permitted to remain' in the country. The breach of the contract mandated their removal and there was no violation of the principles of fundamental justice by virtue of the deportation required to effect that removal. This means that the *Chiarelli* decision never ruled on whether deportation constituted a deprivation of liberty. Instead, Sopinka J skipped to the principles of fundamental justice, possibly because he 'assumed without deciding' that that deportation engaged section 7.[86]

This order of analysis is flawed. It changes the structure of section 7, which amounts to an end-run around the constitutional right to life, liberty and security of the person when aliens are involved. There are two reasons for this. First, while the Court had established the relevance of the immigration context to the principles of fundamental justice, there is no reason to presume that the immigration context is particularly relevant to the deprivation of liberty. On its face, the fact of non-citizenship is not relevant to the deprivation of liberty. Section 7 applies to everyone physically present. By working backwards from the fundamental principles, the Court frontloads the alien/citizen distinction into the deprivation analysis. This is why later courts are able to find that deportation is not a deprivation of liberty *because* non-citizens have no right to enter or remain. Indeed, this is the true legacy of *Chiarelli*: the legal end-run over deprivation.

Second, the ordering of the provision and contextual nature of the principles of fundamental justice suggests that it is essential to know the content of the deprivation of liberty in order to know the fundamental principles that might apply. The nature of the deprivation, in other words, is part of the context. The setting for that deprivation, whether criminal, immigration, administrative, or security, will determine which fundamental principles apply and affect the calibration of the individual and societal interest. Justice Sopinka's order of analysis amounts to finding that the

84 *Chiarelli*.

85 Ibid.

86 Stewart, *Principles of Fundamental Justice*, 279. See also Heckman, 'Revisiting the Application'.

deprivation was in accordance with the principles of fundamental justice so there was no breach of section 7; but it is not possible to know the fundamental principles or the correct balancing of interests until the deprivation is named. As Kelley writes, to consider the principles of fundamental justice without considering 'whether and to what extent Chiarelli's right to liberty was at stake . . . rendered it easier for the Court to find that his deportation . . . was not a disproportionate response'.[87]

The legacy of *Chiarelli,* and particularly its sequencing, is obvious in *Medovarski* v. *Canada* in 2005.[88] In *Medovarski,* the Supreme Court directly addressed the possibility that deportation could implicate the rights to liberty and security. It extrapolated from *Chiarelli*'s finding that non-citizens do not have the right to enter or remain:

> Thus the deportation of a non-citizen in itself cannot implicate the liberty and security interests protected by s. 7 of the *Charter.*

This is a 'remarkable extrapolation'.[89] As Stewart summarises: 'deportation in itself does not engage life, liberty, or security of the person; consequently, deportation as such does not have to comply with the principles of fundamental justice'.[90] The outstanding issue is that *Chiarelli* did not decide whether citizen status is a relevant consideration for the deprivation branch of section 7 analysis, and yet this has become standard dictum in immigration law cases. Indeed, it has become the restatement of the philosophical and political foundation for the constitution's external face towards people inside Canadian state territory.

2 ***Suresh*** **[2002]** In *Suresh* v. *Canada,* the individual interests implicated in the principles of fundamental justice met national security interests on post-9/11 terrain. Manickavasagam Suresh was a Convention refugee from Sri Lanka who had filed for permanent resident status when the Canadian government detained him and commenced deportation proceedings on national security grounds.[91] The issue in *Suresh* was whether the Canadian government could deport a refugee to a country

[87] Kelley, 'Rights in the Balance', 266.

[88] [2005] 2 SCR 539.

[89] Donald Galloway and Jamie Liew, *Immigration Law*, 2nd ed. (Toronto, Irwin Law, 2015), 656; see also Heckman, 'Revisiting the Application', 329–30.

[90] Stewart, *Principles of Fundamental Justice,* 279.

[91] [2002] 1 SCR 3; The term 'Convention refugee' refers to the refugee status designation under the international Refugee Convention, UN General Assembly, Convention Relating to the Status of Refugees, 28 July 1951, 189 UNTS 137, available at www.refworld.org/docid/3be01b964.html.

where he faced the risk of torture. After determining that the Canadian government would still be responsible for torture carried out by another government, the Supreme Court turned to the principles of fundamental justice. The government conceded that 'deportation to torture may deprive a refugee of liberty, security and perhaps life'.[92] While deportation *on its own* could not amount to a deprivation of liberty, deportation *to face torture* could constitute such a deprivation. 'The only question is whether this deprivation is in accordance with the principles of fundamental justice.'[93]

Reiterating the contextual approach to principles of fundamental justice, the Court confirmed that context meant attention to 'the nature of the decision to be made. . . . The approach is essentially one of balancing.'[94] Here, Canada's national security interest in fighting terrorism must be weighed against Suresh's individual interest in not being deported to torture. The Court never named the context for the Suresh decision, as it had in *Chiarelli*, even though it was clearly adjudicating the constitutionality of the Immigration and Refugee Protection Act.[95] That omission may be attributable to the hybridity of the post-9/11 landscape, in which immigration matters blur into national security matters. The Court then further blurs the context by analogising deportation to extradition. There are, noted the Court, a 'variety of phrases' used to describe conduct that would violate fundamental principles.[96] Those phrases came from extradition cases.

It is difficult to say what ultimately turned on the analogy to extradition. In some respects, the alignment helped Suresh. The Court's analogy between torture and the death penalty (the latter had previously been found clearly disproportionate under the balancing test) and its reliance on extradition cases establishing section 7's extension to the consequences of removal both cast a broad protective net.[97] Yet, in other respects, placing the deportation to torture inquiry in the extradition context is precisely what permitted the Court to take the otherwise broad prohibition against torture and locate its exceptions. Specifically, the Court infamously found that deportation to face torture might be

[92] Ibid., at para. 44.
[93] Ibid.
[94] Ibid., at para. 45.
[95] Dauvergne, 'How the Charter Has Failed Non-citizens'.
[96] *Suresh*, at [49].
[97] Ibid., at [54].

justified 'in exceptional circumstances'.[98] It is beyond the scope of this chapter to explore all of the differences between extradition and deportation, but it is worth noting that they are initiated by different states (home state versus host state) and they occur in different contexts (criminal context versus immigration context), and that these differences might matter for their relationship with the constitution.

Drawing from a string of extradition cases that described conduct that violates fundamental justice as 'conduct that would shock the Canadian conscience', the Court queried: 'is the conduct fundamentally unacceptable to our notions of fair practice and justice?'[99] One of those extradition cases, *Burns,* focused on the Canadian public perception of the death penalty in order to locate the collective conscience of the Canadian people.[100] Although hesitant to draw a straight line between public opinion and the principles of the fundamental justice, the Supreme Court equivocated in *Suresh*:

> [T]he fact that successive governments and Parliaments have refused to inflict torture and the death penalty surely reflects a fundamental Canadian belief about the appropriate limits of a criminal justice system.[101]

The constitutional test is whether it would 'shock the Canadian conscience' to deport the person on national security grounds.[102] Relying on Canada's complete rejection of torture, the Charter's section 12 prohibition on cruel and unusual punishment or treatment, and judicial precedent that extraditing someone to face torture would be inconsistent with fundamental justice, the Court found that Canadians do not accept torture as 'fair or compatible with justice'.[103] The problem with this framework is twofold. First, it creates its own balancing test by enfolding *both* the deportation to torture inquiry and the national security inquiry. In the extradition context, there is only the extradition to death penalty inquiry; there is no national security aspect. The addition of the national security aspect significantly changes the test in part because of the particular features of that context, several of which are not publicly available. Second, the trouble with the Canadian conscience is that it

98 Ibid., at [78].
99 Ibid., at [49].
100 Macfarlane, 'Thomas Hobbes on Section 7 of the Charter', 8.
101 *Suresh,* [50].
102 Kelley, 'Rights in the Balance', 281.
103 The SCC also addressed the constitutionality of the Ministerial procedures but that is not examined in this chapter.

makes the principles of fundamental justice relative.[104] It is not that extradition to the death penalty or deportation to torture are objectively offensive to fundamental justice; rather, it is whether the Canadian people find those practices objectionable. Constitutionally, this meant that the balancing in the contextual approach was informed by public perception. This transposed extradition framework meant that Suresh could not quite come into view for the internal face of the constitution.

The *Suresh* decision, seemingly magnanimous in its stance against deportation to torture in most circumstances, in fact set immigration law back in terms of its relationship with constitutional law through its analytical frameworks. The Supreme Court elaborated the context at play in the principles of fundamental justice in ways that further devalued the context of the alien. The decision built on the scaffolding from *Chiarelli* that set immigration law apart by likening the immigration context to the extradition context and incorporating a test from the latter that is both parochial and relative. As a result of this test, the citizens who see only the constitution's internal face are partly adjudicating the reach of its external face.

3 ***Charkaoui*** **[2007]** In *Charkaoui* v. *Canada (Citizenship and Immigration)*, the Court shifted from the substantive question of whether section 7 permitted deportation to torture to the question of what process protections are contemplated by the principles of fundamental justice.[105] Adil Charakoui is a permanent resident of Canada who was detained under a Canadian security certificate. The security certificate system is a special immigration regime for national security concerns. Such certificates are an immigration tool that allow the Canadian government to detain and deport non-citizens whom it deems to be a threat to national security.[106] The regime has been present in in Canada's immigration legislation since 1978. Over time, security certificates have become the government's 'policy instrument of choice' in the war against terror.[107]

One of the key features of the regime is that the allegations and evidence against detainees are never fully revealed and significant parts of their trials are held in secret. In *Charkaoui*, the Court had to determine

[104] Macfarlane, 'Thomas Hobbes on Section 7 of the Charter', at 9.

[105] [2007] 1 SCR 350.

[106] Audrey Macklin, *The Canadian Security Certificate Regime*, Centre for European Policy Studies Special Report (March 2009), available at https://www.ceps.eu/system/files/book/1819.pdf, accessed August 6, 2019.

[107] Ibid., 1.

the constitutionality of the security certificate regime, specifically the processes for determining their reasonableness as well as for the detention and release of subjects. The first issue was about the disclosure of secret evidence vital to national security interests. The second was what to do with individuals who cannot be deported. *Charkaoui* further developed the *Chiarelli* and *Medovarski* holdings in the deportation setting, softening their edges to clarify:

> While the deportation of a non-citizen in the immigration context may not *in itself* engage s.7 of the Charter, some features associated with deportation, such as detention in the course of the certificate process or the prospect of deportation to torture, may do so.[108]

The Court found that 'the individual interests at stake suggest that s. 7 of the Charter . . . is engaged'.[109] The deprivation of liberty in this case was located in the 'features' of deportation, notably the detention procedures – not in deportation itself. The individual security interest was also engaged. The Court then went on to consider whether that deprivation was in accordance with the principles of fundamental justice, which turned out to be the decisive inquiry. The case turned on 'the overarching principle of fundamental justice that . . . before the state can detain people for significant periods of time, it must accord them a fair judicial process'.[110] The Court noted that the principles include a 'guarantee of procedural fairness'.[111] Ultimately, the Court found that the security certificate processes did not meet the requirements of the principles of fundamental justice.[112]

For those concerned with the curtailment of civil liberties in national security matters, *Charkaoui* marks a welcome return to limits and a retreat from the relative standards of the Canadian conscience in the substantive sphere. Yet it is worth interrogating the particulars of the contextual approach here, as well as the consequences for the double-facing constitution. In *Suresh,* the Court located the principles of

108 *Charkaoui,* [17] (emphasis in original). The second *Charkaoui* case concerned the narrower issue of the remedy for destruction of documents and late disclosure of information.
109 Ibid., at [16].
110 Ibid., [28].
111 Ibid., [19]. See also James Stribopoulos, 'Charkaoui: Beyond Anti-Terrorism, Procedural Fairness, and Section 7 of the Charter' (2007) 16(1) *Constitutional Forum* 15–20.
112 *Charkaoui,* [31]; specifically, the regime failed on these two requirements: 'that the judge make a judicial decision based on the facts and the law; and finally, that the named person be afforded an opportunity to meet the case put against him or her by being informed of that case and being allowed to question or counter it'.

fundamental justice in a hybrid immigration–national security context. With *Charkoui*, the Court pivots to a wholesale national security context. The Court confirms 'the procedures required to conform to the principles of fundamental justice *must reflect the exigencies of the security context*'.[113] This is immediately concerning for aliens, who arguably receive even fewer rights protections under national security law than under immigration law proper.[114]

There are also larger repercussions. First, the Court relies on the jurisprudential legacy of the Vattel distinction to create an artificial distinction between the *act* of deportation and the *procedures* of deportation. The notion that deportation *itself* cannot violate the constitution leads the Court to find that 'the context is the detention, incidental to their removal or an attempt to remove them from the country, of permanent residents and foreign nationals who the ministers conclude pose a threat to national security'.[115] This sets odd parameters for the principles of fundamental justice, which cannot be invoked to stop forcible physical removal itself but may protect the processes surrounding it. It is similar to setting constitutional limits on the arrest procedures in criminal law without setting any limits on imprisonment itself. Second, the *Charkaoui* decision rests on the *Chiarelli* finding that immigration is the most important part of context for the principles of fundamental justice and thus, according to *Medavorski*, deportation does not violate section 7. The problem is that *Charkaoui* is a *national security* context where immigration status is important only for triggering the security certificate regime – not for understanding or adjudicating the terrorism allegations. The Court transplanted the legacy of the Vattel distinction from the immigration-constitution context into the national security context. Indeed, that distinction is the reason that the Court heavily focuses on procedural justice, permitting it to ignore that the detention is in service of deportation.

In short, the Court made a solid effort to retrieve the perimeter of the deportation setting for constitutional protection but, by refiguring the context, it arguably made the principles of fundamental justice even less protective. In the immigration – national security matrix, the state often seems to be seeking more and different ways to employ the external face of the constitution. Yet, as *Charakoui* shows, the Court is somewhat

[113] Ibid., [27] (emphasis added).
[114] Dauvergne, 'How the Charter Has Failed Non-citizens'.
[115] *Charkaoui*, [24].

constrained by the constitution's internal face. The reach of constitutional rights and subjectivity cannot be wholly withheld from aliens. The next section explores the nuanced narrative that emerges and its implications for the double-facing constitution.

D Context and Narrative in the Principles of Fundamental Justice

The Vattel distinction is a crucial part of the relationship between immigration and constitutional law. The 'most fundamental principle of immigration law' is its direct derivation. As set out above, the genealogy of the internal/external distinction reveals a point of rupture whereby only the broad sovereign right to exclude is incorporated into immigration law. The sovereign obligation to admit, even exceptionally, disappears. The constitutional landscape for aliens turns on an immigration law principle that is a distorted derivation from the eighteenth century international law publicists, and this oddly has implications for constitutional identity and rights.

The influence of that distinction for section 7 jurisprudence lies in the judicial resort to context. Typically, the incorporation of context is lauded for connecting laws to society. But here, 'the nature of the decision', 'factual circumstances', and 'the applicable principles and policies that have animated legislative and judicial practice in the field' are sites of constitutional exclusion for aliens. The contextual approach embodies the tension between the internal and external faces of the constitution. In immigration cases, the principles of fundamental justice embody a circuit wherein the internal constitution of the legal order (who receives constitutional protection, who may claim constitutional rights, the content of that protection and those rights) is modulated by principles and laws directed externally, towards aliens. The 'most fundamental principle of immigration law' is used in these cases to ground constitutional content, thus crystallising an external projection that loops back into delimiting the internal constitution.

These cases demonstrate the complicated position of the alien in the constitutional order: someone whom the constitution seeks to address and subject but not to fully protect. Indeed, it is possible to see the deprivation of liberty shifting in the periphery even as the centre continues to hold. In *Chiarelli*, it was not necessary to locate that deprivation at all. The Court in *Medavorski* interpreted *Chiarelli* to hold that deportation was not a deprivation of liberty. In *Suresh*, the deprivation of liberty was deportation *to face torture*. In *Charkaoui*, the deprivation of liberty was the possibility of *indefinite detention preceding* deportation. In all of these cases, the Court hesitates to name the thing itself – deportation – as a deprivation of liberty because of the heft of alienage and the legacy of the Vattel distinction. Yet the Court is not engaged in wholesale exclusion. The cases tell a more complex story about the evolution of the alien from stranger to the constitution to its partial subject. Although the alien is not constitutionally protected against deportation itself, s/he may be constitutionally protected against violations in its orbit: deportation to torture or indefinite detention. Indeed, glimmers of the natural law obligation from Vattel's writings seem to reappear.[116] The suggestion that there might be a moral imperative to admit aliens into the circle of constitutional protection in egregious circumstances seems to underwrite the Court's stance on torture and detention in the shadow of deportation.

How might we explain the resurfacing of this moral commitment, itself reminiscent of natural law? One explanation is that the Supreme Court found itself in a difficult bind. Once *Re BC Motor Vehicle Act* opened up the principles of fundamental justice to procedure and substance, the Court lacked a ready limit on deprivations of life, liberty, and security of the person. The resulting framework for aliens hangs on an omission (the Court having never squarely worked out if deportation deprives an individual of the right to life, liberty, and security of the person) and an interpretative sleight of hand (the Court having incorporated the limiting immigration law context into the content of the principles of fundamental justice). This framework likely emerged from concern that finding otherwise would trigger innumerable judicial reviews that would undermine the immigration control regime.[117]

It is possible, however, that hewing to a procedural interpretation of fundamental justice and the current Supreme Court jurisprudence on deportation bring us to the same place. The difficult bind may be partly a result of the early substantive interpretation of the principles of fundamental justice. As it stands, some procedural aspects of deportation are not in accordance with the principles of fundamental justice. Arguably, the problem with the immigration cases is that the Supreme Court had to contort its analysis in order to confine its holdings. The broader protection conferred by the substantive dimensions of fundamental justice prompted the Court to limit section 7 in the immigration context

[116] I am grateful to David Dyzenhaus for this insight.

[117] On this point of floodgates if the Court finds deportation to violate section 7, see also Heckman, 'Revisiting the Application', 353.

through its end-run around the deprivation of liberty and by resort to the context of the relevant field of law.

In an almost complete circle, a natural justice interpretation may have provided the limit that would have left the Vattel distinction out of the fundamental principles of justice. While there are obvious disadvantages to this procedural understanding of fundamental justice, it is possible that this interpretation would have lent coherence to the judicial approach. Limiting fundamental justice to procedural principles is a hard case to make, especially when the distinction between procedure and substance is untenable.[118] But, if Stewart's recent observation holds, then 'the project of recognizing substantive norms of fundamental justice has reached its limit'.[119] If the Supreme Court could hold that deportation *does* violate the right to life, liberty, and security of the person but that the deprivation could be justified by the principles of natural justice – *i.e.* when proper procedures are followed – without ceding their ground, there would be some potential benefits. The structural logic of section 7 would be preserved and courts and litigants could reason honestly and factually into that logic. Deportation, at least in some circumstances, is a prima facie deprivation of liberty and security of the person. As well, the variability of fundamental justice according to statutory context would be removed and the Vattel distinction could drop out of section 7 analysis. From there, it would be up to immigration advocates and scholars to push the boundary between procedure and substance from this new terrain, where deportation is a recognised deprivation of life, liberty, and security of the person.

III Conclusion: Opposition and Balance

All constitutions hold opposing values in some sort of balance. Some of these are higher order equilibriums woven through the constitutional text, such as the tension between the collective and the individual. Others are more specific, such as the tension between unity and diversity in the Canadian constitution.[120] To return to Pitkin's prescription to look at

[118] Hogg, *Constitutional Law of Canada*, 47–23.

[119] Hamish Stewart, 'R v Khawaja: At the Limits of Fundamental Justice' (2013) 63 *Supreme Court Law Review* 403, 416.

[120] See Jeremy Webber's work on agonistic constitutions, e.g., 'Contending Sovereignties', in Peter Oliver, Patrick Macklem and Nathalie Des Rosiers (eds.), *The Oxford Handbook of the Canadian Constitution* (Oxford: Oxford University Press, 2017), 281.

specific oppositions held in tension by a specific concept: the constitution materialises the oppositions between internal/citizen and external/alien through the principles of fundamental justice. The contextual approach to those principles is the constitutional concept that holds the tension between internal and external in equipoise. The story of that equipoise goes all the way back to Vattel, then lurches forward into the early immigration cases, and finally lands on the principles of fundamental justice. By tracing the genealogy of immigration law's location in the bosom of executive discretion, locating the source of that discretion, and then following its incorporation into section 7, the connections between the constitutional order and membership questions rise quickly to the surface. It becomes apparent that immigration and the constitution work *together* to cull the masses for membership. The framework concept of the double-facing constitution exposes both the configuration of particular fields of law and the limits that run inside the constitutional order itself.

The external face of the constitutional order – whether turned towards foreign policy or immigration or conflicts of laws – is outside of the normal purview of the constitution, only exceptionally folded into it. In the case of immigration law, this division has stakes and direction. Immigration constitutes the constitutional order in the most basic sense: it gives the order its boundaries, members, and legal concepts of inclusion (in the form of citizenship). Immigration law polices the boundaries and members of the constitutional order at least partly, if not mostly, outside of the confines of public law. This placement turns on the internal/external distinction crystallised by Vattel and appears in modified form as the sovereign executive discretion over immigration law. Constitutional law in turn relies upon the contemporary contorted version of this distinction. That lineage has sustained the characterisation that immigration law faces externally and functions at some remove from the internal norms of the constitutional order. Constitutional law understands the immigration cases as having *already decided* who is an alien so that it may begin from a pure citizenship place. In other words, constitutional law denies constitutional subjectivity to aliens based on a principle from another field of law, which means issues of constitutional justification are never on the table. In this way, the constitutional order relies on immigration law for its own coherence, identity, and constituency. This theoretical and disciplinary division of labour is the source of constitutional coherence.

There is still another layer to the relationship between immigration and the constitution, one that rests on the ambulation of the double-facing constitution. This layer focuses on what it means for the internal and external faces of the constitution to acknowledge the internal constitutional order is always shifting, not only along the lines of birth and death, but also along the lines of immigration. The constitutional order pulls immigrants from outside, who it then internalises as the people. Those people remake the constitutional order in their own image and re-project it externally. Immigration ultimately brings new members to the constitution and presses on constitutional inclusion, thus altering the rules for new entrants and members. The Canadian self, then, is in motion, shape shifting as immigration changes the constitutional population. The population of the immigrant state is in constant revision and that revision changes constitutional identity and subjectivity; in other words, it is brought about by a constant melding of internal and external faces of the constitution. This relationship between the internal and external faces of the constitution also reveals its partial faces. Immigration laws are conceived as external projections, but they feed back into the internal constitutional order *through principles of constitutional interpretation* such as the contextual approach to the principles of fundamental justice. Parts of the constitution turn on an immigration law principle that is a distorted derivation from the classical international law publicists – and the contours of this relationship reveals the partiality of the constitution when it is turned towards aliens.

PART III

The Foreign in Foreign Relations Law

11

Double-Facing Administrative Law: State Prerogatives, Cities and Foreign Affairs*

GENEVIÈVE CARTIER

Introduction

When one thinks about cities and the law, one usually thinks of administrative law, as cities get their legal authority from statutes. But this chapter asks you to think of cities as both subjects and agents on the international stage, where the law is at the same time constitutional and international, as well as administrative. Moreover, it asks you to understand cities as actors in an area that is ordinarily understood as the preserve of the state – foreign relations. In other words, it seeks to understand the place of cities in the double-facing constitution – the idea that constitutional orders are delimited by membranes that face both outwards and inwards, with both faces not independent but closely related. I shall argue that the place of cities is best understood as participants in an institutional dialogue, nested within a particular, double-facing conception of administrative law.

A number of contributions have documented various ways in which cities intervene on the international stage, a phenomenon sometimes

* This research was supported by the Social Sciences and Humanities Research Council of Canada. I thank David Dyzenhaus and Karen Knop for their invitation to participate in their *Foreign Affairs Law* course at the University of Toronto in November 2017, where I first reflected on the topic of this chapter. Katrina Longo, then student in that class, shared written ideas that have much in common with the general themes that I take up in detail in the following pages. I had the privilege to write most of this chapter while I was Herbert Smith Freehills Visitor to the Faculty of Law of the University of Cambridge and Visiting Fellow at Clare Hall in early 2018. Clare Hall provided an inspiring environment for my work and I am grateful to all the College members who contributed to making my stay a memorable moment. I thank the editors of this book for the invitation to contribute and David Dyzenhaus in particular, for his patience, inspiration and support.

referred to as '"local" foreign policy'.[1] The picture is extremely complex and varied, ranging from the naming of streets after famous foreign dissidents or heroes, the conclusion of sister-cities agreements and the establishment of procurement processes aimed at excluding wicked states, to the emergence of sanctuary cities and the creation of networks between the world's largest cities in the fight against climate change.[2] Enquiries have also highlighted how different forms of pragmatic arrangements between cities and the state in which they are located seem to make local foreign policy possible on the ground. For example, central states may choose not to intervene when cities' actions do not directly hinder their policies, or they may conduct consultations and encourage discussion on issues of state interest that also affect local governments, or they may even indirectly encourage cities to act with them in a coordinated way.[3]

While there is no denying that these and other examples attest to cities' actual involvement in matters loosely associated to foreign relations and policy, the legal foundation for this involvement is far from clear.[4] Of course, cities' actions may at times be purely symbolic, but they may also purport to produce actual, adverse consequences on third parties. In such

[1] Michael Taggart, 'Globalization, "Local" Foreign Policy, and Administrative Law', in Grant Huscroft and Michael Taggart (eds.), *Inside and Outside Administrative Law – Essays in Honour of David Mullan* (Toronto: University of Toronto Press, 2006), 259, 259. The distinction between 'foreign policy', 'foreign relations' and 'foreign affairs' is subtle and the literature does not seem to follow a consistent use of these terms. Based on the Merriam-Webster Dictionary, 'foreign policy' focuses on the guiding principles that one sovereign state adopts in its interactions with other sovereign states. 'Foreign relations' designate the actual interaction between states, the result of the foreign policy previously articulated. 'Foreign affairs' consist in 'matters having to do with international relations and with the interests of the home country in foreign countries' (www.merriam-webster.com/dictionary/foreign%20policy; www.merriam-webster.com/dictionary/foreign%20relations; www.merriam-webster.com/dictionary/foreign%20affairs, accessed 19 December 2018). Unless specific distinctions are necessary, I will use the terms interchangeably to designate either policy or action based on that policy in the context of international relations.

[2] Taggart, 'Globalization, "Local" Foreign Policy, and Administrative Law', 262–63. See also Michael J. Glennon and Robert D. Sloane, *Foreign Affairs Federalism: The Myth of National Exclusivity* (New York: Oxford University Press, 2016), 60ff.

[3] Helmut Philipp Aust, 'Foreign Affairs', in Rainer Grote, Frauke Lachenmann and Rüdiger Wolfrum (gen. eds.), *Max Planck Encyclopedia of Comparative Constitutional Law* (Oxford: Oxford University Press, 2017) para. 23. See also Taggart, 'Globalization, "Local" Foreign Policy, and Administrative Law', 261.

[4] This is pointed out, for example, by Judith Resnik, 'Law's Migration: American Exceptionalism, Silent Dialogues, and Federalism's Multiple Ports of Entry' (2005–2006) 115 *Yale Law Journal* 1564, 1634.

cases, cities cannot dispense with establishing a legal foundation and authority for their actions.[5]

Such legal foundation potentially mobilises three fields of law – international, constitutional and administrative/local government law – but in their traditional instantiation, each field seems anathema to local foreign policy. International law recognises sovereign states only and it requires that states speak with one voice in international debate. Constitutional law in Anglo-American and most Commonwealth jurisdictions establishes that the executive branch of central states speaks in this single voice, silencing sub-national entities, including cities. Administrative law – and its particular manifestation, local government law – conceives cities as statutory creations, subordinated to a legislative framework that they have no power to alter, and focused on purely local matters. Therefore, cities that intervene in foreign policy seem to be acting in a purely political, not legal, capacity. I will argue that alternative trends in these three fields of law point to a different conclusion and that administrative law plays the leading role in this reconfiguration.

In Section I, I present an overview of traditional understandings of particular aspects of international, constitutional and administrative/local government law, and I briefly discuss some of the critiques they attract and some changes that seem to be emerging. This discussion is important because it highlights substantial sites of legal resistance to cities' action on the international stage, while at the same time suggesting how to overcome such resistance.

This sets the stage for Section II, where I put forward a double-facing conception of administrative law. To determine whether cities have legal authority to act in matters of foreign policy, there needs to be a form of 'normative mediation'[6] between the various legal fields that have something to say in these matters. This mediation is difficult under a traditional understanding of administrative law, conceived as a hermetic space in which the legal limits of cities' powers are based on formal interpretation of statutes by judges. Under such a view, administrative law only looks

[5] See notably Joost Pauwelyn, Ramses A. Wessel and Jan Wouters, 'When Structures Become Shackles: Stagnation and Dynamics in International Lawmaking' (2014) 25 *European Journal of International Law* 733, 745–46, where the authors refer to the fundamental importance of accountability. See also Helmut Philipp Aust, 'Shining Cities on the Hill? The Global City, Climate Change, and International Law' (2015) 26 *European Journal of International Law* 255, 269.

[6] The inspiration for this expression is Yishai Blank, 'The City and the World' (2006) 44 *Columbia Journal of Transnational Law* 868, 892. However, Blank refers to cities as being the normative mediators, while I take administrative law to be that mediator.

inward, so that emerging conceptions of international and constitutional law can have little concrete impact on the development of cities' legal power in foreign affairs. Stated differently, these emerging conceptions would have little influence if they collided with the hermetic seal of a traditional conception of domestic administrative law.

By contrast, a double-facing conception of administrative law provides the required normative mediation between international, constitutional and local government law. Such a conception of administrative law views legal boundaries surrounding administrative entities – including cities – as being more porous than is usually assumed. More precisely, it views the determination of the legal contours of cities' powers as a cooperative endeavour between various components of the state – judicial, executive and legislative – and citizens. Cities thus become participants in an institutional dialogue where a plurality of understandings of cities' role in the world can be shared, contrasted and contested. And among these understandings figure emerging conceptions of international and constitutional law that point towards a form of legal recognition of cities' action in foreign affairs. The result is a destabilisation of the traditional legal framework that virtually denies cities' legal existence on the international scene, opening up the way for the development of a legal basis for local foreign policy. In other words, administrative law conceived as double-facing suggests that cities' practices on the international stage can have legal significance.

***

As alluded to above, the manifestations of cities' action on the international scene are manifold and not easy to categorise neatly. The same is true with the vocabulary associated with the field. Michael Taggart uses the expression 'local foreign policy' to designate cities taking position on contentious public matters abroad.[7] Andrew Kirby and Sallie Marston refer to 'the municipal foreign policy movement' to describe the collective effort of local governments engaging on international issues.[8] Their view includes both 'local efforts to take positions with respect to the foreign policies of their host nations' and 'the local effort to internalize aspects of international law itself'.[9] Michael Shuman divides municipal

[7] Taggart, 'Globalization, "Local" Foreign Policy, and Administrative Law', 262.

[8] Andrew Kirby and Sallie Marston with Kenneth Seasholes, 'World Cities and Global Communities: The Municipal Foreign Policy Movement and New Roles for Cities', in Paul L. Knox and Peter J. Taylor (eds.), *World Cities in a World-System* (Cambridge: Cambridge University Press, 1995) 267.

[9] Gerald Frug and David Barron, 'International Local Government Law' (2006) 38 *The Urban Lawyer* 1, 28. See also Nick Clarke, 'In What Sense "Spaces of Neoliberalism"? The

foreign policies into 'consciousness-raising measures, unilateral measures, and bilateral measures'.[10] The first kind of measures embrace education, research and lobbying. The second cover activities conducted 'through unilateral use of policing, zoning, contracting, and investing powers'.[11] The third include the thousands of bilateral agreements between cities situated in different countries, often aiming at accomplishing things that contradict official foreign policy positions.[12]

In this chapter, I do not – and could not – address each of these cases. But at times, I refer to one manifestation of Shuman's second category: selective procurement practices. In this kind of case, cities purport to condition the choice of contracting parties on factors seemingly related to foreign affairs considerations, such as the relations that potential contracting parties entertain with political regimes that violate human rights. We thus have cities making unilateral decisions – through either regulations or resolutions – purporting ultimately to influence situations abroad that have to do with the application of international human rights norms, and that affect the rights of private parties – those who want to contract with cities. Under the dominant paradigms of international, constitutional and administrative/local government law, such action belongs to the exclusive jurisdiction of sovereign states. It is therefore instructive to see how this particular expression of local foreign policy can illustrate a possible application of a double-facing conception of administrative law. In turn, highlighting the relevant aspects of that kind of case has the potential to guide us in resolving challenges posed in the other kinds of situations referred to above.

As we shall see, parts of my argument focus on Canadian law. But I hope to show that it is relevant for any jurisdiction where cities lack constitutional protection and therefore act only under the authority of statutory delegations of power.

I Context

The starting point for my argument is a 2006 trilogy of papers that marked the emergence of a line of scholarship underlining various

New Localism, the New Politics Of Scale, And Town Twinning' (2009) 28 *Political Geography* 496, 498, who refers to the expression 'bottom-up localism'.

10 Michael H. Shuman, 'Dateline Main Street: Local Foreign Policies' (1986–1987) 65 *Foreign Policy* 154, 159.

11 Ibid., 160.

12 Ibid., 161.

aspects of the transformation of the role of cities on the international stage and the challenges that this poses to their legal status, both domestically and internationally.[13]

First, Gerald Frug and David Barron argued that a new conception of cities is emerging, which views them as 'simultaneously subordinate to domestic governments *and* independent international actors'.[14] This conception makes 'domestic local government law . . . a subject of international concern',[15] because international institutions and those who influence them want to shape the relationship between states and cities. Their argument builds on 'examples of cities' own attempts to intervene in world affairs', on 'ways in which international efforts to promote good governance and human rights are affecting local government organization, policies, and powers' and on 'cases that examine the legality of city actions under international agreements' in matters of city powers over land use. They observe that:

> '[i]nternational law is increasingly penetrating the nation-state in order to regulate directly the actions of subnational governments. In doing so, [international law] is also attempting to redefine the legal position of cities *vis à vis* both higher-level sub national governments and the nation-state itself. In other words, international law is beginning to treat the city as a distinct level of government that may be separately targeted for legal transformation.[16]

[13] For some time now, the role of cities on the international stage has been the subject of much attention in the fields of international relations, urban planning, geography and diplomacy. See, among many other examples, Paul L. Knox and Peter J. Taylor (eds.), *World Cities in a World-System* (Cambridge: Cambridge University Press, 1995); Simon Curtis (ed.), *The Power of Cities in International Relations* (New York: Routledge, 2014); Benjamin Barber, *If Mayors Ruled the World. Rising Cities, Declining Nation States* (New Haven: Yale University Press, 2013); Rodrigo Tavares, *Paradiplomacy. Cities and States as Global Players* (Oxford: Oxford University Press, 2016). By contrast, the interest of legal academics for the subject is more recent, but is now steadily growing. Of particular interest figure Helmut Philipp Aust, 'Shining Cities on the Hill? The Global City, Climate Change, and International Law'; Janne E. Nijman, 'The Future of the City and the International Law of the Future', in Sam Muller et al. (eds.), *Law of the Future and the Future of Law* (Torkel Opsahl EPublisher, 2011), 215; and Janne E. Nijman, 'Renaissance of the City as Global Actor. The Role of Foreign Policy and International Law Practices in the Construction of Cities as Global Actors', in Gunther Hellmann, Andreas Fahrmeir and Milos Vec (eds.), *The Transformation of Foreign Policy. Drawing and Managing Boundaries From Antiquity to the Present* (Oxford: Oxford University Press, 2016), 209.

[14] Frug and Barron, 'International Local Government Law', 11 (emphasis in original).

[15] Ibid., 11.

[16] Ibid., 21.

Second, Yishai Blank claimed that cities have become '*normative mediators*' because of a 'combination between their domestic legal powers and . . . emerging global schemes of decentralizations'. Through a number of examples, Blank illustrates how 'localities become bearers of international rights, duties, and powers', 'objects of international and transnational regulation', enforcers of 'international norms and standards' and parts of 'global networks'. As a result, cities become 'nodal points for radically distinct governance projects that have as their common goal to transform cities from mere subdivisions of sovereign states into legally empowered entities, able to advance goals and values that are different from their states'.[17]

Third, Michael Taggart suggested that globalisation might well invigorate local authorities because '[t]he problems of the world are [now] both too big and too small for states to handle, and the latter are being dispatched increasingly to sub-national levels of government'.[18] He reflected more specifically on the capacity of local authorities to adopt and enforce local foreign policy, by which he meant local authorities 'taking a public stand in relation to an issue of concern in another country or region'.[19] In his view, these challenges 'turned ultimately on questions of administrative law',[20] although he thought that the administrative law 'tether of *ultra vires* is the principal restraint on local authorities that wish to take a stand on matters of foreign policy'.[21] Stated differently, Taggart suggested that administrative law was both the main contender for a legal basis for local foreign policy and the main reason for its underdevelopment.

Taken together, these contributions prompt two observations. On the one hand, they highlight the fact that cities are playing roles that are ever more complex: they remain responsible for local matters, but they are now involved, on their own initiative or as instruments of other actors and institutions, in matters that have transnational, international or global ramifications. On the other hand, such roles do not concord

[17] Blank, 'The City and the World', 892 (emphasis in original).

[18] Taggart, 'Globalization, "Local" Foreign Policy, and Administrative Law', 259. Taggart echoes what Michael H. Shuman expressed 20 years before, discussing federal tolerance towards municipalities intervening in foreign affairs in the USA: 'Washington may be recognizing that international affairs, like many domestic issues, have become too complicated to run effectively as a monopoly': Michael H. Shuman, 'Dateline Main Street. Local Foreign Policy', 170.

[19] Taggart, 'Globalization, "Local" Foreign Policy, and Administrative Law', 262.

[20] Taggart, 'Globalization, "Local" Foreign Policy, and Administrative Law', 283.

[21] Ibid., 262.

with the traditional understanding of the legal fields potentially applicable to cities in such contexts. Stated differently, it is puzzling to see that cities remain legally invisible on the international scene even though legitimate actors on that scene seem to recognise the legitimacy of cities' involvement, at least partially.

Following up on Taggart's intuition, this chapter suggests that domestic administrative law has the potential to provide a way out of this puzzle.

II Changing Frameworks

As alluded to in the introduction, traditional, and still highly influential understandings of international, constitutional and administrative law combine to deny cities any form of legal recognition in the domain of foreign policy. My objective in this section is to show that these traditional conceptions coexist with important counter-influences that point towards a redefinition of cities' legal status, and with it a transformed conception of their role on the world stage.

A International Law

Prevailing accounts of international law revolve around concepts of statehood and sovereignty.[22] International law here assumes a grouping of formally equal and uniform subjects – unitary states – each speaking through the single voice of central government agents.[23] Under this model, states alone are sovereign and, with few exceptions, states alone are subjects of international law.[24] To be a state, an entity must fulfil a number of requirements, which typically include a defined territory,

[22] See, among many other sources, James Crawford, *Brownlie's Principles of Public International Law*, 8th ed. (Oxford: Oxford University Press, 2012), 12–13; and Hugh M. Kindred, Phillip M. Saunders and Robert J. Currie (gen. eds.), *International Law Chiefly as Interpreted and Applied in Canada*, 8th ed. (Toronto: Emond Montgomery Publications, 2014), ch. 2.

[23] 'International law has assumed states to be unitary actors, amenable to representation by unitary governmental agents. In this world, states talked only to one another, and only to one another as such. Their communications were highly stylised in the form of diplomacy, the traditional model of which admits only to centralised expression of state interests through the sovereign and his representatives to other states (in the form of ambassadors and the rest of the diplomatic apparatus)': Peter J. Spiro, 'Globalization and the (Foreign Affairs) Constitution' (2002) 63 *Ohio State Law Journal* 649, 667.

[24] Frédéric Mégret suggests that these exceptions only reinforce the monopoly of states as subjects of international law: '[L]es États conservent le monopole de la qualité de sujet' du

a permanent population, a government and a capacity to enter into relations with other states.[25] A related and debated question is whether meeting these conditions is sufficient to satisfy the requirements of international law – the declaratory theory – or whether a candidate for statehood needs the recognition of existing states to join the international legal community – the constitutive theory.[26] Even absent clear endorsement of either theory, there seems to exist a consensus that some form of recognition has clear political significance.[27]

Once acquired, statehood entails sovereignty,[28] that is, exclusive jurisdiction over territory and people on this territory. Sovereign states conduct their domestic affairs autonomously, without foreign interference: 'members of the international system have no right to pierce the veil of statehood'.[29] The resulting picture is that of an international scene filled with unitary, impermeable entities, where clear boundaries exist between internal or domestic matters and external or foreign affairs. This suggests two main corollaries. One is that states decide the extent to which international law is binding upon them: 'the general consent of states creates rules of general application'.[30] The other corollary is that states assume responsibility for the conduct of their component parts: states cannot both claim absolute control over domestic affairs and invoke domestic considerations to escape international responsibilities.[31]

Most international lawyers would certainly view this description as a caricature of the contemporary system of international law.[32] Various

droit international': Frédéric Mégret, 'L'étatisme spécifique du droit international' (2011) 24 *Revue Québécoise de droit international* 105, 113.

25 Montevideo Convention on the Rights and Duties of States (1934) 28 *American Journal of International Law* Supp 75, Art. 1.

26 This is the debate between declaratory and constitutive theories of statehood. Crawford, *Brownlie's Principles of Public International Law*, 144–45.

27 Ibid., 144ff.

28 Crawford, *Brownlie's Principles of Public International Law*, 12–13; Kindred, Saunders and Currie, *International Law Chiefly as Interpreted and Applied in Canada*, 104.

29 Anne-Marie Slaughter, *A New World Order* (Princeton and Oxford: Princeton University Press, 2004), 12.

30 See, e.g., Duncan B. Hollis, 'Why State Consent Still Matters – Non-state Actors, Treaties, and the Changing Sources of International Law' (2005) 23 *Berkeley Journal of International Law* 137, 141.

31 Crawford, *Brownlie's Principles of Public International Law*, 542–43.

32 One example might be the following: '[E]ven if this were ever true, it no longer applies in the modern international legal system. International humanitarian law regulates conflicts between States and non-State actors; international human rights law gives rights to individuals within States, and international criminal law gives individuals obligations which are internationally judiciable (even if a State has not consented to the jurisdiction

non-state entities now enjoy some form of legal status – for example, international organisations and individuals.[33] The emergence of 'sovereignty-limiting doctrines' – for example, the responsibility to protect – weakened the view that states have exclusive jurisdiction on internal or domestic matters.[34] And '[t]he communications revolution and economic integration . . . have suggested a diluted significance to territorial control and the very meaning of national boundaries'.[35] Notwithstanding these reservations, the main components of the orthodox description suggested above still inform the general framework and narratives of international law, so that 'sovereignty and statehood remain the basic units of currency'.[36]

This state-centred framework not only makes it clear that cities are not subjects of international law, but also makes it very difficult to see how cities could ever have some form of legal status or significance in that field.[37] I suggest that alternative conceptions of international law and international relations question not so much the existence and importance of both statehood and sovereignty, as their centrality, indispensability or exclusivity within the architecture of international law,[38] which opens up spaces for cities to make their international presence felt.

As we saw above, there is increasing recognition that states now coexist with other actors that affect the underlying forces at play on the international stage and in the course of international affairs.[39] Indeed, a number

of the ICC, its citizens and those within its territory can be judged by ad-hoc tribunals established by the Security Council); international investment law regulates the interactions between States and foreign corporations': European Research Council, *Supra-State Order: International Law and National Law*, www.federalism.eu/assets/2016/10/Supra-State-Order_IntNatLaw.pdf, accessed 2 September 2018.

33 See, e.g., Crawford, *Brownlie's Principles of Public International Law*, 115ff.

34 See, e.g., Rosa Brooks, 'Strange Bedfellows: The Convergence of Sovereignty-Limiting Doctrines in Counterterrorist and Human Rights Discourse' (2012) *Georgetown Journal of International Affairs* 125, 126ff.

35 Spiro, 'Globalization and the (Foreign Affairs) Constitution', 649.

36 Crawford, *Brownlie's Principles of Public International Law*, 17.

37 See, e.g., Aust, 'Shining Cities on the Hill? The Global City, Climate Change, and International Law', 270: 'Under traditional doctrines of sources and subjects of international law, the activities of cities in transnational networks . . . are hard to accommodate.' See also Mégret, 'L'étatisme spécifique du droit international', 118: '. . . comme si la pensée juridique internationale peinait fondamentalement à prendre en compte des phénomènes ne correspondant pas à son paradigme dominant'.

38 'States still exist in this world; indeed, they are crucial actors. But they are "disaggregated"', Slaughter, *A New World Order*, 5.

39 'The shift has brought a variety of new actors – some governmental, many not – into the realm of international decision-making. No longer do foreign ministries, or even states,

of contributions highlight that the effect of 'globalisation' is the development of interactions between numerous governmental subunits and non-state constituencies, which together create webs of networks that cut across or circumvent traditional, centralised state channels. Anne-Marie Slaughter describes this phenomenon through the notion of 'disaggregation':

> Stop imagining the international system as a system of states . . . subject to rules created by international institutions that are apart from, 'above' these states. Start thinking about a world of governments, with all the different institutions that perform the basic functions of governments – legislation, adjudication, implementation – interacting both with each other domestically and also with foreign and supranational counterparts. States still exist in this world; indeed they are crucial actors. But they are 'disaggregated.' They relate to each other not only through the Foreign Office, but also through regulatory, judicial, and legislative channels.[40]

Cities fit nicely with this model, which locates them in complex networks of actors active internationally.[41] But the notion of 'disaggregated states' does not, in and of itself, accommodate, or take account of, the *legal* significance of cities in international law, since most if not all of the actors in those networks lack the quality of legal subjects under the dominant paradigm of international law.[42] However, when one combines the idea

enjoy an unchallenged monopoly on the course of international affairs', Spiro, 'Globalization and the (Foreign Affairs) Constitution', 649.

40 Slaughter, *A New World Order*, 5. See also Anne-Marie Slaughter, 'Global Government Networks, Global Information Agencies, and Disaggregated Democracy' (2003) 24 *Michigan Journal of International Law* 1041.

41 But see Aust, 'Shining Cities on the Hill? The Global City, Climate Change, and International Law', 269, for the view that this model does not highlight the democratic nature of cities.

42 '[Q]ui dit acteur ne veut pas – surtout pas en droit international – dire sujet, et dans la pratique deux discours cohabitent de manière sophistiquée sans jamais se rejoindre' ('He who says actor does not – especially in international law – mean subject, and in practice, both discourses stand side by side without ever joining themselves'), Mégret, 'L'étatisme spécifique du droit international', 117. Frédéric Mégret goes as far as saying that 'les juristes reconnaissent peut-être d'autant plus volontiers le rôle croissant des acteurs non-étatiques que celui-ci ne semble pas impliquer de conséquences formelles' ('jurists recognize all the more readily the increasing role of non-state actors because such a role does not seem to imply formal consequences') and that 'l'influence réelle voire déterminante des entités non-étatiques est loin de se traduire par une reconnaissance correspondante de leur qualité de sujet, conçue plus comme une propriété formelle du système juridique que comme un brevet de pertinence sociale réelle' ('the real if not determining influence of non-state entities is far from translating into a corresponding recognition of their quality as subject, conceived more as a formal quality of the legal system than as a license of actual social relevance'), ibid., 117–18.

of disaggregation with an interactional account of international law, put forward by Jutta Brunnée and Stephen Toope,[43] one can see that cities are more than influential political forces. They are legal actors who participate in the construction and articulation of international legal norms.

Brunnée and Toope's general argument is that international law 'is made through the interactions of a variety of actors, including elites, the media, NGOs and "ordinary" citizens'.[44] They take inspiration from Lon L. Fuller, who viewed 'law as a purposive enterprise that is both shaped by human interaction and aimed at guiding that interaction in distinctive ways'.[45]

Under an interactional account of international law, legitimate legal norms emerge from the combination of three elements. The first is that 'states and other international actors must build up shared understandings of what they want to accomplish through law',[46] or of 'what they are doing and why'.[47] This process generates social norms and these norms 'help shape how actors see themselves, their world and . . . their interests'.[48] The second element is that, for these social norms to become legal norms, they must comply with the requirements of legality, expressed through the criteria that together form what Fuller termed the 'internal morality of law'.[49] Meeting the criteria induces 'fidelity to law', or the 'self-bindingness of law', so that a legal obligation is 'an internalized commitment and not . . . an externally imposed duty matched with a sanction for non-performance'.[50]

The third element is that:

> [s]hared understandings and rules that meet the criteria of legality must be continuously reinforced through a robust practice of legality. In other words, law is created and maintained through interaction. It is interaction

[43] Jutta Brunnée and Stephen J. Toope, *Legitimacy and Legality in International Law. An Interactional Account* (Cambridge: Cambridge University Press, 2010).

[44] Ibid., 5.

[45] Ibid., 7.

[46] Ibid., 55.

[47] Ibid., 13.

[48] Ibid.

[49] Fuller articulated eight such criteria: rules must exist, be prospective, published, intelligible, not contradictory, allow compliance, not be constantly changing, and there must be congruence between the rules as declared and the rules as applied by officials: Lon L. Fuller, *The Morality of Law*, rev. ed. (New Heaven and London: Yale University Press, 1969), 39.

[50] Brunnée and Toope, *Legitimacy and Legality in International Law. An Interactional Account*, 27.

that makes this relationship 'horizontal' and 'reciprocal', and is the core of 'legal' legitimacy.[51]

For Brunnée and Toope then, '[c]itizens in domestic systems, and states *and other actors* at the international level are [. . .] active agents in the continuing enterprise of law-making, through the elaboration of custom, treaty and soft-law'.[52]

An interactional account of international law provides a more convincing explanation of cities' legal role on the international stage than the dominant paradigm presented above, for a number of reasons. Firstly, this model 'explains how diverse actors can interact through law and accommodates both the continuing pre-eminence of states in the international legal system and the rise of non-state actors'.[53] As such, it aligns well with the notion of 'disaggregated states', where a number of networks connect a wide variety of constituents, and where interactions prevail over status.

Secondly, the constructivist foundation of an interactional account of international law exposes cities' capacity to alter the parameters of international law. Constructivism not only views social structures as both constraining and enabling social action, it also highlights how social action in turn affects and potentially alters the parameters of social structures.[54] When cities put forward interpretations of their legal powers that purport to give them some form of jurisdiction on the international stage, they cause friction against the parameters of the structure of international law[55] whose dominant understandings restrict such jurisdiction to formal legal subjects and to central states in particular. Cities' interpretations of their legal powers do not necessarily prevail, because they inevitably confront the interpretation put forward by other constituencies, such as central states and judges. Hence, some parameters of the structure will probably remain intact, such as those surrounding typical high-policy, foreign affairs decisions like decisions to go to war. However, a constructivist perspective suggests that cities,

[51] Ibid., 54.

[52] Ibid., 55 (emphasis added). See also Aust, 'Shining Cities on the Hill? The Global City, Climate Change, and International Law', 273.

[53] Brunnée and Toope, *Legitimacy and Legality in International Law. An Interactional Account*, 8.

[54] Ibid., 14.

[55] '[S]tructures constrain social action, but they also enable action and in turn are affected and potentially altered by the *friction of social action against the parameters of the structure*': ibid., 14 (emphasis added).

because they have the potential to affect the parameters of the legal structure of international law, cannot have their contributions to the debates surrounding their legal capacity on the international stage ruled out as irrelevant as a matter of principle.

Thirdly, as cities increasingly gain recognition as international actors,[56] they inevitably participate in the building of shared understandings, a core element of an interactional account of international law and a crucial component in the articulation of international legal norms. As sub-state institutions and as members of transgovernmental or transnational networks of actors, cities are also part of learning communities. When they interact and communicate with members of these domestic and non-domestic networks, they increase their knowledge of international issues, express their own positions on such issues and become more conscious of the impact of their action on the international stage. As a result, they progressively contribute to building shared understandings of what international law should accomplish, and such understandings are constitutive of international law.[57]

Fourthly, the interactional account of international law relies in part on a process of 'internalisation' – whereby international norms penetrate into the domestic sphere – and cities can be significant actors in this process. Internalisation is necessary because central states do not control all the matters covered by their international engagements and they sometimes need to rely on components of the apparatus of state to live up to these engagements. This requires that the components engage with norms. For this to occur, 'relevant communities of practice must expand to engage domestic actors in their shared legal understandings. In turn, domestic engagement with norms is likely to have feedback effects back into the international arena.'[58] Now '[i]nternalization into the domestic sphere can occur through a variety of processes – social (the public legitimacy of a norm results in widespread obedience), political (elites

[56] See, among numerous contributions: Blank, 'The City and the World'; Frug and Barron, 'International Local Government Law'; Aust, 'Shining Cities on the Hill? The Global City, Climate Change, and International Law'; and Nijman, 'Renaissance of the City as Global Actor. The Role of Foreign Policy and International Law Practices in the Construction of Cities as Global Actors'.

[57] See also Nijman, 'Renaissance of the City as Global Actor. The Role of Foreign Policy and International Law Practices in the Construction of Cities as Global Actors' 238: 'The active engagement of cities with international law . . . not only constitutes the city as a global actor, it also transforms foreign policy and international law . . .'.

[58] Brunnée and Toope, *Legitimacy and Legality in International Law. An Interactional Account*, 118.

accept an international norm and adopt it as government policy), and legal (incorporation of the norm into the domestic legal system).'[59] Cities can thus play a key role in processes of internalisation, because they have the capacity to act through all three processes. They are therefore important channels of internalisation, a consideration that may affect the power relations between central states and cities.

Hence, Brunnée and Toope's interactional account of international law shatters law's resistance to accommodate international action by cities. Such an account suggests how evolving practices of cities have the potential to transform both the structure of international law that determines who can and cannot accede the circle of legal actors, and the norms of that part of the law.

This account of international law aligns well with what Antje Wiener describes as processes of constitution, contestation and re-constitution of norms in the field of international relations.[60] Wiener suggests that in a global society, affected stakeholders inevitably dispute the meaning of fundamental norms. However, under the orthodox framework of international relations, stakeholders may not be able to access processes whereby they can actually contest norms and participate in their re-constitution.[61] Wiener wants to highlight practices of norm validation that allow affected stakeholders to move beyond formal constraints and frameworks to engage in dialogue or 'multilogue' with other stakeholders on the meaning of fundamental norms.[62] I suggest that cities form part of the potential sites of dialogue or multilogue that can facilitate stakeholder engagement, which in turn generate novel, common organising principles that form the basis for action on the international stage.[63] In other words, when cities deploy legal instruments, like by-laws or resolutions, to support action that has an international impact, they express their understanding of fundamental norms – like human rights protections – and as such participate in reconstituting the meaning of those norms.

In sum, these contributions highlight that prevailing conceptions of statehood and sovereignty are controversial and that their orthodox meaning may not reflect contemporary practices of legality on the

[59] Ibid., 117.

[60] Antje Wiener, *Contestation and Constitution of Norms in Global International Relations* (Cambridge: Cambridge University Press, 2018).

[61] Ibid., 9.

[62] Her book examines 'affected stakeholders' practices of norm validation and . . . critically scrutinis[es] the conditions that shape them', ibid., 1.

[63] Ibid., 5.

international stage. They also propose alternative frameworks that integrate better the evolving roles and relationships of cities and states on that stage. Perhaps most importantly for the purposes of the present collection, they radically question the plausibility of clear boundaries between domestic and international affairs, and between domestic and international actors.

B *Constitutional Law*

In a way similar to international law, prevailing accounts of the constitutional law of many states deny cities' competence in foreign affairs. Focusing here on the common law tradition, the constitutional framework of foreign affairs builds on the Hobbesian idea that 'the constitutional State exists to protect itself and its citizens from the chaos of relations beyond its borders'.[64] This implies the existence of two distinct realms of state action – the internal and the external – that exhibit fundamentally different characteristics. The internal realm, constituted by law, establishes structures and institutions that provide for the making, adjudication and enforcement of public judgements, which iron out the differences in private opinion that threaten peace.[65] It is thus through law that those differences are settled. Law, by contrast, does not govern the external realm of state action, which remains in a state of nature. Hence, the fundamental assumptions underlying the constitutional treatment of foreign affairs in common law jurisdictions trade on a strict dichotomy 'between the regime of peace and order that inhere to the constituted order on the one hand, and the external relations between states, which remain in natural conditions of a-legality or pre-legality'[66] or 'between domestic legality and external a-legality'.[67]

Now, in Locke's terms, the external realm of state power is the realm of the 'federative power', that is the authority over external affairs, which concern 'war and peace, leagues and alliances'.[68] In Locke's view, the

[64] Campbell A. McLachlan, 'Five Conceptions of the Function of Foreign Relations Law', 2 October 2017. Draft on file with author, 7.

[65] Thomas Poole, 'The Constitution and Foreign Affairs' (2016) 69 *Current Legal Problems* 142, 148.

[66] Ibid., 149.

[67] Ibid., 150.

[68] John Locke, *Two Treatises of Government*, ed. Peter Laslett (Cambridge, Cambridge University Press, 1967), [147]. For a more detailed discussion of the Lockean idea of federative power, see Thomas Poole, 'The Idea of the Federative', Chapter 3 of this volume.

particular nature of the matters covered in the federative power implies two conditions. One is that it cannot be divided, because '[a]ny division of the federative power internally "would be apt sometime or other to cause disorder and ruine"'.[69] The other is that only prudence and wisdom can guide the exercise of the federative power: 'Locke [. . .] plainly understood the necessities which marked the vicissitudes of foreign affairs, explaining that matters of war and peace could not be directed by "antecedent, standing, positive laws" and must be dealt with through the exercise of prudence and wise judgment.'[70] Stated differently, since the external realm of state action is the site of existential decisions over war, peace, leagues and alliances, only one voice must speak in that realm, and it must speak free of legal rules. Translated into the legal language of the common law, this unique and free voice is that of the executive branch, acting through the prerogative power over foreign affairs.[71]

This kind of constitutional framework makes it very difficult to find a legal basis for cities' involvement in foreign affairs. First, the Lockean notion of foreign affairs involves existential issues about the preservation of the integrity of the state – war, peace, leagues, alliances – seemingly unrelated to cities' concerns, at least in their traditional instantiation. Secondly, traditionally conceived, cities are statutory creations subordinated to both legislation and judicial review. As such, they possess neither the freedom of action, nor the freedom from control, that Locke considered essential in the domain of foreign affairs, which he thought required 'Prudence and Wisdom' undirected by 'antecedent, standing, positive Laws'. In other words, cities must conform to legal constraints incompatible with the leeway that is necessary to deal with the existential challenges that arise in the realm external to the state. Thirdly, participation of cities in foreign affairs, like participation of other sub-state actors,

[69] McLachlan, 'Five Conceptions of the Function of Foreign Relations Law', 7, quoting Locke, *Two Treatises of Government,* [147 and 148]. See also Poole, 'The Constitution and Foreign Affairs', 149.

[70] James Richard Broughton, 'Judicializing Federative Power' (February 2007) 1, 1, available at SSRN, https://ssrn.com/abstract=963158, accessed 6 August 2019.

[71] One of the 'essential structural features of foreign relations law [. . .] is the central importance of the executive branch within constitutional system in the actual conduct of foreign relations', McLachlan, 'Five Conceptions of the Function of Foreign Relations Law', 10. Referring more specifically to the situation in the USA, Richard Bilder argues that a 'major purpose of the Constitution was to place control of foreign relations firmly in the hands of the national Government', Richard B. Bilder, 'Distribution of Constitutional Authority – The Role of States and Cities in Foreign Policies' (1983) 83 *The American Journal of International Law* 821, 821.

clashes with the one-voice requirement. Efficient and credible management of external affairs, some would argue, requires that the executive branch alone be authorised to speak. States cannot afford to accommodate the multiple different voices that cities would speak were they allowed to do so. This constitutional rule is the mirror image of the orthodox understanding of international law, which views states as unitary entities each with a unitary voice.[72] In sum, the only possible conclusion to draw from the framework just described seems to be that no constitutional foundation supports cities' action in foreign affairs.

However, this framework builds on questionable assumptions. One is that discussion beyond state boundaries is limited to existential questions of the war, peace and treaty category. Yet, the external realm of state action is the scene of a significant variety of relationships that have nothing to do with such issues, and that therefore might not imply the conditions that this framework imposes on the exercise of foreign affairs powers.

The framework also assumes that prerogative powers confer unrestricted leeway to the executive branch. However, there is no question today that executive exercises of the prerogative are amenable to judicial review, even though the extent of this control is hotly debated and controversial. This does not suggest that courts can legitimately supervise every executive decision in foreign affairs. It rather suggests that it is increasingly difficult to assume that only institutions uncontrolled by law can make decisions in foreign affairs.

A third assumption is that foreign affairs matters require that the state speak with one voice. Authors, particularly in the US context, have argued that this requirement is a fiction and that the executive has always composed with multiple interveners.[73] Others have pointed out that legislatures increasingly play a role in the conduct of foreign affairs, affecting the relative weight of central government agents in such affairs.[74] However, the rationale behind Locke's reasoning is that the one-voice requirement makes sense when external action needs coherence, which perhaps applies only when the very existence of the state is threatened. If this is so, when variations are legitimate and sometimes

[72] McLachlan, 'Five Conceptions of the Function of Foreign Relations Law', 8.

[73] See, e.g., Sarah H. Cleveland, 'Crosby and the One-Voice Myth in U.S. Foreign Relations' (2001) 46 Villanova Law Review 975.

[74] 'In practice, however, the picture today is much more nuanced, and most constitutional systems give the legislative some role in the conduct of foreign affairs', Aust, 'Foreign Affairs', para. 14.

necessary (for example, in the fight against climate change), it would be acceptable for the executive to speak with more than one voice. Stated differently, to say that one directive voice is necessary to avoid falling back on the state of nature is also to admit that a plurality of voices is permissible when no such threat exists. These elements together challenge the assumption that multiple voices necessarily weaken exercises of power in foreign affairs.

Perhaps more fundamentally, the prevailing conceptions of the constitutional framework of foreign affairs do not account for the actual presence of cities internationally, nor do they make sense of a number of changes in the relationship between cities and the executive branch. Cities are actually interested, concerned and engaged in matters that arise beyond their state's border and this brings into question the explanatory value of the prevailing framework.

However, different perspectives may pave the way for alternative views of cities in constitutional law, and therefore potentially on the constitutionality of cities' action in foreign affairs. I argue that Thomas Poole provides one such alternative, through what he terms the 'mutually constitutive model' of the relationship between external and internal faces of the constitution. He suggests that domestic and international legal orders are interrelated, through a process of mutual recognition:

> [T]he status of the state as sovereign is confirmed – arguably even conferred – through its recognition of a legal order external to itself. And the authority of that external or international order is itself confirmed – or conferred – by virtue of its acceptance by the states that constitute it, most crucially in the moment by which those states appeal to that external order for recognition.[75]

Poole 'alerts us to the dynamic and purposive essence of constitutional development', suggesting that '[a]ction within constitutions is at once ineluctably both a backward- and forward-looking affair'.[76]

This model suggests that cities may not inherently lack legitimacy on the international stage, because recognition of the legitimacy depends on processes that somehow escape the formal constitutional constraints that structure their exclusion. It suggests that, in line with constructivist approaches of the kind alluded to in the preceding section, practices eventually generate norms, so that continued presence of cities on the international stage, coupled with recognition of this presence from states

[75] Poole, 'The Constitution and Foreign Affairs', 150
[76] Ibid., 151.

either through the development of actual interaction or implicit acquiescence might lead to concrete changes in the constitutional structure. In turn, this could be articulated through a renewed structure of international law of the kind suggested in the preceding section.

To view the process as one of mutual recognition would also better explain that not all action by cities on the international stage qualifies as legally legitimate action. For example, cities' intervention on environmental matters might benefit from the explicit or implicit recognition from states, while assertions of imperial powers would not. More generally, Poole's model suggests a reassessment of the justification for excluding cities from foreign relations, as presented above.

C *Administrative and Local Government Law*

In most common law jurisdictions, not only do cities lack constitutional protection, but also they are generally viewed as 'mere statutory creations' exercising delegated powers with no inherent authority:[77]

> Cities are not free to do whatever they please. They can exercise power only within the legal frameworks that others have created for them. These legal frameworks are called local government law. Traditionally, the content of local government law has been determined either by national governments directly (as in the United Kingdom and South Africa) or by subnational governments (such as the states in the United States). . . . Domestic politics and domestic legal rules, in short, largely determine the legal status of cities, and these rules have a major influence on both the experience of city life and the practice of local self-government.[78]

In the USA, the idea that municipalities are 'creatures' is expressed through 'Dillon's rule', after the name of Iowa Supreme Court Judge who pronounced it in an 1868 decision: 'the power of the legislature over [municipal] corporations is supreme and transcendent: it may erect, change, divide, and even abolish them, at pleasure, as it deems the public good to require'.[79]

[77] See, among many other sources: Taggart, 'Globalization, "Local" Foreign Policy, and Administrative Law', 261; Gerald E. Frug, 'The City as a Legal Concept' (1980) 93 *Harvard Law Review* 1059, 1062; Craig Forcese, 'Municipal Buying Power and Human Rights in Burma: The Case for Canadian Municipal "Selective Purchasing" Policies' (1998) 56 *University of Toronto Faculty of Law Review* 251, 263; and Warren Magnusson, 'Urbanism, cities and local self-government' (2005) 48 *Canadian Public Administration / Administration Publique du Canada* 96, 111.

[78] Frug and Barron, 'International Local Government Law', 1.

[79] John F. Dillon, *Commentaries On The Law Of Municipal Corporations*, 3rd ed. (Boston: Little Brown, 1881), 75.

The evolution of localities' status in Canada, the USA and the UK followed a similar path, which can be summed up as a transformation from self-government to subordinated creatures. In Canada, fears that cities might 'encourage dissent and disloyalty to the British Crown'[80] seem to have influenced their legal treatment over the years. In the US context, Joan C. Williams suggested that the subordinated status of cities was in fact the result of judges and commentators projecting their 'apprehension about the potential for abuse in powerful government'.[81] Michael Taggart's overview of the British version of that history indicates that while localities were 'pretty much the only government that mattered . . . until the nineteenth century', they met with 'a considerable growth in centrally generated local legislation' from the eighteenth century, which triggered a 'slow process of local subservience to Parliament'.[82]

The subordinated status of cities solidified through traditional understandings of administrative law and judicial review of administrative action. Prevailing accounts of administrative law outline a story of boundaries built on the notion of jurisdiction and the doctrine of *ultra vires*. That doctrine is still highly influential in common law traditions of administrative law. It states that executive and administrative agencies acting under a delegating statute cannot go beyond or alter the terms of their mandate, and that judges are uniquely equipped to determine the meaning of those terms.[83] The *ultra vires* doctrine participates in what Mark Walters termed a 'linear theory of authority', one that assumes 'that the authority of legal norms can be traced back along a line of increasingly higher norms until an originating source is located'.[84] This 'suppose[s] that the values and principles have to be attributed to the

[80] Luis Silva, *Escaping From the Straightjacket that Baffled Houdini – An Analysis of the Myths and Realities of Empowering Toronto Through a City Charter*, MPA Research Report, submitted to The Local Government Program, Department of Political Science, The University of Western Ontario, London, Ontario, Canada, 2005, 28.

[81] Joan C. Williams, 'The Constitutional Vulnerability of American Local Government: The Politics of City Status in American Law' (1986) 83 *Wisconsin Law Review* 83, 150.

[82] Taggart, 'Globalization, "Local" Foreign Policy, and Administrative Law', 260

[83] David Dyzenhaus, 'The Politics of Deference: Judicial Review and Democracy', in Michael Taggart (ed.), *The Province of Administrative Law* (Oxford: Hart Publishing, 1997), 279, 281 and 303.

[84] Mark Walters, 'The Unwritten Constitution as a Legal Concept', in David Dyzenhaus and Malcolm Thorburn (eds.), *Philosophical Foundations of Constitutional Law* (Oxford: Oxford University Press, 2016), 33, 34.

tacit will of some lawmaker',[85] relying on a doctrine of actual legislative intent.[86]

In the field of local government law, judges have consistently interpreted municipal statutes in light of a legislative intent that expressed a restrictive view of 'municipal purposes' as limited to the provision of basic services to the inhabitants of a city. One typical example is Sopinka J majority opinion in the Supreme Court of Canada decision in *Shell Canada Products* v. *Vancouver*.[87] At a time when the apartheid regime was still formally entrenched and brutally applied in South Africa, Vancouver adopted two resolutions stating that it would stop doing business with Shell until the company withdraws and disinvests from the country. Shell challenged the resolutions.

Speaking for the majority, Sopinka J considers that the purpose of the resolutions is 'to influence Shell to divest in South Africa by expressing moral outrage against the apartheid regime and to join the alleged international boycott of its subsidiaries and products until Shell "completely withdraws from South Africa"'.[88] But as creatures of statutes, municipalities must 'stay within the powers conferred to them by the provincial legislature'.[89] They can only act for municipal purposes, that is 'those that are expressly stated [and] those that are compatible with the purpose and objects of the enabling statute'.[90] Since no specific provision of the enabling statute authorises the resolutions, they must fall under the general power to 'provide for the good rule and government of the city'. Reflecting on the legislative intent behind the constitutive statute of the City of Vancouver and referring to Ian Rogers, the leading commentator on municipal law in Canada, Sopinka J writes:

> In most cases, as here, the problem arises with respect to the exercise of a power that is not expressly conferred but is sought to be implied on the basis of a general grant of power. It is in these cases that the purposes of the enabling statute assume great importance. The approach in such circumstances is set out in the following excerpt in Rogers, *The Law of Canadian Municipal Corporations, supra*, § 64.1, at p. 387, with which I agree:

[85] David Dyzenhaus, 'The Idea of a Constitution. A plea for Staatsrechtslehre', in David Dyzenhaus and Malcolm Thorburn (eds.), *Philosophical Foundations of Constitutional Law* (Oxford: Oxford University Press, 2016)9, 24.

[86] Ibid., 30.

[87] *Shell Canada Products Ltd* v. *Vancouver (City)*, [1994] 1 SCR 231 (*Shell*).

[88] Ibid., 277.

[89] Ibid., 273.

[90] Ibid., 275.

> In approaching a problem of construing a municipal enactment a court should endeavour firstly to interpret it so that the powers sought to be exercised are in consonance with the purposes of the corporation. The provision at hand should be construed with reference to the object of the municipality: to render services to a group of persons in a locality with a view to advancing their health, welfare, safety and good government.
>
> Any ambiguity or doubt is to be resolved in favour of the citizen especially when the grant of power contended for is out of the 'usual range'.[91]

For Sopinka J, '[t]his places a territorial limit on Council's jurisdiction' and it does not 'include the imposition of a boycott based on matters external to the interests of the citizens of the municipality'.[92] In this case, the purpose of the resolutions is extraterritorial as it seeks 'to influence the international political situation'.[93]

Overall, such conceptions of administrative and local government law project a view of cities as locally focused entities to control and restrain, which have no independent and legitimate role to play in foreign affairs. However, I suggest that another conception of administrative law has the potential to better account for cities' actual presence on the world stage and for cities' evolving understanding of their own role on that stage.

This alternative conception of administrative law finds expression through a particular approach to judicial review. It takes its roots in a deferential attitude that judges must manifest towards administrative determinations of legal questions, and more specifically in the theory of 'deference as respect' put forward by Etienne Mureinik and David Dyzenhaus.[94]

The idea of deference as respect is located within the larger idea of a 'legal culture of justification',[95] which conditions the legitimacy of any exercise of public power on its being adequately justified to the

[91] Ibid., 276–77.
[92] Ibid., 279.
[93] Ibid., 283.
[94] The following three paragraphs are taken from Geneviève Cartier, 'Deliberative Ideals and Constitutionalism in the Administrative State', in Ron Levy, Hoi Kong, Graeme Orr and Jeff King (eds.), *The Cambridge Handbook of Deliberative Constitutionalism* (Cambridge: Cambridge University Press, 2018), 57, 67.
[95] Etienne Mureinik, 'A Bridge to Where?: Introducing the Interim Bill of Rights' (1994) 10 *South African Journal of Human Rights* 31 and David Dyzenhaus, 'Law as Justification: Etienne Mureinik's Conception of Legal Culture' (1998) 14 *South African Journal of Human Rights* 11.

individuals in relation to which the power is applied.[96] Public decisions are justified if they meet the requirements of legality, that is, if they are based on reasons that qualify as law. But law is here viewed, not as having a predetermined meaning existing as a matter of fact, which judges are uniquely equipped to discover. Law is rather conceived as an interpretative exercise aimed at finding 'the *single* answer that shows the legal order in its best light given its underlying moral and political values'.[97]

Finding that single, best answer requires being attentive to the interpretative context within which the issue of interpretation arises. In cases of judicial review of administrative interpretation of legal questions, this interpretative context is necessarily shaped by the administrative decision at issue, and most especially, the arguments and reasoning that support it.[98] Courts faithful to an interpretative conception of law and to the rule of law as justification must therefore express 'deference as respect' in relation to administrative interpretations of legal questions. Courts must adopt this attitude because, since administrative decision-makers have experience, expertise and are closest to the issues as they concretely arise, their decisions potentially have great significance on the interpretative context and therefore on the determination of the best answer to a legal question.

Courts express deference as respect when they manifest 'respectful attention to the reasons offered or which could be offered'[99] in support of a disputed decision and limit their intervention to cases where they are 'prepared to discharge the onus of showing, not that [they] would have reached a different conclusion, but that the decision reached is not reasonably supportable'.[100] Now 'reasonable' here does not mean that 'there could reasonably have been another resolution of that issue', suggesting that a number of equally acceptable solutions coexist and that either of them can be chosen by the decision-maker. Rather, a decision is reasonable when the reasons that the decision-maker invokes to sustain the decision 'do in fact or in principle support the conclusion reached'.[101]

[96] Mark D. Walters, 'Respecting Deference as Respect: Rights, Reasonableness and Proportionality in Canadian Administrative Law', in Hanna Wilberg and Mark Elliott (eds.), *The Scope and Intensity of Substantive Review: Traversing Taggart's Rainbow* (Oxford: Hart Publishing, 2015), 395, 418.

[97] Ibid., 420 (emphasis in original).

[98] Dyzenhaus, 'The Politics of Deference: Judicial Review and Democracy', 303: 'the tribunal's interpretation makes a difference to the structure of the interpretative context'.

[99] David Dyzenhaus, 'Developments in Administrative Law: the 1992–93 Term' (1994) 5 (2d) *The Supreme Court Law Review* 189, 190.

[100] Dyzenhaus, 'The Politics of Deference: Judicial Review and Democracy', 304.

[101] Ibid.

Thus, the notion of deference is grounded on a conception of law and legal interpretation that radically departs from those founding the *ultra vires* doctrine: it does not assume that statutes have a single, predetermined answer that only judges are competent to discover. It rather makes both courts and executive decision-makers collaborators in the search for the best answer to any given issue of legal interpretation. Consequently, there is a shared, collaborative practice of accountability between state institutions that makes it difficult to identify an epicentre of legal justification.

In Canadian law, the dissenting opinion from McLachlin J – as she then was – in *Shell* clearly aligns with this kind of approach. In that decision. McLachlin J points out that while procurement decisions are subject to judicial review, a 'deferential' approach to the review of municipal decisions is preferable to a 'narrow' one, 'having regard both to the authorities and to the modern conception of cities and municipalities'.[102] For McLachlin J, 'it is important that the courts not unduly confine municipalities in the responsible exercise of the powers which the legislature has conferred on them'.[103] They must respect the responsibility of elected municipal bodies to serve the people who elected them and exercise caution to avoid substituting their views of what is best for the citizens for those of municipal councils. A deferential approach is 'more in keeping with the true nature of modern municipalities', which 'should be free to define for themselves, as much as possible, the scope of their statutory authority. Excessive judicial interference in the decisions of elected municipal councils may . . . have the effect of confining modern municipalities in the straitjackets of tradition.'[104] She writes that a 'generous approach' to the control of municipal decisions is 'more in keeping with the flexible, more deferential approach this Court has adopted in recent cases to the judicial review of administrative agencies' and that '[t]here can be little justification for holding decisions on the welfare of the citizens by municipal councillors to a higher standard of review than the decisions of non-elected statutory boards and agencies'.[105] In her view, the wording of Vancouver's enabling statute does not restrict City's powers to 'the provision of services' but 'encompass expression of community concerns about what is happening outside the community's boundaries. Collective expression through elected

[102] *Shell*, 238.
[103] Ibid., 241.
[104] Ibid.
[105] Ibid., 246–47.

representatives may be seen as a proper function of "government".'[106] While Sopinka J considers that municipal purposes 'cannot extent to include the imposition of a boycott based on matters external to the interests of the citizens of the municipality', McLachlin J considers that 'the changing nature and role of municipal government in Canada' affects the meaning of 'municipal purposes' and 'external to the interests of citizens'.[107]

There are clear indications that McLachlin J's dissent in *Shell* has now become the position of the Supreme Court.[108]

In sum, administrative law so conceived recognises the legitimacy of cities' voice in the cooperative enterprise of articulating the contours of their legal powers. If cities are legitimate participants in such articulation, they will necessarily build on their own understanding of their role in the world to make sense of the statutory frameworks that confer them the power to act.

III Articulating a Double-Facing Conception of Administrative Law

We saw above that particular conceptions of international and constitutional law have the potential to reconfigure the legal framework of foreign affairs and of cities' place within that framework. But for these conceptions to fully unlock their potential, they have to connect with a compatible conception of domestic administrative law. I think this is what Michael Taggart may have been suggesting in his contribution on local foreign policy:

> It may be that cities have more involvement in international trade and the like nowadays, but it does not necessarily follow that they will be allowed to have more power to shape the course of international events. This turns ultimately on questions of administrative law.[109]

In this section, I argue that the conception of administrative law outlined in Section I has a double-facing nature that allows its connection with international and constitutional law. More precisely, a double-facing conception of administrative law suggests how the legal fields relevant to the determination cities' legal authority in foreign affairs intersect.

[106] Ibid., 253.
[107] Ibid., 254.
[108] For a clear example, see *Catalyst Paper Corp* v. *North Cowichan (District)*, [2012] 1 SCR 5.
[109] Taggart, 'Globalization, "Local" Foreign Policy, and Administrative Law', 282.

Questions of borders and openness to the 'foreign', which figure at the heart of this collection, are relevant to both administrative law and constitutional law. Indeed, the language of borders permeates orthodox conceptions of administrative law: judicial pronouncements and doctrinal discourse have traditionally constructed administrative agencies' powers around the notion of jurisdiction, understood as a statutorily delimited space that agencies cannot cross.

Applying the metaphor of boundaries to administrative law, one would think that its traditional conceptual edifice is made of hermetic frontiers. Under the traditional view of that part of the law outlined in Section I, Parliament alone, acting within the internal confines of the constitution, decides on the location of administrative frontiers through statutory enactments, with courts elucidating its word and intent only when they are unclear. External influences – be they expressed through norms, principles, policies – do not penetrate the frontiers unless Parliament allows them to so travel, shielding administrative constituencies, agencies, institutions from them. Administrative agencies therefore appear to be working inside a sealed container, constructed by Parliament and courts.

From such a perspective, cities seem required to cross two sets of borders to reach the international scene. The first set is composed of the statutory rules that delimit the legal authority of cities within the constitutional order and at the same time delimit the legal authority of other institutions within that order. The second set of borders is composed of constitutional norms, which trace the line between domestic and international matters. Under this dominant view however, cities can never reach the constitutional border because administrative and local government law build a hermetic first set of membranes, preventing cities from acting beyond their territorial jurisdiction. The first challenge is therefore to cross that first border. As suggested above, it is possible to meet this challenge with a conception of administrative law that both moves away from a theory of *ultra vires* and endorses a conception of deference as respect.

The second challenge is to cross the second border, the constitutional one. Traditionally, beyond state borders is a conversation among sovereign states governed by international and constitutional law rules and principles that close the door to cities. However, the conceptions of international and constitutional law that we discussed in Section I suggest that cities' actual presence in the networks that exist on the international stage express practices that can ultimately transform both the structure of these legal fields and the legal norms themselves. As a result, acting beyond the constitution's borders may become legally possible for cities.

If both challenges are met, that is if cities can cross both sets of borders, the way is clear for a double-facing view of administrative law. Such a view suggests, on the one hand, that cities' actions in matters of foreign policy potentially alter the domestic, interpretative context – or 'field of legal meaning'[110] – that informs the determination of their legal powers. That is, cities' own understanding of their legitimate role in the world – shaped by their concrete experiences – weighs in on the interpretation of the extent of their powers. From this perspective, external influences affect the content of internal norms, opening up the way for the legal recognition of cities' role in foreign policy matters. On the other hand, this evolution suggests that cities, relying on such legal recognition to act on the international stage, bring with them an understanding of the legitimate limits to exercises of cities' power, including general principles about exercises of administrative action. From this perspective, internal influences project themselves beyond state boundaries, affecting the interpretative context that informs exercises of public power on the international stage.

This continuous movement of mutual influences illustrates the double-facing nature of administrative law,[111] which in turn highlights the extent to which it is permeable to the influence of constitutional and international law, particularly when these legal fields are articulated along the lines suggested in the preceding section.

Hence, taking the perspective of Brunnée and Toope's interactional account of international law outlined in Section I, one can see how *Shell*, essentially focused on administrative law questions, takes on a different meaning. In that case, the city council passed the resolutions after hearing representations from both a group of citizens supporting the boycott and Shell arguing against it, the company also submitting written observations. Council members voted on the proposed resolutions in the usual public setting. Hence, the municipal, democratic processes and the judicial proceedings involved in *Shell* may together be viewed as sites where a variety of stakeholders – citizens, corporations, municipal councillors, municipal councils, judges – exchange knowledge allowing the emergence of shared understandings on the appropriate role of cities on the

110 See David Dyzenhaus, 'The Janus-Faced Constitution', Chapter 2 of this volume.

111 Aust, 'Shining Cities on the Hill? The Global City, Climate Change, and International Law', 260: 'it is not only the international that is piercing through the outer layers of the state, but it is also the inside of the state which is pushing its way outwards'.

international stage. We thus have a concrete case of friction of social action against the parameters of a dominant legal structure of international and local government law. Where the dominant paradigm of international law would see in Vancouver's resolutions a political attempt by a non-state actor to influence the situation in South Africa, the interactional account sees an attempt to develop shared understandings on what cities want to accomplish through law on the international scene and why. Subject to complying with criteria of legality and to a robust practice of legality, the development of shared understandings is a crucial step towards law-making in international law. Besides, to borrow from Wiener, the processes and deliberation of the city council and in the Supreme Court form parts of dialogues, or multilogues about the understanding of the role of cities in international affairs. They allowed Vancouver to participate in both the contestation of the norms of international law that restrict access to norm validation to formal legal subject – states – and the re-constitution of these norms.

These processes also illustrate the challenges that lay ahead in building such understandings. The Vancouver City Council adopted the resolutions, in a narrow vote – 6 against 5. Shell challenged the resolutions, and a divided Supreme Court – 5 to 4 – found in its favour. Given the narrow margin of both outcomes – municipal and judicial – one could hardly have concluded, back in 1994, that stakeholders shared an understanding of a legitimate role for cities in conditioning the legality of procurement decisions to the adoption of a particular behaviour in another part of the world. As we saw however, the dissenting opinion in *Shell* took centre stage in the following years in cases concerning the appropriate approach to judicial review of municipal decisions generally, suggesting that, should the Court today hear a case similar to *Shell*, the shared understanding might be different. This echoes Helmut Aust's observation of the evolving nature of that kind of transformation:

> I argue for the observation of processes by which cities (and other actors) assert themselves as internationally relevant actors, together with an analysis of how the established structures of international law respond to these processes. It might not be possible to identify a precise tipping point where the assertion of authority is successful, but in this way the plausibility of claims to participation in the international legal system may be assessed gradually. The assessment of the evolution of the international legal system is thereby never frozen in time, but can only provide snapshots of its development at a respective point in time.[112]

[112] Ibid., 273.

That kind of case can also be examined from the perspective of Poole's mutually constitutive model of the relationship between external and internal faces of the constitution alluded to in Section I. Following this model, the continued presence of Vancouver and of other cities on the international stage through the boycott against Shell, coupled with the recognition of this presence from states, could have affected the constitutional structure and eventually the constitutional norms relating to cities' jurisdiction to act in foreign affairs. Vancouver adopted the resolutions in a context where many states had imposed economic sanctions on South Africa with a view to pressuring the country to transform radically its political regime. Vancouver's move also figured among an international movement of protest from numerous non-state constituencies. Those included cities and other kinds of organisations, like universities that decided to disinvest from companies doing business in that country. There was thus continued presence of cities on the international stage. But one could also suggest that there had been at least implicit acquiescence from states to that form of action by cities, potentially affecting the constitutional framework concerning foreign affairs.

In sum, under a double-facing conception of administrative law, cities' actions in foreign affairs trigger a process in which a number of actors implicitly deliberate on the determination of the contours of cities' legal powers. When coupled with particular alternative conceptions of constitutional and international law, the result is a destabilisation of the traditional legal framework that virtually denies cities' legal existence on the international scene, opening the way for the development of a legal basis for local foreign policy. In other words, a double-facing conception of administrative law suggests that *political* actions of cities on the international stage can have *legal* significance.

IV Conclusion

The alternative view of administrative law that I propose highlights the idea that cities' concrete actions in matters of local foreign policy – for instance, a decision to adopt selective procurement practices to exclude companies that do business in wicked states – are not only a way of taking a political stand on matters outside their geographical limits. Cities so acting also take a legal stand on the interpretation of the normative framework that establishes the extent of their jurisdiction.[113] Stated differently, they assert their authority as internationally relevant actors.[114] My suggestion is that a double-facing conception of administrative law provides processes whereby one can assess the extent to which local government law, constitutional law and international law respond to cities' assertions of authority.

The search for a legal basis for local foreign policy does not assume that local foreign policy is inherently good. Michael Taggart, for one, seemed to view local government action as such: 'Local governments around the world increasingly want to lend support in making the world a better place both for those within and without their territorial boundaries.'[115] However, authors have expressed more nuanced positions and even scepticism at times.[116] My perspective is not to find ways to justify any city action on the underlying assumption that they do things better than their states. It is rather that any exercise of public power must rely on proper legal justification. Cities' action on the international stage raises the fundamental question of the legitimacy of public power. Cities cannot interfere with rights without appropriate justification, nor can central states. Recent actions by cities may seem to some observers a manifestation of democratic, progressive and to some extent unthreatening exercise of power, and in fact a welcome counterbalance of powerful, unthoughtful centre powers. Yet, cities' actions are as much in need of justification as any other exercise of public power.

The place of cities in the double-facing constitution is that of participants to a process that includes more players than orthodox conceptions of international and constitutional law used to allow. In my view, administrative law's capacity to bring various perspectives to bear on the legality of executive action generally has the potential to translate into administrative

113 'When cities enter the international sphere on their own, they do so recognizing the extent of the power that national and sub-national governments exercise over them. Cities' international activities are designed, in part, to change these existing central-local relationships by expanding the scope of cities' authority', Frug and Barron, 'International Local Government Law', 23.

114 Aust, 'Shining Cities on the Hill? The Global City, Climate Change, and International Law', 273.

115 Taggart, 'Globalization, "Local" Foreign Policy, and Administrative Law', 263. See also generally Barber, *If Mayors Ruled the World. Rising Cities, Declining Nation States.*

116 See, among others, Blank, 'The City and the World' 924ff; Frug and Barron, 'International Local Government Law', 54 and Jean Galbraith, 'Cooperative and Uncooperative Foreign Affairs Federalism' (2017) 130 *Harvard Law Review* 2131, 2132–33.

law's capacity to mediate between the normative legal influences and standards more specifically involved in the legality of local foreign policy. Administrative law rules and principles neither always prevail over international or constitutional legal standards, nor always give way to them. Rather, administrative law provides the framework in which all legitimate participants, including cities themselves, cooperate to make sense of the complex nexus of legal standards involved in contemporary city action, and to articulate the best interpretation of cities' power.

12

The Democratic Challenge to Foreign Relations Law in Transatlantic Perspective

HELMUT PHILIPP AUST*

Introduction: Foreign Relations Law and the 'Globalisation Paradox'

Is international cooperation compatible with sovereignty and democracy? Harvard economist Dani Rodrik has suggested one possible answer in his analysis of the development of the global free trade regime. Rodrik discussed how societies face a conundrum of how to square participation in free trade regimes with national sovereignty and democracy – he calls this the 'globalization paradox'.[1] In a nutshell, he argued that we face a trilemma insofar as 'we cannot have hyperglobalization, democracy and national self-determination all at once. We can have at most two out of the three.'[2]

As with any catchy categorisation, the devil is in the details. Of course, Rodrik does not argue that the three categories are crystal clear and exist as fixed parameters which can only interact in one specific way. Instead, it makes more sense to conceive of them as variables which can be fuzzy around the edges. Democracy can certainly mean different things to different people. Sovereignty is a good candidate for being the single most contested notion of political theory. It may also be a vehicle for protecting national democracy. At the same time, the exercise of sovereignty can be an expression of democratic decision-making processes. And free trade can take many different forms as the current rows over the imposition of tariffs and the respective threats and virtues of protectionism

* I would like to thank Alexander Silke for research assistance as well as critical engagement with the text during the writing process. Further thanks are due to the editors, as well as Curtis Bradley, Jean Galbraith, Thomas Kleinlein, Georg Nolte and Mehrdad Payandeh for comments on various earlier drafts. Any errors and misconceptions are mine. Comments are welcome at helmut.aust@fu-berlin.de.

1 Dani Rodrik, *The Globalization Paradox* paperback ed. (New York: W. W. Norton, 2012).

2 Ibid., 200.

might come to show. Nonetheless, Rodrik's trilemma captures the essence of a current debate which views international cooperation increasingly as an encroachment on the domestic political process. His take is also helpful as it captures the types of decisions to be made with respect to foreign relations law. Traditionally, the greater leeway given to the executive in this field was meant to enable the executive to play an effective role at the international level. If we think of this narrative, it ties in with Rodrik's view that you can combine international cooperation and sovereignty. Allowing the executive to act with a more or less free hand at the international level is hence seen as strengthening sovereignty. From a democratic perspective, the reverse might be true. Giving the executive a free hand might undermine the democratic legitimacy of political processes.

Indeed, Rodrik's analysis touches upon core questions of what constitutional lawyers call foreign relations law. With respect to many jurisdictions, the field of foreign relations law is a relatively recent creation.[3] True, the legal questions which permeate this field are not new. Foreign relations law is generally concerned with the relationship between the outside of a state and its interior[4] and is thus very much an expression of the double-facing constitution in the sense of this volume.[5] It focuses on the interaction between international and domestic norms and regulates the competences that state organs enjoy when they act with international repercussions. As such, any given state will have some kind of foreign relations law, at least to the extent that its constitution or other relevant legal sources provide for guidance on exactly these questions. What is fairly novel, however, is the field of foreign relations law as an academic discipline, at least if we look beyond the United States. A proper field of foreign relations law has not even materialised in all constitutional systems. Traditionally, foreign relations law was seen as some kind of specialty of US constitutional law.[6] This overlooks, however, that *Äußeres Staatsrecht* was

[3] See further Helmut Philipp Aust, 'Foreign Affairs', in Rainer Grote, Frauke Lachenmann and Rudiger Wolfrum (eds.), *Max Planck Encyclopedia of Comparative Constitutional Law* (Oxford: Oxford University Press, 2017), para. 7; Curtis Bradley, 'What Is Foreign Relations Law?' in Curtis Bradley (ed.), *Oxford Handbook of Comparative Foreign Relations Law* (Oxford: Oxford University Press, 2019), 3, 8.

[4] Campbell McLachlan, 'Five Conceptions of the Function of Foreign Relations Law', in Bradley (ed.), *Oxford Handbook of Comparative Foreign Relations Law*, text accompanying footnote 6.

[5] See David Dyzenhaus, 'The Janus-Faced Constitution', Chapter 2 of this volume.

[6] On the reasons for this state of affairs, see Anthea Roberts, *Is International Law International?* (Oxford: Oxford University Press, 2017), at 104–05; on the particular

a term prevalent for quite some time in late nineteenth-century Germany.[7] It has also recently been rediscovered, although its current day usage does not automatically align with its nineteenth-century roots.[8]

This essay discusses how foreign relations law and domestic notions of democracy relate to each other. To that extent, it engages in a comparative exercise which looks primarily at discourses about foreign relations law in a specific transatlantic context, i.e. in the United States and in Germany; two jurisdictions in which a specific subfield of foreign relations law has been in existence for quite some time. This contribution is sketched with a broad brush, looking for general trends in the field. The impetus for this exercise stems from the changing political environment in which we are currently living. Across a number of states, we are seeing authoritarian and populist movements on the rise.[9] The election of Donald Trump as President of the United States and the popular vote for 'Brexit' are only the most conspicuous signs of a development which aims at 'taking back control' and snubs a so-called ideology of 'globalism'.[10] Already in the preface to the 2016 paperback edition of *The Court and the World*, US Supreme Court Justice Stephen Breyer noted that

tradition of foreign relations law as an 'ersatz' international law in the United States, see Campbell McLachlan, *Foreign Relations Law* (Cambridge: Cambridge University Press, 2014), para. 1.30; the British tradition of foreign relations law reaches further back, an important starting point being Frederick Alexander Mann, *Foreign Affairs in English Courts* (Oxford: Clarendon Press, 1986).

[7] See further on this Helmut Philipp Aust, 'Fundamental Rights of States: Constitutional Law in Disguise?' (2016) 5 *Cambridge Journal of International and Comparative Law* 521, 523.

[8] Frank Schorkopf, *Das Staatsrecht der internationalen Beziehungen* (Munich: C. H. Beck, 2017); see also Volker Röben, *Außenverfassungsrecht* (Tübingen: Mohr Siebeck, 2007).

[9] See, for helpful conceptual clarifications, Jan-Werner Müller, *What is Populism?* (Philadelphia: University of Pennsylvania Press, 2016); more specifically, from the perspective of international law and human rights Philip Alston, 'The Populist Challenge to Human Rights Law' (2017) 9 *Journal of Human Rights Practice* 1.

[10] David Goodhart, *The Road to Somewhere: The Populist Revolt and the Future of Politics* (London: Hurst and Company, 2017). US President Trump has recently set out his vision of international cooperation most clearly in his Remarks to the 73rd Session of the UN General Assembly, 25 September 2018. Inter alia, he emphasised that 'America will always choose independence and cooperation over global governance, control and domination. . . . We will never surrender America's sovereignty to an unelected, unaccountable, global bureaucracy. America is governed by Americans. We reject the ideology of globalism, and we embrace the doctrine of patriotism', available at www.whitehouse.gov, accessed 2 October 2018.

> it has become more popular to ignore transnational problems or turn inward in an effort to find solutions. Many citizens seem ever more likely to understand the word 'globalization' as descriptive of a problem, not a solution.[11]

The crucial question is taking back control 'from whom'? There is certainly not a clear-cut answer in this regard. Both the developments in the United States and in the United Kingdom, but also the electoral successes of right-wing parties in France, Germany and other European states, indicate that a previous latent feeling of frustration about globalisation and an ensuing alienation have translated into political momentum. Causes for this development have been analysed in some detail elsewhere.[12] One facet of 'taking back control' relates to the conditions under which states can continue to participate in forms of international cooperation. Railing against free trade was a staple in the campaign speeches of Donald Trump. The North American Free Trade Agreement (NAFTA) was singled out as a target, as was the planned Trans-Pacific Partnership Agreement (TPP).[13] It is noticeable that there was considerable convergence between these discourses in the United States and a simultaneously mounting level of frustration with and protest against new free trade and investment agreements on the other side of the Atlantic.[14] In particular in Germany, concerns about the

[11] Stephen Breyer, *The Court and the World. American Law and the New Global Realities* paperback ed. (New York: Vintage Books, 2016), ix; for an earlier discussion of the relationship between globalisation and democracy, see Armin von Bogdandy, 'Demokratie, Globalisierung, Zukunft des Völkerrechts – eine Bestandsaufnahme' (2003) 63 *Zeitschrift für ausländisches öffentliches Recht und Völkerrecht* 853, 860–63.

[12] For a take on the related question of how the changing political climate affects international law see James Crawford, 'The Current Political Discourse Concerning International Law' (2018) 81 *Modern Law Review* 1; see also Heike Krieger and Georg Nolte, 'The International Rule of Law – Rise or Decline? Points of Departure' *KFG Working Paper Series No. 1* (2016), available at https://papers.ssrn.com/sol3/papers.cfm?abstract_id=2866940 accessed 28 August 2018; for a useful conceptualisation of the current backlash (against human rights) see Leslie Vinjamuri, 'Human Rights Backlash', in Stephen Hopgood, Jack Snyder and Leslie Vinjamuri (eds.), *Human Rights Futures* (Cambridge: Cambridge University Press, 2017), 114, at 120–23.

[13] On the US–Mexican dynamics in this regard see Alejandro Rodiles, 'After TPP is Before TPP: Mexican Politics for Economic Globalization and the Lost Chance for Reflection', in Benedict Kingsbury et al. (eds.), *Megaregulation Contested: Global Economic Ordering After TPP* (Oxford: Oxford University Press, 2019), 606.

[14] For a comparison of the legal debates see Thomas Kleinlein, 'TTIP and the Challenges of Investor-State-Arbitration: An Exercise in Comparative Foreign Relations Law', in Anna-Bettina Kaiser, Niels Petersen and Johannes Saurer (eds.), *US Constitutional Law in the Obama Era: A Transatlantic Perspective* (Baden-Baden: Nomos/Routledge, 2019).

Transatlantic Trade and Investment Partnership (TTIP) and the Comprehensive Economic and Trade Agreement (CETA) between the European Union and its Member States, on the one hand, and Canada, on the other, were voiced. With a new intensity, people took to the street to protest, inter alia, against so-called shadow tribunals (in legal technical terms: investor-state dispute settlement mechanisms, ISDS) and concerns about the impact that such agreements might have on domestic democracy.[15] In the eyes of the general public, these are of course not debates about arcane issues of foreign relations law. Rather, they concern issues of vital interest for the public as a whole. This is noteworthy in its own right as the questions underlying these debates are hitting right at the heart of foreign relations law: who gets to decide on the international commitments of a state? Who is negotiating these agreements? Under which institutional constraints? How is the domestic separation of powers affected? These concerns are all of a sudden in the centre of political attention, without necessarily being brought out in the open as such.

Accordingly, it is time for a closer look at how different conceptions of foreign relations law impact on these debates and on the possibilities of states to cooperate internationally. To this end, the next section will first briefly describe the legal context in which these debates take place. This context is characterised by changing perceptions of 'the international' which is increasingly viewed as encroaching upon the domestic policy space. The chapter will then identify two possible variants of foreign relations law: one leaning more towards a 'closed' conception of this field, the other one emphasising the virtues of being 'open'. On the one hand, the predominant approach of US foreign relations law is increasingly turning inwards, leaning towards a closed conception of foreign relations law. On the other hand, I will look at how German constitutional law has for quite some time maintained that a fundamental principle of the Basic Law was its openness to international cooperation. The contribution will then discuss how this traditional openness is now also coming under pressure in the German context. I will argue that this is a consequence of a growing democratic

15 For a sophisticated argument on the possible impacts on domestic democracy see Eyal Benvenisti, 'Democracy Captured: The Mega-Regional Agreements and the Future of Global Public Law' (2016) 23 *Constellations* 58, 61 (analysing ISDS as a countermove against assertive domestic courts); for a thoughtful analysis of the debate on ISDS see also Ntina Tzouvala, 'The academic debate about mega-regionals and international lawyers: legalism as critique?' (2018) 6 *London Review of International Law* 189.

challenge to foreign relations law in the German context, which, to some extent, mimics the state of affairs in the United States – however, without the central actors in the judiciary and academia openly acknowledging this move. In a final substantive section I will turn to a comparative assessment of these developments, highlighting some structural differences between the two jurisdictions. A brief conclusion follows.

I Changing Perceptions of International Law and Cooperation

Among Western states, there is a growing level of discontent with the way that the external sphere is impacting on the internal. This wish to become less open intensifies as a society aspires to stabilise the categories of the internal and the external. This trend might have to do with changing perceptions of what international law regulates and for whom. The development of international law from 'co-existence to co-operation'[16] has entailed new forms of regulation of matters which were previously considered to fall into the domestic jurisdiction of states. This development has taken place in a number of fields, most prominently in human rights law and in the law of international investment protection. In some ways, this is a process of international law 'coming of age'. It is no longer just seen as a horizontal law of coordination which does not impact on domestic regulatory questions. Human rights law has pervaded domestic legal systems and domestic courts have, to varying degrees, responded to the need to implement human rights and interpret domestic law in accordance with the international obligations of their respective state.[17] This has occurred despite the different legal techniques and strategies which can be deployed to shield a domestic legal order from international influences.[18] For instance, there is no requirement under international human rights law as such to provide for the direct effect of its

[16] Wolfgang Friedmann, *The Changing Structure of International Law* (London: Stevens & Sons, 1964), 60–73.

[17] For an account of the trajectory of the European Convention on Human Rights see Mikael Rask Madsen, 'The Protracted Institutionalization of the Strasbourg Court: From Legal Diplomacy to Integrationist Jurisprudence', in Jonas Christofferson and Michael Rask Madsen (eds.), *The European Court of Human Rights between Law and Politics* (Oxford: Oxford University Press, 2011), 43, 54–59.

[18] On these avoidance techniques see Eyal Benvenisti, 'Judicial Misgivings Regarding the Application of International Law: An Analysis of the Attitudes of National Courts' (1993) 4 *European Journal of International Law* 159, 161.

provisions.[19] International law traditionally leaves it to states *how* to implement their international legal obligations.[20] This leeway is one of the core sites for foreign relations law, to the extent that the rules in a given constitution can grant international law a certain rank and effect domestically. Yet, it is of course also true that domestic courts are state organs. Their jurisprudence can therefore give rise to state responsibility if the courts misjudge what international law requires of them.[21] Not surprisingly then, domestic courts have embraced techniques with regard to taking into account international law even when they may not be formally required to do so under their domestic legal framework.[22] Over time, such processes consolidate – and what has started as policy in order to avoid conflicts with international institutions can turn into more or less fixed expectations that international human rights obligations are to be taken into account.[23] With this development, the potential for conflict also increases as requirements under human rights law can come into conflict with other legally protected goods. This then requires constitutional courts to enter into more or less open balancing games – and to identify limits for the openness of a given constitutional system towards international (and, where applicable, EU) law.

It can be debated to what extent this really is a new phenomenon or rather a continuation of forms of the exercise of power which international law always featured. What is new is the perception among wider parts of the population in Western states that international law is 'hitting home'. Human rights law and international investment law are no longer

[19] See further Mathias Forteau, 'The Role of the International Rules of Interpretation for the Determination of Direct Effect of International Agreements', in Helmut Philipp Aust and Georg Nolte (eds.), *The Interpretation of International Law by Domestic Courts – Uniformity, Diversity, Convergence* (Oxford: Oxford University Press, 2016), 96, 99.

[20] Alfred Verdross and Bruno Simma, *Universelles Völkerrecht – Theorie und Praxis*, 3rd ed. (Berlin: Duncker & Humblot, 1984), para. 848.

[21] This a traditional core of the international law pertaining to the reparation for injuries to aliens, see only Jan Paulsson, *Denial of Justice in International Law* (Cambridge: Cambridge University Press, 2005), 38–44.

[22] Doctrinally, this will turn on variants of 'consistent interpretation', see further André Nollkaemper, *National Courts and the International Rule of Law* (Oxford: Oxford University Press, 2011), 139–57.

[23] An example is the development of the case law of the German Federal Constitutional Court on the role of the European Convention on Human Rights for the interpretation of the fundamental rights of the German Basic Law, see on this development and the broader European picture Nico Krisch, *Beyond Constitutionalism: The Pluralist Structure of Postnational Law* (Oxford: Oxford University Press, 2010), ch. 4.

regulating merely situations in the 'Global South'.[24] Human rights law is no longer just about preventing the worst atrocities in faraway dictatorships. International investment protection is no longer just a one-way insurance contract for investors from Western states. In both fields, domestic constituencies have felt that policy space has become limited by international norms.[25]

This feeling of a shrinking policy space leads to a reevaluation of the way that foreign relations law allows international rules and principles to impact on domestic legal systems. Out of consideration for the protection of domestic democracy it is questioned whether the executive should continue to enjoy more leeway in conducting a state's foreign affairs. In the political and legal debates, it is noticeable that this form of objection to the traditional prerogatives of the executive in the field of foreign affairs comes from different points on the political spectrum. In the case of widespread protests against so-called 'mega-regionals', such as TTIP and CETA, there was both 'resistance' from a nationalist left and from the political right – both challenging the way in which these agreements would endanger domestic democracy. Indeed, the challenges against free trade regimes seems to be at the point where previous political opposites seem to converge and coalesce around a political distinction primarily based on open v. closed conceptions of politics.

II Two Conceptions of Foreign Relations Law

Political commentators have for some time now maintained that the defining political fracture of our times would no longer be between the right and the left, but rather be 'open' against 'closed'.[26] Across the previous political spectrum, it would be possible to categorise debates along these lines. The distinction itself goes back to the work of philosopher of science Karl Popper, in particular his 1945 book on *The Open Society and its Enemies*.[27] One may wonder to what extent the recent reappropriation of

[24] On these origins see Sundhya Pahuja, *Decolonising International Law – Development, Economic Growth and the Politics of Universality* (Cambridge: Cambridge University Press, 2011), 99.

[25] Peter-Tobias Stoll, Till Patrik Holterhus and Henner Gött, *Investitionsschutz und Verfassung* (Tübingen: Mohr Siebeck, 2017), 12–14.

[26] N. N., 'Drawbridges up – The new divide in rich countries is not between left and right but between open and closed', *The Economist*, 30 July 2016, available at www.economist.com; also on this divide in the context of foreign relations law Schorkopf, *Staatsrecht*, § 9, para. 41.

[27] Karl Popper, *The Open Society and its Enemies* (London: Routledge, 1945).

the division between 'open' and 'closed' is analytically coherent. In particular, it strikes me as questionable whether these two notions lend themselves to being generalised. Rather, they will come in different gradations, with some proponents of an 'open' system of trade favouring a 'closed' conception in the sector of migration and vice versa. The field of foreign relations law could of course be conceptualised without paying much attention to this division. But whether one comes down on the open or closed sides of the spectrum impacts on the spin one will give to this field.[28] Proponents of an 'open' foreign relations law might be tempted to preserve the special character of this field and interpret domestic constitutional law so that it can embrace international law effectively. Those arguing with more of a 'closed' mindset will aim to conceptualise foreign relations law as a bulwark against unwanted outside interference. With these observations in mind, it is now time to turn to the jurisdictions of the United States and Germany and to test the value of the categories of open v. closed as parameters of analysis for the field of foreign relations law.

A *From Exceptionalism to Sovereigntism? The Case of the United States*

In the United States, the study of foreign relations law took off to an early start with the first specialist monograph on the topic, authored by Quincy Wright, a towering figure in international law in the interwar United States.[29] His book was written very much in an internationalist spirit. Wright was no sceptic of international law. Quite to the contrary, his interwar writings constantly expanded the boundaries of international law, towards a loosening of the ties of state consent and towards the recognition that international law was not just translating such consent into norms, but also about regulating 'community interests', long before this term became a staple of the international law discourse in the 1990s.[30]

[28] McLachlan, 'Five Conceptions', text accompanying footnote 11.

[29] Quincy Wright, *The Control of American Foreign Relations* (New York: Macmillan, 1922); on Wright's contribution to international law see Hatsue Shinohara, *US International Lawyers in the Interwar Era – A Forgotten Crusade* (Cambridge: Cambridge University Press, 2012), 27–29, 64–66, 148–53.

[30] See, for instance, Quincy Wright, 'The Legal Nature of Treaties' (1916) 10 *American Journal of International Law* 706, 717 (for a very early emphasis that individuals hold rights under international agreements); Quincy Wright, 'Collective Rights and Duties' (1932) *Proceedings of the American Society of International Law* 101; later the concept of community interests was fully developed by Bruno Simma, 'From Bilateralism to Community Interest in International Law' (1994-VI) 250 *Recueil des cours* 217; for the

Louis Henkin's book on *Foreign Affairs and the US Constitution* shared a similar internationalist ethos.[31] It led to a re-emergence of the field some 50 years after Wright wrote the first monograph on the topic. Henkin's book first appeared right after the Vietnam War and then again, in a second edition, in the early 1990s. Published in markedly different times – right after the US defeat in Vietnam and after the vindication of the United States as the 'winner' of the Cold War, the book is characterised by a decidedly enlightened stance towards international law. Henkin was an internationalist, too.[32] He famously said that 'almost all nations comply with almost all of their international obligations almost all of the time'[33] and also proclaimed from the late 1970s onwards that the world had entered an 'age of rights'.[34] At the same time, he was worried about the degree of US absence from the development of large parts of the human rights treaty regime and characterised the US role as a 'flying buttress', not a pillar of the international human rights system.[35] All this informed both his monograph on foreign affairs as well as his work as Rapporteur for the American Law Institute for which he saw to completion the Restatement, third, on Foreign Relations Law which was published in the late 1980s. As Georg Nolte has remarked, the Restatement coincided with a progressive '*Zeitgeist*'.[36] It is fair to say that Henkin's positions were taken very seriously indeed. At the same time, his internationalist outlook did probably not capture the prevalent mood among a majority of US *constitutional* law scholars.[37] In particular, his important treatise on the domestic legal ramifications of US

most recent exposition, see the contributions in Eyal Benvenisti and Georg Nolte (eds.), *Community Interests Across International Law* (Oxford: Oxford University Press, 2018).

31 Louis Henkin, *Foreign Affairs and the US Constitution*, 2nd ed. (Oxford: Clarendon Press, 1996).

32 See the conversation between Henkin and Antonio Cassese, reprinted in Antonio Cassese, *Five Masters of International Law* (Hart: Oxford, 2011), 189–224.

33 Louis Henkin, *How Nations Behave: Law and Foreign Policy* 2nd ed. (New York: Council on Foreign Relations, 1979), 47.

34 Louis Henkin, *The Age of Rights* (New York: Columbia University Press, 1990); on the development of Henkin's scholarship in this regard see Samuel Moyn, *The Last Utopia – Human Rights in History* (Cambridge, MA: Harvard University Press, 2010), 201–07.

35 Louis Henkin, 'Rights: American and Human' (1979) 79 *Columbia Law Review* 405, at 421; see further Georg Nolte and Helmut Philipp Aust, 'European Exceptionalism?' (2013) 2 *Global Constitutionalism* 407, 419.

36 Georg Nolte, 'Remarks: The Fourth Restatement of Foreign Relations Law of the United States' (2014) 108 *Proceedings of the American Society of International Law*, 27, 28.

37 For criticism in this regard, see Curtis A. Bradley and Jack L. Goldsmith, 'Customary International Law as Federal Common Law: A Critique of the Modern Position' (1997) 110 *Harvard Law Review* 815, 835–36.

participation in forms of international cooperation did not pay a lot of attention to the substance of the democratic process. Henkin wrote extensively about the separation of powers in the field of foreign relations law, i.e. the partition of roles between President and Congress and the role that courts have to play in this arena.[38] Yet, throughout the treatise there is barely a mention of sovereignty or democracy as legal goods or principles that would need protection against a hollowing out effected by international cooperation.[39]

This state of affairs changed markedly with a new generation of scholars that appeared in the late 1990s. In retrospect, an article by Curtis Bradley and Jack Goldsmith can be identified as a game changer.[40] In their 1997 piece on customary international law as federal common law, Bradley and Goldsmith sought to limit the impact of customary international law within the US legal system. Among their arguments a concern for 'American representative democracy' took pride of place. Arguably, their more cautious position towards the effects of international law on the US domestic legal system was more in line with a mainstream position in the US constitutional law scholarship.[41] Nonetheless, their work and the contribution of other more sceptical authors such as Julian Ku or Eric Posner stirred a heated debate[42] about 'the new sovereigntists', as Peter Spiro characterised them in an essay in *Foreign Affairs*.[43] Spiro was outspoken in his critique. He saw an 'anti-

[38] Henkin, *Foreign Affairs*, 83–130.

[39] Note that Henkin was not ignorant about these issues. In the published version of his 1988 Cooley Lectures he notes in the conclusion that 'In foreign affairs, it has become important to rededicate ourselves to the principles of constitutionalism – to limited, checked, balanced government and respect for the rule of law and individual rights. In foreign affairs we are particularly susceptible to the claims of "efficiency" at the expense of other values, to pleas that we repose full faith in "the experts", to demands of individual sacrifice, including the sacrifice of our obligation to scrutinise and criticise, and sacrifice individual rights. In foreign affairs we are particularly susceptible to becoming bemused by assertion of "leadership", by appeal to false patriotism, by play on our fears of appearing divided before the world.' Louis Henkin, *Constitutionalism, Democracy, and Foreign Affairs* (New York: Columbia University Press, 1990), 108.

[40] Bradley and Goldsmith, 'Customary International Law'.

[41] See now also Ingrid Wuerth, 'The Future of the Federal Common Law of Foreign Relations' (2018) 106 *Georgetown Law Journal* 1825, 1831.

[42] Eric Posner and Cass R. Sunstein, '*Chevronizing* Foreign Relations Law' (2006) 116 *Yale Law Journal* 1170; Julian Ku and John Yoo, '*Globalization and Sovereignty*' (2013) *Berkeley Journal of International Law* 210; Peter J. Spiro, '*Sovereigntism's Twilight*' (2013) *Berkeley Journal of International Law* 307.

[43] Peter J. Spiro, 'The New Sovereigntists – American Exceptionalism and its False Prophets' (2000) 79(6) *Foreign Affairs*, 9.

internationalism' at work that would seek to develop a 'coherent blueprint for defending American institutions against the alleged encroachment of international ones'.[44] This debate has not abated since. The more sceptical position towards international law which might emanate from the new Restatement[45] can also point to the development of the case law of the US Supreme Court. As has been observed by David Sloss and others, the case law of the Court has become more inward-looking over time.[46] At the time that Quincy Wright was writing, the heyday of 'good faith' interpretation and a liberal inclination to pre-empt local courts from overly parochial attitudes were still not that far away. This line of jurisprudence has receded into the distance, however, with avoidance doctrines of various sorts becoming more regular features of the Court's case law.[47]

This case law lends itself easily to an explanation in the light of the sovereigntist position as identified and critiqued by Spiro. A key text in this regard is a contribution by Julian Ku and John Yoo on 'Globalization and Sovereignty' that appeared in a 2013 special issue of the *Berkeley Journal of International Law* (alongside two contributions by Spiro). The noteworthy feature of this article is that Ku and Yoo do not purport to fend off international law to protect state sovereignty as such. Rather, they distinguish between what they call 'Westphalian sovereignty', i.e. an outdated form of state sovereignty that much of international law has sought to overcome, and 'popular sovereignty' which would need to be shielded from overreaching international institutions.[48] Popular sovereignty taps into the legacy of the American Revolution and has thus an immediately more positive ring to it than what the authors portray as a rigid and formalist concept dating back to seventeenth century Europe.

[44] Ibid., 9.

[45] See also Nolte, 'Remarks', at 28: 'Given the uncertain status of international law in the United States, and the complicated decision making process within the American Law Institute, the new Restatement will probably not produce results that will be criticized as being too progressive.'

[46] David L. Sloss, Michael D. Ramsey and William S. Dodge, 'Conclusion: Continuity and Change over Two Centuries', in David Sloss, Michael Ramsey and William Dodge (eds.), *International Law in the US Supreme Court – Continuity and Change* (Cambridge: Cambridge University Press, 2011), 589, 604–05; see also Helmut Philipp Aust, Alejandro Rodiles and Peter Staubach, 'Unity or Uniformity? Domestic Courts and Treaty Interpretation' (2014) 27 *Leiden Journal of International Law* 75, at 86.

[47] For a thorough analysis of the shifting lines of debate in the 1920s and 1930s see G. Edward White, 'The Transformation of the Constitutional Regime of Foreign Relations Law' (1999) 85 *Virginia Law Review* 1, 77 et seq.

[48] Ku and Yoo, 'Globalization and Sovereignty', 232–33.

(We can leave aside here whether their depiction of the Westphalian notion of sovereignty is convincing.) One cannot help but notice an ironic twist in the US debate about democracy v. international law. A lot of what is portrayed as the 'new international law' by the sovereigntist authors is not binding on the United States. Many human rights treaties have not been ratified, individual complaints procedures not activated. In a way, the sovereigntist position is thus a preemptive shield against a potentially overreaching international law and seeks to fortify the status quo.[49]

Arguably, this move inwards also finds support in the case law of the Supreme Court of the United States. Ganesh Sitaraman and Ingrid Wuerth have recently described the development of the case law in the field of foreign relations as one of 'normalization'.[50] By this they mean that the Court has gradually abandoned its stance that foreign relations law is a decidedly different field from 'ordinary' constitutional law. Foreign affairs exceptionalism would be a thing of the past, having given way to an understanding of this body of law as 'ordinary'. In particular, separation of powers cases would no longer automatically see the executive win. And cases supposedly pertaining to deference to the executive would be decided on the same basis as in domestic administrative law contexts where this doctrine also has a key role to play.[51] This move towards 'normalization' can be understood in different ways. At first sight, it seems to do away with the kind of foreign affairs exceptionalism that is often understood to be one of the root causes for a lack of international engagement of the United States. Seen from this perspective, American exceptionalism on the international level is mirrored by the peculiar constitutional structures and traditions on the internal level. Yet, this perspective risks overlooking that part of the foreign affairs exceptionalism might actually have been in place to secure the national executive leeway *for* engaging on the international level. In

[49] On the, at times, bewildering fixation on sovereignty in the US foreign policy debate, see Bruce Jones, 'American Sovereignty is Safe from the UN', *Foreign Affairs*, 28 September 2018, available at www.foreignaffairs.com, accessed 2 October 2018; see further Vicki C. Jackson, 'The U.S. Constitution and International Law', in Mark Tushnet, Mark A. Graber and Sanford Levinson (eds.), *The Oxford Handbook of the U.S. Constitution* (Oxford: Oxford University Press, 2015), 921, at 939.

[50] Gatesh Sitaraman and Ingrid Wuerth, 'The Normalization of Foreign Relations Law' (2015) 128 *Harvard Law Review* 1897; for a related endeavour, see Harlan Grant Cohen, 'Formalism and Distrust: Foreign Affairs and the Roberts Court' (2015) 83 *The George Washington Law Review* 380, at 385 in footnote 25.

[51] Emblematic of this move: Posner and Sunstein, '*Chevronizing* Foreign Relations Law'.

other words, exceptionalism has different foci when assessed with respect to the US position towards international cooperation and the internal division of powers in the field of foreign affairs. At least in some cases, the gradual abandonment of foreign affairs exceptionalism now risks limiting the possibility of the United States to engage in forms of international cooperation. This is not an entirely novel insight. Already in 1964, Richard Falk formulated that:

> [m]any lawyers allege that it is a progressive tendency to encourage substantive review by domestic courts because this tends to increase the application of international norms. Rules of deference – such as act of state – are seen as regressive.[52]

Falk rejected this simplistic claim and insisted that the calculus could be much more complex.[53]

An illustration of this point from recent US judicial practice concerns the domestic effects of decisions by the International Court of Justice (ICJ). This question arose in the aftermath of several rulings of the ICJ against the United States[54] which involved the right to consular notification under Article 36 of the Vienna Convention on Consular Relations (VCCR)[55] and the potential conflict between this right and the so-called 'procedural default' rule of US criminal law which bars the invocation of procedural errors past a certain point in court proceedings.[56] The *Avena* judgment of the ICJ went further into the consequences of a violation of Article 36 VCCR and specified as a legal consequence that the United States should offer a possibility for 'review and reconsideration' of the verdict in some cases.[57] Subsequently, US President George W. Bush issued a memorandum in which he directed state courts to provide review and reconsideration in the cases addressed by the ICJ in *Avena* with a view to ensuring compliance

[52] Richard Falk, *The Role of Domestic Courts in the International Legal Order* (New York: Syracuse University Press, 1964), 75.

[53] Ibid.

[54] *LaGrand* (*Germany* v. *United States*), Judgment of 27 June 2001, ICJ Rep 2001, 466; *Case Concerning Avena and other Mexican Nationals* (*Mexico* v. *United States*), Judgment of 31 March 2004, ICJ Rep 2004, 12.

[55] Vienna Convention on Consular Relations, adopted on 24 April 1963, entered into force 19 March 1967, 596 UNTS 261.

[56] For a vivid description of this conflict see Breyer, *The Court and the World*, 199–218; see also – from the perspective of international law – Bruno Simma and Carsten Hoppe, 'The *LaGrand* Case: A Story of Many Miscommunications', in John Noyes, Laura Dickinson and Mark Janis (eds.), *International Law Stories* (New York: Foundation Press, 2007), 371.

[57] *Avena*, paras. 130 et seq.

with the ICJ judgment. This move was eventually not successful as a case brought by one of the persons whose prior conviction formed part of the *Avena* case went up to the US Supreme Court. In *Medellin*, the Court found that there was no basis in the UN Charter for ICJ decisions to have immediate effect in the US domestic legal order.[58] What is important in our context is that the US Supreme Court did not consider the *Medellin* case to warrant any special privilege for the US President in order to ensure US compliance with its international obligations.[59] Instead, the Court insisted on upholding the ordinary constitutional framework.[60]

The Court has been more forthcoming also in other contexts to allow a 'normal' form of judicial review over governmental conduct with international implications. A good illustration is provided by the two *Bond* cases in which the Court affirmed that an individual had standing to challenge a statute implementing the Chemical Weapons Convention on the grounds of the Tenth Amendment.[61] Traditional doctrines of foreign relations law which might have impeded the Court from exercising judicial review here – such as the political questions doctrine, act of

[58] Charter of the United Nations, adopted on 26 June 1945, entered into force 24 October 1945, 892 UNTS 119. See *Medellin* v. *Texas*, 552 US 491, 508 (2008). The question turned on whether the ICJ's judgment in *Avena* was binding on state courts by virtue of the President's February 28, 2005 Memorandum. In the proceedings, the US government contended that while the *Avena* judgment would not of its own force require domestic courts to set aside ordinary rules of procedural default, 'that judgment became the law of the land with precisely that effect pursuant to the President's Memorandum and his power "to establish binding rules of decision that preempt contrary state law." … In this case, the President seeks to vindicate US interests in ensuring the reciprocal observance of the Vienna Convention, protecting relations with foreign governments, and demonstrating commitment to the role of international law. These interests are plainly compelling. Such considerations, however, do not allow us to set aside first principles. The President's authority to act, as with the exercise of any governmental power, "must stem either from an act of Congress or from the Constitution itself." … The President has an array of political and diplomatic means available to enforce international obligations, but unilaterally converting a non-self-executing treaty into a self-executing one is not among them. The responsibility for transforming an international obligation arising from a non-self-executing treaty into domestic law falls to Congress' (Chief Justice Roberts delivering the Opinion of the Court).

[59] See also Ingrid Wuerth, 'Foreign Official Immunity Determinations in U.S. Courts: The Case Against the State Department' (2011) 51 *Virginia Journal of International Law* 1, at 15.

[60] Jackson, 'The U.S. Constitution', 932.

[61] *Bond* v. *United States I*, 564 US 211 (2010); *Bond* v. *United States II*, 572 US ____ (2014) (slip op); Convention on the Prohibition of the Development, Production, Stockpiling and Use of Chemical Weapons and on their Destruction, adopted on 3 September 1992, entered into force on 29 April 1997, 1975 UNTS 45.

state, deference – did not play a role.[62] To the contrary, the Court established a presumption that Congress would not have authorised 'a stark intrusion into traditional state authority' when giving advice and consent to the ratification of the Chemical Weapons Convention. Although this language indicates that a central issue of the case revolved around issues of federalism – and hence the legacy of *Missouri* v. *Holland*[63] – the opinions strike a chord also with the broader debates about the limits of foreign affairs powers. In his popular book on the Supreme Court and its relation to the world, Justice Breyer accordingly contextualised the *Bond* case by pointing out that *Bond* illustrates a broader concern:

> What are the constitutional limits upon the treaty power, including on Congress's authority to implement a treaty through legislation? What *should* they be, given the Constitution's structural provisions and its concerns with federalism, separation of powers and democratic accountability?[64]

As Breyer also notes, the Court did not give a principled answer in *Bond* and generally shies away from doing so. Nonetheless, there are indications in the case law that the approach of the Court is consolidating around a certain form of distrust of special privileges of the executive in the field of foreign affairs. A most remarkable decision in this regard is *Zivotofsky* v. *Clinton* in which the Court ruled that it could review a decision by the executive not to execute a statute allowing for the registration of 'Jerusalem, Israel' as a birthplace in US official documents. Writing for the majority of the Court, Chief Justice Roberts insisted that '(t)he federal courts are not being asked to supplant a foreign policy decision of the political branches with the courts' own unmoored determination of what United States policy toward Jerusalem should be'. Instead, the case was about the enforcement of a specific statutory right – all in all a 'familiar judicial exercise'.[65] The *Zivotofsky* case is

[62] Sitaraman and Wuerth, 'The Normalization of Foreign Relations Law', 1927.

[63] *Missouri* v. *Holland*, 252 US 416 (1920); this case concerned the reach of the federal treaty making power. On the occasion of the conclusion of an international agreement with Great Britain on the protection of international migratory birds, the Court held that the treaty-making power is not limited to what may be done with an unaided act of Congress.

[64] Breyer, *The Court and the World*, 225.

[65] *Zivotofsky* v. *Clinton*, 566 US 189 (2012); see also the follow-up case *Zivotofsky* v. *Kerry*, 576 US ___ (2015) (slip op) which again involved a win for the executive, yet without a special niche of a foreign affairs power carved out which would be devoid of judicial intervention.

remarkable not because the executive eventually won the case. Rather the case stands out as it marked with very general language that the Roberts court would no longer be inclined to see the subject matter of the case – which pertained to the recognition of a foreign government and related issues – as warranting any special form of treatment such as in the form of an invocation of the political questions doctrine. As Harlan Grant Cohen has observed, in this case Chief Justice Roberts 'announced the return of the courts to foreign affairs'.[66] A broader reading of these cases might even consist in pointing to a generally diminishing possibility to clearly distinguish between purely internal and external situations, a move arguably triggered by both the rising concerns about individual rights and domestic democracy playing out.

B *From Friendliness to Guarded Scepticism? German Foreign Relations Law under the Basic Law*

The development of foreign relations law as a field in Germany has followed a somewhat different trajectory. First, we need to clarify the starting point of this development. In light of the various systemic changes in German politics and constitutional orientation, it is a natural inclination to focus only on the developments which have taken place since the end of the Second World War and hence since the Basic Law took effect in 1949. While this will also be the general thrust of this contribution it is nonetheless apt to briefly remark that different stories of German foreign relations law could also be told, tapping into previous historical layers. Jochen von Bernstorff has recently analysed how German constitutional law doctrine dealt with the imperial ambitions of the German Reich in the period between 1871 and 1918, for instance.[67] In this regard, it is intriguing how the conceptualisation of the relationship between the international and domestic in the form of dualism as developed by Heinrich Triepel[68] might have been shaped by the imperial ambitions of a nation state that was in many ways a latecomer to the imperial games already undertaken by the other European powers.[69] Yet again a different story might be told for the

66 Cohen, 'Formalism and Distrust', 433.

67 Jochen von Bernstorff, 'Innen und Außen in der Staats- und Völkerrechtswissenschaft des deutschen Kaiserreichs' (2015) 23 *Der Staat (Beiheft)* 137.

68 Heinrich Triepel, *Völkerrecht und Landesrecht* (Leipzig: Hirschfeld, 1899), 111.

69 This relates to Triepel's emphasis on dualism. A strict divide between international law and domestic law arguably gave the political branches more leeway for both external

Weimar Republic, where much German international and public law scholarship was united in the fight against the Versailles peace treaty which was viewed as an unjust and oppressive regime imposed on Germany by the victorious powers in the First World War.[70] And, of course, National Socialist Germany brought about its own form of constitutional law scholarship which emphasised the superiority of the Aryan race and delivered arguments for the realisation of *Lebensraum* and the implementation of the Holocaust, although both endeavours were not mainly driven by legal arguments but rather coyly accompanied by willing opportunists and zealous anti-Semites alike.[71] And even if we only focus on the post–World War II order, it is readily apparent that concentrating on the Basic Law means overlooking the Eastern part of Germany for a period of more than 40 years. The German Democratic Republic was part of the Eastern bloc and accordingly scholarship on 'peaceful co-existence' on the international law level was produced, which translated into constitutional law writings emphasising the ideological leadership of the Soviet Union, mediated through the Communist Party and its East German incarnation.[72] This brief glance at different historical conjectures helps us to see that there is one significant difference between the US and German stories of foreign relations law: on the

expansion and internal consolidation of the Reich. On the current significance of this legacy see also Bardo Fassbender, 'Triepel in Luxemburg. Die dualistische Sicht des Verhältnisses von Europa- und Völkerrecht in der "Kadi-Rechtsprechung" des EuGH als Problem des Selbstverständnisses der Europäischen Union' (2010) 63 *Die Öffentliche Verwaltung* 333, 338.

[70] Michael Stolleis, *Geschichte des öffentlichen Rechts in Deutschland. Dritter Band 1914–1945* (Munich: C. H. Beck, 1999) 86–89. Opposition to the Versailles treaty was common among the entire political spectrum in Weimar Germany, especially with respect to the war guilt clause of Art. 231 and the reparations regime. Also 'progressive' international lawyers generally supportive of the League of Nations joined in the critique, see further Helmut Philipp Aust, 'Zwischen Freirecht und Völkerpsychologie: Hermann Kantorowicz und die völkerrechtliche Kriegsschuldfrage', in Ino Augsberg et al. (eds.), *Hermann Kantorowicz' Begriff des Rechts und der Rechtswissenschaft* (Tübingen: Mohr Siebeck, 2019, in press), available at https://papers.ssrn.com/sol3/papers.cfm?abstract_id=3170835, accessed 2 October 2018; Felix Lange, 'The dream of a *völkisch* colonial empire: international law and colonial law during the National Socialist era' (2017) 5 *London Review of International Law* 343, 348–350.

[71] Detlef Vagts, 'International Law in the Third Reich' (1990) 84 *American Journal of International Law* 661.

[72] See Maria Bauer et al. ('Autorenkollektiv'), *Völkerrecht Teil 1* (Berlin: Staatsverlag der Deutschen Demokratischen Republik, 1973) 21 (with a very prominent affirmation that compliance with, respect and enforcement of international law would be a constitutional principle and objective of the German Democratic Republic, followed by remarks on class structures of the international system, Ibid., 37–45).

United States side, there is much more continuity with respect to the development of the constitutional regime than was the case in Germany, debates in the USA about various constitutional transformations notwithstanding.[73] Comparing the development of foreign relations law under the Basic Law with the development on the other side of the Atlantic is thus a somewhat imbalanced exercise insofar as the American constitutional discourse rests on a longer tradition that has not been interrupted by major systemic changes to the same extent that has been the case in Germany.

Moreover, if we focus on the development of German foreign relations law under the Basic Law, it is apparent that this development was highly contingent on a number of historical conditions. In this regard, the hallmark of German constitutionalism has been its openness for international cooperation and European integration. A whole subfield of constitutional doctrine has developed which is concerned with the possibility of transferring sovereign rights to international organisations and the 'friendliness' of the German constitutional order towards international and EU law, typically labelled *Staatsrecht III* in the curriculum of law schools.[74] The construction of this field was arguably influenced to a large degree by the wish to reintegrate Germany into the community of civilised nations after the Holocaust and World War II. To a large extent, the German international law community devoted its work to this cause and turned away from the theoretical conundrums with which it was occupied in the interwar phase.[75] A pragmatic orientation towards re-establishing Germany as a European nation state, embedded in the ambitious project of European integration, was the order of the day.[76]

[73] See only Bruce Ackerman, 'The Holmes Lectures: The Living Constitution' (2007) 120 *Harvard Law Review* 1737.

[74] Indicating that this subject is usually taught in the third term, following *Staatsrecht I* (general constitutional law, first term) and *Staatsrecht II* (fundamental rights, second term): Christian Calliess, *Staatsrecht III – Bezüge zum Völker- und Europarecht*, 2nd ed. (Munich: C. H. Beck, 2018); for the most recent comprehensive treatment see Schorkopf, *Staatsrecht*.

[75] For a somewhat different view on this focus of the interwar era see Daniel-Erasmus Khan, 'Die Deutsche Gesellschaft für Völkerrecht 1917–1933', in Nina Dethloff, Georg Nolte and August Reinisch (eds.), *Rückblick nach 100 Jahren und Ausblick – Migrationsbewegungen. Berichte der Deutschen Gesellschaft für Internationales Recht* (Heidelberg, C. F. Müller: 2018, 11.

[76] Georg Nolte, 'Zur Zukunft der Völkerrechtswissenschaft in Deutschland' (2007) 67 *Zeitschrift für ausländisches öffentliches Recht und Völkerrecht* 657, 658–59; Felix Lange, *Praxisorientierung und Gemeinschaftskonzeption. Hermann Mosler als Wegbereiter der westdeutschen Völkerrechtslehre nach 1945* (Berlin: Springer, 2017), 167–203.

For the development of foreign relations law, this had a special resonance due to the traditional combination of public law and international law in most law faculties in Germany.[77]

A key text for this development was Klaus Vogel's short 1964 monograph on the openness of the German Basic Law to international cooperation.[78] This text provided the basis for the subsequent canonisation of this principle of openness in the literature. Vogel's contribution consisted in a combined reading of different constitutional provisions which dealt with international cooperation and European integration. Through this reading, he was able to identify a whole that was greater than its parts.[79] This construction made its way into the case law of the German Federal Constitutional Court (FCC) which deduced various consequences from the assemblage of constitutional norms, ranging from the affirmation of a general (if qualified) acceptance of the primacy of EU law over German constitutional law to the influence of the European Convention on Human Rights on the interpretation of the fundamental rights of the Basic Law.[80] Already here it can be noted that the subsequent framing of the discourse about foreign relations law has been driven to a much greater extent by the FCC than by the academic literature, at least in comparison to the respective roles in the US context.

'Open statehood' (*offene Staatlichkeit*) and 'friendliness towards international law' (*Völkerrechtsfreundlichkeit*) have in any case become staples in the business of attempting to transplant parts of German constitutional law along with its open posture towards international cooperation into the global constitutionalist discourse.[81] In more recent years, however, this state of affairs is increasingly contested, not least from the FCC

[77] On this tradition see Eyal Benvenisti, 'The Conception of International Law as a Legal System' (2007) 50 *German Yearbook of International Law* 393, at 394.

[78] Klaus Vogel, *Die Verfassungsentscheidung des Grundgesetzes für die internationale Zusammenarbeit* (Tübingen: Mohr Siebeck, 1964).

[79] Still debated today; see for a critical view Matthias Jestaedt, 'Selbstand und Offenheit der Verfassung', in Josef Isensee and Paul Kirchhof (eds.), *Handbuch des Staatsrechts, Band XII*, 3rd ed. (Heidelberg: C. F. Müller, 2014), § 264, para. 83; contra: Mehrdad Payandeh, 'Völkerrechtsfreundlichkeit als Verfassungsprinzip' (2009) 57 *Jahrbuch des Öffentlichen Rechts, Neue Folge*, 465, 482–83.

[80] See *BVerfGE* 123, 267 – *Lisbon Treaty Case* and *BVerfGE* 111, 307 – Görgülü; 128, 326 – *Security Detention II* respectively.

[81] One notable expression of this tendency are works of German international law scholars who analyse international law from a constitutionalist perspective, see for instance Christian Tomuschat, 'International Law: Ensuring the Survival of Mankind on the Eve of a New Century' (1999) 281 *Recueil des cours* 10; for a thorough analysis of this

itself. Arguably, this is a parallel movement to the realisation that international law can 'hit home' and that therefore a constitutional court should reflect more seriously on the limits of international cooperation.[82]

In the German context, a new line of jurisprudence has materialised in the last ten to fifteen years. These cases have started to incrementally change the traditional openness and friendliness towards international and EU law. They have also sought to at least partly minimise the leeway that the executive used to enjoy in these fields. This came about due to a replication of the Court's previous case law on the limits of European integration for the broader field of foreign relations and international law.[83] With respect to Germany's participation in the European Union, the Court has for quite some time already struck a delicate balance between the affirmation that EU integration is a central goal of the constitutional order and the requirement that it should comply with the fundamental principles of the Basic Law.[84] The development of this jurisprudence has taken place against the background of a 'legal dialogue' with the Court of Justice of the European Union, which has shifted back and forth between offers of cooperation and threats of conflict.[85]

contribution see Armin von Bogdandy, 'Constitutionalism in International Law: Comment on a Proposal from Germany' (2006) 47 *Harvard International Law Journal* 223; see further on constitutionalist discourses in international law, Bardo Fassbender, 'Grund und Grenzen der konstitutionellen Idee im Völkerrecht', in Otto Depenheuer et al. (eds.), *Staat im Wort – Festschrift für Josef Isensee* (Heidelberg: C. F. Müller, 2007), 73; Thomas Kleinlein, 'Between Myths and Norms: Constructivist Constitutionalism and the Potential of Constitutional Principles in International Law' (2012) 81 *Nordic Journal of International Law* 79.

82 See also Frank Schorkopf, 'Von Bonn über Berlin nach Brüssel und Den Haag. Europa- und Völkerrechtswissenschaft in der Berliner Republik', in Thomas Duve and Stefan Ruppert (eds.), *Rechtswissenschaft in der Berliner Republik* (Suhrkamp, 2018), 327, 348 (suggesting more serious reflection on the limits for democratic decision-making resulting from EU and international law).

83 This trajectory becomes quite evident in a recent decision on the fundamental rights limitations for transferring sovereign powers to international organisations under Art. 24, para. 1 of the Basic Law. In a case concerning the so-called 'European schools' (an international organisation in its own right and independent from the EU) and challenges to school fees brought by parents, the Federal Constitutional Court developed the constitutional limitations in this context with an express reference to its earlier case law on fundamental rights protection against the EU, see *BVerfG*, 2 *BvR* 1961/09, decision of 24 July 2018, para. 30 (not yet reported). The case was dismissed for a lack of substantiation by the applicants.

84 See further on this Mattias Wendel, *Permeabilität im Europäischen Verfassungsverbund: Verfassungsrechtliche Integrationsnormen auf Staats- und Unionsebene im Vergleich* (Tübingen: Mohr Siebeck, 2011), at 434–523.

85 Andreas Voßkuhle, 'Multilevel Cooperation of the European Constitutional Courts – *Der Europäische Verfassungsgerichtsverbund*' (2010) 6 *European Constitutional Law Review*

For the longest time, this line of case law did not have repercussions for the general field of foreign relations law, in particular not for cases which concerned Germany's participation in 'ordinary' international treaty regimes. Here, the general discourse of openness and friendliness prevailed, coupled with an affirmation of the broader leeway that the executive would enjoy in these fields.[86] An important exception has developed with respect to the use of the German armed forces abroad where the Court insisted since the early 1990s that their use in situations of armed conflict required an authorisation by the *Bundestag*.[87] The most important distinction between the case law on European integration and the decisions on 'ordinary' international law might be explained by the perceived 'lack of bite' of the latter.[88] International law was not seen as intruding so deeply into the domestic legal order. Accordingly, it was less risky to emphasise the friendliness and openness of the German legal order for this body of law and to accompany that rhetorical move with corresponding interpretations of the provisions of foreign relations law.

This has changed in recent years. Three developments are particularly important in this regard. First, the FCC felt the need to emphasise the limits of openness also with respect to decisions of the European Court of Human Rights (ECtHR).[89] Whereas the general line of openness and friendliness was continued, a 2004 decision on the implementation of

175; see also, especially in historical perspective, Jo Murkens, *From Empire to Union – Conceptions of German Constitutional Law since 1871* (Oxford: Oxford University Press, 2013); for a critical exploration of the case law of the FCC see Sven Simon, *Grenzen des Bundesverfassungsgerichts im europäischen Integrationsprozess* (Tübingen: Mohr Siebeck, 2016).

[86] Heike Krieger, 'Die Herrschaft der Fremden – Zur demokratietheoretischen Kritik des Völkerrechts' (2008) 133 *Archiv des öffentlichen Rechts* 315, 325.

[87] Starting with *BVerfGE* 90, 286 – *AWACS I*, most recently *BVerfGE* 140, 160 – *Pegasus*; on the development of the case law see Georg Nolte 'Germany: Ensuring Political Legitimacy for the Use of Military Forces by Requiring Constitutional Accountability', in Charlotte Ku and Harold Jacobson (eds.), *Democratic Accountability and the Use of Force in International Law* (Cambridge: Cambridge University Press, 2003), 231; Thomas Kleinlein, 'Kontinuität und Wandel in Grundlegung und Dogmatik des wehrverfassungsrechtlichen Parlamentsvorbehalts' (2017) 142 *Archiv des öffentlichen Rechts* 43; Anne Peters 'Between Military Deployment and Democracy: Use of Force under the German Constitution', in Curtis Bradley (ed.), *Oxford Handbook of Comparative Foreign Relations Law* (Oxford: Oxford University Press, 2019), 791.

[88] As opposed to the 'direct effect' of EU law in domestic legal orders, see on this doctrine Bruno de Witte, 'The Continuous Significance of *Van Gend en Loos*', in Miguel Poiares Maduro and Loïc Azoulai (eds.), *The Past and the Future of EU Law* (Oxford: Hart, 2010), 9.

[89] *BVerfGE* 111, 307 – *Görgülü*; 128, 326 – Security Detention II.

a Strasbourg decision concerning parental rights provided the unlikely occasion to restate that the openness of the German Constitution to international law in general and the decisions of the European Court of Human Rights in particular was not limitless, but rather contingent upon respect for the most important principles of the Basic Law. The Constitution would not have reneged on the 'final world' of sovereignty.[90] Arguably, it would not have been necessary to include these remarks in the decision. This message has been received in other member states of the Council of Europe, for instance in Russia, where it played an important role in justifying the introduction of a mechanism by which decisions of the European Court of Human Rights can now be controlled with respect to their compliance with the Russian Constitution.[91] Most recently, the FCC has further developed its theory on the impact of Strasbourg decisions on German law by emphasising the need to contextualise decisions of the ECtHR against other Council of Europe member states when considering their impact for the interpretation of the German Basic Law. Accordingly, it did not incorporate findings the ECtHR made against other states into the German context without reflecting on the applicable differences. Findings of the Strasbourg court would need to be attuned to the peculiarities of the German legal system.[92]

Second, in a case on an arcane matter of tax law, the Court ruled that there was no constitutional barrier to so-called 'treaty overrides'.[93] This term refers to a widely used practice in the field of tax law where the federal legislature enacts changes to the federal income tax code which derogate partially from double taxation agreements binding on the Federal Republic. The outcome of the case was not controversial as such.[94] Treaties and ordinary legislation enjoy the same rank in the

[90] *BVerfGE* 111, 307, 319 – *Görgülü*.

[91] Matthias Hartwig, 'Vom Dialog zum Disput? Verfassungsrecht vs Europäische Menschenrechtskonvention – Der Fall der Russländischen Föderation' (2017) *Europäische Grundrechte-Zeitschrift* 1.

[92] *BVerfG*, Case 2 *BvR* 1738/12, Judgment of 12 June 2018 (not yet in official collection), para. 132 – *Beamtenstreik*. It should be added that this approach will in many cases be in conformity with the European Convention on Human Rights which stipulates that decisions are binding on the state against which a complaint was raised, see Art. 46 of the Convention. That said, an interpretation by the Strasbourg Court could very well be understood to be a particularly authoritative interpretation of the Convention, requiring also other state parties to take it into account (which the FCC did in its above-cited case).

[93] *BVerfGE* 141, 1 – Treaty Override.

[94] For criticism of the decision, see Mehrdad Payandeh, Grenzen der 'Völkerrechtsfreundlichkeit– Der Treaty Override Beschluss des BVerfG' (2016) *Neue Juristische Wochenschrift* 1279.

German legal system.[95] Accordingly, the *lex posterior* rule allows for such a derogation.[96] More noticeable, however, was language in the decision which made rather sweeping statements on the need to allow for such room for manoeuvre in order to protect the freedom of future democratic legislatures.[97] Here again, the Court felt the need to emphasise the remaining policy space of the German political branches, although the case under review did not really call for such general remarks.

Third, the latest battlefield for the limits of foreign relations law now concerns the ongoing constitutional litigation about the CETA agreement. The Court has already passed down two decisions which were concerned with measures of interim protection. In these decisions, there are hints that the Court is of the opinion that the CETA agreement indeed raises fundamental issues for the German constitutional legal order. This contribution is not the right place to enter into a discussion of the highly intricate and technical questions surrounding this agreement which – once it enters into force – will be a so-called mixed agreement, concluded on the one side by Canada and on the other side by the European Union and its Member States jointly.[98] This state of affairs follows from the division of competences between the EU and its Member States and is a common feature of EU treaty practice.[99] In the

[95] See Ferdinand Wollenschläger, 'Art. 25', in Horst Dreier (ed.), *Grundgesetz Kommentar. Band II Artikel 20–82* 3rd ed. (Tübingen: Mohr Siebeck, 2015), para. 52.

[96] On a comparative note it can be observed that similar debates have been held in US constitutional law, see Jackson, 'The U.S. Constitution', 939 with a reference to *Breard* v. *Greene*, 523 US 371, 376 (1998).

[97] *BVerfGE* 141, 1, para. 53. In the decision, the Court emphasised that the principle of democracy implies that future legislations are in a position to revisit previous legislative decisions. This would also apply with respect to the consenting act of the German *Bundestag*.

[98] The CETA and TTIP processes have given rise to a whole flurry of publications on the constitutional implications of these agreements, see only Stoll, Holterhus and Gött, *Investitionsschutz*; Markus Krajewski, 'Umweltschutz und internationales Investitionsschutzrecht am Beispiel der Vattenfall-Klagen und des geplanten Transatlantischen Handels- und Investitionsschutzabkommens' (2014) *Zeitschrift für Umweltrecht* 396; Bernd Greszick, 'Völkervertragsrecht in der parlamentarischen Demokratie – CETA als Präzedenzfall für die demokratischen Anforderungen an völkerrechtliche Verträge' (2016) *Neue Zeitschrift für Verwaltungsrecht* 1753; Björn Schiffbauer, 'Investitionsschutz und Grundgesetz – Bilaterale Investitionsschutzabkommen (BITs) aus verfassungsrechtlicher Perspektive' (2016) *Kölner Zeitschrift für Wirtschaftsrecht* 145; Gertrude Lübbe-Wolff, 'Democracy, Separation of Powers, and International Treaty-Making – The Example of TTIP' (2016) 69 *Current Legal Problems* 175.

[99] For an overview of the legal issues see Piet Eeckhout, *EU External Relations Law*, 2nd ed. (Oxford: Oxford University Press, 2011), 213–22.

CETA case, this adds another layer of complexity and probably also contributes to the impression that the conclusion of this agreement would have particularly severe consequences for domestic democracy as well as the sovereignty of the German Federal Republic. Seen from this perspective, it is not merely an international agreement which sets forth a mechanism of ISDS and creates treaty bodies which can to some extent further develop the economic integration between Canada and the EU. What is more, these features are equipped with the additional bite of supranational EU law, thereby potentially aggravating the consequences that this agreement might have for the domestic legal order.

What, then, are the main arguments of the sceptics against this agreement? Their reasoning is based largely on a transposition of the arguments and categories which are familiar from the context of the German debates on constitutional limits to European integration. In this context, the Federal Constitutional Court has developed over the course of the years a so-called 'right to democracy' which is derived from Article 38, paragraph 1 of the Basic Law.[100] This provision, which concerns the election and status of members of the *Bundestag* (the Federal Parliament) has been interpreted to guarantee as well that Parliament still enjoys a sufficiently wide range of competences so as to make elections to the *Bundestag* meaningful. Article 38, paragraph 1 of the Basic Law can be invoked as a so-called *grundrechtsgleiches Recht* (quasi-fundamental right) in constitutional complaint procedures before the FCC. What is more, its substance was coupled by the Court in a bold argumentative move with the fundamental principle of democracy as set forth by Article 20 of the Basic Law and protected through the so-called 'eternity clause' of Article 79, paragraph 3 of the Basic Law – thus preventing any constitutional amendment as long as the Basic Law is not replaced with a new Constitution under the provision of Article 146.[101]

This set of arguments is then deployed in the CETA context to underline that the agreement would potentially be in breach of this constitutional framework. In particular, decisions reached by the joint committee of CETA would not meet the required standards of democratic

[100] *BVerfGE* 89, 155, 172 – Maastricht; 123, 267, 330 – Lisbon; 134, 366, 391 – OMT I; 142, 123, para. 147 – OMT II.

[101] For a critical analysis of this move see Martin Nettesheim, 'Ein Individualrecht auf Staatlichkeit? Die Lissabon-Entscheidung des BVerfG' (2009) *Neue Juristische Wochenschrift* 2867, 2869; see also Martin Nettesheim, 'Wo endet das Grundgesetz? Verfassungsgebung als grenzüberschreitender Prozess' (2012) 51 *Der Staat* 313.

legitimacy.[102] With respect to decisions reached under the ISDS mechanism, similar concerns are voiced, coupled also with criticism about the conformity of this mechanism with the ideal of the rule of law (*Rechtsstaatsprinzip*) as guaranteed by Article 20 of the Basic Law.[103]

The aims of this critique are at times hard to identify. Whereas some authors seem to be driven by a general scepticism towards free trade as a political and economic idea, in other cases there seems to be a more fundamental form of resistance against potentially harmful impacts of treaty-making processes on domestic democracy. Yet, it can be wondered whether in some instances this new form of opposition against international cooperation does not give rise to a form of democratic fundamentalism which, if decoupled from the CETA context, would in effect speak against many of the already existing treaty obligations of the Federal Republic. For example, many of the arguments deployed against the ISDS mechanism of CETA could also be used to criticise the judges of the European Court of Human Rights as unelected and based on a weak form of democratic legitimacy.

Before moving on to a comparative assessment of the two jurisdictions two brief disclaimers should be added to the above discussion. First, we still need to see what the FCC will eventually decide with respect to the CETA cases. Not too much should be read into early pronouncements at the interim protection state of the proceedings, although the weight of these pronouncements is not formally lower than the one of decisions on the merits. Second, it can be observed that the more sceptical positions in the case law of the FCC towards international cooperation all stem from decisions of the Second Senate. According to the general distribution of business between the two senates of the Court, it is the Second Senate that is tasked with deciding the cases in which fundamental issues of the relationship between German (constitutional) law and EU as well as international law arise.[104] On the other hand, related issues regularly have a role to play as well in the case law of the First Senate. Originally the Senate in place for fundamental rights protection (a division long given up due to the high number of individual constitutional complaint

[102] See the brief for the constitutional complaint raised by Bernhard Kempen on behalf of Roman Huber et al., 106 et seq., available at www.ceta-verfassungsbeschwerde.de/, accessed 8 July 2018.

[103] Ibid., 89 et seq.

[104] On the general allocation of jurisdiction between the two senates see www.bundesverfassungsgericht.de/EN/Verfahren/Geschaeftsverteilung/geschaeftsverteilung_node.html, accessed 28 August 2018.

procedures which necessitate an involvement of both senates), it is apparently the case that the First Senate continues to embrace a more open position towards both EU law and international law. This has been noticeable in recent years with decisions, for instance, involving the standing of legal persons from EU member states to avail themselves of fundamental rights protection in Germany[105] as well as in a decision turning on the importance of decisions of UN human rights treaty bodies for the interpretation of the German Basic Law.[106] This difference in approach and outlook to 'the international' would merit a more in-depth study on the different sociological dynamics in the two senates of the FCC.[107]

III Structural Differences and the Usefulness of Comparisons

What is the significance of these respective developments? And can the comparison between the United States and Germany tell us something relevant for debates about foreign relations law? It is clear that there are obvious limits to comparative exercises of this kind, especially if undertaken on some level of generality. One observation is that the respective case laws of the US Supreme Court and the German Federal Constitutional Court fulfil different functions. A more coherent and case-law oriented picture emerges from the evolution in Germany even though there is no doctrine of *stare decisis* as such.[108] Yet, the style of

[105] *BVerfGE* 129, 78, 96 – *Cassina*; *BVerfGE* 143, 246, paras. 195 et seq. – *Vattenfall*; for academic criticism of these decisions from a Judge of the Second Senate see Peter M. Huber, 'Artikel 19 Abs. 3', in Peter Huber and Andreas Vosskuhle (eds.), *von Mangoldt/Klein/Starck – Grundgesetz-Kommentar, Band 1* 7th ed. (Munich: C. H. Beck, 2018), paras. 307, at 311.

[106] *BVerfGE* 142, at 313, para. 90 – *Forced Medical Treatment* (for a measured discussion about the effects of decisions of UN treaty bodies which identifies limits in this regard without engaging in unnecessary deliberations about fundamentals of German constitutional law).

[107] Some relevant aspects for such a study shine through the magisterial work on the decision-making process of the Court by Uwe Kranenpohl, *Hinter dem Schleier des Beratungsgeheimnisses – Der Willensbildungs- und Entscheidungsprozess des Bundesverfassungsgerichts* (VS Verlag für Sozialwissenschaften: Wiesbaden, 2010). In the early years of the Court's existence, there was widespread discussion about one 'red' and one 'black' senate of the Court, referring to different predominant political attitudes among the judges. This clear-cut division along party-political lines is a thing of the past, see Christoph Schönberger, 'Anmerkungen zu Karlsruhe', in Matthias Jestaedt et al. (eds.), *Das entgrenzte Gericht – Eine kritische Bilanz nach sechzig Jahren Bundesverfassungsgericht* (Berlin: Suhrkamp, 2011), 9, 21–22.

[108] See Antje von Ungern-Sternberg, 'Normative Wirkungen von Präjudizien nach der Rechtsprechung des Bundesverfassungsgerichts' (2013) 138 *Archiv des öffentlichen Rechts* 1.

reasoning of the Court and the centrality it occupies in the German academic discourse has contributed to the effect that much of the academic discourse follows the parameters of the case law of the Court.[109] In addition, the general inclination of the Karlsruhe judges is to set out in a systematic manner the general rationale behind a case before turning to the concrete facts. This is called the '*Maßstäbeteil*' in the literature.[110] It is hence possible to tell the story of the evolution of German foreign relations law largely through the lens of the development of the case law of the Court.

In this regard, a particularity of the German debate is that it can rely on the constitutionally protected principle of democracy. This distinguishes the German context from the situation in the United States.[111] The US Constitution is obviously based on the idea of democracy. However, democracy is not set forth as a constitutional rule or principle as it is the case in Germany. Instead, questions of democracy are operationalised through the system of checks and balances that the US Constitution enshrines.[112] The German Basic Law knows of course its own principle of the separation of powers and sets forth rules which provide for the concrete allocation of competences to flesh this out.[113] Yet, it also adds the principle of democracy as a kind of superstructure which can then be used in constitutional litigation. This provides the Constitutional Court with a (partly self-constructed) reservoir from which to draw general insights into the optimal allocation of powers in the German constitutional system.

[109] For a critical view on this so-called '*Bundesverfassungsgerichtspositivismus*' see Bernhard Schlink, 'Die Entthronung der Staatsrechtswissenschaft durch die Verfassungsgerichtsbarkeit' (1989) 28 *Der Staat* 161, 163; with respect to the case law on EU and international law also (in a positive sense) Schorkopf, 'Von Bonn über Berlin nach Brüssel und Den Haag', 345.

[110] Oliver Lepsius, 'Die maßstabsetzende Gewalt', in Jestaedt et al. (eds.), *Das entgrenzte Gericht*, 159, 168–170; generally this style of reasoning is limited to case law on fundamental rights and is less prevalent in decisions which pertain to other constitutional issues such as competences and federalism issues, see further Helmut Philipp Aust, 'Grundrechtsdogmatik im Staatsorganisationsrecht?' (2016) 141 *Archiv des öffentlichen Rechts* 415.

[111] See, for a similar remark with respect to a comparison between Germany and the United Kingdom, Lübbe-Wolff, 'Democracy', 191.

[112] See Henkin, *Constitutionalism*, 14 (noting that redistributions in the political branches of the United States in the field of foreign relations law did not take place 'according to some theory of democracy').

[113] See, for a comparison between Germany, the United States and the EU, Christoph Möllers, *The Three Branches – A Comparative Model of Separation of Powers* (Oxford: Oxford University Press, 2013).

In comparison, the US Supreme Court has rarely set out a general vision of how foreign relations law would operate. It has also, according to one commentator, so far managed to avoid going into the 'structural constitutional limitations' of the US Constitution for US engagement with international law but has decided cases on narrower grounds.[114] Its case law is much more anecdotal and characterised by the fact that the Court can decide cases not just on the level of constitutional law, but also on the statutory level. This might help explain why the general construction of foreign relations law is a topic of a greater scholarly discourse in the United States as compared to Germany where there is less of a marked dissent against the case law of the FCC.

These structural differences between the debates in the two jurisdictions are not just of academic concern. They have broader political implications. They also point to the limited space for a significant political debate among the issues of foreign relations law in the German context. Or, to be more precise, the limited space for a political debate which is not immediately caught up in the language of constitutional law and the existing 'precedents' of the FCC case law. These occupy such a powerful role in the debate precisely because of the borrowing of language from the case law about the limits of European integration. Here, much of the case law of the Court has been charged with the absolutist language of Articles 20 and 79, paragraph 3 of the Basic Law. These decisions convey the sense that it cannot be any other way. What should be an open and pluralistic debate about the contours of foreign relations law thus turns into a legalistic debate about the leeway under the Karlsruhe case law. What is problematic about the evolution of the jurisprudence of the FCC is that it conveys the sense that European integration and international cooperation can be easily guarded by domestic constitutional courts applying their domestic constitutional frameworks in a responsible manner, allegedly also taking into account the interests of the greater whole. Now the FCC might be in a position to do just that. But a serious problem is that it overlooks the spill-over effects in other European jurisdictions where its case law helps bolster the position that it is legitimate to question the uniformity and primacy of European law as well as international law in the name of domestic democracy.

[114] Curtis A. Bradley, 'The Supreme Court as a Filter Between International Law and American Constitutionalism' (2016) 104 *California Law Review* 1567, at 1578.

IV Conclusion and Outlook

This contribution has argued that gradually the Court-driven discourse in the German context is following the more 'closed' model of foreign relations law which has become prevalent in the US context. It thereby also follows a broader political trend which questions the special character of foreign relations in the name of democracy. The problem with this development is that it is arguably more difficult in the German system to undo previous decisions of the Court due to their linkage with key constitutional principles.

For both jurisdictions, the trend towards a 'closed' conception of foreign relations law risks aggravating a loss of confidence in democratic decision-making processes as well as in the conduct of international relations. At first sight, this is not obvious.[115] The challenge to foreign relations law is undertaken in the name of democracy, with a view to safeguarding domestic democratic procedures. Yet, by making international cooperation more difficult as far as the traditional forms of international law are concerned, the case law of both courts and the accompanying academic discourse might drive executives further towards an embrace of more informal instruments.[116] For too many issues, there is a pressing need for some form of international cooperation. If it becomes ever more difficult, for instance, to enter into a legally binding international agreement, governments may further intensify the turn towards the kind of agreements they can enter into without any form of democratic oversight and participation. This risks strengthening the general distrust in elites and technocratic forms of governance. Seen from this perspective, a little more flexibility with respect to the conduct of foreign relations might be in the longer-term interest of democratic societies, as it allows governments to cooperate in forms of international law which allow for some form of democratic participation.

At the time of writing, there is ample evidence of the drawbacks of the turn to informal mechanisms which we have already been witnessing.[117] In

[115] For a different diagnosis Schorkopf, 'Von Bonn über Berlin nach Brüssel und Den Haag', 347 who emphasises the positive virtues of 'taking back control'.

[116] On the general trend of deformalisation of international cooperation and global governance see Eyal Benvenisti, *The Law of Global Governance* (Leiden: Brill, 2014), 25; Alejandro Rodiles, *Coalitions of the Willing and International Law: The Interplay between Formality and Informality* (Cambridge: Cambridge University Press, 2018).

[117] From the perspective of US constitutional law see Jean Galbraith, 'From Treaties to International Commitments: The Changing Landscape of Foreign Relations Law' (2017) 84 *The University of Chicago Law Review* 1675.

the current political situation in the United States, it has arguably been made easier for President Trump to withdraw (or announce intended withdrawals) from important international agreements like the Paris Agreement on Climate Change[118] and the Joint Plan for Comprehensive Action[119] on the nuclear program of Iran for the precise reason that these two agreements – very different in kind, as they are – did not go through the advice and consent procedure established under the US Constitution for the ratification process of treaties.[120] That did happen for good reasons – as it would have been impossible for President Obama to obtain advice and consent for these agreements in the first place. The flexibility sought in the recourse to executive agreements (in the case of the Paris Agreement) and a mere political agreement (in the instance of the six powers agreement on Iran) then also paves the way for an easy way out of these agreements. If important agreements for the solution of genuine global problems fall victim to such haphazard forms of foreign policy on the go, we risk further undermining the trust and confidence of wider parts of the population in the capability of international law to deliver meaningful results through the established channels of international cooperation. It may not be in the interest of current executives in the United States and beyond to strengthen such beliefs. Yet, for the long-term stability of international relations, a more measured approach to foreign relations law which grants reasonably acting executives enough leeway to engage in the established forms of international law and diplomacy might not be the worst idea.

[118] Paris Agreement on Climate Change of 12 December 2015, entered into force on 4 November 2016, not yet in UNTS; for the statement of President Trump announcing the withdrawal of the United States of 1 June 2017 see www.whitehouse.gov/briefings-statements/statement-president-trump-paris-climate-accord/, accessed 28 August 2018.

[119] For the text of the JCPOA see UN Doc. S/RES/2231 (2015), Annex A; for a transcript of the remarks by President Trump of 8 May 2018 see www.nytimes.com/2018/05/08/us/politics/trump-speech-iran-deal.html, accessed 28 August 2018.

[120] As a matter of law it is very disputed whether the termination of agreements which had undergone the advice and consent procedure require the participation of Congress, see further Jean Galbraith, 'The President's Power to Withdraw the United States from International Agreements at Present and in the Future' (2017) 111 *American Journal of International Law Unbound* 445.

13

The Double-Facing Foreign Relations Function of the Executive and Its Self-Enforcing Obligation to Comply with International Law

CAMPBELL MCLACHLAN*

Introduction

It has been conventional wisdom that the United Kingdom 'takes a fundamentally dualist view of international law. In other words, it sees domestic and international law as operating on different planes'.[1] Yet recent events have shone a searchlight onto a neglected question that is central to an understanding of the operation of the 'double-facing constitution' in a dualist state. The Constitution grants sovereign law-making power within the state to Parliament and at the same time allocates the conduct of foreign relations to the executive. In that context: to what extent and, if so why, is the executive bound to comply with international law obligations that it has contracted on behalf of the state, but which have not been directly incorporated into domestic law?

This question was exposed directly in the controversy sparked in 2015 by a revision to the Ministerial Code that omitted from its statement of ministers' duty to comply with the law the express reference that this includes 'international law and treaty obligations'. The amendment provoked public debate and litigation, eventually resulting in a decision of the Court of Appeal in 2018.[2] The impact of international law on the

* The author thanks Helmut Aust, Sir Franklin Berman QC, Eirik Bjorge, Julian Kulaga, Felix Lange, Rayner Thwaites and the editors of the volume for their invaluable comments on an earlier draft of this chapter and the Berlin-Potsdam research project KFG 'International Rule of Law: Rise or Decline?' for supporting the research for it.

[1] Lord Mance, 'International law in the UK Supreme Court' (King's College London, 13 February 2017) available at www.supremecourt.uk/docs/speech-170213.pdf, accessed 21 January 2019.

[2] *R (Gulf Centre for Human Rights)* v. *Prime Minister* [2018] EWCA Civ 1855.

deliberative process of government has also been exposed to view to an unprecedented extent in that long postmortem into the 2003 invasion of Iraq, the Chilcot Inquiry, which finally reported in 2016.[3] It continues to be controversial. In 2018, Parliament insisted that the Attorney General produce his full legal advice to ministers on the proposed arrangements regarding Northern Ireland in the draft Withdrawal Agreement for exiting the European Union. The advice was produced but only after Parliament had found ministers in contempt for their failure to do so.[4]

The central argument advanced here is simply this: the executive's prerogative power under the Constitution to conduct the foreign relations of the state carries with it an obligation to do so in conformity with the international law obligations of the state, whether or not such obligations are also directly incorporated into domestic law by statute. Such an obligation is a direct consequence of the application of the doctrine of the separation of powers to the foreign affairs power. It does not conflict with the sovereignty of Parliament to make law domestically.

Nor does it necessarily mean that executive decisions may be subjected to judicial scrutiny before domestic courts for their compliance with international law. Much of the scholarly and the public debate about unincorporated international law obligations has tended to conflate the nature of the duty with the extent to which it is justiciable. The latter question implicates a whole different set of considerations, precisely because it engages the role of the judiciary as a separate organ of government in the review of executive decision.

Rather, the distinctive point about the obligation upon the executive to comply with the international law obligations of the state is that it is, to a large degree, self-enforcing. This does not mean that it lacks substance or real legal force. On the contrary, as with many of the most fundamental aspects of a living constitution, it is the internal recognition of the duty by the constitutional actors that matters most. In a largely unwritten constitution, however, such compliance depends upon a continuity of shared understanding as to the operation of the system and the principles that underpin it.

The debate provoked by this amendment is important because it exposed some fundamental misunderstandings about the import of the obligation upon ministers to abide by international law and its

3 United Kingdom House of Commons 'Report of the Iraq Inquiry' (HC 264, 6 July 2016).

4 *Hansard*, HC, vol. 650, col. 728, 4 December 2018, div 273; Attorney General's letter dated 13 November 2018 available at www.assets.publishing.service.gov.uk, accessed 11 December 2018.

application in a dualist state. It is incorrect to state, as some have claimed, that 'Ministers have never been legally bound to obey unincorporated treaty obligations' or that 'if any such legal duty were to become part of our law it would have momentous constitutional consequences, undercutting the supremacy of Parliament over the executive and, contrary to the principle of the rule of law itself, confronting Ministers with inconsistent legal obligations'.[5]

These propositions are neither descriptively nor normatively correct. The duty on ministers to abide by international law is not a recent aberration in constitutional practice. In fact, as this chapter will seek to show, this is an obligation that, together with the concomitant duty of the law officers of the Crown to advise ministers on international law, has at least four centuries of state practice behind it. It is fully coherent with the allocation of functions within the constitution and with the primacy of parliamentary sovereignty, which the concept of dualism seeks to protect. Indeed the dualist approach is justifiable precisely because the executive's foreign affairs function within such a constitution carries with it the obligation to abide by the international law obligations that the executive contracts on behalf of the state.

In any event, by framing the issue as one concerning unincorporated treaty obligations, those that would seek to negate a ministerial obligation to comply with international law on grounds of dualism, omit to consider that in relation to customary international law, the United Kingdom is not, and never has been, a dualist state. On the contrary, the general law of nations is part of the law of England. This, too, is a necessary consequence of the separation of powers within the constitutional compact, and not in derogation from it. It carries real consequences for the conduct of the executive, particularly in those cases in which high foreign policy is engaged.

In order to make these points good it will be necessary to examine, as a matter of practice, the constitutional significance of the role of the legal advisers to the Crown when they advise ministers on international law (Section II). It will then be possible in Section III to evaluate, as a matter of principle, how this fits within a constitutional theory of the separation of powers and a dualist constitution. At the outset, however, Section

[5] Richard Ekins and Guglielmo Verdirame, 'The Ministerial Code and the Rule of Law' UK constitutional law blog (6 November 2015), available at: https://ukconstitutionallaw.org, accessed 11 December 2018.

I outlines the dispute over the amendment to the Ministerial Code in order to see what is at stake.

I International Law in the Ministerial Code

A *Development of the Code*

The Ministerial Code began its life as an informal and confidential document that was issued as guidance by the prime minister to Cabinet at the outset of each new government as *Questions of Procedure for Ministers.* While it was still possible for the Nolan Committee to describe the Code in 1995 as having 'no particular constitutional status',[6] the prominence accorded to the Code in both the Nolan and the Scott Inquiry[7] and its successive reissue has confirmed its status as 'the defining constitutional document on Prime Minister and Cabinet'.[8]

By the 1990s the Code had come to include a reference to ministers' obligation to comply with the law, including international law.[9] The Ministerial Code issued by Tony Blair in 1997 provided in the notes to paragraph 1 that:

> The notes should be read against the background of the duty of Ministers to comply with the law, *including international law and treaty obligations,* and to uphold the administration of justice . . .[10]

The now retitled Ministerial Code is also referred to in *The Cabinet Manual* (2011) as the principal source of 'the principles underpinning the standards of conduct expected of ministers'.[11]

The 2010 edition of the Code provided in paragraph 1.2:

> The Ministerial Code should be read alongside the Coalition Agreement and the background of the overarching duty on Ministers to comply with

6 Lord Nolan, 'Standards in public life: first report of the Committee on Standards in Public Life' Cm 2850 (May 1995), vol. 1, [9].

7 Richard Scott, 'Return to an address of the Honourable the House of Commons dated 15th February 1996 for the report of the inquiry into the export of defence equipment and dual-use goods to Iraq and related prosecutions' HC 115 (HMSO, 15 February 1996).

8 Peter Madgwick and Diana Woodhouse, *The Law and Politics of the Constitution* (Hertfordshire: Harvester Wheatsheaf, 1995).

9 United Kingdom, House of Commons Library 'Questions of Procedure for Ministers' (Research Paper 96/53, 19 April 1996), 8. See also Frank Berman, 'International law and the Ministerial Code' *The Guardian,* 25 October 2015.

10 A. Baker, *Prime Ministers and the Rule Book* (London: Politico's Publishing, 2000), 152.

11 United Kingdom, *The Cabinet Manual,* 1st ed. (Cabinet Office, 2011), [3.46].

> the law *including international law and treaty obligations* and to uphold the administration of justice and to protect the integrity of public life.[12]

The 2011 *Cabinet Manual* is to like effect.[13]

Lord Bingham, writing extra-judicially in his book *The Rule of Law*, described this overarching duty in the Ministerial Code as 'binding on British ministers'.[14]

B *The Amendment*

In 2015, the government amended this paragraph to omit the reference to international law. The revised text stated:

> The *Ministerial Code* should be read against the background of the overarching duty on Ministers to comply with the law and to protect the integrity of public life.[15]

When this amendment was published, it provoked a sharp response, including from former senior lawyers in the Civil Service. Sir Franklin Berman QC (Legal Adviser to the Foreign & Commonwealth Office 1991–99) wrote:[16]

> It is impossible not to feel a sense of disbelief at what must have been the deliberate suppression of the reference to the international law in the new version of the ministerial code. . . .
>
> I claim part of the credit for the previous formula, dating from my time as legal adviser to the Foreign and Commonwealth Office in the 1990s. The clear intention at the time was to avoid any reverse inferences from the earlier mention simply of 'the law of the land' and to ensure that the duty to obey the law was the same for civil servants and for ministers.

Sir Paul Jenkins (Treasury Solicitor and Head of the Government Legal Service 2006–14) added:[17]

> It is disingenuous of the Cabinet Office to dismiss the changes to the ministerial code as mere tidying up. As the government's most senior legal

[12] United Kingdom, *Ministerial Code: A Code of Ethics and Procedural Guidance for Ministers* (Cabinet Office, July 2010), [1.2], emphasis added.

[13] United Kingdom, *The Cabinet Manual*, [3.46].

[14] Tom Bingham, *The Rule of Law* (London: Penguin Press, 2011), ch. 10.

[15] United Kingdom, *Ministerial Code* (2010), [1.3]. This formulation is unchanged in the January 2018 edition.

[16] Frank Berman, 'International law and the ministerial code' *The Guardian*, 25 October 2015.

[17] Paul Jenkins, 'International law and the ministerial code' *The Guardian*, 25 October 2015.

> official I saw at close hand from 2010 onwards the intense irritation these words caused the PM as he sought to avoid complying with our international legal obligations, for example in relation to prisoner voting. Whether the new wording alters the legal obligations of ministers or not, there can be no doubt that they will regard the change as bolstering, in a most satisfying way, their contempt for the rule of international law.

Questions were asked in Parliament about the amendment. In the House of Lords, the responsible Minister, Lord Faulks, was asked whether he would give the House a categorical assurance 'that the amendment to the Ministerial Code will make absolutely no difference to Ministers' existing duty to comply with international law and treaty obligations'.[18] He said:

> My Lords, as the noble Lord will be aware, we have a dualist system rather than a monist system. Neither Parliament nor the courts are bound by international law, but a member of the Executive, including a Minister such as myself, is obliged to follow international law, whether it is reflected in the Ministerial Code or not. All Ministers will be aware of their obligations under the rule of law.

He added later that week:[19]

> Our position is that all Ministers are obliged to abide by the law, including, in so far as it is ascertainable, international law in this country.

Lord Brown of Eaton-under-Heywood asked:

> Am I right in supposing that this amendment is really a prelude to the introduction of a British Bill of Rights in place of the existing Human Rights Act, and is intended principally to clarify the fact that our own domestic primary legislation trumps unincorporated treaty law?

The Minister replied:

> The noble and learned Lord is quite right. He points to the difference between the dualist system, which we have, and the monist system whereby unless law is incorporated in an Act of Parliament, it does not become automatically a part of the law. The question of the amendments to the Bill of Rights, when or if it comes before Parliament, is somewhat separate but he accurately states the necessary constitutional principles.

On being pressed to answer why exactly the government did change the wording, the Minister said:

> I fear that I will be repeating myself but they have changed the wording because it is a simple summary of what is plainly the position, which is

[18] *Hansard*, HL vol. 765 cols. 1170–1, 28 October 2015.
[19] *Hansard*, HL vol. 765 cols. 1523–4, 3 November 2015.

> that Ministers have an obligation to obey the law. The code does not change the obligation that comes from the law; it is simply a summary for Ministers.

The Cabinet Office also confirmed: '"Comply with the law" includes international law.'[20]

Yet the proposition that a change was intended was not without foundation. An important element in the Conservative Party manifesto in 2014 had been to reassert the primacy of the UK Supreme Court and Parliament by introducing a new British Bill of Rights and at the same time to curb what was seen as the excessive role of the European Court of Human Rights.[21] The manifesto added, for good measure:[22]

> We will amend the Ministerial Code to remove any ambiguity in the current rules about the duty of Ministers to follow the will of Parliament in the UK.

C *The Judicial Review Proceedings*

In a bid to clarify whether the government did indeed intend a change in the legal position, the Gulf Centre for Human Rights launched judicial review proceedings seeking an explanation as to why the change had been made.[23]

At first instance, Mitting J rejected the application for judicial review on the grounds that the challenged wording is not part of the operative Ministerial Code. 'It is', thought the learned judge, 'simply a statement of the background against which those obligations should be read'.[24] Since '[t]he challenge to the decision could only be based on its lawfulness. The fact that it might be in breach of an unincorporated provision of international law and that the minister was said to be under a duty to comply with international law would not avail the claimant.'[25]

The claimant appealed against Mitting J's refusal to grant permission for judicial review.[26] Arden LJ granted conditional leave only on the

[20] *The Guardian*, 22 October 2015, cited in HC Library Briefing Paper 'The Ministerial Code and the Independent Adviser on Ministerial Interests' (No. 03750, 17 January 2018), [2.2], 11–12.

[21] UK Conservative Party, 'Protecting human rights in the UK: the Conservatives' proposals for changing Britain's human rights laws'.

[22] Ibid., 7 (emphasis in original).

[23] *R (ex p Gulf Centre for Human Rights)* v. *Prime Minister* [2016] EWHC 1323 (Admin).

[24] Ibid., at [8].

[25] Ibid., [9].

[26] *R (ex p Gulf Centre for Human Rights)* v. *Prime Minister* [2018] EWCA Civ 1855.

question whether there was a change of substance in the two versions of the Code.[27] The Lord Chief Justice, the Master of the Rolls and Hamblen J heard the appeal. The Court held that no change of substance was made. The overarching duty referred to in the Code was not imposed by it. Rather the Code referenced existing duties outside the Code. The Court held that:[28]

> [T]he reference to 'international law and treaty obligations' in the 2010 Code is subsumed within the stated duty 'to comply with the law.' That duty includes those obligations. Whatever the precise meaning of the reference to those obligations, they are not independent obligations but simply part of the 'overarching' duty of compliance with the law.

The government had confirmed this to Parliament in 2015 and again to the Court.[29] In light of these conclusions, the appeal was dismissed.

D *The Arguments Advanced in Support of the Amendment*

Was this, then, nothing more than a peculiarly British storm in a teacup? One might gain that impression from reading the judgments. But the debate in Court was framed, as it had to be, in terms of the scope of judicial review. The outcome of those proceedings (and the earlier Ministerial statements to Parliament) may have usefully confirmed that no change in ministers' obligations was intended. But the decision of the Court of Appeal neatly sidestepped the more fundamental question of exactly what those obligations are, when they arise by virtue of treaties that have not been incorporated into domestic law. The statement that ministers must obey 'the law', while compendious, does little to illuminate the source and nature of the obligation to obey international law.

It is at this point that the obligation as originally formulated faced three more fundamental challenges: the first alleging that the concept of the rule of law itself is really a concept that is only applicable to the internal operation of the domestic legal system of a state; the second based on alleged incompatibility with the two bedrock principles of the Constitution: Parliamentary sovereignty and the rule of law; and the third derived from the separation between the international and the domestic legal spheres. In each case, these arguments proceed

27 Ibid., [13].
28 Ibid., [20].
29 Ibid., [19]-[24].

from the same point of departure: that ministers may be placed in a position of conflicting obligations arising respectively from domestic and international law, which has to be resolved in favour of one source of law or the other.[30] It is necessary to examine precisely the way in which each of these arguments was advanced before considering their tenability.

The first proposition is that we cannot understand the concept of the rule of law as applying to international law, which is 'like it or not, a defective example of law', such that '[i]f we can speak of the Rule of Law in the international domain . . . it is only a Rule by imperfect analogy with the law of the land'.[31] Rather, it is claimed that the concept of the rule of law is 'intimately connected to the institution of the state'.[32] Its application to the international sphere is questionable, and would require substantial qualification.

The second proposition is that: 'When international law conflicts with domestic law, the constitutional principle of the rule of law requires British courts and ministers – and other legal subjects – to follow British law.'[33] Finnis goes further and claims that the idea of a legal obligation upon ministers to abide by international law challenges 'that most fundamental principle of our constitutional law, and thus also challenges the Rule of Law'.[34] He argues that, if ministers were under a legal obligation to abide by international law, the consequence would be that ministers would be entitled to 'change the legal rights or obligations of anyone in the realm simply by entering into or ratifying an international treaty' and, further, that they could 'change the legal rights or duties of present or future Ministers'.[35] In his view, the result is that the obligation on ministers to abide by international law, and to account to their colleagues and to Parliament for the international obligations that they contract is merely an expression of a 'morally grounded UK *policy*'. This may be 'an important principle of responsible government of our constitutional form' but '*none of this* imposes on Ministers (or civil

[30] Mark Elliot, 'The Ministerial Code and international law' *Public law for everyone* blog post (26 October 2015) available at https://publiclawforeveryone.com/2015/10/26/the-ministerial-code-and-international-law/, accessed 10 February 2019.

[31] John Finnis, 'Ministers, international law, and the rule of law' Judicial Power Project (2 November 2015) available at www.judicialpowerproject.org.uk, accessed 10 February 2019.

[32] Ekins and Verdirame, 'The Ministerial Code and the Rule of Law'.

[33] Ekins and Verdirame, 'The Ministerial Code and the Rule of Law'.

[34] Finnis, 'Ministers, international law, and the rule of law'.

[35] Ibid.

servants) anything comparable to their personal obligation as citizens and Ministers to *comply with the law*, that is, with the law of the land'.[36]

The third proposition is that any difficulty that may be posed by any apparent conflict between the UK's international obligations and domestic law is resolved by the fact that 'ultimately these two elements of legal doctrine inhabit different – domestic and international – legal dimensions'.[37] From this separation of realms, critics of the prior formulation derive a separation of the persons subject to legal obligation. Only the state, the United Kingdom, is responsible as a matter of international law, not ministers personally. In turn ministers' obligations arise only under domestic law. As a result: 'Under our constitution, Ministers are incapable of imposing legal obligations on themselves or on their successors by way of the Crown's prerogative to conduct foreign relations.'[38]

These arguments all proceed from a fundamental misunderstanding of the nature and source of the legal obligation upon ministers to abide by the international law commitments of the state. The obligation on ministers is a principle of the British Constitution, not of international law. It is an essential correlative of the exercise by ministers of the Royal prerogative to conduct foreign relations – itself a legal power conferred upon ministers by the Constitution. These points of principle will be developed in Section III. The arguments are not only falsifiable as a matter of principle. They are also contrary to the established constitutional practice of the United Kingdom over (at least) four centuries. Recent events demonstrate that this practice has lost none of its force. In view of the density of this practice, it will be possible only to sketch it in outline, which is the task that Section II will address.

II British State Practice

This section advances five points derived from the practice of the British state that are of more general application to the theme of the present essay. It considers: (a) the constitutional role of the law officers of the Crown in advising on international law; (b) the assumption underlying the seeking of advice as to the determinacy of international law; (c) the significance of international legality to the conduct of British foreign

[36] Ibid. (emphasis in original).

[37] Elliot, 'The Ministerial Code and international law'.

[38] Ekins and Verdirame, 'The Ministerial Code and the Rule of Law'.

policy; (d) even in the exceptional cases where international law was not followed or much disputed; and (e) the accountability of the executive to Parliament for the consistency of its foreign policy with international law.

A Advice of the Law Officers of the Crown on International Law

The governmental legal adviser on matters of international law has a critically important function in the development of the foreign policy of the state. As Berman puts it:[39]

> [T]he main role of the Governmental legal adviser is to 'make' his Government comply with international law . . . .It is a truism to say that the question whether or not to comply with what international law requires is always a question of *policy*. But even the meanest definition of the role of the international legal adviser in government cannot treat that policy question as if it were an entirely neutral one. It must be assumed to be a necessary part of the role that the international legal adviser should be expected to use his gifts of exposition and persuasion to bring those with whom the power of decision lies to use this power to the right result.

Within the British state, this function has over centuries taken on a particular constitutional significance. At least since the sixteenth century, law officers of the Crown have advised the British government as to its obligations and those of other states with whom it is engaged under international law.[40] This practice originated in the taking of advice from the civilians of Doctors' Commons.[41] The evidence from the State Papers establishes that even 'before the period when international law was greatly developed, the English Government was convinced of the necessity of juridical study and advice upon international questions'.[42] From

[39] Frank Berman, 'The Role of the International Lawyer in the Making of Foreign Policy', in Chanaka Wickremasinghe (ed.), *The International Lawyer as Practitioner* (London: British Institute of International and Comparative Law, 2000), 3. Berman served as Principal Legal Adviser to the UK Foreign & Commonwealth Office (FCO), 1991–99.

[40] Arnold McNair, 'The debt of international law in Britain to the Civil Law and the civilians' (1953) 39 *Transactions of the Grotius Society* 183, reprinted in Arnold McNair, *International Law Opinions, Selected and Annotated*, 3 vols. (Cambridge: Cambridge University Press, 1956), App. II; Clive Parry (ed.) (1965) VII *British Digest of International Law* 242–81; Clive Parry, *Law Officers' opinions to the Foreign Office 1793–1860: A reproduction of the manuscript series with index and commentaries* 97 vols. (Westmead: Gregg International Publishers, 1970–1973); Clive Parry, *Great Britain Law Officers' Opinions* (6 micro-film reels, Trans-Media, 1976).

[41] McNair, 'The debt of international law in Britain to the Civil Law and the civilians'.

[42] William Holdsworth, *History of English Law* vol. 5 (Methuen, 1924), 44.

about 1600 until 1872, the Crown's standing adviser on questions of international law was the King's Advocate-General. He was appointed by letters patent and was consulted constantly. This practice continued after the establishment of the Foreign Office as a separate department of state in 1782.[43]

After 1876, the Foreign Office acquired its own legal adviser, who could provide a 'reservoir of specialist expertise'[44] and continuous advice on all matters of international law that arise in the daily work of the Office. But this did not lead to the law officers abandoning their function of advising the Crown on matters of international law that are engaged in the high-level policy decisions of the government. Following the retirement of the last Advocate-General in 1872, this function passed to the Attorney General and Solicitor General as the principal law officers of the Crown.[45] Both of these positions are held by ministers who also sit in Parliament. As such they are called upon to advise Cabinet on issues of both domestic law and international law that may arise.[46] As a consequence, they assume ministerial responsibility for their advice.

Parry, discussing the binding force of law officers' Opinions in the *British Digest of International Law*, published in 1965, notes that, while 'there is not, it would seem, any absolute constitutional duty'[47] on the government to follow the Law Officers' advice, the 'Government has consistently considered itself in practice precluded from ordering "policy" otherwise than as the "law", or rather the exposition of it the Law Officers have given, dictates.'[48] He concludes on that 'at least during the period covered by this volume, a Law Officers' report, if capable of

[43] McNair, vol. III, App. II, *International Law Opinions*, 421–25. The demise of this office may perhaps be partly attributable to the débâcle over delay in advice by the Queen's Advocate on the *Alabama*, the vessel whose provision to Confederate forces in the course of the American Civil War gave rise to the *Alabama* arbitration. A full account is given in Parry (1965) VII *British Digest of International Law* 274–81. See Frank Berman and Michael Wood, 'Submission in response to consultation on the role of the Attorney General' Annex, *The Governance of Britain: A Consultation on the Role of the Attorney General*, Cm 7192 (30 November 2007). At all events, the last holder of the office was Sir Travers Twiss, who retired in 1872.

[44] Berman and Wood, 'Submission in response to consultation on the role of the Attorney General' [7].

[45] John Edwards, *The Law Officers of the Crown* (London: Sweet & Maxwell, 1964); John Edwards, *The Attorney-General: Politics and the Public Interest* (London: Sweet & Maxwell, 1984).

[46] Parry (1965) VII *British Digest of International Law* 249–52.

[47] Parry (1965) VII *British Digest of International Law* 271.

[48] Ibid.

importance of Belgian neutrality, as lynchpin of the system of European order bounded by international law so painstakingly constructed in the pre-war era, as the basis for Britain entering the War.[56] But the importance of the Great War for present purposes is what it demonstrates about the constraints of international law upon the British government's own conduct of the war. The British blockade of shipping was constructed with painstaking consideration of the position under international law and '[t]he cabinet returned to the legal dilemmas again and again'.[57]

The resulting Order in Council was tested upon the requisition of a Swedish neutral ship carrying a cargo of copper in Prize Court in *The Zamora*.[58] The case was appealed to the Privy Council and argued for the Crown by the Attorney General and Solicitor General.[59] Lord Parker of Waddington delivered the judgment of the Board. His Lordship begins with a classic exposition of the separation of powers, in holding that: 'The idea that the King in Council, or indeed any branch of the Executive, has power to prescribe or alter the law to be administered by the Courts of this country is out of harmony with the principles of our Constitution.'[60] But the Prize Court does not administer domestic law. It administers international law. The Board rejected the suggestion that this affects the ability of the executive to prescribe the law applicable in such a court. The Prize Court 'must ascertain and give effect to a law which is not laid down by any particular State, but originates in the practice and usage long observed by civilized nations in their relations towards each other or in express international agreement'.[61] This rule is of particular importance in prize cases, so that a neutral aggrieved by the actions of a belligerent power can be assured that he has a right of recourse to a court which administers international law. The rule requiring exhaustion of local remedies would otherwise 'entirely vanish if a Court of Prize, while nominally administering a law of international obligation, were in reality acting under the direction of the Executive of a belligerent Power'.[62] A Committee assembled by the Attorney General after this decision

[56] Ibid., 16.
[57] Ibid., 161.
[58] *The Zamora* [1916] P 27.
[59] [1917] 2 AC 77.
[60] Ibid., 90.
[61] Ibid., 91–92.
[62] Ibid., 93.

concluded that 'The Government *cannot* by executive act alter international law in its favour.'[63]

Even in time of war when matters of vital national survival were at stake, the British government recognised that international law operated as a constraint upon its actions for which it could be held to account domestically as well as internationally.

D Exceptional Cases

The significance within the national constitution of the principle that the executive is constrained in its exercise of its foreign affairs power by international law, on which it receives advice from the law officers of the Crown is underscored by the constitutional significance of two much-discussed incidents involving the use of force abroad: the Suez Intervention in 1956 and the invasion of Iraq in 2003.

In the first case, the executive deliberately decided not to seek a formal opinion from the law officers, knowing (as the evidence now establishes) that it would not be favourable to the adventure. As the research of Geoffrey Marston from the Foreign Office archives vividly demonstrates,[64] the government proceeded on the basis of advice proffered by the lord chancellor,[65] which was emphatically rejected by the law officers of the Crown. On the eve of the ill-fated Suez intervention, the Attorney General, Sir Reginald Manningham-Buller (later Viscount Dilhorne) wrote to the foreign secretary (copied to the prime minister and lord chancellor):[66]

> It is just not true to say that we are entitled under the Charter to take any measures open to us 'to stop the fighting.' Nor would it be true to say that under international law apart from the Charter we are entitled to do so. Further, it is not true to say that under international law we are entitled to take any measures open to us 'to protect our interests which are threatened by hostilities'.
>
> ....

[63] Report of the 'Zamora' Committee in Malkin Papers, 'Maritime Rights, Prize Orders in Council and Papers relating to Withdrawal of Declaration of London 1914-1917' FO 800/918.

[64] Geoffrey Marston, 'Armed intervention in the 1956 Suez Canal Crisis: the legal advice tendered to the British Government' (1988) 37 *International and Comparative Law Quarterly* 773.

[65] Viscount Kilmuir cited ibid. See *Hansard*, HL, vol. 199, col. 1350, 1 November 1956.

[66] FO 800/749 (1 November 1956) cited in Marston 'Armed intervention in the 1956 Suez Canal Crisis' 803–04 (emphasis added).

> *I feel compelled to write this letter because as the Law Officers are constitutionally the legal advisers of the Government . . . it will be generally assumed that we have been approached for advice as to the legality of what has been done.* In fact we were not consulted on this matter nor were we upon questions relating to the Suez Canal before Israel's attack.

Sir Gerald Fitzmaurice, Legal Adviser to the Foreign Office, wrote a memorandum to his colleagues in the Foreign Office to the same effect.[67]

The decision of the British government to support an armed intervention in Iraq in 2003 also demonstrates the consequences where the constitutional process is not properly followed. As a result of the exhaustive investigation of the Chilcot Inquiry, the process of seeking legal advice in this case has been exposed to public scrutiny.[68] Some elements of this narrative deserve special emphasis for their relevance here.

Following the Security Council's adoption of Resolution 1441 on 8 November 2002, the government decided to delay calling for formal legal advice from the Attorney General, Lord Goldsmith.[69] Lord Goldsmith provided draft advice to the Prime Minister, Mr Blair, on 14 January 2002, which was not shared with Cabinet or the Foreign Secretary, Mr Straw. Lord Goldsmith stated that a further decision by the Security Council would be needed to revive the authorisation to use force contained in Resolution 678 (1990) and that he saw no grounds for self-defence or humanitarian intervention providing the legal basis for military action in Iraq.[70] Despite this advice, Mr Blair continued to say in public that he would not rule out military action if a further resolution in response to an Iraqi breach was vetoed. These statements were at odds with Lord Goldsmith's advice.[71] The Inquiry concluded that: 'Mr Blair's response suggested a readiness to seek any ground on which Lord Goldsmith would be able to conclude that there was a legal basis for military action.'[72]

67 FO 800/748 (1 November 1956) cited in Marston 'Armed intervention in the 1956 Suez Canal Crisis' 806.

68 United Kingdom, House of Commons, 'The Report of the Iraq Inquiry' (HC 264, 6 July 2016) ('Chilcot Inquiry Report'); and see generally the Symposium on the Iraq Inquiry in the *British Yearbook of International Law* (advance articles published 22 September 2018) available at www.bybil.oxfordjournals.org. See, for an earlier account, Philippe Sands, *Lawless World: Making and Breaking Global Rules* 2nd ed. (London: Penguin Publishing, 2006), ch. 12 'This wretched legal advice.'

69 Chilcot Inquiry Report, vol. 5, [903].

70 Ibid., [167]–[170].

71 Ibid., [206]–[208].

72 Ibid., [198].

The Legal Adviser to the Foreign Office, Michael Wood, had given legal advice to the same effect to the Foreign Secretary, Jack Straw on 22–23 January 2003. Mr Straw wrote to Mr Wood on 29 January 2003 stating: '*I note your advice, but I do not accept it.*'[73] Lord Goldsmith wrote to advise Mr Straw that the proper constitutional course where a Minister challenges legal advice he has received is to seek an opinion from the law officers.[74]

On 27 February 2003, after a visit to Washington on 10 February, Lord Goldsmith met officials at Downing Street and advised that 'I am prepared to accept – and I am choosing my words carefully here – that a reasonable case can be made that resolution 1441 is capable of reviving the authorisation in 678 without a further resolution if there are strong factual grounds for concluding that Iraq has failed to take the final opportunity.'[75] He confirmed this advice formally on 7 March 2003.[76] By 13 March 2003, the chiefs of staff of the Armed Forces and the Civil Service pressed him to state his opinion on the legality of the proposed intervention more definitively. Admiral Boyce considered this to be essential because the members of the armed forces, who might otherwise incur personal liability under international criminal law if they were deployed, were entitled to receive an unequivocal assurance as to the legality of the use of force.[77]

In response, Lord Goldsmith confirmed that he was 'satisfied that the proposed military action by the UK would be in accordance with national and international law'.[78] Thereafter Lord Goldsmith provided a written answer to Parliament on the legality of the intervention on 17 March 2003, in which he confirmed: 'It is plain that Iraq has failed so to comply and therefore Iraq was at the time of resolution 1441 and continues to be in material breach. Thus the authority to use force under resolution 678 has revived and so continues today.'[79] A Cabinet meeting on the same day endorsed the use of force in Iraq. Cabinet was provided with a copy of that answer, which set out the government's legal position. It was not provided with the legal basis for the conclusion that Iraq had

73 Ibid., [351], emphasis added.
74 Minute dated 3 February 2003, ibid., [357].
75 Ibid., [461].
76 Minute Goldsmith to Blair dated 7 March 2003, Ibid., [515]–[559].
77 Ibid., [703].
78 Letter Brummell (Legal Secretary to the Law Officers) on behalf of Lord Goldsmith to Hemming (MOD Legal Adviser), 'Iraq–Position of the CDS' (14 March 2003) ibid., [696].
79 *Hansard*, HL vol. 646, col. 482W, 14 March 2003.

failed to take the final opportunity to comply with its disarmament obligations under resolution 1441, nor with a legal opinion that set out the competing arguments.[80] The Inquiry concluded that 'Lord Goldsmith should have been asked to provide written advice which fully reflected the position on 17 March, explained the legal basis on which the UK could take military action and set out the risks of legal challenge.'[81]

On 18 March 2003, Elizabeth Wilmshurst, FCO Deputy Legal Adviser, resigned stating:[82]

> I regret that I cannot agree that it is lawful to use force against Iraq without a second Security Council resolution to revive the authorisation given in SCR 678 . . . . My views accord with the advice that has been given consistently in this Office before and after the adoption of SCR 1441 and with what the Attorney General gave us to understand was his position prior to his letter of 7 March. (The view expressed in that letter has of course changed again into what is now the official line.) I cannot in conscience go along with advice – within the Office or to the public of Parliament – which asserts the legitimacy of military action without such a resolution, particularly since an unlawful use of force on such a scale amounts to the crime of aggression; nor can I agree with such action in circumstances which are so detrimental to the international order and the rule of law.

What are we to make of this débâcle for present purposes? This was, after all, a case in which the Attorney's advice was sought and given. Yet the circumstances were such as to give rise to a major concern that that process had been misused by a government merely intent on finding a legal justification in international law for an action that it was determined to take. Three observations of a rather general character need to be made.

In the first place, the question of international legality was central to the concerns of all the constitutional actors, not just the legal advisers. Secondly, those actors knew the paramount importance of an affirmative opinion of the law officers of the Crown. That is precisely why ministers delayed seeking such an opinion to the eleventh hour. Thirdly, the officers of state that would be responsible for implementation of the government's decision, namely the members of the armed forces, insisted upon definitive advice on legality under international law as a precondition to action.

[80] Ibid., [946].
[81] Ibid., [955].
[82] Letter Wilmshurst to Wood, 18 March 2003.

For them legality under international law is paramount because it is the source of their permission to use lethal force.[83] There was a widespread view both at the time and thereafter that the legal basis cited by the government for the invasion was unsound and that the government had placed the Attorney under intense political pressure to change his opinion to suit the government policy. Those concerns resulted in reviews of both the role of the attorney general in general and the conduct of the decision-making in relation to Iraq.[84] These reviews have served to underscore, and not to undermine, the importance of the requirement upon the executive to undertake foreign policy action in accordance with Britain's international law obligations in accordance with dispassionate advice from the law officers of the Crown.

E *Accountability to Parliament*

A final aspect of the constitutional role of the law officers of the Crown vis-à-vis international law is the extent of their accountability to Parliament for their advice. A review of the position in 1984 noted the inconsistency of government practice with regard to the disclosure to Parliament of the Attorney's advice on international law matters.[85] Harold Wilson maintained in 1963 that:[86]

> The Attorney General, whoever he may be, is not only the legal adviser to the Crown and to the government. He is also a servant of this House. It is, from time to time, his duty to advise the House on legal matters – a duty going beyond his responsibility to this government and the Crown ….

Closer examination of instances involving issues of the compatibility of proposed legislation with the international obligations of the United Kingdom shows some instances where the Attorney's legal advice was disclosed to Parliament[87] and some other instances where disclosure was

[83] David Howarth and Shona Wilson Stark, 'H. L. A. Hart's secondary rules: what do "officials" really think?' (2018) 14 *International Journal of Law in Context* 61, 73–74 develop this point by reference to subsequent interviews with armed forces personnel.

[84] *The Governance of Britain: A Consultation on the Role of the Attorney General* CM 7192 (30 November 2007); Chilcot Inquiry Report, esp. vol. 5.

[85] John Edwards, *The Attorney-General: Politics and the Public Interest* (Sweet & Maxwell, 1984), 210–27.

[86] *Hansard*, HC, vol. 678 col. 994, 27 May 1968.

[87] For example, consistency of the Customs (Import Deposits) Bill 1968 with the UK's obligations under the European Free Trade Agreement (EFTA), where Sir Elwyn Jones AG disclosed his legal opinion: *Hansard*, HC, vol. 943, cols. 793–831, discussed in Edwards, *The Attorney-General*, 211–22.

resisted.[88] Sir Michael Havers AG contended that there was no such duty. He thought this 'would raise conflicts with the primary duty of the Law Officers to advise the Crown on legal questions'.[89]

Erskine May states the principle in terms of a constitutional convention:[90]

> By long-standing convention, observed by successive Governments, the fact of, and substance of advice from, the law officers of the Crown is not disclosed outside government. This convention is referred to in paragraph 2.13 of the Ministerial Code. The purpose of this convention is to enable the government to obtain frank and full legal advice in confidence. Therefore, the opinions of the law officers of the Crown, being confidential, are not usually laid before Parliament, cited in debate or provided in evidence before a select committee, and their production has frequently been refused; but if a Minister deems it expedient that such opinions should be made known for the information of the House, the Speaker has ruled that the orders of the House are in no way involved in the proceeding.

Berman and Wood express the balance between accountability to Parliament and the need to maintain confidentiality of legal advice in the following way:[91]

> [T]he current arrangements also ensure that there is direct Parliamentary accountability in respect of the legal positions which the Government adopts in this vital area. The accountability is of course of a special kind, not identical with that which applies to policy decisions. It has to reflect, amongst other things, the confidentiality that necessarily attaches to advice given by a lawyer to the client, a factor that may be particularly acute when the issue under consideration is a matter of dispute internationally, or may become the subject of judicial proceedings nationally or internationally. All the same, the fact that the Attorney General is a Minister and sits in Parliament at least enables a direct and authoritative explanation to be given of the Government's legal views, allows for

88 Legality of the Immigration Regulations in light of the European Convention on Human Rights: *Hansard*, HC, vol. 975 cols. 256–57, discussed in Edwards, *The Attorney-General*, 213.

89 Law Officers' Department files, letter dated 29 January 1980, cited in Edwards, *The Attorney-General*, 225.

90 Malcolm Jack (ed.), *Erskine May's Treatise on the Law, Privileges, Proceedings and Usages of Parliament* 24th ed. (LexisNexis, 2011), 447 (references omitted). See also: Edwards, *The Attorney-General*, 256–61. On the recent practice see: United Kingdom, House of Lords Library Briefing Paper, 'Publishing Government Legal Advice' (6 December 2018).

91 Berman and Wood, 'Submission in response to consultation on the role of the Attorney General', [11].

> Parliamentary Questions to be posed and answered, and may in appropriate cases also allow for such issues to be knowledgeably debated.

The extent to which Parliament may compel the Attorney to disclose to it his or her advice to the government on the legal effect at *international* law of steps that the government proposes to take has gained prominence in recent years. As has been seen, at the time of the proposed entry into armed conflict in Iraq, the Attorney gave a written statement to the House of Lords on the legal position but did not disclose his written legal advice to the government. A motion that he should be compelled to do so was defeated in the Commons in 2004,[92] but the government subsequently decided, in the face of continuing public controversy, to disclose it voluntarily. In 2015, the point arose again in the context of the government's plan to extend its air strikes against ISIS into Syria. The prime minister gave a statement to the House on the legal position, but both he and the Attorney reiterated the convention against disclosure of the written advice.[93]

The matter came to a head very recently, when Parliament sought clarification of the legal effect of the proposed provisions on Ireland and Northern Ireland in the draft Withdrawal Agreement with the European Union. The Attorney disclosed his legal advice[94] only after an unprecedented contempt motion against the government was passed in the House of Commons.[95]

The point here is that under the British Constitution the Ministry is accountable to Parliament not merely, as Dicey emphasised, for its general conduct of the foreign affairs prerogative.[96] It is also accountable to Parliament for the legality of its exercise of that power under international law. The law officers of the Crown are members of Parliament and can be called upon to explain the government's legal position on its obligations under international law where Parliament so requires. In exceptional cases, they can also be required to produce to Parliament their written legal advice.

In this light, it is now possible in Section III to return to the arguments of principle raised against the proposition that ministers are under an obligation to comply with international law and to consider how those arguments are to be answered.

92 *Hansard*, HC, vol. 418, cols. 1459–60, 9 March 2004.
93 *Hansard* HC, vol. 602, cols. 1467–68, 1489–94, 26 November 2015.
94 Letter Cox AG to Prime Minister, 13 November 2018.
95 *Hansard*, HC, vol. 650, cols. 728–31, 4 December 2018.
96 A. V. Dicey, *Introduction to the Study of the Law of the Constitution* 2nd ed. (London: Macmillan & Co, 1886), 393–94.

III The Obligation in Constitutional Principle

The previous section has sought to demonstrate that the practice of the British state over several centuries supports the proposition that the executive has a constitutional duty to comply with the international law obligations of the state. The present section considers the nature of that obligation in light of the principles that underlie the constitutional compact in its application to the field of foreign relations. It will consider first the relation between the obligation and the constitutional precepts of dualism. Subsection B will then examine in particular the relation between the obligation of the executive and parliamentary sovereignty. Subsection C then turns to the larger frame: the question whether the recognition of such an obligation is consistent with the concept of the rule of law in its application to a particular state.

A Executive Compliance with International Law in a Dualist State

How may the obligation upon ministers to comply with international law be reconciled with the basic premise of dualism that underlies the approach of the Constitution to foreign relations? This premise has two elements: the separation of the international plane from the domestic and the separation of the power to make law binding domestically, which is reserved to Parliament, from the power to conduct foreign affairs – including the power to enter into treaties – which is exercised by the executive under the prerogative.

In considering the impact of international law within the domestic polity, it is first necessary to distinguish between customary international law and treaties. So far as custom is concerned, the United Kingdom cannot be described as a dualist state. On the contrary, custom is a direct source of English law. Blackstone explained the reasons for this principle in a manner that directly confronts the dualist argument:[97]

> In arbitrary states [international] law, wherever it contradicts or is not provided for by the municipal law of the country, is enforced by the royal power: but since in England no royal power can introduce a new law, or suspend the execution of the old, therefore the law of nations (wherever any question arises which is properly the object of its jurisdiction) is here

[97] William Blackstone, *Commentaries on the Law of England* 9th ed. reprint (Oxford: Strahan, Cadell and Prince, 1783), bk IV, 67.

> adopted in its full extent by the common law, and is held to be a part of the law of the land.

In other words, it is precisely *because* the executive cannot change the law of the land by the arbitrary exercise of its own prerogative power that general international law must be directly received into English law. This is not the place to retrace the impact that this principle has had, and continues to have, on the substantive content of English law, which the author has done elsewhere.[98] It suffices for present purposes to observe that, in this context, there can be no separation of realms.[99]

In the case of treaty obligations, the point of departure is the same, but the consequence is different. In this case, the international law obligation does not arise by virtue of general international law. Rather it arises from the deliberate act of the executive on the international plane. The principle that the executive has no power by treaty to change the law of the land is fundamental to the Constitution. In 1892, Lord Herschell held that the proposition that the executive was entitled to justify an invasion of an individual's private rights at home by reference to a treaty obligation that it had assumed in the exercise its foreign affairs prerogative was 'wholly untenable'.[100] This point was central to the ratio of the *Miller* case on withdrawal from the European Union. The Supreme Court held: 'it is a fundamental principle of the Constitution that, unless primary legislation permits it, the Royal prerogative does not enable Ministers to change statute law or the common law'.[101] The Court explained: 'the dualist system is a necessary corollary of Parliamentary sovereignty, or, to put the point another way, it exists to protect Parliament not ministers'.[102]

Nor will the courts *compel* domestic decision-makers to exercise their powers with reference to international law. As Lord Mance put

98 Campbell McLachlan, *Foreign Relations Law* (Cambridge: Cambridge University Press, 2014), ch. 3; See for a contrary account: Roger O'Keefe, 'The Doctrine of Incorporation Revisited' (2008) 79 *British Yearbook of International Law* 7.

99 See, e.g., *R* v. *Bow Street Metropolitan Stipendiary Magistrate, ex p Pinochet Ugarte (No 3)* [2000] 1 AC 147. For further development see Campbell McLachlan, 'Five Conceptions of Foreign Relations Law', in Curtis Bradley (ed.), *Oxford Handbook on Comparative Foreign Relations Law* (Oxford: Oxford University Press, 2019) ch. 2.

100 *Walker* v. *Baird* [1892] AC 491, 497.

101 *R (on the application of Miller)* v. *Secretary of State for Exiting the European Union* [2017] UKSC 5, [2018] AC 61, [50].

102 Ibid., [57], approving McLachlan, *Foreign Relations Law*, [5.20].

it in a case concerning the exercise of a common law power by a lower court:[103]

> The United Kingdom takes a dualist approach to international law . . . . The starting point in this connection is that domestic and international law considerations are separate . . . . [A] domestic decision-maker exercising a general discretion (i) is neither bound to have regard to this country's purely international obligations nor bound to give effect to them, but (ii) may have regard to the United Kingdom's international obligations, if he or she decides this to be appropriate . . . . Neither by reference to the principle of legality, which refers to rights and obligations recognised at a domestic level, nor on any other basis is it possible to limit the domestic court's general discretion by reference to international obligations . . . .

But a proper account of dualism requires not only an explanation of the primary role of Parliament to make domestic law and the limits of the court's powers vis-à-vis unincorporated treaty obligations. It also calls for an account of the legal limits on the exercise of the executive's prerogative power to conduct foreign relations. Lauterpacht addressed this question directly when he considered whether doctrines in domestic law that limit judicial determination in the field of foreign relations are a limitation on the rule of law. In his view, 'limitations upon the freedom of judicial decision, far from amounting to a suspension of the rule of law, are the expression of a differentiation of functions, which for reasons of obvious expediency is unavoidable in the modern State'.[104]

Akande and Bjorge pursue this point in the context of the debate about the Ministerial Code:[105]

> The fact that certain obligations of international law are not enforceable in the courts does not in any way detract from the fact that the Crown is bound by them. Much of the discussion of the relationship between international law and domestic law has focused on the extent to which international law may be applied by the courts. The unfortunate side effect of this concentration on judicial application of international law is that one may lose sight of the point that obligations may still be *legal* obligations binding on parties, although they are not enforceable before domestic courts.

[103] *R (Yam)* v. *Central Criminal Court* [2015] UKSC 76, [2016] AC 771, [35]–[36].

[104] Hersch Lauterpacht, *The Function of Law in the International Community* (Oxford: Oxford University Press, 1933, reprinted 2011), 397.

[105] Dapo Akande and Eirik Bjorge, 'The United Kingdom Ministerial Code and International Law: a Response to Richard Ekins and Guglielmo Verdirame' UK constitutional law blog (10 December 2016) available at https://ukconstitutionallaw.org.

The Constitution vouchsafes to the executive the power of engaging the state through treaty actions on the international plane; 'the making of a treaty is an executive act'.[106] Furthermore, by its acts or omissions, the executive may engage the United Kingdom's international responsibility vis-à-vis other states, since 'most acts giving rise to implications of responsibility will emerge from the executive government, which provides the most direct manifestation of state power'.[107] But it does not follow from this, as has been contended, that the legal obligation, which undoubtedly rests upon the state at international law, has no reach to ministers. In order to consider this question, it is necessary to consider first the role of ministers on the international plane and then, second, to consider the implications of this within the domestic constitution.

Treaties may be concluded by states[108] and bind the states that are parties to them.[109] The state is represented in treaty-making by those persons who have full powers to express the consent of the state to be bound. The first such category, specified in Article 7(2)(a) of the Vienna Convention on the Law of Treaties ('VCLT') is as follows:

> In virtue of their functions and without having to produce full powers, the following are considered as representing their State:
>
> (a) Heads of State, Heads of Government and Ministers for Foreign Affairs for the purpose of performing all acts relating to the conclusion of a treaty;

Once a treaty has entered into force, 'it is binding upon the parties to it and must be performed by them in good faith'.[110] 'A party may not invoke the provisions of its internal law as justification for its failure to perform a treaty.'[111] If the state's internal legislation is not in conformity with its treaty obligation, 'a State which has contracted valid international obligations is bound to make in its legislation such modifications as may be necessary to ensure the fulfilment of the obligations undertaken'.[112]

106 *Attorney General for Canada* v. *Attorney General for Ontario* [1937] AC 326, 347 (PC).

107 James Crawford, *State Responsibility: the General Part* (Cambridge: Cambridge University Press, 2013), 119; Art. 4, Draft Articles on International Responsibility of States for Internationally Wrongful Acts ('ARSIWA') [2001] 2(2) YB ILC 26.

108 Vienna Convention on the Law of Treaties ('VCLT'), signed 23 May 1969, entered into force 27 January 1980, 1155 UNTS 331, Art. 2(a).

109 Ibid., Art. 26.

110 Ibid.

111 Ibid., Art. 27.

112 *Exchange of Greek and Turkish Populations* (Advisory Opinion) (1925) PCIJ Ser. B No. 10, 20.

International law, then, both (a) recognises that heads of government and foreign ministers have the capacity to conclude treaty obligations that bind the state and (b) requires that once such a treaty enters into force the state has the obligation to perform it in good faith, including, where necessary, by bringing its domestic legislation into conformity with the treaty.

How is this responsibility at the international level given effect within the British Constitution? Baroness Chalker of Wallasey stated the position in answer to a written question in the House of Lords in 1994, which enquired whether ministers and civil servants, in discharging their public functions, have a duty to comply with the European Convention on Human Rights and the International Covenant on Civil and Political Rights. She replied:[113]

> International treaties are binding on states and not on individuals. The United Kingdom is party to both treaties and it must comply with its obligations under them. In so far as acts of Ministers and civil servants in the discharge of their public functions constitute acts which engage the responsibility of the United Kingdom, they must comply with the terms of the treaties.

This formulation starts with the general proposition that the international obligations constituted by treaties bind states not individuals. This proposition can be accepted as a general statement. But it is important to keep in mind that there are important contexts in which international law does impose its obligations directly on individuals, notably (though not solely) under international criminal law.[114] As has already been seen,[115] this was a critical consideration in the minds of key constitutional actors in the debate of the legality of the invasion of Iraq in 2003.

The main purpose of Baroness Chalker's statement was to describe the link between obligations that have been assumed by the state and the position of state ministers and officials in the exercise of their public functions. As she put it: 'In so far as acts of Ministers and civil servants

[113] *Hansard*, HL, vol. 559, col. WA 84, 7 December 1994.

[114] Art. 49, Geneva Convention I, signed 12 August 1949, entered into force 21 October 1950, 75 UNTS 31; Art. 50, Geneva Convention II, signed 12 August 1949, entered into force 21 October 1950, 75 UNTS 85; Art. 129, Geneva Convention III, signed 12 August 1949, entered into force 21 October 1950, 75 UNTS 135; Art. 146, Geneva Convention IV, signed 12 August 1949, entered into force 21 October 1950, 75 UNTS 287; Rome Statute of the International Criminal Court, signed 17 July 1998, entered into force 1 July 2002, 2187 UNTS 90.

[115] Above, Section II.D.

in the discharge of their public functions constitute acts which engage the responsibility of the United Kingdom, they must comply with the terms of the treaties.'[116] In other words, since the acts of such officials can engage the responsibility of the state, there is a concomitant obligation upon such persons to comply with the obligations that the executive has itself assumed. As Berman put it, the argument that international law and domestic law are in different spheres '*fails to take into account that governments are comprised of individuals and act through individuals ... [T]he state is the hinge through which international law is transmuted into the domestic context.*'[117]

This does not turn ministers or officials into agents of international law when acting in relation to the international sphere, as George Scelle famously but erroneously proposed in developing his theory of *dédoublement fonctionnel.*[118] On the contrary, they are and remain agents of their state. International law imposes its obligations upon the state as a whole. It is a matter for the internal law of the state to determine how those obligations are to be complied with. So the duty of ministers and officials to comply with the international law obligations of the state is a *consequence* of the state's duty to give effect to its obligations in good faith, but is given effect through a principle of the British Constitution that allocates this responsibility internally to the executive. It flows from the fact that where the executive undertakes an international obligation on behalf of the state, the duty to implement it falls in the first instance on the executive. In a dualist state, that responsibility may include taking steps to introduce legislation into Parliament. But that does not lessen the duty on the executive, whether or not legislation is properly required.

It may be objected that Parliament and the judiciary are also organs of the state, who may engage the state's international responsibility, yet this does not translate into a specific duty upon them to comply with the state's international obligations. In the case of Parliament, there is a presumption that it will not legislate in breach of the international

116 *Hansard*, HL, vol. 559, col. WA 84, 7 December 1994.

117 Bingham Centre for the Rule of Law/All Party Parliamentary Group on the Rule of Law, 'Meeting Report: The Ministerial Code and International Rule of Law' (9 November 2015).

118 Georges Scelle, 'Règles générales du droit de la paix' (1933) 46 *Recueil des cours* 358; on which see James Crawford, 'Chance, Order, Change: the Course of International Law' (2013) 365 *Recueil des cours* 9, ch. VII; Yuval Shany, *Regulating Jurisdictional Relations between National and International Courts* (Oxford: Oxford University Press, 2007).

obligations of the state, the practical effect of which is to create a powerful incentive for Parliament in the formulation of legislation. But this is not such as to call into question Parliament's law-making sovereignty within the domestic sphere. It may choose to legislate in breach of the international obligations assumed for the state on the place of international law. If it does so, it will risk placing the state in breach of international law, a breach for which legality under national law can provide no excuse.[119] But this it is, as a matter of the domestic Constitution, entitled to do.

So too the fact that the courts may by their decisions engage the responsibility of the state does not entail that they are under an obligation, for that reason, to give effect to unincorporated treaty obligations. This is, as Lord Hoffmann put it, 'a fallacy'.[120] Lord Millett developed the point in this way:[121]

> [T]he identification of the judicial and other organs of the state with the state itself is a principle of international law. But it has no place in the domestic jurisprudence of that state. The legal relationships of the different branches of government depend upon its internal constitutional arrangements. In the case of the United Kingdom, the governing principles are the separation of powers, the supremacy of Parliament, and the independence of the judiciary.

The duty of the executive to comply with the international obligations that it has contracted on behalf of the state must be seen as a consequence of the role that the Constitution allocates to it in the field of foreign relations. Since the Constitution, as a matter of the separation of powers, grants the conduct of foreign affairs to the executive, the correlative of the supremacy of Parliament to make law domestically is that the legal obligations that the executive enters into on behalf of the state internationally engage a duty upon the members of the executive to comply with those obligations. Ministers may not be answerable in court for their breach. But that is the result of the limitations on the role of the domestic court in relation to international law. It does not suggest the absence of an obligation *ab initio*.

The existence of such an obligation flows from the fact that the power pursuant to which the executive conducts foreign affairs is a *legal* power, not a licence for the arbitrary exercise of authority. 'It is a limited source of non-statutory administrative power accorded by the common law to

[119] Art. 3 ARSIWA.

[120] *R* v. *Lyons* [2002] UKHL 447, [2003] 1 AC 976, [40] per Lord Hoffmann.

[121] Ibid., [105].

the Crown.'[122] The consequence is that: 'Without these ancient powers, Governments would have to take equivalent authority through primary legislation.'[123]

The nature of this power may now be compared with the powers of Parliament under the principle of parliamentary sovereignty.

B *The Executive Foreign Affairs Power and Parliamentary Sovereignty*

The sovereignty of Parliament carries the consequence that, where Parliament does choose to legislate in the foreign affairs context and establishes a statutory scheme that is inconsistent with the continued exercise of the prerogative, 'it abridges the Royal Prerogative while it is in force to this extent: that the Crown can only do the particular thing under and in accordance with the statutory provisions, and that its prerogative power to do that thing is in abeyance'.[124] In that sense, where Parliament chooses to make specific provision proscribing the powers of ministers in a particular way, ministers are bound to comply. Where however Parliament has not asserted its power in such a manner, the result is not to leave the executive with unlimited discretion in foreign affairs. Rather its powers are legally limited by the international law obligations that it has assumed on behalf of the state.

The British Constitution places the power to make treaties in the hands of the executive. This power is now qualified by the power of Parliament to prevent, save in exceptional cases, the executive from ratifying a treaty if the House of Commons has resolved that it should not be ratified.[125] But Parliament's power to object does not alter the legal source of the treaty-making power. 'Ratification of a treaty is, as a matter of domestic law, an executive act within the prerogative power of the Crown.'[126]

It bears emphasising that, on many occasions, the exercise of the foreign affairs power will not directly collide with domestic law since it relates to the external relations of the state in its relations with other states and to acts outside its territory. A particularly important aspect of this is

[122] *Khadr* v. *Canada (Prime Minister)* 2010 SCC 3, [2010] 1 SCR 44, [34].

[123] United Kingdom; House of Commons Public Administration Select Committee, 'Taming the prerogative: strengthening ministerial accountability to Parliament' (HC 422, 16 March 2004), [8].

[124] *Attorney General* v. *De Keyser's Royal Hotel Ltd* [1920] AC 508, 539–40 (HL).

[125] Ss. 20 & 22 Constitutional Reform and Governance Act 2010.

[126] *R (Wheeler)* v. *Office of the Prime Minister* [2008] EWHC 1409 (DC), [15].

the conduct of armed conflict. This is regulated in the field by the major international humanitarian law conventions that enjoy almost universal adherence.[127] Such conventions apply directly to the conduct of the British armed forces abroad.[128] Grave breaches of such conventions may, as a result of primary legislation, give rise to domestic criminal liability.[129] But the greater part of international humanitarian law simply applies directly to the exercise of the executive function of the armed forces by virtue of the direct operation of international law.[130]

In this field, the invocation of parliamentary sovereignty solves nothing, since neither the executive nor Parliament is competent to change international law. This is the lesson that the executive learned in World War I as a result of *The Zamora* when it realised that 'The Government *cannot* by executive act alter international law.'[131] It also explains the insistence of the chiefs of staff on an unequivocal assurance as to the legality of the UK's intervention in Iraq in 2003.

In this field, the limitation on the power of the executive equally applies to Parliament. Recently published empirical research considered the views of the chiefs of the defence staff ('CDS') as to the status of international law vis-à-vis domestic law in the conduct of UK military operations reports as follows:[132]

> The military, without exception, saw international law as a superior source of law. One former CDS said that he was 'bound by international law' because it was the source of his permission to use lethal force. Another former CDS stated that international law was what 'define[d]' the military. When asked what would happen if parliament passed a statute requiring the government to go to war, contrary to international law, yet another former CDS hesitated – the idea was clearly inconceivable to him – but then he replied: 'I don't think it's possible for parliament to do that. Parliament could pass a Bill, but there would be very serious problems if it was contrary to international law.' One former Army General was confused as to why parliament appeared to be unable to get to grips with international law, considering that he could 'get a Private to understand it.'

[127] Geneva Conventions I-IV, note 114.

[128] United Kingdom, Ministry of Defence, *The Joint Service Manual of the Law of Armed Conflict* (JSP 383, 2004).

[129] Geneva Conventions Act 1957; International Criminal Court Act 2001.

[130] *Armed Activities (DRC* v. *Uganda)* [2005] ICJ Rep. 168, 242.

[131] Report of the 'Zamora' Committee.

[132] David Howarth and Shona Wilson Stark, 'H. L. A. Hart's secondary rules: what do "officials" really think?', 73–74.

Nor can the legality of the actions of ministers in peacetime be determined solely by reference to internal law. In *Belhaj* v. *Straw*,[133] Jack Straw, then British foreign minister, is sued, along with MI6 and officials, for his part in the alleged complicity of the British government in the extraordinary rendition of Mr Belhaj, a prominent Libyan opponent of Gaddafi. The claim is formulated as a civil action in tort for false imprisonment, trespass to the person and misfeasance in public office. The applicable law, determined according to English domestic choice of law rules, is that of the place where the alleged acts took place.[134] But the critical point for present purposes is that the Court was not precluded by the foreign act of state doctrine from scrutinising the acts of the minister because they were alleged to have been carried out in concert with a foreign state. Such acts are 'in breach of peremptory norms of international law'[135] to which overriding effect must be given.

C *The Rule of Law and Compliance with International Obligations*

It is still necessary to address a larger objection to the central proposition that the executive is bound by the international legal obligations that it assumes on behalf of the state. That is the argument that this is inconsistent with the concept of the rule of law. As has been seen, this argument is advanced in two steps. First it is said that the rule of law is intrinsically connected with the law within the state and cannot extend to international law, which is 'a defective example of law'.[136] Second it is submitted that an acceptance of a legal obligation on ministers to comply with international law would necessarily entail the consequence that they could change the legal rights and duties of 'anyone in the realm' contrary to the rule of law.[137] Each of these propositions involves a seriously fallacious reasoning step.

One can accept that there is a serious question about the extent to which conceptions of the rule of law that have been developed by reference to their application to national legal systems can be applied in

133 [2017] UKSC 3, [2017] AC 964.

134 [2014] EWCA Civ 1394, [2017] AC 964, [134]–[160], affirming EWHC 4111 (QB) on this point.

135 *Habib* v. *Commonwealth of Australia* [2010] FCAFC 12, (2010) 265 ALR 50, [114], reasoning approved by Lord Mance in *Belhaj* [2017] AC 964, [81]–[82], as to which see Campbell McLachlan, 'The foreign relations power in the Supreme Court' (2018) 134 *Law Quarterly Review* 380.

136 John Finnis, 'Ministers, international law, and the rule of law'.

137 Ibid.

the same way to the international legal system.[138] But this is not the issue that is raised by the present debate, which concerns the application of treaty obligations voluntarily assumed by the state to the conduct of executive government. In this context, an important function of international law is precisely to contribute to government under the rule of law.

As Arthur Watts put it in considering the concept of the rule of law as applied to international law:[139]

> The rule of law is the counterweight to political power; together they establish a balance in which the exercise of power is subject to legal constraints which ensure that power is not abused. The rule of law is thus at the crossroads of law and politics: '[n]o legal system operates, or can operate, in a political vacuum; no political system can provide good government, ensure justice, or preserve freedom except on the basis of respect for law.'

A central aspect of the rule of law is the control of the exercise of arbitrary power: 'There is indeed a general sense in which other elements comprised within the general concept of the rule of law serve primarily to establish the conditions in which this central element can be realised.'[140]

In this regard, international law concerns itself not merely with the conduct of states on the international plane, but also with matters internal to the state. As James Crawford put it:[141]

> International law is concerned increasingly with matters internal to the state – human rights, the environment, investment protection, criminal law, intellectual property, the conditions of free trade in terms of the WTO, the control of civil conflict and so on. Indeed it is not too much to say that in many of these areas the role of international law is to reinforce, and on occasions to institute, the rule of law internally.

The contribution of international law to the securing of the rule of law within the domestic setting was recognised in the Advisory Opinion of the Permanent Court of International Justice in *Danzig Decrees*.[142] In

[138] Crawford, *Chance, Order, Change*, chs. XI–XV.

[139] Arthur Watts, 'The international rule of law' (1993) 36 *German Yearbook of International Law* 15, 23, citing W. C. Jenks, *The Prospects of International Adjudication* (London: Stevens & Sons, 1964), 757.

[140] Ibid., 32.

[141] James Crawford, 'International law and the rule of law' (2003) 24 *Adelaide Law Review* 3, 7–8.

[142] *Consistency of Certain Danzig Decrees with the Constitution of the Free City* (Advisory Opinion) PCIJ Ser. A/B No .65 (1935).

that case, the Court was asked by the Council of the League of Nations to give its opinion on the consistency with the Danzig Constitution of certain decrees instituted by the new National Socialist administration that amended the Penal Code by inter alia purporting to confer upon the judge the power to deprive a person of his liberty or to convict him for the commission of an act which 'according to sound popular feeling is deserving of penalty'.

The Court decided that it was entitled to render an Opinion since 'though the interpretation of the Danzig Constitution is primarily an internal question of the Free City, it may involve the guarantee of the League of Nations, as interpreted by the Council and the Court'.[143] That is to say, the conformity of measures adopted at the domestic level with the rule of law was a matter which international law could and should address.

At this point, the Court's conception of the rule of law becomes a matter of some importance. It observed:

> [T]he Constitution endows the Free City with a form of government under which all organs of the State are bound to keep within the confines of the law (*Rechtsstaat*, State governed by the rule of law).

This comprises two elements. The first is a requirement that the Senate must always 'keep within the bounds of the Constitution and the law'.[144] The second element is that the Constitution contains fundamental rights of the individual that 'are designed to fix the position of the individual in the community, and to give him the safeguards which are considered necessary for his protection against the State. It is in that sense that the words "fundamental rights" have always been understood.'[145] It is apparent from the Court's reasoning that neither of these elements can be approached by reference to a purely internal understanding of legality.

The Court rejected the submission of the Senate of the Free City that it sufficed that the new provisions had legal force under the law and therefore met the requirement of the Constitution that allowed restrictions on the liberties of individuals to be imposed by law.[146] It required that 'the law itself must define the conditions in which such restrictions are to be imposed'.[147] Here the Court takes an external view of what it is to be

143 Ibid., 50.
144 Ibid., 54.
145 Ibid.
146 Ibid., 55.
147 Ibid., 56.

a 'State governed by the rule of law'. The Senate of Danzig was not entitled to determine this question for itself as a purely internal matter, since, by reason of treaty, the question would be judged by reference to a broader international conception of the rule of law.

As to the second element, the protection of such rights against the abuse of power by the organs of executive government acting at the domestic level is an important function of international law that contributes to the maintenance of the rule of law. Its application is not limited to autocratic states, since, as Hersch Lauterpacht put it in 1949: '*Even in democratic countries, situations may arise where the individual is in danger of being crushed under the impact of reason of State.*'[148]

In this context, the control of arbitrary action by the executive is a central concern of international law, as Arthur Watts rightly recognised. A Chamber of the International Court of Justice ('ICJ') expressed this idea in a case in which it was called upon to decide whether the conduct of public officials constituted a breach of treaty. It held:[149]

> Arbitrariness is not so much something opposed to a rule of law, as something opposed to the rule of law. This idea was expressed by the Court in the *Asylum* case, when it spoke of 'arbitrary action' being 'substituted for the rule of law' (*Asylum Judgment, I.C.J. Reports 1950*, p. 284). It is a wilful disregard of due process of law . . .

There is also a fallacy in the second proposition: that to accept a binding obligation upon the executive to comply with international law would necessarily entail empowering ministers to change the legal rights of others within the realm. The problem with this proposition is that it reverses the object of the legal duty and, in so doing, distorts the nature of that duty. It is certainly correct that ministers may not invoke a treaty commitment to change the legal rights of individuals within the state. That is precisely the import of *Walker* v. *Baird*[150] and of *Miller*.[151] The reason that ministers may not do that is precisely to preserve the sovereignty of Parliament to legislate domestically to determine the

[148] Hersch Lauterpacht, 'The Proposed European Court of Human Rights' (1949) 35 *Transactions of the Grotius Society* 25, 35.

[149] *Elettronica Sicula SpA (ELSI) (United States of America* v. *Italy)* [1989] ICJ Rep. 15, 76, [128].

[150] *Walker* v. *Baird* [1892] AC 491, 497.

[151] *R (on the application of Miller)* v. *Secretary of State for Exiting the European Union* [2018] AC 61.

rights and duties of citizens and to ensure that those rights cannot be taken away by executive fiat.[152]

This principle is not engaged in the present context, since the obligation to comply with international law rests upon ministers themselves. Here the point is simply that, in conducting foreign relations, including entering into treaty relations on behalf of the state, ministers are exercising a legal power – the prerogative foreign relations power – conferred upon them under the Constitution. In so doing they have the capacity to engage the responsibility of the state on the international plane: by their acts and omissions and specifically in the treaty context, by exercise of the power to conclude treaties as representatives of the state. That power to act on behalf of the state carries with it a correlative duty that itself supports the state whom they are appointed to serve: to abide by the international treaty obligations that the executive has assumed.

It is finally objected that this gives a minister the power to bind future ministers. This is precisely the point. The executive power is exercised on behalf of the state as a whole and is enduring. This point was established as long ago as 1764 in the Opinion of Lord Halifax cited above: 'The Sovereign contracts not for himself as a private Person (for that Idea would be injurious to Sovereignty) but as a public One. *In other words, he binds himself, his Successors and his People, as the great Representative of a whole Kingdom, who neither* dies nor changes *in his national Capacity*.'[153]

IV Conclusion

In conclusion, the import of the present chapter has been to demonstrate that, so far from being an aberrant and misplaced instruction, the requirement upon ministers to comply with 'the law, including international law and treaty obligations' is in fact an integral element in the operation of the British Constitution. It is supported by several centuries of consistent practice in which the law officers of the Crown take ministerial responsibility for advice to the government on its obligations under international

[152] In the Brexit debate, Finnis argued *a contrario* that the executive *was* entitled to use the treaty power within the foreign affairs prerogative to alter the rights of citizens on the domestic plane, because Parliament had sanctioned this under the European Communities Act 1972: John Finnis, 'Brexit and the balance of our Constitution' (Judicial Power Project, 1 December 2016) 5. For analysis and critique see McLachlan 'The foreign relations power', 380.

[153] Text in McNair, *International Law Opinions*, vol. I, 4-6 (emphasis added).

law, for which the government, including its law officers are answerable to Parliament. Cases in which this rule has not been followed serve only to highlight its continuing validity and importance.

The omission of the express reference to 'international law and treaty obligations' from the Ministerial Code was a retrograde step away from the clarity with which that obligation had been articulated in a document that is designed to provide important advice in a concise form about the conduct of ministerial government. But the subsequent clarifications provided by ministers to Parliament, now also memorialised in the judgments in the *Gulf Centre* litigation, place again beyond doubt that the compendious reference to 'the law' includes 'international law and treaty obligations'.

This requirement serves an important function in principle. It is not to be reduced to an expression of a 'morally grounded UK *policy*'.[154] It is itself a fundamental tenet of the British dualist Constitution, which, by conferring upon the executive the prerogative power to conduct foreign relations, including by means of the conclusion of treaties, also imposes on the executive the obligation to comply with the international law obligations, which it has assumed. This requirement does not undermine the rule of law; it advances it. Ministers may not thereby change the law of the land or impose obligations upon citizens that interfere with their rights under ordinary domestic law. Rather, the requirement ensures that the state abides by the international law obligations that it has assumed through the persons that contract on its behalf and represent it in its foreign relations.

[154] John Finnis, 'Ministers, international law, and the rule of law'.

14

The Various Faces of Fundamental Rights

DIETER GRIMM

I The Beginnings: Universal Justification – Domestic Realisation

Fundamental rights were double-faced in the beginning. They were proclaimed as universal rights, not confined to national borders, but antedating the state and inherent in every human being: 'All men are by nature equally free and independent and have certain inherent rights' (Virginia Bill of Rights, 1776). 'Les hommes naissent et demeurent libres et égaux en droits' (Déclaration des Droits de l'Homme et du Citoyen, 1789). But they gained the quality of positive law in domestic legal documents valid only on the territory of the state that had enacted them and binding only the government of that state. Their universal character was consummated in the moment of positivisation. As positive rights they were single-faced. They looked inward. What remained of their universality was that some of these rights could by claimed by everybody ('tout homme', 'nul homme'), but not everywhere, while others entitled only citizens ('tous les citoyens').

However, the transformation of a philosophical postulate into positive law in North America and France had an enormous impact abroad. The French Revolution in particular created a demand for constitutions all over Europe, and 'constitution' was equivocal with an elected representation of the people and a bill of rights. But this did not mean that the French Déclaration extended its legal validity to foreign countries. Validity and impact have to be distinguished. Validity is a normative, impact an empirical notion. Every country adopted its own bill of rights whose legal validity was confined to the territory of that country. The rights were single-faced. They were not even double-faced in the sense of the prototypes. Most countries that adopted a bill of rights after the French Revolution did not recognise the natural law origin and the universal character derived therefrom.

The majority of constitutions lacked a revolutionary background. They were voluntarily granted by monarchs, not because of constitution-mindedness, but in the interest of dynastic self-preservation in times of revolutionary threat. As a consequence, they were not based on the principle of popular sovereignty, but maintained monarchical sovereignty. They were acts of self-binding of previously absolute monarchs. This could not remain without consequences for fundamental rights. Like the constitutions, fundamental rights were regarded as voluntary grants by the monarch. As such, they were rights of citizens, not of men. This was true, for example, for all constitutions of the German states in the nineteenth century. Their framers explicitly distanced themselves from the assumption that fundamental rights had their basis in natural law because this idea was regarded as an invitation to revolt and made responsible for the excesses of the French Revolution.

This sheds some light on the historical function of the assumption that human rights were based on natural law and as such universally valid. The break with the existing legal order, undertaken by the American and French revolutionaries after their attempts to reach their goals legally had failed, needed a justification, and this could only come from higher law that transcended the state. This is not to say that human rights were instrumentalised in the interest of other purposes. The existence of universal rights was widely accepted in contemporary philosophy and part of the American colonists' and the French bourgeoisie's belief. In the revolutionary moments of 1776 and 1789, the idea became politically relevant and conveyed legitimacy on the revolutionary action, the destructive as well as the constructive. But in order to become the legal foundation of the new order, higher law had to be transformed into positive law, and in the absence of any supranational legislature this could only be domestic law.

II The Present Situation

A The Emergence of International Human Rights

Fundamental rights remained single-faced until the middle of the twentieth century. The world was a world of sovereign states, their laws were a product of state institutions. The laws were valid within state borders and so were fundamental rights. When people transgressed the borders of a state, they could not take their rights with them. They left one legal regime and entered a different one. Above the states, no political entity or institution existed that could have enacted and guaranteed human rights. Individual rights were a matter of national law. This does not mean that beyond the states a lawless zone extended. Here international law was in force. But international law was law agreed upon by sovereign states. Its purpose was to regulate the external relations among states. It lacked any interior validity. How states treated their inhabitants was of no interest to international law.

The change occurred with the founding of the United Nations (UN) at the end of World War II. Different from the many alliances of the past, different also from the post–World War I League of Nations, the states that founded the UN not only agreed to refrain from using military means to reach their political ends, with the sole exception of self-defence against external aggressors. They also authorised the UN to enforce this obligation in cases of non-compliance. For this purpose they transferred public powers to the UN, which could be exercised vis-à-vis disobedient states independently of their consent and if necessary with military force. The century-old identity between public power and state power dissolved. From now on, there was public power above the states against which they could not assert their sovereignty. This change was not less important than the emergence of the modern state in the sixteenth century and its constitutionalisation in the eighteenth century.

One of the aims of the UN, proclaimed in the Preamble of the UN Charter of 1945, was 'to reaffirm faith in fundamental human rights'. The first step to achieve this end was the drafting of the Universal Declaration of Human Rights. However, the Declaration that was passed in 1948 found the consent of the member states only under the condition that these rights were *not* positive law, but 'a common standard of achievement for all peoples and all nations to the end that every individual and every organ of society, keeping this Declaration constantly in mind, shall strive by teaching and education to promote respect for these rights and freedoms and by progressive measures, national and international, to secure their universal and effective recognition and observance'.

Legally binding human rights were first realised on a regional level by the European Convention on Human Rights (ECHR), adopted 1950 by the Council of Europe. The member states of the Council did not content themselves with enacting these rights, but also created an enforcement mechanism in the form of the European Court of Human Rights (ECtHR). The Convention stayed within the framework of traditional international law insofar as this court was not empowered to annul laws or legal acts of the member states. Rather, the states are obliged under international law to implement the decisions of the Court, but do not have to expect force in case of non-compliance. It broke with traditional international law insofar as not only states are entitled to bring an action, but also individuals. As a matter of fact, actions by one member state against another are extremely rare. The complaints are almost exclusively brought by individuals against their states.

Other regions followed later. In 1969, the American Convention on Human Rights was signed, ten years later the Inter-American Court of Human Rights came into being, but the United States and Canada refused to subject themselves to its jurisdiction. The African Charter on Human and Peoples' Rights followed in 1981; the African Court was agreed upon in 1998 and started to work in 2006. So far, only Asia has no regional human rights agreement and no human rights court. On the universal level, human rights are still not judicially enforceable. The two International Pacts of 1966, one on civil and political rights, the other on economic, social and cultural rights, differ from the Universal Declaration in that they claim legal validity. But they bind only the signatory states, not all states, and the monitoring system, created in order to assess the compliance of the member states, does not provide remedies for individuals.

B National Rights under Pressure of Adaptation to International Standards

This would not have affected the single-faced character of rights if each document had had a separate field of application. But the purpose of enacting international human rights was just the opposite. They were intended to take effect within the states, most of which already had domestic bills of rights. As a consequence, most human beings now enjoy the protection of various bills of rights, a set of rights granted or acknowledged by their state and another set from supranational sources. A German citizen, for example, is protected by the bill of rights of the state Constitution, the bill of rights of the federal Constitution - the Basic Law - the European Convention on Human Rights, the Charter of Fundamental Rights of the European Union and the various universal human rights pacts. All but the universal ones are enforceable by specialised constitutional or human rights courts.

However, the various documents do not add up to a uniform rights picture. The number of rights differs from document to document. Some rights appear in almost every bill or charter. Others can be found only in some documents. But even if the object of protection is the same, the wording may differ and even more will the limitation clauses differ. The differences increase if the interpretation and application of the rights are included in the observation. Interpretation does not just reveal a meaning that was deposited in the text of the norm from the moment of its enactment on. The text of a legal norm is never capable of completely determining its application. The general and abstract norm is in need of being concretised in view of the case at hand. This is the more so if the norm is as vague as fundamental rights usually are. Interpretation therefore does not only ascertain, but to a certain extent also constitutes the meaning of a norm. This is why interpretation must be understood as an independent factor in human rights practice.

This does not mean that interpretation is arbitrary. If done in a responsible and faithful way, it remains closely linked to the text and the purpose of the norm. It is a legal operation guided by specific legal methods. However, the methods of interpretation differ. They differ within one jurisdiction, and they differ even more between various jurisdictions. The question which method is adequate may be highly controversial. Given the vague and open-ended way fundamental rights are framed, the theory of what the source, the purpose, and the function of rights are, plays an important role for the interpretation and application of rights. Theories differ even more than methods. The ways in which fundamental rights are conceptualised, the rights discourse, the style of legal reasoning are deeply rooted in the legal culture of a country and influence judicial behaviour often subconsciously, but all the more effectively.

What does this mean for the faces of rights? The reason behind the adoption of international human rights catalogues was the disregard and even denial of fundamental rights in many states. It is not by chance that the attempts to establish guarantees of human rights on an international level started after the atrocities committed by Nazi Germany and the Soviet Union under Stalin and the devastations of World War II. This led to the conclusion that individuals had to be better protected against their states. Citizens were beneficiaries, states were addressees of international human rights. They had to acknowledge and respect them while the international organisations functioned as guarantors. So, like the constitutional rights within states, international human rights obliging states were single-faced, yet in the opposite direction. They did not look inward, but outward. They transgressed state borders and took effect within the states.

The adoption of legally binding international human rights has changed the conditions under which fundamental rights in state constitutions operate. They are no longer self-sufficient, but coexist with international human rights. The national bills cannot be interpreted and applied anymore in a purely national perspective. As far as the rights from different sources overlap, both have to be taken into account and accommodated. This brings back the double-faced character to national fundamental rights, however different from the prototypes with their natural law background. They are now double-faced within the realm of positive law. Yet, as there is no pre-established harmony between domestic and international rights documents, the two proceed with tensions or even contradictions. National fundamental rights come under pressure from international human rights.

The tension cannot be dissolved without modifications of national fundamental rights. Some may be superseded by human rights. Others will have to be reinterpreted. Gaps in national bills of rights may be filled by international rights, like in Austria whose Constitution contains but a rudimentary bill of rights that dates back to 1867. Enforcement may be strengthened as in Switzerland where federal laws were exempted from judicial review, but may now be reviewed under the ECHR. The UK, which lacked a bill of rights before the Human Rights Act of 1998, incorporated the ECHR into domestic law, so that there is a textual congruence between national and international rights. But this does not mean that the interpretation of the rights has become a purely domestic matter. The congruence does not eliminate the double-faced situation. Rather, British courts have to take the jurisprudence of the ECtHR into account to avoid conflicts between the two levels of protection.

C *International Rights as Threat to National Standards*

All international human rights documents were enacted with the intention of improving the protection of human rights in the various states. And this is what they did in general. In some states, citizens for the first time enjoyed the protection of human rights, in others their scope was extended or their protection intensified. But although improvement is the intention, it is not necessarily the effect. Under certain circumstances international human rights can weaken national fundamental rights. This is felt particularly by states with a high standard of domestic fundamental rights protection. The European situation can demonstrate that. Diminution of a high standard of rights protection is certainly not the purpose of the two European documents, the European Convention on Human Rights and the European Charter of Fundamental Rights. To the contrary, both contain provisions to prevent just this from happening.

Article 53 of the ECHR reads: 'Nothing in this Convention shall be construed as limiting or derogate from any of the human rights and fundamental freedoms which may be ensured under the laws of any High Contracting Party or under any other agreement to which it is a party.' According to this provision, the national rights prevail if they furnish a better protection than the Convention rights. Article 53 was indeed able to fulfill this purpose as long as human rights applied only to the vertical relationship between the individual and the state. This relationship is asymmetric. The individual is the holder of the right, the state is the addressee. It has to respect them. In this constellation, it was rather easy to determine whether the national or the international rights offered superior protection. States with a high standard of fundamental rights protection did not have to fear being convicted in Strasbourg.

Meanwhile the scope of fundamental rights has broadened. They take effect also in the horizontal dimension and influence the relationship between private individuals. However, the horizontal relationship differs fundamentally from the vertical. It is not asymmetric but symmetric. Both parties are protected by fundamental rights. If the rights of both parties to a private law suit have to be considered in the interpretation and application of private law provisions (the so-called indirect horizontal effect), the court has to determine which right prevails in case of a collision between them. This is usually done by way of balancing. Once this was recognised, more and more cases emerged from litigation between private parties. The losing party on the national level claimed that the national court had violated Convention rights. Should the European court find that the balance struck by the national court violates the European Convention, it inevitably diminishes the protection of the right that prevailed on the national level.

A well-known example is the Caroline of Monaco (later of Hannover) cases.[1] Caroline sued German magazines that had published photographs of her without her permission. The pictures showed Princess Caroline at busy public places in everyday activities like shopping in a market place or riding a bicycle. The private law courts in Germany dismissed her claim and so did the German Constitutional Court. The Court balanced Princess Caroline's right to privacy against the publisher's freedom of press. On the one hand, it argued that the right to privacy is not limited to the house and premise of a person or to other private places, but extends to the public space, however, only insofar as the person has a reasonable expectation not to be observed by others. According to the Court, this expectation does not exist if a person visits busy public places. On the other hand, the Court admitted that there is a legitimate interest of the general public in public figures, which the press serves.

The ECtHR, in turn, denied a legitimate public interest in the private behaviour of public figures, politicians excluded. It accepted Princess Caroline's argument that a legitimate interest in publishing photographs of her exists only when she appears officially in her capacity as Princess of Monaco. For the Court, all other photographs serve only the nosiness of the public, whereas the purpose of freedom of press is to protect discussions of serious public concerns. With this argument it turned the balance of the national court around and thereby diminished the guarantee of freedom of the press in the German understanding considerably. Article 53 ECHR was not even mentioned.

The German Constitutional Court used another case to clarify the relationship between the European Convention and German law and between the jurisprudence of the ECtHR and domestic courts.[2] The case concerned a biological father's right to access to his son. The relationship between him and the mother of the child had ended before the child was born. The mother refused the father's wish to be in touch with the child. The German civil courts denied the father a right to access as not being in the best interest of the child. The father won his case in Strasbourg, but the German civil courts argued that they were not bound by the European judgment. An individual complaint of the father gave the

[1] Decisions of the Federal Constitutional Court (*Bundesverfassungsgericht*), *BVerfGE* 101, 361 (1999) – *Caroline I*; European Court of Human Rights, Case 59320/00 (2004); *BVerfGE* 120, 180 (2008) – *Caroline II*.

[2] *BVerfGE* 111, 307 (2008) – *Görgülü*.

Federal Constitutional Court an opportunity to elaborate on the effect of judgments of the ECtHR in Germany.

The Court started from the premise that Germany has ratified the European Convention in the rank of ordinary law. As a consequence, judgments of the ECtHR cannot supersede the German Constitution. However, the openness of the German Basic Law to international law, which has found expression in Articles 23 and 24 BL, requires that the German courts take judgments of the European Court into consideration and follow them as far as possible. This requires in principle a reinterpretation of German law in the light of the jurisprudence of the ECtHR. The obligation to implement the European Court's judgments ends, however, when following them would result in a violation of the Basic Law. It also ends if there is no way to integrate the European ruling into the framework of German law. This is particularly true if following the European judgment would interfere with a carefully calibrated accommodation of various legally protected interests in domestic law.

The danger of a diminution of the national standard of fundamental rights protection is even greater in the EU. This has two reasons. First, differently from the ECtHR whose judgments oblige member states to take action and redress the contravention, judgments of the European Court of Justice (ECJ) bind the national courts directly. National laws that contradict European law lose their applicability. However, like the European Convention, the European Charter of Fundamental Rights contains a rule that follows Article 53 of the Convention. Article 53 of the Charter reads: 'Nothing in this Charter shall be interpreted as restricting or adversely affecting human rights and fundamental freedoms as recognized in their respective fields of application, by Union law and international law and by international agreements to which the Union, or all the Member States are party, including the European Convention for the Protection of Human Rights and Fundamental Freedoms, and by the Member States' constitutions.'

The main difference is that this prohibition protects the national fundamental rights only in their field of application. This field is defined in Article 51 of the Charter. The Article reads: 'The provisions of this Charter are addressed to the institutions, bodies, offices and agencies of the Union . . . and to the Member States only when they are implementing Union law . . .', so that the double-faced character of the Charter flows directly from the text. However, the ECJ interprets 'implementing Union law' as including the implementation of national law, provided that the latter is in some way or other related to Union law.[3] Yet, the degree of entanglement between European law and national law is meanwhile so high that it seems rather easy for the ECJ to discover a relation wherever it wants. At the same time, it opens the doors to subject matters that have not been transferred to the EU although Article 51(2) states that the Charter 'does not extend the field of application of Union law beyond the powers of the Union'.

The second reason lies in the difference between national fundamental rights and Charter rights. The differences are not so much textual. They rather appear on the level of interpretation. Unlike the ECtHR, the ECJ is not primarily a human rights court. Its main concern is the functioning of the Common Market and the primacy, unity and efficacy of EU law. The protection of fundamental rights is subordinated to that goal. In the same vein, the ECJ attributes prevalence to economic rights, especially to the four economic freedoms in Article 26(2) of the Treaty on the Functioning of the European Union (TFEU) (freedom of movement of goods, persons, services and capital), whereas the courts of the member states tend to give more weight to personal and communicative rights. Thus, the rights that are the weakest in the national constitutional order are the strongest in the European legal order.

This imbalance could have been cured had the EU acceded to the ECHR as Article 6(2) of the Treaty on European Union (TEU) stipulates. Already now, the EU recognises the rights set out in the ECHR and accords them the same legal rank as the Treaties (Article 6(1) TEU). Together with the constitutional traditions common to all member states they shall constitute general principles of EU law. The double-faced character of rights thus repeats itself on the international level in the relationship between different international organisations. The difference that the accession of the EU to the ECHR would have made consists in the possibility to challenge judgments of the ECJ before the ECtHR. The ECJ prevented this from happening when it declared the agreement reached between the EU and the Council of Europe incompatible with the European Treaties, in an opinion that seems to be motivated more by institutional self-interest of the ECJ than faithfulness to Article 6 (2) TEU.[4]

[3] ECJ, *Akerberg Fransson*, C-617/10 (2013), ECLI:EU:C:2013:105, [5] and [17]; *Melloni*, C-399/11 (2013), ECLI:EU:C:2013:107, [60].

[4] ECJ, Opinion 2/13 (2014), ECLI:EU:C:2014:2454.

D National Rights as Substitutes for the Lack of Human Rights Protection vis-à-vis International Organisations

These considerations may create the impression that national fundamental rights are always on the passive side, superseded or modified by international rights. But this is not necessarily so. The single-faced character of international human rights that apply only to states leaves a gap of rights protection on the international level, regarding those international organisations that exercise public authority, not only vis-à-vis states, but also vis-à-vis individuals. By far the most advanced organisation in this respect is the EU. This situation troubled the German Constitutional Court in the 1970s. By that time, the ECJ had declared that European law applied directly in the member states and enjoyed primacy over national law, even the highest national law, the national constitutions.[5] But it had failed to sufficiently protect the fundamental rights of individuals against the public power exercised by the then European Communities, albeit understandably as the Treaties did not contain a bill of rights binding the European authorities.

The German Constitutional Court regarded fundamental rights as so crucial for the legitimacy of political rule that it declared its intention to review acts of the European authorities as to their compatibility with the German Bill of Rights as long as ('solange') a sufficient European standard of fundamental rights protection was missing. This gave the judgment its name: the *Solange* decision.[6] The Court's ruling extended the effect of national fundamental rights beyond the territory of the Federal Republic and made them double-faced in a different sense: they could now influence international law. This, in turn, alarmed the ECJ. It denied the German Court the power to review European legal acts against national rights, but at the same time started to develop a set of unwritten European fundamental rights, borrowing from the common standard of the member states and from the ECHR. A genuine Charter of Fundamental Rights of the EU exists only as of 2007.

The *Solange* pattern found followers outside Germany. The ECtHR used it in its *Bosphorus* ruling of 2005.[7] Bosphorus was a Turkish airline

[5] ECJ, *Van Gend & Loos*, Case 62/62 (1963), ECLI:EU:C:1963:1; *Costa* v. *ENEL*, Case 6/64 (1964), ECLI:EU:C:1964:66; *Internationale Handelsgesellschaft*, Case 11/70 (1970), ECLI:EU:C:1970:114.

[6] *BVerfGE* 37, 271 (1974) – *Solange I*.

[7] ECtHR No. 45036/98 (2005), *Bosphorus Hava Yollari Turizm ve Ticaret Anonim Şirketi* v. *Ireland*.

that had leased Yugoslavian airplanes. One of these airplanes was confiscated by Irish authorities who, by doing so, implemented a resolution of the World Security Council, issued during the Yugoslavian crisis, which obliged all UN member states to confiscate Yugoslavian airplanes stationed on their territory. Remedies were not provided. The Irish courts rejected an action by Bosphorus because Ireland had not acted on its own initiative, but executed the UN resolution by which it was bound. The ECtHR ruled that, as long as even minimal guarantees of individual property and the rule of law were not guaranteed at UN level, the Strasbourg Court would review acts implementing UN resolutions against the ECHR.

The ECJ that had to deal with the Bosphorus case before it reached the ECtHR and which denied review of the confiscation, changed sides a few years later in the *Kadi* case.[8] The background of this case was the fight against terrorism after 9/11. Again, the Security Council had issued a resolution obliging all UN member states to freeze the assets of a number of persons who were presumed to support Al Qaida. People who figured on the list had no possibility to defend themselves against the measure. Kadi was one of them. The EU implemented the resolution of the Security Council by enacting a regulation that was binding on the member states. They executed the order and Kadi sought legal protection with the courts of the EU and won his case. While the Court of First Instance had rejected his claim,[9] the ECJ applied the *Solange* ratio that it had criticised when used vis-à-vis the EU by the German Constitutional Court.

The *Solange* reasoning points to a more general problem of international human rights. Single-faced as they are, they address states and their attitude vis-à-vis human rights. They are not concerned about human rights protection on the international level. With the recent exception of the EU, all international organisations, even those whose task it is to improve the protection of human rights on state level, do not submit their own rule to human rights. However, what needs to be constrained by human rights is not the state, but public power. If the states are no longer the exclusive holders of public power but share it with international organisations, these organisations are likewise in need of being submitted to human rights. Rights violations by UN

[8] ECJ, C-84/95 (1996), ECLI:EU:C:1996:312 – *Bosphorus*; C-402/05 (2008), ECLI:EU:C:2008:461 – *Kadi*.

[9] CFI, Case T-315/01(2005), ECLI:EU:T:2005:332.

peacekeeping forces have put the problem on the agenda. *Bosphorus* and *Kadi* show that it is not limited to military activities, but may occur in other areas as well.

Meanwhile, the UN is aware of the issue. Two resolutions of the UN Security Council reveal the development. In 2006, the Security Council still declared that it 'attaches vital importance to promoting peace and the rule of law including respect for human rights'. In 2010, a similar resolution read: 'The Security Council expresses its conviction to ensure that all UN efforts to restore peace and security *themselves* respect and promote the rule of law'.[10] However, until today the measures taken are limited to educational programs and rules of conduct. The human rights documents are still not made binding for the UN itself, let alone accompanied by the establishment of a court that would be authorised to review acts of the UN or their suborganisations as to their compliance with universal human rights.

Today, the *Solange* reasoning could acquire a new meaning because of the democratic and rule of law backsliding that can be observed in some member states of the EU. There, autocratic majorities opened the doors for a system change by paralysing their constitutional courts or bringing them in line with the government. This endangers the standard of domestic fundamental rights protection in these countries, especially insofar as political rights are concerned. This is why scholars suggest a reversed *Solange* approach: as long as national fundamental rights are not sufficiently enforced in the member states, the ECJ should compensate the deficit by applying the European Charter.[11] In the same vein, the Hungarian Constitutional Court, before it was completely filled by judges loyal to the ruling Fidesz Party, ruled that the ECHR forms the red baseline below which the national standard of fundamental rights protection may not fall.[12]

E *Institutional Consequences: Overlapping Rights-Rivalry of Courts*

Finally, the double-faced character of rights has institutional consequences. Just as international and domestic rights overlap, the jurisdictions

[10] UN Doc. S/PRST/2006/28; UN Doc. S/PRST/2010/11 (emphasis added).

[11] See Armin von Bogdandy et al., 'Reverse Solange – Protecting the essence of fundamental rights against EU Member States' (2012) 49 *Common Market Law Review* 489.

[12] Hungarian Constitutional Court, Cases 61/2011; 166/2011; 43, 2012.

of the courts that administer them overlap. If conflicts arise, international courts claim the final say, while national constitutional courts or supreme courts are not prepared to accept this claim unconditionally. The German Constitutional Court with its *Solange* reasoning and the Italian Constitutional Court with its concept of so-called *controlimiti* took the lead.[13] National and European courts assume that European law is neither part of national nor of public international law, but is an independent legal order that flows from an autonomous source. They differ as to the ground of its validity within the member states. While the ECJ sees its validity no longer depending on the will of the member states, the German Constitutional Court argues that it derives its validity in Germany from the sovereign decision of the Federal Republic that orders its applicability in Germany.

Already in *Solange I*, the Court insisted that the very identity of the Basic Law is not negotiable. Hence, the identity is exempted from any transfer of powers and thus forms an unsurmountable barrier for the primacy of EU law. The identity argument as elaborated further in the *Lisbon* Judgment[14] is now at the centre of most national courts' position vis-à-vis the ECJ. It finds its European support in Article (2) TEU according to which the EU respects the 'national identities, inherent in their fundamental structures, political and constitutional'. Still, the current situation entails the possibility of contradicting judgments in the same case and at the same time without a legal solution to the conflict. This could not have happened in strictly separated jurisdictions. There, too, contradicting judgments in one and the same case are possible, but not at the same time. At a given time, only one judgment is valid. Contradictions are solved through the hierarchical order of the judiciary. Such a hierarchy is missing in the overlapping space.

For jurists it is hard to admit that a certain behaviour may simultaneously be allowed and prohibited, a certain norm may, at the same time, be valid and void. But as this situation cannot be excluded, although it happened extremely seldom, legal scholars have begun to discover positive elements in this situation. They call it the 'dialogue of courts'. Dialogue does not mean that judges of competing courts enter into

[13] *BVerfGE* 37, 271 (1974) – *Solange I*; Italian Constitutional Court, Decision 183/73 (1974) – *Frontini*. In 1986, the German Constitutional Court declared that, by now, the standard of fundamental rights protection in Europe is equivalent to the German one, so that it suspended (but not relinquished) its power to review EU acts against the bill of rights of the Basic Law, *BVerfGE* 73, 339 (1986) – *Solange II*.

[14] *BVerfGE* 123, 267 (2009) – *Lissabon*.

a conversation about the solution of a controversial case before they decide. It rather means that the fact that there is no hierarchy will prompt courts to take the jurisprudence of the rival court into account in order to avoid conflicts of that sort. The assumption is that, if no one can act out of a hierarchical position, mutual consideration suggests itself to preserve the trust in the judiciary. To this point, it seems, however, that the willingness to act accordingly is bigger on the side of the national courts than on the side of the ECJ.

III An Outlook on the Effects of Globalisation

Fundamental rights do not only face pressure by other (usually international) rights. They undergo pressure also from factual international developments such as globalisation. A case that the German Constitutional Court had to decide in 1995 may show this.[15] It was not one of the spectacular cases and did not arouse much public interest. But for me as a Justice of the Court at that time, it was alarming. The case dealt with shipping on the high seas. As a rule, German law applies on German ships. This meant that also the high German standard of fundamental rights protection, labour conditions and social security applied to the sailors working on German ships. However, the overwhelming majority of sailors were not Germans but citizens of low wage countries, frequently from the Philippines. Often, just the captain and the first officer came from Germany.

In order to avoid the high labour and social security costs, German ship owners used to flag out their vessels and sail under the flag of a foreign country. The German government wanted to stop the trend to flag out and created a second ship register for international shipping. For ships registered here, the standard of labour protection and social security was considerably lowered for non-German sailors. The law was challenged by way of an abstract norm control by two state governments, Hamburg and Bremen, both important sea ports, and by way of individual complaint by some labour unions. They based their claims on Article 3 I (equal treatment) and Article 9 III (guarantee of unions and the right to fight for adequate wages and labour conditions) and Article 12 (freedom of occupation) of the Basic Law.

The details are of no interest here. The problem is what matters. It posed itself as follows: if one upholds the high German standard of

[15] *BVerfGE* 92, 26 (1995) – *Zweitregister*.

fundamental rights protection, there will be no longer a field of application for it on the high sea. If one wants to have German ships active in international trade, one must give up the high domestic standard of fundamental rights protection. This dilemma is a crucial test for a constitutional court, the more as it was foreseeable that it would not remain a unique case but a constellation that will repeat itself because of continuing globalisation. In the end the Court accepted the lowering of the standard to a certain extent, making it clear that there was no business as globalised as high sea–shipping, but guaranteed all sailors on German ships access to the German courts if they felt that even the remaining standard of rights protection was not kept.

The case has remained singular so far. But it demonstrates that pressure which emanates from worldwide technological and economic developments leave national fundamental rights and national constitutional courts rather helpless behind. The national fundamental rights standard could be upheld only if the national economy were cut off from international commerce, which would not be possible without violating certain fundamental rights. This means that the only remedy that could be expected is from international human rights protection. However, here another problem arises. The case shows that at stake is whether to uphold a comparatively high standard of rights protection. But so far, international human rights documents that apply to a variety of states can only guarantee a minimum standard. Otherwise, there would be no consensus by the states that are subject to these rights. Currently, a maximal standard on the global level seems only possible when a right is considered as absolute so that the question of maximal or minimal protection does not arise. However, the number of such rights is extremely small. It can be more or less reduced to the prohibition of slavery and torture. Insofar, the inward-looking and outward-looking perspectives converge. The much bigger rest remains precarious.

INDEX